16th International Conference on Parsing Technologies (IWPT 2020) and IWPT 2020 Shared Task on Parsing into Enhanced Universal Dependencies

Online
9 July 2020

ISBN: 978-1-7138-1387-3

IWPT 2020

The 16th International Conference on Parsing Technologies and IWPT 2020 Shared Task on Parsing into Enhanced Universal Dependencies

Proceedings of the Conference

July 9, 2020

Organized by SIGPARSE
the ACL Special Interest Group on Natural Language Parsing

Preface

Welcome to the 16th International Conference on Parsing Technologies (IWPT 2020), which this year (for the first time since 2007) is co-located with the Annual Meeting of the Association for Computational Linguistics (ACL). The IWPT meeting series, hosted by the ACL Special Interest Group in Natural Language Parsing (SIGPARSE), has been held biennualy since its inaugual meeting in 1989 in Pittsburgh, PA (USA).

For 2020, the SIGPARSE steering group decided to try out something new, co-location with the main ACL meeting in the form of a reduced one-day IWPT programme. The main motivation for this move was to reduce fragmentation (and travel) and to increase IWPT visibility in the 'mainstream' ACL community (we already know that at least one of these goals was attained). At the same time, IWPT launches its own series of parsing shared tasks this year, which strengthens the experimental and applied perspective on parsing technologies in the conference programme.

The IWPT 2020 shared task focuses on the parsing of Enhanced Universal Dependencies (EUD) over 17 languages. This is the first time that graph-based representations of syntactic structures are evaluated on such a large scale, and we believe it will pave way for research on richer models and representations. The task attracted system submissions from ten teams from around the world and, thus, establishes a highly relevant point of comparison for this line of syntactic analysis. We are very grateful to everyone who contributed to this shared task, starting with the data providers who worked hard to meet our deadline. Thanks to the participant teams who worked tirelessly in a short time period to provide such a set of great and interesting systems!

Owing to the COVID-19 pandemic this year, the meeting will regrettably be held entirely virtual, where for IWPT we have adopted a mostly-asynchronous format: Accepted papers (of three different types: long, short, and shared task) will be presented through pre-recorded talks, which become available on-line for individual viewing before the actual conference day. On the original date of the conference, July 9, there will be a three-hour live session, scheduled so that the timing should be convenient (all things considered) for participants around the world: 14:00–17:00 UTC, which translates, for example, into a starting time at 7:00 in the morning at the US West Coast and wrapping up at 1:00 in the morning in Melbourne, Australia. The live sessions will be devoted exclusively to questions and answers, organized into five thematic sessions. Authors of papers associated with each session will be available to answer questions and disucss their work (possibly also among themselves).

There has been (and to some degree still is) much uncertainty about the format of ACL and IWPT this year, and in a sense we were positively surprised to receive a number of submissions comparable to recent IWPT instances. Out of 24 regular paper submissions, the programme committee accepted 14 for presentation at the conference. The IWPT 2020 programme is complemented by one invited talk, by Paola Merlo of the University of Geneva (to whom we are immensely grateful for honoring her commitment despite the mostly-asynchronous, virtual format) and by an overview paper and ten system descriptions from the IWPT 2020 shared task. We further gratefully acknowledge the work of authors and reviewers, as well as of the ACL workshop chairs, who had to try and shepherd our community through a difficult logistics process.

Copenhagen, Davis, Groningen, Kyoto, Oslo, Paris, Peking, Prague, and Tel Aviv

Gosse Bouma, Yuji Matsumoto, Stephan Oepen, Kenji Sagae, Djamé Seddah,
Weiwei Sun, Anders Søgaard, Reut Tsarfaty, and Dan Zeman

Organizers:

Kenji Sagae, University of California at Davis (General Chair)
Anders Søgaard, University of Copenhagen (Programme Co-Chair)
Weiwei Sun, Peking University (Programme Co-Chair)
Gosse Bouma, University of Groningen (Shared Task Co-Chair)
Djamé Seddah, University Paris-Sorbonne (Shared Task Co-Chair)
Dan Zeman, Charles University in Prague (Shared Task Co-Chair)
Stephan Oepen, University of Oslo (Publicity Chair)

Program Committee:

Željko Agić
Mark Anderson
Miguel Ballesteros
James Barry
Steven Bethard
Anders Björkelund
Gosse Bouma
Marie Candito
Xavier Carreras
John Carroll
Özlem Çetinoğlu
Grzegorz Chrupała
Ryan Cotterell
Miryam de Lhoneux
Mathieu Dehouck
Chris Dyer
Adam Ek
Jennifer Foster
Annemarie Friedrich
Yoav Goldberg
Carlos Gómez-Rodríguez
Han He
Johannes Heinecke
James Henderson
Daniel Hershcovich
Jenna Kanerva
Sandra Kübler
Marco Kuhlmann
Jonathan K. Kummerfeld
Xuezhe Ma
Gabriel Marzinotto
Yusuke Miyao
Mark-Jan Nederhof
Joakim Nivre
Stephan Oepen
Lilja Øvrelid
Barbara Plank
Ines Rehbein

Roi Reichart
Kenji Sagae
Giorgio Satta
Natalie Schluter
Djamé Seddah
Anders Søgaard
Weiwei Sun
Ivan Titov
Gertjan van Noord
Joachim Wagner
Rui Yan
Daniel Zeman
Yi Zhang
Yue Zhang

Invited Speaker:

Paola Merlo, University of Geneva

Table of Contents

Conference Program

July 9, 2020

14:00 UTC–14:15 UTC Session 1: Invited Talk Q&A

Syntactic Parsing in Humans and Machines
Paola Merlo

14:15 UTC–14:40 UTC Session 2: Regular Papers Q&A

Distilling Neural Networks for Greener and Faster Dependency Parsing
Mark Anderson and Carlos Gómez-Rodríguez

End-to-End Negation Resolution as Graph Parsing
Robin Kurtz, Stephan Oepen and Marco Kuhlmann

Integrating Graph-Based and Transition-Based Dependency Parsers in the Deep Contextualized Era
Agnieszka Falenska, Anders Björkelund and Jonas Kuhn

Semi-supervised Parsing with a Variational Autoencoding Parser
Xiao Zhang and Dan Goldwasser

14:40 UTC–15:00 UTC Session 3: Regular Papers Q&A

Memory-bounded Neural Incremental Parsing for Psycholinguistic Prediction
Lifeng Jin and William Schuler

Obfuscation for Privacy-preserving Syntactic Parsing
Zhifeng Hu, Serhii Havrylov, Ivan Titov and Shay B. Cohen

Tensors over Semirings for Latent-Variable Weighted Logic Programs
Esma Balkir, Daniel Gildea and Shay B. Cohen

15:10 UTC–15:35 UTC Session 4: Regular Papers Q&A

Advances in Using Grammars with Latent Annotations for Discontinuous Parsing
Kilian Gebhardt

Lexicalization of Probabilistic Linear Context-free Rewriting Systems
Richard Mörbitz and Thomas Ruprecht

Self-Training for Unsupervised Parsing with PRPN
Anhad Mohananey, Katharina Kann and Samuel R. Bowman

Span-Based LCFRS-2 Parsing
Miloš Stanojević and Mark Steedman

15:35 UTC–16:00 UTC Session 5: Regular Papers Q&A

Analysis of the Penn Korean Universal Dependency Treebank (PKT-UD): Manual Revision to Build Robust Parsing Model in Korean
Tae Hwan Oh, Ji Yoon Han, Hyonsu Choe, Seokwon Park, Han He, Jinho D. Choi, Na-Rae Han, Jena D. Hwang and Hansaem Kim

Statistical Deep Parsing for Spanish Using Neural Networks
Luis Chiruzzo and Dina Wonsever

The Importance of Category Labels in Grammar Induction with Child-directed Utterances
Lifeng Jin and William Schuler

16:10 UTC–17:00 UTC Session 6: Shared Task Q&A

Syntactic Parsing in Humans and Machines

Paola Merlo
Computational Learning and Computational Linguistics,
University of Geneva, Switzerland
`paola.merlo@unige.ch`

[   ]

Abstract

To process the syntactic structures of a language in ways that are compatible with human expectations, we need computational representations of lexical and syntactic properties that form the basis of human knowledge of words and sentences.

Recent neural-network-based and distributed semantics techniques have developed systems of considerable practical success and impressive performance. As has been advocated by many, however, such systems still lack human-like properties. In particular, linguistic, psycholinguistic and neuroscientific investigations have shown that human processing of sentences is sensitive to structure and unbounded relations.

In the spirit of better understanding the structure building and long-distance properties of neural networks, I will present an overview of recent results on agreement and island effects in syntax in several languages. While certain sets of results in the literature indicate that neural language models exhibit long-distance agreement abilities, other finer-grained investigation of how these effects are calculated indicates that that the similarity spaces they define do not correlate with human experimental results on intervention similarity in long-distance dependencies. This opens the way to reflections on how to better match the syntactic properties of natural languages in the representations of neural models.

Proceedings of the 16th International Conference on Parsing Technologies and the IWPT 2020 Shared Task, page 1
Virtual Meeting, July 9, 2020. ©2020 Association for Computational Linguistics

Distilling Neural Networks for Greener and Faster Dependency Parsing

Mark Anderson   **Carlos Gómez-Rodríguez**
Universidade da Coruña, CITIC
FASTPARSE Lab, LyS Research Group,
Departamento de Ciencias de la Computación y Tecnologías de la Información
Campus Elviña, s/n, 15071 A Coruña, Spain
{m.anderson,carlos.gomez}@udc.es

Abstract

The carbon footprint of natural language processing research has been increasing in recent years due to its reliance on large and inefficient neural network implementations. Distillation is a network compression technique which attempts to impart knowledge from a large model to a smaller one. We use *teacher-student* distillation to improve the efficiency of the Biaffine dependency parser which obtains state-of-the-art performance with respect to accuracy and parsing speed (Dozat and Manning, 2017). When distilling to 20% of the original model's trainable parameters, we only observe an average decrease of ~1 point for both UAS and LAS across a number of diverse Universal Dependency treebanks while being 2.30x (1.19x) faster than the baseline model on CPU (GPU) at inference time. We also observe a small increase in performance when compressing to 80% for some treebanks. Finally, through distillation we attain a parser which is not only faster but also more accurate than the fastest modern parser on the Penn Treebank.

1 Introduction

Ethical NLP research has recently gained attention (Kurita et al., 2019; Sun et al., 2019). For example, the environmental cost of AI research has become a focus of the community, especially with regards to the development of deep neural networks (Schwartz et al., 2019; Strubell et al., 2019). Beyond developing systems to be greener, increasing the efficiency of models makes them more cost-effective, which is a compelling argument even for people who might downplay the extent of anthropogenic climate change.

In conjunction with this push for greener AI, NLP practitioners have turned to the problem of developing models that are not only accurate but also efficient, so as to make them more readily deployable across different machines with varying computational capabilities (Strzyz et al., 2019; Clark et al., 2019; Vilares et al., 2019; Junczys-Dowmunt et al., 2018). This is in contrast with the recently popular principle of *make it bigger, make it better* (Devlin et al., 2019; Radford et al., 2019).

Here we explore *teacher-student* distillation as a means of increasing the efficiency of neural network systems used to undertake a core task in NLP, dependency parsing. To do so, we take a state-of-the-art Biaffine parser from Dozat and Manning (2017). The Biaffine parser is not only one of the most accurate parsers, it is the fastest implementation by almost an order of magnitude among state-of-the-art performing parsers.

Contribution We utilise *teacher-student* distillation to compress Biaffine parsers trained on a diverse subset of Universal Dependency (UD) treebanks. We find that distillation maintains accuracy performance close to that of the full model and obtains far better accuracy than simply implementing equivalent model size reductions by changing the parser's network size and training normally. Furthermore, we can compress a parser to 20% of its trainable parameters with minimal loss in accuracy and with a speed 2.30x (1.19x) faster than that of the original model on CPU (GPU).

2 Dependency parsing

Dependency parsing is a core NLP task where the syntactic relations of words in a sentence are encoded as a well-formed tree with each word attached to a head via a labelled arc. Figure 1 shows an example of such a tree. The syntactic information attained from parsers has been shown to benefit a number of other NLP tasks such as relation extraction (Zhang et al., 2018), machine translation (Chen et al., 2018), and sentiment analysis (Poria et al., 2014; Vilares et al., 2017).

Proceedings of the 16th International Conference on Parsing Technologies and the IWPT 2020 Shared Task, pages 2–13
Virtual Meeting, July 9, 2020. ©2020 Association for Computational Linguistics

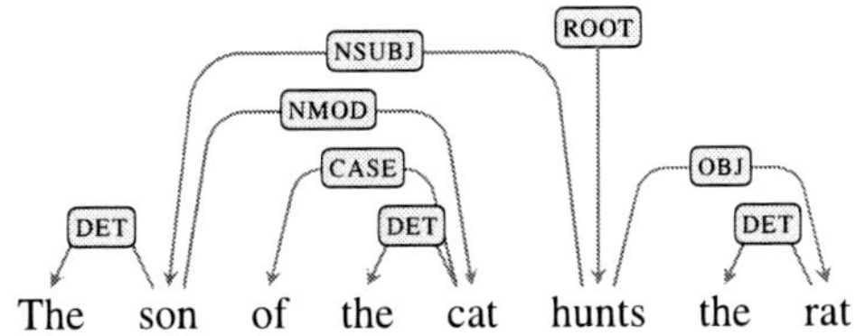

Figure 1: Dependency tree example.

2.1 Current parser performance

Table 1 shows performance details of current state-of-the-art dependency parsers on the English Penn Treebank (PTB) with predicted POS tags from the Stanford POS tagger (Marcus and Marcinkiewicz, 1993; Toutanova et al., 2003). The Biaffine parser of Dozat and Manning (2017) offers the best trade-off between accuracy and parsing speed with the HPSG parser of Zhou and Zhao (2019) achieving the absolute best reported accuracy but with a reported parsing speed of roughly one third of the Biaffine's parsing speed. It is important to note that direct comparisons between systems with respect to parsing speed are wrought with compounding variables, e.g. different GPUs or CPUs used, different number of CPU cores, different batch sizes, and often hardware is not even reported.

We therefore run a subset of parsers locally to achieve speed measurements in a controlled environment, also shown in Table 1: we compare a Py-Torch implentation of the Biaffine parser (which runs more than twice as fast as the reported speed of the original implementation); the UUParser from Smith et al. (2018a) which is one of the leading parsers for Universal Dependency (UD) parsing; a sequence-labelling dependency parser from Strzyz et al. (2019) which has the fastest reported parsing speed amongst modern parsers; and also distilled Biaffine parsers from our implementation described below. All speeds measured here are with the system run with a single CPU core for both GPU and CPU runs.[1]

Biaffine parser is a graph-based parser extended from the graph-based BIST parser (Kiperwasser and Goldberg, 2016) to use a biaffine attention mechanism which pairs the prediction of edges with the prediction of labels. This results in

---

[1]This is for ease of comparability. Parsing can trivially be parallelised by allocating sentences to different cores, so speed per core is an informative metric to compare parsers (Hall et al., 2014).

a fast and accurate parser, as described above, and is used as the parser architecture for our experiments. More details of the system can be found in Dozat and Manning (2017).

3 Network compression

Model compression has been under consideration for almost as long as neural networks have been utilised, e.g. LeCun et al. (1990) introduced a pruning technique which removed weights based on a locally predicted contribution from each weight so as to minimise the perturbation to the error function. More recently, Han et al. (2015) introduced a means of pruning a network up to 40 times smaller with minimal affect on performance. Hagiwara (1994) and Wan et al. (2009) utilised magnitude-based pruning to increase network generalisation. More specific to NLP, See et al. (2016) used absolute-magnitude pruning to compress neural machine translation systems by 40% with minimal loss in performance. However, pruning networks leaves them in an irregularly sparse state which cannot be trivially recast into less sparse architectures. Sparse tensors could be used for network layers to obtain real-life decreases in computational complexity, however, current deep learning libraries lack this feature. Anwar et al. (2017) introduced structured pruning to account for this, but this kernel-based technique is restricted to convolutional networks. More recently Voita et al. (2019) pruned the heads of the attention mechanism in their neural machine translation system and found that the remaining heads were linguistically salient with respect to syntax, suggesting that pruning could also be used to undertake more interesting analyses beyond merely compressing models and helping generalisation.

Ba and Caruana (2014) and Hinton et al. (2015) developed distillation as a means of network compression from the work of Bucilǎ et al. (2006), who compressed a large ensemble of networks into one smaller network. Similar and more recent work, used this method of compressing many models into one to achieve state-of-the-art parsing performance (Kuncoro et al., 2016). *Teacher-student* distillation is the process of taking a large network, the *teacher*, and transferring its knowledge to a smaller network, the *student*. *Teacher-student* distillation has successfully been exploited in NLP for machine translation, language modelling, and speech recognition (Kim and Rush,

	speed (sent/s)			
	GPU	CPU	UAS	LAS
Pointer-TD (Ma et al., 2018)	-	10.2[†]	95.87[†]	94.19[†]
Pointer-LR (Fernández-González and Gómez-Rodríguez, 2019)	-	23.1[†]	96.04[†]	94.43[†]
HPSG (Zhou and Zhao, 2019)	158.7[†]	-	96.09[†]	94.68[†]
BIST - Transition (Kiperwasser and Goldberg, 2016)	-	76±1[‡]	93.9[†]	91.9[†]
BIST - Graph (Kiperwasser and Goldberg, 2016)	-	80±0[‡]	93.1[†]	91.0[†]
Biaffine (Dozat and Manning, 2017)	411[†]	-	95.74[†]	94.08[†]
CM (Chen and Manning, 2014)	-	654[†]	91.80[†]	89.60[†]
SeqLab (Strzyz et al., 2019)	648±20[‡]	101±2[‡]	93.67[‡]	91.72[‡]
UUParser (Smith et al., 2018a)	-	42±1	94.63	92.77
Biaffine (PyTorch)	1003±3	53±0	95.74	94.07
SeqLab	1064±13	99±1	93.46	91.49
Biaffine-D20	1189±4	391±2	92.84	90.73
Biaffine-D40	**1153±3**	**96±0**	**94.59**	**92.64**
Biaffine-D60	1112±6	71±1	94.78	92.86
Biaffine-D80	1033±5	61±0	94.84	92.95

Table 1: Speed and accuracy performance for state-of-the-art parsers and parsers from our distillation method, Biaffine-Dπ compressing to $\pi\%$ of the original model, for the English PTB with POS tags predicted from the Stanford POS tagger. In the first table block, † denotes values taken from the original paper and ‡ from Strzyz et al. (2019). Values with no superscript (corresponding to the models in the shaded area, i.e. the second and third blocks) are from running the models on our system locally with a single CPU core for both CPU and GPU speeds (averaged over 5 runs) and with a batch size of 256 (excluding UUParser which doesn't support batching) with GloVe 100 dimension embeddings.

2016; Yu et al., 2018; Lu et al., 2017). Beyond that it has also been successfully used in conjunction with exploring structured linguistic prediction spaces (Liu et al., 2018). Latterly, it has also been used to distill task-specific knowledge from BERT (Tang et al., 2019).

Other compression techniques have been used such as low-rank approximation decomposition (Yu et al., 2017), vector quantisation (Wu et al., 2016), and Huffman coding (Han et al., 2016). For a more thorough survey of current neural network compression methods see Cheng et al. (2018).

4 Teacher-student distillation

The essence of model distillation is to train a model and subsequently use the patterns it learnt to influence the training of a smaller model. For *teacher-student* distillation, the smaller model, the *student*, explicitly uses the information learnt by the larger original model, the *teacher*, by comparing the distribution of each model's output layer. We use the Kullback-Leibler divergence to calculate the loss between the teacher and the student:

$$\mathcal{L}_{KL} = -\sum_{t \in b} \sum_{i} P(\mathbf{x}_i) \log \frac{P(\mathbf{x}_i)}{Q(\mathbf{x}_i)} \qquad (1)$$

where P is the probability distribution from the teacher's softmax layer, Q is the probability distribution from the student's, and $\mathbf{x}_i$ is input vector to the softmax corresponding to token w_i of a given tree t for all trees in batch b.

For our implementation, there are two probability distributions for each model, one for the arc prediction and one for the label prediction. By using the distributions of the teacher rather than just using the predicted arc and label, the student can learn more comprehensively about which arcs and labels are very unlikely in a given context, i.e. if the teacher makes a mistake in its prediction, the distribution might still carry useful information such as having a similar probability for y_g and y_p which can help guide the student better rather than just learning to copy the teacher's predictions.

In addition to the loss with respect to the teacher's distributions, the student model is also trained using the loss on the gold labels in the training data. We use categorical cross entropy to calculate the loss on the student's predicted head classifications:

$$\mathcal{L}_{CE} = -\sum_{t \in b} \sum_{i} \log p(h_i | \mathbf{x}_i) \qquad (2)$$

where h_i is the true head position for token w_i, corresponding to the softmax layer input vector $\mathbf{x}_i$, of tree t in batch b. Similarly, categorical cross entropy is used to calculate the loss on the predicted arc labels for the student model. The total loss for the student model is therefore:

$$\mathcal{L} = \mathcal{L}_{KL}(T_h, S_h) + \mathcal{L}_{KL}(T_{lab}, S_{lab})$$
$$+ \mathcal{L}_{CE}(h) + \mathcal{L}_{CE}(lab) \qquad (3)$$

where $\mathcal{L}_{CE}(h)$ is the loss for the student's predicted head positions, $\mathcal{L}_{CE}(lab)$ is the loss for the student's predicted arc label, $\mathcal{L}_{KL}(T_h, S_h)$ is the loss between the teacher's probability distribution for arc predictions and that of the student, and $\mathcal{L}_{KL}(T_{lab}, S_{lab})$ is the loss between label distributions. This combination of losses broadly follows the methods used in Tang et al. (2019) but is altered to fit the Biaffine parser.

5 Methodology

We train Biaffine parsers and apply the *teacher-student* distillation method to compress these models into a number of different sizes for a number of Universal Treebanks v2.4 (UD) (Nivre et al., 2019). We use the hyperparameters from Dozat and Manning (2017), but use a PyTorch implementation for our experiments which obtains the same parsing results and runs faster than the reported speed of the original (see Table 1).[2] The hyperparameter values can be seen in Table 7 in the Appendix. During distillation dropout is not used as in earlier experiments with dropout performance was hampered. And subsequent work on distillation which uses dropout also didn't perform well, but it isn't clear if this is the cause of the poorer performance, e.g. different treebanks were used, UPOS tags weren't, and no pre-trained embeddings were used (Dehouck et al., 2020). Beyond lexical features, the model only utilises universal part-of-speech (UPOS) tags. Gold UPOS tags were used for training and at runtime. Also, we used gold sentence segmentation and tokenisation. We opted to use these settings to compare models under homogeneous settings, so as to make reproducibility of and comparability with our results easier.

Data We use the subset of UD treebanks suggested by de Lhoneux et al. (2017) from v2.4, so as to cover a wide range of linguistic features, linguistic typologies, and different dataset sizes. We make some changes as this set of treebanks was

chosen from a previous UD version. We exchange Kazakh with Uyghur because the Kazakh data does not include a development set and Uyghur is a closely related language. We also exchange Ancient-Greek-Proiel for Ancient-Greek-Perseus because it contains more non-projective arcs (the number of arcs which cross another arc in a given tree) as this was the original justification for including Ancient Greek. Further, we follow Smith et al. (2018b) and exchange Czech-PDT with Russian-GSD. We also included Wolof as African languages were wholly unrepresented in the original collection of suggested treebanks (Dione, 2019). Details of the treebanks pertinent to parsing can be seen in Table 2. We use pre-trained word embeddings from FastText (Grave et al., 2018) for all but Ancient Greek, for which we used embeddings from Ginter et al. (2017), and Wolof, for which we used embeddings from Heinzerling and Strube (2018). When necessary, we used the algorithm of Raunak (2017) to reduce the embeddings to 100 dimensions.

For each treebank we then acquired the following models:

i **Baseline 1**: Full-sized model is trained as normal and undergoes no compression technique.

ii **Baseline 2**: Model is trained as normal but with equivalent sizes of the distilled models (20%, 40%, 60%, and 80% of the original size) and undergoes no compression technique. These models have the same overall structure of baseline 1, with just the number of dimensions of each layer changed to result in a specific percentage of trainable parameters of the full model.

iii **Distilled**: Model is distilled using the *teacher-student* method. We have four models were the first is distilled into a smaller network with 20% of the parameters of the original, the second 40%, the third 60%, and the last 80%. The network structure and parameters of the distilled models are the exact same as those of the baseline 2 models.

Hardware For evaluating the speed of each model when parsing the test sets of each treebank we set the number of CPU cores to be one and either ran the parser using that solitary core or using a GPU (using a single CPU core too). The CPU

---

used was an Intel Core i7-7700 and the GPU was an Nvidia GeForce GTX 1080.[3]

Experiment We compare the performance of each model on the aforementioned UD treebanks with respect to the unlabelled attachment score (UAS) which evaluates the accuracy of the arcs, and the labelled attachment score (LAS) which also includes the accuracy of the arc labels. We also evaluate the differences in inference time for each model on CPU and GPU with respect to sentences per second and tokens per second. We report sentences per second as this has been the measurement traditionally used in most of the literature, but we also use tokens per second as this more readily captures the difference in speed across parsers for different treebanks where the sentence length varies considerably. We also report the number of trainable parameters of each distilled model and how they compare to the baseline, as this is considered a good measure of how green a model is in lieu of the number of floating point operations (FPO) (Schwartz et al., 2019).[4]

6   Results and Discussion

Figure 2 shows the average attachment scores across all test treebanks (all results presented in this section are on the test treebanks) for the distilled models and the equivalent-sized base models against the size of the model relative to the original full model. There is a clear gap in performance between these two sets of models with roughly 2 points of UAS and LAS more for the distilled models. This shows that the distilled models do actually manage to leverage the information from the original full model. The full model's scores are also shown and it is clear that on average the model can be distilled to 60% with no loss in performance. When compressing to 20% of the full model, the performance only decreases by about 1 point for both UAS and LAS.

Figures 3a and 3b show the differences in UAS and LAS for the models distilled to 20% and 80% respectively for each treebank when compared to the equivalent sized baseline model and the full baseline model. The distilled models far outperform the equivalent-sized baselines for all treebanks. It is clear that for the smaller model

---

[3]Using Python 3.7.0, PyTorch 1.0.0, and CUDA 8.0.

[4]There exist a number of packages for computing the FPO of a model but, to our knowledge, as of yet they do not include the capability of dealing with LSTMs.

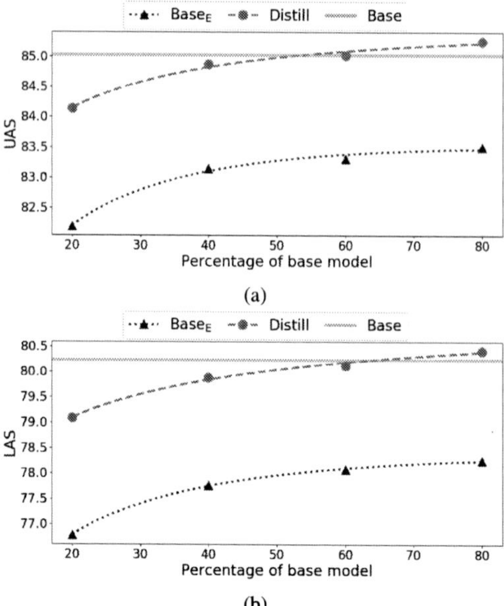

Figure 2: UAS (a) and LAS (a) against the model size relative to the original full-sized model: Base_E, the baseline models of equivalent size to the distilled models; Distill, the distilled models; Base, the performance of the original full-sized model.

some treebanks suffer more when compressed to 20% than others when compared to the full baseline model, e.g. Finnish-TDT and Ancient-Greek-Perseus. These two treebanks have the largest percentage of non-projective arcs (as can be seen in Table 2) which could account for the decrease in performance, with a more powerful model required to account for this added syntactic complexity.

However, the two smallest treebanks, Tamil-TTB and Wolof-WTB, actually increase in accuracy when using distillation, especially Tamil-TTB, which is by far the smallest treebank, with an increase in UAS and LAS of about 4 points over the full base model. This is likely the result of over-fitting when using the larger, more powerful model, so that reducing the model size actually helps with generalisation.

These observations are echoed in the results for the model distilled to 80%, where most treebanks lose less than a point for UAS and LAS against the full baseline, but have a smaller increase in performance over the equivalent-sized baseline. This makes sense as the model is still close in size to the full baseline and still similarly powerful. The increase in performance for Tamil-TTB and Wolof-

	number of trees			average sent length			average arc length			non-proj. arc pct		
	train	dev	test	train	dev	test	train	dev	test	train	dev	test
Ancient-Greek-Perseus	11476	1137	1306	14.9	20.5	17.0	4.1	4.5	4.1	23.9	23.2	23.5
Chinese-GSD	3997	500	500	25.7	26.3	25.0	4.7	4.9	4.7	0.1	0.0	0.3
English-EWT	12543	2002	2077	17.3	13.6	13.1	3.7	3.5	3.6	1.0	0.6	0.6
Finnish-TDT	12217	1364	1555	14.3	14.4	14.5	3.4	3.4	3.4	1.6	1.9	1.8
Hebrew-HTB	5241	484	491	27.3	24.6	26.0	3.9	3.8	3.7	0.8	0.8	0.9
Russian-GSD	3850	579	601	20.5	21.2	19.9	3.5	3.7	3.7	1.1	1.0	1.2
Tamil-TTB	400	80	120	16.8	16.8	17.6	3.5	3.7	3.7	0.3	0.0	0.2
Uyghur-UDT	1656	900	900	12.6	12.8	12.5	3.5	3.5	3.5	1.1	1.3	1.4
Wolof-WTB	1188	449	470	20.8	23.9	23.1	3.5	3.8	3.6	0.4	0.4	0.5

Table 2: Statistics for salient features with respect to parsing difficulty for each UD treebank used: number of trees, the number of data instances; average sent length, the length of each data instance on average; average arc length, the mean distance between heads and dependents; non.proj. arc pct, the percentage of non-projective arcs in a treebank.

	gr		zh		en		fi		he		ru		ta		ug		wo		avg	
	UAS	LAS	UAS	LAS	UAS	LAS	UAS	LAS	UAS	LAS	UAS	LAS	UAS	LAS	UAS	LAS	UAS	LAS	UAS	LAS
Full	75.5	70.4	88.2	85.9	90.8	89.0	90.5	88.6	90.8	88.6	88.9	85.2	76.9	71.0	75.2	58.9	88.5	84.5	85.0	80.2
B-20	70.5	64.4	85.1	82.1	88.6	86.4	86.7	83.6	87.9	85.1	86.3	82.0	76.2	69.9	72.2	55.6	86.1	81.8	82.2	76.8
B-40	72.2	66.4	86.1	83.5	88.9	86.8	87.7	84.8	88.5	85.6	87.1	83.1	78.4	71.8	73.0	55.7	86.5	82.2	83.2	77.8
B-60	72.0	66.4	86.7	84.0	89.5	87.5	88.1	85.5	88.7	86.3	87.1	83.1	77.5	70.9	72.7	55.9	87.5	83.1	83.3	78.1
B-80	71.8	66.2	86.7	84.3	89.1	87.1	88.5	85.9	89.3	86.6	87.1	82.9	78.2	71.5	73.0	56.2	87.8	83.6	83.5	78.3
D-20	72.3	66.4	86.7	84.2	89.5	87.7	87.6	84.9	89.4	86.7	88.2	84.2	80.6	74.7	74.1	57.9	89.0	85.0	84.1	79.1
D-40	74.0	68.3	87.9	85.6	89.9	88.0	89.5	86.9	89.4	87.0	88.4	84.6	80.9	74.7	74.5	58.3	89.4	85.5	84.9	79.9
D-60	74.2	68.7	88.3	85.9	90.1	88.3	89.4	87.1	90.0	87.5	88.6	84.7	80.4	74.5	74.5	58.6	89.5	85.8	85.0	80.1
D-80	75.0	69.6	88.4	86.2	90.1	88.3	89.2	86.9	90.3	88.0	88.8	85.0	81.2	75.4	74.6	58.6	89.6	85.7	85.3	80.4

Table 3: Full attachment scores for each model and for each test treebank where Full means the original sized model, B-X means training a model with X% of the trainable parameters of the original model, and D-X means distilling to a model with X% of the trainable parameters of the original model.

WTB are greater for this distilled model, which suggests the full model doesn't need to be compressed to such a small model to help with generalisation. The full set of attachment scores from our experiments can be seen in Table 3.

With respect to how green our distilled models are, Table 5 shows the number of trainable parameters for each distilled model for each treebank alongside its corresponding full-scale baseline. We report these in lieu of FPO as, to our knowledge, no packages exist to calculate the FPO for neural network layers like LSTMs which are used in our network. These numbers do not depend on the hardware used and strongly correlate with the amount of memory a model consumes. Different algorithms do utilise parameters differently, however, the models compared here are of the same structure and use the same algorithm, so comparisons of the number of trainable model parameters do relate to how much work each respective model does compared to another. Beyond this we offer a nominal analysis of inference energy consumption for each of the model sizes. These measurements can be seen in Table 4. The full baseline uses roughly 33% more than the smallest distilled model. This difference is more pronounced when including the energy used to load the models (which might be a consideration if the parser cannot be kept in memory) as the full baseline almost uses twice as much energy as the smallest distilled model.

	Energy (kJ)			
	Full	**D-80**	**D-60**	**D-40**	**D-20**
inf	0.32	0.31	0.27	0.25	0.24
w/ load	6.91	6.70	6.9	5.95	3.67

Table 4: Total inference energy consumption (inf) used for all test treebanks (8K sentences) and also with the energy consumption used to load each of the 9 models (w/ load). The standard deviation for inference energy consumption was 0.01 exclusively and for the consumption with loading models it ranged from 0.06 to 0.15.

Figures 4 and 5 show the parsing speeds on CPU and GPU for the distilled models and for the full baseline model in sentences and tokens per second, respectively. The speeds are reported for different batch sizes as this obviously affects the speed at which a neural network can make predic-

	gr	zh	en	fi	he	ru	ta	ug	wo
Full	12.28	11.98	12.23	12.77	12.04	11.92	11.22	11.45	11.39
D-20	2.47 (19.7)	2.42 (20.2)	2.44 (19.7)	2.56 (19.7)	2.39 (19.2)	2.36 (19.3)	2.25 (19.6)	2.30 (20.2)	2.27 (19.5)
D-40	4.88 (39.3)	4.79 (39.5)	4.86 (39.3)	5.12 (40.2)	4.80 (40.0)	4.73 (39.5)	4.49 (39.3)	4.60 (40.4)	4.57 (39.8)
D-60	7.35 (59.8)	7.24 (60.5)	7.33 (59.8)	7.66 (59.8)	7.19 (59.2)	7.18 (59.7)	6.71 (59.8)	6.90 (60.5)	6.84 (60.2)
D-80	9.80 (80.3)	9.57 (79.8)	9.75 (79.5)	10.23 (80.3)	9.59 (79.2)	9.52 (79.8)	8.94 (79.5)	9.19 (79.8)	9.12 (80.5)

Table 5: Trainable model parameters ($\times 10^6$) with percentage of full model in parentheses, where Full means the original sized model and D-X means distilling to a model with X% of the trainable parameters of the original model.

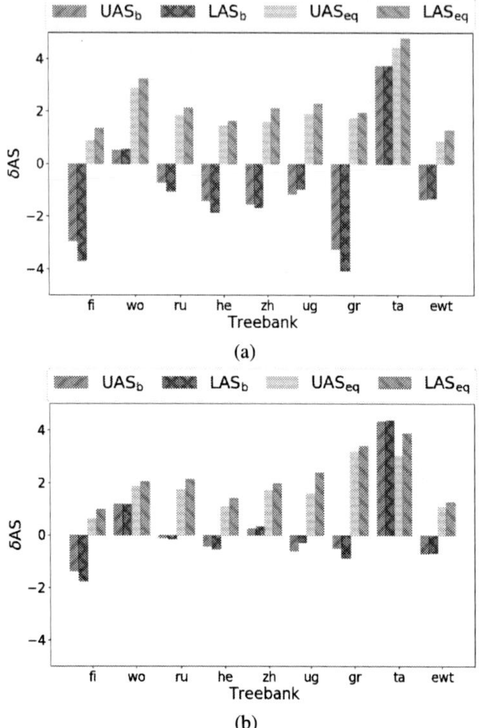

Figure 3: Delta UAS and LAS for when comparing both the original base model and equivalent-sized base models for each treebank for two of our distilled models: (a) D-20, 20% of original model and (b) D-80, 80% of original model.

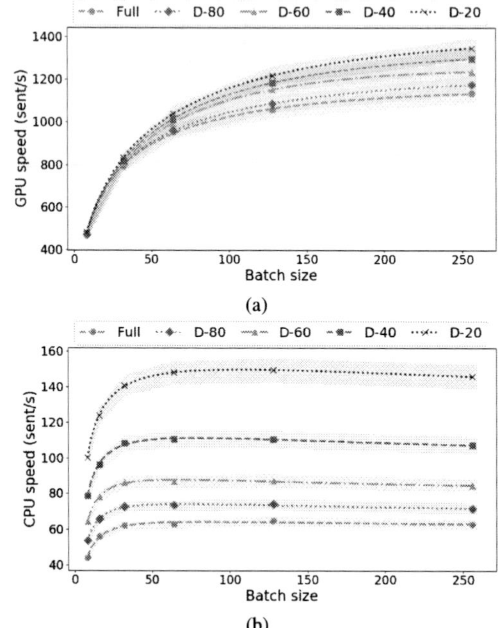

Figure 4: GPU (a) and single core CPU (b) speeds in sentence per second with varying batch sizes for distilled models (D-X) and full-sized base model (Full). Shaded areas show the standard error. Speeds for Tamil-TTB are not included as the test treebank is too small for larger batch sizes.

tions, but the maximum batch size that can be used on different systems varies significantly. As can be seen in Figures 4a and 5a, the limiting factor in parsing speed is the bottleneck of loading the data onto the GPU when using a batch size less than ∼50 sentences. However, with a batch size of 256 sentences, we achieve an increase in parsing speed of 19% over the full baseline model when considering tokens per second.

As expected, a much smaller batch size is required to achieve increases in parsing speed when using a CPU. Even with a batch size of 16 sentences, the smallest model more than doubles the speed of the baseline. For a batch size of 256, the distilled model compressed to 20% increases the speed of the baseline by 130% when considering tokens per second. A full breakdown of the parsing speeds for each treebank and each model when using a batch size of 256 sentences is given in Table 6 in the Appendix.

Figure 6 shows the attachment scores and the corresponding parsing speed against model size for the distilled model and the full baseline model. These plots clearly show that the cost in accu-

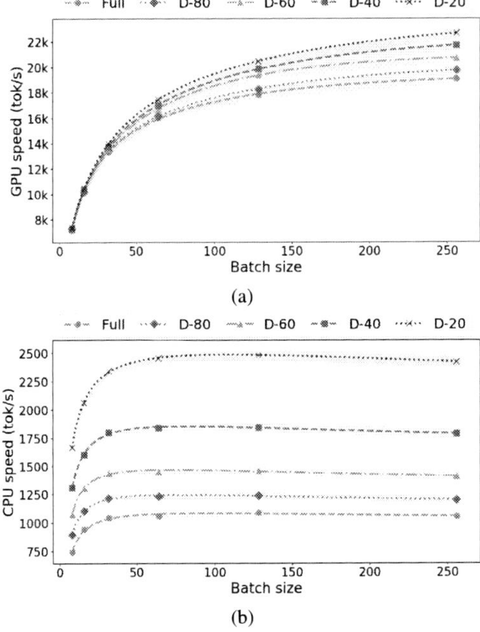

Figure 5: GPU (a) and single core CPU (b) speeds in tokens per second with varying batch sizes for distilled models (D-X) and full-sized base model (Full). Shaded areas show the standard error. Speeds for Tamil-TTB are not included as the test treebank is too small for larger batch sizes.

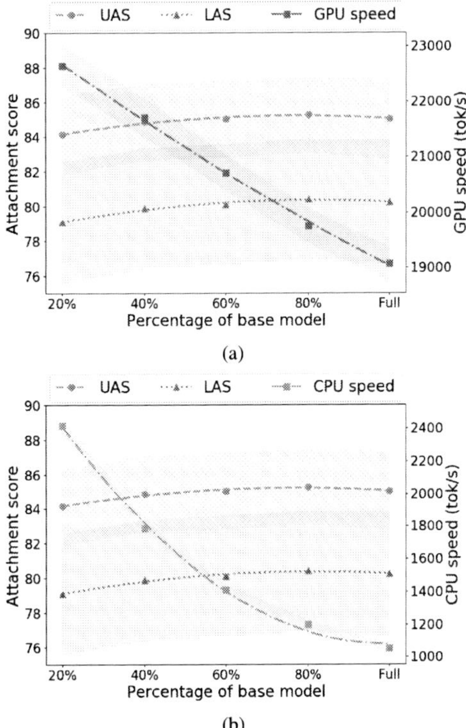

Figure 6: Comparison of attachment scores and percentage increase of speed (tok/s) for different distilled models with batch size 256: speed on GPU (a) and speed on CPU (b). Shaded areas show the standard error. Speeds for Tamil-TTB are not included as the test treebank is too small for larger batch sizes.

racy is neglible when compared to the large increase in parsing speed. So not only does this *teacher-student* distillation technique maintain the accuracy of the baseline model, but it achieves real compression and with it practical increases in parsing speed and with a greener implementation. In absolute terms, our distilled models are faster than the previously fastest parser using sequence labelling, as can be seen explicitly in Table 1 for PTB, and outperforms it by over 1 point with respect to UAS and LAS when compressing to 40%. Distilling to 20% results in a speed 4x that of the sequence labelling model on CPU but comes at a cost of 0.62 points for UAS and 0.76 for LAS compared to the sequence labelling accuracies. Furthermore, the increase in parsing accuracy for the smaller treebanks suggests that distillation could be used as a more efficient way of finding optimal hyperparameters depending on the available data, rather than training numerous models with varying hyperparameter settings.

We also need to consider training costs, an important factor to implement green AI. In this re-

spect, while our full baseline model took 66.4 seconds per epoch to train on English-EWT (the largest treebank used in this analysis), the baseline reduced to 20% trainable parameters required 52.9s per epoch, and the distillation into 20% of the original parameters clocked in at 103.1s per epoch. The distillation process takes longer and must be done after a full model is trained. However, the optimal model when distilling often occurred earlier (about epoch 50, rather than 80-100) suggesting less training is required.

In practice, the intended use of a parser should be considered when evaluating the environmental adequacy of distillation: in systems that will parse at a large scale or be deployed for extended periods of time, the savings at decoding time will offset the increased carbon footprint from training, but this may not be true in smaller-scale scenarios. However, in the latter, distillation can still be useful to reduce hardware requirements of the machine(s) used for decoding, indirectly reducing emissions.

6.1 Future work

There are numerous ways in which this distillation technique could be augmented to potentially retain more performance and even outperform the large baseline models, such as using *teacher annealing* introduced by Clark et al. (2019) where the distillation process gradually secedes to standard training. Beyond this, the structure of the distilled models can be altered, e.g. student models which are more shallow than the teacher models (Ba and Caruana, 2014). This technique could further improve the efficiency of models and make them more environmentally friendly by reducing the depth of the models and therefore the total number of trainable parameters.

Distillation techniques can also be easily expanded to other NLP tasks. Already attempts have been made to make BERT more wieldy by compressing the information it contains into task-specific models (Tang et al., 2019). But this can be extended to other tasks more specifically and potentially reduce the environmental impact of NLP research and deployable NLP systems.

7 Conclusion

We have obtained results that suggest using *teacher-student* distillation for UD parsing is an effective means of increasing parsing efficiency. The baseline parser used for our experiments was not only accurate but already fast, meaning it was a strong baseline from which to see improvements. We obtained parsing speeds 2.30x (1.19x) faster on CPU (GPU) while only losing $\sim$1 point for both UAS and LAS when compared to the original sized model. Furthermore, the smallest model which obtains these results only has 20% of the original model's trainable parameters, vastly reducing its environmental impact.

Acknowledgments

This work has received funding from the European Research Council (ERC), under the European Union's Horizon 2020 research and innovation programme (FASTPARSE, grant agreement No 714150), from the ANSWER-ASAP project (TIN2017-85160-C2-1-R) from MINECO, and from Xunta de Galicia (ED431B 2017/01, ED431G 2019/01).

References

Sajid Anwar, Kyuyeon Hwang, and Wonyong Sung. 2017. Structured pruning of deep convolutional neural networks. *ACM Journal on Emerging Technologies in Computing Systems (JETC)*, 13(3):32.

Jimmy Ba and Rich Caruana. 2014. Do deep nets really need to be deep? In *Advances in Neural Information Processing Systems*, pages 2654–2662.

Cristian Bucilă, Rich Caruana, and Alexandru Niculescu-Mizil. 2006. Model compression. In *Proceedings of the 12th ACM SIGKDD International Conference on Knowledge Discovery and Data Mining*, pages 535–541. ACM.

Danqi Chen and Christopher Manning. 2014. A fast and accurate dependency parser using neural networks. In *Proceedings of the 2014 Conference on Empirical Methods in Natural Language Processing*, pages 740–750.

Kehai Chen, Rui Wang, Masao Utiyama, Eiichiro Sumita, and Tiejun Zhao. 2018. Syntax-directed attention for neural machine translation. In *Thirty-Second AAAI Conference on Artificial Intelligence*.

Yu Cheng, Duo Wang, Pan Zhou, and Tao Zhang. 2018. Model compression and acceleration for deep neural networks: The principles, progress, and challenges. *IEEE Signal Processing Magazine*, 35(1):126–136.

Kevin Clark, Minh-Thang Luong, Urvashi Khandelwal, Christopher D Manning, and Quoc Le. 2019. BAM! Born-again multi-task networks for natural language understanding. In *Proceedings of the 57th Annual Meeting of the Association for Computational Linguistics*, pages 5931–5937.

Mathieu Dehouck, Mark Anderson, and Carlos Gómez-Rodríguez. 2020. Efficient EUD parsing. In *Proceedings of the Enhanced Universal Dependencies (EUD) Shared task at IWPT 2020 (In press)*.

Jacob Devlin, Ming-Wei Chang, Kenton Lee, and Kristina Toutanova. 2019. BERT: Pre-training of deep bidirectional transformers for language understanding. In *Proceedings of NAACL-HLT*, pages 4171–4186.

Cheikh M Bamba Dione. 2019. Developing universal dependencies for wolof. In *Proceedings of the Third Workshop on Universal Dependencies (UDW, SyntaxFest 2019)*, pages 12–23.

Timothy Dozat and Christopher D Manning. 2017. Deep biaffine attention for neural dependency parsing. *Proceedings of the 5th International Conference on Learning Representations*.

Daniel Fernández-González and Carlos Gómez-Rodríguez. 2019. Left-to-right dependency parsing with pointer networks. In *Proceedings of NAACL-HLT*, pages 710–716.

Filip Ginter, Jan Hajic, Juhani Luotolahti, Milan Straka, and Daniel Zeman. 2017. CoNLL 2017 shared task-automatically annotated raw texts and word embeddings. LINDAT/CLARIN digital library at the Institute of Formal and Applied Linguistics, Charles University.

Edouard Grave, Piotr Bojanowski, Prakhar Gupta, Armand Joulin, and Tomas Mikolov. 2018. Learning word vectors for 157 languages. In *Proceedings of the International Conference on Language Resources and Evaluation (LREC 2018)*.

Masafumi Hagiwara. 1994. A simple and effective method for removal of hidden units and weights. *Neurocomputing*, 6(2):207–218.

David Hall, Taylor Berg-Kirkpatrick, and Dan Klein. 2014. Sparser, better, faster GPU parsing. In *Proceedings of the 52nd Annual Meeting of the Association for Computational Linguistics (Volume 1: Long Papers)*, pages 208–217.

Song Han, Huizi Mao, and William J Dally. 2016. Deep compression: Compressing deep neural networks with pruning, trained quantization and huffman coding. *ICLR*.

Song Han, Jeff Pool, John Tran, and William Dally. 2015. Learning both weights and connections for efficient neural network. In *Advances in Neural Information Processing Systems*, pages 1135–1143.

Benjamin Heinzerling and Michael Strube. 2018. BPEmb: Tokenization-free Pre-trained Subword Embeddings in 275 Languages. In *Proceedings of the Eleventh International Conference on Language Resources and Evaluation (LREC 2018)*.

Geoffrey Hinton, Oriol Vinyals, and Jeff Dean. 2015. Distilling the knowledge in a neural network. *arXiv preprint arXiv:1503.02531*.

Marcin Junczys-Dowmunt, Roman Grundkiewicz, Tomasz Dwojak, Hieu Hoang, Kenneth Heafield, Tom Neckermann, Frank Seide, Ulrich Germann, Alham Fikri Aji, Nikolay Bogoychev, et al. 2018. Marian: Fast neural machine translation in C++. In *Proceedings of ACL 2018, System Demonstrations*, pages 116–121.

Yoon Kim and Alexander M Rush. 2016. Sequence-level knowledge distillation. In *Proceedings of EMNLP*, pages 1317–1327.

Eliyahu Kiperwasser and Yoav Goldberg. 2016. Simple and accurate dependency parsing using bidirectional LSTM feature representations. *Transactions of the Association for Computational Linguistics*, 4:313–327.

Adhiguna Kuncoro, Miguel Ballesteros, Lingpeng Kong, Chris Dyer, and Noah A. Smith. 2016. Distilling an ensemble of greedy dependency parsers into one MST parser. In *Proceedings of the 2016 Conference on Empirical Methods in Natural Language Processing*, pages 1744–1753, Austin, Texas. Association for Computational Linguistics.

Keita Kurita, Nidhi Vyas, Ayush Pareek, Alan W Black, and Yulia Tsvetkov. 2019. Measuring bias in contextualized word representations. *Proceedings of the 1st Workshop on Gender Bias in Natural Language Processing*, page 166–172.

Yann LeCun, John S Denker, and Sara A Solla. 1990. Optimal brain damage. In *Advances in neural information processing systems*, pages 598–605.

Miryam de Lhoneux, Sara Stymne, and Joakim Nivre. 2017. Old school vs. new school: Comparing transition-based parsers with and without neural network enhancement. In *TLT*, pages 99–110.

Yijia Liu, Wanxiang Che, Huaipeng Zhao, Bing Qin, and Ting Liu. 2018. Distilling knowledge for search-based structured prediction. In *Proceedings of the 56th Annual Meeting of the Association for Computational Linguistics (Volume 1: Long Papers)*, pages 1393–1402, Melbourne, Australia. Association for Computational Linguistics.

Liang Lu, Michelle Guo, and Steve Renals. 2017. Knowledge distillation for small-footprint highway networks. In *2017 IEEE International Conference on Acoustics, Speech and Signal Processing (ICASSP)*, pages 4820–4824. IEEE.

Xuezhe Ma, Zecong Hu, Jingzhou Liu, Nanyun Peng, Graham Neubig, and Eduard Hovy. 2018. Stack-pointer networks for dependency parsing. In *Proceedings of the 56th Annual Meeting of the Association for Computational Linguistics (Volume 1: Long Papers)*, pages 1403–1414.

Mitchell P Marcus and Mary Ann Marcinkiewicz. 1993. Building a large annotated corpus of English: The Penn Treebank. *Computational Linguistics*, 19(2).

Joakim Nivre, Mitchell Abrams, Željko Agić, et al. 2019. Universal Dependencies 2.4. LINDAT/CLARIN digital library at the Institute of Formal and Applied Linguistics (ÚFAL), Faculty of Mathematics and Physics, Charles University.

Soujanya Poria, Erik Cambria, Grégoire Winterstein, and Guang-Bin Huang. 2014. Sentic patterns: Dependency-based rules for concept-level sentiment analysis. *Knowledge-Based Systems*, 69:45–63.

Alec Radford, Jeffrey Wu, Rewon Child, David Luan, Dario Amodei, and Ilya Sutskever. 2019. Language models are unsupervised multitask learners. *OpenAI Blog*, 1(8).

Vikas Raunak. 2017. Simple and effective dimensionality reduction for word embeddings. *Proceedings of NIPS LLD Workshop*.

Roy Schwartz, Jesse Dodge, Noah A Smith, and Oren Etzioni. 2019. Green AI. *arXiv preprint arXiv:1907.10597*.

Abigail See, Minh-Thang Luong, and Christopher D Manning. 2016. Compression of neural machine translation models via pruning. In *Proceedings of The 20th SIGNLL Conference on Computational Natural Language Learning*, pages 291–301.

Aaron Smith, Bernd Bohnet, Miryam de Lhoneux, Joakim Nivre, Yan Shao, and Sara Stymne. 2018a. 82 treebanks, 34 models: Universal dependency parsing with multi-treebank models. In *Proceedings of the CoNLL 2018 Shared Task: Multilingual Parsing from Raw Text to Universal Dependencies*, pages 113–123.

Aaron Smith, Miryam de Lhoneux, Sara Stymne, and Joakim Nivre. 2018b. An investigation of the interactions between pre-trained word embeddings, character models and pos tags in dependency parsing. In *Proceedings of the 2018 Conference on Empirical Methods in Natural Language Processing*, pages 2711–2720.

Emma Strubell, Ananya Ganesh, and Andrew McCallum. 2019. Energy and policy considerations for deep learning in NLP. *Proceedings of the 56th Annual Meeting of the Association for Computational Linguistics*.

Michalina Strzyz, David Vilares, and Carlos Gómez-Rodríguez. 2019. Viable dependency parsing as sequence labeling. In *Proceedings of NAACL-HLT*, pages 717–723.

Tony Sun, Andrew Gaut, Shirlyn Tang, Yuxin Huang, Mai ElSherief, Jieyu Zhao, Diba Mirza, Elizabeth Belding, Kai-Wei Chang, and William Yang Wang. 2019. Mitigating gender bias in natural language processing: Literature review. *Proceedings of the 57th Annual Meeting of the Association for Computational Linguistics*, pages 1630–1640.

Raphael Tang, Yao Lu, Linqing Liu, Lili Mou, Olga Vechtomova, and Jimmy Lin. 2019. Distilling task-specific knowledge from BERT into simple neural networks. *arXiv preprint arXiv:1903.12136*.

Kristina Toutanova, Dan Klein, Christopher D Manning, and Yoram Singer. 2003. Feature-rich part-of-speech tagging with a cyclic dependency network. In *Proceedings of the 2003 Conference of the North American Chapter of the Association for Computational Linguistics on Human Language Technology-Volume 1*, pages 173–180. Association for computational Linguistics.

David Vilares, Mostafa Abdou, and Anders Søgaard. 2019. Better, faster, stronger sequence tagging constituent parsers. In *Proceedings of the 2019 Conference of the North American Chapter of the Association for Computational Linguistics: Human Language Technologies, Volume 1 (Long and Short Papers)*, pages 3372–3383.

David Vilares, Carlos Gómez-Rodríguez, and Miguel A Alonso. 2017. Universal, unsupervised (rule-based), uncovered sentiment analysis. *Knowledge-Based Systems*, 118:45–55.

Elena Voita, David Talbot, Fedor Moiseev, Rico Sennrich, and Ivan Titov. 2019. Analyzing multi-head self-attention: Specialized heads do the heavy lifting, the rest can be pruned. In *Proceedings of the 57th Annual Meeting of the Association for Computational Linguistics*, pages 5797–5808.

Weishui Wan, Shingo Mabu, Kaoru Shimada, Kotaro Hirasawa, and Jinglu Hu. 2009. Enhancing the generalization ability of neural networks through controlling the hidden layers. *Applied Soft Computing*, 9(1):404–414.

Jiaxiang Wu, Cong Leng, Yuhang Wang, Qinghao Hu, and Jian Cheng. 2016. Quantized convolutional neural networks for mobile devices. In *Proceedings of the IEEE Conference on Computer Vision and Pattern Recognition*, pages 4820–4828.

Seunghak Yu, Nilesh Kulkarni, Haejun Lee, and Jihie Kim. 2018. On-device neural language model based word prediction. In *Proceedings of the 27th International Conference on Computational Linguistics: System Demonstrations*, pages 128–131.

Xiyu Yu, Tongliang Liu, Xinchao Wang, and Dacheng Tao. 2017. On compressing deep models by low rank and sparse decomposition. In *Proceedings of the IEEE Conference on Computer Vision and Pattern Recognition*, pages 7370–7379.

Yuhao Zhang, Peng Qi, and Christopher D Manning. 2018. Graph convolution over pruned dependency trees improves relation extraction. In *Proceedings of the 2018 Conference on Empirical Methods in Natural Language Processing*, pages 2205–2215.

Junru Zhou and Hai Zhao. 2019. Head-driven phrase structure grammar parsing on Penn Treebank. In *Proceedings of the 57th Annual Meeting of the Association for Computational Linguistics*, pages 2396–2408.

A   Appendix

		Full	D-20	D-40	D-60	D-80
gr	CPU (tok/s)	1211 ± 2	2842 ± 3	2086 ± 3	1638 ± 3	1390 ± 1
	CPU (sent/s)	75.4 ± 0.1	177.1 ± 0.2	130.0 ± 0.2	102.1 ± 0.2	86.6 ± 0.0
	GPU (tok/s)	19219 ± 77	21017 ± 142	21296 ± 122	20346 ± 70	19202 ± 147
	GPU (sent/s)	1197.6 ± 4.8	1309.6 ± 8.9	1327.0 ± 7.6	1267.8 ± 4.3	1196.5 ± 9.1
zh	CPU (tok/s)	1124 ± 2	2503 ± 3	1872 ± 2	1490 ± 2	1278 ± 1
	CPU (sent/s)	46.8 ± 0.1	104.2 ± 0.1	77.9 ± 0.1	62.0 ± 0.1	53.2 ± 0.0
	GPU (tok/s)	21255 ± 113	25665 ± 82	24862 ± 134	23567 ± 28	22663 ± 91
	GPU (sent/s)	884.7 ± 4.7	1068.3 ± 3.4	1034.9 ± 5.6	981.0 ± 1.2	943.4 ± 3.8
en	CPU (tok/s)	884 ± 1	2217 ± 10	1548 ± 3	1217 ± 1	1010 ± 7
	CPU (sent/s)	73.2 ± 0.1	183.5 ± 0.8	128.1 ± 0.3	100.7 ± 0.1	83.6 ± 0.6
	GPU (tok/s)	16942 ± 25	20538 ± 60	19739 ± 109	19003 ± 90	17511 ± 57
	GPU (sent/s)	1402.2 ± 2.1	1699.8 ± 5.0	1633.7 ± 9.0	1572.7 ± 7.4	1449.2 ± 4.7
fi	CPU (tok/s)	988 ± 1	2586 ± 3	1767 ± 2	1371 ± 2	1153 ± 0
	CPU (sent/s)	72.9 ± 0.0	190.9 ± 0.2	130.4 ± 0.2	101.2 ± 0.1	85.1 ± 0.0
	GPU (tok/s)	18325 ± 46	22181 ± 50	21408 ± 130	20220 ± 90	19013 ± 33
	GPU (sent/s)	1352.4 ± 3.4	1637.0 ± 3.7	1580.0 ± 9.6	1492.3 ± 6.7	1403.2 ± 2.4
he	CPU (tok/s)	1180 ± 1	2644 ± 3	1964 ± 2	1582 ± 1	1337 ± 1
	CPU (sent/s)	47.2 ± 0.0	105.7 ± 0.1	78.5 ± 0.1	63.3 ± 0.0	53.5 ± 0.0
	GPU (tok/s)	22202 ± 98	26441 ± 150	25418 ± 181	24233 ± 176	22651 ± 89
	GPU (sent/s)	887.4 ± 3.9	1056.8 ± 6.0	1016.0 ± 7.2	968.6 ± 7.1	905.4 ± 3.5
ru	CPU (tok/s)	734 ± 1	1717 ± 3	1237 ± 1	976 ± 1	832 ± 1
	CPU (sent/s)	38.7 ± 0.0	90.6 ± 0.1	65.3 ± 0.1	51.5 ± 0.1	43.9 ± 0.1
	GPU (tok/s)	16383 ± 87	19661 ± 137	18337 ± 44	17901 ± 65	17014 ± 21
	GPU (sent/s)	864.9 ± 4.6	1037.9 ± 7.2	968.0 ± 2.3	944.9 ± 3.4	898.2 ± 1.1
ta	CPU (tok/s)	1110 ± 2	2334 ± 5	1799 ± 1	1464 ± 2	1251 ± 2
	CPU (sent/s)	67.0 ± 0.1	140.8 ± 0.3	108.5 ± 0.1	88.3 ± 0.1	75.5 ± 0.1
	GPU (tok/s)	17188 ± 194	19829 ± 126	19771 ± 106	18540 ± 98	18172 ± 151
	GPU (sent/s)	1037.0 ± 11.7	1196.3 ± 7.6	1192.8 ± 6.4	1118.6 ± 5.9	1096.4 ± 9.1
ug	CPU (tok/s)	1058 ± 1	2289 ± 3	1806 ± 2	1404 ± 2	1199 ± 2
	CPU (sent/s)	92.2 ± 0.1	199.4 ± 0.3	157.3 ± 0.2	122.4 ± 0.2	104.5 ± 0.1
	GPU (tok/s)	17974 ± 35	21298 ± 82	21004 ± 93	19738 ± 70	18963 ± 132
	GPU (sent/s)	1566.0 ± 3.0	1855.6 ± 7.2	1829.9 ± 8.1	1719.6 ± 6.1	1652.1 ± 11.5
wo	CPU (tok/s)	1245 ± 2	2559 ± 5	2021 ± 3	1614 ± 2	1398 ± 2
	CPU (sent/s)	56.3 ± 0.1	115.6 ± 0.2	91.3 ± 0.1	72.9 ± 0.1	63.2 ± 0.1
	GPU (tok/s)	20225 ± 74	24361 ± 94	21564 ± 73	20661 ± 102	21059 ± 105
	GPU (sent/s)	913.8 ± 3.4	1100.6 ± 4.2	974.2 ± 3.3	933.4 ± 4.6	951.4 ± 4.7
avg	CPU (tok/s)	1070 ± 21	2440 ± 39	1808 ± 32	1431 ± 26	1218 ± 23
	CPU (sent/s)	63.5 ± 2.1	146.8 ± 5.4	108.1 ± 3.8	85.3 ± 2.9	72.5 ± 2.4
	GPU (tok/s)	18933 ± 243	22503 ± 307	21488 ± 271	20463 ± 251	19666 ± 252
	GPU (sent/s)	1124.7 ± 33.3	1336.3 ± 40.1	1282.8 ± 41.7	1220.4 ± 38.8	1168.2 ± 34.8

Table 6: Speeds with batch size 256.

hyperparameter	value
word embedding dimensions	100
pos embedding dimensions	100
embedding dropout	0.33
BiLSTM dimensions	400
BiLSTM layers	3
arc MLP dimensions	500
label MLP dimensions	100
MLP layers	1
learning rate	0.2
dropout	0.33
momentum	0.9
L2 norm λ	0.9
annealing	$0.75^{(t/5000)}$
ϵ	1×10^{-12}
optimiser	Adam
loss function	cross entropy
epochs	100

Table 7: Hyperparameters for full-sized baseline models.

End-to-End Negation Resolution as Graph Parsing

Robin Kurtz♠, Stephan Oepen♣, Marco Kuhlmann♠
♠ Linköping University, Department of Computer and Information Science
♣ University of Oslo, Department of Informatics
`robin.kurtz@liu.se, oe@ifi.uio.no, marco.kuhlmann@liu.se`

Abstract

We present a neural end-to-end architecture for negation resolution based on a formulation of the task as a graph parsing problem. Our approach allows for the straightforward inclusion of many types of graph-structured features without the need for representation-specific heuristics. In our experiments, we specifically gauge the usefulness of syntactic information for negation resolution. Despite the conceptual simplicity of our architecture, we achieve state-of-the-art results on the Conan Doyle benchmark dataset, including a new top result for our best model.

1 Introduction

Negation resolution (NR), the task of detecting negation and determining its scope, is relevant for a large number of applications in natural language processing, and has been the subject of several contrastive research efforts (Morante and Blanco, 2012; Oepen et al., 2017; Fares et al., 2018). In this paper we cast NR as a graph parsing problem. More specifically, we represent negation *cues* and corresponding *scopes* as a bi-lexical graph and learn to predict this graph from the tokens. Under this representation, we may apply any dependency graph parser to the task of negation resolution. The specific parsing architecture that we use in this paper extends that of Dozat and Manning (2018).

Contributions This work (a) rationally reconstructs the previous state of the art in negation resolution; (b) develops a novel approach to the problem based on general graph parsing techniques; (c) proposes and evaluates different ways of integrating 'external' grammatical information; (d) gauges the utility of morpho-syntactic pre-processing at different levels of accuracy; (e) shifts experimental focus (back) to a complete, end-to-end perspective on the task; and (f) reflects on un-

certainty in judging experimental findings, including thorough significance testing.

Paper Structure In the following Section 2, we review selected related work on negation resolution. Section 3 describes the specific NR task that we address in this paper. In Section 4 we present our new encoding of negations and our parsing model, followed by the description of our experiments and results in Section 5. We discuss these results in Section 6 and summarize our findings in Section 7.

2 Related Work

While there exist a variety of datasets that annotate negation (Jiménez-Zafra et al., 2020), the Bio-Scope (Szarvas et al., 2008) and Conan Doyle datasets (ConanDoyle-neg; Morante and Daelemans, 2012) are most commonly used for evaluation. The latter was created for the shared task at *SEM 2012 (Morante and Blanco, 2012), where competing systems needed to predict both negation *cues* (linguistic expressions of negation) and their corresponding *scopes*, i.e. the part of the utterance being negated. Cues can be simple negation markers (such as *not* or *without*), but may also consist of multiple words (i.e. *neither ... nor*), or be mere affixes (i.e. *in*frequent or clue*less*). In contrast to other datasets, ConanDoyle-neg also annotates negated *events* that are part of the scopes.

The analysis of negation is divided into two related sub-tasks, *cue detection* and *scope resolution*. While cue detection is mostly dependent on lexical or morphological features, relating cues to scopes is a structured prediction problem and will likely benefit from an analysis of morpho-syntactic or surface-semantic properties. The UiO$_2$ system SHERLOCK (Lapponi et al., 2012), the winner of the open track of the *SEM 2012 shared task, uses morpho-syntactic parts of speech and syntactic dependencies to classify tokens as either

14

Proceedings of the 16th International Conference on Parsing Technologies and the IWPT 2020 Shared Task, pages 14–24
Virtual Meeting, July 9, 2020. ©2020 Association for Computational Linguistics

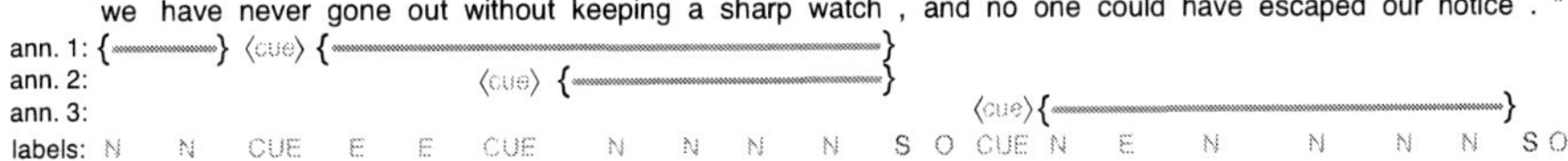

Figure 1: An example of how overlapping ConanDoyle-neg annotations are converted to flat sequences of labels in SHERLOCK. In this example, an in-scope token is labelled with N, a cue with CUE, a negated event with E, a negation stop with S, and an out-of-scope token with O. Illustration taken from Lapponi et al. (2017).

in-scope or out-of-scope using a conditional random field (CRF). Another CRF further classifies scope tokens as events, and a heuristic is applied to distribute scope tokens to their respective cues. The SHERLOCK system was subsequently used by Elming et al. (2013) to evaluate various dependency conversions, and similarly served as one of three reference 'downstream' applications in the 2017 Extrinsic Parser Evaluation initiative (EPE; Oepen et al., 2017). The best results from this evaluation define the state of the art in NR.

Deviating from the original *SEM 2012 setup, Packard et al. (2014) simplified the task to only evaluate the performance on finding scope tokens, assuming gold-standard information about negation cues. Fancellu et al. (2016, 2018) continued this trend, additionally treating each negation instance separately, and successfully used BiLSTM (bidirectional Long Short-Term Memory recurrent neural networks; Hochreiter and Schmidhuber, 1997). Recently, Sergeeva et al. (2019) used pre-trained transformers (Vaswani et al., 2017), namely BERT (Devlin et al., 2019), to further improve performance, albeit on a derivative of the original dataset (Liu et al., 2018). Using BERT in a two-stage sequence-labelling approach on the original ConanDoyle-neg corpus and other relevant negation corpora, Khandelwal and Sawant (2020) successfully improved previous results by a considerable margin. The 2018 follow-up to the EPE shared task (Fares et al., 2018) again used SHERLOCK to evaluate parsing performance, this time restricting itself to participating systems in the co-located 2018 CoNLL Shared Task on Universal Dependency Parsing (Zeman et al., 2018).

3 Task and Data

We target the original *SEM 2012 shared task and aim to predict both negation cues and their scopes. We compare our approach with the baseline SHERLOCK system and the state-of-the-art systems identified through the EPE shared tasks.

3.1 Data

The negation data of *SEM 2012 consists of selected Sherlock Holmes stories from the works of Arthur Conan Doyle, and contains 3,644 sentences in the training set, 787 sentences in the development set, and 1,089 sentences in the evaluation set. The corpus annotates a total of 1,420 instances of negation. Several sentences contain two or more instances of negation, while 4,294 sentences do not contain any at all.

Negation instances are annotated as tri-partite structures: Negation *cues* can be full tokens, multiword expressions, or affixal sub-tokens. For each cue, its *scope* is defined as the possibly discontinuous sequence of (sub-)tokens affected by the negation. Additionally, a subset of in-scope tokens can be marked as negated *events* (or *states*), provided that the sentence is factual and the events in question did not take place. For sentences containing multiple negation instances, their respective scope and event spans may nest or overlap.

The systems submitted to the EPE 2017 and 2018 tasks work on 'raw', unsegmented text, and apply different segmentation strategies. To evaluate these systems in the context of negation resolution, the gold-standard negation annotations have to be retrofitted to each system's output. Each system is then tested against their own 'personalized' gold standard. For more information on this projection procedure, we refer to Lapponi et al. (2017).

3.2 Baseline System

As in the EPE shared tasks, our baseline is the SHERLOCK system of Lapponi et al. (2012, 2017), which approaches NR as a token-based sequence labelling problem and uses a Conditional Random Field (CRF) classifier (Lavergne et al., 2010). The token-wise negation annotations contain multiple layers of information. Tokens may or may not be negation cues; they can be in or out of scope for a specific cue; in-scope tokens may or may not be negated events. Moreover, as already stated, multiple negation instances may be (partially or fully)

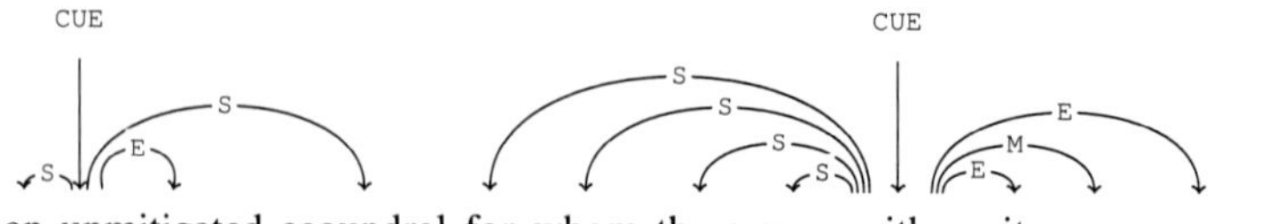

... an unmitigated scoundrel for whom there was neither pity nor excuse .

Figure 2: An example of how ConanDoyle-neg annotations are converted to a dependency-style graph structure. We omit the special root node r_0 and mark roots instead with vertical arcs. The arcs are labelled for scope (S), event (E), and multi-word-cue (M).

overlapping. Before presenting the CRF with the annotations, SHERLOCK 'flattens' all negation instances in a sentence, assigning a six-valued extended begin–inside–outside labelling scheme, as indicated in Figure 1. After classification, hierarchical (overlapping) negation structures are reconstructed using a set of post-processing heuristics.

The features of the classifier include different combinations of token-level observations, such as surface forms, part-of-speech tags, lemmas, and dependency labels. In addition, SHERLOCK employs features encoding both token and dependency distance to the nearest cue, together with the full shortest dependency paths. In the EPE context, gold-standard negation cues were provided as input to SHERLOCK.[1]

4   Approach

In this section we define our graph-based encoding of negation structures, and present our parsing system and training procedure.

4.1   Negation Graphs

Instead of labelling each token sequentially with cue, scope or event markers, we reformulate NR as a parsing task, creating dependency-style *negation graphs* with lexicalized nodes and bilexical arcs $i \rightarrow j$ between a *head i* and a *dependent j* as target structures. This formulation allows us to more naturally encode the relationship between tokens and their cue(s), while being able to easily differentiate between regular scopes and events.

An example for a negation graph is shown in Figure 2. We adopt a convention from dependency parsing and visualize negation graphs with their nodes laid out as the words of the respective sentence, and their arcs drawn above the nodes. When

transforming negation annotations into graphs, we mark negation cues i by special arcs $r_0 \rightarrow i$ emanating from an artificial root node r_0. Scope and event tokens are marked by appropriately labelled arcs from their respective cue(s). For multi-word cues, only the first cue token is assigned as a root, while the remaining tokens are connected to the first with arcs labelled M. Since we do not split tokens into subtokens, we mark the full token containing an affixal cue as root. The negated part of the token is (by convention) annotated as an event, and thus marked by an appropriately labelled loop.

The resulting graphs thus contain unconnected nodes, multiple structural roots (dependents of the artificial root node r_0), loops, and nodes with multiple incoming arcs. Sentences that do not contain any negations are represented by empty graphs.

4.2   Neural Model

With the translation of the negation annotation into graphs, we can use parsers that learn how to jointly predict cues and their respective scopes, avoiding a cascade of classifiers and heuristics as in the SHERLOCK system. Specifically, we use a reimplementation of the neural parser by Dozat and Manning (2018), which in turn is based on the architecture of Kiperwasser and Goldberg (2016). The parser learns to weigh all possible arcs, and predicts the output graph simply as the collection of all arcs with positive weights. At the heart of this parser is a bidirectional recurrent neural network with Long Short-Term Memory cells (BiLSTM; Hochreiter and Schmidhuber, 1997). Given an input sequence $\vec{x} = x_1, \ldots, x_n$ and corresponding word embeddings $\vec{w}_i$, the network outputs a sequence of context-dependent embeddings $\vec{c}_i$:

$$\vec{c}_1, \ldots, \vec{c}_n = \mathrm{BiLSTM}(\vec{w}_1, \ldots, \vec{w}_n)$$

We augment the input word embeddings $\vec{w}_i$ with additional part-of-speech tag and lemma embeddings, embeddings created by a character-based

---

[1] One main focus of the EPE task was the downstream evaluation of different syntactic representations; but the subtask of cue detection is relatively insensitive to grammatical structure (Velldal et al., 2012).

LSTM, and 100-dimensional GloVe (Pennington et al., 2014) embeddings. Based on the context-dependent embeddings, two feedforward neural networks (FNN) create specialized representations of each word as a potential head and dependent:

$$\vec{h}_i = \text{FNN}_h(\vec{c}_i) \qquad \vec{d}_i = \text{FNN}_d(\vec{c}_i)$$

These new representations are then scored via a bilinear model with weight tensor $\vec{U}$:

$$\text{score}(\vec{h}_i, \vec{d}_j) = \vec{h}_i^\top \vec{U} \vec{d}_j$$

The inner dimension of the tensor $\vec{U}$ corresponds to the number of negation graph labels plus a special NONE label indicating the absence of an arc, and thus predicts arcs and labels jointly.

4.3 Adding External Graph Features

Similarly to SHERLOCK, our neural model is able to process external morpho-syntactic or surface-semantic analyses of the input sentence in the form of dependency graphs. Inspired by Kurtz et al. (2019), we extend the contextualized embeddings that are computed by our parser by information derived from the external graph. For this we use three approaches: (i) attaching the sum of heads; (ii) scaled attention on the heads; and (iii) Graph Convolutional Networks (Kipf and Welling, 2017). In the following, we view the external graph in terms of its $n \times n$ adjacency matrix $\vec{A}$ and the contextualized embeddings as an $n \times d$ matrix $\vec{C}$.

Sum of Heads The first method generalizes that of Kurtz et al. (2019), who concatenate to each contextualized embedding the contextualized embedding of its head. This only works when the graphs are trees, that is, when every node has one incoming arc. When there is more than one incoming arc, we instead sum up all respective contextual embeddings. We express this as a matrix product

$$\text{sumoh}(\vec{A}, \vec{C}) = \vec{A}\vec{C}.$$

Scaled Attention The second approach is inspired by Vaswani et al. (2017), who compute the (scaled) dot product attention $\vec{Q}\vec{K}^\top$ between a matrix of queries $\vec{Q}$ and a matrix of keys $\vec{K}$, and normalize it by a row-wise softmax function, which yields probabilistic weights on potential values. Noting the similarity between this normalized attention matrix and a probabilistic adjacency matrix, we replace $\vec{Q}\vec{K}^\top$ with the matrix $\vec{A}$:

$$\text{scatt}(\vec{A}, \vec{C}) = \text{softmax}\left(\frac{\vec{A}}{\sqrt{d}}\right) \vec{C}$$

Here, d is the size of the contextualized embeddings. In our case, where we merely want to extract features from a given graph, the matrix $\vec{A}$ is known and sparse; but the same scaled attention model could also be used in a multi-task setup to jointly learn to parse syntactico-semantic graphs and negations, in which case $\vec{A}$ would be learned and dense.

Graph Convolutional Networks Graph Convolutional Networks (GCNs; Kipf and Welling, 2017) generalize convolutional networks to graph-structured data. While they were developed with graphs much larger than our negation graphs in mind, Marcheggiani and Titov (2017) showed their usefulness for semantic role labelling. With $\vec{X}^0 = \vec{C}$ at the first level, we compute, for each level $l > 0$, a combined representation of heads (H), dependents (D), and the nodes themselves (S), weighted by layer-specific weight matrices $\vec{W}^l$:

$$\vec{X}^l = \text{ReLU}\left(\left(\vec{A}\vec{W}_H^l + \vec{A}^\top \vec{W}_D^l + \vec{W}_S^l\right)\vec{X}^{l-1}\right)$$

When applying the next layer l, each node is updated with respect to its representation $\vec{X}^{l-1}$ from the previous layer, thus indirectly taking into account grandparents and grandchildren. As this method is the only one that not only uses a node's head but also its dependents, we expect it to benefit the most from external graph features.

5 Experiments

In this section we describe our experiments and review our baselines, methodology, and reported results.

5.1 Training

Our parser is trained with a softmax cross-entropy loss using the Adam optimizer (Kingma and Ba, 2015) and mini-batching. The training objective for our negation parsing system does not directly match the official evaluation measures, but is instead based on labelled per-arc F_1 scores (i.e. the harmonic mean of precision and recall), which measures the amount of (in)correctly predicted arcs and labels. For model selection, we train for 200 epochs and choose the model instance that performs best on the development set.

Our network sizes, dropout rates, and training parameters are shown in Table 1. Despite having less than half as many trainable parameters than the model by Dozat and Manning (2018), our

Network	Embeddings	100
sizes	Char LSTM	1 @ 100
	Char embedding	80
	BiLSTM	3 @ 200
	Arc/Label FNN	200
	GCN Levels	2
Dropout	Embeddings	20%
rates	Char LSTM feedforward	30%
	Char LSTM recurrent	30%
	Char Linear	30%
	BiLSTM feedforward	40%
	BiLSTM recurrent	20%
	Arc FNN	20%
	Arc scorer	20%
	Label FNN	30%
	Label scorer	30%
Training	Epochs	200
parameters	Mini-batch size	50
	Adam β_1	0
	Adam β_2	0.95
	Learning rate	$1 \cdot 10^{-3}$
	Gradient clipping	5
	Interpolation constant	0.025
	L_2 regularization	$3 \cdot 10^{-9}$

Table 1: Network sizes, dropout rates, and training parameters of our neural models.

model is still prone to overfitting, partly due to the rather small size of the training data. Hence we use only slightly smaller dropout rates than Dozat and Manning (2018). Following Gal and Ghahramani (2016), we apply variational dropout sharing the same dropout mask between all time steps in a sequence, and DropConnect (Wan et al., 2013; Merity et al., 2017) on the hidden states of the BiLSTM.

5.2 Evaluation Measures

Standard evaluation measures for the original *SEM 2012 task include scope tokens (ST), scope match (SM), event tokens (ET), and full negation (FN) F_1 scores. ST and ET are token-level scores for in-scope and negated event tokens, respectively, where a true positive is a correctly retrieved token of the relevant class (Morante and Blanco, 2012). FN is the strictest of these measures (and the primary evaluation metric for the NR part of the EPE shared task), counting as true positives only perfectly retrieved full scopes, including an exact match on negated events.

5.3 Baselines

In order to have a fair comparison with the previous results of the 2017 and 2018 EPE shared tasks, we evaluate on the ConanDoyle-neg data as processed by the best-performing systems from the two editions. The best-performing system on the nega-

tion task of the 2017 edition of EPE, STANFORD-PARIS-06 (Schuster et al., 2017), uses enhanced Universal Dependencies (v1) and data from the Penn Treebank (Marcus et al., 1993), the Brown Corpus (Francis and Kučera, 1985) and the GENIA treebank (Tateisi et al., 2005). In contrast to this, the best performing system for the 2018 edition, TURKUNLP (Kanerva et al., 2018), only uses the English training data provided by the co-located UD parsing shared task. Both systems use the parser and hyperparameters of Dozat et al. (2017), the winning submission of the CoNLL 2017 Shared Task on parsing Universal Dependencies.

In the overview paper for the 2018 EPE shared task (Fares et al., 2018), the organizers report that the version of the SHERLOCK negation system that was used for EPE 2017 had a deficiency that could leak gold-standard scope and event annotations into system predictions, leading to potentially inflated scores.[2] The EPE 2018 version of SHERLOCK corrected this problem and added automated hyperparameter tuning, which Fares et al. (2018) suggest largely offset the negative effect on overall scores from the bug fix, at least when averaging over all submissions. They did not, however, rerun the EPE 2017 evaluation with the corrected and enhanced version of SHERLOCK, leaving substantive uncertainty about current state-of-the-art results. We address this problem by applying the improved (i.e. 2018) version of the baseline system, including the exact same tuning procedure described by Fares et al. (2018), to the originally best-performing STANFORD-PARIS dependency graphs. In this replication study, we observe a large (5 points FN F_1) drop in performance compared to the originally reported results. While STANFORD-PARIS still outperforms TURKUNLP, the margin between the two systems is narrowed down to less than 2 points FN F_1.

5.4 Experiments

We report two sets of experiments. For all experiments, we run each of our neural network models 10 times with different random seeds and choose the best performing model with respect to performance on the development set in terms of FN F_1.

Gold-Standard Cues Even though our approach can predict negation cues on its own, for our first set of experiments, we follow the setup of the EPE tasks and predict only scopes and events, adding

---

[2] This problem also applies to Elming et al. (2013).

Data	Model	Extra	Development				Evaluation			
			SM	ST	ET	FN	SM	ST	ET	FN
STANFORD-PARIS	SHERLOCK		80.43	88.82	71.64	61.60°	78.83	88.31	67.09	61.42
	sumoh	w/o syntax	78.70	86.35	73.74	69.43	78.54	89.62	62.10	62.15
		with syntax	74.62	86.86	72.3	64.85	75.19	88.74	63.87	57.68
	scatt	w/o syntax	79.57	88.86	75.92	69.93	78.24	89.35	59.74	58.45
		with syntax	76.92	87.68	70.94	68.94	77.34	88.96	63.32	62.15
	gcn	w/o syntax	76.92	87.53	77.36	68.94	77.04	88.99	66.86	61.05
		with syntax	80.00	88.84	76.85	70.89*	78.54	89.71	65.00	**64.27**
TURKUNLP	SHERLOCK		77.38	87.19	72.36	59.91°	80.48	89.36	65.36	59.74
	sumoh	w/o syntax	79.14	87.36	78.26	71.85	78.43	89.10	61.63	60.48
		with syntax	76.47	87.28	73.73	66.92	75.69	88.90	64.83	57.45
	scatt	w/o syntax	80.85	88.5	75.24	70.89	79.32	89.56	65.61	60.48
		with syntax	80.43	88.76	73.93	68.44*	78.13	89.74	66.46	**61.58**
	gcn	w/o syntax	78.26	87.31	74.75	67.94	77.23	88.89	62.50	60.85
		with syntax	78.26	88.76	76.70	69.43	76.00	88.98	64.17	58.99

Table 2: Results of our NR parser on the STANFORD-PARIS and TURKUNLP versions of the ConanDoyle-neg development and evaluation sets when gold-standard cues are provided. The numerically best results are shown in bold. We compare our *gcn with syntax* model for STANFORD-PARIS and our *scatt with syntax* model for TURKUNLP with the respective SHERLOCK models using bootstrap significance testing. Only the ∗-marked measures are significantly different from their ○-marked counterparts.

Data	Model	Development					Evaluation				
		CUE	SM	ST	ET	FN	CUE	SM	ST	ET	FN
Read et al. (2012)		–	–	–	–	–	91.31	70.39	82.37	67.02	57.63
Packard et al. (2014)		–	77.80	82.40	–	–	91.31	73.10	85.40	–	–
STANFORD-PARIS	no syntax	91.76	73.76	86.57	71.96	65.69	90.98°	75.81	87.69	60.66	**59.40**
	sumoh	91.62	74.10	85.63	69.43	63.39	91.05	68.64	86.66	59.74	52.58
	scatt	91.51	76.16	84.72	70.00	66.42	90.98	72.25	86.09	61.21	57.64
	gcn	93.26	73.11	84.22	72.40	65.19	92.68*	73.83	86.89	63.69	58.07
TURKUNLP	no syntax	92.98	76.22*	85.61	71.11	66.42	90.71	72.09	86.92	59.88	**55.18**
	sumoh	92.49	73.45	85.03	75.35	62.31	90.66	71.73	87.91	60.06	53.19
	scatt	92.54	76.60	85.34	71.03	64.15	90.13	71.85	87.06	57.23	52.08
	gcn	91.02	72.46°	84.90	73.49	63.15	90.98	71.43	86.57	63.40	54.54

Table 3: Results of our NR parser on the STANFORD-PARIS and TURKUNLP versions of the ConanDoyle-neg development and evaluation sets when cues are predicted. The numerically best results are shown in bold. We test for significant differences between our *gcn with syntax* models for STANFORD-PARIS and TURKUNLP and respective models using no additional inputs. Only the ∗-marked measures are significantly different from their ○-marked counterparts.

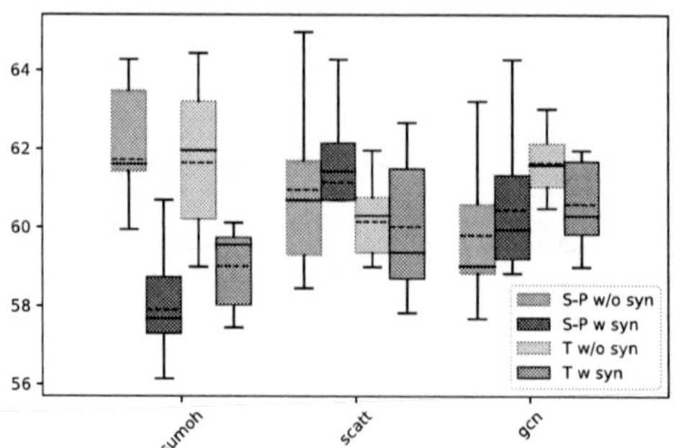

Figure 3: Boxplots visualizing the variance of performance on the evaluation set for the systems using gold cues. We compare the different methods using and not using additional syntactic information.

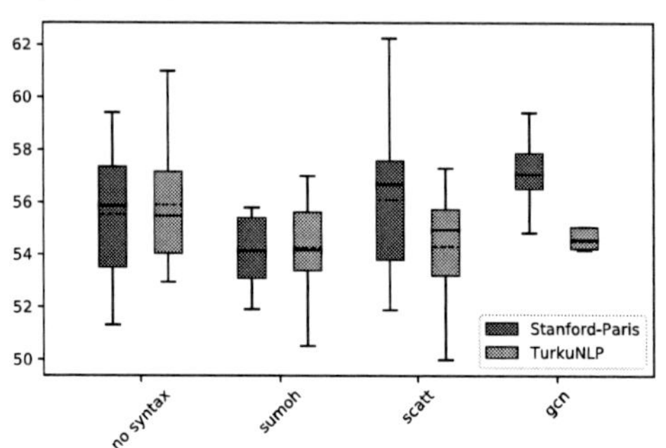

Figure 4: Boxplots visualizing the variance of performance on the evaluation set for the systems additionally predicting cues. We compare the four models using no syntax and using syntax with each of the three methods.

gold-standard cues as external graph features. Overlapping the gold-cue inputs with the additional graph inputs is not optimal but avoids adding more complexity to the model. Similar to SHERLOCK, we handle affixal cues in post-processing, splitting and classifying five known prefixes and one suffix as cues, and the remainder as the negated event. The results for these experiments are reported in Table 2. On the STANFORD-PARIS version of the evaluation data, our model with external syntactic features via GCNs (*gcn with syntax*) outperforms the SHERLOCK baseline by 2.85 FN F_1 points; on the TURKUNLP version, our best model uses syntactic features via scaled attention (*scatt with syntax*), beating the baseline by 1.84 FN F_1 points.

Predicted Cues For the second set of experiments, we also predict negation cues, and additionally report the F_1 for cues (CUE). In order to put these results into perspective, we contrast them

with the winning system of the *SEM 2012 shared task by Read et al. (2012), and also with the MRS Crawler of Packard et al. (2014). The results for these experiments are reported in Table 3. Our best models for both versions of the evaluation data are the ones that do not use external syntactic features at all (*no syntax*), with FN F_1 scores of 59.40 (STANFORD-PARIS) and 55.18 (TURKUNLP), respectively. The former result is 1.77 points higher than the result reported by Read et al. (2012).

Significance Testing Given the rather small size of the dataset, we follow the advice of Dror et al. (2018) and test for signficance using the bootstrap method (Berg-Kirkpatrick et al., 2012). We compare our best-performing system for both STANFORD-PARIS and TURKUNLP with the respective SHERLOCK sytems, resampling the test sets 10^6 times and setting our threshold to 5%, following standard methodology. For the second set of experiments, where we additionally predict negation cues, we compare our best system to our second-best system. We furthermore visualize the variance of performance across all 10 systems on the evaluation sets in Figures 3 and 4.

6 Discussion

In this section we discuss the results of our experiments and place them in the broader context of the research literature on negation resolution.

6.1 Gold Cues

We first discuss our results when using gold-standard cues, as in the EPE tasks.

Effect of Pre-processing Similar to the SHERLOCK baseline system, our system also performs better with STANFORD-PARIS rather than with TURKUNLP processed data (64.27 vs. 61.58 FN F_1), even when no syntactic inputs are used (62.15 vs. 60.48 FN F_1). The tokenization, part-of-speech tagging and lemmatization done by STANFORD-PARIS thus seem to better fit the NR task, and have likely also benefitted from the larger and more diverse data used during training.

Handling Additional Inputs The most efficient method to handle gold cues at input time, it turns out, is our simplest method, concatenating each contextual token with the sum of its heads. A likely explanation for this is that this method is able to directly read off the gold-cue information. This method however is clearly not able to handle additional syntactic inputs (losing 4.47 FN F_1 points for STANFORD-PARIS), motivating the use of either of the more advanced techniques. Combining STANFORD-PARIS syntactic trees with the GCN clearly performs best here, but does not point towards a general trend; the plots in Figure 3 rather show that most of the systems perform similarly, with the exception of the *sum-of-heads* method when using additional syntactic inputs.

6.2 Predicted Cues

When we task our system to also predict cues, as in *SEM 2012, our best system outperforms Read et al. (2012) and Packard et al. (2014) on most measures. Our neural graph parsing approch is clearly better at identifying the relevant scope tokens (ST), due to its pairwise classification approach, respectively gaining 5.32 and 2.29 points in FN F_1. This generally also results in better performance for matching complete scopes (SM). The system does however struggle with telling events and regular scopes apart, and is clearly outperformed by Read et al. (2012) on that measure (6.36 points ET F_1 for STANFORD-PARIS *no syntax*). Our system differentiates between scopes and events using arc labels only, and might not have seen enough data to sufficiently train the labelling part of the network.

One slightly surprising result is that, even though our best systems for both the STANFORD-PARIS and the TURKUNLP version of the evaluation data use syntactic inputs when gold-standard cues were provided, our best systems for also predicting cues do not rely on syntactic inputs at all.

6.3 Significant Learning

While the boxplots in Figures 3 and 4 show the same general trends as our particular systems in Tables 2 and 3, they also illustrate the considerable variance of performance between runs. Choosing the final system with regards to performance on the development sets *may* lead to state-of-the-art performance on the evaluation sets—this is the case for our best performing system using gold cues and additional syntax processed by a GCN, which performs more than two points of FN F_1 better than the average system of its kind. However, we also see examples to the opposite. Our system using gold cues with scaled attention on STANFORD-PARIS for example, performs more than two points FN F_1 *worse* than the average on the evaluation set, even though it performs three points better on the devel-

opment set. Thus, at least in this study, good performance on the development sets is not necessarily and indication for good performance on the final evaluation set. This notion is further reinforced by the lack of significant difference in performance of our best systems, compared to SHERLOCK. For the STANFORD-PARIS version of the data, even nearly three points of FN F_1 (64.27 vs. 61.42) do not constitue a significant difference. The difficulty to confidently analyse the results is also illustrated by the somewhat erratic performance differences across different settings and runs.

The NLP community has recently realized the importance of proper testing in favour of simple comparisons of benchmark scores (Gorman and Bedrick, 2019). This becomes even more pronounced when working with deep learning architectures, where model selection is more complicated (Moss et al., 2019) due to sensitivity to different random seeds. When working with smaller datasets such as ConanDoyle-neg, it is particularly important to thoroughly analyse the results before claiming that a new system improves the state of the art (Dror et al., 2017).

7 Conclusion

We have introduced a novel approach to negation resolution that remodels negation annotations into dependency-style graph structures. These negation graphs directly encode the pairwise cue–scope relationships, and thus enable our neural network to more easily learn them. We extended an already powerful neural graph-parsing approach further to additionally use arbitrary dependency graph structures as inputs. To validate our method, we revisited the EPE 2017 and 2018 shared tasks and the full *SEM 2012 shared task on negation resolution, clearly outperforming each previously best system, albeit none of our results is statistically significant.

We believe that our approach can be used to restructure other tasks as dependency-style graphs in similar fashion, and thus reuse existing systems as general purpose tools. Recasting the negation resolution task as a graph-parsing problem allows us to straightforwardly use a variety of such tools. With most of these now using neural networks, we can extend them to employ massive pre-trained models such as BERT (Devlin et al., 2019) or ELMo (Peters et al., 2018). This would allow us to leverage their general power into more specific tasks that have only limited data available.

References

Taylor Berg-Kirkpatrick, David Burkett, and Dan Klein. 2012. An Empirical Investigation of Statistical Significance in NLP. In *Proceedings of the 2012 Joint Conference on Empirical Methods in Natural Language Processing and Computational Natural Language Learning*, pages 995–1005, Jeju Island, Korea. Association for Computational Linguistics.

Jacob Devlin, Ming-Wei Chang, Kenton Lee, and Kristina Toutanova. 2019. BERT: Pre-training of Deep Bidirectional Transformers for Language Understanding. In *Proceedings of the 2019 Conference of the North American Chapter of the Association for Computational Linguistics: Human Language Technologies, Volume 1 (Long and Short Papers)*, pages 4171–4186, Minneapolis, Minnesota. Association for Computational Linguistics.

Timothy Dozat and Christopher D. Manning. 2018. Simpler but more accurate semantic dependency parsing. In *Proceedings of the 56th Annual Meeting of the Association for Computational Linguistics (Volume 2: Short Papers)*, pages 484–490, Melbourne, Australia. Association for Computational Linguistics.

Timothy Dozat, Peng Qi, and Christopher D. Manning. 2017. Stanford's graph-based neural dependency parser at the CoNLL 2017 shared task. In *Proceedings of the CoNLL 2017 Shared Task: Multilingual Parsing from Raw Text to Universal Dependencies*, pages 20–30, Vancouver, Canada. Association for Computational Linguistics.

Rotem Dror, Gili Baumer, Marina Bogomolov, and Roi Reichart. 2017. Replicability Analysis for Natural Language Processing: Testing Significance with Multiple Datasets. *Transactions of the Association for Computational Linguistics*, 5:471–486.

Rotem Dror, Gili Baumer, Segev Shlomov, and Roi Reichart. 2018. The Hitchhiker's Guide to Testing Statistical Significance in Natural Language Processing. In *Proceedings of the 56th Annual Meeting of the Association for Computational Linguistics (Volume 1: Long Papers)*, pages 1383–1392, Melbourne, Australia. Association for Computational Linguistics.

Jakob Elming, Anders Johannsen, Sigrid Klerke, Emanuele Lapponi, Hector Martinez Alonso, and Anders Søgaard. 2013. Down-stream effects of tree-to-dependency conversions. In *Proceedings of the 2013 Conference of the North American Chapter of the Association for Computational Linguistics: Human Language Technologies*, pages 617–626, Atlanta, Georgia. Association for Computational Linguistics.

Federico Fancellu, Adam Lopez, and Bonnie Webber. 2016. Neural Networks For Negation Scope Detection. In *Proceedings of the 54th Annual Meeting of the Association for Computational Linguistics (Volume 1: Long Papers)*, pages 495–504, Berlin, Germany. Association for Computational Linguistics.

Federico Fancellu, Adam Lopez, and Bonnie Webber. 2018. Neural Networks for Cross-lingual Negation Scope Detection. *arXiv:1810.02156 [cs]*.

Murhaf Fares, Stephan Oepen, Lilja Øvrelid, Jari Björne, and Richard Johansson. 2018. The 2018 Shared Task on Extrinsic Parser Evaluation. On the downstream utility of English Universal Dependency parsers. In *Proceedings of the 22nd Conference on Natural Language Learning*, page 22–33, Brussels, Belgia.

W. Nelson Francis and Henry Kučera. 1985. Frequency Analysis of English Usage: Lexicon and Grammar. *Journal of English Linguistics*, 18(1):64–70.

Yarin Gal and Zoubin Ghahramani. 2016. A Theoretically Grounded Application of Dropout in Recurrent Neural Networks. In *Proceedings of the 30th International Conference on Neural Information Processing Systems*, NIPS'16, pages 1027–1035, Barcelona, Spain. Curran Associates Inc.

Kyle Gorman and Steven Bedrick. 2019. We Need to Talk about Standard Splits. In *Proceedings of the 57th Annual Meeting of the Association for Computational Linguistics*, pages 2786–2791, Florence, Italy. Association for Computational Linguistics.

Sepp Hochreiter and Jürgen Schmidhuber. 1997. Long Short-term Memory. *Neural computation*, 9:1735–80.

Salud María Jiménez-Zafra, Roser Morante, María Teresa Martín-Valdivia, and L. Alfonso Ureña-López. 2020. Corpora annotated with negation: An overview. *Computational Linguistics*, 46(0):1–56. Early access.

Jenna Kanerva, Filip Ginter, Niko Miekka, Akseli Leino, and Tapio Salakoski. 2018. Turku Neural Parser Pipeline: An End-to-End System for the CoNLL 2018 Shared Task. In *Proceedings of the CoNLL 2018 Shared Task: Multilingual Parsing from Raw Text to Universal Dependencies*, pages 133–142, Brussels, Belgium. Association for Computational Linguistics.

Aditya Khandelwal and Suraj Sawant. 2020. NegBERT: A transfer learning approach for negation detection and scope resolution. In *Proceedings of the 12th Language Resources and Evaluation Conference*, pages 5739–5748, Marseille, France. European Language Resources Association.

Diederik P. Kingma and Jimmy Ba. 2015. Adam: A Method for Stochastic Optimization. In *3rd International Conference on Learning Representations, ICLR 2015, San Diego, CA, USA, May 7-9, 2015, Conference Track Proceedings*.

22

Eliyahu Kiperwasser and Yoav Goldberg. 2016. Simple and accurate dependency parsing using bidirectional LSTM feature representations. *Transactions of the Association for Computational Linguistics*, 4:313–327.

Thomas N. Kipf and Max Welling. 2017. Semi-supervised classification with graph convolutional networks. In *5th International Conference on Learning Representations, ICLR 2017, Toulon, France, April 24-26, 2017, Conference Track Proceedings*. OpenReview.net.

Robin Kurtz, Daniel Roxbo, and Marco Kuhlmann. 2019. Improving Semantic Dependency Parsing with Syntactic Features. In *Proceedings of the First NLPL Workshop on Deep Learning for Natural Language Processing*, pages 12–21, Turku, Finland. Linköping University Electronic Press.

Emanuele Lapponi, Stephan Oepen, and Lilja Øvrelid. 2017. EPE 2017: The Sherlock negation resolution downstream application. In *Proceedings of the 2017 Shared Task on Extrinsic Parser Evaluation at the Fourth International Conference on Dependency Linguistics and the 15th International Conference on Parsing Technologies*, page 25 – 30, Pisa, Italy.

Emanuele Lapponi, Erik Velldal, Lilja Øvrelid, and Jonathon Read. 2012. UiO2. Sequence-labeling negation using dependency features. In *Proceedings of the 1st Joint Conference on Lexical and Computational Semantics*, page 319 – 327, Montréal, Canada.

Thomas Lavergne, Olivier Cappé, and François Yvon. 2010. Practical very large scale CRFs. In *Proceedings of the 48th Meeting of the Association for Computational Linguistics*, page 504 – 513, Uppsala, Sweden.

Qianchu Liu, Federico Fancellu, and Bonnie Webber. 2018. NegPar: A parallel corpus annotated for negation. In *Proceedings of the Eleventh International Conference on Language Resources and Evaluation (LREC 2018)*, Miyazaki, Japan. European Language Resources Association (ELRA).

Diego Marcheggiani and Ivan Titov. 2017. Encoding Sentences with Graph Convolutional Networks for Semantic Role Labeling. In *Proceedings of the 2017 Conference on Empirical Methods in Natural Language Processing*, pages 1506–1515, Copenhagen, Denmark. Association for Computational Linguistics.

Mitchell P. Marcus, Beatrice Santorini, and Mary Ann Marcinkiewicz. 1993. Building a large annotated corpus of English: The Penn Treebank. *Computational Linguistics*, 19(2):313–330.

Stephen Merity, Nitish Shirish Keskar, and Richard Socher. 2017. Regularizing and Optimizing LSTM Language Models. *CoRR*, abs/1708.02182.

Roser Morante and Eduardo Blanco. 2012. *SEM 2012 Shared Task. Resolving the scope and focus of negation. In *Proceedings of the 1st Joint Conference on Lexical and Computational Semantics*, page 265 – 274, Montréal, Canada.

Roser Morante and Walter Daelemans. 2012. ConanDoyle-neg: Annotation of negation cues and their scope in Conan Doyle stories. In *Proceedings of the Eighth International Conference on Language Resources and Evaluation (LREC'12)*, pages 1563–1568, Istanbul, Turkey. European Language Resources Association (ELRA).

Henry Moss, Andrew Moore, David Leslie, and Paul Rayson. 2019. FIESTA: Fast IdEntification of State-of-The-Art models using adaptive bandit algorithms. In *Proceedings of the 57th Annual Meeting of the Association for Computational Linguistics*, pages 2920–2930, Florence, Italy. Association for Computational Linguistics.

Stephan Oepen, Lilja Øvrelid, Jari Björne, Richard Johansson, Emanuele Lapponi, Filip Ginter, and Erik Velldal. 2017. The 2017 Shared Task on Extrinsic Parser Evaluation. Towards a reusable community infrastructure. In *Proceedings of the 2017 Shared Task on Extrinsic Parser Evaluation at the Fourth International Conference on Dependency Linguistics and the 15th International Conference on Parsing Technologies*, page 1 – 16, Pisa, Italy.

Woodley Packard, Emily M. Bender, Jonathon Read, Stephan Oepen, and Rebecca Dridan. 2014. Simple negation scope resolution through deep parsing: A semantic solution to a semantic problem. In *Proceedings of the 52nd Meeting of the Association for Computational Linguistics*, page 69 – 78, Baltimore, MD, USA.

Jeffrey Pennington, Richard Socher, and Christopher D. Manning. 2014. GloVe: Global Vectors for Word Representation. In *Empirical Methods in Natural Language Processing (EMNLP)*, pages 1532–1543.

Matthew E. Peters, Mark Neumann, Mohit Iyyer, Matt Gardner, Christopher Clark, Kenton Lee, and Luke Zettlemoyer. 2018. Deep contextualized word representations. In *Proc. of NAACL*.

Jonathon Read, Erik Velldal, Lilja Øvrelid, and Stephan Oepen. 2012. UiO1. Constituent-based discriminative ranking for negation resolution. In *Proceedings of the 1st Joint Conference on Lexical and Computational Semantics*, page 310 – 318, Montréal, Canada.

Sebastian Schuster, Éric Villemonte de la Clergerie, Marie Candito, Benoît Sagot, Christopher Manning, and Djamé Seddah. 2017. Paris and Stanford at EPE 2017: Downstream Evaluation of Graph-based Dependency Representations. In *EPE 2017 - The First Shared Task on Extrinsic Parser Evaluation*, pages 47–59.

Elena Sergeeva, Henghui Zhu, Amir Tahmasebi, and Peter Szolovits. 2019. Neural Token Representations and Negation and Speculation Scope Detection in Biomedical and General Domain Text. In *Proceedings of the Tenth International Workshop on Health Text Mining and Information Analysis (LOUHI 2019)*, pages 178–187, Hong Kong. Association for Computational Linguistics.

György Szarvas, Veronika Vincze, Richárd Farkas, and János Csirik. 2008. The BioScope corpus: Annotation for negation, uncertainty and their scope in biomedical texts. In *Proceedings of the Workshop on Current Trends in Biomedical Natural Language Processing*, pages 38–45, Columbus, Ohio. Association for Computational Linguistics.

Yuka Tateisi, Akane Yakushiji, Tomoko Ohta, and Jun'ichi Tsujii. 2005. Syntax Annotation for the GE-NIA Corpus. In *Companion Volume to the Proceedings of Conference Including Posters/Demos and Tutorial Abstracts*.

Ashish Vaswani, Noam Shazeer, Niki Parmar, Jakob Uszkoreit, Llion Jones, Aidan N. Gomez, Lukasz Kaiser, and Illia Polosukhin. 2017. Attention is all you need. In *NIPS*, pages 5998–6008.

Erik Velldal, Lilja Øvrelid, Jonathon Read, and Stephan Oepen. 2012. Speculation and negation: Rules, rankers, and the role of syntax. *Computational Linguistics*, 38(2):369–410.

Li Wan, Matthew Zeiler, Sixin Zhang, Yann LeCun, and Rob Fergus. 2013. Regularization of Neural Networks Using Dropconnect. In *Proceedings of the 30th International Conference on International Conference on Machine Learning - Volume 28*, ICML'13, pages III–1058–III–1066, Atlanta, GA, USA. JMLR.org.

Daniel Zeman, Jan Hajič, Martin Popel, Martin Potthast, Milan Straka, Filip Ginter, Joakim Nivre, and Slav Petrov. 2018. CoNLL 2018 Shared Task: Multilingual Parsing from Raw Text to Universal Dependencies. In *Proceedings of the CoNLL 2018 Shared Task: Multilingual Parsing from Raw Text to Universal Dependencies*, pages 1–21, Brussels, Belgium. Association for Computational Linguistics.

Integrating Graph-Based and Transition-Based Dependency Parsers in the Deep Contextualized Era

Agnieszka Falenska[1] and **Anders Björkelund**[2] and **Jonas Kuhn**[1]
[1] University of Stuttgart, Institute for Natural Language Processing
[2] Lund University, Department of Astronomy and Theoretical Physics
{falenska,jonas}@ims.uni-stuttgart.de
anders.bjorkelund@thep.lu.se

Abstract

Graph-based and transition-based dependency parsers used to have different strengths and weaknesses. Therefore, combining the outputs of parsers from both paradigms used to be the standard approach to improve or analyze their performance. However, with the recent adoption of deep contextualized word representations, the chief weakness of graph-based models, i.e., their limited scope of features, has been mitigated. Through two popular combination techniques – blending and stacking – we demonstrate that the remaining diversity in the parsing models is reduced below the level of models trained with different random seeds. Thus, an integration no longer leads to increased accuracy. When both parsers depend on BiLSTMs, the graph-based architecture has a consistent advantage. This advantage stems from globally-trained BiLSTM representations, which capture more distant look-ahead syntactic relations. Such representations can be exploited through multi-task learning, which improves the transition-based parser, especially on treebanks with a high ratio of right-headed dependencies.

1 Introduction

Dependency parsers can roughly be divided into two classes: graph-based (Eisner, 1996; McDonald et al., 2005) and transition-based (Yamada and Matsumoto, 2003; Nivre, 2003). The two paradigms differ in their approach to the trade-off between access to contextual features in the output dependency tree and exactness of search (McDonald and Nivre, 2007). The complementary strengths of those paradigms have given grounds to numerous *diversity-based* methods for integrating parsing models (Nivre and McDonald, 2008; Sagae and Lavie, 2006, among others). To date, the methods are commonly used for improving the accuracy of single parsers[1], achieving robust predictions for the silver-standard resource preparation (Schweitzer et al., 2018), or as analysis tools (de Lhoneux et al., 2019).

One of the most significant recent developments in dependency parsing is based on encoding rich sentential context into word representations, such as BiLSTM vectors (Hochreiter and Schmidhuber, 1997; Graves and Schmidhuber, 2005) and deep contextualized word embeddings (Peters et al., 2018; Devlin et al., 2019). Including these representations as features has set a new state of the art for both graph-based and transition-based parsers (Kiperwasser and Goldberg, 2016; Che et al., 2018). However, it also brought the two architectures closer. Kulmizev et al. (2019) showed that after including deep contextualized word embeddings, the average error profiles of graph- and transition-based parsers converge, potentially reducing gains from combining them. On the other hand, the authors also noticed that the underlying trade-off between the parsing paradigms is still visible in their results. Thus, it is an open question to what extent the differences between the parsing paradigms could still be leveraged.

In this paper, we fill the gaps left in understanding the behavior of transition- and graph-based dependency parsers that employ today's state-of-the-art deep contextualized representations. We start from the setting of Kulmizev et al. (2019), i.e., Kiperwasser and Goldberg's (2016) seminal transition-based and graph-based parsers extended with deep contextualized word embeddings. We show that, on average, the differences between BiLSTM-based graph-based and transition-based models are reduced below the level of different random seeds. Interestingly, the diversity needed for a successful integration vanishes al-

---

[1] See results from the CoNLL 2018 shared task on dependency parsing (Zeman et al., 2018)

Proceedings of the 16th International Conference on Parsing Technologies and the IWPT 2020 Shared Task, pages 25–39
Virtual Meeting, July 9, 2020. ©2020 Association for Computational Linguistics

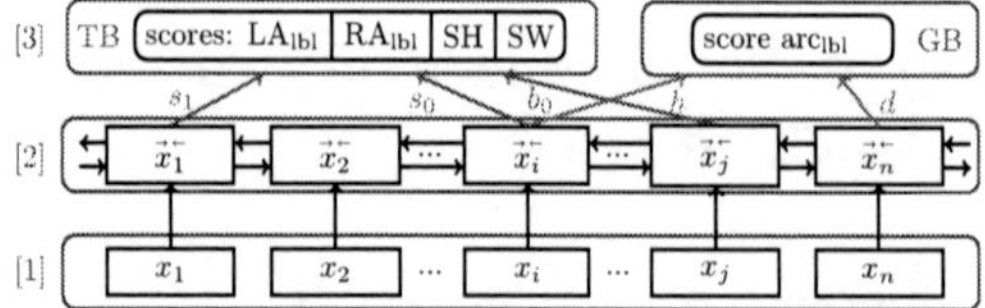

Figure 1: Architectures of BiLSTM-based dependency parsers employed in this work. Layers: [1] word representations, [2] BiLSTMs, [3] multi-layer perceptron.

ready with BiLSTM feature representations and does not change when deep contextualized embeddings are added.

We further consider treebank-specific differences between graph- and transition-based models. Through a set of carefully designed experiments, we show that our graph-based parser has an advantage when parsing treebanks with a high ratio of right-headed dependencies. This advantage comes from globally-trained BiLSTMs and can be exploited by the locally-trained transition-based parser through multi-task learning (Caruana, 1993). This combination improves the performance of the two parsing architectures and narrows the gap between them without requiring additional computational effort at parsing time.

2 Experimental Setup

2.1 Parsing Architecture

We re-implement the basic transition- and graph-based architectures proposed by Kiperwasser and Goldberg (2016) (denoted **K&G**) with a few changes outlined below. We follow Kulmizev et al. (2019) and intentionally abstain from extensions such as Dozat and Manning's (2016) attention layer to keep our experimental setup simple. This enables us to control for all relevant methodological aspects of the architectures. Our hypothesis is that adding more advanced mechanisms would resemble adding contextualized word embeddings, i.e., improve the overall performance but not change the picture regarding parser combination. However, testing this hypothesis is orthogonal to this work.

All the described parsers are implemented with the DyNet library (Neubig et al., 2017).[2] We provide details on used hyperparameters in Appendix A.

---

[2]The code is available for download on the first author's website.

Deep contextualized word representations. The two most popular models of deep contextualized representations are ELMo (Peters et al., 2018) and BERT (Devlin et al., 2019). Both models have been used with dependency parsers, either for multi-lingual applications (Kondratyuk and Straka, 2019; Schuster et al., 2019) or to improve parsing accuracy (Che et al., 2018; Jawahar et al., 2018; Lim et al., 2018). Recently, Kulmizev et al. (2019) analyzed the influence of both of the models on the K&G architecture and showed that they give similar results, BERT being slightly ahead. Since the scope of our experiments is to analyze the influence of contextualized embeddings on parser integration, and not to analyze differences between different embedding models, we use ELMo, which is more accessible.

ELMo representations encode words within the context of the entire sentence. The representations are built from a linear combination of several layers of BiLSTMs pre-trained on a task of language modeling:

$$\text{ELMo}(x_{1:n}, i) = \gamma \sum_{j=1}^{L} s_j \text{BiLSTM}_{LM}^{j}(x_{1:n}, i)$$

We use pre-trained ELMo models provided by Che et al. (2018) and train task-specific parameters s_j and γ together with the parser. The final representations are combinations of $L = 3$ layers and have dimensionality 1024.

Word representations. In both transition- and graph-based architectures input tokens are represented in the same way (see level [1] in Figure 1). For a given sentence with words $[w_1, \ldots, w_n]$ and part-of-speech (POS) tags $[t_1, \ldots, t_n]$ each word representation x_i is built from concatenating: embedding of the word, its POS tag, BiLSTM character-based embedding, and word's ELMo representation:

$$x_i = e(w_i) \circ e(t_i) \circ \text{BiLSTM}_{ch}(w_i) \circ \text{ELMo}(x_{1:n}, i)$$

Word embeddings are initialized with the pre-trained fastText vectors (Grave et al., 2018) and trained together with the model. The representations x_i are passed to the BiLSTM feature extractors (level [2]) and represented by a vector $\overrightarrow{x_i} = \text{BiLSTM}(x_{1:n}, i)$.

Transition-based parser. The part of the architecture that is specific to the transition-based

K&G parser is colored red in Figure 1. For every configuration consisting of a stack, buffer, and the current set of arcs, the parser builds a feature set of three items: the two top-most items of the stack and the first item on the buffer (denoted s_0, s_1, and b_0). Next, it concatenates their BiLSTM vectors and passes on to a multi-layer perceptron (MLP, level [3] in Figure 1). The MLP scores all possible transitions, and the highest-scoring one is applied to proceed to the next configuration.

Our implementation (denoted **TB**) uses the arc-standard transition system extended with the SWAP transition (Nivre, 2009) and can thus handle non-projective trees.[3] We use Nivre et al.'s (2009) lazy SWAP oracle for training. Labels are predicted together with the transitions.

For analysis, we also use variants of TB trained without BiLSTMs. In these cases, vectors x_i are passed directly to the MLP layer (similarly to Chen and Manning (2014)), and the implicit context encoded by the BiLSTMs is lost. We compensate for it by using Kiperwasser and Goldberg's (2016) *extended* feature set, which adds the embedding information of eight additional tokens in the structural context of the parser state.

Graph-based parser. The specific parts of the graph-based K&G parser are highlighted in blue in Figure 1. At parsing time, every pair of tokens $\langle x_i, x_j \rangle$ yields a feature set $\{\overset{\rightharpoonup}{x_i}, \overset{\rightharpoonup}{x_j}\}$. The BiLSTM representations are concatenated and passed to an MLP to compute the score for an arc $x_i \overset{lbl}{\longrightarrow} x_j$ for every possible dependency label lbl (unlike the original K&G implementation, we predict labels together with the arcs). To find the highest-scoring tree, we apply the Chu-Liu-Edmonds algorithm (Chu and Liu, 1965; Edmonds, 1967). We denote this architecture **GB**.

In experiments where GB is trained without BiLSTMs, we extend the feature set with surface features known from classic graph-based parsers, such as distance between head and dependent, and words at the distance of 1 and 2 from heads and dependents (McDonald et al., 2005).

<hr>

[3] We performed multiple experiments within the K&G architecture by differentiating transition-systems (e.g., removing SWAP, using the arc-hybrid system (Kuhlmann et al., 2011), and adding the dynamic oracle (Goldberg and Nivre, 2012, 2013)), graph-decoders (testing Eisner's (1996) algorithm), feature sets (also extended feature set from Kiperwasser and Goldberg (2016)), and word representations. In all the tested scenarios, the general picture was essentially the same. Therefore, we present results only for the best-performing configurations.

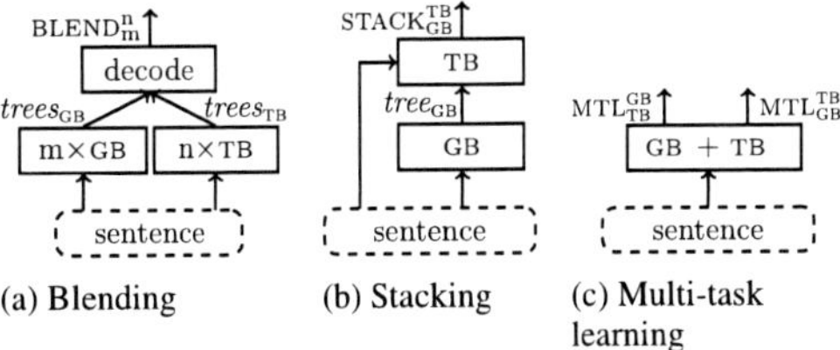

Figure 2: Schematic illustration of the integration methods used in this work.

2.2 Integration Methods

Parser combination approaches can be divided into two categories: methods that integrate base parsers at prediction time and training time. We use one well-established representative from each of the categories, i.e., blending and feature-based stacking, respectively. Additionally, for analysis purposes, we combine the two parsers through multi-task learning.

Blending (see Figure 2a), also known as re-parsing (Sagae and Lavie, 2006), is a parsing-time integration method. It consists of running basic models in separation and combining their outputs into one graph. Weights in this graph depend on how many basic models predicted a particular arc. Finally, a graph-based decoder is used to find the maximum spanning tree in the combined graph.

In our implementation, we use the Chu-Liu-Edmonds algorithm to find the final tree. For every resulting arc, we select the most frequent label across all the labels previously assigned to it. Blending needs at least three basic models to apply the voting scheme. Therefore, we follow Kuncoro et al. (2016) and train multiple instances of models with random seeds and denote **BLEND$_m^n$** a combination of $m{\times}$GB and $n{\times}$TB parsers. For analysis, we vary the ratio of TB and GB models while leaving the total number of models constant at 6 for a fair comparison.

Feature-based stacking (see Figure 2b) was introduced by Nivre and McDonald (2008) and Martins et al. (2008). It involves running two parsers in sequence so that the second (level-1) parser can use the output of the first (level-0) parser as features (denoted **STACK$_{level-0}^{level-1}$**).

To generate training data for the level-1 parser, we apply 10-fold cross-validation on the training sets with the level-0 parser. Then, we follow Ouchi et al. (2014) and extract stacking features from the level-0 parser's predictions in the form of supertags. More precisely, for every word w_i, we build its supertag by filling the template `label/hdir+hasLdep_hasRdep`, where `label` is the dependency relation, `hdir` denotes relative head direction, and `hasLdep/hasRdep` mark presence of left/right dependents. Such supertags are then, similarly to POS tags, represented as embeddings and concatenated with other representations to build x_i. The dimensionality and type of information encoded in the stacking representations were determined in exploratory experiments on the English development data and left unchanged for other languages.

Multi-task learning (see Figure 2c) allows combining the transition- and graph-based K&G parsers by sharing their BiLSTM representations (level [2] in Figure 1). We keep feature extraction and MLP layers separate, and do not enforce any agreement between the two decoders. Effectively this means that training yields two parsers that can be applied independently: one transition-based (denoted $\text{MTL}_{\text{GB}}^{\text{TB}}$) and one graph-based ($\text{MTL}_{\text{TB}}^{\text{GB}}$).

We use a straightforward MTL training protocol: for every sentence, we calculate the BiLSTM representations $\overrightarrow{x_i}$ and collect all local losses from both tasks (TB and GB). Then, the losses are summed and the model parameters are updated through backpropagation. We note in passing that this training protocol leaves many options for improvements, such as adding weights to losses from different tasks (Shi et al., 2017b), sharing representations on different levels of Bi-LSTMs (Søgaard and Goldberg, 2016), or employing stack-propagation (Zhang and Weiss, 2016). We abstain from such extensions as they are orthogonal to the central points of our analysis.

2.3 Data Sets and Preprocessing

We conduct experiments on a selection of thirteen treebanks from Universal Dependencies v2.4 (Nivre et al., 2019): Arabic (ar_padt), Basque (eu_bdt), Chinese (zh_gsd), English (en_ewt), Finnish (fi_tdt), Hebrew (he_htb), Hindi (hi_hdtb), Italian (it_isdt), Japanese (ja_gsd), Korean (ko_gsd), Russian (ru_syntagrus), Swedish (sv_talbanken), and Turkish (tr_imst). This selection was proposed by Kulmizev et al. (2019) and varies in terms of language family, domain, and amount of non-projective arcs.

We use automatically predicted universal POS tags in all the experiments. The tags are assigned using a CRF tagger (Mueller et al., 2013). We annotate the training sets via 5-fold jackknifing.

2.4 Evaluation and Analysis

We evaluate the experiments using Labeled Attachment Score (LAS).[4] We train models for 30 epochs and select the best model based on development LAS. For the results on the test sets, we follow Reimers and Gurevych's (2018) recommendation and report averages and standard deviations from six models trained with different random seeds. We test for significance using the Wilcoxon rank-sum test with p-value < 0.05.

An analysis is carried out on the development sets in order not to compromise the test sets. We follow Kulmizev et al. (2019) and sample the same number of sentences from every development set (484 sentences since this is the size of the smallest one). We then aggregate results from three models trained with different random seeds and present the combined results.

3 Diversity-Based Integration

We start by evaluating the two integration methods (STACK and BLEND) and applying them to our transition- and graph-based parsers (TB and GB).

Average results. The first column in Table 1 gives the average results. In the case of stacking, the performance of combined models is almost the same as that of the baseline models. Small improvements are noticeable for $\text{STACK}_{\text{GB}}^{\text{TB}}$ vs. TB, but they are statistically significant only for one treebank. Comparing $\text{STACK}_{\text{TB}}^{\text{GB}}$ vs. GB we even notice a small average drop of 0.08 LAS. In the case of blending, the method does provide big improvements over single baselines (BLEND_0^0 vs. TB and BLEND_0^0 vs. GB). However, those improvements are not coming from integrating different paradigms since BLEND_3^3 achieves the same average performance as BLEND_0^0, which uses only GB.

There are two possible explanations for lack of gains from integrating parsing paradigms: either (1) in general, the neural models are simply not capable of benefiting from such combination, or (2) feature representations based on the BiLSTMs and the deep contextualized representations bring the architectures too close to each other for the integration to be beneficial. In Section 4, we investigate which of those two situations takes place.

---

[4]The percentage of tokens that received the correct head and label.

	avg.	ar	en	eu	fi	he	hi	it	ja	ko	ru	sv	tr	zh
TB	84.60	82.59	86.61	79.96	86.75	85.57	91.00	90.61	93.47	82.17	90.30	86.52	63.94	80.27
STACK_{GB}^{TB}	84.72	82.59	86.72	80.35	$86.38^{\dagger}$	$85.94^{\dagger}$	91.19	90.83	93.32	81.95	90.60	86.65	64.18	80.71
GB	85.40	82.95	86.97	82.21	87.16	86.55	91.58	91.18	93.34	82.99	90.90	87.09	66.19	81.11
STACK_{TB}^{GB}	85.32	83.02	87.15	81.71	87.47	86.62	$91.32^{\dagger}$	91.22	93.39	82.62	90.83	86.97	66.03	80.80
BLEND_0^6	86.06	83.66	87.85	82.19	88.25	86.87	91.79	91.56	93.92	84.02	91.34	88.10	66.90	82.31
BLEND_6^0	86.63	84.09	87.95	83.98	88.35	87.68	92.16	91.93	93.97	84.41	91.80	88.49	68.52	82.83
BLEND_3^3	86.63	84.08	88.11	83.70	88.61	87.41	92.05	91.95	94.05	84.31	91.85	88.67	68.34	83.01

Table 1: Average (from six runs) parsing results (LAS) on test sets. † marks statistical significance compared to single model baselines (p-value < 0.05). Corresponding standard deviations are provided in Table 4 in Appendix A. Since blending already involves multiple models, we run it only once and do not test the results for significance.

Treebank-specific results. Next, we take a closer look at the treebank-specific accuracy. Comparing single baselines (TB vs. GB), we note that GB has a clear advantage over TB. It surpasses TB on twelve out of thirteen treebanks (all improvements are significant). We reproduce analysis from Kulmizev et al. (2019) and confirm that this advantage is consistent across arcs of different lengths, distances to root, and sentences with different sizes (we provide corresponding plots in Appendix A). Interestingly, the dominance of GB over TB significantly differs across treebanks and is especially prominent for more challenging ones, e.g., with small amounts of training data or a high level of non-projectivity. For instance, the largest difference of 2.25 LAS is visible for Basque, which is the treebank with the largest number of non-projective arcs, and Turkish, which has the smallest training dataset. Moreover, those are the treebanks where STACK_{GB}^{TB} offers small improvements (0.39 LAS and 0.24 LAS, respectively), but both STACK_{TB}^{GB} and BLEND_3^3 cannot make use of the diversity in predictions of the two models and cause the accuracy to drop (comparing STACK_{TB}^{GB} vs. GB and BLEND_3^3 vs. BLEND_0^0). In the case of non-neural parsers, a big gap between the performance of a strong graph-based model and a greedy transition-based model does not prevent the former to learn from the latter (Faleńska et al., 2015). Therefore, the questions arise where those treebank-specific differences come from and why integration methods cannot benefit from them. We address these questions in Section 5.

4 Parsing Architectures and Diversity

In this section, we investigate which aspects of the K&G architecture are responsible for no gains from the integration. For this purpose, we run ablation experiments and apply blending and stacking on models trained with and without BiLSTMs and with and without ELMo representations.

4.1 Feature-based Stacking

We perform stacking with different types of level-0 information. Apart from the standard way, in which TB is stacked on top of GB or vice versa (denoted O; for other) we carry out two types of control experiments: S (for self), where we stack a model on itself, and G (for gold), where gold-standard trees are used as level-0 predictions.

Oracle experiments. Figure 3a displays results for stacking with different level-0 information. We immediately see that scenario G, in which models are stacked on gold-standard trees, exhibits almost perfect performance. Regardless of the level-1 parser and employment of BiLSTMs and ELMo, all models achieve accuracy higher than 95 LAS, proving that they are capable of learning from the stacking representations.

Influence of representations. Next, we consider the models which were trained without BiLSTMs and ELMo (left, lightest bars). Surprisingly, for both TB (green) and GB (blue), small improvements can be noticed in the self-application scenario S, which was not the case for non-neural models (Martins et al., 2008; Faleńska et al., 2015). One explanation for this is the diversity of the models coming with random seeds, which was less prominent in their non-neural versions (Reimers and Gurevych, 2017). However, clearer improvements are visible in scenario O, which combines models of different types. Both STACK_{GB}^{TB} and STACK_{TB}^{GB} surpass both of the single baselines, proving that integration is beneficial when BiLSTMs and ELMo are not used.

Considering the case where BiLSTMs are included (middle) changes the picture. Self-

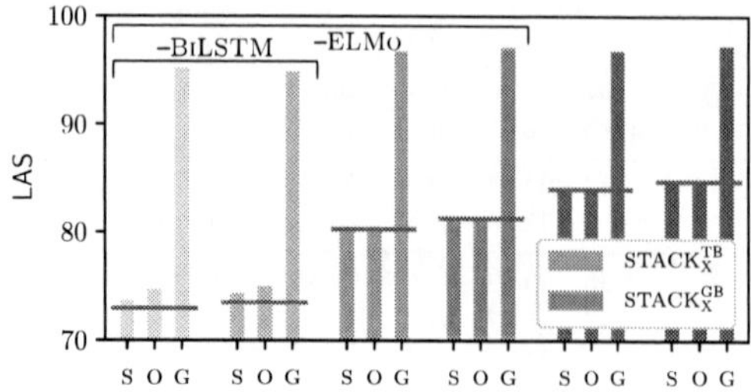

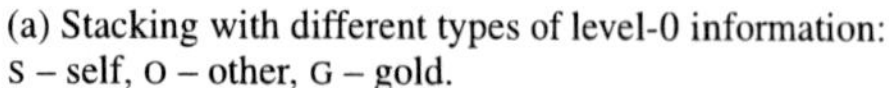

(a) Stacking with different types of level-0 information: S – self, O – other, G – gold.

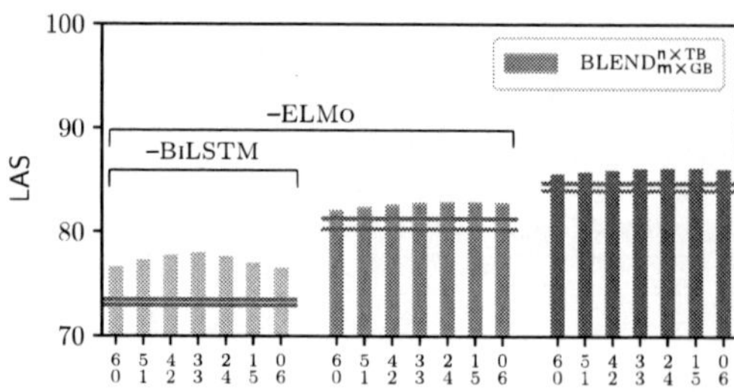

(b) Blending; top line – GB single model, bottom line – TB single model.

Figure 3: Parsing accuracy (average LAS over thirteen treebanks on dev sets) for diversity-based integration methods when models are trained with or without BiLSTMs and with or without ELMo. Red lines mark the average LAS of the single baseline models.

application behaves almost on par with stacking the parsers on each other. The only modest improvement (amounting to 0.18 LAS on average) occurs for STACK_{GB}^{TB}, but it is not enough to surpass a single GB baseline.

As expected, adding ELMo (right, darkest bars) results in big improvements comparing to the models without these representations. However, those improvements do not impact stacking results, and the picture regarding the integration of the architectures stays the same.

4.2 Blending

Figure 3b presents results for blending with different ratios of TB and GB. We start by analyzing models trained without BiLSTMs and ELMo (left). We can observe a pattern we would expect from diverse models: (1) blending always improves over the baselines (signified by red lines); (2) combining models only of one sort (BLEND_6^0 or BLEND_0^6) yields lower scores than when we introduce more diversity into the combination; (3) the best result is obtained by BLEND_3^3, where the same number of TB and GB models is used.

For the models that use BiLSTMs (middle), the gains coming from blending are smaller. For example, BLEND_0^6 improves TB by 1.84 LAS, whereas the corresponding improvement when no BiLSTMs are used is 3.67 LAS. Interestingly, the models show a different pattern when it comes to diversity within the combination. The accuracy of the blend increases with the number of GB models. Although BLEND_4^2 achieves the highest accuracy, it surpasses BLEND_0^6 by only 0.05 LAS. This suggests that TB models do not bring enough diversity into the combination, and the accuracy of BLEND is mostly influenced by GB models.

Finally, for models that use ELMo (right), improvements over baselines are slightly smaller – BLEND_6^0 improves GB by 1.34 LAS comparing to 1.59 LAS when no ELMo is used. However, the picture regarding diversity is the same, and overall performance depends on the number of GB models and not the diversity among combined paradigms.

To conclude, we showed that the performance of TB and GB models can be improved through the traditional diversity-based approaches as long as no BiLSTMs are used. Otherwise, the gains from combination methods decrease considerably. Adding ELMo representations improves the performance of both of the models but has almost no impact on the outcome of the integration.

5 Representations and Treebank-Specific Diversity

In the previous section, we saw that BiLSTMs mitigate average benefits from integration methods. One explanation might be that when both TB and GB use the same feature representations, the diversity between them is much smaller, thus reducing the gains the models could draw from each other. However, when comparing treebank-specific results in Table 1, we noticed that in specific cases the two baselines differ considerably. We now investigate where do those differences come from and if they could be beneficial.

5.1 Representation Analysis

First, we take a closer look at information encoded in representations learned by the transition- and graph-based models.

IMPACT metric. We follow Gaddy et al. (2018) and use derivatives to estimate how sensitive a par-

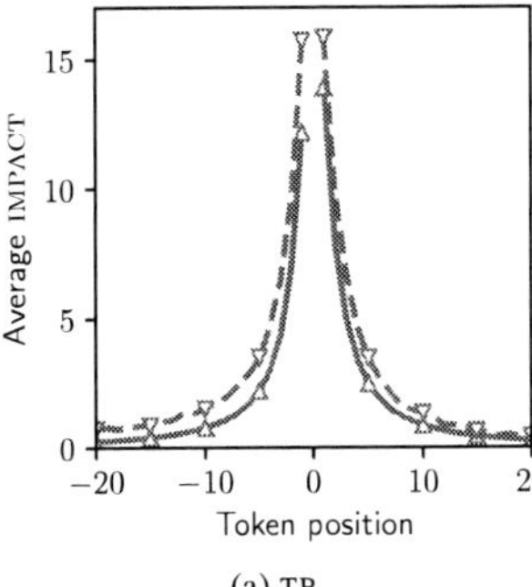
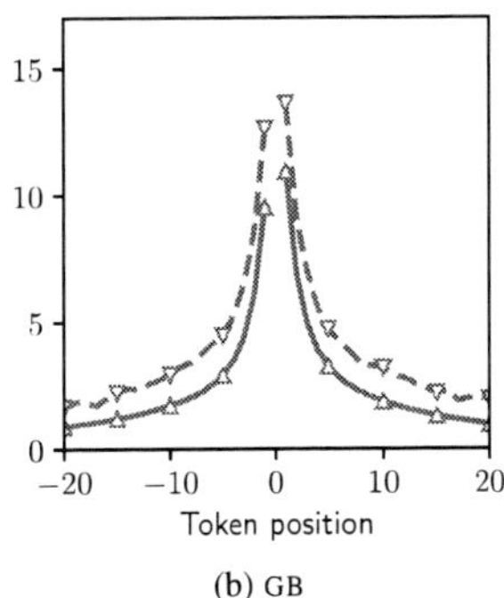
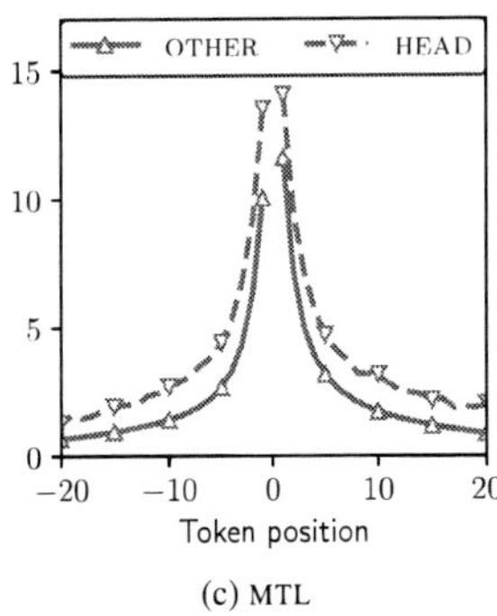

Figure 4: The average IMPACT of tokens on BiLSTM vectors with respect to the token position and the structural (gold-standard) relation between them (heads vs. non-heads of the analyzed vector).

ticular part of the architecture is with respect to changes in input. Specifically, we use our metric IMPACT from Falenska and Kuhn (2019) that measures how every BiLSTM representation $\overrightarrow{x_i}\overleftarrow{}$ is influenced by every word representation x_j from the sentence. Intuitively, IMPACT can be thought of as a percentage distributed over all words of the sentence – the higher the percentage of x_j the more it influenced the representation of $\overrightarrow{x_i}\overleftarrow{}$.

For every sentence from the development set and every vector $\overrightarrow{x_i}\overleftarrow{}$ we calculate IMPACT values of all words x_j on $\overrightarrow{x_i}\overleftarrow{}$ and bucket those values according to the distance between j and i. Figure 4 shows the average impact of tokens at particular positions. We see the same two general patterns as Gaddy et al. (2018): (1) closer words have larger effects on the representations, and (2) even words 15 or more positions away influence the vectors.

Transition-based parser. For representations trained with TB (Figure 4a) the difference in signals coming from heads and other tokens is bigger on the left side than on the right side (see, e.g., positions −15 and 15). de Lhoneux et al. (2019) provided an explanation for this and showed that for greedy *locally-trained* models, the forward LSTMs could be interpreted as rich history-based features while the backward LSTMs could be thought of as look-ahead features. Since the information to the right mostly (i.e., except for the buffer front) comes from backward LSTMs, it contains, as in the case of standard look-ahead features, less structural relations.

Graph-based parser. Representations trained together with GB (Figure 4b) show a slightly different pattern. Compared to TB, the impact of heads is smaller for tokens closeby, but it deterio-

rates slower. Since this model is *globally*-trained, the influence of heads does not depend on the side – the plot is almost symmetrical, suggesting that representations encode as much information about syntactic relations on the left as on the right.

5.2 BiLSTMs Integration

Next, we investigate whether the observed differences in the information encoded in BiLSTM representations can explain the advantage of GB over TB. We train new models where we share those intermediate representations between the two parsers through multi-task learning (MTL). We hypothesize that if the advantage of GB stems from global training and the influence it has on the representations, then MTL will re-balance the representations and, as a result, narrow the gap between the two models. We note in passing that MTL is typically carried out on different tasks, often with different training sets. However, it is perfectly possible to consider graph-based and transition-based dependency parsing as two separate tasks trained on the same training set.

IMPACT analysis. Figure 4c displays the IMPACT statistics for MTL models. The plot shows that the BiLSTM representations draw on the advantages from both locally trained TB and globally-trained GB – the distribution has a slightly stronger peak for closer words as in TB, but flattens out more slowly as in GB. This effect is particularly pronounced when comparing the far right (look-ahead) of TB with the MTL distribution, especially as heads become more influential.

Error analysis. To understand how the changes in representations influence the parsing performance, we break down the LAS by dependency

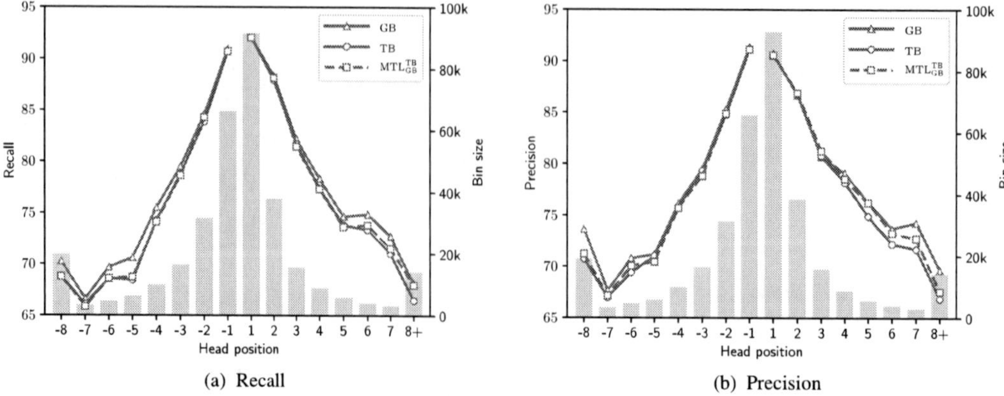

(a) Recall   (b) Precision

Figure 5: Dependency recall and precision relative to the head position on development sets.

length and head direction. Figure 5 shows the dependency recall and precision of models with respect to the positions of the heads.[5]

First, we compare TB (blue) with GB (green) and observe that GB has a consistent advantage. However, when comparing recall and precision, we note an interesting difference. In terms of recall (Figure 5a), the plot is symmetrical and the advantage of GB is roughly the same for heads on the left and on the right side of the token. In terms of precision (Figure 5b), both TB and GB behave identically for heads on the left, but the performance of TB drops faster for heads on positions 3 and more to the right.

Second, we analyze $\mathrm{MTL}_{\mathrm{GB}}^{\mathrm{TB}}$ (red). We notice that sharing representations with GB does not influence TB's recall or precision on heads on the left, while for right-headed dependencies precision improves. The model catches up with GB's performance and starts deteriorating much later, for heads on positions 6 and more to the right.

Treebank-specific improvements. Finally, we look at the treebank-specific accuracy of the MTL models. The two bottom rows in Table 2 show the effects of MTL on GB. Sharing representations between the two architectures has a small influence on GB, and on average, improves its performance by 0.18 LAS. Although for few treebanks bigger improvements can be seen, e.g., Chinese (0.39 LAS) or Swedish (0.35 LAS), none of them is statistically significant. Therefore, it is not clear

if those improvements come from the actual combination of different parsing paradigms, or MTL in this case acts as additional regularization, ultimately reducing overfitting during training.

In the case of TB, the average performance is improved through MTL by 0.42 LAS, with statistically significant differences for four treebanks. The biggest gains are visible for the treebanks, where the difference between TB and GB is greatest, such as Basque (0.94 LAS). Interestingly, among the treebanks with the biggest improvements, we can notice Turkish (1.28 LAS) and Chinese (0.52 LAS), which are the two treebanks with the greatest ratio of right-headed arcs (62.58% and 71.86%, respectively). This result is in line with the results of de Lhoneux et al. (2019), who demonstrated that backward LSTMs are especially important for head-final languages.

To conclude, we saw that the advantage of GB over TB stems from global training. The training increases the impact of tokens (far) to the right as compared to a locally trained TB model and translates into an improved prediction of right-headed dependencies. Thus, the distance between the two models is treebank-related and can be reduced through integration methods such as MTL, especially when parsing more challenging treebanks.

6   Related Work

Traditional integration of dependency parsers. Classical integration methods were initially introduced to take advantage of differences in the strengths of the component parsers. Such differences were usually the result of different parsing paradigms, as in the case of feature-based stack-

---

[5]Dependency recall is defined as the percentage of correct predictions among gold standard arcs with head position p. Precision is the percentage of correct predictions among all predicted arcs. The definitions slightly differ from McDonald and Nivre (2007), who looked at absolute arc lengths.

	avg.	ar	en	eu	fi	he	hi	it	ja	ko	ru	sv	tr	zh
TB	84.60	82.59	86.61	79.96	86.75	85.57	91.00	90.61	93.47	82.17	90.30	86.52	63.94	80.27
$\text{MTL}_{\text{GB}}^{\text{TB}}$	85.02	82.55	86.97	$80.90^\dagger$	87.09	85.90	$91.29^\dagger$	90.97	93.45	82.36	90.58	$87.16^\dagger$	$65.22^\dagger$	80.79
GB	85.40	82.95	86.97	82.21	87.16	86.55	91.58	91.18	93.34	82.99	90.90	87.09	66.19	81.11
$\text{MTL}_{\text{TB}}^{\text{GB}}$	85.58	82.99	$87.24^\dagger$	82.55	87.52	86.68	91.71	91.31	93.47	83.12	91.11	87.44	65.88	81.50

Table 2: Average (from six runs) parsing results (LAS) on test sets. † marks statistical significance compared to single model baselines (p-value < 0.05). Corresponding standard deviations are provided in Table 5 in Appendix A.

ing, blending, or beam search-based transition-based parsers with features strongly inspired by graph-based models (Zhang and Clark, 2008; Bohnet and Kuhn, 2012). However, combining parsers that process input left-to-right and right-to-left (Hall et al., 2007; Attardi and Dell'Orletta, 2009), or even parsers and sequence labelers (Faleńska et al., 2015), was also proposed. Blending was usually applied to a mixture of graph-based and transition-based left-to-right and right-to-left parsers (Sagae and Lavie, 2006; Surdeanu and Manning, 2010; Björkelund et al., 2017, among others). Moreover, in the case of stacking, integrating two parsers of the same type gives at most minor improvements (Martins et al., 2008).

Neural-specific ensemble dependency parsers. Since neural network training can be sensitive to initialization (Reimers and Gurevych, 2017), recent ensemble dependency parsers are rather combining models trained with different random seeds than different paradigms. For example, out of 24 teams participating in the CoNLL 2018 Shared Task on dependency parsing (Zeman et al., 2018), five employed ensemble techniques. However, all of them took advantage of either diversity coming from random seeds or different languages.

Neural parsers of the same type can be combined by taking the sum of their MLP scores (Che et al., 2017), averaging softmax scores (Che et al., 2018), or through re-parsing (Kuncoro et al., 2016). The last authors also showed that such an ensemble could be distilled into a single graph-based parser. Finally, Shi et al. (2017b) used MTL in a similar way to ours. They shared BiLSTMs between three parsers to speed up their training time. However, all the models where globally-trained and the authors did not evaluate if the combination improved their performance.

7 Discussion and Conclusion

In this paper, we investigated the recent advances in dependency parsing from the perspective of the traditional integration methods. These methods are known for exploiting diversity in the strengths and weaknesses of transition- and graph-based parsing paradigms. We found out that when models use BiLSTMs, such diversity is on the level of different random seeds. Adding deep contextualized representations on top of BiLSTMs improves the performance of both parsers but does not change the picture regarding the integration.

Rich-feature sets used to be the advantage of the transition-based parsers. Now that the parsers do not need structural features (Falenska and Kuhn, 2019), the graph-based parsers have an advantage that the locally-trained transition-based parsers cannot make up for. Therefore, improving parsers through combination methods is not as straightforward as it used to be. Such a combination has to take into consideration the specificity of the treebank and depend on whether accuracy or parsing time is the priority. The greatest gains in accuracy can be obtained by blending multiple graph-based models. However, the method comes with the cumbersome overhead of running multiple predictors at application time. When speed is essential and the accuracy can be sacrificed (Gómez-Rodríguez et al., 2017) greedy transition-based parsers or even sequence labelers are the preferable choices (Strzyz et al., 2019). In such cases, alternative integration approaches such as multi-task learning can boost the performance of locally-trained models without requiring additional computational effort at parsing time.

Introduction of BiLSTMs into dependency parsers had another consequence, i.e., it enabled the use of exact search algorithms for transition-based parsers (Shi et al., 2017a; Gómez-Rodríguez et al., 2018). Therefore, it is an interesting question if the error profiles of such parsers are even less distinguishable from the graph-based outputs. We leave this question for future work.

Acknowledgments

This work was in part supported by the Deutsche Forschungsgemeinschaft (DFG) via the SFB 732, project D8. Anders Björkelund was funded by AIR Lund Chest pain (VR; grant no 2019-00198). We would like to thank the anonymous reviewers for their comments. We also thank our colleagues Özlem Çetinoğlu and Xiang Yu for many conversations and comments on this work.

References

Giuseppe Attardi and Felice Dell'Orletta. 2009. Reverse Revision and Linear Tree Combination for Dependency Parsing. In *Proceedings of Human Language Technologies: The 2009 Annual Conference of the North American Chapter of the Association for Computational Linguistics, Companion Volume: Short Papers*, pages 261–264, Boulder, Colorado. Association for Computational Linguistics.

Anders Björkelund, Agnieszka Falenska, Xiang Yu, and Jonas Kuhn. 2017. IMS at the CoNLL 2017 UD Shared Task: CRFs and Perceptrons Meet Neural Networks. In *Proceedings of the CoNLL 2017 Shared Task: Multilingual Parsing from Raw Text to Universal Dependencies*, pages 40–51, Vancouver, Canada. Association for Computational Linguistics.

Bernd Bohnet and Jonas Kuhn. 2012. The Best of Both Worlds – A Graph-based Completion Model for Transition-based Parsers. In *Proceedings of the 13th Conference of the European Chapter of the Association for Computational Linguistics*, pages 77–87, Avignon, France. Association for Computational Linguistics.

Richard Caruana. 1993. Multitask Learning: A Knowledge-Based Source of Inductive Bias. In *Proceedings of the Tenth International Conference on Machine Learning*, pages 41–48. Morgan Kaufmann.

Wanxiang Che, Jiang Guo, Yuxuan Wang, Bo Zheng, Huaipeng Zhao, Yang Liu, Dechuan Teng, and Ting Liu. 2017. The HIT-SCIR System for End-to-End Parsing of Universal Dependencies. In *Proceedings of the CoNLL 2017 Shared Task: Multilingual Parsing from Raw Text to Universal Dependencies*, pages 52–62, Vancouver, Canada. Association for Computational Linguistics.

Wanxiang Che, Yijia Liu, Yuxuan Wang, Bo Zheng, and Ting Liu. 2018. Towards Better UD Parsing: Deep Contextualized Word Embeddings, Ensemble, and Treebank Concatenation. In *Proceedings of the CoNLL 2018 Shared Task: Multilingual Parsing from Raw Text to Universal Dependencies*, pages 55–64, Brussels, Belgium. Association for Computational Linguistics.

Danqi Chen and Christopher Manning. 2014. A Fast and Accurate Dependency Parser using Neural Networks. In *Proceedings of the 2014 Conference on Empirical Methods in Natural Language Processing (EMNLP)*, pages 740–750. Association for Computational Linguistics.

Yoeng-Jin Chu and Tseng-Hong Liu. 1965. On shortest arborescence of a directed graph. *Scientia Sinica*, 14(10):1396–1400.

Jacob Devlin, Ming-Wei Chang, Kenton Lee, and Kristina Toutanova. 2019. BERT: Pre-training of deep bidirectional transformers for language understanding. In *Proceedings of the 2019 Conference of the North American Chapter of the Association for Computational Linguistics: Human Language Technologies, Volume 1 (Long and Short Papers)*, pages 4171–4186, Minneapolis, Minnesota. Association for Computational Linguistics.

Timothy Dozat and Christopher D. Manning. 2016. Deep Biaffine Attention for Neural Dependency Parsing. *CoRR*, abs/1611.01734.

Jack Edmonds. 1967. Optimum branchings. *Journal of Research of the National Bureau of Standards B*, 71(4):233–240.

Jason M. Eisner. 1996. Three New Probabilistic Models for Dependency Parsing: An Exploration. In *COLING 1996 Volume 1: The 16th International Conference on Computational Linguistics*.

Agnieszka Faleńska, Anders Björkelund, Özlem Çetinoğlu, and Wolfgang Seeker. 2015. Stacking or Supertagging for Dependency Parsing – What's the Difference? In *Proceedings of the 14th International Conference on Parsing Technologies*, pages 118–129, Bilbao, Spain. Association for Computational Linguistics.

Agnieszka Falenska and Jonas Kuhn. 2019. The (Non-)Utility of Structural Features in BiLSTM-based Dependency Parsers. In *Proceedings of the 57th Annual Meeting of the Association for Computational Linguistics*, pages 117–128, Florence, Italy. Association for Computational Linguistics.

David Gaddy, Mitchell Stern, and Dan Klein. 2018. What's Going On in Neural Constituency Parsers? An Analysis. In *Proceedings of the 2018 Conference of the North American Chapter of the Association for Computational Linguistics: Human Language Technologies, Volume 1 (Long Papers)*, pages 999–1010. Association for Computational Linguistics.

Yoav Goldberg and Joakim Nivre. 2012. A Dynamic Oracle for Arc-Eager Dependency Parsing. In *Proceedings of COLING 2012*, pages 959–976, Mumbai, India. The COLING 2012 Organizing Committee.

Yoav Goldberg and Joakim Nivre. 2013. Training Deterministic Parsers with Non-Deterministic Oracles. *Transactions of the Association for Computational Linguistics*, 1:403–414.

Carlos Gómez-Rodríguez, Iago Alonso-Alonso, and David Vilares. 2017. How Important is Syntactic Parsing Accuracy? An Empirical Evaluation on Rule-Based Sentiment Analysis. *Artificial Intelligence Review*, pages 1–17.

Carlos Gómez-Rodríguez, Tianze Shi, and Lillian Lee. 2018. Global Transition-based Non-projective Dependency Parsing. In *Proceedings of the 56th Annual Meeting of the Association for Computational Linguistics (Volume 1: Long Papers)*, pages 2664–2675, Melbourne, Australia. Association for Computational Linguistics.

Edouard Grave, Piotr Bojanowski, Prakhar Gupta, Armand Joulin, and Tomas Mikolov. 2018. Learning Word Vectors for 157 Languages. In *Proceedings of the Eleventh International Conference on Language Resources and Evaluation (LREC 2018)*, Miyazaki, Japan. European Language Resources Association (ELRA).

Alex Graves and Jürgen Schmidhuber. 2005. Framewise Phoneme Classification with Bidirectional LSTM and Other Neural Network Architectures. *Neural Networks*, 18(5):602–610.

Johan Hall, Jens Nilsson, Joakim Nivre, Gülsen Eryigit, Beáta Megyesi, Mattias Nilsson, and Markus Saers. 2007. Single Malt or Blended? A Study in Multilingual Parser Optimization. In *Proceedings of the CoNLL Shared Task Session of EMNLP-C oNLL 2007*, pages 933–939, Prague, Czech Republic. Association for Computational Linguistics.

Sepp Hochreiter and Jürgen Schmidhuber. 1997. Long short-term memory. *Neural computation*, 9(8):1735–1780.

Ganesh Jawahar, Benjamin Muller, Amal Fethi, Louis Martin, Éric Villemonte de la Clergerie, Benoît Sagot, and Djamé Seddah. 2018. ELMoLex: Connecting ELMo and Lexicon Features for Dependency Parsing. In *Proceedings of the CoNLL 2018 Shared Task: Multilingual Parsing from Raw Text to Universal Dependencies*, pages 223–237, Brussels, Belgium. Association for Computational Linguistics.

Eliyahu Kiperwasser and Yoav Goldberg. 2016. Simple and Accurate Dependency Parsing Using Bidirectional LSTM Feature Representations. *Transactions of the Association for Computational Linguistics*, 4:313–327.

Dan Kondratyuk and Milan Straka. 2019. 75 Languages, 1 Model: Parsing Universal Dependencies Universally. In *Proceedings of the 2019 Conference on Empirical Methods in Natural Language Processing and the 9th International Joint Conference on Natural Language Processing (EMNLP-IJCNLP)*, pages 2779–2795, Hong Kong, China. Association for Computational Linguistics.

Marco Kuhlmann, Carlos Gómez-Rodríguez, and Giorgio Satta. 2011. Dynamic programming algorithms for transition-based dependency parsers. In *Proceedings of the 49th Annual Meeting of the Association for Computational Linguistics: Human Language Technologies*, pages 673–682, Portland, Oregon, USA. Association for Computational Linguistics.

Artur Kulmizev, Miryam de Lhoneux, Johannes Gontrum, Elena Fano, and Joakim Nivre. 2019. Deep Contextualized Word Embeddings in Transition-Based and Graph-Based Dependency Parsing - A Tale of Two Parsers Revisited. In *Proceedings of the 2019 Conference on Empirical Methods in Natural Language Processing and the 9th International Joint Conference on Natural Language Processing (EMNLP-IJCNLP)*, pages 2755–2768, Hong Kong, China. Association for Computational Linguistics.

Adhiguna Kuncoro, Miguel Ballesteros, Lingpeng Kong, Chris Dyer, and Noah A. Smith. 2016. Distilling an Ensemble of Greedy Dependency Parsers into One MST Parser. In *Proceedings of the 2016 Conference on Empirical Methods in Natural Language Processing*, pages 1744–1753, Austin, Texas. Association for Computational Linguistics.

Miryam de Lhoneux, Miguel Ballesteros, and Joakim Nivre. 2019. "Recursive Subtree Composition in LSTM-Based Dependency Parsing". In *Proceedings of the 2019 Conference of the North American Chapter of the Association for Computational Linguistics: Human Language Technologies, Volume 1 (Long and Short Papers)*, pages 1566–1576, Minneapolis, Minnesota. Association for Computational Linguistics.

KyungTae Lim, Cheoneum Park, Changki Lee, and Thierry Poibeau. 2018. SEx BiST: A Multi-Source Trainable Parser with Deep Contextualized Lexical Representations. In *Proceedings of the CoNLL 2018 Shared Task: Multilingual Parsing from Raw Text to Universal Dependencies*, pages 143–152, Brussels, Belgium. Association for Computational Linguistics.

André Filipe Torres Martins, Dipanjan Das, Noah A. Smith, and Eric P. Xing. 2008. Stacking Dependency Parsers. In *Proceedings of the 2008 Conference on Empirical Methods in Natural Language Processing*, pages 157–166, Honolulu, Hawaii. Association for Computational Linguistics.

Ryan McDonald, Koby Crammer, and Fernando Pereira. 2005. Online Large-Margin Training of Dependency Parsers. In *Proceedings of the 43rd Annual Meeting of the Association for Computational Linguistics (ACL'05)*, pages 91–98. Association for Computational Linguistics.

Ryan McDonald and Joakim Nivre. 2007. Characterizing the Errors of Data-Driven Dependency Parsing Models. In *Proceedings of the 2007 Joint Conference on Empirical Methods in Natural Language Processing and Computational Natural Language Learning (EMNLP-CoNLL)*, pages 122–131, Prague, Czech Republic. Association for Computational Linguistics.

Thomas Mueller, Helmut Schmid, and Hinrich Schütze. 2013. Efficient Higher-Order CRFs for Morphological Tagging. In *Proceedings of the 2013 Conference on Empirical Methods in Natural Language Processing*, pages 322–332. Association for Computational Linguistics.

Graham Neubig, Chris Dyer, Yoav Goldberg, Austin Matthews, Waleed Ammar, Antonios Anastasopoulos, Miguel Ballesteros, David Chiang, Daniel Clothiaux, Trevor Cohn, Kevin Duh, Manaal Faruqui, Cynthia Gan, Dan Garrette, Yangfeng Ji, Lingpeng Kong, Adhiguna Kuncoro, Gaurav Kumar, Chaitanya Malaviya, Paul Michel, Yusuke Oda, Matthew Richardson, Naomi Saphra, Swabha Swayamdipta, and Pengcheng Yin. 2017. DyNet: The Dynamic Neural Network Toolkit. *CoRR*, abs/1701.03980.

Joakim Nivre. 2003. An Efficient Algorithm for Projective Dependency Parsing. In *Proceedings of the Eighth International Workshop on Parsing Technologies (IWPT*, pages 149–160, Nancy, France.

Joakim Nivre. 2009. Non-Projective Dependency Parsing in Expected Linear Time. In *Proceedings of the Joint Conference of the 47th Annual Meeting of the ACL and the 4th International Joint Conference on Natural Language Processing of the AFNLP*, pages 351–359. Association for Computational Linguistics.

Joakim Nivre, Mitchell Abrams, Željko Agić, et al. 2019. Universal Dependencies 2.4. LINDAT/CLARIN digital library at the Institute of Formal and Applied Linguistics (ÚFAL), Faculty of Mathematics and Physics, Charles University.

Joakim Nivre, Marco Kuhlmann, and Johan Hall. 2009. An Improved Oracle for Dependency Parsing with Online Reordering. In *Proceedings of the 11th International Conference on Parsing Technologies (IWPT'09)*, pages 73–76. Association for Computational Linguistics.

Joakim Nivre and Ryan McDonald. 2008. Integrating Graph-Based and Transition-Based Dependency Parsers. In *Proceedings of ACL-08: HLT*, pages 950–958, Columbus, Ohio. Association for Computational Linguistics.

Hiroki Ouchi, Kevin Duh, and Yuji Matsumoto. 2014. Improving Dependency Parsers with Supertags. In *Proceedings of the 14th Conference of the European Chapter of the Association for Computational Linguistics, volume 2: Short Papers*, pages 154–158, Gothenburg, Sweden. Association for Computational Linguistics.

Matthew Peters, Mark Neumann, Mohit Iyyer, Matt Gardner, Christopher Clark, Kenton Lee, and Luke Zettlemoyer. 2018. Deep Contextualized Word Representations. In *Proceedings of the 2018 Conference of the North American Chapter of the Association for Computational Linguistics: Human Language Technologies, Volume 1 (Long Papers)*, pages 2227–2237, New Orleans, Louisiana. Association for Computational Linguistics.

Nils Reimers and Iryna Gurevych. 2017. Reporting Score Distributions Makes a Difference: Performance Study of LSTM-networks for Sequence Tagging. In *Proceedings of the 2017 Conference on Empirical Methods in Natural Language Processing*, pages 338–348, Copenhagen, Denmark. Association for Computational Linguistics.

Nils Reimers and Iryna Gurevych. 2018. Why Comparing Single Performance Scores Does Not Allow to Draw Conclusions About Machine Learning Approaches. *CoRR*, abs/1803.09578.

Kenji Sagae and Alon Lavie. 2006. Parser Combination by Reparsing. In *Proceedings of the Human Language Technology Conference of the NAACL, Companion Volume: Short Papers*, pages 129–132, New York City, USA. Association for Computational Linguistics.

Tal Schuster, Ori Ram, Regina Barzilay, and Amir Globerson. 2019. Cross-Lingual Alignment of Contextual Word Embeddings, with Applications to Zero-shot Dependency Parsing. In *Proceedings of the 2019 Conference of the North American Chapter of the Association for Computational Linguistics: Human Language Technologies, Volume 1 (Long and Short Papers)*, pages 1599–1613, Minneapolis, Minnesota. Association for Computational Linguistics.

Katrin Schweitzer, Kerstin Eckart, Markus Gärtner, Agnieszka Falenska, Arndt Riester, Ina Rösiger, Antje Schweitzer, Sabrina Stehwien, and Jonas Kuhn. 2018. German Radio Interviews: The GRAIN Release of the SFB732 Silver Standard Collection. In *Proceedings of the Eleventh International Conference on Language Resources and Evaluation (LREC 2018)*, Miyazaki, Japan. European Language Resources Association (ELRA).

Tianze Shi, Liang Huang, and Lillian Lee. 2017a. Fast(er) Exact Decoding and Global Training for Transition-Based Dependency Parsing via a Minimal Feature Set. In *Proceedings of the 2017 Conference on Empirical Methods in Natural Language Processing*, pages 12–23. Association for Computational Linguistics.

Tianze Shi, Felix G. Wu, Xilun Chen, and Yao Cheng. 2017b. Combining Global Models for Parsing Universal Dependencies. In *Proceedings of the CoNLL*

2017 Shared Task: Multilingual Parsing from Raw Text to Universal Dependencies, pages 31–39, Vancouver, Canada. Association for Computational Linguistics.

Anders Søgaard and Yoav Goldberg. 2016. Deep multi-task learning with low level tasks supervised at lower layers. In *Proceedings of the 54th Annual Meeting of the Association for Computational Linguistics (Volume 2: Short Papers)*, pages 231–235, Berlin, Germany. Association for Computational Linguistics.

Michalina Strzyz, David Vilares, and Carlos Gómez-Rodríguez. 2019. Viable Dependency Parsing as Sequence Labeling. In *Proceedings of the 2019 Conference of the North American Chapter of the Association for Computational Linguistics: Human Language Technologies, Volume 1 (Long and Short Papers)*, pages 717–723, Minneapolis, Minnesota. Association for Computational Linguistics.

Mihai Surdeanu and Christopher D. Manning. 2010. Ensemble Models for Dependency Parsing: Cheap and Good? In *Human Language Technologies: The 2010 Annual Conference of the North American Chapter of the Association for Computational Linguistics*, pages 649–652, Los Angeles, California. Association for Computational Linguistics.

Hiroyasu Yamada and Yuji Matsumoto. 2003. Statistical Dependency Analysis with Support Vector Machines. In *Proceedings of the Eighth International Conference on Parsing Technologies*, pages 195–206, Nancy, France.

Daniel Zeman, Jan Hajič, Martin Popel, Martin Potthast, Milan Straka, Filip Ginter, Joakim Nivre, and Slav Petrov. 2018. CoNLL 2018 Shared Task: Multilingual Parsing from Raw Text to Universal Dependencies. In *Proceedings of the CoNLL 2018 Shared Task: Multilingual Parsing from Raw Text to Universal Dependencies*, pages 1–21, Brussels, Belgium. Association for Computational Linguistics.

Yuan Zhang and David Weiss. 2016. Stack-propagation: Improved Representation Learning for Syntax. In *Proceedings of the 54th Annual Meeting of the Association for Computational Linguistics (Volume 1: Long Papers)*, pages 1557–1566, Berlin, Germany. Association for Computational Linguistics.

Yue Zhang and Stephen Clark. 2008. A Tale of Two Parsers: Investigating and Combining Graph-based and Transition-based Dependency Parsing. In *Proceedings of the 2008 Conference on Empirical Methods in Natural Language Processing*, pages 562–571, Honolulu, Hawaii. Association for Computational Linguistics.

A Appendix

Word embedding dimension	300
POS tag embedding dimension	20
Character embedding dimension	24
Supertag embedding dimension	30
ELMo representation dimension	1024
Hidden units in MLP	100
BiLSTM layers	2
BiLSTM dimensions	125
BiLSTM dropout	0.33
Character-based BiLSTM dimensions	100
α for word dropout	0.25
Trainer	Adam
Non-lin function	tanh

Table 3: Hyperparameters for the parsers.

	ar	en	eu	fi	he	hi	it	ja	ko	ru	sv	tr	zh
TB	0.089	0.184	0.297	0.162	0.250	0.169	0.201	0.213	0.432	0.116	0.153	0.571	0.495
STACK$_{GB}^{TB}$	0.145	0.180	0.212	0.176	0.136	0.093	0.136	0.158	0.288	0.042	0.209	0.406	0.200
GB	0.159	0.166	0.314	0.216	0.226	0.130	0.159	0.108	0.414	0.064	0.174	0.280	0.261
STACK$_{TB}^{GB}$	0.131	0.143	0.234	0.105	0.339	0.116	0.067	0.105	0.234	0.056	0.171	0.459	0.351

Table 4: Standard deviation for results in Table 1.

	ar	en	eu	fi	he	hi	it	ja	ko	ru	sv	tr	zh
TB	0.089	0.184	0.297	0.162	0.250	0.169	0.201	0.213	0.432	0.116	0.153	0.571	0.495
MTL$_{GB}^{TB}$	0.249	0.144	0.325	0.385	0.368	0.134	0.409	0.167	0.239	0.078	0.167	0.336	0.604
GB	0.159	0.166	0.314	0.216	0.226	0.130	0.159	0.108	0.414	0.064	0.174	0.280	0.261
MTL$_{TB}^{GB}$	0.225	0.058	0.170	0.237	0.356	0.081	0.298	0.157	0.319	0.087	0.152	0.290	0.425

Table 5: Standard deviation for results in Table 2.

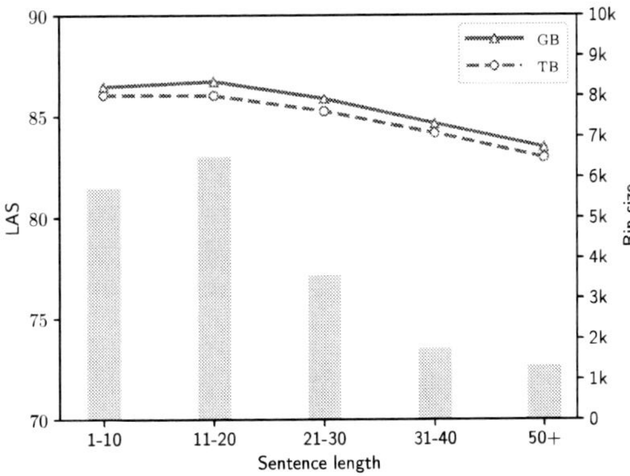

Figure 6: Average LAS relative to sentence length on development sets.

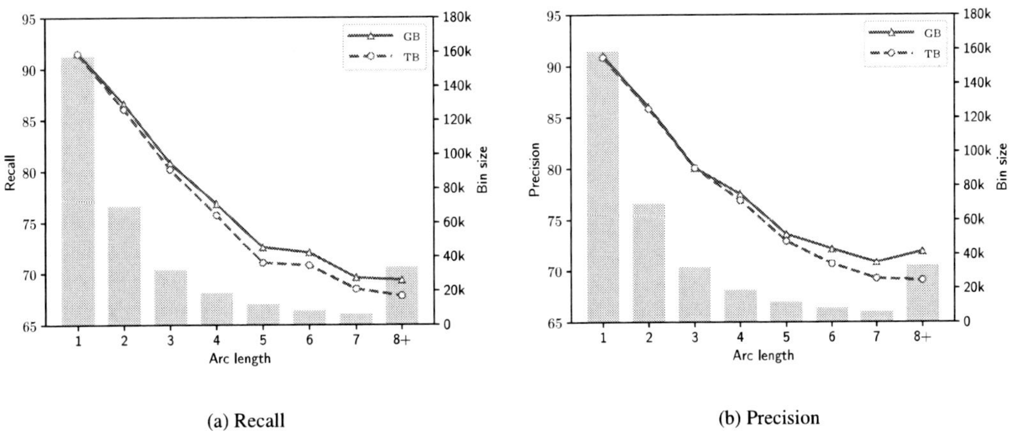

(a) Recall

(b) Precision

Figure 7: The dependency recall and precision relative to arc length on development sets.

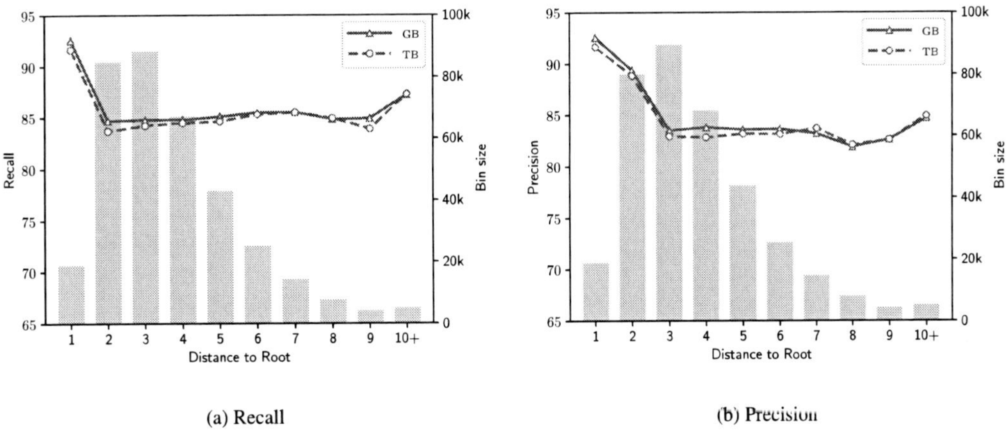

(a) Recall

(b) Precision

Figure 8: The dependency recall and precision relative to the distance to root on development sets.

39

Semi-supervised Parsing with Variational Autoencoding Parser

Xiao Zhang
Department of Computer Science
Purdue University
zhang923@purdue.edu

Dan Goldwasser
Department of Computer Science
Purdue University
dgoldwas@purdue.edu

Abstract

We propose an end-to-end variational autoencoding parsing (VAP) model for semi-supervised graph-based projective dependency parsing. It encodes the input using continuous latent variables in a sequential manner by deep neural networks (DNN) that can utilize the contextual information, and reconstruct the input using a generative model. The VAP model admits a unified structure with different loss functions for labeled and unlabeled data with shared parameters. We conducted experiments on the WSJ data sets, showing the proposed model can use the unlabeled data to increase the performance on a limited amount of labeled data, on a par with a recently proposed semi-supervised parser with faster inference.

1 Introduction

Dependency parsing captures bi-lexical relationships by constructing directional arcs between words, defining a head-modifier syntactic structure for sentences, as shown in Figure 1. Dependency trees are fundamental for many downstream tasks such as semantic parsing (Reddy et al., 2016; Marcheggiani and Titov, 2017), machine translation (Bastings et al., 2017; Ding and Palmer, 2007), information extraction (Culotta and Sorensen, 2004; Liu et al., 2015) and question answering (Cui et al., 2005). Recently, efficient parsers (Kiperwasser and Goldberg, 2016; Dozat and Manning, 2017; Dozat et al., 2017; Ma et al., 2018) have been developed using various neural architectures.

While supervised approaches have been very successful, they require large amounts of labeled data, particularly when neural architectures are used, which usually are over-parameterized. Syntactic annotation is notoriously difficult and requires specialized linguistic expertise, posing a serious challenge for low-resource languages. Semi-supervised

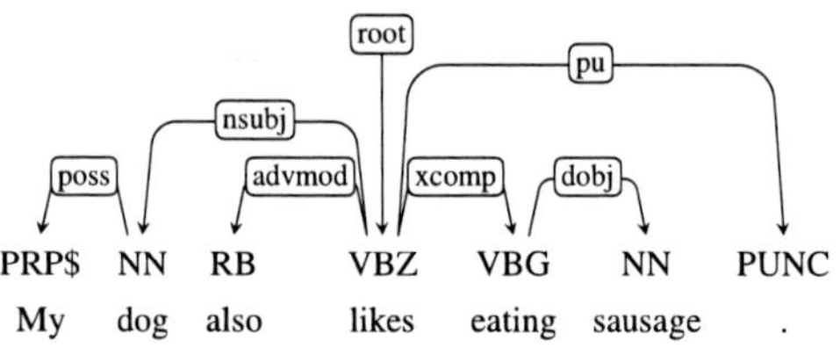

Figure 1: A dependency tree: directional arcs represent head-modifier relation between words.

parsing aims to alleviate this problem by combining a small amount of labeled data and a large amount of unlabeled data, to improve parsing performance on using labeled data alone. Traditional semi-supervised parsers use unlabeled data to generate additional features in order to assist the learning process (Koo et al., 2008), together with different variants of self-training (Søgaard, 2010). However, these approaches are usually pipe-lined and error-propagation may occur.

In this paper, we propose Variational Autoencoding Parser, or VAP, extends the idea of VAE, illustrated in Figure 3. The VAP model uses unlabeled examples to learn continuous latent variables of the sentence, which can be used to support tree inference by providing an enriched representation.

We summarize our contributions as follows:

1. We proposed a Variational Autoencoding Parser (VAP) for semi-supervised dependency parsing;
2. We designed a unified loss function for the proposed parser to deal with both labeled and unlabeled data.
3. We show improved performance of the proposed model with unlabeled data on the WSJ data sets, and the performance is on a par with a recently proposed semi-supervised parser (Corro and Titov, 2019), with faster inference.

2 Related Work

Most dependency parsing studies fall into two major groups: graph-based and transition-based

Proceedings of the 16th International Conference on Parsing Technologies and the IWPT 2020 Shared Task, pages 40–47
Virtual Meeting, July 9, 2020. ©2020 Association for Computational Linguistics

(Kubler et al., 2009). Graph-based parsers (McDonald, 2006) regard parsing as a structured prediction problem to find the most probable tree, while transition-based parsers (Nivre, 2004, 2008) treat parsing as a sequence of actions at different stages leading to a dependency tree.

While earlier works relied on manual feature engineering, in recent years the hand-crafted features were replaced by embeddings and deep neural network architectures were used to learn representation for scoring structural decisions, leading to improved performance in both graph-based and transition-based parsing (Nivre, 2014; Pei et al., 2015; Chen and Manning, 2014; Dyer et al., 2015; Weiss et al., 2015; Andor et al., 2016; Kiperwasser and Goldberg, 2016; Wiseman and Rush, 2016).

The annotation difficulty for this task, has also motivated work on unsupervised (grammar induction) and semi-supervised approaches to parsing (Tu and Honavar, 2012; Jiang et al., 2016; Koo et al., 2008; Li et al., 2014; Kiperwasser and Goldberg, 2015; Cai et al., 2017; Corro and Titov, 2019). It also leads to advances in using unlabeled data for constituent grammar (Shen et al., 2018b,a)

Similar to other structured prediction tasks, directly optimizing the objective is difficult when the underlying probabilistic model requires marginalizing over the dependency trees. Variational approaches are a natural way to alleviate this difficulty, as they try to improve the lower bound of the original objective, and have been applied in several recent NLP works (Stratos, 2019; Chen et al., 2018; Kim et al., 2019b,a). Variational Autoencoder (VAE) (Kingma and Welling, 2014) is particularly useful for latent representation learning, and has been studied in semi-supervised context as the Conditional VAE (CVAE) (Sohn et al., 2015). Note our work differs from VAE as VAE is designed for tabular data but not for structured prediction, as the input towards VAP is the sequence of sentential tokens and the output is the dependency tree.

3 Graph-based Dependency Parsing

A dependency graph of a sentence can be regarded as a directed tree spanning all the words of the sentence, including a special "word"–the ROOT– to originate out. Assuming a sentence of length l, a dependency tree can be denoted as $\mathcal{T} = (< h_1, m_1 >, \ldots, < h_{l-1}, m_{l-1} >)$, where h_t is the index in the sequence of the head word of the dependency connecting the tth word m_t as a modifier.

Our graph-based VAP parser is constructed based on the following standard structured prediction paradigm (McDonald et al., 2005; Taskar et al., 2005). In inference, based on the scoring function $\mathcal{S}_\Lambda$ with parameter Λ, the parsing problem is formulated as finding the most probable directed spanning tree for a given sentence x:

$$\mathcal{T}^* = \arg\max_{\tilde{\mathcal{T}} \in \mathbb{T}} \mathcal{S}_\Lambda(x, \tilde{\mathcal{T}}),$$

where $\mathcal{T}^*$ is the highest scoring parse tree and $\mathbb{T}$ is the set of all valid trees for the sentence x.

It is common to factorize the score of the entire graph into the summation of its substructures–the individual arc scores (McDonald et al., 2005):

$$\mathcal{S}_\Lambda(x, \tilde{\mathcal{T}}) = \sum_{(h,m) \in \tilde{\mathcal{T}}} s_\Lambda(h, m) = \sum_{t=1}^{l} s_\Lambda(h_t, m_t),$$

where $\tilde{\mathcal{T}}$ represents the candidate parse tree, and s_Λ is a function scoring individual arcs. $s_\Lambda(h, m)$ describes the likelihood of an arc from the head h to its modifier m in the tree. Throughout this paper, the scoring is based on individual arcs, as we focus on *first-order* parsing.

3.1 Scoring Function Using Neural Architecture

We used the same neural architecture as that in Kiperwasser and Goldberg (2016)'s study. We first use a bi-LSTM model to take as input $u_t = [p_t; e_t]$ at position t to incorporate contextual information, by feeding the word embedding e_t concatenated with the POS tag embeddings p_t of each word. The bi-LSTM then projects u_t as o_t.

Subsequently a nonlinear transformation is applied on these projections. Suppose the hidden states generated by the bi-LSTM are $[o_{root}, o_1, o_2, \ldots, o_t, \ldots, o_l]$, for a sentence of length l, we compute the arc scores by introducing parameters W_h, W_m, w and b, and transform them as follows:

$$r_t^{h-arc} = W_h o_t; \quad r_t^{m-arc} = W_m o_t,$$
$$s_\Lambda(h, m) = w^\intercal(\tanh(r_h^{h-arc} + r_m^{m-arc} + b)).$$

In this formulation, we first use two parameters to extract two different representations that carry two different types of information: a head seeking for its modifier (h-arc) and a modifier seeking for its head (m-arc). Then a nonlinear function maps them to an arc score.

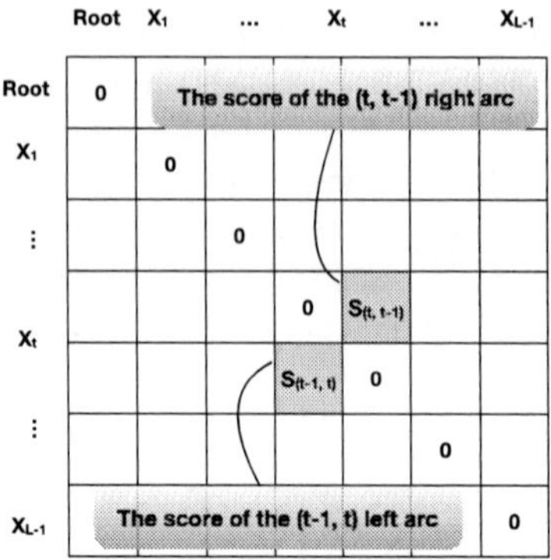

Figure 2: In this illustration of the arc scoring matrix, each entry represents the $(h(head) \rightarrow m(modifier))$ score.

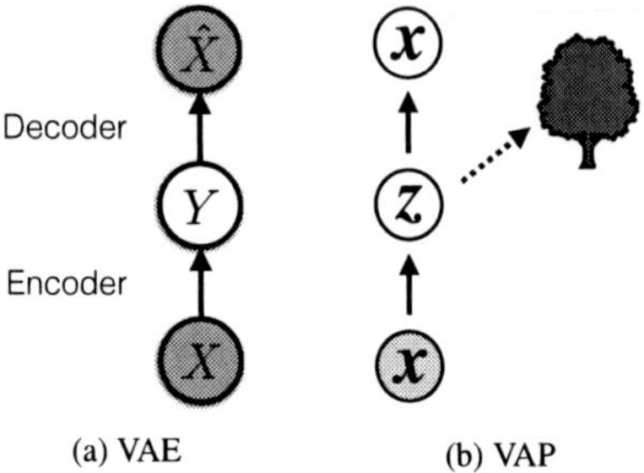

Figure 3: Illustration of variational autoencoder (VAE)(left) and variational autoencoding parser (VAP)(right).

For a single sentence, we can form a scoring matrix as shown in Figure 2, by filling each entry in the matrix using the score we obtained. Therefore, the scoring matrix is used to represent the head-modifier arc score for all the possible arcs connecting two tokens in a sentence (Zheng, 2017). Using this scoring arc matrix, we build our graph-based parser.

4 Variational Autoencoding Parser

VAP (illustrated in Figure 3b) is a semi-supervised parser able to make use of unlabeled data in addition to labeled data, extending the idea of variational autoencoder (VAE, illustrated in Figure 3a) to dependency parsing.

VAP learns, using both labeled and unlabeled data, a continuous latent variables representation, designed to support the parsing task by creating contextualized token-representations that capture properties of the full sentence. Typically, each token in the sentence is represented by its latent variable z_t, which is a high-dimensional Gaussian variable, to be aggregated as a group of latent variables z. This configuration ensures the continuous latent variable retains the contextual information from lower-level neural models to assist finding its head or its modifier; as well as forcing the representation of similar tokens to be closer. The latent variable group z is modeled via $P(z|x)$. In addition, we model the process of reconstructing the input sentence from the latent variable through a generative story $P(x|z)$.

We adjust the original VAE setup in our semi-supervised task by considering examples with labels, similar to recent conditional variational formulations (Sohn et al., 2015; Miao and Blunsom, 2016; Zhou and Neubig, 2017). We propose a full probabilistic model for a given sentence x, with the unified objective to maximize for both supervised and unsupervised parsing as follows:

$$\mathcal{J} = \log P_\theta(x)P_\omega^\epsilon(\mathcal{T}|x), \quad \epsilon = \begin{cases} 1, & \text{if } \mathcal{T} \text{ exists,} \\ 0, & \text{otherwise.} \end{cases}$$

This objective can be interpreted as follows: if the training example has a golden tree $\mathcal{T}$ with it, then the objective is the log joint probability $P_{\theta,\omega}(\mathcal{T},x)$; if the golden tree is missing, then the objective is the log marginal probability $P_\theta(x)$. The probability of a certain tree is modeled by a tree-CRF with parameters ω as $P_\omega(\mathcal{T}|x)$. Given the assumed generative process $P_\theta(x|z)$, directly optimizing this objective is intractable, thus instead we optimize its Evidence Lower BOund (ELBO):

$$\mathcal{J}_{lap} = \underset{z \sim Q_\phi(z|x)}{\mathbb{E}} \left[\log P_\theta(x|z)\right] \\ - \mathbb{KL}(Q_\phi(z|x)||P_\theta(z)) \\ + \epsilon \underset{z \sim Q_\phi(z|x)}{\mathbb{E}} \left[\log P_\omega(\mathcal{T}|z)\right].$$

We show $\mathcal{J}_{lap}$ is the ELBO of J in the appendix A.1.

In practice, similar as VAE-style models, $\underset{z \sim Q_\phi(z|x)}{\mathbb{E}} \left[\log P_\theta(x|z)\right]$ is approximated by $\frac{1}{N}\sum_{j=1}^{N} \log P_\theta(x|z_j)$ and $\underset{z \sim Q_\phi(z|x)}{\mathbb{E}} \left[\log P_\omega(\mathcal{T}|z)\right]$ by $\frac{1}{N}\sum_{j=1}^{N} \log P_\omega(\mathcal{T}|z_j)$, where z_j is the j-th sample of N samples sampled from $Q_\phi(z|x)$. At prediction stage, we simply use μ_z rather than sampling z.

4.1 Incorporating POS and External Embeddings

In previous studies (Chen and Manning, 2014; Dozat and Manning, 2017; Dozat et al., 2017;

Kiperwasser and Goldberg, 2016) exploring parsing using neural architectures, POS tags and external embeddings have been shown to contain important information characterizing the dependency relationship between a head and a child. Therefore, in addition to the variational autoencoding framework taking as input the randomly initialized word embeddings, optionally we can build the same structure for POS to reconstruct tags and for external embeddings to reconstruct words as well, whose variational objectives are $\mathcal{U}_p$ and $\mathcal{U}_e$ respectively. Hence, the final variational objective can be a combination of three: $\mathcal{U} = \mathcal{U}_w$(The original $\mathcal{U}$ in Lemma A.1)$+\mathcal{U}_p+\mathcal{U}_e$ (or just $\mathcal{U} = \mathcal{U}_w + \mathcal{U}_p$ if external embeddings are not used).

5 Experiments

5.1 Experimental Settings

Data sets We compared our models' performance with strong baselines on the WSJ data set, which is the Stanford Dependency conversion (De Marneffe and Manning, 2008) of the Penn Treebank (Marcus et al., 1993). We used the standard section split: 2-21 for training, 22 for development and 23 for testing.

To simulate the low-resource language environment, we used 10% of the whole training set as the annotated, and the rest 90% as the unlabeled.

Input Representation and Architecture We describe the details of the architecture as follows: The internal word embeddings have dimension 100 and the POS embeddings have dimension 25. The hidden layer of the bi-LSTM layer is of dimension 125. The nonlinear layers used to form the head and the modifier representation both have 100 dimension. We also used separate bi-LSTMs for words and POSs.

Training In the training phase, we usedd Adam (Kingma and Ba, 2014) to learn all the parameters in the VAP model. We did not take efforts to tune models' hyper-parameters and they remained the same across all the experiments. To preventing over-fitting, we applied the "early stop" strategy by using the development set.

5.2 Semi-Supervised Dependency Parsing on WSJ Data Set

We evaluated our VAP model on the WSJ data set and compared the model performance with other semi-supervised parsing models, including CRFAE (Cai et al., 2017), which is originally designed for dependency grammar induction but can be adopted for semi-supervised parsing, and "differentiable Perturb-and-Parse" parser (DPPP) (Corro and Titov, 2019). To contextualize the results, we also experiment with the supervised neural margin-based parser (NMP) (Kiperwasser and Goldberg, 2016), neural tree-CRF parser (NTP) and the supervised version of VAP, with only the labeled data. To ensure a fair comparison, our experimental set up on the WSJ is identical as that in DPPP, using the same 100 dimension skip-gram word embeddings employed in an earlier transition-based system (Dyer et al., 2015). We show our experimental results in Table 1.

Model	UAS
DPPP(L)	88.79
DPPP(L+U)	**89.50**
CRFAE(L+U)	82.34
NMP(L)	89.64
NTP (L)	89.63
Self-training (L+U)	87.81
VAP (L)	89.37
VAP (L+U)	**89.49**

Table 1: This table compares the model performance on the WSJ data set with 10% labeled data. "L" means only 10% labeled data is used, while "L+U" means both 10% labeled and 90% unlabeled data are used.

As shown in this table, our VAP model is able to utilize the unlabeled data to improve the overall performance on that with only using labeled data alone. Our VAP model performs slightly worse than the NMP model, which we attribute to the increased model complexity by incorporating extra encoder and decoders to deal with the latent variable. However, our VAP model achieved comparable results on semi-supervised parsing as the DPPP model, while our VAP model is simple and straightforward without inferencing the parse tree if it is unknown. Instead, the DPPP model has to apply Monte Carlo sampling from the posterior of the structure by using a "GUMBEL-MAX trick" to approximate the categorical distribution at each step, which is intensively computationally expensive, in order to form a dependency tree of high probability. Self-training using NMP with both labeled and unlabeled data is also included as a base-line, where the performance is deteriorated without appropriately using the unlabeled data.

6 Conclusion

In this study, we presented Variational Autoencoding Parser (VAP), an end-to-end parser, capable of utilizing the unlabeled data together with labeled data to improve the parsing performance, without any external resources. The proposed VAP model performs on a par with a recently published (Corro and Titov, 2019) semi-supervised parsing system on the WSJ data set, with faster inference, showing its potential for low-resource languages.

References

Daniel Andor, Chris Alberti, David Weiss, Aliaksei Severyn, Alessandro Presta, Kuzman Ganchev, Slav Petrov, and Michael Collins. 2016. Globally normalized transition-based neural networks. In *Proc. of the Annual Meeting of the Association Computational Linguistics (ACL)*.

Joost Bastings, Ivan Titov, Wilker Aziz, Diego Marcheggiani, and Khalil Simaan. 2017. Graph Convolutional Encoders for Syntax-aware Neural Machine Translation. In *Proc. of the Conference on Empirical Methods for Natural Language Processing (EMNLP)*.

Samuel R Bowman, Luke Vilnis, Oriol Vinyals, Andrew M Dai, Rafal Jozefowicz, and Samy Bengio. 2016. Generating Sentences from a Continuous Space. In *Proc. of the International Conference on Learning Representation (ICLR)*.

Jiong Cai, Yong Jiang, and Kewei Tu. 2017. CRF Autoencoder for Unsupervised Dependency Parsing. In *Proc. of the Conference on Empirical Methods for Natural Language Processing (EMNLP)*.

Danqi Chen and Christopher D Manning. 2014. A fast and accurate dependency parser using neural networks. In *Proc. of the Conference on Empirical Methods for Natural Language Processing (EMNLP)*.

Mingda Chen, Qingming Tang, Karen Livescu, and Kevin Gimpel. 2018. Variational sequential labelers for semi-supervised learning. In *Proc. of the Conference on Empirical Methods for Natural Language Processing (EMNLP)*.

Caio Corro and Ivan Titov. 2019. Differentiable Perturb-and-Parse: Semi-Supervised Parsing with a Structured Variational Autoencoder. In *Proc. of the International Conference on Learning Representation (ICLR)*.

Hang Cui, Renxu Sun, Keya Li, Min-Yen Kan, and Tat-Seng Chua. 2005. Question Answering Passage Retrieval Using Dependency Relations. In *Proc. of the International Conference on Research and Development in Information Retrieval (SIGIR)*.

Aron Culotta and Jeffrey Sorensen. 2004. Dependency tree kernels for relation extraction. In *Proc. of the Annual Meeting of the Association Computational Linguistics (ACL)*.

Marie-Catherine De Marneffe and Christopher D Manning. 2008. The Stanford typed dependencies representation. In *Proc. of the International Conference on Computational Linguistics (COLING)*.

Yuan Ding and Martha Palmer. 2007. Machine translation using probabilistic synchronous dependency insertion grammars. In *Proc. of the Annual Meeting of the Association Computational Linguistics (ACL)*.

Timothy Dozat and Christopher D. Manning. 2017. Deep biaffine attention for neural dependency parsing. In *Proc. of the International Conference on Learning Representation (ICLR)*.

Timothy Dozat, Peng Qi, and Christopher D. Manning. 2017. Stanford's graph-based neural dependency parser at the conll 2017 shared task. In *Proceedings of the CoNLL 2017 Shared Task: Multilingual Parsing from Raw Text to Universal Dependencies*.

Chris Dyer, Miguel Ballesteros, Wang Ling, Austin Matthews, and Noah A. Smith. 2015. Transition-Based Dependency Parsing with Stack Long Short-Term Memory. In *Proc. of the Annual Meeting of the Association Computational Linguistics (ACL)*.

Yong Jiang, Wenjuan Han, and Kewei Tu. 2016. Unsupervised Neural Dependency Parsing. In *Proc. of the Conference on Empirical Methods for Natural Language Processing (EMNLP)*.

Yoon Kim, Chris Dyer, and Alexander Rush. 2019a. Compound probabilistic context-free grammars for grammar induction. In *Proc. of the Annual Meeting of the Association Computational Linguistics (ACL)*.

Yoon Kim, Alexander Rush, Lei Yu, Adhiguna Kuncoro, Chris Dyer, and Gábor Melis. 2019b. Unsupervised recurrent neural network grammars. In *Proc. of the Annual Meeting of the North American Association of Computational Linguistics (NAACL)*.

Diederik P. Kingma and Jimmy Ba. 2014. Adam: A Method for Stochastic Optimization. *ArXiv*.

Diederik P Kingma and Max Welling. 2014. Auto-Encoding Variational Bayes. In *Proc. of the International Conference on Learning Representation (ICLR)*.

Eliyahu Kiperwasser and Yoav Goldberg. 2015. Semi-supervised dependency parsing using bilexical contextual features from auto-parsed data. In *Proc. of the Conference on Empirical Methods for Natural Language Processing (EMNLP)*.

Eliyahu Kiperwasser and Yoav Goldberg. 2016. Simple and accurate dependency parsing using bidirectional lstm feature representations. *Transactions of the Association for Computational Linguistics (TACL)*.

Terry Koo, Xavier Carreras, and Michael Collins. 2008. Simple Semi-supervised Dependency Parsing. In *Proc. of the Annual Meeting of the Association Computational Linguistics (ACL)*.

Sandra Kubler, Ryan McDonald, Joakim Nivre, and Graeme Hirst. 2009. *Dependency Parsing*. Morgan and Claypool Publishers.

Zhenghua Li, Min Zhang, and Wenliang Chen. 2014. Ambiguity-aware ensemble training for semi-supervised dependency parsing. In *Proc. of the Annual Meeting of the Association Computational Linguistics (ACL)*.

Yang Liu, Furu Wei, Sujian Li, Heng Ji, Ming Zhou, and Houfeng Wang. 2015. A Dependency-Based Neural Network for Relation Classification. In *Proc. of the Annual Meeting of the Association Computational Linguistics (ACL)*.

Xuezhe Ma, Zecong Hu, Jingzhou Liu, Nanyun Peng, Graham Neubig, and Eduard Hovy. 2018. Stack-Pointer Networks for Dependency Parsing. In *Proc. of the Annual Meeting of the Association Computational Linguistics (ACL)*. Association for Computational Linguistics.

Diego Marcheggiani and Ivan Titov. 2017. Encoding Sentences with Graph Convolutional Networks for Semantic Role Labeling. In *Proc. of the Conference on Empirical Methods for Natural Language Processing (EMNLP)*.

Mitchell P Marcus, Mary Ann Marcinkiewicz, and Beatrice Santorini. 1993. Building a large annotated corpus of English: the penn treebank. *Computational Linguistics*.

Ryan McDonald. 2006. *Discriminative learning and spanning tree algorithms for dependency parsing*. Ph.D. thesis, University of Pennsylvania.

Ryan McDonald, Koby Crammer, and Fernando Pereira. 2005. Online large-margin training of dependency parsers. In *Proc. of the Annual Meeting of the Association Computational Linguistics (ACL)*.

Yishu Miao and Phil Blunsom. 2016. Language as a latent variable: Discrete generative models for sentence compression. In *Proc. of the Conference on Empirical Methods for Natural Language Processing (EMNLP)*.

Joakim Nivre. 2004. Incrementality in deterministic dependency parsing. In *Proceedings of the Workshop on Incremental Parsing: Bringing Engineering and Cognition Together*.

Joakim Nivre. 2008. Algorithms for deterministic incremental dependency parsing. *Computational Linguistics*.

Joakim Nivre. 2014. The inside-outside recursive neural network model for dependency parsing. In *Proc. of the Conference on Empirical Methods for Natural Language Processing (EMNLP)*.

Wenzhe Pei, Tao Ge, and Baobao Chang. 2015. An effective neural network model for graph-based dependency parsing. In *Proc. of the Annual Meeting of the Association Computational Linguistics (ACL)*.

Siva Reddy, Oscar Tackstrom, Michael Collins, Tom Kwiatkowski, Dipanjan Das, Mark Steedman, and Mirella Lapata. 2016. Transforming Dependency Structures to Logical Forms for Semantic Parsing. *Transactions of the Association for Computational Linguistics (TACL)*, pages 127–140.

Yikang Shen, Zhouhan Lin, Chin wei Huang, and Aaron Courville. 2018a. Neural language modeling by jointly learning syntax and lexicon. In *Proc. of the International Conference on Learning Representation (ICLR)*.

Yikang Shen, Shawn Tan, Alessandro Sordoni, and Aaron Courville. 2018b. Ordered neurons: Integrating tree structures into recurrent neural networks. In *Proc. of the International Conference on Learning Representation (ICLR)*.

Anders Søgaard. 2010. Simple semi-supervised training of part-of-speech taggers. In *Proc. of the Annual Meeting of the Association Computational Linguistics (ACL)*.

Kihyuk Sohn, Xinchen Yan, and Honglak Lee. 2015. Learning structured output representation using deep conditional generative models. In *Proc. of the Conference on Advances in Neural Information Processing Systems (NIPS)*.

Karl Stratos. 2019. Mutual Information Maximization for Simple and Accurate Part-Of-Speech Induction. In *Proc. of the Annual Meeting of the North American Association of Computational Linguistics (NAACL)*.

Toshiyuki Tanaka. 1999. A Theory of Mean Field Approximation. In *Proc. of the Conference on Advances in Neural Information Processing Systems (NIPS)*.

Ben Taskar, Vassil Chatalbashev, Daphne Koller, and Carlos Guestrin. 2005. Learning structured prediction models: A large margin approach. In *Proc. of the International Conference on Machine Learning (ICML)*.

Kewei Tu and Vasant Honavar. 2012. Unambiguity regularization for unsupervised learning of probabilistic grammars. In *Proc. of the Conference on Empirical Methods for Natural Language Processing (EMNLP)*.

David Weiss, Chris Alberti, Michael Collins, and Slav Petrov. 2015. Structured training for neural network transition-based parsing. In *Proc. of the Annual Meeting of the Association Computational Linguistics (ACL)*.

Sam Wiseman and Alexander M. Rush. 2016. Sequence-to-sequence learning as beam-search optimization. In *Proc. of the Conference on Empirical Methods for Natural Language Processing (EMNLP)*.

Xiaoqing Zheng. 2017. Incremental graph-based neural dependency parsing. In *Proc. of the Conference on Empirical Methods for Natural Language Processing (EMNLP)*.

Chunting Zhou and Graham Neubig. 2017. Multi-space variational encoder-decoders for semi-supervised labeled sequence transduction. In *Proc. of the Annual Meeting of the Association Computational Linguistics (ACL)*.

A Appendix

A.1 ELBO of LAP's Original Ojective

Given an input sequence x, we prove that $\mathcal{J}_{lap}$ is the ELBO of $\mathcal{J}$:

Lemma A.1. *$\mathcal{J}_{lap}$ is the ELBO (evidence lower bound) of the original objective $\mathcal{J}$, with an input sequence x.*

Denote the encoder Q is a distribution used to approximate the true posterior distribution $P_\phi(z|x)$, parameterized by ϕ such that Q encoding the input into the latent space z.

Proof.

$$\log P_\theta(x) P_\omega^\epsilon(\mathcal{T}|x) = \underbrace{\log P_\theta(x)}_{\mathcal{U}} + \underbrace{\epsilon \log P_\omega(\mathcal{T}|x)}_{\mathcal{L}}$$

$$\mathcal{U} = \log \int_z Q_\phi(z|x) \frac{P_\theta(x)}{Q_\phi(z|x)} d_z$$

$$\geq \mathop{\mathbb{E}}_{z \sim Q_\phi(z|x)} [\log P_\theta(x|z)]$$

$$- \mathop{\mathbb{E}}_{z \sim Q_\phi(z|x)} \left[\log \frac{Q_\phi(z|x)}{P_\theta(x)} \right]$$

$$= \mathop{\mathbb{E}}_{z \sim Q_\phi(z|x)} [\log P_\theta(x|z)]$$

$$- \mathbb{KL}\left(Q_\phi(z|x) || P_\theta(z)\right),$$

$$\text{(ELBO of traditional VAE)}$$

$$\mathcal{L} = \epsilon \log P_\omega(\mathcal{T}|x)$$

$$= \epsilon \log \int_z P_\omega(\mathcal{T}|z) Q_\phi(z|x) d_z$$

$$= \epsilon \log \mathop{\mathbb{E}}_{z \sim Q_\phi(z|x)} [P_\omega(\mathcal{T}|z)]$$

$$\geq \epsilon \mathop{\mathbb{E}}_{z \sim Q_\phi(z|x)} [\log P_\omega(\mathcal{T}|z)].$$

Combining $\mathcal{U}$ and $\mathcal{L}$ leads to the fact:

$$\mathcal{U} + \mathcal{L} \geq \mathop{\mathbb{E}}_{z \sim Q_\phi(z|x)} [\log P_\theta(x|z)]$$

$$- \mathbb{KL}(Q_\phi(z|x) || P_\theta(z))$$

$$+ \epsilon \mathop{\mathbb{E}}_{z \sim Q_\phi(z|x)} [\log P_\omega(\mathcal{T}|z)] = \mathcal{J}_{lap}$$

$\square$

A.2 Mean Field Approximation and Annealing

Directly calculating the the auxiliary posterior $Q_\phi(z|x)$ is difficult due to the complex model structure with deep neural networks, thus we used a mean field approximation (Tanaka, 1999) together with the conditional independence assumption by assuming $Q_\phi(z|x) = \prod_{t=1}^{l} Q_\phi(z_t|x_t)$ to compute it. Similarly, the generative model $P_\theta(x|z)$, acting as a decoder parameterized by θ, tries to regenerate the input x_t at time step t given the latent variable z_t, assuming $P_\theta(x|z) = \prod_{t=1}^{l} P_\theta(x_t|z_t)$. The encoder and the decoder are trained jointly using the traditional variational autoencoder framework, by minimizing the KL divergence between the approximated posterior and the true posterior.

We parameterize the encoder $Q_\phi(z_t|x_t)$ in two steps: First a bi-LSTM is used to obtain a non-linear transformation h_t of the original x_t; then two separate MLPs are used to compute the mean μ_{z_t} and the variance $\sigma_{z_t}^2$. The generative story $P_\theta(x_t|z_t)$ follows such parameterization: we used a MLP of two hidden layers in-between to take z_t as the input, and predict the word (or POS tag) over the vocabulary, such that the reconstruction probability can be measured.

Following traditional VAE training paradigms, we also apply the "re-parameterization" trick (Kingma and Welling, 2014) to circumvent the non-differentiable sampling procedure to sample z_t from the $Q_\phi(z_t|x_t)$. Instead of directly sample from $\mathcal{N}(\mu_{z_t}, \sigma_{z_t}^2)$, we form $z_t = \mu_{z_t} + \epsilon \odot \sigma_{z_t}^2$ by sampling $\epsilon \sim \mathcal{N}(0, \mathbf{I})$. In addition, to avoid hindering learning during the initial training phases, following previous works (Chen et al., 2018; Bowman et al., 2016), we anneal the temperature on the KL divergence term from a small value to 1.

A.3 Empirical Bayesian Treatment

From an empirical Bayesian perspective, it is beneficial to estimate the prior distribution directly from the data by treating prior's parameters part of the model parameters, rather than fixing the prior using some certain distributions. Similar to the approach used in the previous study (Chen et al., 2018), LAP also learns the priors from the data by updating them iteratively. We initialize the priors from a standard Gaussian distribution $\mathcal{N}(0, \mathbf{I})$, where $\mathbf{I}$ is an identity matrix. During the training, the current priors are updated using the last optimized posterior, following the rule:

$$\pi_\theta^k(z) = \sum_x Q_\phi^{k-1}(z|x) P(x),$$

where $P(x)$ represents the empirical data distribution, and k the iteration step. Empirical Bayesian is also named as "maximum marginal likelihood", such that our approach here is to marginalize over the missing observation as a random variable.

Memory-bounded Neural Incremental Parsing for Psycholinguistic Prediction

Lifeng Jin and **William Schuler**
Department of Linguistics
The Ohio State University, Columbus, OH, USA
{jin, schuler}@ling.osu.edu

Abstract

Syntactic surprisal has been shown to have an effect on human sentence processing, and can be calculated from prefix probabilities of generative incremental parsers. Recent state-of-the-art incremental generative neural parsers are able to produce accurate parses and surprisal values, but have unbounded stack memory, which may be used by the neural parser to maintain explicit in-order representations of all previously parsed words, inconsistent with results of human memory experiments. In contrast, humans seem to have a bounded working memory, demonstrated by inhibited performance on word recall in multi-clause sentences (Bransford and Franks, 1971), and on center-embedded sentences (Miller and Isard, 1964). Bounded statistical parsers exist, but are less accurate than neural parsers in predicting reading times. This paper describes a neural incremental generative parser that is able to provide accurate surprisal estimates and can be constrained to use a bounded stack. Results show that accuracy gains of neural parsers can be reliably extended to psycholinguistic modeling without risk of distortion due to unbounded working memory.

1 Introduction

Syntactic surprisal has been shown to have an effect on human sentence processing, and can be calculated from prefix probabilities of generative incremental parsers (Hale, 2001; Levy, 2008), making it a useful baseline predictor when looking for effects of other factors, like limits of memory or attention. Recent work in generative neural network parsing (Dyer et al., 2016; Hale et al., 2018) has shown that generative parsers based on neural networks are more accurate than earlier statistical generative parsers, and can be used for surprisal calculation. Although a typical shift-reduce neural network parser like that used by Hale et al. (2018)

and Crabbé et al. (2019) may be successful in predicting brain imaging data, the depth of its stack memory, the model component where past predicted items are faithfully stored, can be as long as the whole derivational history of the parse (Kuncoro et al., 2018). This potentially sentence-length stack may be used by the neural parser to maintain explicit in-order representations of all previously parsed words. In contrast, humans seem to have a bounded working memory, demonstrated by inhibited performance on word recall in multi-clause sentences (Bransford and Franks, 1971), and on center-embedded sentences (Miller and Isard, 1964).[1] Explicit storage of this long parsing history may improve parsing accuracy, but it also risks distorting the predictions of the model when used as a statistical control in psycholinguistic experiments.

Left-corner parsers (Rosenkrantz and Lewis, 1970; Johnson-Laird, 1983) have been argued to provide human-like limits on working memory, because the stack memory requirements of this kind of parser do not grow unboundedly in linguistically common cases of left- or right recursion, only in linguistically rare cases of center recursion. For example, a left corner parser would require only one memory element to process the right recursive sentence, 'The dog chased the cat that ate the rat that nibbled the malt,' but would require three elements to process the center recursive

---

[1]Specifically, Bransford and Franks (1971) found that subjects were not reliably able to recall word-order information such as whether sentences were in passive or active voice following exposure to sentence stimuli, and Miller and Isard (1964) found that subjects were not able to understand sentences with deeply nested center-embedded structures, such as:

(i) The cart [$_{RC}$ the horse [$_{RC}$ the man bought] pulled] broke.

as easily as non-center-embedded control sentences, despite being composed of familiar rules.

Proceedings of the 16th International Conference on Parsing Technologies and the IWPT 2020 Shared Task, pages 48–61
Virtual Meeting, July 9, 2020. ©2020 Association for Computational Linguistics

sentence, 'The rat that the cat that the dog chased ate nibbled the malt,' consistent with findings that humans have more difficulty understanding the latter sentence. Left-corner parsers also define a fixed set of probabilistic decisions at each word, which naturally paces the surprisal measures produced by the model. Unfortunately, existing left-corner parsers (van Schijndel et al., 2013) are statistical rather than neural, and are therefore substantially less accurate than state-of-the-art neural network parsers.

This paper therefore defines a neural-network left-corner parser with bounded stack memory for parsing and psycholinguistic prediction. Experiments described in this paper show that this generative left-corner neural network parser is competitive with incremental generative parsers that use unbounded stack memory in a parsing task, and outperforms statistical memory-bounded generative left-corner parsers both in parsing accuracy and in fitting human behavioral data on two different datasets, consistent with the conclusion that accuracy gains of neural parsers can be reliably extended to psycholinguistic modeling without risk of distortion due to unbounded working memory.

2 Related work

Incremental generative constituent parsers are able to process sentences in time order and provide psycholinguistically predictive measures like syntactic surprisal and entropy reduction (Levy, 2008; Hale, 2001, 2006), which in turn are used in psycholinguistic experiments for probing effects of syntax on behavioral data (Demberg and Keller, 2008; Demberg et al., 2012; van Schijndel and Schuler, 2015). Statistical incremental parsers like ones proposed by Roark (2001) and van Schijndel et al. (2013) are based on context-free grammars. The Roark (2001) parser builds syntactic structures top-down incrementally and has been used in studies for calculating surprisal (Demberg and Keller, 2008; Roark et al., 2009; Frank, 2009). Left-corner parsers (Rosenkrantz and Lewis, 1970; Johnson-Laird, 1983) are often used to model limits on center embedding (Abney and Johnson, 1991; Gibson, 1991; Resnik, 1992; Stabler, 1994; Lewis and Vasishth, 2005). van Schijndel et al. (2013) proposed an incremental parser that takes working memory constraints into account, and is able to produce probabilistic measures as well as predictions about working memory operations (van Schijndel and Schuler, 2015). Demberg et al. (2013) propose a parser which is also able to produce prefix probabilities for tree-adjoining grammars. All of these statistical parsers lag behind state-of-the-art parsers in parsing accuracy, because of psycholinguistic constraints like incrementality and because they use less expressive statistical models.

State-of-the-art constituency parsers generally are neural network models (Choe and Charniak, 2016; Dyer et al., 2016; Kitaev and Klein, 2018). Dyer et al. (2016) propose a generative neural model for top-down incremental parsing but use it only as a reranker for a discriminative parser. Extensions to the Dyer et al. (2016) model allow the parser to do in-order tree traversal (Liu and Zhang, 2017; Kuncoro et al., 2018).[2] However, the in-order transition system has a bias towards left children of constituents, which is not desirable when the model is used to calculate prefix probabilities. This issue was addressed by using word-synchronous beam search (Stern et al., 2017; Hale et al., 2018) or variable sized beam search (Crabbé et al., 2019) and successfully predict brain imaging data. However, all of these parsers do not limit the number of stack elements the parser has direct access to at any timestep, which in some cases can be equal to number of derivational decisions made up to the current timestep. This behavior of unbounded stack does not match what we know about human working memory and is undesirable for calculating predictors like probabilistically-weighted emdedding depth (Wu et al., 2010). The model described in this paper avoids these problems by using a left-corner transition system, which uses a bounded pushdown store and a fixed set of probabilistic decisions per word. The bounded stack memory not only more closely implements human working memory limits in a model designed to calculate cognitive predictors, other work (Jin et al., 2018) shows that it also helps limit search space for unsupervised grammar acquisition.

---

[2]Kuncoro et al. (2018) calls the in-order tree traversal a left-corner traversal. In order to avoid confusion, we refer to it as in-order tree traversal, and save the name left-corner traversal for the Johnson-Laird (1983) formulation, which traverses trees from left to right with a bounded stack.

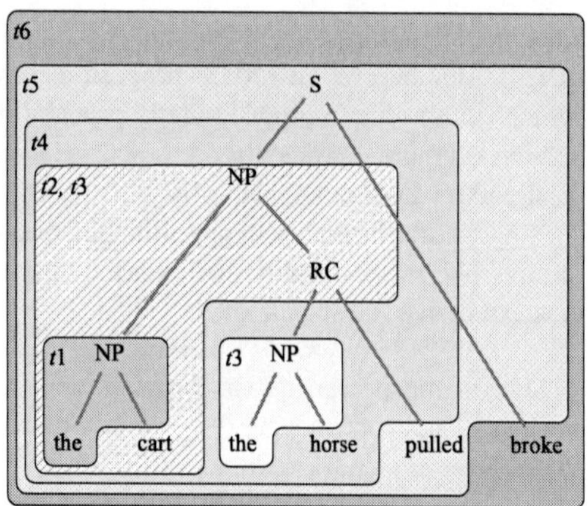

Figure 1: Example of a parse tree for the sentence *the cart the horse pulled broke*. Time step indices are marked inside the derivation fragment built in that time step. A and B nodes are the top and the rightmost node of each derivation fragment. Note that $t3$ has two separate derivation fragments, which indicates that at $t3$ there are two sets of A and B nodes on the stack. At each timestep, A and B nodes of the lowest derivation fragment will be predicted. If they have already been predicted or they do not exist, then the decision will be NULL. POS tags for terminals are omitted.

Step	Stack	Decision
	[ ]	GENERATE-the
1	[the]	PJA-NP
	[NP/NP ⊤]	PJB-NULL
	[NP/NP ⊥]	GENERATE′-cart
2	[NP]	PJA-NP
	[NP/NP ⊤]	PJB-RC
	[NP/RC]	GENERATE-the
3	[NP/RC the]	PJA-NP
	[NP/RC NP/NP ⊤]	PJB-NULL
	[NP/RC NP/NP ⊥]	GENERATE′-horse
4	[NP/RC NP]	PJA-NULL
	[NP/RC ⊤]	PJB-NULL
	[NP/RC ⊥]	GENERATE′-pulled
5	[NP]	PJA-S
	[S/S ⊤]	PJB-NULL
	[S/S ⊥]	GENERATE′-broke
6	[S]	PJA-NULL
	[⊤]	PJB-T
	[ ]	

Table 1: Parser decisions and stack states for the sentence "*the cart the horse pulled broke*" shown in Figure 1 using the simple left-corner transition system. It shows that the stack grows only when there is a new center embedded clause within the clause being processed.

3 Incremental left corner transition system with bounded working memory

This paper introduces a neural left-corner transition system for incremental constituency parsing with minimal working memory requirements. This system defines a fixed set of parser decisions at each time step. Following these parsing decisions, the parser incrementally generates each word in a sentence and the syntactic structures associated with that word, in time order. Because the parser needs space on the stack only when there is center-embedding in the sentence, this transition system uses much less stack memory than other shift-reduce transition systems (Kuncoro et al., 2018), modeling the psycholinguistic phenomenon that center-embedding is rare and hard for humans to process.

3.1 Types of nodes in left-corner parsing

A left-corner parser maintains a pushdown store of one or more derivation fragments A/B, each of which consists of a top node of category A lacking a bottom node of category B yet to come. The parser generates each word in a sentence at each time step, and then makes predictions about the top nonterminal category of the current derivation fragment and the bottom rightmost unfinished nonterminal category. This process uses stored states only within center-embedded structures, reflecting the difficulty of center-embedding for humans. For example, in processing the sentence *The cart the horse pulled broke* (see Figure 1), in timestep $t2$ immediately after the word *cart* is generated, the derivation fragment is NP/RC, shown in the figure with an orange-yellow striped plate. The top nonterminal category, or the A category, of this derivation fragment is NP and the bottom rightmost unfinished nonterminal category, or the B category, is RC. At $t3$ when a center-embedded structure appears, a new derivation fragment is created and stored in the stack memory, making $t3$ a timestep with two derivation fragments: NP/RC and NP/NP.

3.2 Parser decisions

Figure 2 defines the set of parser decisions that the parser must make at each time step. They consist of the following:

GENERATE: First a word must be generated given the current state of the parser and pushed onto the stack. There are two rules associated with GENERATE decisions, and they have different stack configurations when the push operation happens. If the stack has a derivation fragment X/Y at its head, then the word is pushed onto the top of the stack without further operation (GENERATE-W). If the top of the stack has a fragment followed by a $\perp$ sign, then the word is first merged with the bottom node Y and then the merged Y node is merged with X. In the end only the top node X remains (GENERATE'-w). The parser deterministically decides which rule to use based on the state of the stack.

PJA : Next a nonterminal top node must be projected onto the head of the stack. The set of possible top nodes include all the nonterminal categories in the training data X as well as a special category NULL. The PJA-x decision projects a nonterminal top node X together with a place-holding bottom node with the same category onto the stack, and appends the stack with a $\top$ sign. PJA-NULL merges the final node Y on the stack, which is often a terminal, with the closest bottom node, and appends the $\top$ sign to the stack.

PJB : Finally a nonterminal bottom node must be projected onto the head of the stack. The set of possible bottom nodes includes all the nonterminal categories in the training data X as well as a special category NULL and discourse level category T. The PJB-x decision merges the last bottom node Y to the bottom node with the predicted category X. PJA-NULL changes the $\top$ sign to the $\perp$ sign at the head of stack.

Table 1 shows how the sentence in Figure 1 is parsed with this left-corner transition system. The state of the stack in the parser in the beginning is implicitly [T/T], which represents the top-level discourse structure which has a top node of T and bottom node of T. We omit this initial fragment in the table for brevity. After parsing the whole sentence, the state of the parser will be [ ], again omitting the top level discourse nodes.

The relationship between a parse tree and a sequence of decisions generated by the transition system is bijective. Trees produced with this system are all binary-branching.

3.3 Use of stack memory

Stack memory depth increases only when a left nonterminal child of a right child is generated (Schuler et al., 2010) as a center-embedded structure is generated. In the current transition system, the PJB decision at the previous time step (PJB_{t-1}) and the PJA decision at the current time step (PJA_t) together decide how depth of a parse will change:

- if PJB_{t-1} = NULL and PJA_t = NULL, then the

$$\text{GENERATE-}W \quad \frac{[\,\sigma \cdot X/Y,\, i\,]}{[\,\sigma \cdot X/Y \cdot W,\, i+1\,]}$$

$$\text{GENERATE'-}W \quad \frac{[\,\sigma \cdot X/Y \cdot \perp,\, i\,]}{[\,\sigma \cdot X,\, i+1\,]}$$

$$\text{PJA-}X \quad \frac{[\,\sigma \cdot Y,\, i\,]}{[\,\sigma \cdot X/X \cdot \top,\, i\,]}$$

$$\text{PJA-NULL} \quad \frac{[\,\sigma \cdot Y,\, i\,]}{[\,\sigma \cdot \top,\, i\,]}$$

$$\text{PJB-}X \quad \frac{[\,\sigma \cdot Z/Y \cdot \top,\, i\,]}{[\,\sigma \cdot Z/X,\, i\,]}$$

$$\text{PJB-NULL} \quad \frac{[\,\sigma \cdot X/Y \cdot \top,\, i\,]}{[\,\sigma \cdot X/Y \cdot \perp,\, i\,]}$$

Figure 2: The generative incremental left-corner transition system. Adding a buffer to the system yields a discriminative transition system.

depth of the sentence will decrease by 1.

- if PJB_{t-1} $\neq$ NULL and PJA_t $\neq$ NULL, then the depth of the sentence will increase by 1.

- in all other cases, the depth remains the same as the previous time step.

The depth of the stack memory for a parse is closely related to the well-formedness of a parse. As Figure 1 shows, a valid parse starts at depth 0, stays at larger depths during parsing the sentence, and returns to depth 0 at the end of the sentence. The figure also shows that the depth of the stack memory only increases when a center embedding is being parsed at $t3$. The average stack memory depth for the transition system in these parsing experiments is 2, which means that on average there are 4 tree nodes in stack memory, much smaller than 12 which is the average number of items for the top-down system used in Hale et al. (2018). This shows that the left-corner transition system makes much more parsimonious use of stack memory than a typical shift-reduce system. The left-corner model evaluated in the experiments also applies bounding to the stack memory and uses a relatively liberal maximum depth of 5 derivation fragments (10 tree nodes), reflecting the fact that remembering more than 10 items faithfully at once is highly unlikely in sentence processing due to working memory limits in humans.

There are two sets of constraints for different use cases for the parser to prune parses on the beam.[3] The basic set only drops a parse when the

---

[3] Please see the supplemental materials for details.

parse reaches depth 0 before the end of the sentence. This set is used by the parser when psycholinguistic measures are needed. The extended set provides information to the parser about the length of the sentence currently parsing, guiding the parser to drop parses with stack memory too deep or too shallow while parsing. Because this set provides some forward context, it is only used when the parser is used to find best parses in linguistic evaluation.

4 Parsing model

This section defines a memory-bounded neural incremental generative parser as a generative probability model for surprisal calculation using the proposed left-corner transition system. In the description below, all LSTMs are stack-LSTMs (Dyer et al., 2016) with coupled input and forget gates (Greff et al., 2017) and all FFs are feed-forward neural networks.

Surprisal at a word w_t is defined as the negative log of the probability of that word given its preceding words $w_{1..t-1}$ under some model θ. This can be computed by marginalizing over the final hidden state of a sequence:

$$-\log \mathsf{P}_\theta(w_t \mid w_{1..t-1}) = -\log \frac{\sum_{q_t} \mathsf{P}_\theta(q_t\, w_{1..t})}{\sum_{q_t w_t} \mathsf{P}_\theta(q_t\, w_{1..t})} \tag{1}$$

then decomposing the marginalized term into a recurrence of marginalized transition-observation probabilities:

$$\mathsf{P}_\theta(q_t\, w_{1..t}) = \sum_{q_{t-1}} \mathsf{P}_\theta(w_t\, q_t \mid q_{t-1}) \cdot \mathsf{P}_\theta(q_{t-1}\, w_{1..t-1}) \tag{2}$$

using $\mathsf{P}_\theta(q_0\, w_0) = 1$ for some start-of-sentence word w_0 and initial state q_0.

The hidden states q_t of the model described in this paper consist of:

- cell and hidden vectors $\mathbf{c}_t, \mathbf{h}_t \in \mathbb{R}^n$ for a word LSTM,
- a preterminal decision $p_t \in C$ over category labels C,
- a top decision $a_t \in C \cup \{\bot\}$ over labels and null results $\bot$,
- a bottom decision $b_t \in C \cup \{\bot\}$ over labels and null results,
- a top vector $\mathbf{a}_t^d \in \mathbb{R}^n$ for each depth $d \in \{1..D\}$,

- a bottom vector $\mathbf{b}_t^d \in \mathbb{R}^n$ for each depth $d \in \{1..D\}$, and
- cell and hidden vectors $\mathbf{c}_t', \mathbf{h}_t' \in \mathbb{R}^n$ for a decision LSTM.

Probabilities for observing a word and transitioning to a new hidden state at each time step t, given a hidden state at the previous time step $t-1$, can then be decomposed into terms for each individual decision and resulting vector:

$$\mathsf{P}(w_t\, \mathbf{c}_t\, \mathbf{h}_t\, p_t\, a_t\, b_t\, \mathbf{a}_t^{1..D}\, \mathbf{b}_t^{1..D}\, \mathbf{c}_t'\, \mathbf{h}_t' \mid \mathbf{c}_{t-1}\, \mathbf{h}_{t-1}\, \mathbf{a}_{t-1}^{1..D}\, \mathbf{b}_{t-1}^{1..D}\, \mathbf{c}_{t-1}'\, \mathbf{h}_{t-1}')$$
$$= \mathsf{P}(w_t \mid \mathbf{c}_{t-1}\, \mathbf{h}_{t-1}\, \mathbf{a}_{t-1}^{1..D}\, \mathbf{b}_{t-1}^{1..D}\, \mathbf{c}_{t-1}'\, \mathbf{h}_{t-1}')$$
$$\cdot\ \mathsf{P}(\mathbf{c}_t\, \mathbf{h}_t \mid \mathbf{c}_{t-1}\, \mathbf{h}_{t-1}\, \mathbf{a}_{t-1}^{1..D}\, \mathbf{b}_{t-1}^{1..D}\, \mathbf{c}_{t-1}'\, \mathbf{h}_{t-1}'\, w_t)$$
$$\cdot\ \mathsf{P}(p_t \mid \mathbf{c}_{t-1}\, \mathbf{h}_{t-1}\, \mathbf{a}_{t-1}^{1..D}\, \mathbf{b}_{t-1}^{1..D}\, \mathbf{c}_{t-1}'\, \mathbf{h}_{t-1}'\, w_t\, \mathbf{c}_t\, \mathbf{h}_t)$$
$$\cdot\ \mathsf{P}(a_t \mid \mathbf{c}_{t-1}\, \mathbf{h}_{t-1}\, \mathbf{a}_{t-1}^{1..D}\, \mathbf{b}_{t-1}^{1..D}\, \mathbf{c}_{t-1}'\, \mathbf{h}_{t-1}'\, w_t\, \mathbf{c}_t\, \mathbf{h}_t\, p_t)$$
$$\cdot\ \mathsf{P}(b_t \mid \mathbf{c}_{t-1}\, \mathbf{h}_{t-1}\, \mathbf{a}_{t-1}^{1..D}\, \mathbf{b}_{t-1}^{1..D}\, \mathbf{c}_{t-1}'\, \mathbf{h}_{t-1}'\, w_t\, \mathbf{c}_t\, \mathbf{h}_t\, p_t\, a_t)$$
$$\cdot\ \mathsf{P}(\mathbf{a}_t^{1..D} \mid \mathbf{c}_{t-1}\, \mathbf{h}_{t-1}\, \mathbf{a}_{t-1}^{1..D}\, \mathbf{b}_{t-1}^{1..D}\, \mathbf{c}_{t-1}'\, \mathbf{h}_{t-1}'\, w_t\, \mathbf{c}_t\, \mathbf{h}_t\, p_t\, a_t\, b_t)$$
$$\cdot\ \mathsf{P}(\mathbf{b}_t^{1..D} \mid \mathbf{c}_{t-1}\, \mathbf{h}_{t-1}\, \mathbf{a}_{t-1}^{1..D}\, \mathbf{b}_{t-1}^{1..D}\, \mathbf{c}_{t-1}'\, \mathbf{h}_{t-1}'\, w_t\, \mathbf{c}_t\, \mathbf{h}_t\, p_t\, a_t\, b_t\, \mathbf{a}_t^{1..D})$$
$$\cdot\ \mathsf{P}(\mathbf{c}_t'\, \mathbf{h}_t' \mid \mathbf{c}_{t-1}\, \mathbf{h}_{t-1}\, \mathbf{a}_{t-1}^{1..D}\, \mathbf{b}_{t-1}^{1..D}\, \mathbf{c}_{t-1}'\, \mathbf{h}_{t-1}'\, w_t\, \mathbf{c}_t\, \mathbf{h}_t\, p_t\, a_t\, b_t\, \mathbf{a}_t^{1..D}\, \mathbf{b}_t^{1..D}) \tag{3}$$

The probability of observing a word depends on bounded representations of the store, the decision sequence and the word sequence:

$$\mathsf{P}(w_t \mid \mathbf{a}_{t-1}^{1..D}\, \mathbf{b}_{t-1}^{1..D}\, \mathbf{c}_{t-1}'\, \mathbf{h}_{t-1}'\, \mathbf{c}_{t-1}\, \mathbf{h}_{t-1}) =$$
$$\delta_{w_t}{}^\top \textsc{SoftMax}(\mathrm{FF}_{\theta_{\mathrm{W}}}[\, \mathbf{q}_{t-1}, \mathbf{h}_{t-1}', \mathbf{h}_{t-1}\,]) \tag{4}$$

where δ_i is a Kronecker delta vector, consisting of a one at element i and zeros elsewhere, and $\mathbf{q}_t$ is a summary of the current stack:

$$\mathbf{q}_t = \mathrm{LSTM}_{\theta_{\mathrm{Q}}}[\, \mathbf{a}_t^1, \mathbf{b}_t^1, \ldots, \mathbf{a}_t^D, \mathbf{b}_t^D\,]. \tag{5}$$

This probability term defines a distribution over GENERATE decisions.

The probability of a cell and hidden vector of the word LSTM is deterministic given the preceding operations, and is modeled as an indicator equal to one when the vectors are as defined by the corresponding LSTM model, zero otherwise:

$$\mathsf{P}(\mathbf{c}_t\, \mathbf{h}_t \mid \mathbf{a}_{t-1}^{1..D}\, \mathbf{b}_{t-1}^{1..D}\, \mathbf{c}_{t-1}'\, \mathbf{h}_{t-1}'\, \mathbf{c}_{t-1}\, \mathbf{h}_{t-1}\, w_t) =$$
$$[\![\, \mathbf{c}_t, \mathbf{h}_t = \mathrm{LSTM}_{\theta_{\mathrm{H}}}[\, \mathbf{c}_{t-1}, \mathbf{h}_{t-1}; \mathbf{w}_t\,]\,]\!], \tag{6}$$

where:

$$\mathbf{w}_t = \mathrm{FF}_{\theta_{\mathrm{W}'}}[\, \mathbf{e}_t, \mathbf{e}_t', \mathbf{E}'\, \textsc{SoftMax}(\mathrm{FF}_{\theta_{\mathrm{W}''}}[\, \mathbf{q}_{t-1}, \mathbf{h}_{t-1}, \mathbf{h}_{t-1}', \mathbf{e}_t, \mathbf{e}_t'\,])] \tag{7}$$

and $\mathbf{e}_t = \mathbf{E}''\, \delta_{w_t}$ is a trained word embedding, and $\mathbf{e}_t' = \mathbf{E}'''\, \delta_{w_t}$ is a pre-trained word embedding.

Similarly for the cell and hidden states of the decision LSTM:

$$P(\mathbf{c}'_t\,\mathbf{h}'_t \mid \mathbf{a}^{1..D}_{t-1}\,\mathbf{b}^{1..D}_{t-1}\,\mathbf{c}'_{t-1}\,\mathbf{h}'_{t-1}\,\mathbf{c}_{t-1}\,\mathbf{h}_{t-1}\,w_t) =$$
$$[\![\,\mathbf{c}'_t,\mathbf{h}'_t = \mathrm{LSTM}_{\theta_M}[\,\mathbf{c}'_{t-1},\mathbf{h}'_{t-1};\mathbf{m}_{t-1}\,]\,]\!],\quad (8)$$

where $\mathbf{m}_{t-1}$ is a trainable embedding for the decision made at timestep $t-1$. Note that there are three timesteps for $\mathbf{m}$ corresponding to three decisions, compared to one timestep for $\mathbf{w}$. Figure 3 shows an illustration of how the model works to predict the GENERATE-the decision at timestep 3 in Table 1. In the illustration, the decision LSTM takes all previous decisions $\mathbf{m}_1,\mathbf{m}_2,\dots$, and generates a hidden state $\mathbf{h}'_2$ which represent the decision history (Equation 8). The word LSTM takes the words which have already been generated, and produces a hidden state $\mathbf{h}_2$ which represents the word history (Equation 6). The stack composer composes all top and bottom categories on the stack represented by the vectors, and produces the representation of the stack (Equation 5). Finally, all three representations of different kinds of information are processed by the GENERATE feedforward network FF$_{\theta_W}$, which makes a prediction about which word is next (Equation 4). Other decisions are made in a similar fashion as shown below.

The probability of a preterminal category decision depends on a bounded representation of the word sequence at the current time step, and a bounded representation of the decision sequence and the store at the previous time step, and the trained and untrained pre-trained word embeddings:

$$P(p_t \mid \mathbf{c}_{t-1}\,\mathbf{h}_{t-1}\,\mathbf{a}^{1..D}_{t-1}\,\mathbf{b}^{1..D}_{t-1}\,\mathbf{c}'_{t-1}\,\mathbf{h}'_{t-1}\,w_t\,\mathbf{c}_t\,\mathbf{h}_t) =$$
$$\delta_{p_t}^{\ \top}\mathrm{SOFTMAX}(\,\mathrm{FF}_{\theta_P}[\,\mathbf{h}_t,\mathbf{h}'_{t-1},\mathbf{q}_{t-1},\mathbf{e}_t,\mathbf{e}'_t\,]\,)\quad (9)$$

This term defines a distribution over preterminal (part of speech) decisions.

The probability of a top category decision depends on a bounded representation of the word sequence at the current time step and a bounded representation of the decision sequence and the store at the previous time step:

$$P(a_t \mid \mathbf{c}_{t-1}\,\mathbf{h}_{t-1}\,\mathbf{a}^{1..D}_{t-1}\,\mathbf{b}^{1..D}_{t-1}\,\mathbf{c}'_{t-1}\,\mathbf{h}'_{t-1}\,w_t\,\mathbf{c}_t\,\mathbf{h}_t\,p_t) =$$
$$\delta_{a_t}^{\ \top}\mathrm{SOFTMAX}(\,\mathrm{FF}_{\theta_A}[\,\mathbf{h}_t,\mathbf{h}'_t,\mathbf{q}_{t-1}\,]\,)\quad (10)$$

This term defines a distribution over PJA decisions.

The probability of a bottom category decision depends on a bounded representation of the word

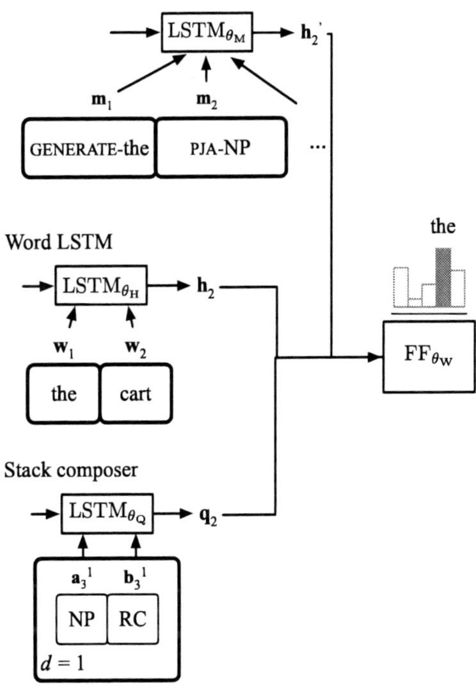

Figure 3: The model makes the prediction for the GENERATE-the decision at timestep 3 in Table 1.

sequence at the current time step and decision sequence including the current top decision and the store at the previous time step:

$$P(b_t \mid \mathbf{c}_{t-1}\,\mathbf{h}_{t-1}\,\mathbf{a}^{1..D}_{t-1}\,\mathbf{b}^{1..D}_{t-1}\,\mathbf{c}'_{t-1}\,\mathbf{h}'_{t-1}\,w_t\,\mathbf{c}_t\,\mathbf{h}_t\,p_t\,a_t) =$$
$$\delta_{b_t}^{\ \top}\mathrm{SOFTMAX}(\,\mathrm{FF}_{\theta_B}[\,\mathbf{h}_t,\mathbf{h}'_{t-.5},\mathbf{q}_{t-1}\,]\,)\quad (11)$$

where $\mathbf{c}'_{t-.5},\mathbf{h}'_{t-.5} = \mathrm{LSTM}_{\theta_{H'}}[\,\mathbf{c}'_{t-1},\mathbf{h}'_{t-1};\delta_{a_t}\,]$ is the result of adding the bottom decision to the decision LSTM. This term defines a distribution over PJB decisions.

The probability of a top vector is deterministic given the preceding operations, and is modeled as an indicator function equal to one when the vectors are as defined by a set of LSTMs over dependent top and bottom store vectors, depending on the previous bottom category and current top category decisions:

$$P(\mathbf{a}^{1..D}_t \mid \mathbf{c}_{t-1}\,\mathbf{h}_{t-1}\,\mathbf{a}^{1..D}_{t-1}\,\mathbf{b}^{1..D}_{t-1}\,\mathbf{c}'_{t-1}\,\mathbf{h}'_{t-1}\,w_t\,\mathbf{c}_t\,\mathbf{h}_t\,p_t\,a_t\,b_t)=$$
$$\begin{cases} [\![\mathbf{a}^{\bar{d}-1}_t=\mathbf{a}^{\bar{d}-1}_{t-1}]\!]\cdot\phi_{\bar{d}-1} & \text{if } b_{t-1}{=}\bot,a_t{=}\bot \\[4pt] [\![\mathbf{a}^{\bar{d}}_t=\mathrm{LSTM}_{\theta_{Q'}}[\,\mathbf{w}_t,\mathbf{a}^{\bar{d}}_{t-1},\mathbf{E}\,\delta_{a_t}\,]]\!]\cdot\phi_{\bar{d}} & \text{if } b_{t-1}{=}\bot,a_t{\neq}\bot \\[4pt] [\![\mathbf{a}^{\bar{d}}_t=\mathbf{a}^{\bar{d}}_{t-1}]\!]\cdot\phi_{\bar{d}} & \text{if } b_{t-1}{\neq}\bot,a_t{=}\bot \\[4pt] [\![\mathbf{a}^{\bar{d}+1}_t=\mathrm{LSTM}_{\theta_{Q'}}[\,\mathbf{w}_t,\mathbf{E}\,\delta_{a_t}\,]]\!]\cdot\phi_{\bar{d}+1} & \text{if } b_{t-1}{\neq}\bot,a_t{\neq}\bot \end{cases}\quad (12)$$

where $\bar{d} = \text{argmax}_d\{\mathbf{a}_{t-1}^d \neq \mathbf{0}\}$ is the previous store depth, and $\phi_d = [\![\mathbf{a}_t^{1..d-1} = \mathbf{a}_{t-1}^{1..d-1}, \mathbf{a}_t^{d+1..D} = \mathbf{0}]\!]$ is a maintenance constraint on stores. These stack operations related to the top category are illustrated in Figure 5 in the appendix.

The probability of a bottom vector is also deterministic and modeled as an indicator function equal to one when the vectors are as defined by a set of LSTMs over dependent top and bottom store vectors, depending on the previous bottom category and current top category decisions:

$$P(\mathbf{b}_t^{1..D}|\mathbf{c}_{t-1}\,\mathbf{h}_{t-1}\,\mathbf{a}_{t-1}^{1..D}\,\mathbf{b}_{t-1}^{1..D}\,\mathbf{c}_{t-1}'\,\mathbf{h}_{t-1}'\,w_t\,\mathbf{c}_t\,\mathbf{h}_t\,p_t\,a_t\,b_t\,\mathbf{a}_t^{1..D}) =$$

$$\begin{cases} [\![\mathbf{b}_t^{\bar{d}-1}=\text{LSTM}_{\theta_{Q'}}[\,\mathbf{w}_t,\mathbf{a}_{t-1}^{\bar{d}},\mathbf{b}_{t-1}^{\bar{d}-1},\mathbf{E}\,\delta_{b_t}\,]\!] \cdot \psi_{\bar{d}-1} & \\ \qquad\qquad\qquad\qquad\qquad\qquad \text{if } b_{t-1}=\perp,a_t=\perp & \\ [\![\mathbf{b}_t^{\bar{d}}=\mathbf{E}\,\delta_{b_t}]\!] \cdot \psi_{\bar{d}} & \text{if } b_{t-1}=\perp,a_t\neq\perp \\ [\![\mathbf{b}_t^{\bar{d}}=\text{LSTM}_{\theta_{Q'}}[\,\mathbf{w}_t,\mathbf{b}_{t-1}^{\bar{d}},\mathbf{E}\,\delta_{b_t}\,]\!] \cdot \psi_{\bar{d}} & \text{if } b_{t-1}\neq\perp,a_t=\perp \\ [\![\mathbf{b}_t^{\bar{d}+1}=\mathbf{E}\,\delta_{b_t}]\!] \cdot \psi_{\bar{d}+1} & \text{if } b_{t-1}\neq\perp,a_t\neq\perp \end{cases} \quad (13)$$

where $\bar{d} = \text{argmax}_d\{\mathbf{a}_{t-1}^d \neq \mathbf{0}\}$ is the previous store depth, and $\psi_d = [\![\mathbf{b}_t^{1..d-1} = \mathbf{b}_{t-1}^{1..d-1}, \mathbf{b}_t^{d+1..D} = \mathbf{0}]\!]$ is a maintenance constraint on stores.

Finally, the probability of a cell and hidden vector of the decision LSTM is also deterministic and modeled as an indicator equal to one when the vectors are as defined by the corresponding LSTM model, zero otherwise:

$$P(\mathbf{c}_t'\,\mathbf{h}_t'|\mathbf{c}_{t-1}\,\mathbf{h}_{t-1}\,\mathbf{a}_{t-1}^{1..D}\,\mathbf{b}_{t-1}^{1..D}\,\mathbf{c}_{t-1}'\,\mathbf{h}_{t-1}'\,w_t\,\mathbf{c}_t\,\mathbf{h}_t\,p_t\,a_t\,b_t\,\mathbf{a}_t^{1..D}\,\mathbf{b}_t^{1..D}) =$$

$$[\![\mathbf{c}_t',\mathbf{h}_t'=\text{LSTM}_{\theta_{\text{H}}}[\,\mathbf{c}_{t-1}',\mathbf{h}_{t-1}';\delta_{a_t},\delta_{b_t}\,]\!] \quad (14)$$

4.1 Training and Parsing

The proposed model here is a generative model for sequence prediction with no forward context, therefore ideally it should be trained with a structured training scheme (Weiss et al., 2015). However since it is expensive to search a wide beam in training with a neural network, this model uses a two-stage training scheme. The model is first trained to minimize a cross-entropy loss objective with an l_2 regularization term, defined by:

$$L_\theta(w_{1..T}\,q_{1..T}) = -\log P_\theta(w_{1..T}\,q_{1..T}) + \frac{\lambda}{2}\|\theta\|^2 \tag{15}$$

where $P_\theta(w_{1..T}\,q_{1..T}) = \prod_t P_\theta(w_t\,q_t\,|\,q_{t-1})$, and λ is an l_2 regularization strength hyper-parameter.

Training with the local cross-entropy objective quickly leads to overfitting, because the left-corner parsing decisions can be ambiguous at early parts of the sentence, and the objective drives the model to make such decisions perfectly by memorizing the training data. This model therefore stops the cross-entropy training when parsing performance starts to decrease on a development set, and switches to use the REINFORCE algorithm (Williams, 1992; Le and Fokkens, 2017) to fine-tune the model with sequence level supervision. The loss becomes:[4]

$$L_\theta'(w_{1..T}\,q_{1..T}) = \frac{\lambda}{2}\|\theta\|^2 - \mathbb{E}_{q_{1..T}'\sim P_\theta(q_{1..T}'|w_{1..T})}$$

$$(F(q_{1..T}', q_{1..T}) - \hat{b})\log P_\theta(q_{1..T}'\,|\,w_{1..T}) \quad (16)$$

where $P_\theta(q_{1..T}'\,|\,w_{1..T}) = \frac{P_\theta(w_{1..T}\,q_{1..T}')}{\sum_{q_{1..T}} P_\theta(w_{1..T}\,q_{1..T})}$, F is a function from gold and hypothesized decision sequences to parsing F-scores, and $\hat{b}$ is a global running average of F scores of all sampled trees.

After the model is trained, the parser uses beam search to find the approximate best parse. A large beam width is desirable because it provides more accurate parses and straightforward ways to calculate psycholinguistic measures like surprisal which requires marginalization.

5 Experiments

A first set of experiments compare the linguistic accuracy of the bounded neural parser to other generative incremental parsers using bracketing F1 scores on the Penn Treebank (Marcus et al., 1994). A second set of experiments then compare the psycholinguistic accuracy of the bounded neural parsing model against an equivalently bounded non-neural parsing model by regressing syntactic surprisal derived from each model to self-paced reading times from the Natural Stories Corpus (Futrell et al., 2018) and eye-tracking fixation durations of newspaper article reading from the Dundee Eye-tracking Corpus (Kennedy et al., 2003).

The neural parser used in all experiments is trained on Sections 02 - 21 of the Wall Street Journal part of the Penn Treebank. Hyper-parameters of the parser are tuned on the development set, WSJ Section 22. The cross-entropy objective is used for about 9 epochs before accuracy on the development set starts to decrease, with stochastic gradient descent (SGD) using initial learning rate = 0.1 and gradually decreasing the learning

---

[4]This term does not include p_t because preterminal (POS) decisions are soft, and F scores provide no supervision to POS tagging accuracy. To increase efficiency in sampling, GENERATE decisions are not sampled.

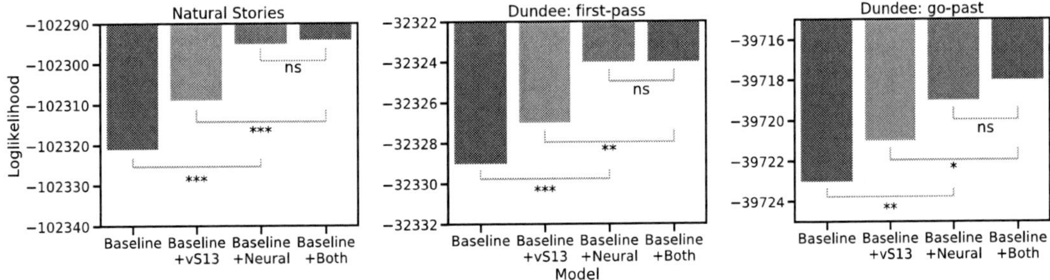

Figure 4: Goodness of fit of the regression model with different surprisal values calculated by the incremental left-corner parser in van Schijndel et al. (2013) and the incremental neural parser to human reading times and eye tracking data. Likelihood ratio tests are conducted to obtain p values. *** : $p < 1 \times 10^{-4}$, ** : $p < 1 \times 10^{-3}$, * : $p < 1 \times 10^{-2}$, ns: $p > 0.05$.

rate to be 0.001, and $\lambda = 1 \times 10^{-6}$. Training then switches to the REINFORCE objective until the parser reaches the maximum F1 score (about 3 epochs), with SGD using learning rate = 5×10^{-3} and $\lambda = 1 \times 10^{-5}$. Using REINFORCE adds 0.3 F1 points on the development set. The pretrained English word embeddings are from Liu and Zhang (2017). Dropout is applied to input to all layers.

Experiments first evaluate model performance on Section 22 of WSJ as the development set and Section 23 as the test set for linguistic accuracy evaluation with a beam width of 2000. These experiments use the extended set of constraints for parsing WSJ for efficiency. This evaluation reports EVALB F scores on both datasets. Trees in the training set are binarized with left-branching constituents and the unary nodes are removed from gold trees following van Schijndel et al. (2013).

The trained model then is used to calculate surprisal for sentences in the Natural Stories Corpus and the Dundee Corpus for psycholinguistic accuracy evaluation. These experiments only use the exploratory set of both corpora. Corpus cleaning follows van Schijndel and Schuler (2013). The parser uses the basic set of constraints to parse the Natural Stories and Dundee corpora, only rejecting parses that would lead to premature termination of the parsing process while doing beam search, with width 2000.

5.1 Linguistic accuracy evaluation

A linguistic accuracy evaluation compares the performance of the bounded neural parser with the published results of generative incremental parsers that are able to calculate psycholinguistic predictors. These experiments first compare parsing scores of the current parser on the develop-

Model	F_1	
	dev	test
memory-bounded parsers		
Demberg et al. (2013)	-	78.7
Roark (2001)	-	85.7
van Schijndel et al. (2013)	-	87.8
this work	90.1	**89.5**
memory-unbounded parsers		
Hale et al. (2018)	**91.3**	-

Table 2: Parsing results (%) on development data, WSJ section 22 and test data, WSJ section 23 for memory-bounded and unbounded generative incremental parsers.

ment set of WSJ with results reported in Hale et al. (2018) in Table 2. Results show that there is a 1.2 point difference between this parser and the parser used in Hale et al. (2018). This decrease may be attributable to the bounded stack losing information about past parsing decisions. Table 2 also shows labeled bracketing F1 scores of the current parser compared with other generative incremental parsers widely used for calculating surprisal predictors, especially van Schijndel et al. (2013) which is the previous state-of-the-art memory-bounded generative incremental parser, on the test set. The neural parser is more accurate than all of the published results of the memory-bounded parsers.

5.2 Psycholinguistic accuracy evaluation

The psycholinguistic accuracy of the parser is evaluated by comparing surprisal predictors calculated by the neural left-corner model against surprisal predictors from the statistical left-corner parser of van Schijndel et al. (2013), which is the memory-bounded generative incremental parser with current state-of-the-art linguistic accuracy. This evaluation uses linear mixed effects models in lme4[5] to regress to both reading time (how long a word is read) data in the Natural Stories Corpus and first-pass (how long a word is first fixated) and go-past (how long before a subsequent word is fixated) fixation durations in the Dundee Corpus, with all four combinations of the neural psycholinguistic (referred to as Neural) and van Schijndel et al. (2013) (referred to below as vS13) surprisal predictors in a diamond ANOVA.[6] All the models also have random intercepts for subject-sentence interaction and word, and random by-subject slopes for all fixed effects. Since this evaluation uses ablative testing to determine whether a fixed effect significantly improves the fit of a model compared to that model without that fixed effect, all models also include random slopes for all fixed effects, even if that particular fixed effect is not used in that model.

Psycholinguistic evaluation results are shown in Figure 4 in terms of model fit to human behavioral data. Results show that surprisal values derived from the bounded neural parser explain behavioral data better than the bounded statistical parser. First, the results show that the neural parser produces more human-like surprisal values than the vS13 parser in all three experiments. This is shown by the fact that adding vS13 to a model which already has Neural (Baseline+Both vs. Baseline+Neural) yields no significant improvement in model fit. The other comparison in which Neural surprisal values are added on top of vS13 surprisal values (Baseline+Both vs. Baseline+vS13) also shows this effect, because significant improvement in model fit is observed. Second, both surprisals derived from memory-bounded generative incremental parsers significantly increase model fit, showing that surprisal is a reliable predictor of both reading times and fixation durations, but in all three experiments, the results show that Baseline+Neural achieves much better model fit to the data than Baseline+vS13 with larger loglikelihood improvements compared to Baseline.

---

[5]https://cran.r-project.org/web/packages/lme4/index.html
[6]Please see the supplemental materials for detailed independent variable description and lmer formulae.

6 Conclusion

This paper proposes a new incremental left-corner transition system that can calculate surprisal and other psycholinguistic predictors, and a new neural generative incremental parser to use this transition system to do memory-bounded incremental generative parsing. Experiments described in this paper show that this generative left-corner neural network parser is competitive with incremental generative parsers that use unbounded stack memory in a parsing task, and outperforms statistical memory-bounded generative left-corner parsers both in parsing accuracy and in fitting human behavioral data on two different datasets, showing that accuracy gains of neural parsers can be reliably extended to psycholinguistic modeling without risk of distortion due to unbounded working memory.

References

Steven P Abney and Mark Johnson. 1991. Memory Requirements and Local Ambiguities of Parsing Strategies. *J. Psycholinguistic Research*, 20(3):233–250.

J D Bransford and J J Franks. 1971. The Abstraction of Linguistic Ideas. *Cognitive Psychology*, 2:331–350.

Do Kook Choe and Eugene Charniak. 2016. Parsing as Language Modeling. In *Proceedings of the Conference on Empirical Methods in Natural Language Processing*.

Benoit Crabbé, Murielle Fabre, and Christophe Pallier. 2019. Variable beam search for generative neural parsing and its relevance for the analysis of neuroimaging signal. In *EMNLP-IJCNLP*, pages 1150–1160. Association for Computational Linguistics.

Vera Demberg and Frank Keller. 2008. Data from eye-tracking corpora as evidence for theories of syntactic processing complexity. *Cognition*, 109(2):193–210.

Vera Demberg, Frank Keller, and Alexander Koller. 2013. Incremental, Predictive Parsing with Psycholinguistically Motivated Tree-Adjoining Grammar. *Computational Linguistics*, 39(4):1025–1066.

Vera Demberg, Asad B Sayeed, Philip J Gorinski, and Nikolaos Engonopoulos. 2012. Syntactic surprisal affects spoken word duration in conversational contexts. In *Proceedings of the 2012 Joint Conference on Empirical Methods in Natural Language Processing and Computational Natural Language Learning*, pages 356–367.

Chris Dyer, Adhiguna Kuncoro, Miguel Ballesteros, and Noah A. Smith. 2016. Recurrent Neural Network Grammars. *Proceedings of the 54th Annual*

Meeting of the Association for Computational Linguistics, 3(2013).

Stefan Frank. 2009. Surprisal-based comparison between a symbolic and a connectionist model of sentence processing. *Proceedings of the 31st annual conference of the cognitive science society*, pages 1139–1144.

Richard Futrell, Edward Gibson, Harry J . Tily, Idan Blank, Anastasia Vishnevetsky, Steven Piantadosi, and Evelina Fedorenko. 2018. The Natural Stories Corpus. In *Proceedings of the 11th International Conference on Language Resources and Evaluation*, Paris, France.

Edward Gibson. 1991. *A computational theory of human linguistic processing: Memory limitations and processing breakdown*. Ph.D. thesis, Carnegie Mellon.

Klaus Greff, Rupesh K Srivastava, Jan Koutnik, Bas R Steunebrink, and Jurgen Schmidhuber. 2017. LSTM: A Search Space Odyssey. *IEEE Transactions on Neural Networks and Learning Systems*, 28(10):2222–2232.

John Hale. 2001. A probabilistic earley parser as a psycholinguistic model. In *Proceedings of the Second meeting of the North American Chapter of the Association for Computational Linguistics on Language technologies*, pages 1–8.

John Hale. 2006. Uncertainty about the rest of the sentence. *Cognitive Science*, 30(4):643–672.

John Hale, Chris Dyer, Adhiguna Kuncoro, and Jonathan R. Brennan. 2018. Finding Syntax in Human Encephalography with Beam Search. In *Proceedings of the 56st Annual Meeting of the Association for Computational Linguistics*.

Kenneth Heafield, Ivan Pouzyrevsky, Jonathan H Clark, and Philipp Koehn. 2013. Scalable modified Kneser-Ney language model estimation. In *Proceedings of the 51st Annual Meeting of the Association for Computational Linguistics*, pages 690–696, Sofia, Bulgaria.

Lifeng Jin, William Schuler, Finale Doshi-Velez, Timothy A Miller, and Lane Schwartz. 2018. Unsupervised Grammar Induction with Depth-bounded PCFG. *Transactions of the Association for Computational Linguistics (TACL)*.

Philip N Johnson-Laird. 1983. *Mental models: Towards a cognitive science of language, inference, and consciousness*. Harvard University Press, Cambridge, MA, USA.

Alan Kennedy, James Pynte, and Robin Hill. 2003. The Dundee Corpus. In *Proceedings of the 12th European conference on eye movement*.

Nikita Kitaev and Dan Klein. 2018. Constituency Parsing with a Self-Attentive Encoder. In *Proceedings of the 56st Annual Meeting of the Association for Computational Linguistics*.

Adhiguna Kuncoro, Chris Dyer, John Hale, Dani Yogatama, Stephen Clark, and Phil Blunsom. 2018. LSTMs Can Learn Syntax-Sensitive Dependencies Well, But Modeling Structure Makes Them Better. In *Proceedings of the 56st Annual Meeting of the Association for Computational Linguistics*, pages 1–11.

Minh Le and Antske Fokkens. 2017. Tackling Error Propagation through Reinforcement Learning: A Case of Greedy Dependency Parsing. In *Proceedings of the 15th Conference of the European Chapter of the Association for Computational Linguistics*, volume 1, pages 677–687.

Roger Levy. 2008. Expectation-based syntactic comprehension. *Cognition*, 106(3):1126–1177.

Richard L Lewis and Shravan Vasishth. 2005. An activation-based model of sentence processing as skilled memory retrieval. *Cognitive Science*, 29(3):375–419.

Jiangming Liu and Yue Zhang. 2017. In-Order Transition-based Constituent Parsing. *Transactions of the Association for Computational Linguistics*.

Mitchell Marcus, Grace Kim, Mary Ann Marcinkiewicz, Robert MacIntyreand Ann Bies, Mark Ferguson, Karen Katz, and Britta Schasberger. 1994. The Penn Treebank: Annotating predicate argument structure. In *Proceedings of the ARPA Human Language Technology Workshop*.

George A. Miller and Stephen Isard. 1964. Free recall of self-embedded english sentences. *Information and Control*, 7(3):292–303.

Philip Resnik. 1992. Probabilistic tree-adjoining grammar as a framework for statistical natural language processing. In *Proceedings of the Fourteenth International Conference on Computational Linguistics*, pages 418–424, Nantes, France.

Brian Roark. 2001. Probabilistic top-down parsing and language modeling. *Computational Linguistics*, 27(2):249–276.

Brian Roark, Asaf Bachrach, Carlos Cardenas, and Christophe Pallier. 2009. Deriving lexical and syntactic expectation-based measures for psycholinguistic modeling via incremental top-down parsing. In *Proceedings of the 2009 Conference on Empirical Methods in Natural Langauge Processing*, pages 324–333.

D J Rosenkrantz and P M Lewis. 1970. Deterministic left corner parsing. In *11th Annual Symposium on Switching and Automata Theory (swat 1970)*, pages 139–152.

Marten van Schijndel, Andy Exley, and William Schuler. 2013. A Model of Language Processing as Hierarchic Sequential Prediction. *Topics in Cognitive Science*, 5(3):522–540.

Marten van Schijndel and William Schuler. 2013. An Analysis of Memory-based Processing Costs using Incremental Deep Syntactic Dependency Parsing. In *Proceedings of the Workshop on Cognitive Modeling and Computational Linguistics*, pages 37–46.

Marten van Schijndel and William Schuler. 2015. Hierarchic syntax improves reading time prediction. In *Proceedings of Human Language Technologies: The 2015 Annual Conference of the North American Chapter of the ACL*, pages 1597–1605. Association for Linguistics.

William Schuler, Samir AbdelRahman, Tim Miller, and Lane Schwartz. 2010. Broad-coverage parsing using human-Like memory constraints. *Computational Linguistics*, 36(1):1–30.

Edward Stabler. 1994. The finite connectivity of linguistic structure. In *Perspectives on Sentence Processing*, pages 303–336. Lawrence Erlbaum.

Mitchell Stern, Daniel Fried, and Dan Klein. 2017. Effective Inference for Generative Neural Parsing. In *Proceedings of the 2017 Conference on Empirical Methods in Natural Langauge Processing*.

David Weiss, Chris Alberti, Michael Collins, and Slav Petrov. 2015. Structured Training for Neural Network Transition-Based Parsing. In *Proceedings of the 53rd Annual Meeting of the Association for Computational Linguistics and the 7th International Joint Conference on Natural Language Processing*, pages 323–333.

Ronald J Williams. 1992. Simple Statistical Gradient-Following Algorithms for Connectionist Reinforcement Learning. *Machine Learning*, 8(3-4):229–256.

Stephen Wu, Asaf Bachrach, Carlos Cardenas, and William Schuler. 2010. Complexity Metrics in an Incremental Right-corner Parser. In *Proceedings of the 48th Annual Meeting of the Association for Computational Linguistics*, pages 1189–1198.

A Illustration for the stack operations for the top category

Figure 5 shows the four kinds of stack manipulations for the top category described in Equation 12. The stack manipulations for the bottom category are similar to those illustrated here. At each depth of the stack, there are top and bottom categories, as well as vectors representing them. Figure 5 only shows stack depths with non-empty elements, as well as the stack depth the parser is currently at. Because Equation 12 only deals with the top category, only top categories are shown in the illustration. For all operations, the current working depth is 2. When both the bottom decision at the previous timestep b_{t-1} and the top decision at the current time step a_t are NULL, the parser returns to the stack depth above, copying the top category a^1_{t-1} and its vector $\mathbf{a}^1_{t-1}$ from the stack at the previous timestep to the new stack, shown in Figure 5.1. If the bottom category is NULL, but the top category at the current timestep is predicted to be a real category, the parser copies the categories from the stack depths above and generates a new vector $\mathbf{a}^2_t$ for the newly predicted top category a_t using the top category from the depth above $\mathbf{a}^2_{t-1}$, the current word $\mathbf{w}_t$ and the embedding of the predicted top category a_t as input to $\mathrm{LSTM}_{\theta_{Q'}}$, shown in Figure 5.2. If the bottom category from the previous timestep is not NULL, but the current top category is NULL, the parser copies top categories from all depths into the new stack, shown in Figure 5.3. Finally, if the bottom category and the top category are not NULL, the parser first copies all top categories and vectors, and then generates a new embedding $\mathbf{a}^3_t$ using the current word $\mathbf{w}_t$ and the category embedding of the new top category for the top category a_t in the stack depth below the current depth, creating a new derivational fragment, shown in Figure 5.4.

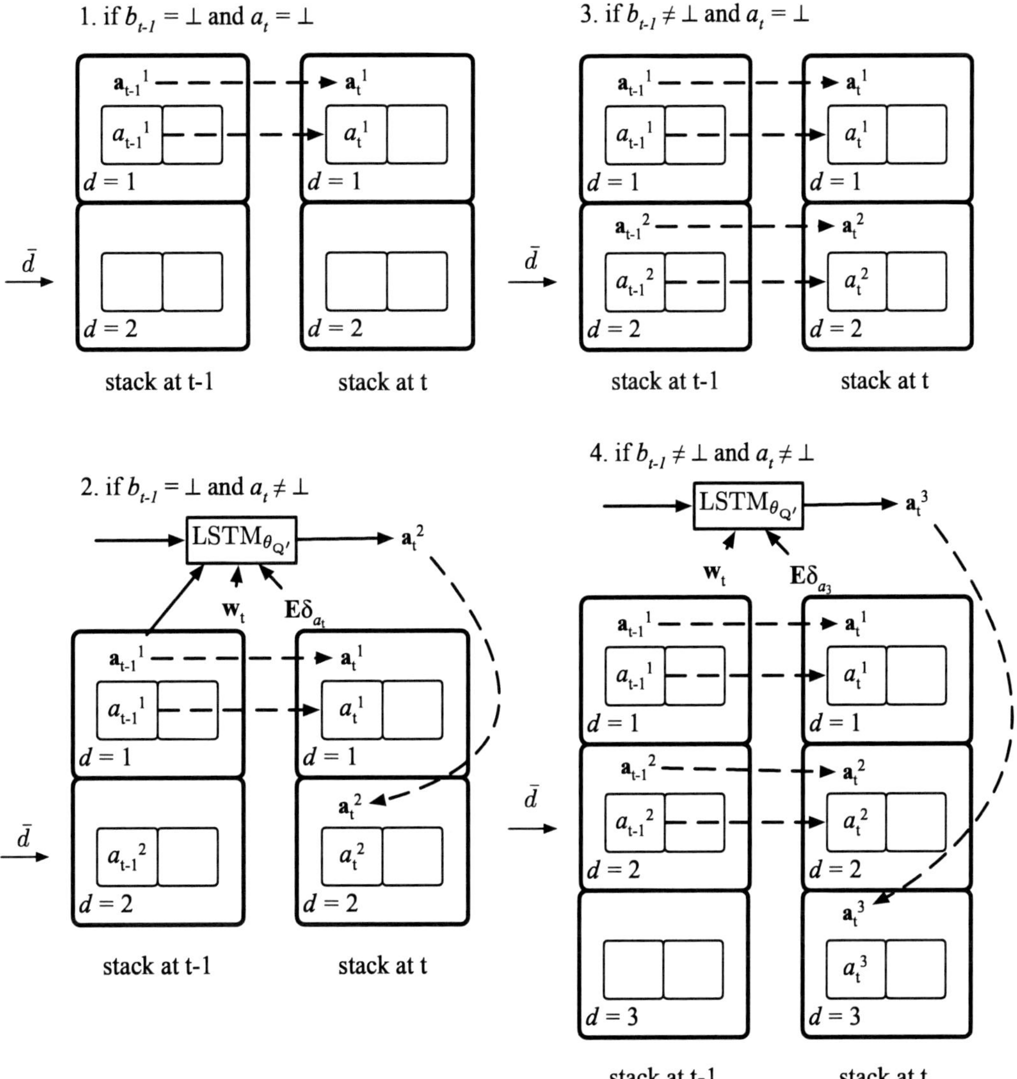

Figure 5: The stack operations for the top categories described in Equation 12.

B Constraint sets for parsing

There are two sets of constraints for different use cases for the parser to prune parses on the beam.

Basic set is the set of constraints used when psycholinguistic measures are needed. It includes two constraints: the first PJA must not be NULL, and all parses with $d = 0$ are removed from the beam while parsing.

Extended set is the set of constraints used when searching for a best parse. It guarantees that all parses on the beam to be valid parses. Let n be the length of the sentence, d the depth at the current time step and o be the offset of the current word at i to the end of the sentence, we can use the following constraints to ensure well-formed parses:

1. if $d = o - 1$, then both PJA$_t$ and PJB$_t$ must be NULL.

2. if $d = 1$ and $o > 1$, then PJA$_t$ and PJB$_t$ cannot be NULL at the same time.

3. if $d = o - 2$, if constraint 2 is also true, then PJA$_t$ and PJB$_t$ cannot be both NULL and both x, otherwise PJA$_t$ and PJB$_t$ cannot be both x.

The parser with the extended set can be seen as the parser with the basic set and a wider beam if it is used for getting the best parse. If a parse is at the top of the beam with the extended set, then it will be also at the top of beam with the basic set provided that it is not lost in beam search and a better one is not found due to using a wider beam.

Hyper-parameter	Value
LSTM layer	2
Word embedding dim	80
English pretrained word embedding dim	100
POS tag embedding dim	48
Decision embedding dim	50
Stack-LSTM input dim	256
Stack-LSTM hidden dim	256
Dropout	0.3
Feed-forward layer	2

Table 3: Hyper-parameters of the model used in the evaluations.

C Hyperparameters

Table 3 shows the hyperparameters the model use for all experiments. These values are tuned on the development set.

D lmer formulae for psycholinguistic experiments

The following sections record the lmer formulae for all psycholinguistic experiments mentioned in the paper. The independent variables included in all models are: word length (wlen), unigram probability (unigram) and 5-gram forward probability of the current word given the preceding context (fwprob5surp). All independent variables are centered and scaled before being added to each model. The 5-gram probabilities are interpolated 5-grams computed over the Gigaword corpus using KenLM (Heafield et al., 2013). Regressions to eye tracking data also include word position (wdelta) as well as whether the previous word was fixated on (prevwasfix). For regressing to go-past durations, one-position spillover measures for unigram (unigramS1) and 5-gram forward probability (fwprob5surpS1) are also added.

D.1 Natural stories

The lmer formula for regression to reading times in the Natural Stories Corpus is:

log(reading times) ~ z.(wlen) + z.(unigram) + z.(fwprob5surp) + z.(neuralsurp) + z.(vssurp) + (1 + z.(wlen) + z.(unigram) + z.(fwprob5surp) + z.(neuralsurp) + z.(vssurp) | subject) + (1 | word) + (1 | sentid:subject).

The difference between four evaluated models is whether each surprisal variable is used as a fixed effect or not. This is true for all the experiments.

D.2 Dundee: first pass

The lmer formula for regression to first pass fixation durations in the Dundee Corpus is:

log(first pass fixation duration) ~ z.(sentpos) + z.(wlen) + z.(wdelta) + z.(prevwasfix) + z.(fwprob5surp) + z.(cumfwprob5surp) + z.(totsurp) + z.(cumtotsurp) + z.(totsurpNeural) + (1 + z.(sentid) + z.(sentpos) + z.(wlen) + z.(wdelta) + z.(prevwasfix) + z.(fwprob5surp) + z.(cumfwprob5surp) + z.(vssurp) + z.(cumtotsurp) + z.(neuralsurp) | subject) + (1 | word) + (1 | sentid).

D.3 Dundee: go past

The lmer formula for regression to go past fixation durations in the Dundee Corpus is:

log(go past fixation duration) ~ z.(wlen) + z.(wdelta) + z.(prevwasfix) + z.(unigram) + z.(unigramS1) + z.(cumfwprob5surp) + z.(cumfwprob5surpS1) + z.(totsurpNeural) + z.(totsurp) + (1 + z.(wlen) + z.(wdelta) + z.(prevwasfix) + z.(unigram) + z.(unigramS1) + z.(cumfwprob5surp) + z.(cumfwprob5surpS1) + z.(neuralsurp) + z.(vssurp) | subject) + (1 | word) + (1 | sentid:subject)

Obfuscation for Privacy-preserving Syntactic Parsing

Zhifeng Hu[♠][*]   **Serhii Havrylov**[◇]   **Ivan Titov**[◇♡]   **Shay B. Cohen**[◇]

[♠]School of Computer Science, Fudan University, Shanghai 201203, China
[◇]School of Informatics, University of Edinburgh, Edinburgh EH8 9AB, UK
[♡]ILLC / FNWI, University of Amsterdam, Amsterdam 1098XG, Netherlands
`zfhu16@gmail.com, s.havrylov@ed.ac.uk`
`ititov@inf.ed.ac.uk, scohen@inf.ed.ac.uk`

Abstract

The goal of homomorphic encryption is to encrypt data such that another party can operate on it without being explicitly exposed to the content of the original data. We introduce an idea for a privacy-preserving transformation on natural language data, inspired by homomorphic encryption. Our primary tool is *obfuscation*, relying on the properties of natural language. Specifically, a given English text is obfuscated using a neural model that aims to preserve the syntactic relationships of the original sentence so that the obfuscated sentence can be parsed instead of the original one. The model works at the word level, and learns to obfuscate each word separately by changing it into a new word that has a similar syntactic role. The text obfuscated by our model leads to better performance on three syntactic parsers (two dependency and one constituency parsers) in comparison to an upper-bound random substitution baseline. More specifically, the results demonstrate that as more terms are obfuscated (by their part of speech), the substitution upper bound significantly degrades, while the neural model maintains a relatively high performing parser. All of this is done without much sacrifice of privacy compared to the random substitution upper bound. We also further analyze the results, and discover that the substituted words have similar syntactic properties, but different semantic content, compared to the original words.

1   Introduction

We consider the case in which there is a powerful server with NLP technology deployed on it, and a set of clients who would like to access it to get output resulting from input text taken from problems such as syntactic parsing, semantic parsing and machine translation. In such a case, the server models

---

* Work done at the University of Edinburgh.

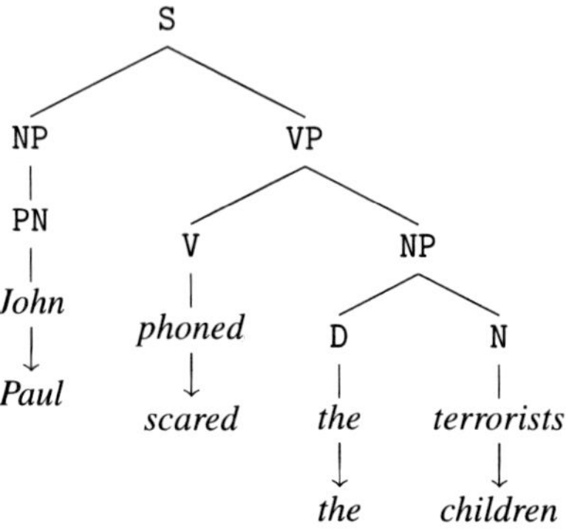

Figure 1:   An example of a sentence (words on top) and an obfuscated version of the sentence (words at bottom), both having identical syntactic structure. The obfuscated sentence hides the identity of the person who performs the action and the action itself.

may have been trained on large amounts of data, yielding models that cannot be deployed on the client machines either for efficiency or licensing reasons. We ask the following question: how can we use the NLP server models while minimizing the exposure of the server to the original text? Can we exploit the fact we work with natural language data to reduce such exposure?

Conventional encryption schemes, including public-key cryptography which is the one widely used across the Internet, are not sufficient to answer this question. They encrypt the input text before it is transferred to the server side. However, once the server decrypts the text, it has full access to it. This might be unacceptable if the server itself is not necessarily trustworthy.

The cryptography community posed a similar question much earlier, in the 1970s (Rivest et al., 1978) with partial resolutions proposed to solve it in later research (Sander et al., 1999; Boneh et al., 2005; Ishai and Paskin, 2007). These solutions al-

Proceedings of the 16th International Conference on Parsing Technologies and the IWPT 2020 Shared Task, pages 62–72
Virtual Meeting, July 9, 2020. ©2020 Association for Computational Linguistics

low the server to perform computations directly on encrypted data to get the desired output without ever decrypting the data. This cryptographic protocol is known as *homomorphic encryption*, where a client encrypts a message, then sends it to a server which performs potentially computationally intensive operations and returns a new data, still encrypted, which only the client can decipher. All of this is done without the server itself ever being exposed to the actual content of the encrypted input data. While solutions for generic homomorphic encryption have been discovered, they are either computationally inefficient (Gentry, 2010) or have strong limitations in regards to the depth and complexity of computation they permit (Bos et al., 2013).

In this paper, we consider a softer version of homomorphic encryption in the form of *obfuscation* for natural language. Our goal is to identify an efficient function that stochastically transforms a given natural language input (such as a sentence) into another input which can be further fed into an NLP server. The altered input has to preserve intra-text relationships that exist in the original sentence such that the NLP server, depending on the task at hand, can be successfully applied on the transformed data. There should be then a simple transformation that maps the output on the obfuscated data into a valid, accurate output for the original input. In addition, the altered input should hide the private semantic content of the original data.

This idea is demonstrated in Figure 1. The task at hand is syntactic parsing. We transform the input sentence *John phoned the terrorists* to the sentence *Paul scared the children* – both of which yield identical phrase-structure trees. In this case, the named entity *John* is hidden, and so are his actions. In the rest of the paper, we focus on this problem for dependency and constituency parsing.

We consider a neural model of obfuscation that operates at the word level. We assume access to the parser at training time: the model learns how to substitute words in the sentence with other words (in a stochastic manner) while maintaining the highest possible parsing accuracy. This learning task is framed as a latent-variable modeling problem where the obfuscated words are treated as latent. Direct optimization of this model turns out to be intractable, so we use continuous relaxations (Jang et al., 2016; Maddison et al., 2017) to avoid explicit marginalization.

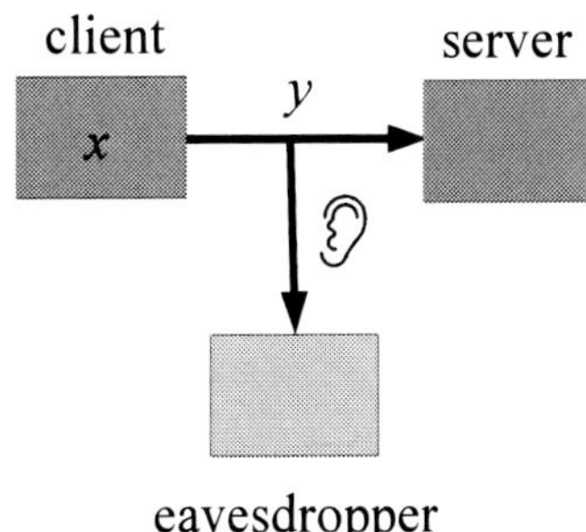

Figure 2: General setting illustration (figure adapted from Coavoux et al. 2018). An NLP client encrypts an x into y through obfuscation and y is sent to an NLP server. The NLP server (potentially even a legacy one) does not need to be modified to de-obfuscate y. An eavesdropper (a possibly malicious channel listener) only has access to y which is needed to be de-obfuscated to gain any information about x.

Our experimental results on English demonstrate that the neural model performs better than a strong random-based baseline (an upper bound; in which a word is substituted randomly with another word with the same part-of-speech tag). We vary the subset of words that are hidden and observe that the higher the obfuscation rate of the words, the harder it becomes for the parser to retain its accuracy. Degradation is especially pronounced with the random baseline and is less severe with our neural model. The improved results for the neural obfuscator come at a small cost to the accuracy of the attacker aimed at recovering the original obfuscated words. We also observe that the neural obfuscator is effective when different parsers or even different syntactic formalisms are used in training and test time. This relaxes the assumption that the obfuscator needs to have access to the NLP server at training time. Our results also suggest that the neural model tends to replace words with ones that have similar syntactic properties.

2 Homomorphic Obfuscation of Text

Our problem formulation is rather simple, demonstrated in generality in Figure 2. Let $\mathcal{T}$ be some natural language task, such as syntactic parsing, where $\mathcal{X}$ is the input space and $\mathcal{Z}$ is the output space. Let $f_{\mathcal{T}} \colon \mathcal{X} \to \mathcal{Z}$ be a trained decoder that maps x to its corresponding structure according to $\mathcal{T}$. Note that f is trained as usual on labeled data. Given a sentence $x = x_1 \cdots x_n$, we aim to learn a function that stochastically transforms x

into $y = y_1 \cdots y_n$ such that $f_{\mathcal{T}}(x)$ is close, if not identical, to $f_{\mathcal{T}}(y)$, or at the very least, we would like to be able to recover $f_{\mathcal{T}}(x)$ from $f_{\mathcal{T}}(y)$ using a simple transformation.

To ground this in an example, consider the case in which $\mathcal{T}$ is the problem of dependency parsing and $\mathcal{Z}$ is the set of dependency trees. If we transform a sentence x to y in such a way that it preserves the syntactic relationship between the indexed words in the sentences, then we can expect to easily recover the dependency tree for x from a dependency tree for y.

Note that we would also want to stochastically transform x into a y in such a way that it is *hard* to recover a certain type of information in x from y (otherwise, we could just set $y \leftarrow x$). Furthermore, we are interested in hiding information such as named entities or even nouns and verbs. In our formulation, we also assume that the sentence x comes with a function $t(x)$ that maps each token in the sentence with its corresponding part-of-speech tag (predicted using a POS tagger).

3   Neural Obfuscation Model

In this section we describe the neural model used to obfuscate the sentence. We note that the model has to be simple and efficient, as it is being run by the obfuscating party. If it is more complicated than parsing the text, for example, then the obfuscating party might as well directly parse the text.[1]

3.1   The Main Model

Our model operates by transforming a subset of the words in the sentence into new words. Each of these words is separately transformed in a way that maintains the sentence length after the transformation. Let x be the original sentence $x = x_1 \cdots x_n$ and let y be the output, $y = y_1 \cdots y_n$. From a high-level point of view, we have a conditional model:

$$p(y \mid x, \theta) = \prod_{i=1}^{n} p(y_i \mid x, \theta). \qquad (1)$$

The selection of words to obfuscate depends on their part of speech (POS) tags – only words that are associated with specific POS tags from the set $\mathcal{P}$ are obfuscated under our model. Let t_i be the

POS tag of the ith word in the sentence. In our basic model, we apply a bidirectional Long Short-Term Memory network (BiLSTM) to the sentence to get a latent representation h_i for each word x_i (see Section 3.2).

We assume conditional independence between the sequence $x_1 \cdots x_{i-1} x_{i+1} \cdots x_n$ and y_i given h_i (which is a function of x), and as such, our probability distribution $p(y_i \mid x, \theta)$ is given by:

$$p(y_i = y \mid x_i, h_i, \theta) = \begin{cases} 1 & t_i \notin \mathcal{P}, y = x_i \\ p_y & t_i \in \mathcal{P}, y \in \mathcal{V}_{t_i} \setminus \{x_i\} \\ 0 & otherwise. \end{cases} \quad (2)$$

Here, $\mathcal{V}_{t_i}$ is the set of word types appearing at least once with tag t_i in the training set, and p_y is predicted with a softmax function, relying on the BiLSTM state h_i. More specifically, we define p_y as follows:

$$p_y = \frac{\exp(w_{t_i,y}^\top h_i)}{\sum_{y' \in \mathcal{V}_{t_i}, y' \neq x_i} \exp(w_{t_i,y'}^\top h_i)},$$

where $w_{t,y} \in \mathbb{R}^{1024}$ are vectors of parameters associated with every tag-word pair (t, y), $y \in \mathcal{V}_t$. Note that the above probability distribution never transforms a word x_i to an identical word if $t_i \in \mathcal{P}$. This is a hard constraint in our model.

3.2   Embedding the Sentence

The BiLSTM that encodes the sentence requires an embedding per word, which we create as follows. We first map each token x_i to three embedding channels e_i^k, $k \in \{1, 2, 3\}$. The first channel is a randomly initialized embedding for each part-of-speech tag. Its dimension is 100. The second channel is a pre-trained GloVe embedding for the corresponding token. The vector e_i^3 is a character-level word embedding (Kim et al., 2016) which first maps each character of the word into an embedding vector of dimension 100 and then uses unidimensional convolution over the concatenation of the embedding vectors of each character. Finally, max-pooling is applied to obtain a single feature. This process is repeated with 100 convolutional kernels so that $e_i^3 \in \mathbb{R}^{100}$.

The three embedding channels $\{e_i^1, e_i^2, e_i^3\}$ are then concatenated and used in the BiLSTM encoder. We use a three-layer BiLSTM with Bayesian dropout (Gal and Ghahramani, 2016). The hidden state dimensionality is 512 for each direction.

---

[1] In the general case, there is a caveat to this statement. It might be the case that the training cost for the server's model is high, and that the model is proprietary. In that case, even if the model can be run on the client side, it might not be possible to do so.

4 Training

In our experiments, we focus on obfuscation for the goal of syntactic parsing. We assume the existence of a conditional parsing model $p_0(z \mid x)$ where z is a parse tree and x is a sentence. This is the base model which is trained offline, and to which we have read-only access and cannot change its parameters. As we will see in experiments, the obfuscator can be trained using a different parser from the one used at test time (i.e. from the one hosted at the NLP server).

Let $(x^{(1)}, z^{(1)}), \ldots, (x^{(n)}, z^{(n)})$ be a set of training examples which consists of sentences and their corresponding parse trees. Considering Eq. 1, we would be interested in maximizing the following log-likelihood objective with respect to θ:

$$\mathcal{L}_0 = \sum_{i=1}^{n} \log \left(\sum_{y} p(y \mid x^{(i)}, \theta) p_0(z^{(i)} \mid y) \right).$$

This objective maximizes the log-likelihood of the parsing model with respect to the obfuscation model. Maximizing the objective $\mathcal{L}_0$ is intractable due to summation over all possible obfuscations. We use Jensen's inequality[2] to lower-bound the cost function $\mathcal{L}_0$ by the following objective:

$$\mathcal{L} = \sum_{i=1}^{n} \sum_{y} p(y \mid x^{(i)}, \theta) \log p_0(z^{(i)} \mid y)$$

$$= \sum_{i=1}^{n} \mathbb{E}_{p(\cdot \mid x^{(i)}, \theta)} \left[\log p_0(z^{(i)} \mid y) \right].$$

Intuitively, the objective function maximizes the accuracy of an existing parser while using as an input the sentences after their transformation. Note that the accuracy is measured with respect to the gold-standard dependency parse tree.[3] This is possible because the sentence length of the original sentence and the obfuscated sentence are identical, and the mapping between the words in each version of the sentence is bijective.

To encourage stochasticity, we also tried including an entropy term that is maximized with respect

to θ in the following form:

$$H_i(\theta, \lambda) = -\lambda \sum_{y} p(y \mid x^{(i)}, \theta) \log p(y \mid x^{(i)}, \theta).$$

However, in our final experiments we omitted that term because (a) it did not seem to affect the model stochasticity to a significant degree; (b) the performance has become very sensitive to the entropy weight λ.

While we can estimate the objective $\mathcal{L}$ using sampling, we cannot differentiate through samples to estimate the gradients with respect to the obfuscator parameters θ. In order to ensure end-to-end differentiabilty, we use a continuous relaxation, the Gumbel-Softmax estimator (Jang et al., 2016; Maddison et al., 2017), and the reparamterization trick (Kingma and Welling, 2014; Rezende et al., 2014).

More formally, the i-th token is represented by the random variable with categorical probability distribution $\mathrm{Cat}(p_i)$ that has support $\mathcal{V}_{t_i}$. To sample the word we first draw $u_k \sim \mathrm{Uniform}(0, 1)$ and transform it to the Gumbel noise $g_k = -\log(-\log(u_k))$, then we calculate

$$y' = \mathrm{onehot} \left\{ \arg\max_{k \in \mathcal{V}_{t_i}} [g_k + \log(p_{i,k})] \right\}$$

as the sampled discrete choice of substitution from $\mathcal{V}_{t_i}$ and

$$y_k = \frac{\exp\left((g_k + \log(p_{i,k})/\tau)\right)}{\sum_{k'} \exp\left((g_{k'} + \log(p_{i,k'})/\tau)\right)}$$

as the "relaxed" differentiable proxy for this choice, where τ denotes the temperature. When it approaches 0, the vector $(y_1, \ldots, y_{|\mathcal{V}_{t_i}|})$ is close to a one-hot vector sampled from the given categorical distribution.[4]

We use the Straight-Through version of the estimator (Bengio et al., 2013): the discrete sampled choice is fed into the parser in the forward computation but the relaxed differentiable surrogate is used when computing partial derivatives on the backward pass.

During the training of our neural model, the parser only backpropagates the gradient from the objective of maximizing the parsing accuracy (i.e. minimum cross-entropy loss of the correct head and label for each word), and hence its parameters are always fixed and are not updated during the optimization.

---

[2]Jensen's inequality states that for a non-negative random variable Z and its probability distribution q it holds that $\log(\mathbb{E}_q[Z]) \geq \mathbb{E}_q[\log Z]$.

[3]In principle, we may not need access to gold-standard annotation when training the obfuscator. Instead, we could train the model to agree with the parser predictions for the original sentence, i.e. $z^{(i)} = \arg\max_z p_0(z \mid x^{(i)})$.

[4]In practice, we anneal the temperature from 1.0 to 0.5 over the course of training.

5 Attacker Approaches

We test the efficiency of our obfuscation model by developing two independent attacker models. Their goal is to recover the original words by inspecting only the obfuscated sentence. The attacker models may have access to all data that the parser and the obfuscator models were trained and developed on. This is perhaps unlike other scenarios in which the training set is assumed to be inaccessible to any attacker.

We note that ideally, we would want to show that our obfuscation model retains privacy universally for *any* attacker. However, this is quite a difficult task, and we follow Coavoux et al. (2018) in presenting two strong attackers which may represent possible universal attackers.

In our attacker experiments, we assume that it is known which words in the sentence are obfuscated. As such, the results we provide for attacking our obfuscation are an upper bound. In practice, an attacker would also have to identify which words were substituted for new words, which may lead to a small decrease in its accuracy.

5.1 Trained Attacker

Our first attacker works by first encoding the obfuscated sentence with a BiLSTM network. We then try to predict original words by using a feed-forward neural network on each of the hidden representations obtained from the encoder model. The architecture is identical to that of the obfuscation model (see Section 3.1), with the only difference that there is a softmax over the entire vocabulary $\mathcal{V}$ instead of restricting it to $V_{t_i} \setminus \{x_i\}$, as in Eq. 2.

5.2 Pretrained Attacker

In addition to a trained attacker, we also use a conditional language model, BERT (Devlin et al., 2019).[5] BERT is based on the Transformer model of Vaswani et al. (2017), and uses a bidirectional encoder to obtain "contextual" embeddings for each word in a given sentence. We use the BERT model by masking out each obfuscated word, and then predicting the masked word similar to the "masked language task" that is mentioned by Devlin et al. (2019). This means that the embeddings in each position are fed into a softmax function to predict the missing word. We use the `bert-base-uncased` model among the available BERT models.

We note that this attacker is not trained by us. Its main weakness is that it is trained on the non-obfuscated text. However, its strength is that it is trained on large amounts of data (we use the model that is trained on 3.3 billion tokens). In addition, in some settings that we consider the obfuscation of the sentence is done in such a way that much of the context by which we predict the obfuscated word remains intact.

6 Experiments

In this section, we describe our experiments with our obfuscation model. We first describe the experimental setting and then turn to the results.[6]

6.1 Experimental Setting

In our experiments, we test the obfuscation model on two parsers. The first parser is used during the training of our model. This is the bi-affine dependency parser developed by Dozat and Manning (2017). To test whether our obfuscation model also generalizes to syntactic parsers that were not used during its training, the constituency parser that is included in the AllenNLP software package (Gardner et al., 2018) was used.[7]

For our dependency parser, we follow the canonical setting of using pre-trained word embedding, 1D convolutional character level embedding and POS tag embedding, each of 100 dimensions as the input feature. We also use a three-layer bidirectional LSTM with Bayesian dropout (Gal and Ghahramani, 2016) as the encoder. We use the bi-affine attention mechanism to obtain the prediction for each head, and also the prediction for the edge labels.

We use the English Penn Treebank (PTB; Marcus et al. 1993) version 3.0 converted using Stanford dependencies for training the dependency parser. We follow the standard parsing split for training (sections 01–21), development (section 22) and test sets (section 23). The training set portion of the PTB data is also used to train our neural obfuscator model.

We also create a spectrum over the POS tags to decide on the set $\mathcal{P}$ for each of our experiments (see Section 3.1). This spectrum is described in Table 1.

---

[5]We use the implementation available at `https://github.com/huggingface/pytorch-pretrained-BERT`.

[6]Our code is available at `https://github.com/ichn-hu/Parsing-Obfuscation`.

[7]We used version 0.8.1.

i	Category description	$\mathcal{P}_i$
1	Named entities	NNP, NNPS
2	Nouns	NN, NNS
3	Adjectives	JJ, JJR, JJS
4	Verbs	VB, VBN, VBD, VBZ, VBP, VBG
5	Adverbs	RB, RBR, RBS

Table 1: A spectrum of part-of-speech tags to obfuscate. In the jth experiment, we set $\mathcal{P} = \cup_{i=1}^{j} \mathcal{P}_i$.

Let the ith set in that table be $\mathcal{P}_i$ for $i \in [5]$[8]. In our jth experiment, $j \in [5]$, we obfuscate the set $\mathcal{P} = \cup_{i=1}^{j} \mathcal{P}_i$. This spectrum of POS tags describes a range from words that are highly content-bearing for privacy concerns (such as named entities) to words that are less of a privacy concern (such as adverbs).

We compare our model against a (privacy) upperbound baseline which is found to be rather strong. With this baseline, a word x with a tag $t \in \mathcal{P}$ is substituted with another by a word that appeared with the same tag in the training data from the set $\mathcal{V}_t$. The substituted words are uniformly sampled. This random baseline serves as an *upper* bound for the privacy level achieved, not a lower bound. Randomly substituting a word with another makes it difficult to recover the original word. However, in terms of parsing accuracy, as we see below, there is a significant room for improvement over that baseline. There are words, which when substituted by other group of words, yield altogether better parsing accuracy.

We evaluate the model through three different principal metrics. The first metric is the accuracy of the parser (Unlabeled Attachment Score or Labeled Attachment Score, depending on the context[9]), the second is the mean reciprocal rank (MRR) of the attacker on the relevant method. With each of the attacker methods, we obtain a distribution q over the possible true outputs recovered from the obfuscated word. We use this distribution to calculate the MRR, the average inverse rank of the correct word according to q. More precisely, the score we calculate is:

$$\text{MRR} = \frac{100}{N} \sum_{i=1}^{N} \frac{1}{r_i},$$

where $r_i \in \mathbb{N}$ is the rank of the ith word (in the whole corpus) according to q (the distribution over possible output words for that word).[10] The result we report is attacker error, or $100 - \text{MRR}$ (the higher it is, the more privacy is maintained). Finally, we also report the ratio between the accuracy of the parser[11] and the accuracy of an attacker (MRR). This metric provides a way to measure the amount of accuracy we gain for each point of privacy we lose, in the form of $\dfrac{\text{accuracy}}{\text{breach}}$ units.

All neural experiments were run on a single GeForce GTX 1080 Ti GPU. The time to run each of the experiments was in the range of 13.3 hours to 25.2 hours.

6.2 Results with Dependency Parsing

In our first set of experiments, we compare the random substitution model to the neural model of obfuscation on the dependency parsing model that was used during training. As is seen in Table 2(a), both the neural model and the random model, with their substitutions, do not significantly harm the accuracy of the parser for the first three experiments (corresponds to rows in the table). However, as the number of obfuscated words increases (with the categories of verbs and adverbs), the accuracy of the parser significantly drops, significantly more for the random model than the neural model.

The attacker error is in the range of the 70%–80% for all experiments. As expected, the random model, given its inherent unpredictability, makes it more difficult for the attacker to identify the original words. That leads to the ratio between accuracy and intrrusion level often being better with the random model. In general, it also seems that the BERT attacker gives similar results to the trained attacker for the random baseline, and worse results with the neural model. Finally, it is evident that as we obfuscate more terms, the attacker's accuracy decreases, with the BERT attacker consistently outperforming the trained attacker.

We next turn to inspect the problem of dependency parsing without a parser that was trained

---

[8]For an integer k, we denote by $[k]$ the set $\{1, ..., k\}$.

[9]The unlabeled/labeled distinction refers to whether the label of the edge in the dependency tree is taken into account when computing the accuracy.

[10]Note that we have a multiplier of 100 in our MRR score definition. This deviates from the standard definition of this score.

[11]The accuracy is labeled attachment score in the case of dependency parsing.

(a)

	Obf. terms	Random (baseline)					Neural model				
			trained		BERT			trained		BERT	
		acc (U L)		prv	ratio	prv	ratio	acc (U L)		prv	ratio	prv	ratio
trained dep.	Named ent.	94.1	93.0	68.3	2.97	66.9	2.84	94.3	92.9	68.4	2.98	66.4	2.81
	+Nouns	93.7	92.9	70.7	3.20	70.3	3.15	94.1	92.4	69.7	3.11	69.4	3.08
	+Adjectives	93.1	92.4	71.9	3.31	72.3	3.36	93.6	91.7	70.5	3.17	70.1	3.13
	+Verbs	85.2	80.4	68.1	2.67	80.2	4.30	87.3	78.7	65.3	2.52	78.1	3.99
	+Adverbs	86.4	78.7	67.2	2.63	81.2	4.60	88.6	76.6	64.2	2.47	77.5	3.94
	No obf.	95.0/93.5 (U/L)										
AllenNLP dep.	Named ent.	91.9	89.7	68.3	2.90	66.9	2.78	92.2	90.1	68.4	2.92	66.4	2.74
	+Nouns	91.5	89.2	70.7	3.12	70.3	3.08	91.5	89.4	69.7	3.02	69.4	2.99
	+Adjectives	90.8	88.5	71.9	3.23	72.3	3.28	91.2	89.0	70.5	3.09	70.1	3.05
	+Verbs	78.2	75.3	68.1	2.45	80.2	3.95	82.2	79.4	65.3	2.37	78.1	3.75
	+Adverbs	76.7	73.5	67.2	2.34	81.2	4.08	82.0	78.9	64.2	2.29	77.5	3.64
	No obf.	94.2/92.6 (U/L)										

(b)

	Obf. terms	Random (baseline)					Neural model				
			trained		BERT			trained		BERT	
		acc (F_1)	prv	ratio	prv	ratio	acc (F_1)	prv	ratio	prv	ratio
AllenNLP const.	Named ent.	92.4	68.3	2.91	66.9	2.79	92.5	68.4	2.93	66.4	2.75
	+Nouns	88.2	70.1	2.95	70.3	2.97	89.0	69.7	2.94	69.4	2.91
	+Adjectives	86.8	71.9	3.09	72.3	3.13	88.1	70.5	2.99	70.1	2.95
	+Verbs	79.2	68.1	2.48	80.2	4.00	82.5	65.3	2.38	78.1	3.77
	+Adverbs	76.8	67.2	2.34	81.2	4.09	79.5	64.2	2.22	77.5	3.53
	No obf.	93.7									

Table 2: (a) Results of parsing accuracy and attacker error for two different dependency parsers. "acc" denotes accuracy (Unlabeled Attachment Score/Labeled Attachment Score for the dependency parsers), "prv" denotes the attacker error (trained attacker and BERT attacker as described in Section 5.1 Section 5.2) and "ratio" is the ratio between the parser accuracy and the attacker error. Two parsers are considered: a parser that participates in the obfuscation model optimization (top part), and offline-trained parsers from the AllenNLP for dependency (bottom part). Two obfuscation models are considered: neural (Section 3.1) and a random baseline. "No obf." are parsing results without obfuscation. See Table 1 for a description of each category of obfuscation terms.. Note that the categories are expanded in the cumulative fashion: e.g., "+Adjectives" refers to the union of named entities, nouns and adjectives. "acc" and "prv" are better when they are higher. (b) Results of parsing accuracy and attacker error for the AllenNLP constituency parser. "acc" denotes accuracy (F_1 PARSEVAL). The constituency parser does not participate in the obfuscation model optimization. *The results demonstrate how quickly the parsers degrade when more terms obfuscated with the random baseline, while retaining a much higher accuracy with the neural system (acc. column).*

with the neural obfuscation model (bottom part of Table 2(a)). We see similar trends there as well, in which the first three experiments give a reasonable performance for both the neural and the random model with a significant drop in performance for the two experiments that follow. We also see that the differences between the neural obfuscation model and the random model are smaller (though still significant), pointing to the importance of using the dependency model during the training of the neural model.

6.3 Results with Constituency Parsing

Table 2(b) describes the results for constituency parsing with the AllenNLP constituency parser as described in Section 6.1. The results point to a similar direction as was described for dependency parsing. While the ratio between accuracy and privacy is slightly better for the random model, there is a significant drop in performance for the fourth and fifth experiments when comparing random model to the neural model.

6.4 Analysis of Syntactic Preservation

Table 3 presents five sentences and their obfuscated versions both by the neural model and the random model. In general, when we inspected the results for the two models, we found that the neural model tends to replace words by others that have a functional syntactic role that is closer to the original. For example, in the examples we present, *was* is replaced with *were* and *n't* is replaced with *not*. The random model, however, does not adhere to any syntactic similarity between the original word

original	I	*do*	*n't*	*feel*	*very*	*ferocious*	.
random	I	*liberalize*	*Usually*	*spin*	*firsthand*	*undistinguished*	.
neural	I	*have*	*not*	*choose*	*even*	*Preliminary*	.
POS	PRP	VBP	RB	VB	RB	JJ	.

original	*Individuals*	can	*always*	*have*	their	*hands*	*slapped*	.
random	*drugstores*	can	*secretly*	*galvanize*	their	*persons*	*hurt*	.
neural	*brokerages*	can	*even*	*get*	their	*Outflows*	*vetoed*	.
POS	NNS	MD	RB	VB	PRP$	NNS	VBN	.

original	*Analysts*	*do*	*n't*	*see*	it	that	*way*	.
random	*carpenters*	*merge*	*unilaterally*	*undertake*	it	that	*wind*	.
neural	*brokerages*	*have*	*not*	*choose*	it	that	*direction*	.
POS	NNS	VBP	RB	VB	PRP	DT	NN	.

original	The	*device*	*was*	*replaced*	.
random	The	*admiral*	*echoed*	*blunted*	.
neural	The	*insulation*	*were*	*vetoed*	.
POS	DT	NN	VBD	VBN	.

original	"	That	*was*	*offset*	by	*strength*	*elsewhere*	.
random	"	That	*produced*	*flawed*	by	*professionalism*	*near*	.
neural	"	That	*were*	*vetoed*	by	*direction*	*even*	.
POS	"	DT	VBD	VBN	IN	NN	RB	.

Table 3: Example of five sentences obfuscated with the random and neural models. Words in italics are the ones being substituted (or the substitutes). The obfuscated terms are named entities, nouns, adjectives, verbs and adverbs.

and its substituted version beyond them having been seen in the training data with the same part-of-speech tag.

To further test whether the neural model preserves other syntactic similarities between the original and obfuscated sentences, we took all verbs from Propbank (Kingsbury and Palmer, 2002) and created a signature for each one: the list of argument types it can appear with. For example, the signature for *yield* is *01,012*, which means that "yield" appears with two frames in Propbank, one with two arguments and the other with three arguments. We then calculated for each verb[12] that appears in the original sentence the overlap between its signature and the signature of the verb in the obfuscated sentence (neural or random). This overlap is counted as the size of the intersection of the frame signatures of the two verbs. For example, the signature of *advocate* might be *012* while the signature of *affect* is *012,01*. Therefore, their overlap is 1.

There was a stark difference between the two averages of the overlap sizes. For the random baseline model, the average was 1.46 (over 5,680 tokens) and for the neural model the average was 1.80. The difference between these two averages is statistically significant with p-value < 0.05 in a one-sided t-test.

7   Related Work

There has been a significant increase in interest in the topic of privacy in the NLP community in recent years. For example, Reddy and Knight (2016) focused on obfuscation of gender features from social media text, while Li et al. (2018), Coavoux et al. (2018) and Elazar and Goldberg (2018) focused on the removal of private information from neural representations such as named entities and demographic information. Unlike the latter work, we are interested in preserving the privacy of the *inputs* themselves, while requiring no extra work from deployed NLP software which processes these

---

[12] The verbs were lemmatized first using the WordNet lemmatizer available in NLTK.

inputs. Marujo et al. (2015), for example, perform multi-document summarization on an approximate version of the original documents.

Differential privacy (Dwork, 2008) which aims to protect the privacy of information contained in a dataset has also been actively researched. Recent research brings differential privacy into natural language processing, for example, the work by Fernandes et al. (2019) that targets the removal of authorship identity in a text classification dataset.

With homomorphic encryption being a long-standing important topic in cryptography, it has also made its way into the field of privacy in machine learning, particularly in terms of designing neural networks which enable homomorphic operations over encrypted data (Hesamifard et al., 2017; Bourse et al., 2018). For example, Gilad-Bachrach et al. (2016) designed a fully homomorphic encrypted convolutional neural network that was able to solve the MNIST dataset with practical efficiency and accuracy. The scheme of direct homomorphic encryption (Brakerski et al., 2014) is constrained by the multiplication depth degree in the circuit, which makes deep models intractable. Other schemes were developed in recent years (Cheon et al., 2017; Fan and Vercauteren, 2012; Dathathri et al., 2018), but achieving satisfactory performance is still a challenge. To the best of our knowledge, no prior work has demonstrated that homomorphic encryption could be directly applied to the design of recurrent neural networks or discrete tokens as input.

8   Conclusions

We presented a model and an empirical study for obfuscating sentences so that the obfuscated sentences transfer syntactic information from the original sentence. Our neural model outperforms in parsing accuracy a strong random baseline when many of the words in the sentence are obfuscated. In addition, the neural model tends to replace words in the original sentence with words which have a closer syntactic function to the original word than a random baseline.

Acknowledgments

The authors thank Marco Damonte and the anonymous reviewers for feedback and comments on a draft of this paper. This research was supported by a grant from Bloomberg, an ERC Starting Grant BroadSem 678254 and the Dutch National Science Foundation NWO VIDI grant 639.022.518.

References

Yoshua Bengio, Nicholas Léonard, and Aaron C. Courville. 2013. Estimating or propagating gradients through stochastic neurons for conditional computation. *CoRR*, abs/1308.3432.

Dan Boneh, Eu-Jin Goh, and Kobbi Nissim. 2005. Evaluating 2-dnf formulas on ciphertexts. In *Theory of Cryptography Conference*, pages 325–341. Springer.

Joppe W. Bos, Kristin E. Lauter, Jake Loftus, and Michael Naehrig. 2013. Improved security for a ring-based fully homomorphic encryption scheme. In *Cryptography and Coding - 14th IMA International Conference, IMACC 2013, Oxford, UK, December 17-19, 2013. Proceedings*, pages 45–64.

Florian Bourse, Michele Minelli, Matthias Minihold, and Pascal Paillier. 2018. Fast homomorphic evaluation of deep discretized neural networks. In *Advances in Cryptology - CRYPTO 2018 - 38th Annual International Cryptology Conference, Santa Barbara, CA, USA, August 19-23, 2018, Proceedings, Part III*, volume 10993 of *Lecture Notes in Computer Science*, pages 483–512. Springer.

Zvika Brakerski, Craig Gentry, and Vinod Vaikuntanathan. 2014. (leveled) fully homomorphic encryption without bootstrapping. *TOCT*, 6(3):13:1–13:36.

Jung Hee Cheon, Andrey Kim, Miran Kim, and Yong Soo Song. 2017. Homomorphic encryption for arithmetic of approximate numbers. In *Advances in Cryptology - ASIACRYPT 2017 - 23rd International Conference on the Theory and Applications of Cryptology and Information Security, Hong Kong, China, December 3-7, 2017, Proceedings, Part I*, volume 10624 of *Lecture Notes in Computer Science*, pages 409–437. Springer.

Maximin Coavoux, Shashi Narayan, and Shay B. Cohen. 2018. Privacy-preserving neural representations of text. In *Proceedings of the 2018 Conference on Empirical Methods in Natural Language Processing, Brussels, Belgium, October 31 - November 4, 2018*, pages 1–10. Association for Computational Linguistics.

Roshan Dathathri, Olli Saarikivi, Hao Chen, Kim Laine, Kristin E. Lauter, Saeed Maleki, Madanlal Musuvathi, and Todd Mytkowicz. 2018. CHET: compiler and runtime for homomorphic evaluation of tensor programs. *CoRR*, abs/1810.00845.

Jacob Devlin, Ming-Wei Chang, Kenton Lee, and Kristina Toutanova. 2019. BERT: pre-training of deep bidirectional transformers for language understanding. In *Proceedings of the 2019 Conference of the North American Chapter of the Association for Computational Linguistics: Human Language Technologies, NAACL-HLT 2019, Minneapolis, MN, USA, June 2-7, 2019, Volume 1 (Long and Short Papers)*, pages 4171–4186. Association for Computational Linguistics.

Timothy Dozat and Christopher D. Manning. 2017. Deep biaffine attention for neural dependency parsing. In *5th International Conference on Learning Representations, ICLR 2017, Toulon, France, April 24-26, 2017, Conference Track Proceedings*. OpenReview.net.

Cynthia Dwork. 2008. Differential privacy: A survey of results. In *Theory and Applications of Models of Computation, 5th International Conference, TAMC 2008, Xi'an, China, April 25-29, 2008. Proceedings*, volume 4978 of *Lecture Notes in Computer Science*, pages 1–19. Springer.

Yanai Elazar and Yoav Goldberg. 2018. Adversarial removal of demographic attributes from text data. In *Proceedings of the 2018 Conference on Empirical Methods in Natural Language Processing, Brussels, Belgium, October 31 - November 4, 2018*, pages 11–21. Association for Computational Linguistics.

Junfeng Fan and Frederik Vercauteren. 2012. Somewhat practical fully homomorphic encryption. *IACR Cryptol. ePrint Arch.*, 2012:144.

Natasha Fernandes, Mark Dras, and Annabelle McIver. 2019. Generalised differential privacy for text document processing. In *Principles of Security and Trust - 8th International Conference, POST 2019, Held as Part of the European Joint Conferences on Theory and Practice of Software, ETAPS 2019, Prague, Czech Republic, April 6-11, 2019, Proceedings*, volume 11426 of *Lecture Notes in Computer Science*, pages 123–148. Springer.

Yarin Gal and Zoubin Ghahramani. 2016. A theoretically grounded application of dropout in recurrent neural networks. In *Advances in Neural Information Processing Systems 29: Annual Conference on Neural Information Processing Systems 2016, December 5-10, 2016, Barcelona, Spain*, pages 1019–1027.

Matt Gardner, Joel Grus, Mark Neumann, Oyvind Tafjord, Pradeep Dasigi, Nelson F. Liu, Matthew E. Peters, Michael Schmitz, and Luke Zettlemoyer. 2018. Allennlp: A deep semantic natural language processing platform. *CoRR*, abs/1803.07640.

Craig Gentry. 2010. Computing arbitrary functions of encrypted data. *Commun. ACM*, 53(3):97–105.

Ran Gilad-Bachrach, Nathan Dowlin, Kim Laine, Kristin E. Lauter, Michael Naehrig, and John Wernsing. 2016. Cryptonets: Applying neural networks to encrypted data with high throughput and accuracy. In *Proceedings of the 33nd International Conference on Machine Learning, ICML 2016, New York City, NY, USA, June 19-24, 2016*, volume 48 of *JMLR Workshop and Conference Proceedings*, pages 201–210. JMLR.org.

Ehsan Hesamifard, Hassan Takabi, and Mehdi Ghasemi. 2017. Cryptodl: Deep neural networks over encrypted data. *CoRR*, abs/1711.05189.

Yuval Ishai and Anat Paskin. 2007. Evaluating branching programs on encrypted data. In *Theory of Cryptography, 4th Theory of Cryptography Conference, TCC 2007, Amsterdam, The Netherlands, February 21-24, 2007, Proceedings*, volume 4392 of *Lecture Notes in Computer Science*, pages 575–594. Springer.

Eric Jang, Shixiang Gu, and Ben Poole. 2016. Categorical reparameterization with Gumbel-Softmax. *CoRR*, abs/1611.01144.

Yoon Kim, Yacine Jernite, David Sontag, and Alexander M. Rush. 2016. Character-aware neural language models. In *Proceedings of the Thirtieth AAAI Conference on Artificial Intelligence, February 12-17, 2016, Phoenix, Arizona, USA.*, pages 2741–2749.

Diederik P. Kingma and Max Welling. 2014. Autoencoding variational bayes. In *2nd International Conference on Learning Representations, ICLR 2014, Banff, AB, Canada, April 14-16, 2014, Conference Track Proceedings*.

Paul R. Kingsbury and Martha Palmer. 2002. From treebank to propbank. In *Proceedings of the Third International Conference on Language Resources and Evaluation, LREC 2002, May 29-31, 2002, Las Palmas, Canary Islands, Spain*. European Language Resources Association.

Yitong Li, Timothy Baldwin, and Trevor Cohn. 2018. Towards robust and privacy-preserving text representations. In *Proceedings of the 56th Annual Meeting of the Association for Computational Linguistics, ACL 2018, Melbourne, Australia, July 15-20, 2018, Volume 2: Short Papers*, pages 25–30. Association for Computational Linguistics.

Chris J. Maddison, Andriy Mnih, and Yee Whye Teh. 2017. The concrete distribution: A continuous relaxation of discrete random variables. In *5th International Conference on Learning Representations, ICLR 2017, Toulon, France, April 24-26, 2017, Conference Track Proceedings*. OpenReview.net.

Mitchell P. Marcus, Beatrice Santorini, and Mary Ann Marcinkiewicz. 1993. Building a large annotated corpus of english: The penn treebank. *Comput. Linguistics*, 19(2):313–330.

Luís Marujo, José Portêlo, Wang Ling, David Martins de Matos, João P Neto, Anatole Gershman, Jaime Carbonell, Isabel Trancoso, and Bhiksha Raj. 2015. Privacy-preserving multi-document summarization. *arXiv preprint arXiv:1508.01420.*

Sravana Reddy and Kevin Knight. 2016. Obfuscating gender in social media writing. In *Proceedings of the First Workshop on NLP and Computational Social Science, NLP+CSS@EMNLP 2016, Austin, TX, USA, November 5, 2016*, pages 17–26. Association for Computational Linguistics.

Danilo Jimenez Rezende, Shakir Mohamed, and Daan Wierstra. 2014. Stochastic backpropagation and approximate inference in deep generative models. In *Proceedings of the 31th International Conference on Machine Learning, ICML 2014, Beijing, China, 21-26 June 2014*, volume 32 of *JMLR Workshop and Conference Proceedings*, pages 1278–1286. JMLR.org.

Ronald L Rivest, Len Adleman, Michael L Dertouzos, et al. 1978. On data banks and privacy homomorphisms. *Foundations of secure computation*, 4(11):169–180.

Tomas Sander, Adam Young, and Moti Yung. 1999. Non-interactive cryptocomputing for nc/sup 1. In *40th Annual Symposium on Foundations of Computer Science (Cat. No. 99CB37039)*, pages 554–566. IEEE.

Ashish Vaswani, Noam Shazeer, Niki Parmar, Jakob Uszkoreit, Llion Jones, Aidan N. Gomez, Lukasz Kaiser, and Illia Polosukhin. 2017. Attention is all you need. In *Advances in Neural Information Processing Systems 30: Annual Conference on Neural Information Processing Systems 2017, 4-9 December 2017, Long Beach, CA, USA*, pages 5998–6008.

Tensors over Semirings for Latent-Variable Weighted Logic Programs

Esma Balkır[1]   Daniel Gildea[2]   Shay B. Cohen[1]

[1]ILCC, School of Informatics, University of Edinburgh
[2]Department of Computer Science, University of Rochester

esma.balkir@ed.ac.uk
gildea@cs.rochester.edu scohen@inf.ed.ac.uk

Abstract

Semiring parsing (Goodman, 1999) is an elegant framework for describing parsers by using semiring weighted logic programs. In this paper we present a generalization of this concept: latent-variable semiring parsing. With our framework, any semiring weighted logic program can be *latentified* by transforming weights from scalar values of a semiring to rank-n arrays, or tensors, of semiring values, allowing the modeling of latent variables within the semiring parsing framework. Semiring is too strong a notion when dealing with tensors, and we have to resort to a weaker structure: a partial semiring.[1] We prove that this generalization preserves all the desired properties of the original semiring framework while strictly increasing its expressiveness.

1 Introduction

Weighted Logic Programming (WLP) is a declarative approach to specifying and reasoning about dynamic programming algorithms and chart parsers. WLP is a generalization of bottom-up logic programming where proofs are assigned weights by combining the weights of the axioms used in the proof, and the weight of a theorem is in turn calculated by combining the weights of all its possible proof paths. The combinatorial nature of this procedure makes weighted logic programs highly suitable for specifying dynamic programming algorithms. In particular, Goodman (1999) presents an elegant abstraction for specifying and computing parser values based on WLP where the values could be drawn from any complete semiring. This generalizes the case of Boolean decision problems, probabilistic grammars with Viterbi search and other quantities of interest such as the best derivation or

the set of all possible derivations. It is then possible to derive a general formulation of inside and outside calculations in a way that is agnostic to the particular semiring chosen.

Latent variable models have been an important component in the NLP toolbox. The central assumption in latent variable models is that the correlations between observed variables in the training data could be explained by unobserved, hidden variables. Latent variables have been used with grammars such as Probabilistic Context-Free Grammars (PCFGs), where each node in the parse tree is represented using a vector of latent state probabilities that further extend the expressiveness of the grammar (Matsuzaki et al., 2005).

The approach of adding latent variables to formal grammars have proven to be a fruitful one: in the context of PCFG parsing, Matsuzaki et al. (2005) show that latent variable PCFGs (L-PCFGs) perform on par with models hand-annotated with linguistically motivated features. Cohen et al. (2013) report that on the Penn Treebank dataset, L-PCFGs trained with either EM or a spectral algorithm provide a 20% increase in F1 over PCFGs without latent states. Gebhardt (2018) shows that the benefits of latent variables are not limited to PCFGs by successfully enriching both Linear Context-Free Rewriting Systems and Hybrid Grammars with latent variables, and demonstrates their applicability on discontinuous constituent parsing.

Given the usefulness of latent variables, it would be desirable to have a generic inference mechanism for any latent variable grammar. WLPs can represent inference algorithms for probabilistic grammars effectively. However, this does not trivially extend to latent-variable models because latent variables are often represented as vectors, matrices and higher-order tensors, and these taken together no longer form a semiring. This is because in the semiring framework, values for deduction items

---

[1]Our definition of a partial semiring is slightly different than those in the abstract algebra literature e.g. Steenstrup (1985).

Proceedings of the 16th International Conference on Parsing Technologies and the IWPT 2020 Shared Task, pages 73–90
Virtual Meeting, July 9, 2020. ©2020 Association for Computational Linguistics

and for rules must all come from the same set, and the semiring operations must be defined over all pairs of values from this set. This does not allow for letting different grammar nonterminals be represented by vectors of different sizes. More importantly, it does not allow for a rule's value to be a tensor whose dimensionality depends on the rule's arity, as is generally the case in latent variable frameworks.

In this paper we start with a broad interpretation of latent variables as tensors over an arbitrary semiring. While a set of tensors over semirings is no longer a semiring, we prove that if the set of tensors have certain matching dimensions for the set of grammar rules they are assigned to, then they fulfill all the desirable properties relevant for the semiring parsing framework. This paves the way to use WLPs with latent variables, naturally improving the expressivity of the statistical model represented by the underlying WLP. Introducing a semiring framework like ours makes it easier to seamlessly incorporate latent variables into any execution model for dynamic programming algorithms (or software such as Dyna, Eisner et al. 2005, and other Prolog-like/WLP-like solvers).

We focus on CFG parsing, however the same latent variable techniques can be applied to any weighted deduction system, including systems for parsing TAG, CCG and LCFRS, and systems for Machine Translation (Lopez, 2009). The methods we present for inside and outside computation can be used to learn latent refinements of a specified grammar for any of these tasks with EM (Dempster et al., 1977; Matsuzaki et al., 2005), or used as a backbone to create spectral learning algorithms (Hsu et al., 2012; Bailly et al., 2009; Cohen et al., 2014).

2   Main Results Takeaway

We present a strict generalization of semiring weighted logic programming, with a particular focus on parser descriptions in WLP for context-free grammars. Throughout, we utilize the correspondence between axioms and grammar rules, deductive proofs and grammar derivations, and derived theorems and strings.

We assume that axioms/grammar rules come equipped with weights in the form of tensors over semiring values. The main issue with going from semirings to tensors over semiring values is that these weights need to be *well defined* in that any

valid derivation should correspond to a sequence of well defined semiring operations. For CFGs, we give a straightforward condition that ensures this is the case. This essentially boils down to making sure that each non-terminal corresponds to a fixed vector space dimension. For example, if A corresponds to a space of d_1 dimensions, B to d_2 and C to d_3, then a rule $A \rightarrow B\ C$ would have a tensor weight in $d_2 \times d_3 \times d_1$.

As long as the weights are well defined, the standard definitions for the value of a grammar derivation and a string according to a semiring weighted grammar extend to the case of tensors of semirings. Weighted logic programming provides the means to declaratively specify an efficient algorithm to obtain these values of interest. In line with Sikkel (1998) and Goodman (1999) we present precise conditions for when a partial-semiring WLP describes a correct parser.

The value of the WLP formulation of parsing algorithms is that it provides a unified fashion in which dynamic programming algorithms can be extracted from the program description. This relies on the ability of a WLP to decompose the value of a proof to a combination of the values of the sub-proofs. Specifically, given a derivation tree, a WLP description automatically provides algorithms for calculating the inside and outside values. We provide analogous algorithms for calculating the inside and outside values for partial-semiring WLPs. Our outside formulation addresses the non-commutative nature of tensors themselves, and could be extended to cases where the underlying semiring is non-commutative using the techniques presented by Goodman (1998).

3   Related Work

"Parsing as deduction" (Pereira and Warren, 1983) is an established framework that allows a number of parsing algorithms to be written as declarative rules and deductive systems (Shieber et al., 1995), and their correctness to be rigorously stated (Sikkel, 1998). Goodman (1999) has extended the parsing as deduction framework to arbitrary semirings and showed that various different values of interest could be computed using the same algorithm by changing the semiring. This led to the development of Dyna, a toolkit for declaratively specifying weighted logic programs, allowing concise implementation of a number of NLP algorithms (Eisner et al., 2005).

The semiring characterization of possible values to assign to WLPs gave rise to the formulation of a number of novel semirings. One novel semiring of interest for purposes of learning parameters is the *generalized entropy semiring* (Cohen et al., 2008) which can be used to calculate the KL-divergence between the distribution of derivations induced by two weighted logic programs. Other two semirings of interest are *expectation* and *variance* semirings introduced by Eisner (2002) and Li and Eisner (2009). These utilize the algebraic structure to efficiently track quantities needed by the expectation-maximization algorithm for parameter estimation. Their framework allows working with parameters in the form of vectors in $\mathbb{R}^n$ for a fixed n, coupled with a scalar in $\mathbb{R}_{\geq 0}$. The semiring value of a path is roughly calculated by the multiplication of the scalars and (appropriately weighted) *addition* of the vectors. This is in contrast with our framework where weights could be tensors of arbitrary rank rather than only vectors, and the values of paths are calculated via tensor multiplication.

Finally, Gimpel and Smith (2009) extended the semiring framework to a more general algebraic structure with the purpose of incorporating non-local features. Their extension comes at the cost that the new algebraic structure does not obey all the semiring axioms. Our framework differs from theirs in that under reasonable conditions, tensors of semirings do behave fully like regular semirings.

4 Background and Notation

Our formalism could be used to enrich any WLP that implements a dynamic programming algorithm, but for simplicity, we follow Goodman (1999) and focus our presentation on parsers with a context-free backbone.[2]

4.1 Context-free Grammars

Formally, a Context-Free Grammar (CFG) is a 4-tuple $\langle N, \Sigma, \mathcal{R}, S \rangle$. The set of N denotes the non-terminals which will be denoted by uppercase letters A, B etc., and S is a non-terminal that is the special start symbol. The set of Σ denotes the terminals which will be denoted by lowercase letters a, b etc. $\mathcal{R}$ is the set of rules of the form $A \rightarrow \alpha$ consisting of one non-terminal on the left hand side

(lhs), and a string $\alpha \in (N \cup \Sigma)^*$ on the right hand side (rhs). We will use $\alpha \Rightarrow \beta$ if β could be derived from α with the application of one grammar rule. We will say that a sentence $\sigma \in \Sigma^+$ could be derived from the non-terminal A if σ could be generated by starting with A and repeatedly applying rules in $\mathcal{R}$ until the right hand side contains only terminals, and denote this as $A \overset{*}{\Rightarrow} \sigma$. We will denote the language that a grammar G defines by $\mathcal{L}(G) = \{\sigma | S \overset{*}{\Rightarrow} \sigma\}$.

CFG derivations can naturally be represented as trees. We will use the notation $\langle r : T_1 \ldots T_k \rangle$ to represent a tree that has the node r as its root and $T_1, \ldots, T_k$ as its direct subtrees. We will use $\mathcal{D}_G$ to denote the set of all derivation trees that can be constructed with the grammar G, and $\mathcal{D}_G(\sigma)$ for all valid derivation trees that generate the sentence σ in G.

4.2 Semirings

A semiring is an algebraic structure similar to a ring, except that it does not require additive inverses.

Definition 1. *A **semiring** is a set $\mathbb{S}$ together with two operations $+$ and $\times$, where $+$ is commutative, associative and has an identity element 0. The operation of $\times$ is associative, has an identity element 1 and distributes over $+$.*

The set of non-negative integers together with the usual $\times, +, 0, 1$ is a semiring, and so are probability values in $[0, 1]$. Booleans {TRUE, FALSE} also form a semiring with $\times := \vee, + := \wedge, 0 :=$ FALSE and $1 :=$ TRUE.

There are a few less common semirings that provide useful values in parsing. The *Viterbi* semiring calculates the probability of the best derivation. It has values in $[0, 1]$, $+ :=$ max and $\times, 0, 1$ as standard. The *Derivation forest, Viterbi derivation* and *Viterbi n-best* semirings calculate the set of all derivations, the best derivation and the n-best derivations respectively. Unlike the previous examples, the $\times$ operation of these semirings is not commutative. In general, if the $\times$ operation in a semiring is commutative, we refer to it as a *commutative semiring*, and otherwise it is referred to as *non-commutative*. For precise definitions and detailed descriptions of these semirings see Goodman (1999).

---

[2]Note that given a grammar G in a formalism F and a string α, it is possible to construct a CFG grammar $c(G, w)$ from G and α (Nederhof, 2003). This construction is possible even for range concatenation grammars (Boullier, 2004) which span all languages that could be parsed in poly-time.

4.3 Weighted Logic Programming

A logic program consists of *axioms* and *inference rules* that could be applied iteratively to prove theorems. Inference rules are expressed in the form $\frac{A_1 \dots A_k}{B}$ where $A_1 \dots A_k$ are antecedents from which B can be concluded. Axioms are inference rules with no antecedents.

One way to express dynamic programming algorithms such as CKY is as logic programs. This approach takes the point of view of *parsing as deduction*: terms consist of grammar rules and *items* in the form of $[i, A, j]$ that correspond to the intermediate entries in the chart. Grammar rules are taken to be axioms, and the description of the parser is given as a set of inference rules. These can have both grammar rules and items as antecedents and an item as the conclusion. A logic program in this form includes a special designated goal item that stands for a successful parse.

Continuing with the example of CKY, consider the procedural description for how to obtain a chart item from smaller chart items if we have the rule $A \rightarrow B\ C$ in the grammar:

$$chart[i, A, j] := chart[i, A, j] \ \vee$$
$$(chart[i, B, k] \ \wedge \ chart[k, C, j])$$

The corresponding inference rule in a logic program would be:

$$\frac{A \rightarrow B\ C \quad [i, B, k] \quad [k, C, j]}{[i, A, j]}$$

Note that in the inference rule above, $A \rightarrow B\ C$ is a rule template with free variables A, B, C. In general, the terms in inference rules can contain free variables, however for a logic program to describe a valid dynamic algorithm, every free variable in the conclusion of an inference rule must appear in its antecedents as well.

A *weighted* logic program is a logic program where terms are assigned values from a semiring. When paired with semiring operations, inference rules provide the description of how to compute the value of the conclusion given the values of the antecedents. The result of an application of a particular inference rule is the semiring multiplication of all the antecedents. The value of a term B is then calculated as the semiring sum of values obtained from inference rules that have B as their conclusion.

4.4 Semiring Parsing

In the context of parsing, Goodman (1999) presents a framework where a grammar G comes equipped with a function w that maps each rule in G to a semiring value. Then, a grammar derivation string E consisting of the successive applications of rules $e_1, \dots, e_n$ is defined to have the value $V_G(E) = \prod_{i=1}^{n} w(e_i)$, and the value of a sentence $\sigma \in \mathcal{L}(G)$ is defined as $V_G = \sum_{j=1}^{k} V_G(E_j)$ where $E_1, E_2, \dots, E_k$ are the derivations of σ in G.

A parser specification is given in the form of a weighted logic program, referred to as *item-based description*. From these, the value of a derivation D is calculated recursively as follows:

$$V(D) = \begin{cases} w(D) & \text{if } D \text{ is a rule} \\ \prod_{i=1}^{k} V(D_i) & \text{if } D = \langle b : D_1, \dots, D_k \rangle \end{cases}$$

where $\prod$ is the semiring product.

Let $inner(x)$ represent the set of all derivation trees headed by the item x. Then the value of x is:

$$V(x) = \sum_{D \in inner(x)} V(D)$$

where $\sum$ is the semiring addition. The value of a sentence is then equal to $inner(goal)$.

Given the definitions of value according to the grammar and the parser, Goodman (1999) provides a theorem for conditions of correctness:

Theorem 4.1. *(Goodman 1999, Theorem 1; informal) An item-based description I is correct if for every grammar G there exists a one-to-one correspondence between the grammar and item derivations, and these derivations get the same value regardless of weight function used.*

One caveat with calculating based on item-based derivations is that there is an ordering of items: we cannot compute the value of an item unless the values of all its children are computed already. For this, Goodman (1999) assumes that each item is assigned to a *bucket* so that if an item b depends on a, then $bucket(a) \leq bucket(b)$. If a bucket depends on itself, then it is considered a special *looping* bucket. For all the formulas we present in this the main paper we assume that the items belong to non-looping buckets. The formulas for looping buckets are provided in Appendix B.

For an item x, calculating its value might require summing over exponentially many derivation trees.

To address this, it is possible to provide a general formula that efficiently computes the inner value for an item (Goodman 1999, Theorem 2):

$$V(x) = \sum_{a_1,\ldots,a_k \text{ s.t. } \frac{a_1,\ldots,a_k}{x}} \prod_{i=1}^{k} V(a_i)$$

The other important value associated with an item x is its *outside* value $Z(x)$, which is the sum of values of derivation trees, modified so that x is removed with all its subtrees. This value is complementary to the inside values $V(x)$ (Goodman 1999, Theorem 4):

$$V(x) \times Z(x) = \sum_{D \text{ a derivation}} V(D)C(D,x)$$

where $C(D,x)$ is the count of the occurrences of item x in derivation D.

$Z(x)$ can likewise be calculated using a recursive formula if the values are from a commutative semiring (Goodman 1999, Theorem 5):

$$Z(x) = \sum_{\substack{j,a_1,\ldots,a_k,b \text{ s.t.} \\ \frac{a_1\ldots a_k}{b} \text{ and } x=a_j}} Z(b) \times \prod_{i=1}^{j-1} V(a_i) \times \prod_{i=j+1}^{k} V(a_i)$$

4.5 Tensor Notation

We use the term *tensor* to refer to an n-dimensional array of semiring values. We use $\mathbb{S}$ to denote a semiring and $\mathbf{A}, \mathbf{B}$ etc. to denote tensors. The element $\mathbf{A} \in \mathbb{S}^{a_1 \times a_2 \times \ldots \times a_n}$ will denote that $\mathbf{A}$ is a rank-n tensor of values drawn from $\mathbb{S}$, with the ith rank having dimension a_i. The entry in index $k_1,\ldots,k_n$ will be denoted with subscripts $\mathbf{A}_{k_1,\ldots,k_n}$.

5 Latent-variable Parsing as Tensor Weighted Logic Programs

For semiring parsing to work for latent-variable models it should allow weights to be vectors, matrices and tensors. In this section we present a framework that generalizes that of Goodman (1999), and is able to capture tensors over semirings as weights. Note that this includes scalars as a special case.

5.1 Semiring Operations

The main reason why tensors over semirings are not semirings is that with tensor weights, $\oplus$ and $\otimes$ become partially defined – not all elements can naturally be added or multiplied to any other element anymore. We refer to these structures as *partial semirings*. With some reasonable constraints,

we show that $\oplus$ and $\otimes$ obey the semiring axioms in cases that are relevant for the semiring parsing framework.

Let $\mathbb{S}$ be the chosen underlying semiring, $+, \times$ to be the semiring operations and $\mathbf{0}, \mathbf{1}$ be the additive and multiplicative identity of the semiring respectively. The set of possible weights are defined as $\{\mathbb{S}^{d_1 \times \ldots \times d_n}\}$ for $n \in \mathbb{N}$, and $d_i \in \mathbb{N}$ for all $i \leq n$. $\oplus$ is a partial addition that is defined on two tensors $\mathbf{A}, \mathbf{B} \in \mathbb{S}^{d_1 \times \ldots \times d_n}$ as long as the dimensions of each of their ranks match. Then, the addition is defined component-wise:

$$(\mathbf{A} \oplus \mathbf{B})_{i_1,\ldots,i_n} := \mathbf{A}_{i_1,\ldots,i_n} + \mathbf{B}_{i_1,\ldots,i_n}$$

The additive identity is now a class of tensors, one for each unique list of tensor dimensions. The additive identity for any $\mathbf{A} \in \mathbb{S}^{d_1 \times \ldots \times d_n}$ is the tensor $\mathbf{Z} \in \mathbb{S}^{d_1 \times \ldots \times d_n}$ with $\mathbf{0}$ in every entry.

Multiplication is defined as the contraction of an index between two tensors with arbitrary number of ranks. Specifically, we consider the family $\otimes_{[k;l]}$ which contracts the kth rank of the first tensor with the lth rank of the second tensor. This is only defined if the two ranks to be contracted have the same dimension, as follows:

$$\left(\mathbf{A} \otimes_{[k;l]} \mathbf{B}\right)_{\substack{i_1,\ldots,i_{k-1},j_1,\ldots,j_{l-1}, \\ j_{l+1},\ldots,j_m,i_{k+1},\ldots,i_n}}$$
$$:= \sum_{i_k,j_l} \delta(i_k,j_l) \mathbf{A}_{i_1,\ldots,i_n} \times \mathbf{B}_{j_1,\ldots,j_m},$$

where δ is the identity function that is equal to $\mathbf{1}$ if $i_k = j_l$ and $\mathbf{0}$ otherwise. Note that the ranks corresponding to $\mathbf{B}$ which are not contracted over go in between the ranks of $\mathbf{A}$, replacing where the contracted rank of $\mathbf{A}$ was. We will use $\otimes_j$ as a shorthand of $\otimes_{[j;1]}$, and in cases where $j = l = 1$, we will omit the subscript on $\otimes$ altogether.

More generally, we will allow multiplication operations that contract multiple consecutive dimensions. $\mathbf{A} \otimes^r_{[k;l]} \mathbf{B}$ will denote contracting rank k of $\mathbf{A}$ with rank l of $\mathbf{B}$, rank $k+1$ of $\mathbf{A}$ with rank $l+1$ of $\mathbf{B}$ and so forth until rank $k+r-1$ of $\mathbf{A}$ and $l+r-1$ of $\mathbf{B}$. Formally:

$$\left(\mathbf{A} \otimes^r_{[k;l]} \mathbf{B}\right)_{\substack{i_1,\ldots,i_{k-1},j_1,\ldots,j_{l-1}, \\ j_{l+r},\ldots,j_m,i_{k+r},\ldots,i_n}} :=$$
$$\sum_{\substack{i_k,\ldots,i_{k+r-1} \\ j_l,\ldots,j_{l+r-1}}} \left(\prod_{p=0}^{r-1} \delta\left(i_{k+p},j_{l+p}\right)\right) \mathbf{A}_{i_1,\ldots,i_n} \mathbf{B}_{j_1,\ldots,j_m}$$

We will use the notation $\mathbf{A} \otimes^* \mathbf{B}$ as a shorthand for $\mathbf{A} \otimes^{rank(\mathbf{A})} \mathbf{B}$ if $rank(\mathbf{A}) < rank(\mathbf{B})$ and $\mathbf{A} \otimes^{rank(\mathbf{B})} \mathbf{B}$ otherwise.

To make the presentation clearer, we will also use the notation $X \otimes [A_1, A_2, \ldots, A_k]$ to denote contraction of A_1 with the first rank of X, A_2 with the second and so forth. In other words $X \otimes [A_1, \ldots, A_n]$ is equivalent to $X \otimes_n A_n \otimes_{n-1} A_{n-1} \ldots \otimes_1 A_1$.

The multiplicative identity for $\mathbf{A} \in \mathbb{S}^{d_1 \times \ldots \times d_n}$ and $\otimes_k$ is the identity matrix $\mathbf{I} \in \mathbb{S}^{d_k \times d_k}$ where the diagonal entries are the multiplicative identity from the underlying semiring, and the non-diagonals are the additive identity. For $\mathbf{A} \in \mathbb{S}^{d_1 \times \ldots \times d_n}$ and $\otimes_k^r$ the multiplicative identity is a rank-$2r$ tensor $\mathbf{I} \in \mathbb{S}^{d_k \times \ldots \times d_{k+r-1} \times d_k \times \ldots \times d_{k+r-1}}$ and is defined as follows:

$$\mathbf{I}_{d_1, \ldots, d_r} = \prod_{i=0}^{\frac{n}{2}} \delta\left(d_i, d_{\frac{r}{2}+i}\right)$$

Lastly, as the higher order analogue of the transpose operator, we will define a permutation operator $\mathbf{A}^\pi$ where $\pi = [\pi_1, \pi_2, \ldots, \pi_r]$ is a permutation of $[1 \ldots r]$ and r is the rank of $\mathbf{A}$. The π_ith rank of $\mathbf{A}^\pi$ is equal to ith rank of $\mathbf{A}$.

The key property of semirings for purposes of efficient calculation of item values is the distributive property. This property also holds for tensors over semirings.

Lemma 5.1. *For any k, l, $\otimes_{[k;l]}$ distributes over $\oplus$*

A proof can be found in Appendix A.

5.2 Grammar Derivations

For a grammar G with a function w that provides a mapping from rules to tensor weights, we will define a value of a derivation via the derivation tree:

Definition 2. *Given a grammar G and a weight function w, the value of a derivation tree T is:*

$$V_G^w(T) = \begin{cases} w(r) \\ \quad if\ T = \langle r \rangle \\ w(r) \otimes [V_G^w(T_1), \ldots, V_G^w(T_k)] \\ \quad if\ T = \langle r : T_1, \ldots, T_k \rangle \end{cases}$$

Note that there is no guarantee that this equation is defined for any arbitrary w. We will call a weight function w *well defined* for a grammar G if for all valid derivation trees T in G, $V_G^w(T)$ is defined. For CFGs there is a straightforward method to ensure that w is well defined:

Tensor dimensions of grammar rules:

$$w(S \to AA) \in \mathbb{S}^{A \times A \times S} \quad w(A \to AA) \in \mathbb{S}^{A \times A \times A}$$
$$w(A \to a) \in \mathbb{S}^{A}$$

Grammar derivation tree:

$$w(S \to AA)/\mathbb{S}^S$$

at the left: $w(A \to a)/\mathbb{S}^A$ and at the right: $w(A \to AA)/\mathbb{S}^A$

with children $w(A \to a)/\mathbb{S}^A \quad w(A \to a)/\mathbb{S}^A$

The value of the tree is given by the equation:

$$w(S \to AA) \otimes (w(A \to a),$$
$$(w(A \to AA) \otimes (w(A \to a), w(A \to a))))$$

Grammar derivation string:

$$S \xrightarrow[\mathbb{S}^{A \times A \times S}]{S \to AA} AA \xrightarrow[\mathbb{S}^{A \times S}]{A \to a} aA \xrightarrow[\mathbb{S}^{A \times A \times S}]{A \to AA} aAA$$
$$\xrightarrow[\mathbb{S}^{A \times S}]{A \to a} aaA \xrightarrow[\mathbb{S}^S]{A \to a} aaa$$

The value of the string is given by the equation:

$$w(S \to AA) \otimes w(A \to a) \otimes (A \to AA)$$
$$\otimes (A \to a) \otimes (A \to a)$$

Figure 1: Example derivation for the string "aaa". We illustrate the initial dimensions of the tensor values for the rules and also show the intermediate tensor dimensions during the calculation of the value of the grammar tree and the grammar string.

Lemma 5.2. *A set of weights w for a given CFG is well defined if there exist consistent dimensions d_i for each nonterminal A_i such that for all grammar rules $R : A_n \to \alpha_1 A_1 \alpha_2 \ldots \alpha_{n-2} A_{n-1} \alpha_n$, $w(R) \in \mathbb{S}^{d_1 \times \ldots \times d_n}$*

Proof is given together with Lemma 5.3.

Note that if a weight function for CFG is well defined, then the rank for the weights of rules with no non-terminals on their rhs is always 1.

Given a grammar derivation tree T, let us call the list of derivation rules $E : R_1, R_2, \ldots, R_n$ appearing in T ordered via depth-first, left-to-right manner a **grammar derivation string**.

Definition 3. *Given a CFG with tensor weights w, the value of a grammar derivation string is defined as:*

$$V_G^w(E) = \bigotimes_i w(R_i)$$

where the application of $\otimes$ proceeds from left to right as is standard.

For semirings, since the bracketing does not affect the final value of an expression, it is straightforward to show that the value of a grammar derivation tree corresponds to that of a grammar derivation string. With tensors over semirings this might fail with an arbitrary formalism F, and in the general we require the value of a derivation to be calculated with the bracketing induced by the derivation tree. However, for the special case of CFGs, the value of the grammar derivation tree and the value of its corresponding grammar derivation string are always equal. This means that for the computation of the value of the derivation, it is possible to replace the bracketing induced by the derivation tree by left-to-right bracketing without affecting the final value. Figure 1 demonstrates the calculation of the value of the tree and the string for the same derivation together with how the tensor dimensions of the intermediate results evolve with each step of the calculation.

Lemma 5.3. *Given a CFG G and a weight function w that fulfills the condition in Lemma 5.2, then w is well defined and $V_G^w(T) = V_G^w(E)$ for any grammar derivation tree T and corresponding grammar derivation string E.*

Proof. We will proceed by induction on the derivation tree. If T consists of only one rule r, then $V_G^w(T) = V_G^w(E)$. Furthermore, r does not have any non-terminals on its rhs, so $V_G^w(T) \in \mathbb{S}^{do}$ with $\mathbb{S}^{do}$ corresponding to the lhs non-terminal in r.

Otherwise, T has a labeled node r and the subtrees $T_1, \ldots, T_k$. Notice that if $A_0 \in \mathbb{S}^{d_1 \times \ldots \times d_n \times d_0}$, $A_1 \in \mathbb{S}^{d_2}, \ldots, A_n \in \mathbb{S}^{d_n}$, then $A_0 \otimes [A_1, \ldots, A_n] = A_0 \otimes A_1 \otimes \ldots \otimes A_n$ due to all arguments within $[\ldots]$ being rank-1.

Because w fulfills the condition in Lemma 5.2, $w(r) \in \mathbb{S}^{d_1 \times \ldots \times d_k \times d_0}$ for some d_i where $\mathbb{S}^{do}$ is the space corresponding to the non-terminal on the lhs of r, and $\mathbb{S}^{d_i}$ is the space corresponding to the ith non-terminal appearing in the rhs of r for $i = 1, \ldots, k$. Then to complete the proof, it suffices to show that $V_G^w(T_i) \in \mathbb{S}^{d_i}$ for all subtrees T_i. This already holds for the base case. For each $T_i : \langle r_i : T_1', .., T_k' \rangle$, if $w(r_i) \in \mathbb{S}^{d_1^i \times \ldots \times d_k^i \times d_0^i}$ then by induction $V_G^w(T_i) \in \mathbb{S}^{d_0^i}$, where $\mathbb{S}^{d_0^i}$ is the space corresponding to the non-terminal in the lhs of R_i. For the derivation to be valid, this non-terminal needs to match the ith non-terminal in the rhs of R, hence $\mathbb{S}^{d_0^i} = \mathbb{S}^{d_i}$ $\qquad\square$

5.3 Item-based Descriptions

Item-based descriptions are formal descriptions of various parsers for context-free grammars. Item-based descriptions consist of a set of deduction rules of the form $\frac{T_1 \ldots T_k}{Q} P_1 \ldots P_j$ where upper case letters could either be grammar rule templates (e.g. if $T_1 : A \rightarrow B\ C$ then any non-terminals from the grammar can be substituted for A, B, C) or for **items**. $T_1 \ldots T_k$ are referred to as antecedents, Q as the conclusion and $P_1 \ldots P_j$ are side conditions that the parser requires to execute the rule, but doesn't use the values of. Items correspond to chart elements in procedural descriptions of parsers, and are placeholders for intermediate results which can be combined to obtain the final result. The item-based description also provides a special **goal item** which is variable-free, and does not occur as a condition of any other inference rules.

Definition 4. *Given a grammar G and an item-based description I, a valid **item derivation tree** is defined as follows:*

- *For all $r \in G$, $\langle r \rangle$ is an item derivation tree.*

- *If $D_{a_1}, \ldots, D_{a_k}$ and $D_{c_1}, \ldots, D_{c_j}$ are derivation trees headed by $a_1, \ldots, a_k$ and $c_1, \ldots, c_j$ respectively, and $\frac{a_1 \ldots a_k}{b} c_1, \ldots, c_j$ is the instantiation of a deduction rule in I, then $\langle b : D_{a_1}, \ldots, D_{a_k} \rangle$ is also an item derivation tree.*

$inner_\sigma(x)$ denotes the set of all trees headed by x that occur in parses for σ. Formally, $D \in inner_\sigma(x)$ if D is headed by x and is a subtree of some $D' \in \mathcal{D}_{I(G)}(\sigma)$. The value of a derivation tree is calculated similarly to that of a grammar tree:

$$V_{I(G)}^w(D) =$$
$$\begin{cases} w(D) & \text{if } D \text{ is a rule} \\ V_{I(G)}^w(D_1) \otimes [V_{I(G)}^w(D_2), \ldots, V_{I(G)}^w(D_n)] & \\ \qquad \text{if } D = \langle b : D_1, \ldots, D_n \rangle \end{cases}$$

Notice that unlike the definition from Goodman (1999), the first antecedent in the inference rule has a special role in the calculation. Intuitively, our framework treats the value of the first antecedent as a *function*, and the trailing ones as the arguments. The interaction between the trailing antecedents is thus moderated through the value of the first antecedent, which corresponds to the requirement that

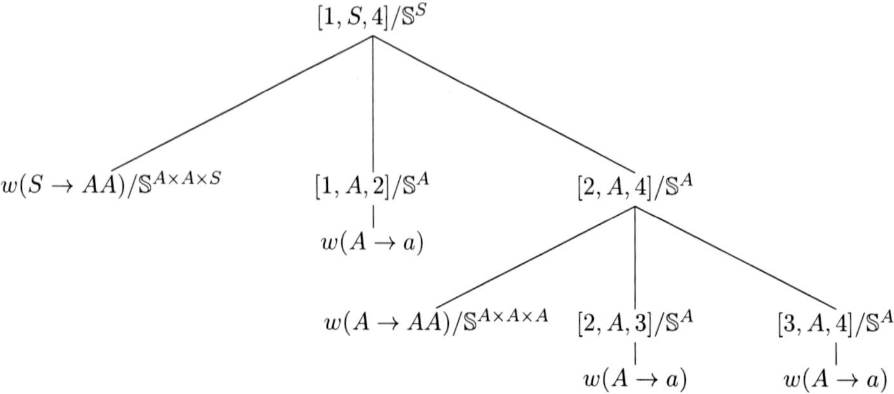

Figure 2: Item derivation corresponding to the derivation given in Figure 1 using the item-based description of CKY in Figure 3.

$$\frac{w(A \to w_i)}{[i, A, j]}$$

$$\frac{w(A \to BC) \quad [i, B, k] \quad [k, C, j]}{[i, A, j]}$$

Figure 3: Item-based description for CKY

the children nodes be independent of each other given the parent node.

Definition 5. *If for any $\sigma \in \mathcal{L}(G)$ and any $T, T' \in inner_\sigma(x)$, $V^w_{I(G)}(T)$ and $V^w_{I(G)}(T')$ are defined and $dim(V^w_{I(G)}(T)) = dim(V^w_{I(G)}(T'))$, then the weights w are well defined.*

Given an item-based derivation I, a grammar G, a well defined weight function w and a target sentence σ, the value of an item x is defined to be the sum of all its possible derivations. Formally:

$$V^w_{I(G)}(x, \sigma) = \bigoplus_{D \in inner_\sigma(x)} V^w_{I(G)}(D)$$

Definition 6. *For a given grammar G and item-based description I, the value of a sentence σ is equal to the value of the goal item which spans σ:*

$$V^w_{I(G)}(\sigma) = V^w_{I(G)}(goal, \sigma)$$

Definition 7. *An item-based description is **correct** if for all grammars G, complete semirings $\mathbb{S}$, well defined weight functions w and sentences σ, $V^w_{I(G)}(\sigma) = V^w_G(\sigma)$*

Now we are ready to state the equivalent theorem to Theorem 4.1. Let us introduce a special symbol $\perp$ and extend V^w_G and $V^w_{I(G)}$ to any weight function w so that if w is not-well defined for G, then $V^w_G(\sigma) = \perp$ and likewise for $V^w_{I(G)}$.

Theorem 5.4. *An item-based description I is correct if*

- *For every grammar G, the mapping g : $\mathcal{D}_{I(G)} \to \mathcal{D}_G$ that maps $d' \in \mathcal{D}_{I(G)}$ to the corresponding $d \in \mathcal{D}_G$ is a bijection with an inverse function f.*

- *For any complete semiring $\mathbb{S}$ and weight function w, g and f preserve the values assigned to a derivation:*

$$V^w_G(d) = V^w_{I(G)}(f(d)) \text{ and}$$
$$V^w_{I(G)}(d') = V^w_G(g(d'))$$

Proof proceeds similarly to that in (Goodman, 1999) and can be found in Appendix A.

6 Inside and Outside Calculations

In the following, we will omit the sentence σ from $inner_\sigma(x)$ and refer to this as $inner(x)$. Let $inner(\frac{a_1,\dots,a_k}{x})$ the set of derivation trees where the root note is x, and the direct children of x are $a_1, \dots, a_k$.

For efficient computation of this value, we will assume that there is a partial order b on the items so that if the item y depends on x, then $b(x) \leq b(y)$.

Theorem 6.1.

$$V(x) = \bigoplus_{\substack{[a_1,\dots,a_k] \\ s.t. \frac{a_1,\dots,a_k}{x}}} V(a_1) \otimes [V(a_2), \dots, V(a_k)]$$

The proof uses the distributive property and follows that of Goodman (1999). It can be found in Appendix A.

For the notion of a value of a derivation to extend to outside trees, we will have to do some modifications. This is because an outside tree will have one subtree $\langle b : A_1, \ldots, A_n \rangle$, such that $V(A_1) \otimes [V(A_2), \ldots, V(A_n)]$ will potentially not be defined since one of the subtrees A_k will be missing. Note that the missing A_k will be headed by an item. We will say the a tree $T \in outer(x)$ if T can be obtained by taking a tree T' headed by the goal item and removing any of its subtrees headed by the item x. Outer value $Z(T_k)$ is defined recursively as follows:

If T_k is headed by the goal item then $Z(T_k) = I_{d_S}$. Else, it has a direct parent tree T such that $T = \langle b : T_1, \ldots, T_k, \ldots, T_n \rangle$. In this case, $Z(T_k) =$

$$\left(V(T_1) \otimes_k [I_{T_k \times d_S}, V(T_{k+1}), \ldots, V(T_n)] \right)^{\pi}$$
$$\otimes [V(T_2), \ldots, V(T_{k-1})] \otimes^* Z(T)$$

where $I_{T_k \times d_S}$ is the identity tensor for the space $\mathbb{S}^{d_1 \times \ldots \times d_i \times d_S}$, $T_k \in \mathbb{S}^{d_1 \times \ldots \times d_i}$, and d_s is the dimension assigned for the terminal symbol S. The permutation π is defined as follows:

$$[1, 2, \ldots, i, j+1, j+2, \ldots, n, i+1, i+2, \ldots, j]$$

where $i = k + \text{rank}(T_k) - 1$ and $j = k + 2 \times \text{rank}(T_k) + 1$

To understand the function of π it is useful to consider the dimensions of the term before and after it is applied. Let the term $V(T_0) \otimes_k [I_{T_k \times d_S}, V(T_{k+1}), \ldots, V(T_n)]$ have dimensions:

$$e_1 \times \ldots \times e_{k-1}, d_1 \times \ldots \times d_i \times d_S \times$$
$$e_k \times d_1 \times \ldots \times d_i \times d_S \times d'_n \times \ldots \times d'_m$$

Here $e_1, \ldots, e_{k-1}$ are the dimensions that will be contracted with $V(T_1), \ldots, V(T_{k-1})$ with the second multiplication operation, and $d'_n, \ldots, d'_m$ are the dimensions that were either introduced by the contraction with $V(T_{k+1}), \ldots, V(T_n)$ or were trailing dimensions from $V(T_1)$. The result of the contraction with $I_{T_k \times d_S}$ are the dimensions in the middle: $d_1, \ldots, d_i, d_S, e_k, d_1, \ldots, d_i, d_S$. Unlike the original definition of I there is one dimension e_k missing from the beginning of the sequence since it got used up during the contraction operation. What the permutation does is to move one section of the dimensions introduced by I to the very end. The dimensions become:

$$e_1 \times \ldots \times e_{k-1}, d_1 \times \ldots \times d_i \times$$
$$d'_n \times \ldots \times d'_m \times d_S \times e_k \times d_1 \times \ldots \times d_i \times d_S$$

Note that this has no effect on the next contraction with $V(T_1), \ldots, V(T_{k-1})$ since the first $k-1$ ranks

are left in place. However, changing the order of the ranks allow the last contraction with $Z(T)$ to be well defined.

Lemma 6.2. *Let V and Z be defined on a commutative semiring $\mathbb{S}$ and let $O \in outer_\sigma(x)$ and $T \in inner_\sigma(x)$. If combining O and T in the obvious way results in the complete derivation D,*

$$V(D) = V(T) \otimes^* Z(O)$$

Proof. (Sketch) We proceed by induction on the parse tree. Base case is where $x = goal$, $T = D$ and O is empty. Then $V(T) = V(D)$ and $Z(O) = I_S$. $V(D) \otimes^* I_S = V(D)$ by the definition of I_S which proves the statement.

Otherwise T has a parent tree $T_p = \langle y : T_1, \ldots, T_n \rangle$ where $T = T_k$. Furthermore, $T_p \in inner_\sigma(y)$, $O_p \in outer_\sigma(y)$ and by the induction hypothesis $V(D) = V(T_p) \otimes^* Z(O_p)$.

Since $T_p \in inner_\sigma(y)$ we know that

$$V(T_p) = V(T_1) \otimes [V(T_2), \ldots, V(T_m)]$$

$$V(D) =$$

$$(V(T_1) \otimes [V(T_2), \ldots, V(T_m)]) \otimes^* Z(O_p)$$

The proof progresses by calculating the value for $[V(D)]_i$ based on the above term and shows that this is equal to the value of $[V(T) \otimes^* Z(O)]_i$. Full proof can be found in Appendix A. $\square$

In the general case, Goodman (1999) defines the reverse value of x as the sum of all its outer trees.

$$Z(x) = \bigoplus_{T \in outer(x)} Z(T)$$

We will see that for a well defined weight function w, any $D \in outer_\sigma(x)$ will be assigned a value with dimensions $d_1 \times \ldots \times d_n \times d_S$ where d_S is the dimension assigned to the start symbol S, and $d_1, \ldots, d_n$ are the dimensions for $inner_\sigma(x)$.

Lemma 6.3. *Let $C(D, x)$ represent the number of times x occurs in a derivation D. Then,*

$$V(x) \otimes^* Z(x) = \bigoplus_{D \in \mathcal{D}(\sigma)} V(D) C(D, x)$$

Proof.

$$V(x) \otimes^* Z(x) = \bigoplus_{T \in inner(x)} V(T) \otimes^* \bigoplus_{O \in outer(x)} Z(O)$$

$$= \bigoplus_{T \in inner(x)} \bigoplus_{O \in outer(x)} V(T) \otimes^* Z(O)$$

By Lemma 6.2, $Z(O) \otimes^* V(T) = V(D)$. For an item x, any $O \in outer(x)$ and $T \in inner(x)$ can be combined to form a successful derivation tree containing x, and thus the number $C(D, x)$ corresponds exactly to the number of derivation trees containing x. Hence,

$$V(x) \otimes^* Z(X) = \bigoplus_{\substack{T \in inner(x) \\ O \in outer(x)}} V(T) \otimes^* Z(O)$$

$$= \bigoplus_{D \in \mathcal{D}(\sigma)} V(D)C(D, x) \quad \square$$

Now we are ready to state how to calculate the outside value of an item. Following Goodman (1999) we will extend the notation for the set of outer trees and introduce $outer\left(k, \frac{a_1 \dots a_n}{b}\right) \subseteq outer(a_k)$ to mean the subset of the outer trees in $outer(a_k)$ where a_k has parent b and the siblings a_i. In other words, this is the set of all outer trees where the rule from which a_k is removed is $\frac{a_1 \dots a_n}{b}$.

Theorem 6.4. *If x is the goal item, then $Z(x) = I_s$. Else, $Z(x) =$*

$$\bigoplus_{\substack{j, a_1, \dots, a_k, b \text{ s.t.} \\ \frac{a_1 \dots a_k}{b} \text{ and } x = a_j}} (V(a_1) \otimes_k [I_{a_k}, V(a_{k+1}), \dots, V(a_n)])^{\pi}$$

$$\otimes [V(a_2), \dots, V(a_{k-1})] \otimes^* Z(b)$$

Proof. (sketch) $Z(x) = \bigoplus_{D \in outer(x)} Z(D)$. Either x is a goal item, in which case $Z(x) = I_S$.

Otherwise the outer trees $outer(x)$ could be written as the union of outer trees $outer\left(k, \frac{a_1 \dots a_n}{b}\right)$ for each rule $\frac{a_1 \dots a_n}{b}$ where $a_k = x$ for some k. Hence:

$$Z(x) = \bigoplus_{\substack{j, a_1, \dots, a_k, b \text{ s.t.} \\ \frac{a_1 \dots a_k}{b} \text{ and } x = a_j}} \bigoplus_{D \in outer\left(k, \frac{a_1 \dots a_n}{b}\right)} Z(D)$$

Using the distributive property of the partial semiring, the inside part of the equation becomes:

$$\bigoplus_{D \in outer\left(k, \frac{a_1 \dots a_n}{b}\right)} Z(D) =$$

$$(V(a_1) \otimes_k [I_{a_k}, V(a_{k+1}), \dots, V(a_n)])^{\pi}$$

$$\otimes [V(a_2), \dots, V(a_{k-1})] \otimes^* Z(b)$$

Replacing the inner part of the previous equation with this term gives the desired equality. $\square$

7 Conclusion

We have presented a general extension of the semiring parsing framework where the weights for the grammar rules are tensors of semiring values, with the motivation of extending semiring parsing framework to latent variable models. We hope that this work will enable streamlined development of EM-based or spectral learning algorithms for latent refinements of a number of grammar formalisms.

Acknowledgments

The authors thank the anonymous reviewers for feedback and comments on a draft of this paper, and acknowledge the support of NSF grant IIS-1813823.

References

Raphaël Bailly, François Denis, and Liva Ralaivola. 2009. Grammatical inference as a principal component analysis problem. In *Proceedings of the 26th Annual International Conference on Machine Learning*, pages 33–40.

Pierre Boullier. 2004. Range concatenation grammars. In *New Developments in Parsing Technology*, pages 269–289. Springer.

Shay B Cohen, Robert J Simmons, and Noah A Smith. 2008. Dynamic programming algorithms as products of weighted logic programs. In *International Conference on Logic Programming*, pages 114–129.

Shay B Cohen, Karl Stratos, Michael Collins, Dean P Foster, and Lyle Ungar. 2013. Experiments with Spectral Learning of Latent-Variable PCFGs. In *Proceedings of the 2013 Conference of the North American Chapter of the Association for Computational Linguistics: Human Language Technologies*, pages 148–157, Atlanta, Georgia. Association for Computational Linguistics.

Shay B Cohen, Karl Stratos, Michael Collins, Dean P Foster, and Lyle Ungar. 2014. Spectral learning of latent-variable PCFGs: Algorithms and sample complexity. *The Journal of Machine Learning Research*, 15(1):2399–2449.

Arthur P Dempster, Nan M Laird, and Donald B Rubin. 1977. Maximum likelihood from incomplete data via the EM algorithm. *Journal of the Royal Statistical Society: Series B (Methodological)*, 39(1):1–22.

Jason Eisner. 2002. Parameter Estimation for Probabilistic Finite-State Transducers. In *Proceedings of the 40th Annual Meeting of the Association for Computational Linguistics*, pages 1–8, Philadelphia, Pennsylvania, USA. Association for Computational Linguistics.

Jason Eisner, Eric Goldlust, and Noah A Smith. 2005. Compiling Comp Ling: Weighted Dynamic Programming and the Dyna Language. In *Proceedings of Human Language Technology Conference and Conference on Empirical Methods in Natural Language Processing*, pages 281–290, Vancouver, British Columbia, Canada. Association for Computational Linguistics.

Kilian Gebhardt. 2018. Generic refinement of expressive grammar formalisms with an application to discontinuous constituent parsing. In *Proceedings of the 27th International Conference on Computational Linguistics*, pages 3049–3063, Santa Fe, New Mexico, USA. Association for Computational Linguistics.

Kevin Gimpel and Noah A Smith. 2009. Cube Summing, Approximate Inference with Non-Local Features, and Dynamic Programming without Semirings. In *Proceedings of the 12th Conference of the European Chapter of the ACL (EACL 2009)*, pages 318–326, Athens, Greece. Association for Computational Linguistics.

Joshua Goodman. 1999. Semiring Parsing. *Computational Linguistics*, 25(4):573–606.

Joshua T Goodman. 1998. *Parsing Inside-Out*. Ph.D. thesis, Harvard University Cambridge, Massachusetts.

Daniel Hsu, Sham M Kakade, and Tong Zhang. 2012. A spectral algorithm for learning hidden Markov models. *Journal of Computer and System Sciences*, 78(5):1460–1480.

Werner Kuich. 1997. Semirings and Formal Power Series: Their Relevance to Formal Languages and Automata. In Rozenberg Grzegorz and Arto Salomaa, editors, *Handbook of Formal Languages: Volume 1 Word, Language, Grammar*, pages 609–677. Springer, Berlin, Heidelberg.

Zhifei Li and Jason Eisner. 2009. First- and Second-Order Expectation Semirings with Applications to Minimum-Risk Training on Translation Forests. In *Proceedings of the 2009 Conference on Empirical Methods in Natural Language Processing*, pages 40–51, Singapore. Association for Computational Linguistics.

Adam Lopez. 2009. Translation as Weighted Deduction. In *Proceedings of the 12th Conference of the European Chapter of the ACL (EACL 2009)*, pages 532–540, Athens, Greece. Association for Computational Linguistics.

Takuya Matsuzaki, Yusuke Miyao, and Jun'ichi Tsujii. 2005. Probabilistic CFG with latent annotations. In *Proceedings of the 43rd Annual Meeting of the Association for Computational Linguistics*, pages 75–82.

Mark-Jan Nederhof. 2003. Weighted Deductive Parsing and Knuth's Algorithm. *Computational Linguistics*, 29(1):135–143.

Fernando C N Pereira and David H D Warren. 1983. Parsing as Deduction. In *Proceedings of the 21st Annual Meeting on Association for Computational Linguistics*, pages 137–144, Cambridge, Massachusetts, USA. Association for Computational Linguistics.

Stuart M Shieber, Yves Schabes, and Fernando C N Pereira. 1995. Principles and implementation of deductive parsing. *The Journal of logic programming*, 24(1-2):3–36.

Klaas Sikkel. 1998. Parsing schemata and correctness of parsing algorithms. *Theoretical Computer Science*, 199(1-2):87–103.

Martha Edmay Steenstrup. 1985. *Sum-Ordered Partial Semirings*. Ph.D. thesis, University of Massachusetts Amherst.

Appendix A - Proofs of Theorems in Main Paper

Lemma 5.1. *For any k, l, $\otimes_{[k;l]}$ distributes over $\oplus$*

Proof. We will proceed by showing that:

$$A \otimes_{[k;l]} (B \oplus C) = (A \otimes_{[k;l]} B) \oplus (A \otimes_{[k;l]} C)$$

Firstly, note that for the left hand side of the equation to be defined, B and C needs to be of matching ranks, and that $B \oplus C$ will be the same rank as both B and C. Therefore, if the left hand side is well defined then both $A \otimes_{[k;l]} B$ and $A \otimes_{[k;l]} C$ is defined and has matching ranks. So the right hand side is defined if and only if the left hand side is defined as well.

$$
\begin{aligned}
[A &\otimes_{[j;k]} (B \oplus C)]_{i_1,\ldots,i_{k-1},j_1,\ldots,j_{l-1},j_{l+1},\ldots,j_m,i_{k+1},\ldots,i_n} \\
&= \sum_{i_k,j_l} \delta(i_k, j_l) A_{i_1,\ldots,i_n} \times (B \oplus C)_{j_1,\ldots,j_m} \\
&= \sum_{i_k,j_l} \delta(i_k, j_l) A_{i_1,\ldots,i_n} \times (B_{j_1,\ldots,j_m} + C_{j_1,\ldots,j_m}) \\
&= \sum_{i_k,j_l} \delta(i_k, j_l)(A_{i_1,\ldots,i_n} \times B_{j_1,\ldots,j_m}) + \delta(i_k, j_l)(A_{i_1,\ldots,i_n} \times C_{j_1,\ldots,j_m}) \\
&= [(A \otimes_{[k;l]} B) \oplus (A \otimes_{[k;l]} C)]_{i_1,\ldots,i_{k-1},j_1,\ldots,j_{l-1},j_{l+1},\ldots,j_m,i_{k+1},\ldots,i_n}
\end{aligned}
$$

$\square$

Theorem 5.4. *An item-based description I is correct if*

- *For every grammar G, the mapping $g : \mathcal{D}_{I(G)} \to \mathcal{D}_G$ that maps $d' \in \mathcal{D}_{I(G)}$ to the corresponding $d \in \mathcal{D}_G$ is a bijection with an inverse function f.*

- *For any complete semiring S and weight function w, g and f preserve the values assigned to a derivation:*
$$V_G^w(d) = V_{I(G)}^w(f(d)) \text{ and } V_{I(G)}^w(d') = V_G^w(g(d'))$$

Proof.

$$V_{I(G)}^w(\alpha) = V_{I(G)}^w(goal, \alpha) = \bigoplus_{D \in \text{inner}_\alpha(goal)} V_{I(G)}^w(D) = \bigoplus_{D \in \mathcal{D}_{I(G)}(\alpha)} V_G^w(g(D))$$

Observe that $D \in \mathcal{D}_{I(G)}(\alpha)$ iff $g(D) \in \mathcal{D}_G(\alpha)$ since the rules that appear in the leaves of D, applied from left to right, determines the grammar derivation tree $g(D)$ uniquely via g, and vice versa. Hence,

$$V_{I(G)}^w(\alpha) = \bigoplus_{g(D) \in \mathcal{D}_G(\alpha)} V_G^w(g(D)) = V_G^w(\alpha)$$

$\square$

Theorem 6.1.

$$V(x) = \bigoplus_{\substack{[a_1,\ldots,a_k] \\ s.t. \frac{a_1,\ldots,a_k}{x}}} V(a_1) \otimes [V(a_2),\ldots,V(a_k)]$$

Proof. Recall that by definition, $V(x) = \bigoplus_{D \in inner(x)} V(D)$. For any item derivation D, D is either an axiom or there is some $a_1, \ldots, a_k, b$ s.t. $D \in inner(\frac{a_1 \ldots a_k}{b})$. If D is an axiom, then $inner(D)$ is just a single rule a, and so $V(D) = V(a)$. Else, for each rule $\frac{a_1 \ldots a_k}{x}$

$$\bigoplus_{D \in inner(\frac{a_1 \ldots a_k}{x})} V(D) = \bigoplus_{\substack{D_{a_1} \in inner(a_1), \ldots, \\ D_{a_k} \in inner(a_k)}} V(D_{a_1}) \otimes [V(D_{a_2}), \ldots, V(D_{a_k})]$$

$$= \left(\bigoplus_{D_{a_1} \in inner(a_1)} V(D_{a_1}) \right) \otimes \left(\bigoplus_{\substack{D_{a_2} \in inner(a_2), \ldots, \\ D_{a_k} \in inner(a_k)}} \bigotimes_{i=2}^{k} V(D_{a_i}) \right)$$

$$= \left(\bigoplus_{D_{a_1} \in inner(a_1)} V(D_{a_1}) \right) \otimes \left(\bigoplus_{D_{a_2} \in inner(a_2)} V(D_{a_2}), \ldots, \bigoplus_{D_{a_k} \in inner(a_k)} V(D_{a_k}) \right)$$

$$= V(a_1) \otimes [V(a_2), \ldots, V(a_k)]$$

Where the last step holds due to the distributive property of the partial semiring.

Since the set $inner(x) = \bigcup_i D_i$ where $D_i \in inner(\frac{a_1 \ldots a_k}{x})$ for all inference rules $\frac{a_1 \ldots a_k}{x}$, we can write the summation over $D \in inner(x)$ as:

$$V(x) = \bigoplus_{D \in inner(x)} V(D)$$

$$= \bigoplus_{\substack{[a_1, \ldots, a_k] \\ \text{s.t.} \frac{a_1, \ldots, a_k}{x}}} \bigoplus_{D \in inner(\frac{a_1 \ldots a_k}{x})} V(D)$$

$$= \bigoplus_{\substack{[a_1, \ldots, a_k] \\ \text{s.t.} \frac{a_1, \ldots, a_k}{x}}} V(a_1) \otimes [V(a_2), V(a_3), \ldots, V(a_k)]$$

Where the last line is obtained by replacing the inner part of the expression with the equality obtained from the previous part of the proof. $\square$

Lemma 6.2. *Let V and Z be defined on a commutative semiring $\mathbb{S}$ and let $O \in outer_\alpha(x)$ and $T \in inner_\alpha(x)$. If combining O and T in the obvious way results in the complete derivation D then*

$$V(D) = V(T) \otimes^* Z(O)$$

Proof. To simplify notation of the indices, let $\mathbf{i}$ stand for a list of indices $i_1, \ldots, i_n$ for some n. We will also use $\mathbf{d}^i$ to denote a list $d_1^i, \ldots d_{n_i}^i$ and $\mathbf{d}$ to denote $\mathbf{d}^1, \ldots, \mathbf{d}^n$. $\delta(\mathbf{i}, \mathbf{j}) = \prod_{k=1}^{n} \delta(i_k, j_k)$.

We will proceed by induction on the parse tree. Base case is where $x = goal$, $T = D$ and O is empty. Then $V(T) = V(D)$ and $Z(O) = I_S$. $V(D) \otimes^* I_S = V(D)$ by the definition of I_S which proves the statement.

Otherwise T has a parent tree $T_p = \langle y : T_1, \ldots, T_n \rangle$ where $T = T_k$. Furthermore, $T_p \in inner_\alpha(y)$, $O_p \in outer_\alpha(y)$ and by induction hypothesis $V(D) = V(T_p) \otimes^* Z(O_p)$.

Since $T_p \in inner_\alpha(y)$ we know that

$$V(T_p) = V(T_1) \otimes [V(T_2), \ldots, V(T_m)]$$

So

$$V(D) = (V(T_1) \otimes [V(T_2), \ldots, V(T_m)]) \otimes^* Z(O_p)$$

The proof progresses by calculating the value for $[V(D)]_i$ based on the above term and shows that this is equal to the value of $[V(T) \otimes^* Z(O)]_i$.

Let:

$$V(T_1) \in \mathbb{S}^{\mathbf{e},\mathbf{f}} \qquad\qquad V(T_i) \in \mathbb{S}^{e_i,\mathbf{d}^i}$$
$$Z(O_p) \in \mathbb{S}^{\mathbf{d},\mathbf{f},s} \qquad\qquad V(D) \in \mathbb{S}^s$$

Then:

$$V[(T_p)]_{\mathbf{d},\mathbf{f}} = [V(T_1) \otimes (V(T_2),\ldots,V(T_m))]_{\mathbf{d},\mathbf{f}}$$

$$= \sum_{\mathbf{e},\mathbf{e}'} V(T_1)_{\mathbf{e},\mathbf{f}} \times \prod_{i=2}^{m} \delta(e_i,e_i')V(T_i)_{e_i',\mathbf{d}^i}$$

$$[V(D)]_s = [V(T_p) \otimes^* Z(O_p)]_s =$$

$$\sum_{\mathbf{e},\mathbf{e}',\mathbf{d},\mathbf{d}'\mathbf{f},\mathbf{f}'} V(T_1)_{\mathbf{e},\mathbf{f}} \times \left(\prod_{i=2}^{m} \delta(e_i,e_i')V(T_i)_{e_i,\mathbf{d}^i} \right)$$
$$\times \delta(\mathbf{d},\mathbf{d}')\delta(\mathbf{f},\mathbf{f}')Z(O_p)_{\mathbf{d},\mathbf{f},s}$$

Now we will proceed to prove that this term is equal to $V(T_k) \otimes^* Z(O)$. Let $I_{T_k} \in \mathbb{S}^{e_k',\mathbf{d}^k,s,e_k,\mathbf{d}^k,s}$. We will calculate the value of the outside term in sections. Let $A = V(T_1) \otimes_k (I_{T_k},V(T_{k+1}),\ldots,V(T_n))$. Then,

$$A_{e_1,\ldots,e_{k-1},\mathbf{d}^k,s,\hat{e}_k,\hat{\mathbf{d}}_k,\hat{s},\mathbf{d}^{k+1},\ldots,\mathbf{d}^n,\mathbf{f}} =$$
$$A^{\pi}_{e_1,\ldots,e_{k-1},\mathbf{d}^k,\mathbf{d}^{k+1},\ldots,\mathbf{d}^n,\mathbf{f},s,\hat{e}_k,\hat{\mathbf{d}}_k,\hat{s}} =$$

$$\sum_{\substack{e_k,\ldots,e_n \\ e_k',\ldots,e_n'}} V(T_1)_{\mathbf{e},\mathbf{f}} \times \delta(e_k,e_k')\delta(\mathbf{d}^k,\hat{\mathbf{d}}^k)\delta(s,\hat{s}) \times \prod_{i=k+1}^{m} \delta(e_i,e_i')V(T_i)_{e_i',\mathbf{d}^i}$$

$$[A^{\pi} \otimes (V(T_2),\ldots,V(T_{k-1}))]_{\mathbf{d},\mathbf{f},s,\hat{e}_k,\hat{\mathbf{d}}^k,\hat{s}} =$$

$$\sum_{\mathbf{e},\mathbf{e}'} V(T_1)_{\mathbf{e},\mathbf{f}} \times \prod_{\substack{i=2 \\ i \neq k}}^{n} V(T_i)_{e_i',\mathbf{d}^i} \times$$

$$\delta(\mathbf{e},\mathbf{e}') \times \delta(e_k,\hat{e}_k) \times \delta(\mathbf{d}^k,\hat{\mathbf{d}}^k) \times \delta(s,\hat{s})$$

$$[Z(O)]_{\hat{e}_k,\hat{\mathbf{d}}^k,\hat{s}} = \sum_{\substack{\mathbf{e},\mathbf{e}',\mathbf{d},\mathbf{d}' \\ \mathbf{f},\mathbf{f}',s,s'}} V(T_1)_{\mathbf{e},\mathbf{f}} \times \prod_{\substack{i=2 \\ i \neq k}}^{n} V(T_i)_{e_i',\mathbf{d}^i} \times Z(O_p)_{\mathbf{d}',\mathbf{f}',s'}$$
$$\times \delta(\mathbf{e},\mathbf{e}') \times \delta(e_k,\hat{e}_k) \times \delta(\mathbf{d}^k,\hat{\mathbf{d}}^k) \times \delta(s,\hat{s})$$
$$\times \delta(\mathbf{d},\mathbf{d}') \times \delta(\mathbf{f},\mathbf{f}') \times \delta(s,s')$$

$$[V(T_k) \otimes^* Z(O)]_{\hat{s}} =$$

$$\sum_{\substack{\mathbf{e},\mathbf{e}',\mathbf{d},\mathbf{d}' \\ \mathbf{f},\mathbf{f}',s,s' \\ \hat{e}_k,\hat{\mathbf{d}}^k,e_k'',\mathbf{d}^{k''}}} V(T_k)_{e_k'',\mathbf{d}^{k''}} \times V(T_1)_{\mathbf{e},\mathbf{f}} \times \prod_{\substack{i=2 \\ i \neq k}}^{n} V(T_i)_{e_i',\mathbf{d}^i} \times Z(O_p)_{\mathbf{d}',\mathbf{f}',s'}$$

$$\times \delta(\mathbf{e},\mathbf{e}') \times \delta(e_k,\hat{e}_k) \times \delta(\mathbf{d}^k,\hat{\mathbf{d}}^k) \times \delta(s,\hat{s})$$
$$\times \delta(\mathbf{d},\mathbf{d}') \times \delta(\mathbf{f},\mathbf{f}') \times \delta(s,s') \times \delta(e_k'',\hat{e}_k) \times \delta(\mathbf{d}^{k''},\hat{\mathbf{d}}^k)$$

$$= \sum_{\mathbf{e},\mathbf{e}',\mathbf{d},\mathbf{d}'\mathbf{f},\mathbf{f}'} V(T_1)_{\mathbf{e},\mathbf{f}} \times \prod_{i=2}^{m} V(T_i)_{e_i,\mathbf{d}^i} \times Z(O_p)_{\mathbf{d},\mathbf{f},\hat{s}}$$

$$\times \delta(\mathbf{e},\mathbf{e}') \times \delta(\mathbf{d},\mathbf{d}') \times \delta(\mathbf{f},\mathbf{f}')$$

Which completes the proof. The last simplification step is obtained by replacing $\hat{e}_k$ and e_k'' with e_k, $\hat{\mathbf{d}}^k$ and $\mathbf{d}^{k''}$ with $\mathbf{d}^k$ and s and s' with $\hat{s}$ since these need to be equal for any term to contribute to the final sum. The commutativity of $\mathbb{S}$ then allows $V(T_k)_{e_k,\mathbf{d}^k}$ to be moved to its place in the sequence.

$\square$

Theorem 6.4. *If x is the goal item, then $Z(x) = I_s$. Else,*

$$Z(x) = \bigoplus_{\substack{j,a_1,..,a_k,b \ s.t. \\ \frac{a_1...a_k}{b} \ and \ x=a_j}} (V(a_1) \otimes_k [I_{a_k}, V(a_{k+1}), \ldots, V(a_n)])^{\pi}$$

$$\otimes \left(V(a_2), \ldots, V(a_{k-1})\right) \otimes^* Z(b)$$

Proof. by definition $Z(x) = \bigoplus_{D \in outer(x)} Z(D)$. Either x is a goal item, in which case $Z(x) = Z() = I_S$.

Otherwise the outer trees $outer(x)$ could be written as the union of outer trees $outer\left(k, \frac{a_1...a_n}{b}\right)$ for each rule $\frac{a_1...a_n}{b}$ where $a_k = x$ for some k. Hence:

$$Z(x) = \bigoplus_{\substack{j,a_1,..,a_k,b \ s.t. \\ \frac{a_1...a_k}{b} \ and \ x=a_j}} \bigoplus_{D \in outer\left(k, \frac{a_1...a_n}{b}\right)} Z(D)$$

For the inner part of this equation we have:

$$\bigoplus_{D \in outer\left(k, \frac{a_1...a_n}{b}\right)} Z(D) =$$

$$\bigoplus_{\substack{D_b \in outer(b)}} \bigoplus_{\substack{D_{a_1} \in inner(a_1),..., \\ D_{a_{k-1}} \in inner(a_{k-1})}} \bigoplus_{\substack{D_{a_{k+1}} \in inner(a_{k+1}),..., \\ D_{a_n} \in inner(a_n)}}$$

$$\left(V(D_{a_1}) \otimes_k \left[I_{D_{a_k} \times d_S}, V(D_{a_{k+1}}), \ldots, V(D_{a_n})\right]\right)^{\pi}$$

$$\otimes \left(V(D_{a_2}), \ldots, V(D_{a_{k-1}})\right) \otimes^* Z(D_b)$$

Since $\oplus$ distributes over $\otimes$, this can rewritten as

$$\bigoplus_{D \in outer\left(k, \frac{a_1...a_n}{b}\right)} Z(D) =$$

$$\left(\bigoplus_{\substack{D_{a_1} \in \\ inner(a_1)}} V(D_{a_1}) \otimes_k \left[I_{D_{a_k}}, \bigoplus_{\substack{D_{a_{k+1}} \in \\ inner(a_{k+1})}} V(D_{a_{k+1}}), \ldots, \bigoplus_{\substack{D_{a_n} \in \\ inner(a_n)}} V(D_{a_n})\right]\right)^{\pi}$$

$$\otimes \left(\bigoplus_{D_{a_2} \in inner(a_2)} V(D_{a_2}), \ldots, \bigoplus_{D_{a_{k-1}} \in inner(a_{k-1})} V(D_{a_{k-1}})\right)$$

$$\otimes^* \bigoplus_{D_b \in outer(b)} Z(D_b)$$

And since $V(a_i)$ and $Z(D_b)$ are defined as the summation of their inner and outer trees respectively

$$\bigoplus_{D \in outer\left(k, \frac{a_1...a_n}{b}\right)} Z(D) =$$

$$(V(a_1) \otimes_k [I_{a_k}, V(a_{k+1}), \ldots, V(a_n)])^{\pi} \otimes (V(a_2), \ldots, V(a_{k-1})) \otimes^* Z(b)$$

Replacing the inner part of the previous equation with this term gives us the desired equality, completing the proof. $\qquad\square$

Appendix B - Inside and Outside Calculations for Looping Buckets

In computing the inside and outside values with an item-based description, we assume a pre-computed ordering over items in the form of *buckets*. For items x and y, we write $bucket(x) \leq bucket(y)$ if the value of y depends on the value of x. So far we have assumed that items could be simply sorted so that no item directly or indirectly depends on itself, and given the inside and outside formulas accordingly. In this section we give the equivalent formulas for items in *looping buckets*. Items in a looping bucket depend on each other and computing their values might require an infinite sum. Our presentation and proofs both follow that of Goodman (1998).

For an item x in a looping bucket B, let the *generation* of a derivation tree x to be the maximum number of items in B that could appear in a single path from the root to a leaf. This intuitively provides an ordering for processing a potentially infinite number of trees by starting from generation 0 and incrementally adding larger and larger trees. We will denote the set of inner trees of x with generation at most g with $inner_{\leq}(x, B)$ Adding up the values of all inner trees of x that have generation at most g then gives us an approximation for the true inner value of x, and the approximation gets better as g gets larger. Formally, we define a *g generation value* for an item x in bucket B as:

$$V_{\leq g}(x, B) = \bigoplus_{D \in inner_{\leq g}(x,B)} V(D)$$

For ω-continuous semirings, the infinite sum is equal to the supremum of the partial sums (Kuich 1997, 613), hence (Goodman 1999, 589):

$$V(x) = \bigoplus_{D \in inner(x)} V(D) = \sup_g V_{\leq g}(x, B)$$

Fortunately, tensors of semirings of set dimensions are ω-continuous as long as the underlying semiring is ω-continuous. We give the necessary definitions to establish this property:

Definition 8. *(Kuich 1997, 611) A semiring is **naturally ordered** if there is a partial ordering $\sqsubseteq$ such that $x \sqsubseteq y$ iff there is a z s.t. $x \oplus z = y$.*

Definition 9. *(Kuich 1997, 612) A naturally ordered complete semiring is ω-continuous if for any sequence $x_1, x_2, \ldots$ and for any constant y, if for all n, $\bigoplus_{0 \leq i \leq n} x_i \sqsubseteq y$ then $\bigoplus_i x_i \sqsubseteq y$*

Notice that for the set of tensors in $\mathbb{S}^\mathbf{d}$ where $\mathbf{d}$ is an arbitrary list of positive integers, if the underlying semiring has a natural ordering then this could be extended straightforwardly to $\mathbb{S}^\mathbf{d}$ by the following rule: $\mathbf{X} \sqsubseteq \mathbf{Y}$ iff $\mathbf{X_i} \sqsubseteq \mathbf{Y_i}$ for all indices $\mathbf{i}$. It is straightforward to check that if the underlying semiring is ω-continuous, then $\mathbb{S}^\mathbf{d}$ is ω-continuous as well.

Goodman (1999) gives a formula for $V_{\leq g}(x, B)$ in order to compute or approximate the supremum. Below we give the analogous formula for partial semirings:

Theorem B.1. *For items x in a looping bucket B and the generation $g \geq 1$*

$$V_{\leq g}(x, B) = \bigoplus_{\substack{[a_1,\ldots,a_k] \\ s.t. \frac{a_1,\ldots,a_k}{x}}} K_g(a_1, B) \otimes [K_g(a_2, B), \ldots, K_g(a_k, B)]$$

Where

$$K_g(a, B) = \begin{cases} V(a) & \text{if } a \notin B \\ V_{\leq g-1}(a, B) & \text{if } a \in B \end{cases}$$

Proof.

$$V_{\leq g}(x, B) = \bigoplus_{D \in inner_{\leq g}(x,B)} V(D)$$

$$= \bigoplus_{\substack{[a_1,\ldots,a_k] \\ \text{s.t.} \frac{a_1\ldots a_k}{x}}} \bigoplus_{\substack{D_{a_1} \in inner_{\leq g-1}(a_1,B),\ldots, \\ D_{a_k} \in inner_{\leq g-1}(a_k,B)}} V\left(\langle x : D_{a_1}, \ldots D_{a_k} \rangle\right)$$

$$= \bigoplus_{\substack{[a_1,\ldots,a_k] \\ \text{s.t.} \frac{a_1\ldots a_k}{x}}} \bigoplus_{\substack{D_{a_1} \in inner_{\leq g-1}(a_1,B),\ldots, \\ D_{a_k} \in inner_{\leq g-1}(a_k,B)}} V(D_{a_1}) \otimes [V(D_{a_2}), \ldots, V(D_{a_k})]$$

$$= \bigoplus_{\substack{[a_1,\ldots,a_k] \\ \text{s.t.} \frac{a_1\ldots a_k}{x}}} \bigoplus_{D_{a_1} \in inner_{\leq g-1}(a_1,B)} V(D_{a_1})$$

$$\otimes \left[\bigoplus_{D_{a_2} \in inner_{\leq g-1}(a_2,B)} V(D_{a_2}), \ldots, \bigoplus_{D_{a_k} \in inner_{\leq g-1}(a_k,B)} V(D_{a_k}) \right]$$

$$= \bigoplus_{\substack{[a_1,\ldots,a_k] \\ \text{s.t.} \frac{a_1\ldots a_k}{x}}} V_{\leq g-1}(a_1, B) \otimes [V_{\leq g-1}(a_2, B), \ldots, V_{\leq g-1}(a_k, B)]$$

Note that if a_i is not in the bucket B then $V_{\leq g-1}(a_i, B) = V(a_i)$, hence $V_{\leq g-1}(a_i, B)$ can be replaced with $K_g(a_i, B)$, completing the proof. $\square$

We will follow a similar strategy for computing the outside values of items that belong to a looping bucket. The only difference is the slight difference in the definition of the generation of of the tree. If $D \in outer(x)$ where x belongs to a looping bucket B, then the generation of D is maximum number of items that could appear in a single path from the root to x, where x is included in the count. Let

$$Z_{\leq g}(x, B) = \bigoplus_{D \in outer_{\leq g}(x,B)} Z(D)$$

Theorem B.2. *For items x in a looping bucket B and the generation $g \geq 1$*

$$Z_{\leq g}(x, B) = \bigoplus_{\substack{j,a_1,\ldots,a_k,b \text{ s.t.} \\ \frac{a_1\ldots a_k}{b} \text{ and } x=a_j}} (V(a_1) \otimes_k [I_{a_k}, V(a_{k+1}), \ldots, V(a_n)])^\pi$$

$$\otimes [(V(a_1), \ldots, V(a_{k-1})] \otimes^* H_g(b, B)$$

Where π is defined as in Theorem 6.4 and

$$H_g(b, B) = \begin{cases} Z(b) & \text{if } b \notin B \\ Z_{\leq g-1}(b, B) & \text{if } b \in B \end{cases}$$

Proof.

$$Z_{\leq g}(x, B) = \bigoplus_{D \in outer_{\leq g}(x,B)} Z(D)$$

$$= \bigoplus_{\substack{j,a_1,..,a_k,b \text{ s.t.} \\ \frac{a_1...a_k}{b} \text{ and } x=a_j}} \bigoplus_{D \in outer_{\leq g-1}\left(k, \frac{a_1...a_n}{b}\right)} Z(D)$$

$$= \bigoplus_{\substack{j,a_1,..,a_k,b \text{ s.t.} \\ \frac{a_1...a_k}{b} \text{ and } x=a_j}} \bigoplus_{D_b \in outer_{\leq g-1}(b)} \bigoplus_{\substack{D_{a_1} \in inner(a_1),..., \\ D_{a_{k-1}} \in inner(a_{k-1})}} \bigoplus_{\substack{D_{a_{k+1}} \in inner(a_{k+1}),..., \\ D_{a_n} \in inner(a_n)}}$$

$$\left(V(D_{a_1}) \otimes_k \left[I_{D_{a_k} \times d_S}, V(D_{a_{k+1}}), \ldots, V(D_{a_n})\right]\right)^{\pi}$$

$$\otimes \left(V(D_{a_2}), \ldots, V(D_{a_{k-1}})\right) \otimes^* Z_{\leq g}(D_b, B)$$

$$= \bigoplus_{\substack{j,a_1,..,a_k,b \text{ s.t.} \\ \frac{a_1...a_k}{b} \text{ and } x=a_j}} \left(\bigoplus_{\substack{D_{a_1} \in \\ inner(a_1)}} V(D_{a_1}) \otimes_k \left[I_{D_{a_k}}, \bigoplus_{\substack{D_{a_{k+1}} \in \\ inner(a_{k+1})}} V(D_{a_{k+1}}), \ldots, \bigoplus_{\substack{D_{a_n} \in \\ inner(a_n)}} V(D_{a_n})\right]\right)^{\pi}$$

$$\otimes \left(\bigoplus_{D_{a_2} \in inner(a_2)} V(D_{a_2}), \ldots, \bigoplus_{D_{a_{k-1}} \in inner(a_{k-1})} V(D_{a_{k-1}})\right)$$

$$\otimes^* \bigoplus_{D_b \in outer_{\leq g-1}(b)} Z_{\leq g-1}(D_b, B)$$

$$= \bigoplus_{\substack{j,a_1,..,a_k,b \text{ s.t.} \\ \frac{a_1...a_k}{b} \text{ and } x=a_j}} \left(V(a_1) \otimes_k \left[I_{a_k}, V(a_{k+1}), \ldots, V(a_n)\right]\right)^{\pi}$$

$$\otimes \left[(V(a_2), \ldots, V(a_{k-1})\right] \otimes^* Z_{\leq g-1}(b, B)$$

Like the inner case, note that for an item b not in the looping bucket b, $Z_{\leq g-1}(b, B) = Z(b)$, hence we can replace $Z_{\leq g-1}(b, B)$ with $H_g(b, B)$, completing the proof. $\qquad\square$

Advances in using
Grammars with Latent Annotations
for Discontinuous Parsing

Kilian Gebhardt
Department of Computer Science
Technische Universität Dresden
D-01062 Dresden, Germany
`kilian.gebhardt@tu-dresden.de`

Abstract

We present new experiments that transfer techniques from Probabilistic Context-free Grammars with Latent Annotations (PCFG-LA) to two grammar formalisms for discontinuous parsing: linear context-free rewriting systems and hybrid grammars. In particular, Dirichlet priors during EM training, ensemble models, and a new nonterminal scheme for hybrid grammars are evaluated. We find that our grammars are more accurate than previous approaches based on discontinuous grammar formalisms and early instances of the discriminative models but inferior to recent discriminative parsers.[1]

1 Introduction

Many tasks in natural language processing, such as machine translation, information extraction, and sentiment analysis, benefit from syntactic analysis (Culotta and Sorensen, 2004; Ding and Palmer, 2005; Duric and Song, 2011). Often syntax is represented by means of constituents. Languages with a flexible word order such as German require constituents that are *discontinuous*, i.e., constituents that cover words which do not constitute a continuous interval in the sentence. To this end, generalizations of context-free grammars such as tree adjoining grammars (Joshi et al., 1975) and *linear context-free rewriting systems* (LCFRS, Vijay-Shanker et al., 1987) have been proposed. Although the parsing complexity with these formalisms is polynomial in the length of the input sentence (for a fixed grammar), they are often considered too slow to be practically useful. Also the accuracy of LCFRS-based parsers does not match up to their continuous counterparts.

Instead, a wide range of models that either apply transition systems with a reordering mecha-

nism or are based on a dependency-to-constituency transformation have been proposed in recent years (Hall and Nivre, 2008; Versley, 2014a; Maier, 2015; Fernández-González and Martins, 2015; Coavoux and Crabbé, 2017; Corro et al., 2017; Stanojević and Garrido Alhama, 2017; Coavoux and Cohen, 2019; Fernández-González and Gómez-Rodríguez, 2020). There are two notable exceptions: van Cranenburgh et al. (2016) considers a discontinuous extension of the data-oriented parsing approach. Gebhardt (2018) studies the extension of two grammar formalisms with latent annotations: LCFRS and hybrid grammars (Nederhof and Vogler, 2014), which is a synchronous grammar formalism that couples a string generating grammar (specifically: LCFRS) and a tree generating grammar (specifically: simple definite clause programs; Deransart and Małuszyński, 1989). In particular, Gebhardt (2018) analyses the effect of a generalization of Petrov et al.'s split/merge procedure (2006), which adaptively refines the grammar's nonterminals by automatic splitting and merging. Although this refinement strategy showed vast improvements over the respective unrefined grammar, some choices in the experimental setup of Gebhardt (2018) can be enhanced:

(i) The *expectation maximization algorithm* (EM, Baker, 1979), which is a subroutine of the split/merge procedure, utilizes a likelihood-based objective that is prone to overfitting.

(ii) Ensemble-models obtained by running the split/merge procedure with different random seeds were successfully applied for continuous parsing (Petrov, 2010) but not considered in Gebhardt (2018).

(iii) Gebhardt (2018) supposes that the initial granularity of the grammar's nonterminals matters as the state-refinement procedure does not fully recover them.

---

[1]The implementation is available at `https://github.com/kilian-gebhardt/panda-parser/`.

91

Proceedings of the 16th International Conference on Parsing Technologies and the IWPT 2020 Shared Task, pages 91–97
Virtual Meeting, July 9, 2020. ©2020 Association for Computational Linguistics

In this work, we address the above points by (i) comparing the likelihood-based objective to a *Maximum-a-Posteriori* (MAP) objective, (ii) evaluating ensemble models, and (iii) proposing a new nonterminal naming scheme for hybrid grammars. We hypothesize that these steps are complementary in improving the accuracy of the parsing model. Although we do not expect to reach or even surpass the performance of recent discriminative approaches (in particular those utilizing neural nets), we suppose that these experiments foster the understanding of the limits of the different architectures.

2 Model

We consider models based on LCFRS and hybrid grammars. Vijay-Shanker et al. (1987) and Gebhardt et al. (2017) give formal definitions of these formalisms, respectively. *Baseline grammars* are induced from the training data using the induction techniques of Kallmeyer and Maier (2013) and Gebhardt et al. (2017), respectively. LCFRS are either binarized right-to-left ($r2\ell$) or head-outward (ho) with vertical and horizontal Markovization set to 1. For hybrid grammars the induction is parametrized such that the LCFRS-component has fanout 2.

The baseline grammars are refined using a variant of Petrov et al.'s split/merge algorithm (2006), which is described in Gebhardt (2018). This algorithm consists of multiple split/merge cycles in each of which the EM algorithm is used to fit the rule weights to the training data. To obtain MAP training, we modify the EM algorithm by including a Dirichlet prior (see Johnson et al., 2007, Sec. 2.3). This is implemented by incrementing each rule count by a non-negative default value in the "expectation" phase.

Gebhardt (2018) reports that LCFRS outperform hybrid grammars but conjectures that this might be an artifact of the choice of nonterminals in the baseline grammar. The nonterminal naming schemes *child* and *strict labeling* for hybrid grammars (originally introduced by Nederhof and Vogler, 2014) name a nonterminal based on the subset of tree nodes U^2 that is generated by the nonterminal. As illustrated in fig. 1, in strict labeling the roots of maximum subtrees formed by U are used in the label, where consecutive sibling nodes are joined. In child labeling, sequences of sibling nodes of length

---

[2]How these nonterminals/subsets are determined is described in Gebhardt et al. (2017).

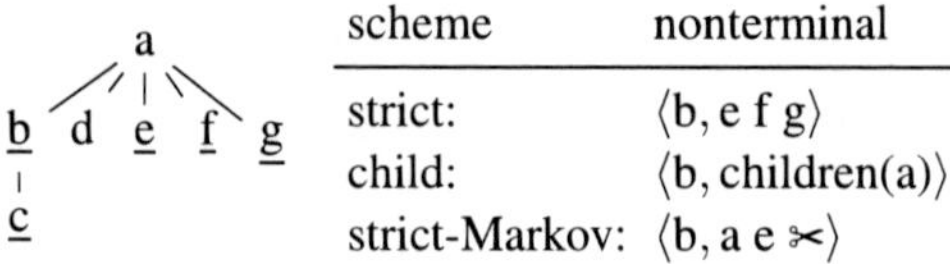

Figure 1: A tree, a subset of its nodes (underlined), and the nonterminals created for this subset according to different nonterminal labeling schemes.

> 1 are replaced by the "children(p)" where p is the parent node. Gebhardt (2018) supposes that these strategies either lead to a number of nonterminals that is too small or too large for favorable automatic refinement. We explore a trade-off by *Markovizing* (cf. Klein and Manning, 2003) the strict labeling strategy. Where strict labeling uses sequences $s = n_1 \cdots n_k$ of sibling nodes in nonterminal labels such that $k > 1$, we now use the parent node p of $n_1 \cdots n_k$, the first node n_1, and a cut-off marker $\bowtie$. Each nonterminal label then consists of sequences $s' = p\, n_1 \bowtie$.

After split/merge refinement, the grammars are used to parse unseen sentences. Since exact parsing is NP-hard already for PCFG-LA (see Matsuzaki et al., 2005), we follow the literature and apply an approximate tractable objective called *max-rule-product* (short: mrp, which projects weights from the refined grammar to a sentence-specific coarse one and computes the the most probable derivation of the latter, see Petrov and Klein, 2007).

Petrov (2010) presents experiments with ensemble models, where different PCFG-LA are obtained from the same training data by changing the random seed. During parsing the mrp objective is applied where each rule weight of the coarse grammar is set to the product of the weights that result from projecting with the individual grammars. This ensemble grammar showed significantly improved accuracy over the best single grammar. We instantiate this approach for LCFRS and hybrid grammars using 4 random seeds.

3 Experiments

Data. We present experiments on the German TIGER (Brants et al., 2004) and NEGRA (Skut et al., 1997) corpora. For TIGER, we use the SPMRL split (Seddah et al., 2014, short: SPMRL) and the split by Hall and Nivre (2008, short: HN08) but optimize hyperparameters solely on HN08. For NEGRA we use the split by Dubey and Keller (2003). For evaluation we compute the labelled

grammar	TIGER HN08				NEGRA			
	NTs	coverage dev. set	parse fails	F1 (≤ 40)	NTs	coverage dev. set	parse fails	F1 (≤ 40)
LCFRS$_{ho}$	767	86.9%	4	68.29	716	88.2%	4	68.88
LCFRS$_{r2\ell}$	817	84.7%	4	70.36	787	82.7%	8	70.07
hybrid child	288	92.5%	11	63.19	279	93.5%	2	62.06
hybrid strict-Markov	1,783	81.9%	108	72.18	1,623	81.1%	42	71.34
hybrid strict	32,281	50.0 %	166	69.90	20,766	53.9%	34	68.82

Table 1: Statistics for the baseline grammars induced from NEGRA and TIGER (after likelihood-based training). For the dev. set we report: *coverage*, i.e., the percentage of gold parse trees that can be derived with the grammar; *parse fails*, i.e., the number of sentences for which the grammar cannot derive any parse tree; labeled F1 for the parse tree with the most probable derivation.

grammar	HN08				NEGRA			
	F1	*(ens.)*	Disc. F1	*(ens.)*	F1	*(ens.)*	Disc. F1	*(ens.)*
Likelihood-based training								
LCFRS$_{ho}$	78.85 $\pm$0.34	79.91	32.57 $\pm$1.91	33.81	80.14 $\pm$0.54	81.35	39.57 $\pm$2.00	41.09
LCFRS$_{r2\ell}$	79.25 $\pm$0.15	79.93	33.82 $\pm$0.21	34.19	78.74 $\pm$0.43	80.25	38.01 $\pm$1.64	39.49
hybrid child	77.82 $\pm$0.24	78.52	30.64 $\pm$0.28	31.15	80.38 $\pm$0.33	82.06	40.73 $\pm$0.86	**44.52**
hybrid strict-Markov	79.66 $\pm$0.23	80.55	45.56 $\pm$0.55	47.65	77.51 $\pm$0.32	78.17	39.27 $\pm$1.96	42.18
MAP training (default count: 1.0)								
LCFRS$_{ho}$	79.03 $\pm$0.42	79.83	30.98 $\pm$0.53	33.00	80.88 $\pm$0.23	82.27	40.40 $\pm$2.27	41.96
LCFRS$_{r2\ell}$	80.01 $\pm$0.16	81.02	34.15 $\pm$0.22	35.70	79.38 $\pm$0.79	80.79	40.92 $\pm$2.48	43.04
hybrid child	78.56 $\pm$0.23	79.36	32.15 $\pm$0.61	33.36	81.75 $\pm$0.26	**83.33**	40.31 $\pm$0.68	43.06
hybrid strict-Markov	80.54 $\pm$0.16	**81.75**	47.32 $\pm$0.96	**49.82**	77.62 $\pm$0.12	78.60	40.23 $\pm$0.89	42.52

Table 2: (Average) F1-scores on the dev. set (length ≤ 40) after training for 4 s/m cycles at 50% merge rate (HN08) and 6 s/m cycles at 80% merge rate (NEGRA). Columns labeled *(ens.)* show scores for the ensemble models.

F1 and labelled discontinuous F1 using *discodop*[3] (van Cranenburgh et al., 2016) with the included `proper.prm` parameter file. In the tables we list average F1 scores and standard deviation over 4 grammars with different random seeds, except for ensemble experiments where we execute just one run combining those 4 grammars.

Properties of baseline grammars. We induce baseline grammars from the training data and display their properties in table 1. We see that Markovizing the strict labels effectively reduces the number of nonterminals (NTs) and leads to the most accurate baseline grammars. Still, this approach comes at the cost of reduced coverage in comparison to the child labeling hybrid grammar and the LCFRS. On NEGRA we see an increase in parse failures also in comparison to strict labeling. This is due to the addition of vertical context

(i.e., the parent node) that is not present in strict labeling.

Training objective. We use the split/merge algorithm to refine the baseline grammars using both a likelihood-based and a MAP-based objective with default count 1.0 during EM training[4]. Differences between both training modes are displayed in table 2 for HN08 and NEGRA. MAP training in many settings improves the accuracy. In particular, using non-ensemble grammars the average F1 score on all constituents always improves. The average F1

---

[4]Next to the default count the training has other hyperparameters, e.g., the rate of splits that is merged or the number of s/m cycles. In early experiments we found default count values around 1.0 to work best. Also, an increase of the merge rate from 50% to e.g. 80% or 90% often does not harm the accuracy and allows for smaller grammars or the execution of additional split/merge cycles. We used such an optimized setting for NEGRA (and for TIGER on the test set). An exhaustive grid search that optimizes these parameters for all considered grammars and corpora is computationally expensive and beyond the scope of this article.

[3]https://github.com/andreasvc/disco-dop

	NEGRA			SPMRL		HN08
	F1 (≤ 40)	F1	Disc. F1	F1	Disc. F1	F1 (≤ 40)
this work						
hybrid grammar (average of 4 grammars)	81.1	80.3	40.7	76.7	38.9	80.7
hybrid grammar (ensemble)	82.5	81.7	43.5	77.7	40.7	81.6
chart-based approaches						
Kallmeyer and Maier (2013) ○	75.8[†]	-	-	-	-	-
van Cranenburgh et al. (2016) ○	76.8	-	-	-	-	78.2◉
Versley (2016) ○◉	-	-	-	79.5	-	82.9
Gebhardt (2018) ○	-	-	-	75.1	-	79.3
Corro (2020) ◉ ⁄ (without pre-trained word embeddings)	-	**86.2**	54.1	**85.5**	53.8	-
Corro (2020) ◉ ⁄ (with BERT, Devlin et al., 2019)	-	**91.6**	66.1	**90.0**	**62.1**	-
dependency-to-constituency conversions						
Hall and Nivre (2008)	-	-	-	-	-	79.9
Fernández-González and Martins (2015)	81.1	80.5	-	-	-	85.5
Corro et al. (2017) ⁄	-	-	-	81.6	-	-
Fernández-González and Gómez-Rodríguez (2020) ⁄	-	86.1	59.9	86.3	60.7	-
transition systems						
Versley (2014a,b)	-	-	-	-	-	74.2
Maier (2015)	77.0[†]	-	19.8[†]	74.7	18.8	79.5
Maier and Lichte (2016)	-	-	-	76.5	16.3	80.0
Coavoux and Crabbé (2017)	82.8	82.2	50.0	81.6	49.2	85.1
Stanojević and Garrido Alhama (2017) ⁄	83.4	82.9	-	81.6	-	85.3
Coavoux and Cohen (2019) ◉ ⁄	-	83.2	56.3	82.5	55.9	-
Coavoux et al. (2019) ◉ ⁄	-	83.2	54.6	82.7	55.9	-

Table 3: Test results with gold POS tags (systems/scores with ◉ use predicted tags; †: sentence length ≤ 30 and no discounting of root notes in F1-score; ○: grammar-based model; ⁄: neural scoring component).

score on only discontinuous constituents does not adhere to this trend in two cases. Note however that the prediction of discontinuous constituents seems to be comparably unstable (cf. the high variance). This indicates that a larger sample size is needed to reliably judge the influence of MAP training on the discontinuous F1. Also in case of ensemble models there are two grammars where the ensemble model trained with the MAP objective is less accurate.

Ensemble models. Comparing the (Disc.) F1-scores of the ensemble model with the averages of the individual grammars, we always see an improvement, which in many cases is also well above the standard deviation.

Selection of grammars. For HN08 we obtain the best results with hybrid grammars with the Markovized strict labeling, which also outperform LCFRS in contrast to the experiments by Gebhardt (2018). In experiments with NEGRA we see that the child nonterminal scheme is more accurate than the Markovized strict one. This might be explained by the smaller corpus size which may lead to sparsity

problems if nonterminal granularity is higher. The hybrid grammar with child labeling scores better than the LCFRS.

External comparison. Test set results are given in table 3. For NEGRA we apply the child labeling scheme and train for 7 s/m cycles using a merge rate of 80% and the MAP objective. For TIGER we apply the Markovized strict labeling scheme and train for 5 s/m cycles using a merge rate of 90% and the MAP objective. The comparison with results from the literature indicates that the ensemble of hybrid grammars performs better than other grammar-based approaches except for the pseudo-projective approach by Versley (2016). They are also more accurate than early dependency-to-constituency and transition-based approaches[5]. However, recent models, in particular those utilizing neural nets, are far more accurate than the hybrid grammars.

---

[5] Interestingly, the model by Fernández-González and Martins (2015) is superior on TIGER but inferior on NEGRA (which has a smaller training set).

4 Discussion and conclusions

The experiments provide further evidence that the split/merge method is applicable and effective beyond PCFG. The use of priors and ensembles of grammars is mostly beneficial and complementary. From the performance differences between child labeling and Markovized strict labeling, we can surmise that the initial nonterminal granularity matters as the split/merge method cannot fully recover important splits or at least during parsing the mrp objective relies on guidance by the baseline nonterminal structure. More generally, the performance differences between the considered grammars indicate that a careful choice of the grammar formalism and the extraction algorithm is not redundant despite split/merge refinement.

Interestingly, the pseudo-projective approach by Versley (2016) outperforms our strictly discontinuous one. He uses a linguistically motivated (de)projectivization strategy[6] that seems to address the sparsity of discontinuous constituents in the data very well. Hence, we may conjecture that true discontinuous grammar formalisms that make available a large number of discontinuous productions (based on scarce evidence) may rarely benefit from the additional expressiveness. To substantiate this claim certainly a controlled experiment is necessary as differences may as well be artefacts of the handling of lexical and fall-back rules by Versley (2016). However, a similar observation was made concerning (discontinuous) tree substitution grammars (van Cranenburgh et al., 2016). Also a recent study by Corro (2020) finds that a very restricted mode of discontinuity, which can be simulated by a series of continuous combinations, is more accurate than more expressive modes.

The research on discontinuous parsing with latent variable grammars may also be extended by considering spectral algorithms (cf. Cohen, 2017, for an overview). In particular, Louis and Cohen (2015) use latently annotated LCFRS obtained by spectral algorithms to parse the topical structure of forum threads. Yet, the application of spectral algorithms for *discontinuous syntactic* parsing has not been investigated.

Acknowledgements

The author thanks the anonymous reviewers, Shay Cohen, Richard Mörbitz, and Thomas Ruprecht for helpful comments on drafts of this paper.

---

[6]Boyd (2007) found that discontinuous trees that actually occur in treebanks can be (de)projectivized without losses.

References

James K. Baker. 1979. Trainable grammars for speech recognition. In *Speech Communication Papers for the 97th Meeting of the Acoustical Society of America*, pages 547–550.

Adriane Boyd. 2007. Discontinuity revisited: An improved conversion to context-free representations. In *Proceedings of the Linguistic Annotation Workshop*, pages 41–44, Prague, Czech Republic.

Sabine Brants, Stefanie Dipper, Peter Eisenberg, Silvia Hansen-Schirra, Esther König, Wolfgang Lezius, Christian Rohrer, George Smith, and Hans Uszkoreit. 2004. Tiger: Linguistic interpretation of a german corpus. *Research on Language and Computation*, 2(4):597–620.

Maximin Coavoux and Shay B. Cohen. 2019. Discontinuous constituency parsing with a stack-free transition system and a dynamic oracle. In *Proceedings of the 2019 Conference of the North American Chapter of the Association for Computational Linguistics: Human Language Technologies, Volume 1 (Long and Short Papers)*, pages 204–217, Minneapolis, Minnesota.

Maximin Coavoux and Benoît Crabbé. 2017. Incremental discontinuous phrase structure parsing with the gap transition. In *Proceedings of the 15th Conference of the European Chapter of the Association for Computational Linguistics: Volume 1, Long Papers*, pages 1259–1270, Valencia, Spain.

Maximin Coavoux, Benoît Crabbé, and Shay B. Cohen. 2019. Unlexicalized transition-based discontinuous constituency parsing. *Transactions of the Association for Computational Linguistics*, 7:73–89.

Shay Cohen. 2017. Latent-variable PCFGs: Background and applications. In *Proceedings of the 15th Meeting on the Mathematics of Language*, pages 47–58, London, UK.

Caio Corro. 2020. Span-based discontinuous constituency parsing: a family of exact chart-based algorithms with time complexities from $\mathcal{O}(n^6)$ down to $\mathcal{O}(n^3)$.

Caio Corro, Joseph Le Roux, and Mathieu Lacroix. 2017. Efficient discontinuous phrase-structure parsing via the generalized maximum spanning arborescence. In *Proceedings of the 2017 Conference on Empirical Methods in Natural Language Processing*, pages 1644–1654, Copenhagen, Denmark.

Andreas van Cranenburgh, Remko Scha, and Rens Bod. 2016. Data-oriented parsing with discontinuous constituents and function tags. *Journal of Language Modelling*, 4(1):57–111.

Aron Culotta and Jeffrey Sorensen. 2004. Dependency tree kernels for relation extraction. In *Proceedings of the 42nd Annual Meeting on Association for Computational Linguistics*, ACL '04, Stroudsburg, PA, USA.

Pierre Deransart and Jan Małuszyński. 1989. A grammatical view of logic programming. In *Programming Languages Implementation and Logic Programming*, pages 219–251, Berlin, Heidelberg.

Jacob Devlin, Ming-Wei Chang, Kenton Lee, and Kristina Toutanova. 2019. BERT: Pre-training of deep bidirectional transformers for language understanding. In *Proceedings of the 2019 Conference of the North American Chapter of the Association for Computational Linguistics: Human Language Technologies, Volume 1 (Long and Short Papers)*, pages 4171–4186, Minneapolis, Minnesota.

Yuan Ding and Martha Palmer. 2005. Machine translation using probabilistic synchronous dependency insertion grammars. In *Proceedings of the 43rd Annual Meeting on Association for Computational Linguistics*, ACL '05, pages 541–548, Stroudsburg, PA, USA.

Amit Dubey and Frank Keller. 2003. Probabilistic parsing for German using sister-head dependencies. In *Proceedings of the 41st Annual Meeting of the Association for Computational Linguistics*, pages 96–103, Sapporo, Japan.

Adnan Duric and Fei Song. 2011. Feature selection for sentiment analysis based on content and syntax models. In *Proceedings of the 2nd Workshop on Computational Approaches to Subjectivity and Sentiment Analysis (WASSA 2.011)*, pages 96–103, Portland, Oregon.

Daniel Fernández-González and André F. T. Martins. 2015. Parsing as reduction. In *Proceedings of the 53rd Annual Meeting of the Association for Computational Linguistics and the 7th International Joint Conference on Natural Language Processing (Volume 1: Long Papers)*, pages 1523–1533, Beijing, China.

Daniel Fernández-González and Carlos Gómez-Rodríguez. 2020. Discontinuous constituent parsing with pointer networks.

Kilian Gebhardt. 2018. Generic refinement of expressive grammar formalisms with an application to discontinuous constituent parsing. In *Proceedings of the 27th International Conference on Computational Linguistics*, pages 3049–3063, Santa Fe, New Mexico, USA.

Kilian Gebhardt, Mark-Jan Nederhof, and Heiko Vogler. 2017. Hybrid grammars for parsing of discontinuous phrase structures and non-projective dependency structures. *Computational Linguistics*, 43(3):465–520.

Johan Hall and Joakim Nivre. 2008. Parsing discontinuous phrase structure with grammatical functions. In *Advances in Natural Language Processing*, pages 169–180, Berlin, Heidelberg.

Mark Johnson, Thomas Griffiths, and Sharon Goldwater. 2007. Bayesian inference for PCFGs via Markov chain Monte Carlo. In *Human Language Technologies 2007: The Conference of the North American Chapter of the Association for Computational Linguistics; Proceedings of the Main Conference*, pages 139–146, Rochester, New York.

Aravind K. Joshi, Leon S. Levy, and Masako Takahashi. 1975. Tree adjunct grammars. *J. Comput. Syst. Sci.*, 10(1):136–163.

Laura Kallmeyer and Wolfgang Maier. 2013. Data-driven parsing using probabilistic linear context-free rewriting systems. *Computational Linguistics*, 39(1):87–119.

Dan Klein and Christopher D. Manning. 2003. Accurate unlexicalized parsing. In *Proceedings of the 41st Annual Meeting on Association for Computational Linguistics - Volume 1*, pages 423–430, Sapporo, Japan.

Annie Louis and Shay B. Cohen. 2015. Conversation trees: A grammar model for topic structure in forums. In *Proceedings of the 2015 Conference on Empirical Methods in Natural Language Processing*, pages 1543–1553, Lisbon, Portugal.

Wolfgang Maier. 2015. Discontinuous incremental shift-reduce parsing. In *Proceedings of the 53rd Annual Meeting of the Association for Computational Linguistics and the 7th International Joint Conference on Natural Language Processing (Volume 1: Long Papers)*, pages 1202–1212, Beijing, China.

Wolfgang Maier and Timm Lichte. 2016. Discontinuous parsing with continuous trees. In *Proceedings of the Workshop on Discontinuous Structures in Natural Language Processing*, pages 47–57, San Diego, California.

Takuya Matsuzaki, Yusuke Miyao, and Jun'ichi Tsujii. 2005. Probabilistic CFG with latent annotations. In *Proceedings of the 43rd Annual Meeting on Association for Computational Linguistics*, pages 75–82, Ann Arbor, Michigan.

Mark-Jan Nederhof and Heiko Vogler. 2014. Hybrid grammars for discontinuous parsing. In *Proceedings of COLING 2014, the 25th International Conference on Computational Linguistics: Technical Papers*, pages 1370–1381, Dublin, Ireland.

Slav Petrov. 2010. Products of random latent variable grammars. In *Human Language Technologies: The 2010 Annual Conference of the North American Chapter of the Association for Computational Linguistics*, pages 19–27, Los Angeles, California.

Slav Petrov, Leon Barrett, Romain Thibaux, and Dan Klein. 2006. Learning accurate, compact, and interpretable tree annotation. In *Proceedings of the 21st International Conference on Computational Linguistics and the 44th Annual Meeting of the Association for Computational Linguistics*, pages 433–440, Sydney, Australia.

Slav Petrov and Dan Klein. 2007. Improved inference for unlexicalized parsing. In *Human Language Technologies 2007: The Conference of the North American Chapter of the Association for Computational Linguistics; Proceedings of the Main Conference*, pages 404–411, Rochester, New York.

Djamé Seddah, Sandra Kübler, and Reut Tsarfaty. 2014. Introducing the SPMRL 2014 shared task on parsing morphologically-rich languages. In *Proceedings of the First Joint Workshop on Statistical Parsing of Morphologically Rich Languages and Syntactic Analysis of Non-Canonical Languages*, pages 103–109, Dublin, Ireland.

Wojciech Skut, Brigitte Krenn, Thorsten Brants, and Hans Uszkoreit. 1997. An annotation scheme for free word order languages. In *Fifth Conference on Applied Natural Language Processing*, pages 88–95, Washington, DC, USA.

Miloš Stanojević and Raquel Garrido Alhama. 2017. Neural discontinuous constituency parsing. In *Proceedings of the 2017 Conference on Empirical Methods in Natural Language Processing*, pages 1666–1676, Copenhagen, Denmark.

Yannick Versley. 2014a. Experiments with easy-first nonprojective constituent parsing. In *Proceedings of the First Joint Workshop on Statistical Parsing of Morphologically Rich Languages and Syntactic Analysis of Non-Canonical Languages*, pages 39–53, Dublin, Ireland.

Yannick Versley. 2014b. Incorporating semi-supervised features into discontinuous easy-first constituent parsing.

Yannick Versley. 2016. Discontinuity (re)^2-visited: A minimalist approach to pseudoprojective constituent parsing. In *Proceedings of the Workshop on Discontinuous Structures in Natural Language Processing*, pages 58–69, San Diego, California.

Krishnamurti Vijay-Shanker, David J. Weir, and Aravind K. Joshi. 1987. Characterizing structural descriptions produced by various grammatical formalisms. In *Proceedings of the 25th Annual Meeting of the Association for Computational Linguistics*, pages 104–111, Stanford, California, USA.

Lexicalization of Probabilistic Linear Context-free Rewriting Systems

Richard Mörbitz and **Thomas Ruprecht**
Faculty of Computer Science
Technische Universität Dresden
01062 Dresden, Germany
{richard.moerbitz,thomas.ruprecht}@tu-dresden.de

Abstract

In the field of constituent parsing, probabilistic grammar formalisms have been studied to model the syntactic structure of natural language. More recently, approaches utilizing neural models gained lots of traction in this field, as they achieved accurate results at high speed. We aim for a symbiosis between probabilistic linear context-free rewriting systems (PLCFRS) as a probabilistic grammar formalism and neural models to get the best of both worlds: the interpretability of grammars, and the speed and accuracy of neural models. A combination of these two could be achieved by applying supertagging to PLCFRS. This approach requires lexical grammar formalisms. Here, we present a procedure which turns any PLCFRS G into an equivalent lexical PLCFRS G'. Moreover, we show how the derivations in G' can be transformed to obtain their corresponding original derivations in G. Our construction for G' preserves the probability assignment and does not increase parsing complexity compared to G.

1 Introduction

Constituency parsing is a syntactical analysis in NLP that aims to enhance sentences with, usually tree-shaped, phrase structures (for an example cf. the left of Fig. 1). Formalisms such as context-free grammars (CFG) are used in this setting because they are conceptually simple, interpretable, and parsing is tractable (cubic in sentence length).

Discontinuous constituents span non-contiguous sets of positions in a sentence. The resulting phrase structures do not take the shape of a tree anymore, as they contain crossing branches (cf. the left of Fig. 1), and cannot be modeled by CFG. As a countermeasure, many corpora (e.g., the Penn Treebank (PTB)) denote these phrase structures as trees nevertheless and introduce designated notations for

discontinuity, which is then often ignored in parsing. However, discontinuity occurs in about 20 % of the sentences in the PTB, and parsing discontinuous constituents can improve accuracy (Evang and Kallmeyer, 2011). For this, so-called "mildly context-sensitive" grammar formalisms have been investigated, e.g., tree-adjoining grammars (TAG; Joshi et al., 1975) and linear context-free rewriting systems (LCFRS; Vijay-Shanker et al., 1987). Their increased expressiveness comes at the cost of a higher parsing complexity: given a sentence of length n, parsing is in $O(n^6)$ for TAG and $O(n^{3 \cdot \text{fanout}(G)})$ for an LCFRS G. The fanout is grammar-specific and reflects the degree of discontinuity in the rules of G. The expressiveness of TAG equals that of LCFRS with fanout 2. An LCFRS derivation of a discontinuous phrase is shown in the right of Fig. 1.

Supertagging has been used for more efficient parsing with lexical TAG (Bangalore and Joshi, 1999). A TAG is lexical if each rule contains one word. A supertagger selects for each position of the input sentence a subset of the rules of the TAG; these are the so-called supertags. Parsing is then performed with the much smaller grammar of supertags. Recently, the performance of supertagging has been improved by using neural classifiers for the selection of supertags (Vaswani et al., 2016). The goal of our research is to use supertagging for parsing with LCFRS, because they are more expressive than TAG.

In this paper, we lay the theoretical foundations for a supertagging-based LCFRS parser. As LCFRS obtained from corpora such as the PTB are usually not lexical, we employ a lexicalization procedure. It can be seen as an instance of the technique for lexicalization of multiple context-free tree grammars (Engelfriet et al., 2018). However, our approach is more concise and does not increase the fanout of the grammar (thus preserving parsing

Proceedings of the 16th International Conference on Parsing Technologies and the IWPT 2020 Shared Task, pages 98–104
Virtual Meeting, July 9, 2020. ©2020 Association for Computational Linguistics

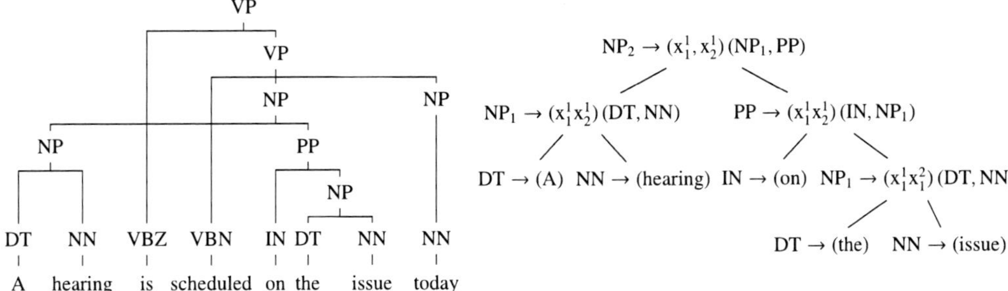

Figure 1: Left: a discontinuous phrase structure tree of the sentence *A hearing is scheduled on the issue today.* Right: an LCFRS derivation of the discontinuous noun phrase *A hearing on the issue.*

complexity). Moreover, the approach is extended to account for probabilistic parsing. Furthermore, we introduce a procedure which recovers from each derivation of a lexicalized LCFRS all corresponding derivations of the original grammar.

This short paper is to be seen as a report on our approaches to lexicalization and recovery of derivations. An implementation of the supertagger and experimental evaluation are currently work in progress.

2 Preliminaries

The set of *non-negative* (resp. *positive*) *integers* is denoted by $\mathbb{N}$ (resp. $\mathbb{N}_+$). We abbreviate $\{1, ..., n\}$ by $[n]$ for each $n \in \mathbb{N}$. Let A be a set; the *set of (finite) strings over A* is denoted by A^*. An *alphabet* is a finite and non-empty set.

Let S be some set whose elements we call *sorts*. An *S-sorted set* is a tuple $(A, sort)$ where A is a set and *sort*$: A \to S$. Usually, we identify $(A, sort)$ with A, and denote *sort* by $sort_A$ and $sort^{-1}(s)$ by A_s for each $s \in S$. The usual notation for sets $(\in, \subseteq, \cup, \ldots)$ is used with sorted sets in the intuitive manner. Now let A be an $(S^* \times S)$-sorted set. The *set of trees over A* is the S-sorted set T^A where $T^A_s = \{a(t_1, \ldots, t_k) \mid k \in \mathbb{N}, s_1, \ldots, s_k \in S, a \in A_{(s_1 \cdots s_k, s)}, t_1 \in T^A_{s_1}, \ldots, t_k \in T^A_{s_k}\}$ for each $s \in S$. A *ranked set A* is an $(S^* \times S)$-sorted set where $S = \{s\}$; the notation $rk_A(a) = k$ abbreviates $sort_A(a) = (s^k, s)$, and A_k abbreviates $A_{(s^k, s)}$. If we use a usual set B in place of a ranked set, we will silently assume $rk_B(b) = 0$ for each $b \in B$. Let X be a set. We let $A(X) = \{a(x_1, \ldots, x_k) \mid k \in \mathbb{N}, a \in A_k, x_1, \ldots, x_k \in X\}$.

LCFRS. *Linear context-free rewriting systems* extend the rule-based string rewriting mechanism of CFG to string tuples; we describe the gener-

ation process by *compositions*. Let $k \in \mathbb{N}$ and $s_1, \ldots, s_k, s \in \mathbb{N}_+$; a *$\Sigma$-composition* is a tuple $(u_1, \ldots, u_s)$ where each $u_1, \ldots, u_s$ is a non-empty string over Σ and variables of the form x_i^j where $i \in [k]$ and $j \in [s_i]$. Each of these variables must occur exactly once in $u_1 \cdots u_s$ and they are ordered such that x_i^1 occurs before x_{i+1}^1 and x_i^j occurs before x_i^{j+1} for each $i \in [k-1]$ and $j \in [s_i - 1]$. We denote the set of Σ-compositions by $C^\Sigma_{(s_1 \cdots s_k, s)}$; we drop the superscript in the case $\Sigma = \emptyset$ (then $C_{(s_1 \cdots s_k, s)}$ is finite); we drop the subscript if we admit any configuration of k, $s_1, \ldots, s_k$ and s. We associate with each composition $(u_1, \ldots, u_s) \in C^\Sigma_{(s_1 \cdots s_k, s)}$ a function from k string tuples, where the i-th tuple is of length s_i, to a string tuple of length s. This function is denoted by $[\![(u_1, \ldots, u_s)]\!]$. Intuitively, it replaces each variable of the form x_i^j in $u_1, \ldots, u_s$ by the j-th component of the i-th argument.

An *LCFRS* is a tuple $G = (N, \Sigma, S, R)$ where $\bullet$ N is a finite $\mathbb{N}_+$-sorted set (*non-terminals*), $\bullet$ Σ is an alphabet (*terminals*), $\bullet$ $S \in N_1$ (*initial non-terminal*), and $\bullet$ R is a finite $(N^* \times N)$-sorted set (*rules*). Each rule is of the form $A \to c(B_1, \ldots, B_k)$, where $k \in \mathbb{N}$, $A, B_1, \ldots, B_k \in N$, and $c \in C^\Sigma_{(sort_N(B_1) \cdots sort_N(B_k), sort_N(A))}$. The sort of the rule is $(B_1 \cdots B_k, A)$; we call A the *left-hand side (lhs)*, $B_1, \ldots, B_k$ the *right-hand side (rhs)* and c the rule's *composition*. We drop the parentheses around the rhs if $k = 0$. We call rules of the form $\bullet$ $A \to c$ where $A \neq S$ *terminating*, $\bullet$ $A \to c(B)$ *monic*, and $\bullet$ $A \to c(B_1, ..., B_k)$ where $k \geq 2$ *branching*, and denote the set of these rules in R by $R^{(T)}$, $R^{(M)}$ and $R^{(B)}$, respectively. A rule is called *lexical*, if its composition contains *at least* one terminal. The lcfrs G is called *lexical*, if each rule is lexical. The *set of (complete) derivations in G* is $D^G = T^R_S$. Let $w \in \Sigma^*$ and $d = r(d_1, \ldots, d_k) \in T^R$

with $r = A \rightarrow c(B_1, \ldots, B_k)$. The *yield of d* is
$\mathrm{yd}(d) = [\![c]\!](\mathrm{yd}(d_1), \ldots, \mathrm{yd}(d_k))$.

PLCFRS. A *probabilistic LCFRS* is a tuple (G, μ) where $G = (N, \Sigma, S, R)$ is an LCFRS and $\mu: R \rightarrow [0, 1]$ maps each rule to a probability. The *weight of a derivation* $d = r(d_1, \ldots, d_k) \in \mathrm{T}^R$ is $\mathrm{wt}(d) = \mu(r) \cdot \mathrm{wt}(d_1) \cdots \mathrm{wt}(d_k)$.

Top-down Tree Transducers. A *top-down tree transducer (TT)* is a tuple $A = (Q, \Sigma, \Delta, q_\mathrm{i}, \delta)$ where • Q is a finite set (*states*), • Σ and Δ are ranked alphabets (*input* and *output alphabet*), • $q_\mathrm{i} \in Q$ (*initial state*), and • δ is a finite set (*transitions*). Each transition is of the form $q(\sigma(\mathsf{x}_1, \ldots, \mathsf{x}_k)) \rightarrow t$, where $\sigma \in \Sigma_k$ and $t \in \mathrm{T}^{\Delta \cup Q((\mathsf{x}_1, \ldots, \mathsf{x}_k))}$. We call a transition *linear* (resp. *non-deleting*) if each variable in $\{\mathsf{x}_1, \ldots, \mathsf{x}_k\}$ occurs at most once (resp. at least once) in t. We call A deterministic if, for each $q \in Q$ an $\sigma \in \Sigma$, there is at most one transition of the form $q(\sigma(\mathsf{x}_1, \ldots, \mathsf{x}_k)) \rightarrow t$ in δ. We call it *linear* (resp. *non-deleting*) if each transition is linear (resp. non-deleting).

In a *TT with ε-rules (εTT)*, the set δ may also contain transitions of the form $q(\mathsf{x}_1) \rightarrow t$ where $t \in \mathrm{T}^{\Delta \cup Q((\mathsf{x}_1))}$ and $q \in Q$. We treat them analogously to transitions where $k = 1$.

The transduction of A is expressed in terms of the binary derivation relation $\Rightarrow_A$ over $\mathrm{T}^{\Delta \cup Q(\mathrm{T}^\Sigma)}$. We write $s \Rightarrow_A t$ if there is a subtree $q(\sigma(s_1, \ldots, s_k))$ in s and a transition $q(\sigma(\mathsf{x}_1, \ldots, \mathsf{x}_k)) \rightarrow t'$ such that t is obtained by replacing $q(\sigma(s_1, \ldots, s_k))$ in s by t' and replacing x_i by s_i for each $i \in [k]$. The *transduction of A* is the relation $[\![A]\!] = \{(s, t) \in \mathrm{T}^\Sigma \times \mathrm{T}^\Delta \mid q_\mathrm{i}(s) \Rightarrow_A^* t\}$. If A is deterministic, we consider $[\![A]\!]$ a function.

TTs are a special case of TTs with regular lookahead (TT^R) that were used by Engelfriet et al. (2018). For an excellent overview on tree transducers, we refer to Maletti (2010).

Equivalence of (P)LCFRS. Two LCFRS G and G' are called *ldTT^R-equivalent* if there are two linear and deterministic TT^R, T and T', such that • $[\![T]\!](d) \in \mathrm{D}^{G'}$ and $\mathrm{yd}([\![T]\!](d)) = \mathrm{yd}(d)$ for each $d \in \mathrm{D}^G$, and • $[\![T']\!](d') \in \mathrm{D}^G$ and $\mathrm{yd}([\![T']\!](d')) = \mathrm{yd}(d')$ for each $d' \in \mathrm{D}^G$. Two PLCFRS (G, μ) and (G', μ') are called *ldTT^R-equivalent* if G and G' are ldTT^R-equivalent and • $\mathrm{wt}([\![T]\!](d)) \geq \mathrm{wt}(d)$ for each $d \in \mathrm{D}^G$, and • $\mathrm{wt}([\![T']\!](d')) \geq \mathrm{wt}(d')$ for each $d' \in \mathrm{D}^{G'}$.

$[\![T]\!]$, as well as $[\![T']\!]$, may map multiple derivations to one single derivation. The relation between the weights assures that this mapped derivation assumes the greatest of the original derivations' weights.

3 Lexicalizing LCFRS

For the remainder, we assume (without loss of generality; cf. Seki et al., 1991) a PLCFRS (G, μ) where $G = (N, \Sigma, S, R)$ is *terminal-* and *initial-separated*, i.e. each rule is either of the form $A \rightarrow (\sigma)$ with $\sigma \in \Sigma$ or $A \rightarrow c(B_1, \ldots, B_k)$ where $c \in C$ (i.e. c contains no terminal symbols) and none of $B_1, \ldots, B_k$ is S. Starting with (G, μ), we incrementally construct a lexical PLCFRS in three steps:

1. Monic rules are removed.

2. Terminating rules are removed and, for each branching rule, each subset of rhs nonterminals is replaced with lexical symbols of matching terminating rules. This construction obtains terminating rules with at least two lexical symbols and each constructed monic rule contains at least one lexical symbol.

3. A terminal is cut from each terminating rule and pasted into a remaining non-lexical branching rule if a derivation with the branching rule reaches the terminating rule at some point. At the end of this step, each rule contains at least one terminal.

The first two steps are direct instances of the lexicalization for multiple context-free tree grammars as introduced by Engelfriet et al. (2018).

Step 1 (<u>De</u>chain). In the first step, we remove each monic rule and chain its composition with the composition of each other reachable rule.

Definition 1. Let $k \in \mathbb{N}$, $s, s', s_1, \ldots, s_k \in \mathbb{N}_+$, $c \in \mathrm{C}_{(s_1 \cdots s_k, s)}$ and $c' \in \mathrm{C}_{(s, s')}$. We denote the composition $[\![c']\!](c) \in \mathrm{C}_{s_1 \cdots s_k, s'}$ by $c' \circ c$. □

The set of rules R_dc is the smallest set $\hat{R}$ such that • $R \setminus R^{(\mathrm{M})} \subseteq \hat{R}$ • for each $A \rightarrow c_1(B) \in R^{(\mathrm{M})}$ and $B \rightarrow c_2(C_1, ..., C_k) \in \hat{R}$, the rule $A \rightarrow c_1 \circ c_2 (C_1, ..., C_k)$ is in $\hat{R}$. We define the function $\mu_\mathrm{dc}: R_\mathrm{dc} \rightarrow [0, 1]$ such that, for each rule $r = A \rightarrow c(C_1, ..., C_k) \in R_\mathrm{dc}$, the value is

$$\mu_\mathrm{dc}(r) = \max \{\mu(r)\} \cup$$
$$\{\mu(r_1) \cdot \mu_\mathrm{dc}(r_2) \mid r_1 = A \rightarrow c_1(B) \in R^{(\mathrm{M})},$$
$$r_2 = B \rightarrow c_2(C_1, ..., C_k) \in R_\mathrm{dc}: c_1 \circ c_2 = c\}.$$

The set R_dc, as well the function μ_dc, can be efficiently computed with an instance of the algorithm by Aho et al. (1974, alg. 5.5), cf. alg. 1 in app. A.

$$
\begin{array}{c}
\text{PP} \to (x_1^1 x_2^1)\,(\text{IN}, \text{NP}_1) \\
\rho(1) = \text{on} \\
\text{IN} \to (\text{on}) \quad \text{NP}_1 \to (x_1^1 x_1^2)\,(\text{DT}, \text{NN}) \\
\rho(1) = \text{the} \qquad \rho(2) = \text{issue} \\
\text{DT} \to (\text{the}) \quad \text{NN} \to (\text{issue})
\end{array}
\qquad
\begin{array}{c}
\text{PP} \to (\text{on}\ x_1^1)\,(\text{NP}_1) \\
| \\
\text{NP}_1 \to (\text{the issue})
\end{array}
$$

Figure 2: Fusing of terminals. Left: derivation of G_{dc}. Right: corresponding derivation of G_{ft}, where the terminals of the leaves are inserted into their parent rules.

Step 2 (<u>Fu</u>se <u>T</u>erminals). In this step, the symbols of the terminating rules are inserted into non-terminating (terminal-free) rules. The intuition is given in Fig. 2. For the formal definition we first introduce the insertion operation.

Definition 2. Let $A \to c(B_1, \ldots, B_k)$ be a rule, $\pi \subseteq \{i \in [k] \mid B_i \in N_1\}$ and $\rho \colon \pi \to \Sigma$. Moreover, let $i_1, \ldots, i_{k-|\pi|}$ be the indices in $[k] \setminus \pi$ in ascending order. The composition $c[\rho]$ is obtained from c by replacing each variable of the form $x_i^j \bullet$ by $\rho(i)$ if $i \in \pi$, or $\bullet$ by x_ℓ^j if $i_\ell = i$. We denote $A \to c[\rho](B_{i_1}, \ldots, B_{i_{k-|\pi|}})$ by $A \to c(B_1, \ldots, B_k)[\rho]$. □

For each rule $r = A \to c(B_1, \ldots, B_k)$, we define the set $F(r) = \{\rho \colon \pi \to \Sigma \mid \pi \subseteq [k], \forall i \in \pi \colon B_i \to (\rho(i)) \in R_{dc}^{(T)}\}$. It contains each function that replaces a subset of r's rhs nonterminals with terminal symbols respecting the terminating rules; we use it to define the set of rules R_{ft} and the function $\mu_{ft} \colon R_{ft} \to [0, 1]$:

$$R_{ft} = \{r[\rho] \mid r \in R_{dc} \setminus R_{dc}^{(T)}, \rho \in F(r)\},$$

$$\mu_{ft}(r') = \max \Big\{ \mu_{dc}(r) \cdot \prod_{i \in \pi} \mu_{dc}(B_i \to (\rho(i)))$$
$$\mid r \in R_{dc} \setminus R_{dc}^{(T)}, \rho \in F(r) \colon r[\rho] = r' \Big\}.$$

Step 3 (<u>P</u>ropagate <u>T</u>erminals). In this final step, terminal symbols are inserted into the remaining non-lexical branching rules. Intuitively, one terminal symbol is *cut* from each terminating rule, which now has at least two occurrences of terminal symbols. This symbol is then *pasted* into a non-lexical branching rule that reaches the rule it was cut from via its second right-hand side nonterminal. If there are rules between the terminating rule the symbol was cut from and the rule it shall be pasted into, then the information that a terminal can be pasted through these rules is propagated via the nonterminals. For this we extend the set of nonterminals to $N_{pt} = N \cup N \times \Sigma$, where $(A, \sigma) \in N \times \Sigma$ indicates that σ was cut from a rule with left-hand side A ($\text{sort}_{N_{pt}}(A, \sigma) = \text{sort}_N(A)$ for each $(A, \sigma) \in N \times \Sigma$).

Fig. 3 shows an example of how the terminal symbols are propagated through a derivation.

Definition 3. Let $\sigma \in \Sigma$ and r be a rule of the form $A \to (\sigma u_1, u_2, \ldots, u_s)(B_1, \ldots, B_k)$. We denote $(A, \sigma) \to (u_1, \ldots, u_s)(B_1, \ldots, B_k)$ by $\text{cut}(r)$. □

Definition 4. Let $r = A \to c(B_1, \ldots, B_k)$ be a rule and $i \in [k]$. We obtain c' from c by replacing the variable x_i^1 with σx_i^1 and denote $A \to c'(B_1, \ldots, (B_i, \sigma), \ldots, B_k)$ by $\text{paste}_\sigma^i(r)$. □

Let $R_{ft}^{(\Sigma)}$ denote the set of rules in $R_{ft}^{(B)}$ without terminals. We define the sets of rules

$$R' = \{\text{paste}_\sigma^2(r) \mid r \in R_{ft}^{(\Sigma)}, \sigma \in \Sigma\} \cup (R_{ft}^{(B)} \setminus R_{ft}^{(\Sigma)})$$

$$R_{pt} = (R_{ft} \setminus R_{ft}^{(B)}) \cup R'$$
$$\cup \{\text{cut}(A \to c) \mid A \to c \in R_{ft}^{(T)}\}$$
$$\cup \{\text{cut}(\text{paste}_\sigma^1(r)) \mid r \in R' \cup R_{ft}^{(M)}, \sigma \in \Sigma\}.$$

Note that, in contrast to Engelfriet et al. (2018), we do not need to split the rules' compositions, because we always cut the first symbol. Therefore, the fanout of the grammar is unchanged.

The applications of cut and paste that led to a rule in R_{pt} are unambiguously determined from the lhs and rhs nonterminals in $N \times \Sigma$. These operations are unambiguously reversible; for each $r' \in R_{pt}$, there is a rule in $r \in R_{ft}$ uniquely determined such that r' is exactly one of $\bullet\ r$, $\bullet\ \text{paste}_\sigma^2(r)$, $\bullet\ \text{cut}(r)$, $\bullet\ \text{cut}(\text{paste}_\sigma^1(r))$, or $\bullet\ \text{cut}(\text{paste}_{\sigma_1}^1(\text{paste}_{\sigma_2}^2(r)))$. We define the function $\mu_{pt} \colon R_{pt} \to [0, 1]$ such that $\mu_{pt}(r') = \mu_{ft}(r)$ for each $r' \in R_{pt}$.

Theorem 5. The PLCFRS $((N_{pt}, \Sigma, S, R_{pt}), \mu_{pt})$ and (G, μ) are ldTT^R-equivalent.

4 Unlexicalizing Derivations

The ultimate goal of parsing is to obtain derivations of the original grammar (G, μ), which are quite different from the derivations of the transformed grammar $((N_{pt}, \Sigma, S, R_{pt}), \mu_{pt})$. Therefore we seek a transformation from $T^{R_{pt}}$ to T^R.

Engelfriet et al. (2018) have introduced deterministic linear and non-deleting TT^R from $T^{R_{pt}}$ to $T^{R_{ft}}$, from $T^{R_{ft}}$ to $T^{R_{dc}}$, and from $T^{R_{dc}}$ to T^R; they were used to show ldTT^R-equivalence of the corresponding grammars. The composition of these transducers yields a transduction from $T^{R_{pt}}$ to T^R. However, for recovering derivations, these transducers are not adequate, as a derivation in $T^{R_{ft}}$ or $T^{R_{dc}}$ may have multiple possible originals in $T^{R_{dc}}$ or T^R, respectively. We want to be able to obtain all of these derivations, as this may be beneficial for

$$NP_2 \rightarrow (x_1^1, x_2^1)(NP_1, PP)$$

$$NP_1 \rightarrow (A\ hearing) \qquad PP \rightarrow (on\ x_1^1)(NP_1)$$

$$NP_1 \rightarrow (the\ issue)$$

$$NP_2 \rightarrow (x_1^1, on\ x_2^1)(NP_1, (PP, on))$$

$$NP_1 \rightarrow (A\ hearing) \qquad (PP, on) \rightarrow (the\ x_1^1)((NP_1, the))$$

$$(NP_1, the) \rightarrow (issue)$$

Figure 3: Propagation of terminals. Left: derivation of a (partly lexicalized) LCFRS before the application of step 3. Right: derivation after step 3, where *the* is propagated from the leaf to the PP rule and *on* is propagated from there to the NP_2 rule, thus lexicalizing it.

later stages of an application (e.g., when selecting k best derivations is desired).

For this, we employ two approaches. We map each derivation in $T^{R_{\mathrm{pt}}}$ to its unique original derivation by using the transducer of (Engelfriet et al., 2018); we denote this transducer by $T_{\overleftarrow{\mathrm{pt}}}$. It realizes a deterministic tree relabeling which is already indicated at the end of the previous section. For the other two transductions, we define novel non-deterministic tree transducers.

Transduction $T^{R_{\mathrm{ft}}} \rightarrow T^{R_{\mathrm{dc}}}$. Let $r = A \rightarrow c(B_1, ..., B_k) \in R_{\mathrm{ft}}$, $\pi \subseteq \{i \in [k] \mid B_i \in N_1\}$, $\rho \colon \pi \rightarrow \Sigma$ and $i_1, \ldots, i_{k-|\pi|}$ be the elements of $[k] \setminus \pi$ in ascending order. We denote the tree $r(d_1, \ldots, d_k)$, where $d_i = B_i \rightarrow (\rho(i))$ if $i \in \pi$ and $d_i = *(x_\ell)$ if $i = i_\ell$, by $r(x_1, \ldots, x_k)[\rho]$.

We define the linear and non-deleting TT $T_{\overleftarrow{\mathrm{ft}}} = (\{*\}, R_{\mathrm{ft}}, R_{\mathrm{dc}}, *, \delta)$, where δ is the smallest set such that, for each rule $r = A \rightarrow c(B_1, ..., B_k) \in R_{\mathrm{dc}} \setminus R_{\mathrm{dc}}^{(\mathrm{T})}$ and $\rho \in F(r)$, the transition $*(r[\rho](x_1, ..., x_{k-|\pi|})) \rightarrow r(x_1, ..., x_k)[\rho]$ is in δ.

Transduction $T^{R_{\mathrm{dc}}} \rightarrow T^R$. Let us denote the composition $(x_1, ..., x_{\mathrm{sort}_N(A)})$ by id_A for each $A \in N$. We define the linear and non-deleting εTT $T_{\overleftarrow{\mathrm{dc}}} = (Q, R_{\mathrm{dc}}, R, (S, \mathrm{id}_S), \delta)$ where $Q = \bigcup_{A,B \in N}\{B\} \times C_{(\mathrm{sort}_N(B), \mathrm{sort}_N(A))}$ and δ is the smallest set that contains,

- for each $(B, c) \in Q$, $r = B \rightarrow c'(B_1, \ldots B_k) \in R \setminus R^{(\mathrm{M})}$ and $A \in N$, the transition

$$(B, c)(A \rightarrow c \circ c'(B_1, ..., B_k)(x_1, ..., x_k))$$
$$\rightarrow r((B_1, \mathrm{id}_{B_1})(x_1), ..., (B_k, \mathrm{id}_{B_k})(x_k)),$$

- for each $(A, c) \in Q$ and $r = A \rightarrow c'(B) \in R^{(\mathrm{M})}$, the transition $(A, c)(x_1) \rightarrow r((B, c \circ c')(x_1))$.

The transduction $[\![T_{\overleftarrow{\mathrm{dc}}}]\!] \circ [\![T_{\overleftarrow{\mathrm{ft}}}]\!] \circ [\![T_{\overleftarrow{\mathrm{pt}}}]\!] \colon T^{R_{\mathrm{pt}}} \rightarrow T^R$, i.e., the composition of the three transductions introduced in this section, is the inverse of the transduction $[\![T]\!]$ from the proof of Theorem 5 (cf. App. B, p. 7). Therefore, the k best derivations in (G, μ) must be among the transductions of the

k best derivations in $((N_{\mathrm{pt}}, \Sigma, S, R_{\mathrm{pt}}), \mu_{\mathrm{pt}})$, which benefits the enumeration of k best derivations.

5 Conclusion

Based on Engelfriet et al. (2018), we have introduced a procedure which constructs for every PLCFRS G an equivalent lexicalized PLCFRS G'. Moreover, we have described how to recover from each derivation of G' all corresponding derivations of G. In future work, we will use our approach to implement a supertagging-based LCFRS parser.

Acknowledgements

We thank our colleague Kilian Gebhardt as well as the anonymous reviewers for their insightful comments on drafts of this paper.

References

Alfred V Aho, John E. Hopcroft, and Jeffrey D. Ullman. 1974. *The design and analysis of computer algorithms*. Pearson Education India.

Srinivas Bangalore and Aravind K. Joshi. 1999. Supertagging: An approach to almost parsing. *Computational linguistics*, 25(2):237–265.

Joost Engelfriet, Andreas Maletti, and Sebastian Maneth. 2018. Multiple context-free tree grammars: Lexicalization and characterization. *Theoretical Computer Science*, 728:29–99.

Kilian Evang and Laura Kallmeyer. 2011. PLCFRS parsing of English discontinuous constituents. In *Proceedings of the 12th International Conference on Parsing Technologies*, pages 104–116, Dublin, Ireland. Association for Computational Linguistics.

Aravind K. Joshi, Leon S. Levy, and Masako Takahashi. 1975. Tree adjunct grammars. 10(1):136–163.

Andreas Maletti. 2010. Survey: Tree transducers in machine translation. In *NCMA*, pages 11–32. Citeseer.

Andreas Maletti and Giorgio Satta. 2009. Parsing algorithms based on tree automata. In *Proceedings of *the 11th International Conference on Parsing Technologies*, IWPT '09, pages 1–12, Stroudsburg, PA, USA. Association for Computational Linguistics.

Hiroyuki Seki, Takashi Matsumura, Mamoru Fujii, and Tadao Kasami. 1991. On multiple context-free grammars. 88(2):191–229.

Ashish Vaswani, Yonatan Bisk, Kenji Sagae, and Ryan Musa. 2016. Supertagging with LSTMs. In *Proceedings of the 2016 Conference of the North American Chapter of the Association for Computational Linguistics: Human Language Technologies*, pages 232–237.

Krishnamurti Vijay-Shanker, David Jeremy Weir, and Aravind K. Joshi. 1987. Characterizing structural descriptions produced by various grammatical formalisms. In *Proceedings of the 25th Annual Meeting on Association for Computational Linguistics*, ACL '87, pages 104–111, Stroudsburg, PA, USA. Association for Computational Linguistics.

A Supplemental Algorithms

Algorithm 1 COMPS shows an instance of the alg. by (Aho et al., 1974, alg. 5.5) that we use to compute R_{dc} and μ_{dc} efficiently.

Require: terminal-separated PLCFRS (G, μ) where $G = (N, \Sigma, S, R)$
Ensure: DECHAIN$(N, R, \mu) = (R_{dc}, \mu_{dc})$

1: max $v \leftarrow w$ denotes $v \leftarrow \max(v, w)$
2: **function** COMPS(N, R, μ)
3:     let $(m_{A \to c(B)} = 0 \mid A, B \in N, c \in C)$
4:     $m_r \leftarrow \mu(r) \quad \forall r \in R^{(M)}$
5:     $m_{A \to \mathrm{id}_A(A)} \leftarrow 1 \quad \forall A$
6:     **for** $B \in N$ **do**
7:         **for** $A, C \in N \setminus \{B\}$ **do**
8:             **for** $c_1, c_2 \in C$ **do**
9:                 $w' \leftarrow m_{A \to c_1(B)} \cdot m_{B \to c_2(C)}$
10:                max $m_{A \to c_1 \circ c_2(C)} \leftarrow w'$
11:     **return** m
12: **function** DECHAIN(N, R, μ)
13:     $m \leftarrow$ COMPS(N, R, μ)
14:     let $(\hat{\mu}_{A \to c(B_1, \ldots, B_k)} = 0 \mid A, B_1, \ldots, B_k \in N, c \in C)$
15:     $R' \leftarrow R \setminus R^{(M)}$
16:     $\hat{\mu}_{r'} = \mu(r') \quad \forall r' \in R'$
17:     **for** $r = B \to c_2(C_1, \ldots, C_k) \in R \setminus R^{(M)}$ **do**
18:         **for** $A \in N, c_1 \in C : m_{A \to c_1(B)} \neq 0$ **do**
19:             $r' \leftarrow A \to c_1 \circ c_2(C_1, \ldots, C_k)$
20:             $R' \leftarrow R' \cup \{r'\}$
21:             max $\hat{\mu}_{r'} \leftarrow m_{A \to c_1(B)} \cdot \mu(r)$
22:     let $\mu \colon R' \to [0, 1]$ with $\mu'(r') = \hat{\mu}_{r'} \, \forall r' \in R'$
23:     **return** (R', μ')

B Supplemental Proofs

We prove thm. 5 in two steps.

First lem. 7 shall prove that the (unweighted) underlying grammars, G and $(N_{pt}, \Sigma, S, R_{pt})$ are ldTT^R-equivalent. As linear and deterministic TT^R are closed under composition, the idea is to construct two of them for each step, one that transduces derivations in the original to derivations in the constructed grammar and vice versa. The three transducers for each direction are then composed to obtain transductions from derivations in G to derivations in $(N_{pt}, \Sigma, S, R_{pt})$ and vice versa.

Thm. 5 additionally proves the preservation of the weights. Similarly to the above, we show that the PLCFRS constructed in each of the three steps are ldTT^R-equivalent. The property is clearly transitive.

Definition 6. A TT^R is a tuple $A = (Q, \Sigma, \Delta, q_i, \delta)$ where Q, Σ, Δ and q_i are as in TT, and transitions in δ are of the form $q(\sigma(x_1 \colon L_1, \ldots, x_k \colon L_k) \colon L_0) \to t$ where $q \in Q$, $\sigma \in \Sigma_k$, $t \in \mathrm{T}^{\Delta \cup Q((x_1, \ldots, x_k))}$ and $L_0, \ldots, L_k$ are regular tree languages.[1] We omit some of the languages $L_0, \ldots, L_k$ if they are T^Σ. We define the binary relation $\Rightarrow_A$ over $\mathrm{T}^{\Delta \cup Q(\mathrm{T}^\Sigma)}$ such that $s \Rightarrow_A t$ if there is a subtree $q(\sigma(s_1, \ldots, s_k))$ in s and a transition $q(\sigma(x_1 \colon L_1, \ldots, x_k \colon L_k) \colon L_0) \to t'$ such that $\bullet$ $\sigma(s_1, \ldots, s_k) \in L_0$, $s_1 \in L_1, \ldots, s_k \in L_k$, and $\bullet$ t is obtained by replacing $q(\sigma(s_1, \ldots, s_k))$ in s by t' and replacing x_i by s_i for each $i \in [k]$. $\square$

Lemma 7. The LCFRS G and $(N_{pt}, \Sigma, S, R_{pt})$ are ldTT^R-equivalent.

Proof. The first two steps are instances of lems. 32 and 37 by Engelfriet et al. (2018), therefore we will only show the third step.

Step 3. For the construction, we consider R_{ft} and R_{pt} as *ranked* sets. For each $\hat{R} \in \{R_{ft}, R_{pt}\}$ and rule of the form $r = A \to c(B_1, \ldots, B_k) \in \hat{R}$, we let $\mathrm{rk}_{\hat{R}}(r) = k$.

Let, for each $\sigma \in \Sigma$, R_σ and R_X be the sets of all rules in R_{ft} of the form $A \to c(B_1, \ldots, B_k)$ where c is of the form $(\sigma u_1, u_2, \ldots, u_s)$ and $(x_1^1 u_1, u_2, \ldots, u_s)$, respectively. To decide whether a terminal symbol may be propagated through a derivation, we define the look-ahead language L_σ

---

[1] Regular tree languages are recognized by regular tree automata. We refer to Maletti and Satta (2009) for an overview.

for each $\sigma \in \Sigma$ as the smallest set L such that

$$L = \{r(d_1, \ldots, d_k) \mid r \in R_\sigma, d_1, \ldots, d_k \in T^{R_{ft}}\}$$
$$\cup \{r(d_1, \ldots, d_k) \mid r \in R_x, d_1 \in L,$$
$$d_2, \ldots, d_k \in T^{R_{ft}}\}.$$

Observation 8. Let $d \in T^{R_{ft}}$ and $\sigma \in \Sigma$. The following are equal: 1. $d \in L_\sigma$, and 2. $\mathrm{yd}(d)$ is of the form $(\sigma u_1, u_2, \ldots, u_s)$.

We define the ldTT^R $T_{pt} = (\{p, *\}, R_{ft}, R_{pt}, *, \delta)$ where δ contains the following transitions

1. $*(r(x_1, \ldots, x_k)) \rightarrow r(*(x_1), \ldots, *(x_k))$ for each $r \in R_{ft} \setminus R_{ft}^{(\mathcal{I})}$,

2. for each $r \in R_{ft}^{(\mathcal{I})}$, $*(r(x_1, x_2 \colon L_\sigma, x_3, \ldots, x_k))$ $\rightarrow \mathrm{paste}_\sigma^2(r)(*(x_1), p(x_2), *(x_3), \ldots, *(x_k))$,

3. $p(r) \rightarrow \mathrm{cut}(r)$ for each $r \in R_{ft}^{(T)}$,

4. for $r \in R_{ft}^{(M)} \cup (R_{ft}^{(B)} \setminus R_{ft}^{(\mathcal{I})})$ and $\sigma \in \Sigma$, $p(r(x_1 \colon L_\sigma, x_2, \ldots, x_k))$ $\rightarrow \mathrm{cut}(\mathrm{paste}_\sigma^1(r))(p(x_1), *(x_2), \ldots, *(x_k))$, and

5. for each $r \in R_{ft}^{(\mathcal{I})}$ and $\sigma_1, \sigma_2 \in \Sigma$, $p(r(x_1 \colon L_{\sigma_1}, x_2 \colon L_{\sigma_2}, x_3, \ldots, x_k))$ $\rightarrow r'(p(x_1), p(x_2), *(x_3), \ldots, *(x_k))$ where $r' = \mathrm{cut}(\mathrm{paste}_{\sigma_1}^1(\mathrm{paste}_{\sigma_2}^2(r)))$.

Let us have a close look at some constructions in these transitions. Let $r = A \rightarrow c(B_1, \ldots, B_k)$ be a rule and $(v_i \in (\Sigma^*)^{\mathrm{fo}(B_i)} \mid i \in [k])$. We denote the composition of $\mathrm{cut}(r)$ by $\mathrm{cut}(c)$ and the composition of $\mathrm{paste}_\sigma^i(r)$ by $\mathrm{paste}_\sigma^i(c)$.

Observation 9. Let $\mathrm{cut}(c)$ be defined, then $[\![\mathrm{cut}(c)]\!](v_1, \ldots, v_k) = \mathrm{cut}([\![c]\!](v_1, \ldots, v_k))$.

Observation 10. Let v_i be of the form $(\sigma u_1, u_2, \ldots, u_s)$ for $i \in [k]$ and $\sigma \in \Sigma$. $[\![\mathrm{paste}_\sigma^i(c)]\!](v_1, \ldots, \mathrm{cut}(v_i), \ldots, v_k) = [\![c]\!](v_1, \ldots, v_k)$.

Using the observations 8–10 one can easily show that, for each $d \in T^{R_{ft}}$ and $d' \in T^{R_{pt}}$: 1. if $*(d) \Rightarrow_{T_{pt}}^* d'$, then $\mathrm{yd}(d) = \mathrm{yd}(d')$, and 2. if $p(d) \Rightarrow_{T_{pt}}^* d'$, then $\mathrm{yd}(d') = (u_1, \ldots, u_s)$ and $d \in L_\sigma$ where $(\sigma u_1, \ldots, u_s) = \mathrm{yd}(d)$. This concludes the proof in the direction $T^{R_{ft}} \rightarrow T^{R_{pt}}$.

For the other direction, we observe that the applications of cut and paste to obtain the rules in R_{pt} can easily be determined by the occurrences of the nonterminals in $N \times \Sigma$. The transduction $T^{R_{pt}} \rightarrow T^{R_{ft}}$ is thus a deterministic relabeling and can be implemented by a deterministic top-down

tree transducer. Engelfriet et al. (2018, lem. 42, pg. 39) came to the same conclusion for their construction. ∎

Theorem 5. The PLCFRS $((N_{pt}, \Sigma, S, R_{pt}), \mu_{pt})$ and (G, μ) are ldTT^R-equivalent.

Proof sketch. We split the proof into the two remaining properties to show:

1. $\mathrm{wt}([\![T]\!](d)) \geq \mathrm{wt}(d)$ for each $d \in T^R$, and

2. $\mathrm{wt}([\![T']\!](d')) \geq \mathrm{wt}(d')^2$ for each $d' \in T^{R_{pt}}$.

(item 1) The weight functions in sec. 3 are obviously defined in such a way that the weight of a constructed rule is the greatest product of weights for all involved rules in the construction. For each step, the transducer T replaces the rules in the derivation d with an unambiguous constructed rule (this follows from the inductive structure of the previous proof). Therefore, the weight $\mathrm{wt}([\![T]\!](d))$ must be greater than $\mathrm{wt}(d)$.

(item 2) For each step, the transducer T' gives us some derivation that contains the rules that were used to construct the rules in d'. The construction of T' for the steps 1 and 2 is ambiguous, so that we can choose any combination of rules used to construct r' for each rule r' in d'. $[\![T']\!](d')$ then contains each rule in these combinations. Intuitively, we choose the combination of rules with greatest product of weights. Then the weight $\mathrm{wt}([\![T']\!](d'))$ is $\mathrm{wt}(d')$. ∎

---

[2]More specifically, we prove $\mathrm{wt}([\![T']\!](d')) = \mathrm{wt}(d')$ for each $d' \in T^{R_{pt}}$.

Self-Training for Unsupervised Parsing with PRPN

Anhad Mohananey[1][*][†] **Katharina Kann**[2][*] **Samuel R. Bowman**[1]
[1]New York University
[2]University of Colorado Boulder
{anhad,bowman}@nyu.edu
katharina.kann@colorado.edu

Abstract

Neural unsupervised parsing (UP) models learn to parse without access to syntactic annotations, while being optimized for another task like language modeling. In this work, we propose *self-training* for neural UP models: we leverage aggregated annotations predicted by copies of our model as supervision for future copies. To be able to use our model's predictions during training, we extend a recent neural UP architecture, the PRPN (Shen et al., 2018a), such that it can be trained in a semi-supervised fashion. We then add examples with parses predicted by our model to our unlabeled UP training data. Our self-trained model outperforms the PRPN by 8.1% F1 and the previous state of the art by 1.6% F1. In addition, we show that our architecture can also be helpful for semi-supervised parsing in ultra-low-resource settings.

1 Introduction

Unsupervised parsing (UP) models learn to parse sentences into unlabeled constituency trees without the need for annotated treebanks. Self-training (Yarowsky, 1995; Riloff et al., 2003) consists of training a model, using it to label new examples and, based on a confidence metric, adding a subset to the training set, before repeating training. For supervised parsing, results with self-training have been mixed (Charniak, 1997; Steedman et al., 2003; McClosky D, 2006). For unsupervised dependency parsing, Le and Zuidema (2015) obtain strong results by training a supervised parser on outputs of unsupervised parsing. UP models show low self-agreement between training runs (Kim et al., 2019a), while obtaining parsing performances far above chance. Supervising one run with confident

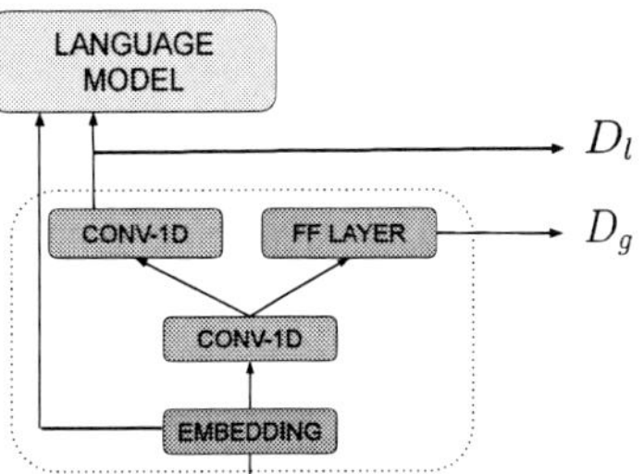

Figure 1: Our parser, represented by the dotted box, outputs syntactic distances D_g and D_l. Both D_g and D_l can be supervised, but D_l can also be learned in a latent manner.

parses from the last could combine their individual strengths. Thus, we ask the question: *Can UP benefit from self-training?*

In order to answer this question, we propose SS-PRPN, a semi-supervised extension of the UP architecture PRPN (Shen et al., 2018a), which can be trained jointly on language modeling and supervised parsing. This enables our model to leverage silver-standard annotations obtained via self-training for supervision. Our approach draws on the idea of *syntactic distances*, which can be learned both as latent variables (Shen et al., 2018a) and as explicit supervision targets (Shen et al., 2018b). We use both of these, leveraging annotations obtained via UP to supervise the two different outputs of the parser, in addition to standard UP training.

SS-PRPN, in combination with self-training, improves over its original version by 8.1% F1 and over the previous state of the art (Kim et al., 2019a) by 1.6% F1, when trained and evaluated on the English PTB (Marcus et al., 1999): *UP can indeed benefit from self training.* We further perform an analysis of our self-training procedure, finding that longer sentences benefit most from self-training.

Although our primary motivation for the de-

*Equal contribution.
†Now at Electronic Arts.

Proceedings of the 16th International Conference on Parsing Technologies and the IWPT 2020 Shared Task, pages 105–110
Virtual Meeting, July 9, 2020. ©2020 Association for Computational Linguistics

velopment of a semi-supervised architecture is to enable self-training, we further hypothesize that, since language modeling and parsing annotations seem to provide complementary information, UP should aid low-resource supervised parsing. As a proof of concept, we employ SS-PRPN for semi-supervised training. In extremely-low-data regimes with no more than 250 labeled parses, SS-PRPN outperforms supervised and unsupervised baselines in most settings on unlabeled parsing, and in all settings on labeled constituency parsing.

Related Work Following the line of research on non-neural UP models (Clark, 2001; Klein and Manning, 2002; Bod, 2006), early approaches to neural UP (Yogatama et al., 2017; Choi et al., 2018) obtain improved performance on downstream tasks, yet show highly inconsistent behavior in parsing (Williams et al., 2018).

Recently, Shen et al. (2018a) introduce the first high performing neural UP model (Htut et al., 2018). Dyer et al. (2019) raise concerns that PRPN's parsing methodology is biased towards English trees. Though these concerns are serious, they are largely orthogonal to our research question regarding the helpfulness of self-training for UP.

Several models have been introduced since: Shen et al. (2019) propose an architecture consisting of an LSTM (Hochreiter and Schmidhuber, 1997) with a modified update function for the LSTM cell state, Kim et al. (2019a)—the current state-of-the-art—introduce a model based on a mixture of probabilistic context-free grammars, Kim et al. (2019b) present unsupervised learning of recurrent neural networks grammars, Li et al. (2019) combine PRPN with imitation learning, and Drozdov et al. (2019) employ a recursive autoencoder. Kim et al. (2020) examine tree induction from pretrained models.

2 Model

Syntactic Distances In order to parse a sentence, a computational model needs to output some kind of variables representing a unique tree structure. The variables we use are *syntactic distances* as introduced by Shen et al. (2018a). They represent the syntactic relationships between all successive pairs of words in a sentence. If the distance between two neighboring words is large, they belong to different subtrees, and, thus, their traversal distance in the tree is large. A parse tree can be created by finding the maximum syntactic distance, splitting

---

Algorithm 1: Tree to latent distances D_l

```
 1  D_l ← [1] * leaves_tree      ▷ leaves_tree :leaf count of tree
 2  b ← 0
 3  max ← 100          ▷ max: max possible depth of tree
 4  Function  DISTANCE (tree, b, max)
 5      DISTANCE (tree_l, b, max-1)
 6      x ← tree_r               ▷ tree_r: right child of tree
 7      while True do
 8          if x_l is empty then
 9              D_l[b + leaves_tree_l] ← max
10              break
11          end
12          x ← x_l              ▷ x_l: left child of x
13      end
```

the sentence into sub-trees there, and repeating this process recursively for each sub-tree until a single token is left.

Two different formulations of syntactic distance have been proposed to realize this basic intuition: The first, which we refer to as D_l, is introduced by Shen et al. (2018a) as a latent variable in their UP model. Since, for self-training, we supervise D_l with values predicted by our model, we introduce Algorithm 1, which is used to convert a tree to distances D_l. The second kind of distance, denoted here as D_g, is introduced by Shen et al. (2018b) as labels for direct supervision. We use their algorithms to map trees to distances D_g and vice versa, and ask readers to refer to Shen et al. (2018b) for details.

We design our parser in such a way that it can predict both. We treat the decision whether D_g or D_l are used at test time as a hyperparameter. The reasons why we employ both types of distances are two-fold: D_g, unlike D_l, cannot be learned in an unsupervised fashion, which is critical for a semi-supervised architecture. Empirically, supervising purely on D_l performs poorly.

The Parser Our parser, cf. Figure 1, consists of an embedding layer and a convolutional layer which are followed by two different components: a linear output layer that predicts D_g and a second convolutional layer that predicts D_l.

Formally, given an input sentence $s = t_0, t_1, \ldots, t_{n-1}$, our parser predicts D_g as:

$$h_i = ReLU\left(W_c \begin{bmatrix} t_{i-L_1} \\ t_{i-L_1+1} \\ \ldots \\ t_i \end{bmatrix} + b_c\right) \quad (1)$$

$$d_i = ReLU(W_d h_i + b_d) \quad (2)$$

Model	F1(μ)
PRPN	39.8 (5.6)
PRPN (ours)	46.3 (6.3)
C-PCFG	52.8 (3.8)
URNNG	44.8 (4.1)
SS-PRPN	**54.4 (0.6)**
Left Branching (LB)	13.1
Right Branching (RB)	16.5
Random	21.4

Table 1: Results on the English PTB test set, with the model tuned on the dev set. LB, RB and Random baselines are taken as-is from Htut et al. (2018). Since evaluation of C-PCFG, PRPN and URNNG is done against binary gold trees, results might differ from the original papers.

Algorithm 2: Self-training for UP

1 Unlabeled data X_U
2 Training set $X_T \leftarrow \emptyset$
3 Train n_c UP models on X_U
4 **for** $s_i \in X_U$ **do**
5    $n_a \leftarrow$ number of models agreeing on parse $p(s_i)$
6   **if** $n_a \geq \mu n_c$ **then**
7       $X_T \leftarrow X_T \cup p(s_i)$ ▷ add confident parse
8   **end**
9 **end**
10 Train model on X_U and X_T

---

where W_c are the weights of the first convolutional layer, W_d are the weights of the output layer corresponding to D_g, and b_c and b_d are bias vectors. L_1 is the filter size. D_l involves similar computations, but is the output of the second layer.

Distance Loss When we have silver-standard annotations from self-training available, we compute the loss for both syntactic distances directly. Since the relative ranking between distances—rather than absolute values—defines the tree structure, we train our parser with a hinge ranking loss following Shen et al. (2018b). Our distance loss L_r is the weighted sum of the distance losses corresponding to D_l (L_{sl}) and D_g (L_{sg}):

$$L_r = \alpha L_{sg} + (1 - \alpha)L_{sl} \qquad (3)$$

Language Modeling Loss In order to optimize the parameters of our parser without direct supervision, we further feed its output—the predictions for D_l—into a language model, following Shen et al. (2018a).

Multi-Task Training Our parser is trained in a semi-supervised fashion with losses corresponding to (i) learning the distances in a latent manner through *language modeling*, and (ii) supervising directly on *distances*. We sample batches from both objectives at random.

Self-Training For self-training, cf. Algorithm 2, we first train n_c models on the unlabeled PTB training set X_U. We then have them predict parse trees for all sentences in X_U. If more than $\mu *$ n_c models (with μ as a hyperparameters) agree on the same parse, we add it as a silver-standard *labeled* example to the parsing training set X_T. We use Algorithm 1 and the respective algorithm by Shen et al. (2018b) to convert consensus trees into distances D_l and D_g. We then train a new model on both X_U and X_T.

3 Experimental Design

Data and Metrics We experiment on the English Penn Treebank Marcus et al. (PTB; 1999). For evaluation, we compute the F1 score of the output parses against binarized gold parses following Williams et al. (2018). The code for our model is published online[1].

Baselines We compare against an unsupervised recurrent neural network grammar (URNNG; Kim et al., 2019b), a compound probabilistic context free grammar (C-PCFG; Kim et al., 2019a), and Shen et al. (2018a)'s PRPN. We re-implement and tune PRPN in our code base.

Hyperparameters We tune our hyperparameters on the development set. Hidden states and word embeddings have 300 and 100 dimensions, respectively. We set the weight $\alpha = 0.5$. For self-training, we obtain best results with $\mu = 60\%$ and $n_c = 15$. We further experiment with converting either D_l or D_g into final parse trees, and find that D_l works best.

4 Results and Analysis

Unsupervised Parsing Performance Table 1 shows our results. SS-PRPN outperforms all baselines: our model obtains a 1.6% higher F1 score than the strongest baseline. It further improves substantially over comparable non-self-trained baselines: by 14.6% over PRPN and by 8.1% over our reimplementation of it. SS-PRPN also shows a much lower variance. This demonstrates that self-training is indeed a viable approach for UP.

---

[1] https://github.com/anhad13/SelfTrainingAndLRP

	Av. Length	Av. Depth	Av. F1	#sents
Self-training	7.0	3.3	82.2	1897
PTB gold	20.9	10.6	100.0	39701

Table 2: Statistics of our best self-training annotations compared to PTB.

Length	0 - 10	10 - 20	20 - 30	30 - 40	> 40
Ex.	115	573	613	295	94
% Ex. improved	20%	36.8%	49.7%	52.8%	55.3%

Table 3: Percentage of development examples improved by SS-PRPN in comparison to PRPN, listed by sentence length.

Analysis of Self-Training We interpret agreement rate as our confidence value for self-training, with the hypothesis that, as agreement among models increases, there is a higher likelihood that the parse is correct. In Figure 2, we show that, as expected, the F1 score increases as more models agree, for the best self-training run (15 individual models, or the second last row in Table 1).

Additionally, Figure 2 and Table 2 show that self-training annotations consist of shorter sentences and shallower trees than our dataset's average, i.e., mostly of easier sentences.

Our final hypothesis is that self-training helps mostly for longer sentences, since models often agree on shorter ones anyways and, trivially, longer sentences leave more room for error. Table 3 shows the development set performance and the number of examples for varying sentence lengths. As expected, self-training yields the greatest gains for longer sentences.

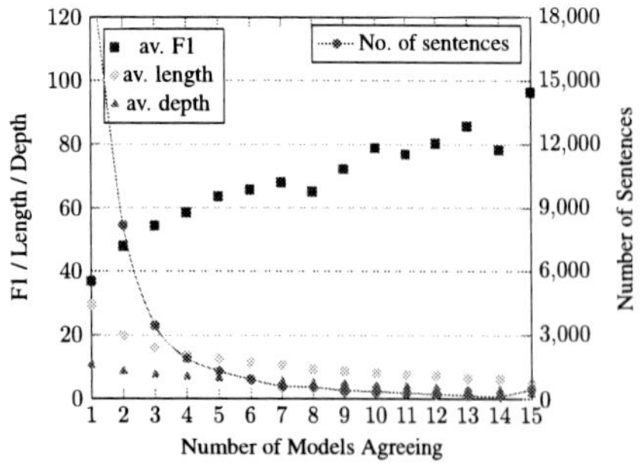

Figure 2: Statistics for self-training ($n_c = 15$): As agreement among UP models goes up, parsing F1 improves, and average depth and length go down.

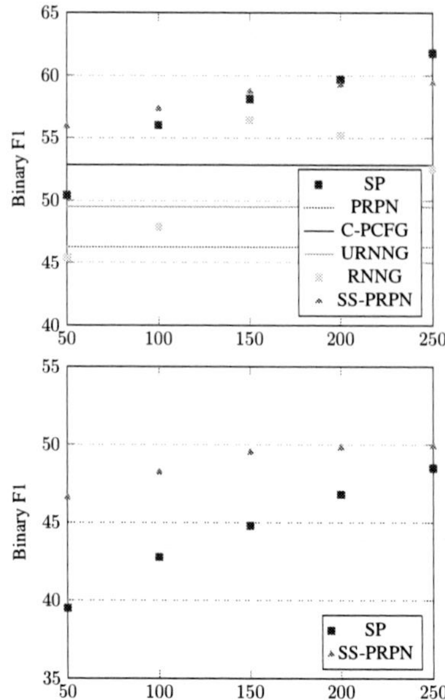

Figure 3: Low-resource parsing on the PTB. The first and second plots show unlabeled and labeled F1 respectively, plotted against the training data size.

Low-Resource Parsing Performance We further investigate how SS-PRPN performs when limited gold parses are available in addition to unlabeled data. To predict constituency labels, we add and train an additional linear output layer after the first convolutional layer. We find that, on the development set, converting D_g into parse trees works better for low-resource parsing than D_l. As supervised baselines, we employ Dyer et al. (2016)'s recurrent neural network grammar (RNNG) and a supervised parser (SP) based on syntactic distances (Shen et al., 2018b). Figure 3 shows results for 50 to 250 annotated examples. The upper part shows the *unlabeled* parsing performance in comparison to the UP baselines. We outperform all baselines for 50 to 150 examples, while SP performs slightly better with more annotations. When looking at *labeled* F1 in the lower part of Figure 3, SS-PRPN clearly outperforms SP, which indicates that unlabeled data can be leveraged in the low-resource setting.

5 Conclusion

We introduce a semi-supervised neural architecture, SS-PRPN, which is capable of UP via self-training. Our self-trained models strongly outperform comparable baselines, and advance the state of the art on PTB by 1.6% F1. Analyses show that our approach yields most gains for longer sentences. Our architecture can also leverage limited amounts of parsing supervision when available. We conclude that it is beneficial to develop better UP models for semi-supervised settings.

6 Acknowledgements

This work has benefited from support of Samsung Research through the project *Improving Deep Learning using Latent Structure* and the donation of Titan V GPU by NVIDIA Corporation.

References

Rens Bod. 2006. An all-subtrees approach to unsupervised parsing. In *Proceedings of the 21st International Conference on Computational Linguistics and 44th Annual Meeting of the Association for Computational Linguistics*.

Eugene Charniak. 1997. Statistical parsing with a context-free grammar and word statistics. *AAAI/IAAI*, 2005.

Jihun Choi, Kang Min Yoo, and Sang-goo Lee. 2018. Learning to compose task-specific tree structures. In *Thirty-Second AAAI Conference on Artificial Intelligence*.

Alexander Clark. 2001. Unsupervised induction of stochastic context-free grammars using distributional clustering. In *Proceedings of the 2001 workshop on Computational Natural Language Learning*. Association for Computational Linguistics.

Andrew Drozdov, Patrick Verga, Mohit Yadav, Mohit Iyyer, and Andrew McCallum. 2019. Unsupervised latent tree induction with deep inside-outside recursive auto-encoders. In *Proceedings of the North American Chapter of the Association for Computational Linguistics*.

Chris Dyer, Adhiguna Kuncoro, Miguel Ballesteros, and Noah A Smith. 2016. Recurrent neural network grammars. In *Proceedings of the North American Chapter of the Association for Computational Linguistics*.

Chris Dyer, Gábor Melis, and Phil Blunsom. 2019. A critical analysis of biased parsers in unsupervised parsing. *arXiv:1909.09428*.

Sepp Hochreiter and Jürgen Schmidhuber. 1997. Long short-term memory. *Neural computation*.

Phu Mon Htut, Kyunghyun Cho, and Samuel Bowman. 2018. Grammar induction with neural language models: An unusual replication. In *Proceedings of the 2018 Conference on Empirical Methods in Natural Language Processing*.

Taeuk Kim, Jihun Choi, Daniel Edmiston, and Sang-goo Lee. 2020. Are pre-trained language models aware of phrases? simple but strong baselines for grammar induction. In *ICLR*.

Yoon Kim, Chris Dyer, and Alexander Rush. 2019a. Compound probabilistic context-free grammars for grammar induction. In *Proceedings of Association for Computational Linguistics*. Association for Computational Linguistics.

Yoon Kim, Alexander M Rush, Lei Yu, Adhiguna Kuncoro, Chris Dyer, and Gábor Melis. 2019b. Unsupervised recurrent neural network grammars. In *Proceedings of the North American Chapter of the Association for Computational Linguistics*.

Dan Klein and Christopher D Manning. 2002. A generative constituent-context model for improved grammar induction. In *Proceedings of Association for Computational Linguistics*. Association for Computational Linguistics.

Phong Le and Willem Zuidema. 2015. Unsupervised dependency parsing: Let's use supervised parsers. *arXiv preprint arXiv:1504.04666*.

Bowen Li, Lili Mou, and Frank Keller. 2019. An imitation learning approach to unsupervised parsing. *arXiv:1906.02276*.

Mitchell Marcus et al. 1999. Treebank-3 ldc99t42 web download. *Philidelphia: Linguistic Data Consortium*.

Johnson M McClosky D, Charniak E. 2006. Effective self-training for parsing. *North American Chapter of the Association of Computational Linguistics*.

Ellen Riloff, Janyce Wiebe, and Theresa Wilson. 2003. Learning Subjective Nouns using Extraction Pattern Bootstrapping. In *Proceedings of CoNLL*.

Yikang Shen, Zhouhan Lin, Chin-Wei Huang, and Aaron Courville. 2018a. Neural language modeling by jointly learning syntax and lexicon. In *ICLR*.

Yikang Shen, Zhouhan Lin, Athul Paul Jacob, Alessandro Sordoni, Aaron Courville, and Yoshua Bengio. 2018b. Straight to the tree: Constituency parsing with neural syntactic distance. In *Proceedings of the Association for Computational Linguistics*.

Yikang Shen, Shawn Tan, Alessandro Sordoni, and Aaron Courville. 2019. Ordered neurons: Integrating tree structures into recurrent neural networks. In *ICLR*.

Mark Steedman, Miles Osborne, Anoop Sarkar, Stephen Clark, Rebecca Hwa, Julia Hockenmaier, Paul Ruhlen, Steven Baker, and Jeremiah Crim. 2003. Bootstrapping statistical parsers from small datasets. In *Proceedings of European chapter of the Association for Computational Linguistics*. Association for Computational Linguistics.

Adina Williams, Andrew Drozdov, and Samuel R Bowman. 2018. Do latent tree learning models identify meaningful structure in sentences? *Transactions of the Association for Computational Linguistics*.

David Yarowsky. 1995. Unsupervised Word-Sense Disambiguation Rivaling Supervised Methods. In *Proceedings of ACL*.

Dani Yogatama, Phil Blunsom, Chris Dyer, Edward Grefenstette, and Wang Ling. 2017. Learning to compose words into sentences with reinforcement learning. In *ICLR*.

Span-Based LCFRS-2 Parsing

Miloš Stanojević
School of Informatics
University of Edinburgh
m.stanojevic@ed.ac.uk

Mark Steedman
School of Informatics
University of Edinburgh
steedman@inf.ed.ac.uk

Abstract

The earliest models for discontinuous constituency parsers used mildly context-sensitive grammars, but the fashion has changed in recent years to grammar-less transition-based parsers that use strong neural probabilistic models to greedily predict transitions.

We argue that grammar-based approaches still have something to contribute on top of what is offered by transition-based parsers. Concretely, by using a grammar formalism to restrict the space of possible trees we can use dynamic programming parsing algorithms for exact search for the most probable tree.

Previous chart-based parsers for discontinuous formalisms used probabilistically weak generative models. We instead use a span-based discriminative neural model that preserves the dynamic programming properties of the chart parsers. Our parser does not use an explicit grammar, but it does use explicit grammar formalism constraints: we generate only trees that are within the LCFRS-2 formalism. These properties allow us to construct a new parsing algorithm that runs in lower worst-case time complexity of $\mathcal{O}(l\,n^4+n^6)$, where n is the sentence length and l is the number of unique nonterminal labels. This parser is efficient in practice, provides best results among chart-based parsers, and is competitive with the best transition based parsers.

We also show that the main bottleneck for further improvement in performance is in the restriction of fan-out to degree 2. We show that well-nestedness is helpful in speeding up parsing, but lowers accuracy.

1   Introduction

Most constituency parsers are designed to predict a projective (or continuous) tree representation. This type of tree representation is not expressive enough to model (structurally) long-range dependencies that are a major concern of most syntactic theories. Take for instance the sentence in Figure 1. It contains a long range dependency between "on" and "what". This is represented differently across syntactic theories. In dependency parsing, there would be a direct arc between these two words that would cause the dependency tree to be non-projective, i.e. there would be crossed dependencies (Nivre et al., 2016). In constituency treebanks this is modelled either by using *traces* that are co-indexed with the moving element, as in English Penn treebank (Marcus et al., 1993), or by having a direct discontinuous constituent, as in German Negra and Tiger treebanks (Brants et al., 2004).

Here we adopt the discontinuous constituency approach because of its well defined formal properties, but the results are also relevant for other representations. The Penn treebank *trace* representation can be converted to a discontinuous representation (Evang and Kallmeyer, 2011)[1] and non-projective dependency trees can be interpreted as lexicalised versions of discontinuous constituency trees (Kuhlmann and Möhl, 2007).

There are two different approaches to predicting discontinuous constituency structure directly.[2] The first approach, usually grammar-based chart parsing, limits the type of trees that are acceptable (for example TAG (Joshi, 1985) or LCFRS (Vijay-Shanker et al., 1987; Seki et al., 1991)) and searches for the best tree with an exact search algorithm like CKY. The second approach, usually transition-based, does not limit the type of trees but searches for the best tree only approximately

---

[1]This is a lossy conversion because the discontinuous representation does not contain information about the initial location of the constituent before it was displaced, nor the attachment point in the surface tree.

[2]Indirect approaches work by conversion to some other simpler formalism, parsing in the simpler formalism, and then converting the result back. They are not the focus of this article but their results are reported in the Section 5.4.

Proceedings of the 16th International Conference on Parsing Technologies and the IWPT 2020 Shared Task, pages 111–121
Virtual Meeting, July 9, 2020. ©2020 Association for Computational Linguistics

with a beam search. Lately, with the success of neural models, transition-based parsers have been preferred to grammar-based approaches because transition-based models do not need to make any independence assumptions and strong neural models can be used to their full potential. Grammar-based methods have more difficulty incorporating rich probabilistic models due to the necessary independence assumptions needed for exact dynamic programming algorithms like CKY. Another disadvantage of grammar based models is that, even though their parsing algorithms are polynomial, they are significantly slower in practice due the high polynomial degrees and a large grammar constant.

In this work we try to improve both speed and accuracy of chart-based parsers. The accuracy is improved by using a modified version of neural span-based scoring of non-terminal nodes (Cross and Huang, 2016; Stern et al., 2017) which does not break the independence assumptions needed for efficient parsing. Speed is improved by restricting the set of acceptable trees to the ones recognizable with an LCFRS-2 grammar formalism, but no explicit grammar is used, removing the grammar constant from the worst-case complexity.[3] Additionally, the parser is implemented using an imperative approach to Viterbi CKY parsing (as opposed to deductive approach), similar to standard CFG CKY implementations with embedded loops. By avoiding the usage of standard *weighted deductive parsing* (Shieber et al., 1995; Nederhof, 2003). we avoid the need to maintain *heap property* of the agenda, further reducing the worst-case parsing complexity.

This results in a fast chart-based LCFRS-2 parser that outperforms all previous chart-based parsers for discontinuous structures, and gives performance that is on par with the best transition-based parsers.

2 LCFRS-2 Trees

LCFRS (Vijay-Shanker et al., 1987; Seki et al., 1991; Kallmeyer, 2010) is a grammar formalism that works in a similar way to CFG: it applies a series of recursive rewriting rules that eventually generate a sentence. What makes it different from CFG is that it allows each non-terminal node in the

---

[3]Note that not having explicit LCFRS-2 grammar but only explicit set of non-terminals is equivalent to having an LCFRS-2 grammar that overgenerates. This is prevented with a strong span-based probabilistic model.

derivation tree to contain more than one continuous span of words.

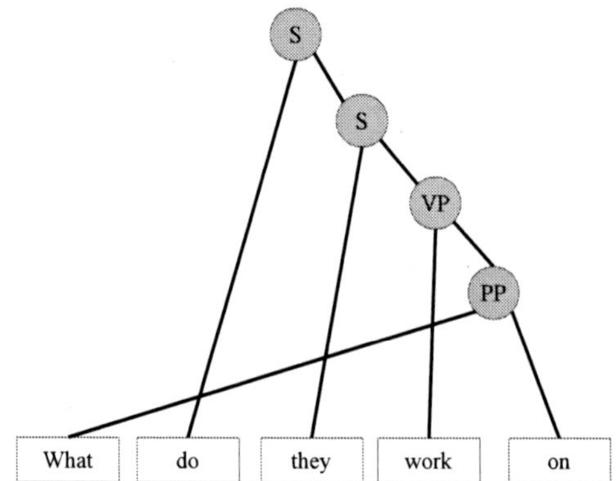

Figure 1: Discontinuous tree example.

For instance, if we look back at the example from Figure 1, we can represent the discontinuous PP as PP*(what, on)*, or in terms of spans $\mathrm{PP}\big((0,1),(4,5)\big)$. An LCFRS rule that forms this constituent can be expressed as:

$$\mathrm{PP}(X,Y) \;\rightarrow\; \mathrm{WH}(X)\; \mathrm{P}(Y)$$

These individual spans are often called components and the number of them per non-terminal is called the fan-out of the non-terminal. The fan-out of an LCFRS grammar is defined by the maximal fan-out of its non-terminals.

The fan-out of the grammar has significant consequences to its expressivity and the parsing complexity. For binary LCFRS the worst-case parsing complexity is $\mathcal{O}(G \cdot n^{3\phi})$ where G is the grammar constant (total number of LCFRS rules) and ϕ is the grammar's fan-out (Seki et al., 1991; Kallmeyer, 2013). If fan-out is 1 we get only the power of a standard CFG and a very efficient parser. If the fan-out is unrestricted (as big as the sentence being parsed), we could process any discontinuous structure but will get a non-polynomial parser.

Clearly, we need to restrict fan-out to some small constant number. Maier et al. (2012) suggested that restricting fan-out to 2 is sufficient to process a large portion of discontinuous structures in German treebanks. We adopt this proposal and show the consequences of it in the experiments section. We will refer to this grammar as LCFRS-2.

Another useful restriction of LCFRS is a *well-nestedness* property (Kuhlmann and Nivre, 2006; Maier and Lichte, 2009). For any LCFRS rule which contains some non-terminals A and B on its right-hand side we say that it is well-nested if there are no components A_1 and A_2 from A, and B_1 and B_2 from B that form a linear order $A_1 < B_1 < A_2 < B_2$. This property allows for efficient parsing (Gómez-Rodríguez et al., 2010), but in our case of a binary LCFRS with fan-out 2, the effect of well-nestedness will be only proportional to some constant. Maier and Lichte (2009) state that well-nestedness holds for the majority of constituents in German treebanks. We will test it in our experiments. We will refer to this type of grammar as LCFRS-wn-2. Tree-Adjoining Grammars (TAG) (Joshi, 1985) are weakly equivalent to LCFRS-wn-2.

3 Neural Span-Based Model

We borrow and modify some ideas already popular in CFG parsing to improve LCFRS-2 chart parsing. In particular, span-based scoring is a popular approach for modelling scoring of parse trees without breaking the dynamic programming assumptions of chart parsers (Cross and Huang, 2016; Stern et al., 2017; Gaddy et al., 2018; Kitaev and Klein, 2018a,b).

In this approach words are first encoded with bi-LSTM (Hochreiter and Schmidhuber, 1997; Graves et al., 2005). These word encodings are afterwards used to score spans. For each span we take encodings of two words that are at its borders and pass them through feed-forward (Cross and Huang, 2016; Gaddy et al., 2018) or bi-affine classifier (Dozat and Manning, 2017; Stern et al., 2017) that predicts the score for each possible label (non-terminal) occupying that span. Unaries are all collapsed into a single non-terminal to simplify scoring. The score of a whole tree is defined as a sum of the scores all of its nodes. These scores are often optimised for max-margin loss (Taskar et al., 2004a) by decoding the currently best tree according to the model and minimising the margin violation in case the predicted tree is not the gold tree.

Stern et al. (2017) show that span labelling and span combination (parsing) part can be done independently for this model because the best label for each span does not depend on the span's children nodes, unlike the standard PCFG. Computing optimal labels for each span takes $\mathcal{O}(l\, n^2)$ for sentence of length n and l labels (non-terminals).

There are a couple of things that need to be addressed before this approach can be used for LCFRS-2 parsing. First is that non-terminals in LCFRS-2 can have two spans and applying the approach of Stern et al. (2017) would give labelling algorithm that runs in $\mathcal{O}(l\, n^4)$ which is prohibitively large considering the hidden constant factor of matrix multiplication done by the neural scoring layer.

To reduce the computational complexity of span scoring we introduce independence assumption that score of some discontinuous constituent with label X and spans $\big((a, b), (c, d)\big)$ is:

$$\begin{aligned}
\text{score}(X\big((a,b),(c,d)\big)) = {} & \text{score}(X_{left}(a,b))+ \\
& \text{score}(X_{gap}(b+1,c-1))+ \\
& \text{score}(X_{right}(c,d))
\end{aligned}$$

where X_{left}, X_{gap}, X_{right} are newly created non-terminals for each X. This decomposes the discontinuous constituent scoring as scoring of three continuous constituents. The labelling complexity with l labels is still $\mathcal{O}(l\, n^4)$ but the neural matrix multiplication will be done only $\mathcal{O}(n^2)$ times just like in CFG case of Stern et al. (2017). In Section 5.3 we will show that most of the time is spent in the neural component and span combination, and that the labelling component takes a negligible proportion of time.

The second aspect of span-based models that we needed to change is the objective function. The original max-margin parsing objective proposed by Taskar et al. (2004b) maximised the margin between the gold tree and all other trees. Because that approach was too slow in practice it is usually approximated by maximising only the margin between the gold and the highest scoring tree, in case highest scoring tree is not the gold tree. This approach gave good results in CFG parsing (Stern et al., 2017), but it was very unstable in our tests. The reason for this may be in the difference between the number of possible hypotheses between CFG and LCFRS-2 which increases quadratically from the order of $\mathcal{O}(n^3)$ to $\mathcal{O}(n^6)$. In this case, optimising for just a single margin violation may be a too weak learning signal. Decreasing the scores of one bad tree alone may increase the score of another bad tree.

That is why instead of the structured max-margin training we used an alternative method where we treat each triple *(span start, span end, label)* as a binary classification task and train the model to predict the probability of that triple being part of the gold tree. For training we use not only the triples from the gold tree but all possible triples for a given sentence. We consider the probability of the tree to be the product of probabilities of the triples coming from each of its nodes. This probability model is obviously making some independence assumptions that are not correct. For instance, the probability of a constituent with a span $(1, 3)$ does not inform the probability of a constituent with a span $(2, 5)$ even though it is clear that both constituents cannot exist at the same time. This model may nevertheless give good parsing results because the optimal result of these classifications would give the optimal tree.

This method is much more stable in comparison to the max-margin approach of Stern et al. (2017) because the gradient takes into consideration the components of all possible trees at the same time instead of only the highest scoring one. In comparison to Max-Margin Markov Networks method of Taskar et al. (2004b) which also considers all trees, our approach is much faster because it does not need to build chart for each training instance.

As mentioned before, we collapse all unary chains into a single non-terminal which contains sufficient information to be unchained after parsing. Nodes that have more than 2 children are binarized with the same method as Stern et al. (2017) by labelling all new sub-nodes as $\varnothing$. Again, there are some aspects to consider before applying the method of Stern et al. (2017). First, binarization of LCFRS, unlike binarization of CFG, can increase the generative power by increasing the fan-out (Kallmeyer, 2010). If we have a tree that can be generated with LCFRS-2 and arbitrarily choose binarization method, the binarised tree may turn out not to be within the strong generative power of LCFRS-2. Hence, choosing the right binarization is important. Second, different binarizations actually correspond to different latent derivations of the tree we are modelling. These latent derivations will have different probabilities and its not easy to see which one of them should be used. The approach we will pursue is to model all of them by treating every possible triple that can be extracted from every possible binarization of a gold tree to be a positive class.

4 Direct CKY Parsing Algorithm

The algorithms for LCFRS are usually presented, and implemented, as deductive rules. These deductive rules, combined with a deduction engine of Shieber et al. (1995) can form a conceptually simple mechanism for parsing. In case of *weighted deductive rules* the modification of Nederhof (2003)

can be used. It modifies the method of search to explore the most probable search space first by implementing the *agenda* as a priority queue. Almost all Probabilistic LCFRS (PLCFRS) parsers have been implemented in this way (Kallmeyer and Maier, 2010; Maier et al., 2012; van Cranenburgh et al., 2016).

However, there are many reasons not to use this approach with our span-based model. First, implementing the agenda as a priority queue adds a $\mathcal{O}(\log n)$ multiplicative term to the worst-case complexity. Second, the multiplicative grammar constant that exists in PLCFRS approaches does not exist in ours since there is no explicit grammar, and the optimal label for each span is independent of the other spans. Third, because of the difficulty of implementing optimal chart lookup under deductive approaches means that most PLCFRS parsers optimise lookup only on the non-terminal labels and not on span indices, representing a serious bottleneck.

The parsing approach we propose has instead worst-case complexity $\mathcal{O}(l\, n^4 + n^6)$ because it does not use an explicit grammar, nor priority queue, and it has very straightforward lookup based on indices. It consists of two parts. First part takes the scores from the neural model and computes the optimal score for each possible LCFRS-2 combination of spans of which there are n^4. That makes its complexity $\mathcal{O}(l\, n^4)$ where l is the number of distinct non-terminals. The second part does the actual parsing by combining these scores to form the best tree. It is a generalisation of how non-deductive CFG CKY algorithm works by having multiple embedded *for* loops and a multi-dimensional array to represent a chart. Both chart and loops have to be adapted to LCFRS.

We have two data structures involved that are both indexed by the span: a lookup table for optimal span label (and its score), and a lookup table for the optimal backpointer to children nodes (and its score). We will refer to the first one as labChart and to the second one as chart. Each one of them could be used for looking up continuous spans (only 2 indices) or discontinuous spans (4 indices). We can implement them with multi-dimensional arrays that provide constant lookup.

To find which loops are needed we borrow Table 1 from Maier et al. (2012) who have found all possible rule shapes for binary LCFRS-2. We augment this table with the worst-case complexity for each rule given in the fourth column. This complexity can be easily derived using the method of McAllester (2002) which states that the computational complexity of each rule depends on the number of free variables on the left-hand side of the rule, assuming rules are non-deleting. For instance, for CFG rule #3 there are three free variables: index at the start of X, index between X and Y and index at the end of Y. Therefore its complexity is $\mathcal{O}(n^3)$. Each of these indices requires an embedded *for* loop.

ID	Type	counts	$\mathcal{O}(.)$
#1	A(X) → B(X)	49	$\mathcal{O}(n^2)$
#2	A(X, Y) → B(X, Y)	1	$\mathcal{O}(n^4)$
#3	A(XY) → B(X) C(Y)	14,430	$\mathcal{O}(n^3)$
#4	A(X,Y) → B(X) C(Y)	1,644	$\mathcal{O}(n^4)$
#5	A(XYZ) → B(X,Z) C(Y)	621	$\mathcal{O}(n^4)$
#6	A(X,YZ) → B(X,Y) C(Z)	100	$\mathcal{O}(n^5)$
#7	A(X,YZ) → B(X,Z) C(Y)	142	$\mathcal{O}(n^5)$
#8	A(XY,Z) → B(X,Z) C(Y)	172	$\mathcal{O}(n^5)$
#9	A(XY,Z) → B(X) C(Y,Z)	582	$\mathcal{O}(n^5)$
#10	A(XY,ZU) → B(X,Z) C(Y,U)	7	$\mathcal{O}(n^6)$
#11	A(XY,ZU) → B(X,U) C(Y,Z)	0	$\mathcal{O}(n^6)$
#12	A(X,YZU) → B(X,Z) C(Y,U)	12	$\mathcal{O}(n^6)$
#13	A(XYZ,U) → B(X,Z) C(Y,U)	12	$\mathcal{O}(n^6)$
#14	A(XYZU) → B(X,Z) C(Y,U)	13	$\mathcal{O}(n^5)$

Table 1: LCFRS-2 rule instances from (Maier et al., 2012) with frequency counts from Tiger sentences of length 30.

This is simple when we have only one rule shape as in the case of CFG, but with LCFRS we need to make sure that all rules are tested in the right order. We know that bigger spans are always composed of smaller spans. Therefore we can have a top *for* loop that would iterate over the total span size. The *for* loop below it would split that total span size between left and right span in case of rules that produce discontinuous constituents. These top loops are needed only to ensure that constituents are built in a bottom-up topological order. Further loops are used only to compute all other needed indices for each rule. The space in this paper is not sufficient to present the implementation for all 14 rules but the example in Algorithm 1 for rule #6 should be sufficient to show how the rest of the algorithm works. The number of embedded *for* loops for this rule clearly corresponds to its computational complexity.

By designing which rules from this schema we use we can get different generative power accompanied with a different computational complexity.

Algorithm 1 Direct CKY LCFRS-2 Parsing

```
for sizeSpan in [1 ... n] do
    ...
    for a in [0 ... n − sizeSpan − 1] do
        b ← a + sizeSpan
        // processing a continuous constituent
        // with the span (a, b)
        // using rules 3, 5 and 14
    ...
    for sizeLeft in [1 ... sizeSpan − 1] do
        sizeRight ← sizeSpan − sizeLeft
        ...
        for a in [0 ... n − sizeSpan − 1] do
            b ← a + sizeLeft
            for c in [b + 1 ... n − sizeRight] do
                d ← c + sizeRight
                best ← −∞
                // processing a discontinuous
                // constituent with two components
                // (a, b) and (c, d)
                // finding best solution with
                // discontinuous rules 2, 4, 6,
                // 7,8,9,10,11,12,13
                ...
                // rule 6: A(X, YZ) → B(X,Y)C(Z)
                // X=(a, b), Y=(c, e), Z=(e, d)
                for e in [c + 1 ... d − 1] do
                    score ← chart[a, b, c, e] +
                                        chart[e, d]
                    if score > best then
                        best ← score
                ...
                chart[a, b, c, d] ← best +
                                    labChart[a, b, c, d]
```

If we use only rule #3 we get a CFG parser that can be run in $\mathcal{O}(n^3)$. If we use all of the rules we get LCFRS-2 parser with complexity $\mathcal{O}(n^6)$. However, there are interesting subsets of rules in between full LCFRS-2 and CFG. Well-nested LCFRS-2 is one of those subsets. It includes all LCFRS-2 rules except #10, #12, #13 and #14. Well-nested LCFRS-2 still has the same complexity as a full LCFRS-2 because it contains rule #11 that is $\mathcal{O}(n^6)$. If we look at its counts in the Negra treebank we can see that that rule never appears. Therefore we find it also interesting to try well-nested LCFRS-2 without the rare rule. We will refer to it as LCFRS-wn-nr-2. LCFRS-wn-nr-2 can be parsed in $\mathcal{O}(n^5)$. We will not use rule types #1 and #2 in any of the approaches because we handle unary rules in a different way as previously described.

5 Experiments

The parser is implemented in Scala using DyNet (Neubig et al., 2017) and is available on github.[4] Experiments are conducted on German and English discontinuous constituency treebanks. The reported development results are on the German Negra treebank. The test set results, in addition to German Negra, also contain German Tiger treebank (Brants et al., 2004) and English Discontinuous Penn Treebank (DPTB) (Evang and Kallmeyer, 2011). The treebanks were preprocessed using standard practice described in (Maier, 2015) by using the *treetools*[5] package. For evaluation we have used the *discodop*[6] package with the standard settings (van Cranenburgh et al., 2016).

parameter	value
word-embeddings dim.	32
char bi-lstm dim.	100
sentence-level bi-lstm layers	2
sentence-level bi-lstm dim.	200
compression MLP layers	2
compression MLP dim.	200
Adam optimiser lr.	0.001
batch size	1 sentence

Table 2: Hyper-parameters.

The architecture and hyper-parameters of the neural model are chosen to be the same as in (Coavoux and Cohen, 2019) to obtain a relatively fair comparison. That is, we use a combination of character bi-LSTM to embed each word. This embedding is concatenated with the lookup table embedding for each word and passed through a two-layer bi-LSTM that runs over the whole sentence. In case of MLP model we score labels for each span by passing two bi-LSTM vectors at borders of the spans through a two-layer MLP. In the case of the bi-affine model we compress bi-LSTM vectors with a specialised MLP for left and right index, analogous to the specialisation for head and dependent vector in Dozat and Manning (2017), and then score labels through a bi-affine layer.

5.1 What is the right objective function and classification layer?

First we test if our new objective function that *locally* optimises span labelling is better than the

parser		all F1	disc F1
MLP	*margin*	20.75	0.00
bi-affine	*margin*	77.85	32.85
MLP	*local*	82.49	38.62
bi-affine	*local*	**84.16**	**48.83**

Table 3: Comparison on Negra dev set of different objectives and label classifiers.

max-margin approach of Stern et al. (2017) in the context of discontinuous parsing. Table 3 shows the results in which we can see that *local* model gives much better results. This is especially true for the version of the model that as its top layer uses MLP which completely fails when trained with max-margin but gives reasonable results when trained with more stable objective that takes into consideration all possible trees.

Therefore in further experiments we are going to use only the bi-affine version of the model trained with the *local* objective.

5.2 Is restriction to LCFRS-2 a good approach?

A particularly interesting point of reference is the work of Coavoux and Cohen (2019) which also uses span-based scoring, but in transition-based setting. Our model can be seen as a dynamic programming alternative to their parser.

Dynamic programming (i.e. chart parsing) provides us with an exact search mechanism, unlike the approximate greedy search used by Coavoux and Cohen (2019). However, that benefit does not come for free. The development set results shown in Table 4 show that in a comparable setting (same hyper-parameters of the encoder) there are aspects in which each of the chart-based and transition-based approaches has an advantage. Why is that?

One explanation could be that the setting in which two parsers are tested is not *fully* comparable. What we mean by that is that there are algorithmic reasons why the neural architecture cannot be exactly the same. Let us take a constituent with a gap as an example where the left component is a span (a, b) and the right component is (c, d). Coavoux and Cohen (2019) predict the probability of the next transition by encoding the gap constituent with all 4 embeddings together as (a, b, c, d). In our case we had to split the decision on the label into three independent decisions: the first one that takes (a, b), the second one for (b, c) and the final one for (c, d). This independence as-

parser	all			disc		
	F1	P	R	F1	P	R
Coavoux and Cohen (2019)	84.00	—	—	**54.00**	—	—
CFG	82.86	84.50	81.29	—	—	—
LCFRS-wn-nr-2	83.99	85.21	82.80	45.04	66.24	34.12
LCFRS-wn-2	83.99	85.21	82.80	45.04	66.24	34.12
LCFRS-2	**84.16**	**85.34**	**83.02**	48.83	**67.21**	**38.34**

Table 4: Development set results on Negra treebank. The column *all* contains the results computed over all constituents, both continuous and discontinuous, while *disc* are results on the discontinuous constituents alone.

sumption is necessary because otherwise we would need to run the MLP layer $\mathcal{O}(n^4)$ times. This is not an issue for Coavoux and Cohen (2019) because they consider only a subset of spans needed in greedy search.

However, we think that the main property that distinguishes these two models is expressive power, i.e. the set of trees that they can generate. While the transition-based parser could generate any discontinuous tree, our chart-based parser can generate only trees that are within the LCFRS-2 formalism. To find evidence for the importance of this property we modified the search to explore the different levels of complexity in between CFG and LCFRS-2 while keeping the exactly same parameters of the neural scoring model. From Table 4 we can see that the higher we get on the complexity hierarchy the better are results on the development set, both for discontinuous constituents and all constituents. In comparison to Coavoux and Cohen (2019), we get better results overall but for discontinuous constituents alone the transition-based parser still has an edge.

parser with	all		disc	
ideal scorer	F1	R	F1	R
CFG	97.53	95.19	—	—
LCFRS-wn-nr-2	99.29	98.60	82.95	70.88
LCFRS-wn-2	99.35	98.71	83.04	71.01
LCFRS-2	99.69	99.39	93.32	87.48

Table 5: Oracle parsing results with an *ideal* scorer that always assigns correct probabilities.

If we look at the results for discontinuous constituents carefully we can see that precision is significantly greater than recall. The reason for this could be that the parser is good when the gold tree is within the reach of the LCFRS-2 formalism, but for discontinuous constituents that is sometimes not the case.

To test the limitations that the formalism puts on our model further we did oracle experiments that would show what would results be if we had an

ideal scoring model that always gives perfect probability 1 to correct span labellings and probability 0 to incorrect ones. The results for the oracle experiments are shown in Table 5. If we compare results over F1 of *all* types of constituents then there is very little difference among the discontinuous formalisms. However, if we evaluate only on the discontinuous constituents, the change in coverage (recall) when we remove the well-nestedness constraint of LCFRS-wn-2 to LCFRS-2 is very large, around 16%.

The recall of 87% for our most expressive formalism LCFRS-2, seem to suggest that if we want further increases in accuracy of chart-based discontinuous constituency parsers we will need more than LCFRS-2 generative power. Furthermore, this more expressive formalism will need to be able to generate trees that are not well-nested.

This is not to be confused with requirements for well-nestedness of *dependencies*. The need for ill-nested dependencies was established in the work of Chen-Main and Joshi (2010). However, grammar formalisms like CCG can model ill-nested dependencies without having ill-nested derivations (Koller and Kuhlmann, 2009). Our statement about the need of increasing fan-out and for allowing ill-nested rules applies only to the prediction of discontinuous constituency structures of the kind found in the Negra treebank.

5.3 Parsing speed

Chart parsers have often been avoided for expressive formalisms like LCFRS because of their high worst-case complexity. Most previous work using them has either constrained sentences to those less than 30 words in length, or used length filtering in combination with heavy pruning (Evang and Kallmeyer, 2011; van Cranenburgh and Bod, 2013; van Cranenburgh et al., 2016; Ruprecht and Denkinger, 2019) it is therefore important to compare our parser with previous approaches not only in accuracy but also in speed.

	parser		DPTB		Tiger		Negra	
			all	disc	all	disc	all	disc
LCFRS	**this work**		90.5	67.1	83.4	53.5	83.6	50.7
	Evang and Kallmeyer (2011)	≤ 25 gold POS	79.0		81.6			
	van Cranenburgh et al. (2016)	≤ 40	87.0				74.8	
	Ruprecht and Denkinger (2019)	≤ 30 gold POS					69.0	
transition-based	Coavoux and Cohen (2019)		90.9	67.3	82.5	55.9	83.2	56.3
	Coavoux et al. (2019)		**91.0**	**71.3**	82.7	55.9	83.2	54.6
	Stanojević and G. Alhama (2017)				77.0			
	Stanojević and G. Alhama (2017)	gold POS			81.6		82.9	
	Maier (2015)	gold POS			74.7	18.8	77.0	19.8
	Coavoux and Crabbé (2017)	gold POS			81.6	49.2	82.2	50.0
conversion	Corro et al. (2017)		89.2					
	Corro et al. (2017)	gold POS	90.1		81.6			
	Versley (2016)				79.5			
	Fernández-González and Martins (2015)				77.3			
	Fernández-González and Gómez-Rodríguez (2020)				**85.3**	**59.1**	**85.4**	**58.8**

Table 6: Test set results.

In theory our parser is certainly an improvement because it runs in $\mathcal{O}(l\,n^4 + n^6)$ while other parsers in the worst-case use $\mathcal{O}(G\,n^6 \log n)$. To test if the same holds in practice we ran the parser on Negra dev set sentences of different length without using any pruning techniques. The results up to length 50 are shown in Figure 2.

The neural component (mostly bi-LSTM) and labelling component (with complexity $\mathcal{O}(l\,n^4)$) are shared across all parsing approaches we have tried. The labelling component, despite its theoretical complexity, has a very small influence on the overall parsing speed even for long sentences.

Stern et al. (2017) state that in their experiments the neural component took most of the time. While in our experience that is true for CFG search, the same conclusion does not hold for LCFRS for sentences longer than 35 words.

Instead, parsing time for long sentences is dominated by the chart parsing component. The well-nested version that excludes the rare rule (LCFRS-wn-nr) is the fastest, as predicted by its complexity of $\mathcal{O}(n^5)$. As we have seen in previous sections, excluding the rare rule #11 does not affect outcome, but it does affect speed significantly.

The more powerful, and accurate, formalism of full LCFRS-2 changes the dynamics of parsing: speed quickly decreases for sentences longer than 30 words. Nevertheless, parsing time stays under 1 second for all sentences under 45 words without any need for pruning. This is significantly faster than speeds reported for all previous chart-based parsers that do not use pruning (see *ddl-cfrs*, *rparse* and *GF* in Figure 4 in Ruprecht and

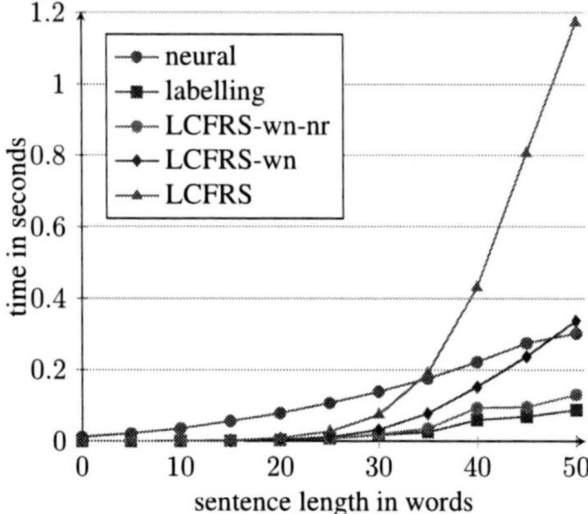

Figure 2: Parsing speed on Negra.

Denkinger (2019)). The only parsers that could compare in speed are heavily pruned versions of *DiscoDOP* (van Cranenburgh and Bod, 2013) and *OP* (Ruprecht and Denkinger, 2019) that get much lower accuracy than our parser (see Table 6).

For sentences longer than 50 words (not visible on the plot) parsing is significantly slower, but it is still tractable. For our test set results we use no pruning up to sentence length 60: for the rare sentences above 60, we use the same model, but with only well-nested parse search.

5.4 Test set results

Test set results for English and German are shown in Table 6. Compared to previous chart-based LCFRS parsers our parser provides the best results on all measures for both English and German.

Compared to transition based parsers, it is competitive over all constituencies, but has slightly lower score on discontinuous constituents alone.

The recent parser by Fernández-González and Gómez-Rodríguez (2020) outperforms both LCFRS and transition-based parsers. It treats discontinuous constituency parsing as a diconstinuous dependency parsing with slightly enriched labels that allow conversion back to the discontinuous constituency structure. However, it is not easy to see how to compare this approach to the ones discussed above.

6   Conclusion

We have presented a span-based LCFRS-2 parser that outperforms all previous LCFRS parsers. It is in addition competitive with the best transition-based parsers, outperforming them in all-constituency evaluation for both German treebanks.

The results from this paper also indicate that the strong generative power of the grammar formalism is correlated with the accuracy. LCFRS-2 power is a great improvement over formalisms that are lower in the complexity hierarchy, but is still inadequate for complete coverage of discontinuity. Our results also show that well-nestedness significantly limiting the coverage that could be achieved even with an ideal scoring model.

Acknowledgments

We thank Maximin Coavoux for providing us access to DPTB dataset. This work was supported by ERC H2020 Advanced Fellowship GA 742137 SEMANTAX grant.

References

Sabine Brants, Stefanie Dipper, Peter Eisenberg, Silvia Hansen-Schirra, Esther König, Wolfgang Lezius, Christian Rohrer, George Smith, and Hans Uszkoreit. 2004. TIGER: Linguistic Interpretation of a German Corpus. *Research on Language and Computation*, 2(4):597–620.

Joan Chen-Main and Aravind K. Joshi. 2010. Unavoidable ill-nestedness in natural language and the adequacy of tree local-MCTAG induced dependency structures. In *Proceedings of the 10th International Workshop on Tree Adjoining Grammar and Related Frameworks (TAG+10)*, pages 53–60, Yale University. Linguistic Department, Yale University.

Maximin Coavoux and Shay B Cohen. 2019. Discontinuous constituency parsing with a stack-free transition system and a dynamic oracle. In *Proceedings of NAACL-HLT*, pages 204–217.

Maximin Coavoux and Benoît Crabbé. 2017. Incremental discontinuous phrase structure parsing with the GAP transition. In *Proceedings of the 15th Conference of the European Chapter of the Association for Computational Linguistics: Volume 1, Long Papers*, pages 1259–1270, Valencia, Spain. Association for Computational Linguistics.

Maximin Coavoux, Benoît Crabbé, and Shay B Cohen. 2019. Unlexicalized transition-based discontinuous constituency parsing. *Transactions of the Association for Computational Linguistics*, 7:73–89.

Caio Corro, Joseph Le Roux, and Mathieu Lacroix. 2017. Efficient discontinuous phrase-structure parsing via the generalized maximum spanning arborescence. In *Proceedings of the 2017 Conference on Empirical Methods in Natural Language Processing*, pages 1644–1654, Copenhagen, Denmark. Association for Computational Linguistics.

Andreas van Cranenburgh and Rens Bod. 2013. Discontinuous parsing with an efficient and accurate dop model. In *Proceedings of The 13th International Conference on Parsing Technologies (IWPT 2013)*, pages 7–16.

Andreas van Cranenburgh, Remko Scha, and Rens Bod. 2016. Data-oriented parsing with discontinuous constituents and function tags. *Journal of Language Modelling*, 4(1):57–111.

James Cross and Liang Huang. 2016. Span-based constituency parsing with a structure-label system and provably optimal dynamic oracles. In *Proceedings of the 2016 Conference on Empirical Methods in Natural Language Processing*, pages 1–11.

Timothy Dozat and Christopher D. Manning. 2017. Deep biaffine attention for neural dependency parsing. In *5th International Conference on Learning Representations, ICLR 2017, Toulon, France, April 24-26, 2017, Conference Track Proceedings*.

Kilian Evang and Laura Kallmeyer. 2011. PLCFRS Parsing of English Discontinuous Constituents. In *Proceedings of the 12th International Conference on Parsing Technologies*, IWPT '11, pages 104–116, Stroudsburg, PA, USA. Association for Computational Linguistics.

Daniel Fernández-González and Carlos Gómez-Rodríguez. 2020. Discontinuous constituent parsing with pointer networks. *arXiv preprint arXiv:2002.01824*.

Daniel Fernández-González and André F. T. Martins. 2015. Parsing as reduction. In *Proceedings of the 53rd Annual Meeting of the Association for Computational Linguistics and the 7th International Joint Conference on Natural Language Processing (Volume 1: Long Papers)*, pages 1523–1533, Beijing, China. Association for Computational Linguistics.

David Gaddy, Mitchell Stern, and Dan Klein. 2018. What's going on in neural constituency parsers? an analysis. In *Proceedings of the 2018 Conference of the North American Chapter of the Association for Computational Linguistics: Human Language Technologies, Volume 1 (Long Papers)*, pages 999–1010.

Carlos Gómez-Rodríguez, Marco Kuhlmann, and Giorgio Satta. 2010. Efficient parsing of well-nested linear context-free rewriting systems. In *Human Language Technologies: The 2010 Annual Conference of the North American Chapter of the Association for Computational Linguistics*, pages 276–284. Association for Computational Linguistics.

Alex Graves, Santiago Fernández, and Jürgen Schmidhuber. 2005. Bidirectional LSTM Networks for Improved Phoneme Classification and Recognition. In *Proceedings of the 15th International Conference on Artificial Neural Networks: Formal Models and Their Applications - Volume Part II*, ICANN'05, pages 799–804, Berlin, Heidelberg. Springer-Verlag.

Sepp Hochreiter and Jürgen Schmidhuber. 1997. Long short-term memory. *Neural Computation*, 9(8).

Aravind K. Joshi. 1985. *Tree adjoining grammars: How much context-sensitivity is required to provide reasonable structural descriptions?*, Studies in Natural Language Processing, page 206–250. Cambridge University Press.

Laura Kallmeyer. 2010. *Parsing Beyond Context-Free Grammars*. Springer, NY.

Laura Kallmeyer. 2013. Linear context-free rewriting systems. *Language and Linguistics Compass*, 7(1):22–38.

Laura Kallmeyer and Wolfgang Maier. 2010. Data-driven parsing with probabilistic linear context-free rewriting systems. In *Proceedings of the 23rd International Conference on Computational Linguistics*, pages 537–545. Association for Computational Linguistics.

Nikita Kitaev and Dan Klein. 2018a. Constituency parsing with a self-attentive encoder. In *Proceedings of the 56th Annual Meeting of the Association for Computational Linguistics (Volume 1: Long Papers)*, pages 2676–2686.

Nikita Kitaev and Dan Klein. 2018b. Multilingual constituency parsing with self-attention and pre-training. *arXiv preprint arXiv:1812.11760*.

Alexander Koller and Marco Kuhlmann. 2009. Dependency Trees and the Strong Generative Capacity of CCG. In *Proceedings of the 12th Conference of the European Chapter of the Association for Computational Linguistics*, EACL '09, pages 460–468, Stroudsburg, PA, USA. Association for Computational Linguistics.

Marco Kuhlmann and Mathias Möhl. 2007. Mildly context-sensitive dependency languages. In *Proceedings of the 45th Annual Meeting of the Association of Computational Linguistics*, pages 160–167, Prague, Czech Republic. Association for Computational Linguistics.

Marco Kuhlmann and Joakim Nivre. 2006. Mildly Non-projective Dependency Structures. In *Proceedings of the COLING/ACL on Main Conference Poster Sessions*, COLING-ACL '06, pages 507–514, Stroudsburg, PA, USA. Association for Computational Linguistics.

Wolfgang Maier. 2015. Discontinuous Incremental Shift-reduce Parsing. In *Proceedings of the 53rd Annual Meeting of the Association for Computational Linguistics and the 7th International Joint Conference on Natural Language Processing (Volume 1: Long Papers)*, pages 1202–1212, Beijing, China. Association for Computational Linguistics.

Wolfgang Maier, Miriam Kaeshammer, and Laura Kallmeyer. 2012. Data-driven PLCFRS parsing revisited: Restricting the fan-out to two. In *Proceedings of the Eleventh International Conference on Tree Adjoining Grammars and Related Formalisms (TAG+11)*, Paris, France.

Wolfgang Maier and Timm Lichte. 2009. Characterizing discontinuity in constituent treebanks. In *International Conference on Formal Grammar*, pages 167–182. Springer.

Mitchell P. Marcus, Beatrice Santorini, and Mary Ann Marcinkiewicz. 1993. Building a large annotated corpus of English: The Penn Treebank. *Computational Linguistics*, 19(2):313–330.

David McAllester. 2002. On the complexity analysis of static analyses. *J. ACM*, 49(4):512–537.

Mark-Jan Nederhof. 2003. Weighted deductive parsing and knuth's algorithm. *Computational Linguistics*, 29(1):135–143.

Graham Neubig, Chris Dyer, Yoav Goldberg, Austin Matthews, Waleed Ammar, Antonios Anastasopoulos, Miguel Ballesteros, David Chiang, Daniel Clothiaux, Trevor Cohn, Kevin Duh, Manaal Faruqui, Cynthia Gan, Dan Garrette, Yangfeng Ji, Lingpeng Kong, Adhiguna Kuncoro, Gaurav Kumar, Chaitanya Malaviya, Paul Michel, Yusuke Oda, Matthew Richardson, Naomi Saphra, Swabha Swayamdipta, and Pengcheng Yin. 2017. Dynet: The dynamic neural network toolkit. *arXiv preprint arXiv:1701.03980*.

Joakim Nivre, Marie-Catherine De Marneffe, Filip Ginter, Yoav Goldberg, Jan Hajic, Christopher D Manning, Ryan McDonald, Slav Petrov, Sampo Pyysalo, Natalia Silveira, et al. 2016. Universal dependencies v1: A multilingual treebank collection. In *Proceedings of the Tenth International Conference on Language Resources and Evaluation (LREC'16)*, pages 1659–1666.

Thomas Ruprecht and Tobias Denkinger. 2019. Implementation of a chomsky-schützenberger n-best parser for weighted multiple context-free grammars. In *Proceedings of the 2019 Conference of the North American Chapter of the Association for Computational Linguistics: Human Language Technologies, Volume 1 (Long and Short Papers)*, pages 178–191.

Hiroyuki Seki, Takashi Matsumura, Mamoru Fujii, and Tadao Kasami. 1991. On multiple context-free grammars. *Theoretical Computer Science*, 88(2):191–229.

Stuart M Shieber, Yves Schabes, and Fernando CN Pereira. 1995. Principles and implementation of deductive parsing. *The Journal of logic programming*, 24(1-2):3–36.

Miloš Stanojević and Raquel G. Alhama. 2017. Neural discontinuous constituency parsing. In *Proceedings of the 2017 Conference on Empirical Methods in Natural Language Processing, EMNLP 2017, Copenhagen, Denmark, September 9-11, 2017.*

Mitchell Stern, Jacob Andreas, and Dan Klein. 2017. A minimal span-based neural constituency parser. In *Proceedings of the 55th Annual Meeting of the Association for Computational Linguistics (Volume 1: Long Papers)*, volume 1, pages 818–827.

Ben Taskar, Carlos Guestrin, and Daphne Koller. 2004a. Max-margin markov networks. In *Advances in neural information processing systems*, pages 25–32.

Ben Taskar, Dan Klein, Mike Collins, Daphne Koller, and Christopher Manning. 2004b. Max-margin parsing. In *Proceedings of the 2004 Conference on Empirical Methods in Natural Language Processing*, pages 1–8.

Yannick Versley. 2016. Discontinuity re^2-visited: A minimalist approach to pseudoprojective constituent parsing. In *Proceedings of the Workshop on Discontinuous Structures in Natural Language Processing*, pages 58–69, San Diego, California. Association for Computational Linguistics.

Krishnamurti Vijay-Shanker, David J Weir, and Aravind K Joshi. 1987. Characterizing structural descriptions produced by various grammatical formalisms. In *Proceedings of the 25th annual meeting on Association for Computational Linguistics*, pages 104–111. Association for Computational Linguistics.

Analysis of the Penn Korean Universal Dependency Treebank (PKT-UD): Manual Revision to Build Robust Parsing Model in Korean

Tae Hwan Oh♠, Ji Yoon Han♠, Hyonsu Choe♠, Seokwon Park♠, Han He,◇
Jinho D. Choi◇, Na-Rae Han♣, Jena D. Hwang♡, Hansaem Kim♠

♠Yonsei University, Seoul, South Korea
◇Emory University, Atlanta GA 30322, USA
♣University of Pittsburgh, Pittsburgh PA 15260, USA
♡Allen Institute For Artificial Intelligence, Seattle WA 98103, USA

{ghks10604,clinamen35,choehyonsu,pswon27}@yonsei.ac.kr, han.he@emory.edu
jinho.choi@emory.edu, naraehan@pitt.edu, jenah@allenai.org, khss@yonsei.ac.kr

Abstract

In this paper, we first open on important issues regarding the Penn Korean Universal Treebank (PKT-UD) and address these issues by revising the entire corpus manually with the aim of producing cleaner UD annotations that are more faithful to Korean grammar. For compatibility to the rest of UD corpora, we follow the UDv2 guidelines, and extensively revise the part-of-speech tags and the dependency relations to reflect morphological features and flexible word-order aspects in Korean. The original and the revised versions of PKT-UD are experimented with transformer-based parsing models using biaffine attention. The parsing model trained on the revised corpus shows a significant improvement of 3.0% in labeled attachment score over the model trained on the previous corpus. Our error analysis demonstrates that this revision allows the parsing model to learn relations more robustly, reducing several critical errors that used to be made by the previous model.

1 Introduction

In 2018, Chun et al. (2018) published on three dependency treebanks in Korean that followed the latest guidelines from the Universal Dependencies (UD) project, that was UDv2. These treebanks were automatically derived from the existing treebanks, the Penn Korean Treebank (PKT; Han et al. 2001), the Google UD Treebank (McDonald et al., 2013), and the KAIST Treebank (Choi et al., 1994), using head-finding rules and heuristics.

This paper first addresses the known issues in the original Penn Korean UD Treebank, henceforth PKT-UD v2018, through a sampling-based analysis (Section 3), and then describes the revised guidelines for both part-of-speech tags and dependency relations to handle those issues (Section 4). Then, a transformer-based dependency parsing approach using biaffine attention is introduced (Section 5) to

experiment on both PKT-UD v2018 and the revised version, henceforth PKT-UD v2020 (Section 6). Our analysis shows a significantly reduced number of mispredicted labels by the parsing model developed on PKT-UD v2020 compared to the one developed on PKT-UD v2018, confirming the benefit of this revision in parsing performance. The contributions of this work are as follows:

1. Issue checking in PKT-UD v2018.

2. Revised annotation guidelines for Korean and the release of the new corpus, PKT-UD v2020.

3. Development of a robust dependency parsing model using the latest transformer encoder.

2 Related Works

2.1 Korean UD Corpora

According to the UD project website,[1] three Korean treebanks are officially registered and released: the Google Korean UD Treebank (McDonald et al., 2013), the Kaist UD Treebank (Choi et al., 1994), and the Parallel Universal Dependencies Treebank (Zeman et al., 2017). These treebanks were created by converting and modifying the previously existing treebanks. The Korean portion of the Google UD Treebank had been re-tokenized into the morpheme level in accordance with other Korean corpora, and systematically corrected for several errors (Chun et al., 2018). The Kaist Korean UD Treebank was derived by automatic conversion using head-finding rules and linguistic heuristics (Chun et al., 2018). The Parallel Universal Dependencies Treebank was designed for the CoNLL 2017 shared task on Multilingual Parsing, consisting of 1K sentences extracted from newswires and Wikipedia articles.

The Penn Korean UD Treebank and the Sejong UD Treebank were registered on the UD website

---

[1]https://universaldependencies.org

Proceedings of the 16th International Conference on Parsing Technologies and the IWPT 2020 Shared Task, pages 122–131
Virtual Meeting, July 9, 2020. ©2020 Association for Computational Linguistics

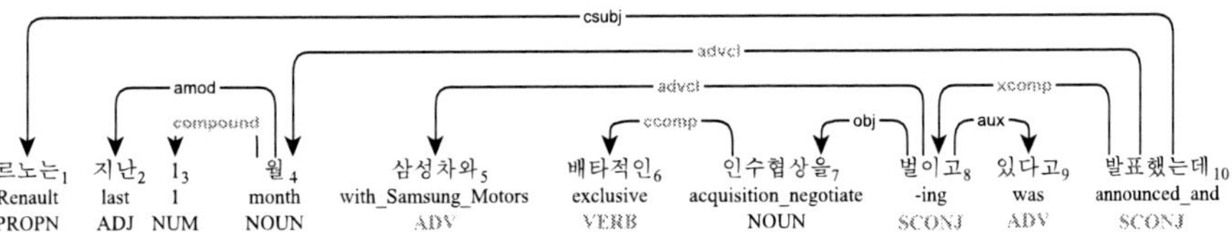

(a) Example from v2018 where the labels in revision are indicated by the red bold font.

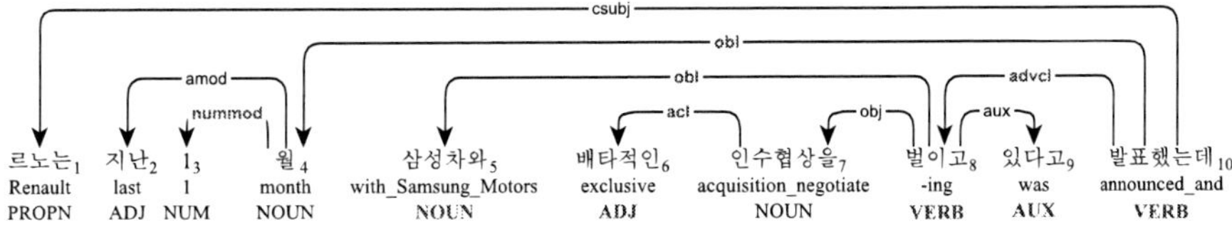

(b) Example from v2020 where the revised labels are indicated by the blue bold font.

Figure 1: Example from v2018 and v2020, that translates to *"Renault announced last January that it was negotiating an exclusive acquisition with Samsung Motors, and ..."*. This example continues in Figure 2.

as well but unreleased due to their license issues. Similar to the Kaist UD Treebank, the Penn Korean UD Treebank[2] was automatically converted into UD structures from phrase structure trees (Chun et al., 2018). The Sejong UD Treebank was also automatically converted from the Sejong Corpus, a phrase structure Treebank consisting of 60K sentences from 6 genres (Choi and Palmer, 2011).

Treebank	GKT	KTB	PUD	PKT	Sejong
Sentences	6k	27k	1k	5k	60k
Tokens	80k	350k	16k	132k	825k
Released	O	O	O	X	X
Unit	Eojeol	Eojeol	Eojeol	Eojeol	Eojeol
Genre	Blog, News	Litr, News, Acdm, Mscr	Blog, News	News	Litr, News, Acdm, Mscr

Table 1: Korean UD Treebanks. Each abbreviations indicate genres of source texts: webblogs(Blog), newswire(News), literatures(Litr), academic(Acdm), manuscripts(Mscr).

In a related effort, the Electronic and Telecommunication Research Institute (ETRI) in Korea conducted a research on standardizing dependency relations and structures (Lim et al., 2015). This effort resulted in the establishment of standard annotation guidelines of Korean dependencies, giving rise to various related efforts that focused on the establishment of Korean UD guidelines that better represent the unique Korean linguistic features. These studies include Park et al. (2018) who focused on the mapping between the UD part-of-speech (POS) tags

and the POS tags in the Sejong Treebank, and Lee et al. (2019) and Oh (2019) who provided in-depth discussions of applicability and relevance of UD's dependency relation to Korean.

2.2 Penn Korean UD Treebank

As mentioned in Section 2.1, the Penn Korean UD Treebank (PKT-UD v2018) was automatically derived from phrase-structure based the Penn Korean Treebank and the results were published by Chun et al. (2018). Even so, it currently does not number among the Korean UD treebanks officially released corpora under the UD project website.

Our effort to officially release Chun et al. (2018)'s PKT-UD v2018 has uncovered numerous mechanical errors caused by the automatic conversion and few other unaddressed issues, leading us to a full revision of this corpus. PKT-UD v2018 made targeted attempts at addressing a number of language-specific issues regarding complex structures such as empty categories, coordination structures, and allocation of POS tags with respect to dependency relations. However, the efforts were limited, leaving other issues such as handling of copulas, proper allocation of verbs according to their verbal endings, and grammaticalized multi-word expressions were unanswered. Thus, this paper aims to address those remaining issues while revising PKT-UD v2018 to clearly represent phenomena in Korean.

3 Observations in PKT-UD v2018

The Penn Korean Treebank (PKT) was originally published as a phrase-structure based treebank by Han et al. (2001). PKT consists of 5,010 sentences

---

[2]The annotation with the word-forms of the Penn Korean UD Treebank can be found here: https://github.com/emorynlp/ud-korean.

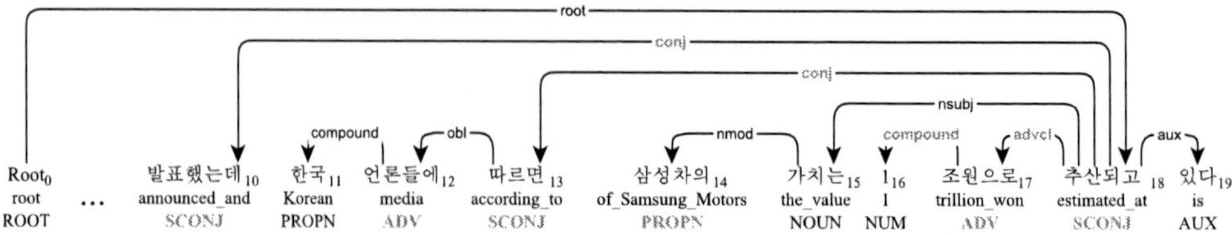

(a) Example from v2018 where the labels in revision are indicated by the red bold font.

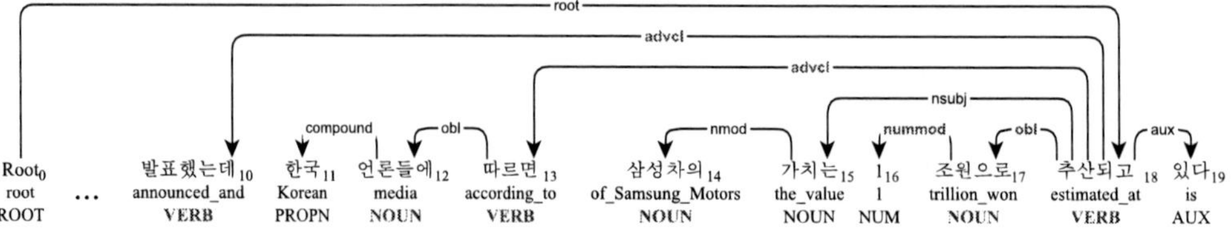

(b) Example from v2020 where the revised labels are indicated by the blue bold font.

Figure 2: Continuing example from Figure 1 that translates to "*... announced ..., and according to Korean media, the value of Samsung Motors is estimated at 1 trillion won*".

from Korean newswire including 132,041 tokens.[3] Following the UDv2 guidelines, Chun et al. (2018) systematically converted PKT to PKT-UD v2018. While this effort achieved a measure of success at providing phrase-structure-to-dependency conversion in a manner consistent across three different treebanks with distinct grammatical frameworks, it stopped short of addressing more nuanced issues that arise from aligning grammatical features of Korean, that is a heavily agglutinative language, to the universal standards put forth by UDv2. In building PKT-UD v2018, the POS tags were largely mapped in a categorical manner from the Penn Korean POS tagset. The dependency relations on the other hand were established via head-finding rules that relied on Penn Korean Treebank's existing function tags, phrasal tags, and morphemes.

Chun et al. (2018) did make a few targeted attempts at teasing apart more fine-grained nuances of grammatical functions. For example, the PKT POS tag (XPOS) *DAN* was subdivided into the UD POS tag (UPOS) DET for demonstrative prenominals (e.g., 이 (*this*), 그 (*the*), and the UPOS ADJ for attributive adjectives (e.g., 새 (*new*), 헌 (*old*)) in the recognition that the XPOS *DAN*, focusing primarily on grammatical distribution, conflated two semantically distinct elements. However, such efforts were limited in scope, and the project did not examine the full breadth of language-specific issues.

Moreover, the converted annotation was found

to contain a share of mechanical errors. A case in point, what should have been 5,010 sentences were found to contain 5,036 roots, suggesting low-level parsing errors. Additionally, a manual examination of the first five sentences in the corpus uncovered a variety of syntactic errors that raised an alarm. The worst of the five examined sentences is shown in Figure 1 (and continued in Figure 2) with errors in both the UPOS and the dependency relation labels (DEPREL). While we will not delve into particulars of each error seen in this example, the example provides a general sense for the extent of errors existent that merited our attention.

These observed issues inspired us to revise PKT-UD v2018, with the aim of producing cleaner syntactic annotations that would be more faithful to the Korean grammar. The following section provides specifics of the revision content.

4 PKT-UD Revisions

4.1 UPOS Revision

Revision of the UPOS portion of the resource was done from the ground up. That is, instead of correcting PKT-UD v2018's UPOS annotations, we implemented a new mapping from XPOS to UPOS after a careful re-examination of the original mapping schema. In particular, we consulted the POS mapping guidelines by Park et al. (2018) whose morphological tagset, carried over from the Sejong Project (Kim, 2006), differs from PKT's in some key aspects. However, we found their nuanced view of grammatical characteristics and typology of Korean in reference to the UDv2 very much applicable.

---

[3]While most Korean resources have what is known as *Eojeol* representing a token and white space is used as delimiter, PTK tokenizes apart symbols, punctuation and even occasional morphemes where strictly required by syntactic structure.

The followings illustrate key ideas of of our UPOS revision approach. Below and throughout this paper, we italicize XPOS labels (e.g., *DAN*) so they are visually distinct from UPOS labels (e.g., ADJ).

Copulas mapped to ADJ   One major target of revision was the scope of the UPOS adjective label ADJ in Korean, which includes typical predicative adjectives such as '예쁘-' (*pretty*) and '다르-' (*different*). As mentioned in Section 3, PKT-UD v2018 already extended the ADJ label to include the closed class of adjectives whose distribution is limited to pre-nominal, attributive use which had been grouped together with the determiner category *DAN* in the original PKT. In our current work, we further extend the ADJ label to encompass the copula: *CO* ('-이-' (*be*)). In Korean, '-이-' (*be*) is a copula particle that attaches to a nominal to produce a predicate, much like the English '*be*'. However, such copula-derived predicates in Korean are known to share semantic and syntactic traits with adjectives rather than verbs, chief among which being their inability to take on the present/habitual aspect verbal ending '-는다' (*do*) which is only allowed on verbs. In light of this, we made a decision to map all instances of XPOS' *CO* to UPOS' ADJ.

Consistent NOUN focusing on morpheme roles   Korean is well-known as an agglutinative language, and *Josa*s (postpositions) are extremely common nominal suffixes that can indicate a variety of syntactic roles of the whole Eojeol unit (Figure 3). For example, when an adverbial case particle ('에', *PAD*) attaches to a noun, the resulting Eojeol serves the syntactic role of an adverb. When a conjunctive particle ('와', *PCJ*) is used, the Eojeol functions as a noun conjunct. Consequently, PKT-UD v2018 mapped ADV to the former and CCONJ to the latter.

학교   학교+에   학교+와
hakkyo   *hakkyo+**PAD***   *hakkyo+**PCJ***
(*school*)   (**at** *school*)   (*school **and***)

Figure 3: Korean postpositions, marked in bold.

However, this distinction underscores a syntactic role rather than a morphological one: while the syntactic role changes with the attachment of the postposition, the POS of the noun itself remains unaffected. UPOS, as a marker that solely demonstrates morphological characteristics of Eojeol rather than its syntactic function, should reflect the morphological status of the nominal. Therefore, we made a decision to allocate the NOUN label to these cases.

Verbal endings signal VERB   Korean has verbal endings on predicates that dictate the syntactic role of Eojeol (Figure 4). In PKT-UD v2018, predicates marked with *ENM* (nominalization verbal ending) and *ECS* (conjunctive ending) are mapped to NOUN and SCONJ, respectively. However, as with the earlier case involving nominals, these verbal ending suffixes should not be treated as fundamentally altering the underlying POS of the predicate itself. This work revises both cases of UPOS to VERB. Extending the same principle, parallel cases with the same verbal endings involving an adjective or a copula were likewise re-assigned to ADJ.

먹+다   먹+기   먹+고
mek+ta   *mek+ki*   *mek+ko*
(*Eat*)   (*Eating*)   (*Eat **and***)

Figure 4: Korean verbal endings, marked in bold.

Statistics of v2018 and v2020   The complete distributions of PKT-UD v2018 and v2020 are listed in Table 2.

UPOS	v2018	v2020	PC
ADJ	3,431	7,034	105.0 ↑
ADP	1,251	1,425	13.9 ↑
ADV	15,174	2,851	81.2 ↓
AUX	2,263	4,060	79.4 ↑
CCONJ	2,453	377	84.6 ↓
DET	685	685	0.0
NOUN	46,866	58,367	24.5 ↑
NUM	7,931	7,602	4.1 ↓
PART	464	290	37.5 ↓
PRON	857	1,142	33.3 ↑
PROPN	12,257	12,769	4.2 ↑
PUNCT	13,428	13,428	0.0
SCONJ	9,780	533	94.6 ↓
SYM	376	376	0.0
VERB	13,855	21,102	52.3 ↑
X	970	0	100.0 ↓
Total	132,041	132,041	0.0

Table 2: Universal POS tagset comparison between the 2018 and 2020 versions of the Penn Universal Dependency Treebank. v2018/v2020: the number of tokens in those versions respectively, PC: percentage change.

4.2   DEPREL Revision

In re-examining PTK-UD v2018's dependency relations, we consulted two existing dependency annotation guidelines for Korean: Lee et al. (2019)

and Oh (2019). They offer a thorough analysis on applicability of the universal dependency relation labels to Korean, and further identify a list of dependency relations such as `iobj`, `xcomp`, `expl`, and `cop` (among others) as not suited for capturing characteristics of Korean grammar. Additionally, where applicable, we took into consideration the UD Japanese Treebank (Asahara et al., 2018), since Japanese exhibits many parallel syntactic phenomena as another strictly head-final agglutinative language (Kanayama et al., 2018).

Reevaluation of `iobj` We turned our attention to `iobj`, the DEPREL label for indirect object. We found PKT-UD v2018's decision to assign nominals with dative case markings to `iobj` questionable, for the following reasons. First, unlike English, where word order distinguishes indirect objects from direct objects (e.g. "She gave me:`iobj` a box:`obj`"), Korean has no such structural constraint that forms the basis for identifying instances of `iobj`. The only potential identifier, then, is dative postpositions such as '-에게'(*to*) and '-한테'(*by*), which correspond roughly to English preposition '*to*' as in "She gave it *to* me". The problem is, these markers do not exclusively encode the dative case, as seen in examples such as "개에게 물렸다" ("*I was bit by a dog*").

Hence, we adopted a new approach of reassigning all instances of `iobj` to the oblique relation `obl`. This move brings language-internal consistency, as postpositions, in many instances, can simply be dropped if contextually recoverable, rendering any such nominals practically indistinguishable from other nominal adverbials that are assigned to `obl`. This overall approach is also in line with UD Japanese Treebank, where `iobj` is categorically absent and 'に (*ni*)', a postposition whose usage largely parallels the two Korean postpositions above, mapping to `obl`.

Standardizing verbal predicates As shown in Figure 5, Korean predicates take on various syntactic functions depending on the attached verbal ending. Predicates with the declarative verbal ending '-다' (*ta*) are assigned to `root`, which is straightforward. Endings '-은' (*un*) and '-을' (*ul*) on the other hand turn the verb into a modifier to an upcoming noun; the `acl` relation therefore is the best fit here. Predicates with endings such as '-어서' (*ese*) and '-게' (*key*) modify other predicates, which calls for an `advcl` assignment. In PKT-UD

v2018, these cases had received an array of inconsistent allocations such as clausal complements (`ccomp`/`xcomp`), auxiliaries (`aux`), and conjuncts (`conj`). These were corrected to `acl` and `advcl`.

먹+다	먹+은/을	먹+어서
mek-ta	*mek-un/ul*	*mek-ese*
(*eat*)	(*ate/to-eat*)	(*eat because*)

Figure 5: Examples of Korean verbal ending.

Orphaned postpositions and verbal endings In Korean, verbal endings and postpositions are bound to verbs and nominals, respectively, and cannot occupy their own Eojeol. In natural text, however, they can occasionally be separated from the constituent they attach to via quotation marks, white spaces, or parentheses. PKT-UD v2018 had assigned such orphaned bound morphemes to UPOS of `PART` (particle) and `ADP` (adposition) with the DEPREL of `mark` (marker) and `case` (case marker), respectively as seen in Figure 6.

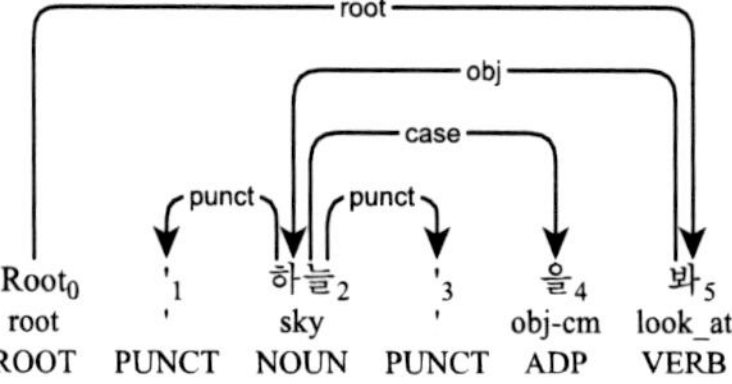

Figure 6: PKT-UD v2018 treatment of separated postposition '-을' (*ul*) in "'하늘'을 봐 (Look at the 'sky')".

However, verbal endings and postpositions can express syntactic function only if they are attached to their modifying predicates and nominals. While PKT-UD v2018's assignment of the UPOS and DEPREL are not categorically incorrect, they address morphological relationship between these morphemes rather than their syntactic relationship. That is, even if these bound morphemes are notationally distanced from their heads by punctuation or white spaces, they form a single syntactic unit with their nominals and postpositions. Hence, `mark` and `case` were updated to `goeswith`, used for divided words as seen in Figure 7, making it clear that the seemingly separate Eojeols (e.g. nominal and postposition) are actually one unit.

Orphaned copulas Similar revisions were applied to copulas. Korean copula morpheme '-이-' (*i*) combines with a nominal on the left and a verbal ending to the right. These copulas too can occasionally be detached via intervening punctuation or white space. To such cases, PKT-UD v2018 had assigned `cop` as the DEPREL. These instances have been updated to `goeswith` in accordance with the treatment given to verbal endings and postpostions.

`roots` and `flats` The number of `root` is adjusted from 5,036 to 5,010 after correcting sentences with zero or more roots. Additionally, DEPREL of Eojeols that used to be incorrectly mapped to `compound` are now assigned to `flat`.

Statistics of v2018 and v2020 The complete DEPREL distributions of PKT-UD v2018 and v2020 are listed in Table 3.

DEPREL	v2018	v2020	PC
acl	1,488	11,210	653.4 ↑
advcl	11,636	5,086	56.3 ↓
advmod	2,964	3,125	5.4 ↑
amod	1,595	1,593	0.1 ↓
appos	1,182	1,173	0.8 ↓
aux	4,807	4,061	15.5 ↓
case	1,548	0	100.0 ↓
ccomp	9,858	1,989	79.8 ↓
cc	785	473	39.7 ↓
compound	28,908	21,433	25.9 ↓
conj	9,960	7,155	28.2 ↓
cop	418	0	100.0 ↓
csubj	8,014	8,012	0.0 ↓
dep	609	10	98.4 ↓
det	685	685	0.0
fixed	528	589	11.6 ↑
flat	18	739	4,005.6 ↑
goeswith	0	2,199	100.0 ↑
iobj	222	0	100.0 ↓
mark	1,003	0	100.0 ↓
nmod	5,555	5,501	1.0 ↓
nsubj	4,012	4,114	2.5 ↑
nummod	154	7,341	4,666.9 ↑
obj	9,823	9,849	0.3 ↑
obl	3,357	16,891	403.2 ↑
orphan	0	9	100.0 ↑
punct	13,073	13,794	5.5 ↑
root	5,036	5,010	0.5 ↓
xcomp	4,803	0	100.0 ↓
Total	132,041	132,041	0.0

Table 3: Universal dependency label comparison between v2018 and v2020 of the Penn Universal Dependency Treebank. v2018/v2020: the number of tokens in those versions respectively, PC: percentage change.

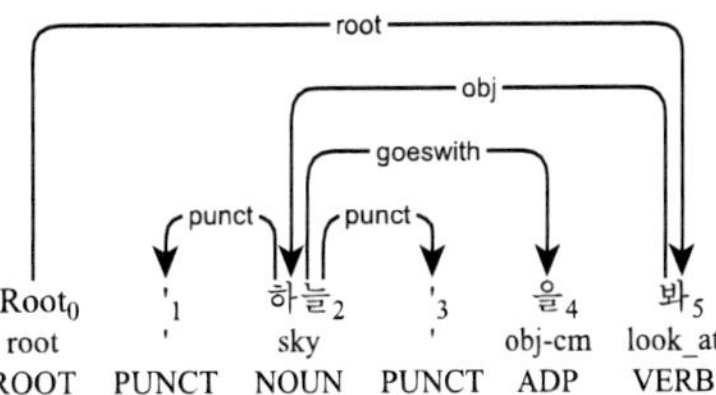

Figure 7: Revision of the DEPREL of the separated postposition 을 at "'하늘'을 봐 (Look at the 'sky')" in PKT-UD v2020, where `case` relation for orphaned postposition revised to `goeswith`.

5 Parsing Approach

Our dependency parsing model is based on the biaffine parser using contextualized embeddings such as BERT (Devlin et al., 2019) that has shown the state-of-the-art results on both syntactic and semantic dependency parsing tasks in multiple languages (He and Choi, 2020). This model is simplified from the original biaffine parser introduced by Dozat and Manning (2017) such that trainable token embeddings are removed and lemmas are used instead of word forms. This section proposes an even more simplified model that no longer uses embeddings from POS tags, so it can be easily adapted to languages that do not have dedicated POS taggers, and drops the Bidirectional LSTM encoder while integrating the transformer layers directly into the biaffine decoder so that it minimizes the redundancy of having multiple encoders for the generation of contextualized embeddings.

Given an input sentence, every token w_i is first segmented into one or more sub-tokens by the SentencePiece tokenizer (Kudo and Richardson, 2018) and fed into a transformer. The output embedding corresponding to the first sub-token of w_i is treated as the embedding representation of w_i, say $\mathbf{e}_i$, and fed into four types of multilayer perceptron (MLP) layers to extract features for w_i being a head (*-h) or a dependent (*-d) for the arc relations (arc-*) and the labels (rel-*) (k and l are the dimensions of the arc and label representations, respectively):

$$\mathbf{h}_i^{\text{(arc-h)}} = \text{MLP}^{\text{(arc-h)}}(\mathbf{e}_i) \in \mathbb{R}^{k \times 1}$$
$$\mathbf{h}_i^{\text{(arc-d)}} = \text{MLP}^{\text{(arc-d)}}(\mathbf{e}_i) \in \mathbb{R}^{k \times 1}$$
$$\mathbf{h}_i^{\text{(rel-h)}} = \text{MLP}^{\text{(rel-h)}}(\mathbf{e}_i) \in \mathbb{R}^{l \times 1}$$
$$\mathbf{h}_i^{\text{(rel-d)}} = \text{MLP}^{\text{(rel-d)}}(\mathbf{e}_i) \in \mathbb{R}^{l \times 1}$$

All feature vectors, $\mathbf{h}_1^*, \ldots, \mathbf{h}_n^*$, from each representation are stacked into a matrix (n is the number

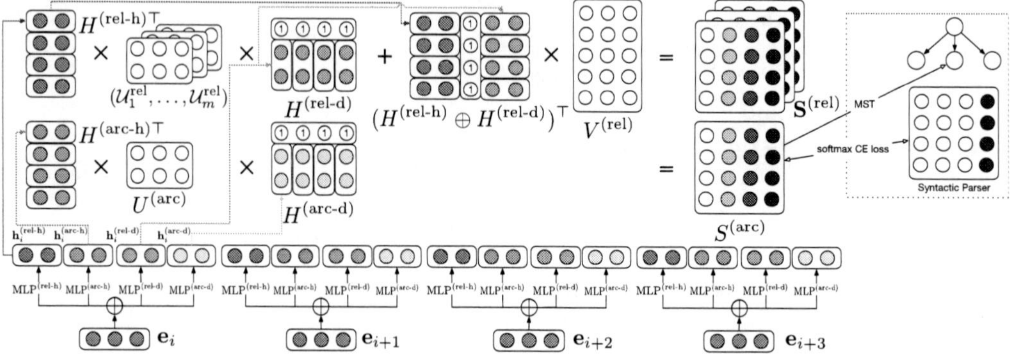

Figure 8: The overview of our transformer-based biaffine dependency parsing model.

of tokens in a sentence); these matrices together are used to predict dependency relations among every token pairs. Note that bias terms are appended to the feature vectors $\mathbf{h}_i^{(*\text{-d})}$ that represent dependent nodes to estimate the likelihood of a certain relation given only the head node:

$$H^{(\text{arc-h})} = (\mathbf{h}_1^{(\text{arc-h})}, \ldots, \mathbf{h}_n^{(\text{arc-h})}) \in \mathbb{R}^{k \times n}$$
$$H^{(\text{arc-d})} = (\mathbf{h}_1^{(\text{arc-d})}, \ldots, \mathbf{h}_n^{(\text{arc-d})}) \oplus \mathbf{1} \in \mathbb{R}^{(k+1) \times n}$$
$$H^{(\text{rel-h})} = (\mathbf{h}_1^{(\text{rel-h})}, \ldots, \mathbf{h}_n^{(\text{rel-h})}) \in \mathbb{R}^{l \times n}$$
$$H^{(\text{rel-d})} = (\mathbf{h}_1^{(\text{rel-d})}, \ldots, \mathbf{h}_n^{(\text{rel-d})}) \oplus \mathbf{1} \in \mathbb{R}^{(l+1) \times n}$$

The bilinear and biaffine classifiers are then used for the arc and label predictions respectively, where $U^{(\text{arc})}$, $U_i^{(\text{rel})}$ and $V^{(\text{rel})}$ are trainable parameters, and m is the number of dependency labels. In particular, a separate weight matrix $U_i^{(\text{rel})}$ is dedicated for the prediction of each label:

$$S^{(\text{arc})} = H^{(\text{arc-h})\top} \cdot U^{(\text{arc})} \cdot H^{(\text{arc-d})} \in \mathbb{R}^{n \times n}$$
$$\mathcal{U}_i^{(\text{rel})} = H^{(\text{rel-h})\top} \cdot U_i^{(\text{rel})} \cdot H^{(\text{rel-d})} \in \mathbb{R}^{n \times n}$$
$$\mathbf{S}^{(\text{rel})} = (\mathcal{U}_1^{(\text{rel})}, \ldots, \mathcal{U}_m^{(\text{rel})})$$
$$+ (H^{(\text{rel-h})} \oplus H^{(\text{rel-d})})^\top \cdot V^{(\text{rel})} \in \mathbb{R}^{m \times n \times n}$$

Once the arc score matrix $S^{(\text{arc})}$ and the label score tensor $\mathbf{S}^{(\text{rel})}$ are generated by those classifiers, the Chu-Liu-Edmond's maximum spanning tree (MST) algorithm is applied to $S^{(\text{arc})}$ for the arc prediction, then the label with largest score in $\mathbf{S}^{(\text{rel})}$ corresponding to the arc is taken for the label prediction:

$$arc = \text{MST}(S^{(\text{arc})})$$
$$label = \text{argmax}(\mathbf{S}^{(\text{rel})}[\text{index}(arc)])$$

6 Experiments

To extrinsically assess the quality of our revision, parsing models are separately developed on PKT-UD v2018 and v2020; in other words, v2018 models are trained and evaluated on PKT-UD v2018 whereas v2020 models are trained and evaluated on PKT-UD v2020. The transformer-based parsing approach in Section 5 is used to develop all models. For each version of the corpus, three models are developed by initializing neural weights with different random seeds and the average accuracy and its standard deviation is reported for each version. The entire corpus is divided into the training (TRN), development (DEV), and evaluation (TST) sets by following the 80/10/10% split (Table 4).

	TRN	DEV	TST
# of Sentences	4,010	501	500
# of Tokens	105,947	13,088	13,023

Table 4: Statistics of the data split.

The multilingual BERT[4] is used as the transformer encoder in our parsing models (Devlin et al., 2019). All models are optimized by the sum of softmax cross-entropy losses on the gold dependency heads and labels. AdamW (Loshchilov and Hutter, 2019) is used as the optimizer with the learning rate of 5e-06 for the BERT weights and 5e-05 for the rest. The learning rate is scheduled as a combination of both linear warm-up and decay phases. The models are trained for 100 epochs with a batch size of 150. Following the standard practice, we evaluate our best models with the unicode punctuation ignored using the unlabeled attachment score (UAS) and the labeled attachment score (LAS).

[4] https://github.com/google-research/bert/blob/master/multilingual.md

128

Table 5 shows the results achieved by the v2018 and v2020 models. The v2020 model shows a significantly improvement of 3.0% in LAS over the v2018 model. This makes sense because the major parts of the revision are dedicated to DEPREL consistency, yielding more robust parsing performance in labeling. The v2020 model also gives a good improvement of 0.6% in finding dependency arcs. The improved parsing results ensure the higher quality annotation in PKT-UD v2020 that is encouraging.

	UAS	LAS
v2018	90.7 (±0.2)	86.0 (±0.1)
v2020	**91.3** (±0.1)	**89.0** (±0.1)

Table 5: Results by the v2018 and v2020 models.

7 Error analysis

PKT-UD v2018 We perform an error analysis on the parsing outputs generated by the v2018 model. Our analysis shows that the head error occurred in 1,360 Eojeols and the label error occurred in 4,292 Eojeols. Table 6 shows the distribution of head and label errors per label based on the revised test set. The relations `advcl`, `nummod`, `acl`, and `obl` have a high error rate, which are due to the inconsistencies seen in the data we handled by establishing clear criteria. Moreover, the labels `goeswith` and `flat` saw 100% error, again, due to the errors we observed during the revision process.

DEPREL	Error	Percentage
obl	1,294	30.15%
acl	961	22.39%
nummod	777	18.1%
advcl	462	10.76%
goeswith	203	4.73%
conj	99	2.31%
compound	96	2.24%
flat	91	2.12%
ccomp	77	1.79%
etc	232	5.41%
Total	4,292	100%

Table 6: DEPREL error of PKT-UD v2018.

There is an observable trend in these errors. For example, a number of error cases report `advcl` as `xcomp`, `conj`, or `ccomp` while `nummod` tends to be wrongly parsed to `compound`, `acl` to `ccomp`, and `obl` to `advcl`. Multiple cases of parsing errors due to errors in the UPOS are also found. Incorrect UPOS appears to commit errors while allocating edge and DEPREL. The annotation guideline based on XPOS is already described in Section 4.

PKT-UD v2020 After revising the data according to the criteria presented in Section 4, many improvements have been made. The error rate of `advcl` decreased from 98.93% to 2.36%, the `nummod` also decreased significantly from 97.37% to 0.5%, and the `acl` error from 86.73% to 0.9%. The error rate of `obl` was also reduced from 79.14% to 5.5%. In addition, the error rate is reduced for `goeswith` and `flat`. In the case of `ccomp`, errors decreased by more than 35% from 44.51% to 8.67%. These results is indicative of the effect of improving training data by ensuring consistency of annotations.

DEPREL	v2018	v2020
obl	1,294	90
acl	961	10
nummod	777	4
advcl	462	11
goeswith	203	3
conj	99	85
compound	96	83
flat	91	34
ccomp	77	15
etc	232	134
Total	4,292	469

Table 7: DEPREL error comparison between PKT-UD v2018 and v2020.

8 Conclusion

In this study, we revise the Penn Korean Universal Dependency Treebank (PKT-UD) and compare parsing performance between models trained on the original and revised versions of PKT. Our new guidelines follow the UDv2 guidelines. UPOS and DEPREL are revised to reflect Korean morphological features and flexible word-order aspects with reference to Korean UD studies such as Park et al. (2018), Lee et al. (2019), and Oh (2019). In UPOS, `ADJ`, `NOUN`, and `VERB` are revised extensively. In DEPREL, `iobj`, `acl`, `advcl`, and `goeswith` are thoroughly revised. The revision results showing the percentage change of each label are presented in Table 2 and Table 3.

As a result of the parsing experiment, the v2020 model improves UAS by 0.6% and LAS by 3.0% over the v2018 model. In particular, `obl`, `acl`, nummod, and advcl errors are significantly reduced. This study, which improves parsing accuracy by applying characteristics of Korean, can also contribute to improve the quality of other Korean UD treebanks. In the future, we will explore the possibility of extending PKT-UD with enhanced dependency types[5] by incorporating empty categories from the original PKT.

References

Masayuki Asahara, Hiroshi Kanayama, Takaaki Tanaka, Yusuke Miyao, Sumire Uematsu, Shinsuke Mori, Yuji Matsumoto, Mai Omura, and Yugo Murawaki. 2018. Universal dependencies version 2 for japanese. In *Proceedings of the Eleventh International Conference on Language Resources and Evaluation (LREC 2018)*.

Jinho D. Choi and Martha Palmer. 2011. Statistical dependency parsing in korean: From corpus generation to automatic parsing. In *Proceedings of the Second Workshop on Statistical Parsing of Morphologically Rich Languages*, pages 1–11. Association for Computational Linguistics.

Key-Sun Choi, Young S Han, Young G Han, and Oh W Kwon. 1994. Kaist tree bank project for korean: Present and future development. In *Proceedings of the International Workshop on Sharable Natural Language Resources*, pages 7–14. Citeseer.

Jayeol Chun, Na-Rae Han, Jena D Hwang, and Jinho D Choi. 2018. Building universal dependency treebanks in korean. In *Proceedings of the Eleventh International Conference on Language Resources and Evaluation (LREC 2018)*.

Jacob Devlin, Ming-Wei Chang, Kenton Lee, and Kristina Toutanova. 2019. BERT: Pre-training of deep bidirectional transformers for language understanding. In *Proceedings of the 2019 Conference of the North American Chapter of the Association for Computational Linguistics: Human Language Technologies, Volume 1 (Long and Short Papers)*, pages 4171–4186, Minneapolis, Minnesota. Association for Computational Linguistics.

Timothy Dozat and Christopher D. Manning. 2017. Deep Biaffine Attention for Neural Dependency Parsing. In *Proceedings of the 5th International Conference on Learning Representations*, ICLR'17.

Chung-hye Han, Na-Rae Han, Eon-Suk Ko, Martha Palmer, and Heejong Yi. 2001. Penn korean treebank: Development and evaluation. In *Proceedings of the 16th Pacific Asia Conference on Language, Information and Computation*, pages 69–78.

Han He and Jinho D. Choi. 2020. Establishing strong baselines for the new decade: Sequence tagging, syntactic and semantic parsing with bert. In *Proceedings of the 33rd International Florida Artificial Intelligence Research Society Conference*, FLAIRS'20.

Hiroshi Kanayama, Na-Rae Han, Masayuki Asahara, Jena D Hwang, Yusuke Miyao, Jinho D Choi, and Yuji Matsumoto. 2018. Coordinate structures in universal dependencies for head-final languages. In *Proceedings of the Second Workshop on Universal Dependencies (UDW 2018)*, pages 75–84.

Hansaem Kim. 2006. Korean national corpus in the 21st century sejong project. In *Proceedings of the 13th NIJL International Symposium*, pages 49–54. National Institute for Japanese Language Tokyo.

Taku Kudo and John Richardson. 2018. SentencePiece: A simple and language independent subword tokenizer and detokenizer for neural text processing. In *Proceedings of the 2018 Conference on Empirical Methods in Natural Language Processing: System Demonstrations*, pages 66–71, Brussels, Belgium. Association for Computational Linguistics.

Chanyoung Lee, Taehwan Oh, and Hansaem Kim. 2019. A study on universal dependency annotation for korean. *Language Fact and Perspectives*, 47(0):1–11.

Joon-Ho Lim, Yongjin Bae, Hyunki Kim, Yunjeong Kim, and Kyu-Chul Lee. 2015. Korean Dependency Guidelines for Dependency Parsing and Exo-Brain Language Analysis Corpus. In *Proceedings of the 27tht Annual Conference on Human and Cognitive Language Technology*.

Ilya Loshchilov and Frank Hutter. 2019. Decoupled weight decay regularization. In *International Conference on Learning Representations*.

Ryan McDonald, Joakim Nivre, Yvonne Quirmbach-Brundage, Yoav Goldberg, Dipanjan Das, Kuzman Ganchev, Keith Hall, Slav Petrov, Hao Zhang, Oscar Täckström, et al. 2013. Universal dependency annotation for multilingual parsing. In *Proceedings of the 51st Annual Meeting of the Association for Computational Linguistics (Volume 2: Short Papers)*, pages 92–97.

Taehwan Oh. 2019. Study on universal dependencies for korean. Master's thesis, Yonsei University, Seoul, Korea.

Hyejin Park, Taehwan Oh, and Hansaem Kim. 2018. Universal pos tagset for korean. *The Korean Society for Language and Information*, 22(3):67–89.

Daniel Zeman, Martin Popel, Milan Straka, Jan Hajič, Joakim Nivre, Filip Ginter, Juhani Luotolahti, Sampo Pyysalo, Slav Petrov, Martin Potthast, Francis Tyers, Elena Badmaeva, Memduh Gokirmak, Anna Nedoluzhko, Silvie Cinková, Jan Hajič jr., Jaroslava Hlaváčová, Václava Kettnerová, Zdeňka

Urešová, Jenna Kanerva, Stina Ojala, Anna Missilä, Christopher D. Manning, Sebastian Schuster, Siva Reddy, Dima Taji, Nizar Habash, Herman Leung, Marie-Catherine de Marneffe, Manuela Sanguinetti, Maria Simi, Hiroshi Kanayama, Valeria de Paiva, Kira Droganova, Héctor Martínez Alonso, Çağrı Çöltekin, Umut Sulubacak, Hans Uszkoreit, Vivien Macketanz, Aljoscha Burchardt, Kim Harris, Katrin Marheinecke, Georg Rehm, Tolga Kayadelen, Mohammed Attia, Ali Elkahky, Zhuoran Yu, Emily Pitler, Saran Lertpradit, Michael Mandl, Jesse Kirchner, Hector Fernandez Alcalde, Jana Strnadová, Esha Banerjee, Ruli Manurung, Antonio Stella, Atsuko Shimada, Sookyoung Kwak, Gustavo Mendonça, Tatiana Lando, Rattima Nitisaroj, and Josie Li. 2017. CoNLL 2017 shared task: Multilingual parsing from raw text to universal dependencies. In *Proceedings of the CoNLL 2017 Shared Task: Multilingual Parsing from Raw Text to Universal Dependencies*, pages 1–19, Vancouver, Canada. Association for Computational Linguistics.

Statistical Deep Parsing for Spanish using Neural Networks

Luis Chiruzzo
Facultad de Ingeniería
Universidad de la República
Montevideo, Uruguay
`luischir@fing.edu.uy`

Dina Wonsever
Facultad de Ingeniería
Universidad de la República
Montevideo, Uruguay
`wonsever@fing.edu.uy`

Abstract

This paper presents the development of a deep parser for Spanish that uses a HPSG grammar and returns trees that contain both syntactic and semantic information. The parsing process uses a top-down approach implemented using LSTM neural networks, and achieves good performance results in terms of syntactic constituency and dependency metrics, and also SRL. We describe the grammar, corpus and implementation of the parser. Our process outperforms a CKY baseline and other Spanish parsers in terms of global metrics and also for some specific Spanish phenomena, such as clitics reduplication and relative referents.

1 Introduction

The syntactic analysis of sentences is one of the key activities within the Natural Language Processing pipeline, and is often seen as a necessary step that must be performed before extracting deeper information such as semantics. Two main paradigms have historically dominated the work on syntactic analysis: constituency parsing, where the sentence is structured as a tree of linguistically motivated segments called constituents; and dependency parsing, where the sentence is structured as a set of bi-lexical dependencies with each word associated to another word that acts as its head.

Throughout the years there have been attempts to create deeper syntactic models that try to combine both syntactic and semantic notions in the same analysis, for example CCG (Steedman, 1996), HPSG (Pollard and Sag, 1994) or TAG (Joshi, 1985). The process of analyzing a sentence in one of these formalisms is often called deep parsing. Over the last years the use of deep neural networks has advanced the state of the art in many NLP tasks, and though some work has been done for performing deep parsing using these architectures (mainly in English and for CCG), few works have

focused on the application of these techniques to other formalisms or other languages. In this work, we present a neural network architecture for deep parsing Spanish sentences using the HPSG formalism.

The rest of the paper is structured as follows: Section 2 describes the grammar and corpus we use. Section 3 introduces our parsing architecture and the baseline we compare it to. Section 4 shows an analysis of results. Section 5 describes relevant related work. Finally, section 6 gives some conclusions and future perspectives.

2 Grammar and Corpus

We use a HPSG style grammar (Pollard and Sag, 1994) adapted to Spanish. HPSG grammars are unification grammars that operate on feature structures. Each word is defined by a feature structure that indicates the combinatorial properties of the word: how it can be combined to other words in order to form phrases. Because of this, these grammars tend to have few rules, which are very generic. When applying a rule, the process of unification validates that both the conditions of the rule and the constraints imposed by the expressions being combined are met, and the resulting phrases inherit some of the features of their children in order to define their own combinatorial properties.

2.1 Feature structure

Our grammar defines morphological, syntactic valence, and semantic role label features, as shown in figure 1. The HEAD feature contains the part-of-speech and the morphological attributes of the word such as number and gender. The VAL feature contains the local syntactic valence features: what are the expected specifier, complements, or modifier that could be associated to the word, and we add a CLITICS feature that is specially important for Spanish as clitic pronouns could act as arguments

Proceedings of the 16th International Conference on Parsing Technologies and the IWPT 2020 Shared Task, pages 132–144
Virtual Meeting, July 9, 2020. ©2020 Association for Computational Linguistics

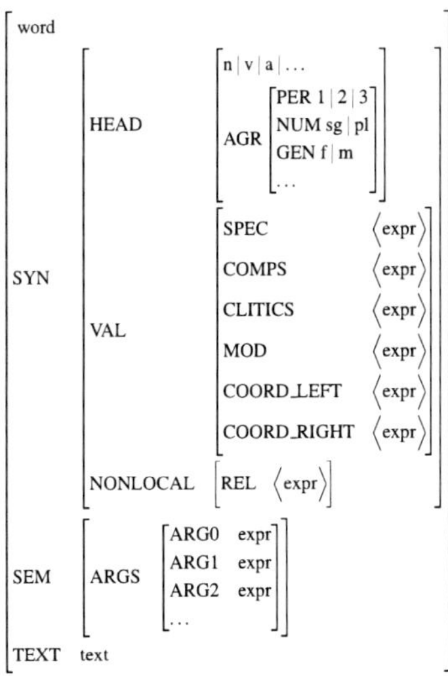

Figure 1: Feature structure for words in our grammar.

of verbs. We also include two features used by conjunctions to guide the analysis of coordinated structures.

In a simplification from the original HPSG theory, the only non-local dependencies modeled in our grammar are the relative clauses that act as modifiers of a noun phrase. This is represented by the REL feature, which allows the grammar to support argument sharing in relative clauses such as *"La manzana que comí" / "The apple I ate"*.

The grammar incorporates semantic features for modeling the semantic role label structure for the sentence. Unlike the way semantics is modeled in standard HPSG (Sag et al., 1999), which uses minimal recursion semantics (Copestake et al., 2005), our approach to semantics uses the simpler Prop-Bank notation (Bonial et al., 2010). The feature SEM includes features derived from PropBank representation: ARG0 for proto-agent, ARG1 for proto-patient, ARGM for modifying adjuncts, etc. Consider, for example, the feature structure for the word *"come" / "eats"* shown in figure 2, which coindexes the syntactic specifier and complement to the corresponding proto-agent and proto-patient semantic arguments.

2.2 Rules

The grammar uses only thirteen combinatorial rules for forming phrases. These rules describe in broad terms how to combine expressions, but the unification process also takes into account the constraints imposed by the expressions as well as the ones

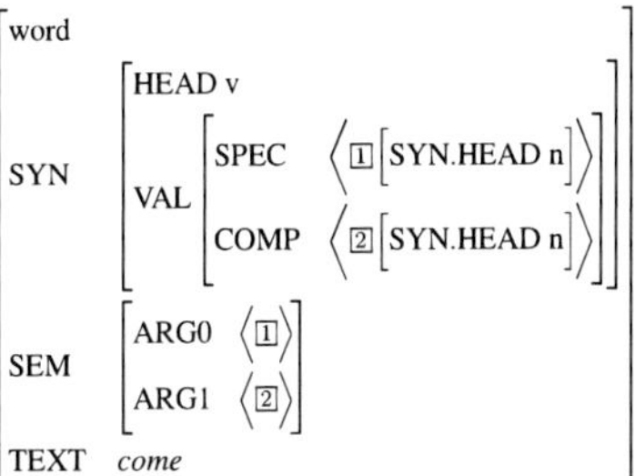

Figure 2: Feature structure for the word *"come" / "eats"*, that expects a noun phrase as specifier (subject) and a noun phrase as complement (direct object), which are also coindexed as proto-agent and proto-patient semantic arguments.

defined in the rules.

For example, consider the `head_comp` rule defined in figure 3. This rule takes the two expressions shown on the left side of the arrow. The left expression (marked as head) expects at least one complement, which is the right expression (shown only as a coindexation box, meaning any expression that unifies with what the left expression expects). The result is the phrase shown on the right side of the arrow: a phrase that will have the same features as the head expression except the COMP feature, which will expect one less complement. This definition is only a description of what this rule does in particular, but the unification process by which the rules are applied will also ensure that the constraints defined within the expressions are held. If we combine the word *"come" / "eats"* as defined in figure 2 with a complement phrase, the rule application will fail (not unify) if the complement is not a noun phrase.

$$(H)\begin{bmatrix}\text{expr}\\ \text{VAL}\ \left[\text{COMP}\ \langle \boxed{1}\ |\ \boxed{2}\rangle\right]\end{bmatrix} + \boxed{1} \rightarrow \begin{bmatrix}\text{phrase}\\ \text{VAL}\ \left[\text{COMP}\ \langle \boxed{2}\rangle\right]\end{bmatrix}$$

Figure 3: Definition of the `head_comp` rule.

All rules in our grammar are binary, and they are designed taking into account that the order of constituents in Spanish is not as strict as in English. For example, even though Spanish is officially an SVO language like English, the sentences *"El tren llegó"* and *"Llegó el tren"* are two equally valid ways of saying *"The train arrived"*, where the second case uses a postponed subject. The thirteen rules in our grammar are the following:

- Two rules for attaching a specifier (or subject) to the left or to the right of a head: `spec_head` and `head_spec`.

- Two rules for attaching a complement to the left or to the right of a head: `comp_head` and `head_comp`.

- One rule for attaching a semantic complement to the right of a head: `head_comp_sem`. This rule is used for building more complex verb phrases such as *"ha ido" / "has gone"* or *"comienza a cantar" / "begins to sing"*.

- Two rules for attaching a modifier to the left or to the right of a head: `mod_head` and `head_mod`.

- One rule for attaching a clitic pronoun to the left of a head: `clitic_head`.

- One rule for attaching a relative clause to the right of a head: `head_rel`.

- Two rules for attaching a punctuation marker to the left or to the right of a head: `punct_head` and `head_punct`.

- Two rules for binarizing coordinated structures: `coord_left` and `coord_right`.

Consider the following sample sentence:

$$[\text{ } \textit{El niño come una manzana roja} \text{ }] \\ (\text{ The boy eats a red apple }) \qquad (1)$$

The parse tree for sentence 1 using our grammar is shown in figure 4. Although the figure shows a simplified version of the tree (with only one expanded node for the main verb and substituting the non-leaf nodes for the name of the applied rule) each node in the tree is a complete feature structure with reentrancies to other parts of the tree that indicate the syntactic and semantic argument structures.

2.3 Composition of the corpus

Our experiments use a corpus of about half a million words annotated with our grammar based on the AnCora (Taulé et al., 2008) Spanish corpus that contains approximately 17,000 sentences labeled with CFG-style syntactic annotations and other information such as the semantic arguments structure. The corpus was transformed semi-automatically into our grammar (Chiruzzo and Wonsever, 2016, 2018). The transformation process involved using

heuristics for identifying heads, binarizing phrases and finding the grammar rules to apply, and reparsing the corpus using unification over feature structures while manually correcting the conversion errors. The training, development and test partitions used in this work are the standard AnCora partitions used for the CoNLL-2009 shared task (Hajič et al., 2009), around 418K words for training, 50K for development and 50K for test.

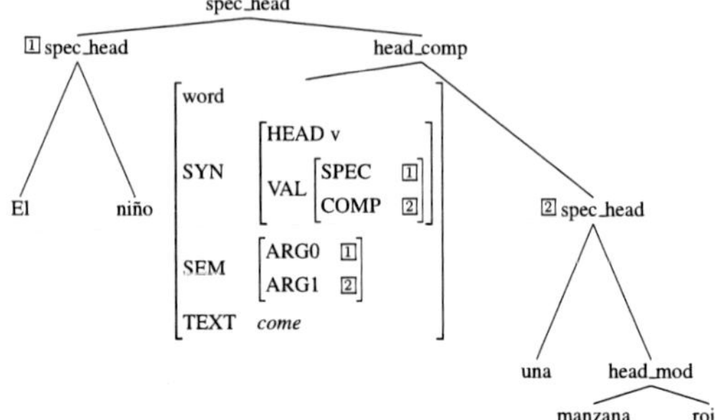

Figure 4: Simplified tree for *"El niño come una manzana roja" / "The boy eats a red apple"*. Only the node for *"come"* is expanded, but each of the nodes in the tree is a feature structure that contains the corresponding combinatorial and semantic information.

3 Parser development

This section describes the LSTM top-down parsing architecture we use in this work and the baselines we compare it to.

3.1 Top-down parser

Our parsing approach divides the parsing process into two steps: first creating a basic binary tree of phrases, where each non-leaf node is annotated with the corresponding rule, and then finding which of the phrases should act as arguments to their respective heads.

3.1.1 Split and rule calculation

The first step is a top-down process that takes as input a sequence of words and decides how to split the sequence in two so that the sub-sequences are valid constituents, indicating which grammar rule should be applied in that node. For example, if we take sentence 1 as input, the output would look like following:

[*El niño*] [*come una manzana roja*]
Rule: `spec_head`

The method proceeds recursively for each constituent that has at least two words. In this case, it will take the sequence *"El niño"* and split it so as to separate the determiner from the noun:

[*El*] [*niño*]

Rule: `spec_head`

The second sub-sequence would be split so as to separate the main verb from the noun phrase complement of the verb, resulting in the following:

[*come*] [*una manzana roja*]

Rule: `head_comp`

This top-down process is iterated until there are no more sub-sequences left to split, effectively transforming the original sentence into a binary tree of words, labeled with the corresponding grammar rules for each non-leaf node. The result is shown in figure 5.

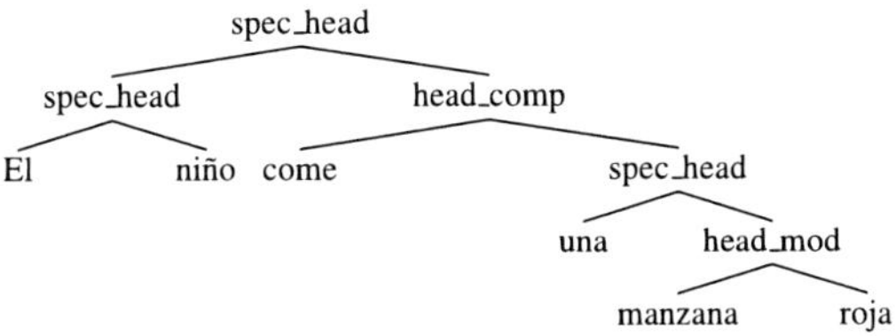

Figure 5: Binary tree with rule labels for the sentence *"El niño come una manzana roja"* / *"The boy eats a red apple"*, result of the first step of the parsing process.

3.1.2 Arguments calculation

Once this basic tree is created, using the calculated rules it is possible to derive the syntactic features and mark the heads for each node in the tree. With the syntactic features in place, the second step tries to determine which of the syntactic arguments of the predicates should also be set as semantic arguments.

This step considers each head that could be taken as predicate (in our case verbs, nouns and adjectives are possible predicates), and each syntactic argument, and calculates if it should be applied as a semantic feature, and which label it should use. In practice, the method takes the following elements as input:

- The sequence of words corresponding to the top-most constituent that includes the predicate, the head, and the argument.

- The candidate argument being classified.

- The word marked as head.

- The feature that relates the head and the candidate argument.

The result of the method could be `none` (if the candidate should not be considered an argument) or a feature between `arg0` and `argM`. The input values and expected outcomes for our example are the following:

[*El niño*$_{SPEC}$ *come*$_{HEAD}$ *una manzana roja*] $\rightarrow$ `arg0`

[*El niño come*$_{HEAD}$ *una manzana roja*$_{COMP}$] $\rightarrow$ `arg1`

[*una manzana*$_{HEAD}$ *roja*$_{MOD}$] $\rightarrow$ `none`

After this step is finished, the tree will look like the one in figure 4.

3.2 Implementation

Both steps of the process are implemented using neural networks. The first step is a neural network whose input is a sequence of words and whose output is the probability of splitting the sentence at each point in the sequence, and the probabilities of rules for each split point. The method proceeds greedily selecting only the split point with maximum probability and the corresponding rule.

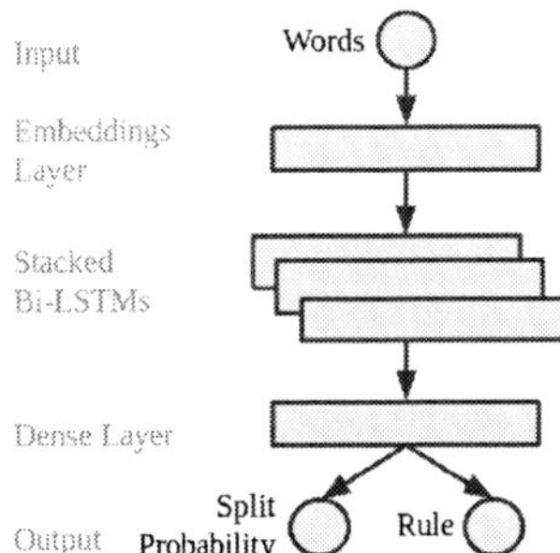

Figure 6: Architecture of the neural network for the sequence split and rule calculation step.

The network (shown in figure 6) is built using stacked bidirectional LSTM layers: the first layer contains a word embeddings model (300 dimensions, trained using `word2vec` for a 6 billion words Spanish corpus); then three layers of stacked bidirectional LSTMs of size 300; then a fully connected layer of size 150; and finally a softmax layer that outputs, for each word in the sequence, the grammar rule to apply or `none` if the word should not be used for splitting in the current step. The probability of the `none` label is used as the probability of splitting at each point in the sequence.

The second step is implemented using a neural network that takes a word (the head), a sequence of words representing the argument to classify, another sequence that represents the outer constituent that contains both the head and the argument, and

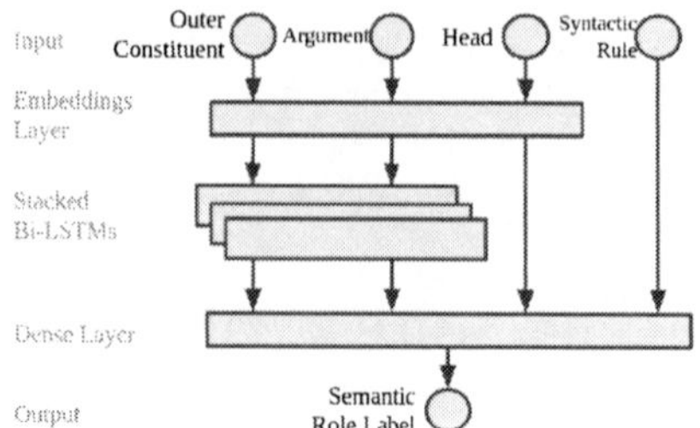

Figure 7: Architecture of the neural network for the argument identification step.

the syntactic rule used to associate the head to the argument. It returns the probability for each argument category (or `none`). The network (as shown in figure 7) has an embeddings layer for the words; then three layers of stacked bidirectional LSTMs of size 150 (in this case they output only one representation for each sequence, instead of one for each word); then a fully connected layer of size 150; and finally a softmax layer that gives the probability distribution for the labels.

We trained several instances of both networks varying the number and sizes of the different layers using `keras` (Chollet, 2015) over `tensorflow` (Abadi et al., 2015), optimizing against the development partition. The number of units for the LSTM and dense layers varied between 150 and 600, and we tried using one, two or three LSTM layers and different values of dropout. Only the results for the best models are reported.

3.3 Baseline CKY parser

In order to compare our parser to more standard HPSG parsing approaches, we implemented another statistical parsing strategy for this grammar, with a bottom-up approach similar to (Matsuzaki et al., 2007): using the CKY algorithm with a probabilistic model to find the best tree. The simplest implementation of the CKY algorithm for HPSG would imply applying all rules to the pairs of expressions found at each step. However, the feature unification method proved to be too slow for doing this in reasonable time, so we relied on a simplification to speed up the process: We designed a set of supertags based on the grammar categories that contain the necessary information to infer the possible rules to apply given a pair of supertags.

Considering sample sentence 1, the main verb of the sentence (*"come" / "eats"*) has a noun phrase specifier to its left (*"El niño" / "The boy"*), which

also acts as `ARG0`, and a noun phrase complement to its right (*"una manzana roja" / "a red apple"*), which also acts as `ARG1`. This will be the information conveyed by the supertag for *come*, which is `v-sna0-x-cna1`. The leftmost character is the part-of-speech of the word and the rest is a description of the use of the word in context, where `x` represents the position of the word. This tag means: a verb that expects a noun phrase acting as specifier on its left (`sn`) coindexed with `ARG0`, plus a noun phrase acting as a complement on its right (`cn`) coindexed with `ARG1`. The corresponding supertags for the whole sentence are the following:

El/`d-x` *niño*/`n-sd-x` *come*/`v-sna0-x-cna1`
una/`d-x` *manzana*/`n-sd-x` *roja*/`a-mn-x`

The possible rules to apply to a pair of words depend on the supertags associated to those words. Once they are combined following a certain rule, the resulting phrase will have a new tag that could be used to continue the parsing process. The tag structure is simple enough so that the possible rules to apply can be predicted in terms of regular expressions over the supertags (much faster than the unification method) but also expressive enough so that the invalid combinations are filtered out.

3.3.1 Probabilistic Model

We created a probabilistic model in a way similar to a PCFG. One way of doing this would be considering each possible supertag as a non terminal, the problem with this approach is that the number of supertags is very large: 4146 different supertags in the training corpus. Consequently, the number of times the combination of a particular pair of supertags appears in the corpus is very low (sparsity problem). To mitigate this, we created simpler models for abstracting the non terminals by reducing the information in the supertags and calculated the rule probabilities based on those abstractions. For example, a supertag `v-sna0-x-cna1-csa2` could have the abstract tag `vcs`, that indicates only the POS (verb) and the features it expects (complements and specifier) but not the finer grained information. Our model uses an average of probabilities calculated over these abstract tags, and assigns a very small probability to unseen tag combinations in order to avoid giving rare examples zero probability. Notice that the abstract tags have no effect in the process of determining the possible rules to apply (the full supertag is used for that), but only for estimating the probability of application of a rule.

3.3.2 Supertagger

The CKY algorithm relies on knowing the exact categories of the words to find the valid rules to apply, but when parsing a sentence from scratch that information would not be available. As the number of possible categories per word is large, we trained a supertagger for calculating the most suitable supertags given a sentence. Its inputs are the sentence words and POS-tags and it returns a sequence of supertags. The architecture for this supertagger is similar to the top-down parser: the first layer contains a word embeddings model (300 dimensions) and a POS embeddings model (5 dimensions); then three layers of stacked bidirectional LSTMs of size 450; then a fully connected layer of size 450; and finally a softmax layer that selects one out of 4146 possible supertags. The network achieves 89.1% accuracy over the development corpus and 88.7% for the test corpus considering the top selected tag.

As the performance is not perfect, the sequence of supertags selected might be invalid for forming a tree according to the grammar rules. To mitigate this problem, if a tree is not found we enable two fallback rules with low probability (`head_none` and `none_head`) that combine two arbitrary nodes and take either the left one or the right one as heads. These rules guarantee that a tree will be found, but they make the process much slower as many more subtrees are tried during parsing.

4 Experimental results

In this section we present the experimental results for our LSTM top-down neural network architecture and the baselines in terms of syntactic parsing and semantic role labeling. We also present an analysis of execution time for the different approaches. We compare our method to the CKY baseline defined before and six well established baselines for Spanish parsing. Three of the baselines are the parsers contained in the FreeLing library (Padró and Stanilovsky, 2012), which include both dependency parsing and SRL: Txala (Batalla et al., 2005), Treeler[1] and a LSTM implementation. The other baselines are the pretrained Spanish models Spanish of spaCy[2] (models `es_core_news_sm` and `es_core_news_md`) and UDPipe (Straka and Straková, 2017) (model `Spanish-AnCora`), which only include dependency parsing but no SRL. We show the perfor-

<hr>

[1]http://treeler.lsi.upc.edu/
[2]https://spacy.io

mance of the (unrealistic) CKY parser using gold supertags as an upper bound for the CKY performance, but also the more realistic CKY using the tags predicted by the supertagger.

4.1 Syntactic parsing

The performance metrics used for the syntactic parsing results are the following:

Constituency F1: The F1 score for the predicted constituents against the expected constituents in a tree. This metric is very strict and penalizes strongly any deviations in the order of application of rules, as swapping the order of only two rules could change many different constituents inside a tree. There are Labeled (L-Cons) or Unlabeled (U-Cons) versions of this metric with or without considering the correct grammar rule.

Dependency Accuracy: As all the rules are binary and they all define a head, it is possible to infer a dependency structure where each word is associated to a corresponding head. This structure contains the same information as the constituent trees except the information about the order of the rules application. This metric calculates the accuracy of assigning each word to its appropriate head, and it is more relaxed compared to constituency F1. Labeled (L-Dep) and Unlabeled (U-Dep) versions of this metric (with or without the grammar rule) are defined.

Model	U-Cons	L-Cons	U-Dep	L-Dep
LSTM Top-down	87.57	82.06	91.32	88.96
CKY Gold tags	77.16	72.72	92.07	92.05
CKY Supertagger	66.08	59.33	83.34	81.03
FreeLing LSTM	-	-	83.15	-
FreeLing Treeler	-	-	83.61	-
FreeLing Txala	-	-	69.75	-
spaCy es_sm	-	-	83.01	-
spaCy es_md	-	-	83.69	-
UDPipe	-	-	82.09	-

Table 1: Results of the syntactic parsing experiments over the test set.

Table 1 shows the performance results for the different experiments. The "CKY Gold tags" model is the unrealistic model that we consider as upper bound for the CKY process, the more realistic version is the "CKY Supertagger". As seen in the table, the best performing model in constituency and dependency metrics is the LSTM top-down approach. The CKY model does not perform well in terms of constituency even when using the gold supertags, probably because it mixes the order of application of rules: it gets only up to 77%, but for the dependency metrics (which ignore the rule application order) it gets around 92%. The CKY using the supertagger, as expected, performs worse than that. On the other hand, the performance of the top-down approach is very robust, outperforming even the CKY with gold supertags for the constituency metrics, and achieving comparable results for the dependency metrics.

The top-down parser also outperforms the external baselines for this corpus. Notice, however, that a direct comparison is difficult given that we are using a different grammar formalism. The only metric that could be considered comparable across the different parsers in this context would be the U-Dep, analogous to the UAS metric in dependency parsing, but even for this not all parsers are trained using the same dependency frameworks and they might have differences in how they determine which words are heads. For example, spacy and UDPipe are trained on corpora annotated using the Universal Dependencies framework (Nivre et al., 2016), which prefers using content words over function words as heads (Alonso and Zeman, 2016). In order to compare to these parsers, we postprocessed the results and transformed the heads of prepositional phrases, copulas and other structures in order to adapt it to our format. Section 4.4 shows other approaches to the evaluation of some aspects of the results, considering some particular phenomena of the language and how well the different parsers deal with them. In these cases it was also necessary to post-process the results to adapt the different ways the parsers represent these phenomena in order to compare them.

4.2 Semantic role labeling

The performance metric used in this case is the F1 measure for SRL taken as bi-lexical dependencies. We report two versions of the metric: the unlabeled version (U-SRL) measures if the argument was correctly matched as a semantic argument of its head regardless of the selected label, while the labeled version (L-SRL) also considers if the appropriate semantic role label was selected.

Table 2 shows the results for the semantic role labeling experiments. In this case, the (unrealistic) CKY using gold tags is the best performing method, and can be seen as an upper bound for performance. Our top-down approach gets almost as good results for the unlabeled metric, but performs a little worse for selecting the correct labels. The

Model	U-SRL	L-SRL
LSTM Top-down	87.68	80.66
CKY Gold tags	88.51	87.51
CKY Supertagger	81.48	75.78
FreeLing LSTM	68.50	60.74
FreeLing Treeler	69.10	61.53
FreeLing Txala	52.17	45.73

Table 2: Results of the semantic role labeling experiments over the test set.

top-down approach also outperforms all the other baselines.

4.3 Execution time

Model	Time (ms)
LSTM Top-down	86.1
CKY Gold tags	288.7
CKY Supertagger	1,237.3
FreeLing LSTM	60.3
FreeLing Treeler	948.5
FreeLing Txala	41.8
spaCy es_sm *(no SRL)*	9.3
spaCy es_md *(no SRL)*	19.8
UDPipe *(no SRL)*	21.8

Table 3: Average time in milliseconds for parsing a sentence in the test set.

Table 3 shows the average time for parsing a sentence in the test set (1,692 sentences) for the different models. The experiments were run on an Intel i7, 2.7GHz, 16GB RAM, without GPU acceleration. The metrics in the table are an average over all sentence lengths, but figure 8 shows a breakdown of execution times for different sentence length ranges (up to 80) for our approaches.

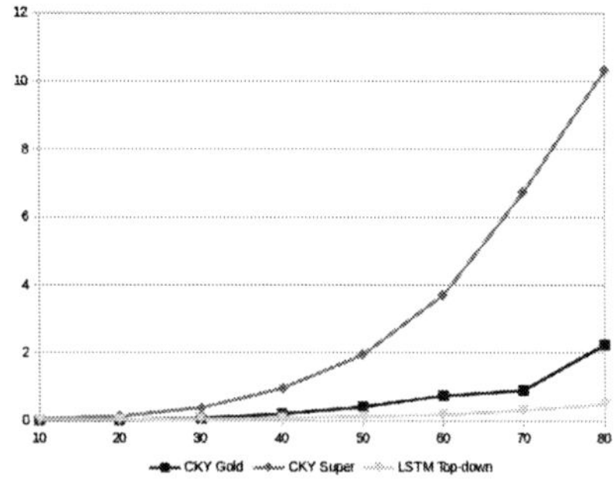

Figure 8: Breakdown of execution time in seconds for different input sizes.

In this case, the parsers based on neural networks seem to have an advantage over the others in terms of speed. The fastest parsers are the spaCy and UDPipe models, but we must take in consideration

138

		LSTM Top-down	CKY Gold	CKY Supert.	Freeling Txala	Freeling LSTM	Freeling Treeler	spaCy es_sm	spaCy es_md	UDPipe
Postponed	P	82.22	99.25	**84.25**	60.00	69.74	74.07	60.11	59.92	57.37
Subjects	R	64.02	98.89	**76.01**	19.92	65.49	62.73	56.45	59.59	52.39
	F	71.99	99.07	**79.92**	29.91	67.55	67.93	58.23	59.75	54.77
Clitics	P	**98.76**	100.	98.71	96.44	78.25	80.67	84.99	83.47	82.33
Identification	R	**99.03**	100.	95.46	85.83	88.58	88.44	97.38	97.93	96.83
	F	**98.90**	100.	97.06	90.82	83.09	84.38	90.76	90.12	89.00
	Acc	**85.28**	95.46	83.63	75.10	80.47	80.88	-	-	-
Clitics	MP	**76.20**	98.46	65.05	72.03	82.67	83.50	-	-	-
Classification	MR	**66.52**	88.18	57.80	44.02	51.51	54.60	-	-	-
	MF	**70.60**	92.78	61.00	49.20	56.37	58.63	-	-	-
Clitics	P	32.69	100.	**75.00**	8.33	22.05	30.23	-	-	-
Reduplication	R	**35.41**	81.25	18.75	2.08	31.25	27.08	-	-	-
	F	**34.00**	89.65	30.00	3.33	25.86	28.57	-	-	-
Relatives	P	90.60	100.	**92.27**	72.84	76.59	78.23	69.16	70.85	66.49
Identification	R	**89.00**	99.72	81.00	54.95	58.61	59.02	55.08	55.35	52.23
	F	**89.80**	99.86	86.27	62.64	66.41	67.28	61.32	62.05	58.51
	Acc	**76.12**	81.14	57.67	4.21	43.15	42.06	-	-	-
Relatives	MP	**64.73**	84.36	54.32	30.54	40.75	40.76	-	-	-
Classification	MR	**55.32**	78.47	37.82	7.63	24.78	24.39	-	-	-
	MF	**59.02**	72.39	43.29	6.54	29.18	28.62	-	-	-
Relative	P	**73.61**	77.68	67.69	37.23	60.46	63.30	54.17	55.53	49.56
Referents	R	**72.32**	77.47	59.43	28.08	46.26	47.76	43.14	43.55	38.94
	F	**72.96**	77.58	63.29	32.01	52.42	54.44	48.03	48.82	43.61
Coordinations	P	**65.49**	74.02	54.92	24.48	56.53	56.09	41.39	42.47	37.22
Identification	R	**65.22**	77.23	48.25	22.20	53.49	53.00	43.85	44.34	39.59
	F	**65.36**	75.59	51.37	23.28	54.96	54.50	42.59	43.38	38.37

Table 4: Results of the experiments for some language phenomena in Spanish. We show precision, recall and F1 score for identification tasks, and accuracy and macro metrics for classification tasks.

that they only perform dependency parsing and not SRL. Our LSTM top-down approach, and FreeLing LSTM and Txala (rule-based) parsers are in intermediate positions, while the CKY approaches and the FreeLing Treeler parser are way behind. If we break down the execution time of our top-down process, we get that there is a balance in the time spent at each step: 54.1 ms for syntactic parsing and 31.9 ms for argument identification. This could be sped up using a unified architecture.

As seen in figure 8, the top-down approach execution time seems to grow close to linearly while for CKY it grows faster, particularly for the CKY with supertagger. This is because, especially for longer sentences, the probability of obtaining a sequence of tags that does not form a correct tree is much higher as the sentence grows, so the fallback rules have to be enabled more frequently, rendering the process much slower.

4.4 Analysis

Besides the global metrics shown so far, we wanted to test the performance of the parsers for some of the Spanish language characteristics that inspired the grammar rules and behavior in the first place (see Section 2.2). We tested the parsers on how well they detect the following phenomena:

Postponed subjects: Identifying a subject that occurs on the right of the verb, as opposed to the more usual left position.

Clitics identification and classification: Detecting the clitic pronouns that accompany a verb and classifying them according to SRL.

Clitics reduplication: In Spanish, clitic pronouns can be used in lieu of an explicit object, but it is also possible to include both the object and the corresponding clitic at the same time. This is called clitic reduplication or clitic doubling.

Relatives identification and classification: Detecting the relative pronouns and expressions that are attached to some verbs creating relative sentences, and classifying them according to SRL.

Relatives referent identification: Besides identifying the relative pronoun and its verb, the parser must also properly identify the nominal referent for the relative pronoun.

Coordinations identification: Finding chains of (two or more) coordinated elements.

Table 4 shows the results for these experiments over the test set for the different parsers. In the results, we can see that the LSTM Top-down parser performs better for most experiments, except for the postponed subject identification where CKY with supertagger performs better. At least for these phenomena, the results seem to indicate that both parsers outperform the other baselines. However, we must take in consideration that, as mentioned in section 4.1, the output of the different parsers had to be post-processed in order to recognize the different phenomena, so there could be some noise in the evaluation introduced by this transformation.

5 Related work

Most of the work over the last years on deep parsing using neural network architectures has been done for the CCG formalism and for English language. For example (Xu et al., 2015) uses a recurrent neural network for improving the supertagging and parsing accuracy for CCG, while (Ambati et al., 2016) describes a neural networks architecture that performs CCG parsing. For HPSG, the work by (Zhou and Zhao, 2019) is very relevant as they try to derive a HPSG grammar from the Penn Treebanks in English and Chinese and use an self-attention based mechanism followed by a CKY decoder to parse them, obtaining very good results. In our work, however, we focus in HPSG for the Spanish language and define a different architecture for parsing: a top-down approach with LSTMs.

Our approach to HPSG development is similar to another relevant statistical parser for HPSG in English, the Enju parser (Matsuzaki et al., 2007; Zhang et al., 2010), which was created by transforming the English Penn Treebank through a set of rules into HPSG format and used this transformed corpus to train a statistical model. Another relevant precedent for HPSG is the LKB (Copestake, 2002) platform together with the PET (Callmeier, 2000) parser, used to define HPSG grammars in English and other languages (in particular the Spanish Resource Grammar (Marimon, 2010)), although they do not use neural networks for the parsing process. We differ from the Spanish Resource Grammar in that we derive the feature structures from a large corpus instead of building them manually, with the aim of building a purely statistical parser that could, for example, handle slightly ungrammatical sentences or out of vocabulary concepts better.

The CKY with supertagging method we compare to in this work follows a similar approach to the parsing methods used for deep syntactic grammars such as CCG (Curran et al., 2006; Lewis and Steedman, 2014), HPSG (Matsuzaki et al., 2007; Dridan, 2009; Zhang et al., 2010) and TAG (Kasai

et al., 2017; Friedman et al., 2017).

Much more work on applying neural network architectures to parsing has been done for the two more classical syntactic paradigms: constituency and dependency parsing. For constituency parsing, (Socher et al., 2013) defines a class of recurrent neural networks that combine pairs of words and builds a tree bottom-up, with the aim of improving sentiment analysis in English sentences. On the other hand, (Vinyals et al., 2015) frames the parsing process as a translation between a sentence in natural language and the bracketed representation of its parse tree. Other authors train neural models to predict the actions to be performed in a transition based shift-reduce constituency parser (Dyer et al., 2016), combining it with a sequence-to-sequence modeling (Liu and Zhang, 2017), or encoding the parsing stack using a recurrent network (Watanabe and Sumita, 2015). In (Cross and Huang, 2016) a transition based constituency parser gets good results for English and French using LSTMs for representing word spans instead of partially derived trees.

Another approach that focuses on determining the word spans in the tree is used in (Stern et al., 2017), which describes a top-down parser that greedily splits a sentence in constituents and assigns labels to them, processing the text spans with LSTMs in order to generate an intermediate representation. This approach is the most similar we found to the one we use, the main differences are that they work for French, they use a standard constituency grammar while ours is a strictly binarized HPSG grammar, and we add a further step for predicting the argument structure of predicates for the generated trees. Related approaches for English include: (Gaddy et al., 2018), that calculates the score and label for each sentence span then uses CKY to find the optimal tree; (Shen et al., 2018), that predicts the syntactic distances for words and builds the tree top-down using these distances.

Compared to English, there are few works that focus on Spanish parsing. For constituency parsing, (Cowan and Collins, 2005) tries two approaches to improve standard PCFG parsers: including morphological information in the probabilistic model, and a reranking method with max-margin criterion trained over a set of global features from the parse trees. Their evaluation against the Cast3LB corpus, a subset of AnCora, achieves a constituent F1 of 83.6 and 85.1 respectively. (Le Roux et al.,

2012) experiments with Spanish parsing using a PCFG with latent annotations with a simplified tagset, achieving 85.47 F1 over the Cast3LB corpus.

There is considerably more work done for dependency parsing and SRL in Spanish, beginning in the CoNLL-X (Buchholz and Marsi, 2006) and CoNLL-2009 (Hajič et al., 2009) shared tasks. The best LAS achieved for Spanish were 82.3 (max span tree approach) and 81.3 (transition based approach). Later on, (Lloberes et al., 2010) describes a dependency grammar and a rule-based dependency parser for Spanish (one of the Freeling parsers (Padró and Stanilovsky, 2012)) transforming the result of a shallow parser, achieving 81.13 UAS and 73.88 LAS. In (Ballesteros et al., 2010) they describe a set of experiments using Malt-Parser (Nivre et al., 2007) to determine how much corpus size, sentence length or other factors contribute to the dependency Spanish parsing performance. The latest efforts in dependency parsing have generally focused on using the Universal Dependencies (Nivre et al., 2016) framework. For example in CoNLL 2017 (Zeman et al., 2017) and CoNLL 2018 (Zeman et al., 2018) shared tasks on multilingual parsing from raw text to Universal Dependencies the best parsers achieve LAS of 87.29 (Dozat et al., 2017) and 90.93 (Che et al., 2018) respectively for Spanish.

6 Conclusions

We presented a statistical deep parser for Spanish that outputs trees in the HPSG formalism. The parser uses a top-down approach for building the tree followed by a second step for calculating the arguments, both steps are implemented using LSTM neural networks. The parser gets good results for performance compared to a CKY baseline and to other parsing baselines in Spanish, achieving 87.57% unlabeled and 82.06% labeled constituency F1, and 91.32% unlabeled and 88.96% labeled dependency accuracy. It also achieves good performance for SRL, getting 87.68% unlabeled and 80.66% labeled F1, and beats the baselines for some particular Spanish phenomena we analyzed.

Although the results improve over the baseline methods, there is still room for improvement, especially in terms of execution time. We plan to build a unified architecture that could perform both the syntactic and the arguments step at the same time, which could help lower the execution times and it

might also help the network generalize better in order to improve the prediction of labels in SRL. It would be also very interesting to try this approach to other languages such as English, and also languages that share some of the characteristics we analyzed such as Italian or French.

References

Martín Abadi, Ashish Agarwal, Paul Barham, Eugene Brevdo, Zhifeng Chen, Craig Citro, Greg S. Corrado, Andy Davis, Jeffrey Dean, Matthieu Devin, Sanjay Ghemawat, Ian Goodfellow, Andrew Harp, Geoffrey Irving, Michael Isard, Yangqing Jia, Rafal Jozefowicz, Lukasz Kaiser, Manjunath Kudlur, Josh Levenberg, Dan Mané, Rajat Monga, Sherry Moore, Derek Murray, Chris Olah, Mike Schuster, Jonathon Shlens, Benoit Steiner, Ilya Sutskever, Kunal Talwar, Paul Tucker, Vincent Vanhoucke, Vijay Vasudevan, Fernanda Viégas, Oriol Vinyals, Pete Warden, Martin Wattenberg, Martin Wicke, Yuan Yu, and Xiaoqiang Zheng. 2015. TensorFlow: Large-Scale Machine Learning on Heterogeneous Systems. Software available from tensorflow.org.

Héctor Martínez Alonso and Daniel Zeman. 2016. Universal dependencies for the ancora treebanks. *Procesamiento del Lenguaje Natural*, 57:91–98.

Bharat Ram Ambati, Tejaswini Deoskar, and Mark Steedman. 2016. Shift-reduce ccg parsing using neural network models. In *Proceedings of the 2016 Conference of the North American Chapter of the Association for Computational Linguistics: Human Language Technologies*, pages 447–453.

Miguel Ballesteros, Jesús Herrera, Virginia Francisco, and Pablo Gervás. 2010. Improving parsing accuracy for spanish using maltparser. *Procesamiento del Lenguaje Natural*, 44.

Jordi Atserias Batalla, Elisabet Comelles Pujadas, and Aingeru Mayor. 2005. Txala un analizador libre de dependencias para el castellano. *Procesamiento del Lenguaje Natural*, 35.

Claire Bonial, Olga Babko-Malaya, Jinho D Choi, Jena Hwang, and Martha Palmer. 2010. PropBank annotation guidelines. *Center for Computational Language and Education Research Institute of Cognitive Science University of Colorado at Boulder*.

Sabine Buchholz and Erwin Marsi. 2006. Conll-x shared task on multilingual dependency parsing. In *Proceedings of the tenth conference on computational natural language learning*, pages 149–164. Association for Computational Linguistics.

Ulrich Callmeier. 2000. Pet–a platform for experimentation with efficient hpsg processing techniques. *Natural Language Engineering*, 6(1):99–107.

Wanxiang Che, Yijia Liu, Yuxuan Wang, Bo Zheng, and Ting Liu. 2018. Towards better UD parsing: Deep contextualized word embeddings, ensemble, and treebank concatenation. In *Proceedings of the CoNLL 2018 Shared Task: Multilingual Parsing from Raw Text to Universal Dependencies*, pages 55–64, Brussels, Belgium. Association for Computational Linguistics.

Luis Chiruzzo and Dina Wonsever. 2016. Transforming the AnCora corpus to HPSG. In *Proceedings of the Joint 2016 Conference on Head-driven Phrase Structure Grammar and Lexical Functional Grammar, Polish Academy of Sciences, Warsaw, Poland*, pages 182–193, Stanford, CA. CSLI Publications.

Luis Chiruzzo and Dina Wonsever. 2018. Spanish HPSG Treebank based on the AnCora Corpus. In *Proceedings of the Eleventh International Conference on Language Resources and Evaluation (LREC-2018)*.

François Chollet. 2015. Keras. `https://github.com/fchollet/keras`.

Ann Copestake. 2002. *Implementing typed feature structure grammars*, volume 110. CSLI publications Stanford.

Ann Copestake, Dan Flickinger, Carl Pollard, and Ivan A Sag. 2005. Minimal recursion semantics: An introduction. *Research on language and computation*, 3(2-3):281–332.

Brooke Cowan and Michael Collins. 2005. Morphology and reranking for the statistical parsing of spanish. In *Proceedings of the conference on Human Language Technology and Empirical Methods in Natural Language Processing*, pages 795–802. Association for Computational Linguistics.

James Cross and Liang Huang. 2016. Span-based constituency parsing with a structure-label system and provably optimal dynamic oracles. In *Proceedings of the 2016 Conference on Empirical Methods in Natural Language Processing*, pages 1–11. Association for Computational Linguistics.

James R Curran, Stephen Clark, and David Vadas. 2006. Multi-tagging for lexicalized-grammar parsing. In *Proceedings of the 21st International Conference on Computational Linguistics and the 44th annual meeting of the Association for Computational Linguistics*, pages 697–704. Association for Computational Linguistics.

Timothy Dozat, Peng Qi, and Christopher D. Manning. 2017. Stanford's graph-based neural dependency parser at the CoNLL 2017 shared task. In *Proceedings of the CoNLL 2017 Shared Task: Multilingual Parsing from Raw Text to Universal Dependencies*, pages 20–30, Vancouver, Canada. Association for Computational Linguistics.

Rebecca Dridan. 2009. *Using lexical statistics to improve HPSG parsing*. Ph.D. thesis, University of Saarland.

Chris Dyer, Adhiguna Kuncoro, Miguel Ballesteros, and Noah A. Smith. 2016. Recurrent neural network grammars. In *Proceedings of the 2016 Conference of the North American Chapter of the Association for Computational Linguistics: Human Language Technologies*, pages 199–209. Association for Computational Linguistics.

Dan Friedman, Jungo Kasai, R. Thomas McCoy, Robert Frank, Forrest Davis, and Owen Rambow. 2017. Linguistically rich vector representations of supertags for TAG parsing. In *Proceedings of the 13th International Workshop on Tree Adjoining Grammars and Related Formalisms*, pages 122–131, Umeå, Sweden. Association for Computational Linguistics.

David Gaddy, Mitchell Stern, and Dan Klein. 2018. What's going on in neural constituency parsers? an analysis. In *Proceedings of the 2018 Conference of the North American Chapter of the Association for Computational Linguistics: Human Language Technologies, Volume 1 (Long Papers)*, pages 999–1010. Association for Computational Linguistics.

Jan Hajič, Massimiliano Ciaramita, Richard Johansson, Daisuke Kawahara, Maria Antònia Martí, Lluís Màrquez, Adam Meyers, Joakim Nivre, Sebastian Padó, Jan Štepánek, Pavel Straňák, Mihai Surdeanu, Nianwen Xue, and Yi Zhang. 2009. The conll-2009 shared task: Syntactic and semantic dependencies in multiple languages. In *Proceedings of the Thirteenth Conference on Computational Natural Language Learning (CoNLL 2009): Shared Task*, pages 1–18. Association for Computational Linguistics.

Aravind Krishna Joshi. 1985. Tree adjoining grammars: How much context-sensitivity is required to provide reasonable structural descriptions?

Jungo Kasai, Robert Frank, R Thomas McCoy, Owen Rambow, and Alexis Nasr. 2017. Tag parsing with neural networks and vector representations of supertags. In *Conference on Empirical Methods in Natural Language Processing*, pages 1712–1722.

Joseph Le Roux, Benoit Sagot, and Djamé Seddah. 2012. Statistical parsing of spanish and data driven lemmatization. In *ACL 2012 Joint Workshop on Statistical Parsing and Semantic Processing of Morphologically Rich Languages (SP-Sem-MRL 2012)*, pages 6–pages.

Mike Lewis and Mark Steedman. 2014. Improved ccg parsing with semi-supervised supertagging. *Transactions of the Association for Computational Linguistics*, 2:327–338.

Jiangming Liu and Yue Zhang. 2017. Encoder-decoder shift-reduce syntactic parsing. In *Proceedings of the 15th International Conference on Parsing Technologies*, pages 105–114, Pisa, Italy. Association for Computational Linguistics.

Marina Lloberes, Irene Castellón, and Lluís Padró. 2010. Spanish freeling dependency grammar. In *LREC*, volume 10, pages 693–699.

Montserrat Marimon. 2010. The spanish resource grammar. In *Proceedings of the International Conference on Language Resources and Evaluation, LREC*, pages 17–23, Valletta, Malta.

Takuya Matsuzaki, Yusuke Miyao, and Jun'ichi Tsujii. 2007. Efficient hpsg parsing with supertagging and cfg-filtering. In *IJCAI*, pages 1671–1676.

Joakim Nivre, Marie-Catherine De Marneffe, Filip Ginter, Yoav Goldberg, Jan Hajic, Christopher D Manning, Ryan McDonald, Slav Petrov, Sampo Pyysalo, Natalia Silveira, et al. 2016. Universal dependencies v1: A multilingual treebank collection. In *Proceedings of the Tenth International Conference on Language Resources and Evaluation (LREC'16)*, pages 1659–1666.

Joakim Nivre, Johan Hall, Jens Nilsson, Atanas Chanev, Gülşen Eryigit, Sandra Kübler, Svetoslav Marinov, and Erwin Marsi. 2007. MaltParser: A language-independent system for data-driven dependency parsing. *Natural Language Engineering*, 13(2):95–135.

Lluís Padró and Evgeny Stanilovsky. 2012. Freeling 3.0: Towards wider multilinguality. In *LREC2012*.

Carl Pollard and Ivan A Sag. 1994. *Head-driven phrase structure grammar*. University of Chicago Press.

Ivan A Sag, Thomas Wasow, Emily M Bender, and Ivan A Sag. 1999. *Syntactic theory: A formal introduction*, volume 92. Center for the Study of Language and Information Stanford, CA.

Yikang Shen, Zhouhan Lin, Athul Paul Jacob, Alessandro Sordoni, Aaron Courville, and Yoshua Bengio. 2018. Straight to the tree: Constituency parsing with neural syntactic distance. In *Proceedings of the 56th Annual Meeting of the Association for Computational Linguistics (Volume 1: Long Papers)*, pages 1171–1180, Melbourne, Australia. Association for Computational Linguistics.

Richard Socher, Alex Perelygin, Jean Wu, Jason Chuang, Christopher D. Manning, Andrew Ng, and Christopher Potts. 2013. Recursive deep models for semantic compositionality over a sentiment treebank. In *Proceedings of the 2013 Conference on Empirical Methods in Natural Language Processing*, pages 1631–1642. Association for Computational Linguistics.

Mark Steedman. 1996. A very short introduction to ccg. *Unpublished paper. http://www. coqsci. ed. ac. uk/steedman/paper. html*.

Mitchell Stern, Jacob Andreas, and Dan Klein. 2017. A Minimal Span-Based Neural Constituency Parser.

In *Proceedings of the 55th Annual Meeting of the Association for Computational Linguistics (Volume 1: Long Papers)*, pages 818–827. Association for Computational Linguistics.

Milan Straka and Jana Straková. 2017. Tokenizing, pos tagging, lemmatizing and parsing ud 2.0 with udpipe. In *Proceedings of the CoNLL 2017 Shared Task: Multilingual Parsing from Raw Text to Universal Dependencies*, pages 88–99, Vancouver, Canada. Association for Computational Linguistics.

Mariona Taulé, M. Antònia Martí, and Marta Recasens. 2008. AnCora: Multilevel Annotated Corpora for Catalan and Spanish. In *Proceedings of the Sixth International Conference on Language Resources and Evaluation (LREC'08)*, Marrakech, Morocco. European Language Resources Association (ELRA). Http://www.lrec-conf.org/proceedings/lrec2008/.

Oriol Vinyals, Lukasz Kaiser, Terry Koo, Slav Petrov, Ilya Sutskever, and Geoffrey Hinton. 2015. Grammar as a foreign language. In *Proceedings of the 28th International Conference on Neural Information Processing Systems - Volume 2*, NIPS'15, pages 2773–2781, Cambridge, MA, USA. MIT Press.

Taro Watanabe and Eiichiro Sumita. 2015. Transition-based neural constituent parsing. In *Proceedings of the 53rd Annual Meeting of the Association for Computational Linguistics and the 7th International Joint Conference on Natural Language Processing (Volume 1: Long Papers)*, pages 1169–1179. Association for Computational Linguistics.

Wenduan Xu, Michael Auli, and Stephen Clark. 2015. Ccg supertagging with a recurrent neural network. In *Proceedings of the 53rd Annual Meeting of the Association for Computational Linguistics and the 7th International Joint Conference on Natural Language Processing (Volume 2: Short Papers)*, pages 250–255.

Daniel Zeman, Jan Hajič, Martin Popel, Martin Potthast, Milan Straka, Filip Ginter, Joakim Nivre, and Slav Petrov. 2018. Conll 2018 shared task: Multilingual parsing from raw text to universal dependencies. In *Proceedings of the CoNLL 2018 Shared Task: Multilingual Parsing from Raw Text to Universal Dependencies*, pages 1–21, Stroudsburg, PA, USA. Association for Computational Linguistics.

Daniel Zeman, Martin Popel, Milan Straka, Jan Hajič, Joakim Nivre, Filip Ginter, Juhani Luotolahti, Sampo Pyysalo, Slav Petrov, Martin Potthast, Francis Tyers, Elena Badmaeva, Memduh Gökırmak, Anna Nedoluzhko, Silvie Cinková, jr. Jan Hajič, Jaroslava Hlaváčová, Václava Kettnerová, Zdeňka Urešová, Jenna Kanerva, Stina Ojala, Anna Missilä, Christopher Manning, Sebastian Schuster, Siva Reddy, Dima Taji, Nizar Habash, Herman Leung, Marie-Catherine de Marneffe, Manuela Sanguinetti, Maria Simi, Hiroshi Kanayama, Valeria de Paiva, Kira Droganova, Héctor Martínez Alonso, Çağrı Çöltekin, Umut Sulubacak, Hans Uszkoreit,

Vivien Macketanz, Aljoscha Burchardt, Kim Harris, Katrin Marheinecke, Georg Rehm, Tolga Kayadelen, Mohammed Attia, Ali Elkahky, Zhuoran Yu, Emily Pitler, Saran Lertpradit, Michael Mandl a! nd Jesse Kirchner, Hector Fernandez Alcalde, Jana Strnadová, Esha Banerjee, Ruli Manurung, Antonio Stella, Atsuko Shimada, Sookyoung Kwak, Gustavo Mendonça, Tatiana Lando, Rattima Nitisaroj, and Josie Li. 2017. Conll 2017 shared task: Multilingual parsing from raw text to universal dependencies. In *Proceedings of the CoNLL 2017 Shared Task: Multilingual Parsing from Raw Text to Universal Dependencies*, pages 1–19, Stroudsburg, PA, USA. Association for Computational Linguistics.

Y. Zhang, Takuya Matsuzaki, and Jun'ichi Tsujii. 2010. Forest-guided supertagger training. In *Proceedings of the 23rd International Conference on Computational Linguistics*, pages 1281–1289. Association for Computational Linguistics.

Junru Zhou and Hai Zhao. 2019. Head-driven phrase structure grammar parsing on Penn treebank. In *Proceedings of the 57th Annual Meeting of the Association for Computational Linguistics*, pages 2396–2408, Florence, Italy. Association for Computational Linguistics.

The Importance of Category Labels in Grammar Induction with Child-directed Utterances

Lifeng Jin and **William Schuler**
Department of Linguistics
The Ohio State University, Columbus, OH, USA
{jin, schuler}@ling.osu.edu

Abstract

Recent progress in grammar induction has shown that grammar induction is possible without explicit assumptions of language-specific knowledge. However, evaluation of induced grammars usually has ignored phrasal labels, an essential part of a grammar. Experiments in this work using a labeled evaluation metric, RH, show that linguistically motivated predictions about grammar sparsity and use of categories can only be revealed through labeled evaluation. Furthermore, depth-bounding as an implementation of human memory constraints in grammar inducers is still effective with labeled evaluation on multilingual transcribed child-directed utterances.

1 Introduction

Recent work in probabilistic context-free grammar (PCFG) induction has shown that it is possible to learn accurate grammars from raw text (Jin et al., 2018b, 2019; Kim et al., 2019), which is significant in addressing the issue of the *poverty of the stimulus* (Chomsky, 1965, 1980) in linguistics. Although phrasal categories and morphosyntactic features can be induced from raw text (Jin and Schuler, 2019; Jin et al., 2019), most unsupervised parsing work has been evaluated using unlabeled parsing accuracy scores (Seginer, 2007; Ponvert et al., 2011; Jin et al., 2018b; Shen et al., 2018, 2019; Shi et al., 2019). This is potentially distortative because children and adults can distinguish categories of phrases and clauses (Tomasello and Olguin, 1993; Valian, 1986; Kemp et al., 2005; Pine et al., 2013), and much of acquisition modeling research has been directed at simulating the development of abstract linguistic categories in first language acquisition (Bannard et al., 2009; Perfors et al., 2011; Kwiatkowski et al., 2012; Abend et al., 2017; Jin et al., 2018b).

Recent work proposed a labeled parsing accuracy evaluation metric called Recall-V-Measure (RVM) as a method for evaluating unsupervised grammar inducers (Jin et al., 2019), but this metric counts categories as incorrect if they are finer-grained than reference categories or if they represent binarizations of n-ary branches in reference trees, which may be linguistically acceptable. We therefore further modify it to Recall-Homogeneity (RH) calculated as the homogeneity (Rosenberg and Hirschberg, 2007) of the labels of matching constituents of the induced and gold trees, weighted by unlabeled recall. This work uses transcribed child-directed utterances from multiple languages as input to a grammar inducer with hyperparameters tuned using either unlabeled F1 or labeled RH. Results show that: (1) the induced grammars capture the preference of sparse concentrations in human grammars only when using labeled evaluation; (2) grammar accuracy increases as the number of labels grows only when using labeled evaluation; (3) depth-bounding (Jin et al., 2018a, limiting center embedding) is still effective when tuned to maximize labeled parsing accuracy.

2 Model

All experiments described in this paper use a Bayesian Dirichlet-multinomial model (Jin et al., 2018a) to induce PCFGs without assuming any language specific knowledge. This model defines a Chomsky normal form (CNF) PCFG with C non-terminal categories as a matrix $\mathbf{G}$ of binary rule probabilities which is first drawn from the Dirichlet prior with a concentration parameter β:

$$\mathbf{G} \sim \text{Dirichlet}(\beta) \tag{1}$$

Trees for sentences $1..N$ in a corpus are then drawn from a PCFG parameterized by $\mathbf{G}$:

$$\tau_{1..N} \sim \text{PCFG}(\mathbf{G}), \tag{2}$$

Proceedings of the 16th International Conference on Parsing Technologies and the IWPT 2020 Shared Task, pages 145–150
Virtual Meeting, July 9, 2020. ©2020 Association for Computational Linguistics

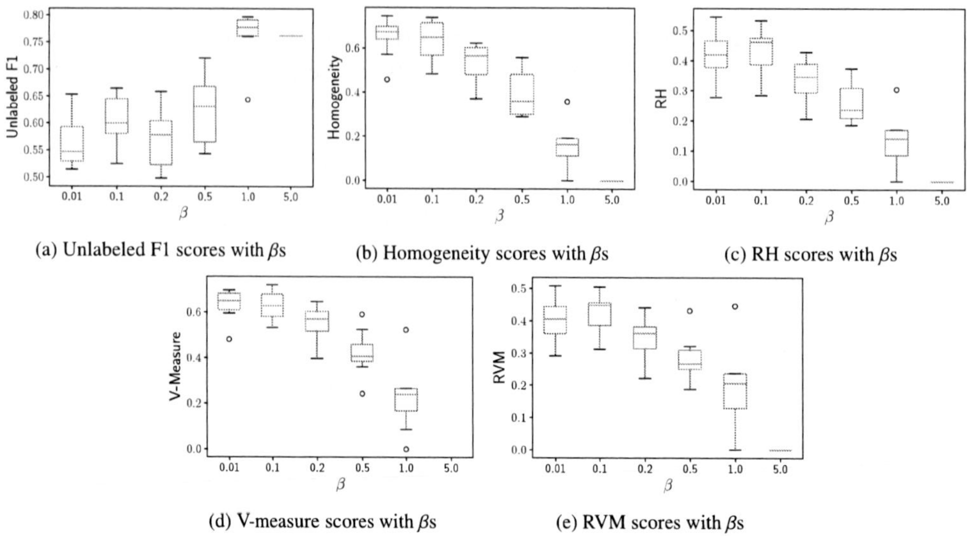

(a) Unlabeled F1 scores with βs   (b) Homogeneity scores with βs   (c) RH scores with βs

(d) V-measure scores with βs   (e) RVM scores with βs

Figure 1: Different evaluation metrics on the Adam dataset with different β values.

and each tree τ is a set $\{\tau_\epsilon, \tau_1, \tau_2, \tau_{11}, \tau_{12}, \tau_{21}, ...\}$ of category node labels τ_η where $\eta \in \{1, 2\}^*$ defines a path of left or right branches from the root to that node. Category labels for every pair of left and right children $\tau_{\eta 1}, \tau_{\eta 2}$ are drawn from a multinomial distribution defined by the grammar $\mathbf{G}$ and the category of the parent τ_η:

$$\tau_{\eta 1}, \tau_{\eta 2} \sim \text{Multinomial}(\delta_{\tau_\eta}{}^\top \mathbf{G}) \qquad (3)$$

where δ_x is a Kronecker delta function equal to 1 at value x and 0 elsewhere. Terminal expansions are treated as expanding into a terminal node followed by a special null node.

Inference in this model uses Gibbs sampling to produce samples of grammars and trees with the most probable parses obtained with the Viterbi algorithm.

3 Data and hyperparameters

Experiments here use transcribed child-directed utterances from the CHILDES corpus (Macwhinney, 1992) in three languages with more than 15,000 sentences each. English hand-annotated constituency trees are taken from the Adam and Eve portions of the Brown Corpus (Brown, 1973). Mandarin (Tong, Deng et al., 2018) and German (Leo, Behrens, 2006) data are collected from CHILDES with reference trees automatically generated using the state-of-the-art Kitaev and Klein (2018) parser. Disfluencies are removed, and only sentences spoken by caregivers are kept in the data. Models are run 10

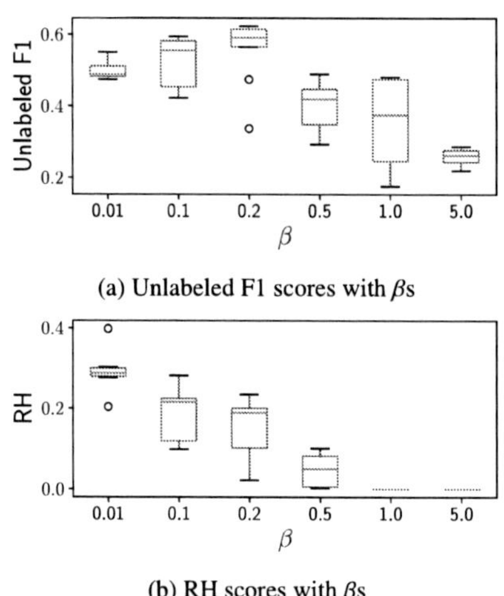

(a) Unlabeled F1 scores with βs

(b) RH scores with βs

Figure 2: Different evaluation metrics on the WSJ20Dev dataset with different β values.

times with 700 iterations with random seeds following previous work (Jin et al., 2018a). The last sampled grammar is used to generate Viterbi parses for all sentences. All punctuation is retained during induction and then removed in evaluation. Significance testing uses permutation tests on concatenations of Viterbi trees from all test runs. We use Adam for exploratory experiments and the other three sets for confirmatory experiments.

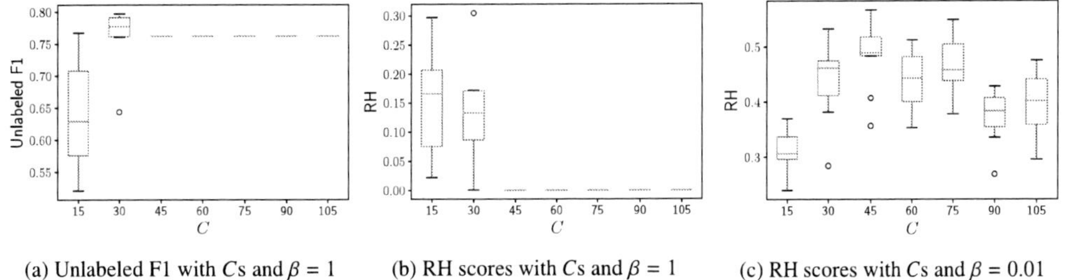

<table>
<tr><td align="center">(a) Unlabeled F1 with Cs and β = 1</td><td align="center">(b) RH scores with Cs and β = 1</td><td align="center">(c) RH scores with Cs and β = 0.01</td></tr>
</table>

Figure 3: Different evaluation metrics on the Adam dataset with different C values at high and low βs.

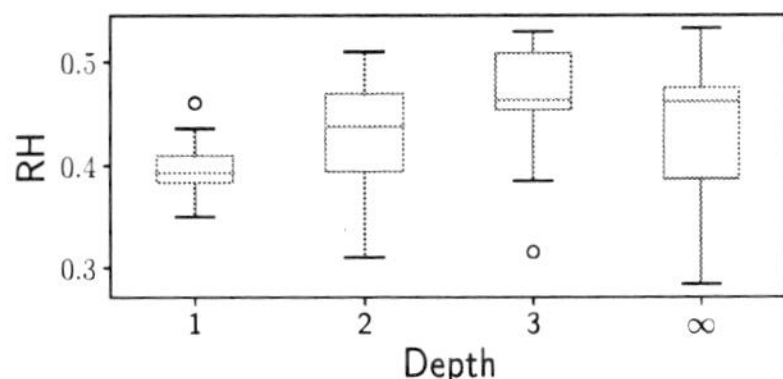

Figure 4: Depth-bounding on Adam

3.1 Recall-Homogeneity

RH is calculated by multiplying unlabeled recall of bracketed spans in the predicted Viterbi trees with the homogeneity score (Rosenberg and Hirschberg, 2007) of the predicted labels of the matching spans, This is different from RVM (Jin et al., 2019), which is the product of unlabeled recall and V-measure. The metric is insensitive to the branching factor of the grammar by the use of unlabeled recall. Unlike RVM, it is also insensitive to the precision of predicted labels to gold labels, indicating that models are not penalized by hypothesizing more refined categories, as long as these categories all fall into the confines of a gold category. RVM, on the other hand, would penalize both underproposing and overproposing categories compared to the ones in the annotation, but the gold categories, like nouns and verbs, are defined on a very high level that languages almost always further specify, represented usually as subcategories or features in linguistic theories. Unary branches in gold and predicted trees are removed, and the top category is used as the category for the constituent.

4 Experiments

4.1 Experiment 1: Labeled evaluation shows preference of grammar sparsity

Human grammars are sparse (Johnson et al., 2007; Goldwater and Griffiths, 2007). For example, in the

Penn Treebank (Marcus et al., 1993), there are 73 unique nonterminal categories. In theory, there can be more than 28 million possible unary, binary and ternary branching rules in the grammar. However, only 17,020 unique rules are found in the corpus, showing the high sparsity of attested rules. In other frameworks like Combinatory Categorial Grammar (Steedman, 2002) where lexical categories can be in the thousands, the number of attested lexical categories is still small compared to all possible ones.

The Dirichlet concentration hyperparameter β in the model controls the probability of a sampled multinomial distribution concentrating its probability mass on only a few items. Previous work using similar models usually sets this value low (Johnson et al., 2007; Goldwater and Griffiths, 2007; Graça et al., 2009; Jin et al., 2018b) to prefer sparse grammars (i.e. grammars in which most of the probability mass is allocated to a small number of rules), with good results. The prediction based on the preference of sparsity is that the best β value should be much lower than 1.

Figure 1a shows unlabeled F1 scores with different β values on Adam.[1] Contrary to the prediction, grammar accuracy peaks at high values for β when measured using unlabeled F1. However, these grammars with high unlabeled F1 are almost purely right-branching grammars, which performs very well on English child-directed speech in unlabeled parsing evaluation, but the right-branching grammars have phrasal labels that do not correlate with human annotation when evaluated with Homogeneity, shown in Figure 1b. This indicates that instead of capturing human intuitions about syntactic structure, such grammars have only captured broad branching tendencies. The same grammars are evaluated again with RH, shown in Figure 1c.

---

[1] The results shown in the figure use C=30. We also tested other C values from 15 to 105 and the trend is almost identical.

When both structural and labeling accuracy is taken into account, results correctly capture the intuition that grammar accuracy has a low peaking concentration hyperparameter. Figure 1d and 1e shows the same experiments evaluated with the labeled evaluation metric RVM. Because of the sensitivity to labeling accuracy, results in VM and RVM also show the similar trend as Homogeneity and RH where labeling quality decreases as β increases. Jin et al. (2018b) noted that induced grammars high in unlabeled bracketing scores are low in NP discovery scores, which is a category-specific evaluation metric. This can also be explained by the induced grammars with high bracketing scores only capture a broad right-branching bias without accurately clustering words and phrases based on their distributional properties.

Figure 2 shows the same experiments on a corpus of formal English written text, the WSJ20dev[2] dataset. The pattern is similar but less extreme than on CHILDES. The higher βs at the range of 0.1-0.2 still show better performance on unlabeled F1 than the sparser models, consistent with previous results in Jin et al. (2018b). However RH scores reveal that the labels induced by the denser models are less accurate, manifesting as the overall lower peak for β using RH than using unlabeled F1.

4.2 Experiment 2: Performance increases with the number of categories

Previous research (Jin et al., 2018a) also reported that the number of categories C used by the induction models was relatively low compared to the number of categories in human annotation. For example, there are 63 unique tags in the Adam dataset. This is in contrast to 30 or fewer categories used in previous induction work. The bias brought by high β values and unlabeled evaluation together may be masking the real relationship between the number of categories and grammar accuracy.

Figures 3a and 3b show unlabeled and labeled evaluation on different grammars induced with the best performing β on Adam tuned by unlabeled F1. With F1, increasing the number of categories beyond 30 yields no improvement as most of the induced grammars are purely right-branching grammars. RH results confirm this: as grammars approach the pure right-branching solution when C increases, the similarity between induced and gold labels of constituents deteriorates quickly. RH scores from grammars induced with $\beta = 0.01$ are more indicative of the interaction between the number of categories and grammar accuracy. Grammar accuracy increases as C gets larger initially and peaks at $C = 75$. The results confirm the importance of labeled evaluation, because the trend from labeled evaluation shows that there should be a sufficient number of categories to account for different syntactic structures, and models with small numbers of categories are limited in their ability to do this.

4.3 Experiment 3: Depth-bounding is still effective with RH

Previous work showed that depth-bounding is effective in helping grammar inducers induce more accurate grammars (Shain et al., 2016; Jin et al., 2018a), because it removes the parse trees with deeply nested center-embeddings, which cannot be produced by humans due to memory constraints (Chomsky and Miller, 1963), from grammar induction inference. However the unlabeled evaluation metric used in previous work may lead to unhelpful conclusions. In order to revisit this claim with labeled evaluation, experiments are first conducted on Adam exploring the interaction between depth and labeled performance, and subsequently on the Eve (English), Tong (Chinese Mandarin) and Leo (German) portions of the CHILDES corpus. All experiments use hyperparameters tuned with RH.[3]

Figure 4 shows the interaction between depth and RH scores on Adam. Performance of the unbounded models can be lower than all bounded models, showing that unbounded inducers can induce grammars inconsistent with human memory constraints. The labeled performance peaks at depth 3, which is significantly more accurate ($p < 1 \times 10^{-3}$) than unbounded models. This is consistent with previous results that over 97% of trees in English contain 3 or fewer nested center embeddings (Schuler et al., 2010).

Experiments on Eve, Tong and Leo replicate this result. Figure 5 shows that the models bounded at depth 3 are more accurate than unbounded models with both unlabeled and labeled evaluation metrics. Significance testing with unlabeled F1[4] shows the

---

[2]The first half of the Wall Street Journal part of the Penn Treebank with sentences with 20 words or fewer.

[3]The optimal C is 75 from previous experiments, but we used 30 in all depth-bounding experiments due to hardware constraints at high depth bounds.

[4]Neither RH nor RVM were used in permutation significance testing, because labels with the same values from different induced grammars may represent different linguistic categories, therefore two parses of the same sentence from

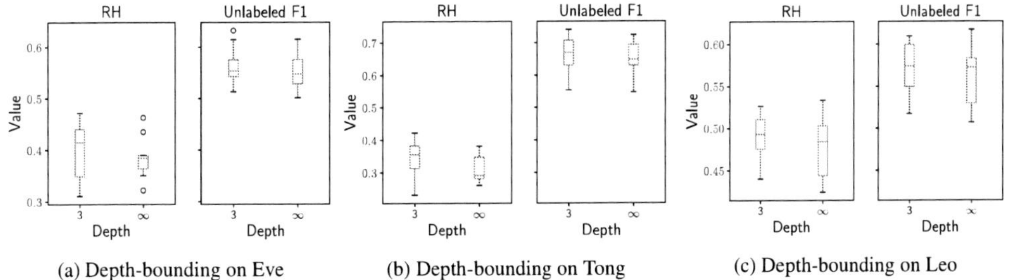

(a) Depth-bounding on Eve   (b) Depth-bounding on Tong   (c) Depth-bounding on Leo

Figure 5: Comparison of labeled and unlabeled evaluation of grammars bounded at depth 3 and unbounded grammars on English (Eve), Chinese Mandarin (Tong) and German (Leo) datasets from CHILDES.

performance differences across three datasets are all highly significant ($p < 0.001$). Therefore, the claim that depth-bounding is effective in grammar induction is still supported when the models are developed and evaluated with labeled evaluation.

5 Conclusion

Unlabeled evaluation has been used in grammar induction, but experiments presented in this paper show that unlabeled evaluation can reveal unexpected bias in the data which may lead to unhelpful conclusions compared to labeled evaluation. Results show that trends of preference of sparsity and use of categories that are consistent with linguistic annotation can only be discovered with labeled evaluation. Furthermore, human memory constraints are still effective in grammar induction when labeled evaluation is used throughout all stages of development.

References

Omri Abend, Tom Kwiatkowski, Nathaniel J. Smith, Sharon Goldwater, and Mark Steedman. 2017. Bootstrapping language acquisition. In *Cognition*, volume 164, pages 116–143. Elsevier B.V.

Colin Bannard, Elena Lieven, and Michael Tomasello. 2009. Modeling children's early grammatical knowledge. *Proceedings of the National Academy of Sciences of the United States of America*, 106(41):17284–9.

Heike Behrens. 2006. The input–output relationship in first language acquisition. *Language and Cognitive Processes*, 21(1-3):2–24.

Roger Brown. 1973. *A first language: The early stages.* Harvard U. Press.

Noam Chomsky. 1965. *Aspects of the Theory of Syntax.* MIT Press, Cambridge, MA.

Noam Chomsky. 1980. On cognitive structures and their development: A reply to Piaget. In Massimo Piattelli-Palmarini, editor, *Language and learning: the debate between Jean Piaget and Noam Chomsky*, chapter 49, pages 751–755. Harvard University Press.

Noam Chomsky and George A Miller. 1963. Introduction to the formal analysis of natural languages. In *Handbook of Mathematical Psychology*, pages 269–321. Wiley, New York, NY.

Xiangjun Deng, Virginia Yip, Brian Macwhinney, Stephen Matthews, Mai Ziyin, Zhong Jing, and Hannah Lam. 2018. A Multimedia Corpus of Child Mandarin: The Tong Corpus. *The Journal of Chinese Linguisticsvol*, 46(1):69–92.

Sharon Goldwater and Tom Griffiths. 2007. A fully Bayesian approach to unsupervised part-of-speech tagging. *Proceedings of the 45th Annual Meeting of the Association of Computational Linguistics*, pages 744–751.

João V. Graça, Kuzman Ganchev, Taskar Ben, and Fernando Pereira. 2009. Posterior vs. Parameter sparsity in latent variable models. In *Advances in Neural Information Processing Systems*, pages 664–672.

Lifeng Jin, Finale Doshi-Velez, Timothy Miller, Lane Schwartz, and William Schuler. 2019. Unsupervised Learning of PCFGs with Normalizing Flow. In *ACL*.

Lifeng Jin, Finale Doshi-Velez, Timothy A Miller, William Schuler, and Lane Schwartz. 2018a. Depth-bounding is effective: Improvements and evaluation of unsupervised PCFG induction. In *Proceedings of the Conference on Empirical Methods in Natural Language Processing*.

Lifeng Jin, Finale Doshi-Velez, Timothy A Miller, William Schuler, and Lane Schwartz. 2018b. Unsupervised Grammar Induction with Depth-bounded PCFG. *Transactions of the Association for Computational Linguistics*.

Lifeng Jin and William Schuler. 2019. Variance of average surprisal: a better predictor for quality of grammar from unsupervised PCFG induction. In *ACL*.

different runs are not exchangeable.

Mark Johnson, Thomas L. Griffiths, and Sharon Goldwater. 2007. Bayesian Inference for PCFGs via Markov chain Monte Carlo. *Proceedings of Human Language Technologies: The Conference of the North American Chapter of the Association for Computational Linguistics*, pages 139–146.

Nenaugh Kemp, Elena Lieven, and Michael Tomasello. 2005. Young Children's Knowledge of the "Determiner" and "Adjective" Categories. *Journal of Speech, Language, and Hearing Research*, 48(June):592–609.

Yoon Kim, Chris Dyer, and Alexander M Rush. 2019. Compound Probabilistic Context-Free Grammars for Grammar Induction. In *ACL*.

Nikita Kitaev and Dan Klein. 2018. Constituency Parsing with a Self-Attentive Encoder. In *ACL*.

Tom Kwiatkowski, Sharon Goldwater, Luke Zettlemoyer, and Mark Steedman. 2012. A probabilistic model of syntactic and semantic acquisition from child-directed utterances and their meanings. *Proceedings of the 13th Conference of the European Chapter of the Association for Computational Linguistics*, pages 234–244.

Brian Macwhinney. 1992. *The CHILDES Project: Tools for Analyzing Talk*, third edition. Lawrence Elrbaum Associates, Mahwah, NJ.

Mitchell P. Marcus, Beatrice Santorini, and Mary Ann Marcinkiewicz. 1993. Building a large annotated corpus of English: The Penn Treebank. *Computational Linguistics*, 19(2):313–330.

Amy Perfors, Joshua B Tenenbaum, and Terry Regier. 2011. The learnability of abstract syntactic principles. *Cognition*, 118:306–338.

Julian M. Pine, Daniel Freudenthal, Grzegorz Krajewski, and Fernand Gobet. 2013. Do young children have adult-like syntactic categories? Zipf's law and the case of the determiner. *Cognition*, 127(3):345–360.

Elias Ponvert, Jason Baldridge, and Katrin Erk. 2011. Simple unsupervised grammar induction from raw text with cascaded finite state models. In *Proceedings of the Annual Meeting of the Association for Computational Linguistics*, pages 1077–1086.

Andrew Rosenberg and Julia Hirschberg. 2007. V-measure: A conditional entropy-based external cluster evaluation measure. In *Proceedings of the 2007 joint conference on empirical methods in natural language processing and computational natural language learning (EMNLP-CoNLL)*.

William Schuler, Samir AbdelRahman, Tim Miller, and Lane Schwartz. 2010. Broad-coverage parsing using human-Like memory constraints. *Computational Linguistics*, 36(1):1–30.

Yoav Seginer. 2007. Fast Unsupervised Incremental Parsing. In *Proceedings of the Annual Meeting of the Association of Computational Linguistics*, pages 384–391.

Cory Shain, William Bryce, Lifeng Jin, Victoria Krakovna, Finale Doshi-Velez, Timothy Miller, William Schuler, and Lane Schwartz. 2016. Memory-bounded left-corner unsupervised grammar induction on child-directed input. In *Proceedings of the International Conference on Computational Linguistics*, pages 964–975.

Yikang Shen, Zhouhan Lin, Chin-Wei Huang, and Aaron Courville. 2018. Neural Language Modeling by Jointly Learning Syntax and Lexicon. In *ICLR*.

Yikang Shen, Shawn Tan, Alessandro Sordoni, and Aaron Courville. 2019. Ordered Neurons: Integrating Tree Structures into Recurrent Neural Networks. In *ICLR*.

Haoyue Shi, Jiayuan Mao, Kevin Gimpel, and Karen Livescu. 2019. Visually Grounded Neural Syntax Acquisition. In *ACL*.

Mark Steedman. 2002. Formalizing Affordance. In *Proceedings of the Annual Meeting of the Cognitive Science Society*.

Michael Tomasello and Raquel Olguin. 1993. Twenty-three-month-old children have a grammatical category of noun. *Cognitive Development*, 8(4):451–464.

Virginia Valian. 1986. Syntactic Categories in the Speech of Young Children. *Developmental Psychology*, 22(4):562–579.

Overview of the IWPT 2020 Shared Task on Parsing into Enhanced Universal Dependencies

Gosse Bouma[*] **Djamé Seddah**[†] **Daniel Zeman**[°]

[*]University of Groningen, Centre for Language and Cognition
[†]INRIA Paris
[°]Charles University in Prague, Faculty of Mathematics and Physics, ÚFAL
g.bouma@rug.nl, djame.seddah@inria.fr
zeman@ufal.mff.cuni.cz

Abstract

This overview introduces the task of parsing into enhanced universal dependencies, describes the datasets used for training and evaluation, and evaluation metrics. We outline various approaches and discuss the results of the shared task.

1 Introduction

Universal Dependencies (UD) (Nivre et al., 2020) is a framework for cross-linguistically consistent treebank annotation that has so far been applied to over 90 languages. UD defines two levels of annotation, the basic trees and the enhanced graphs (EUD).

In 2017 (Zeman et al., 2017) and 2018 (Zeman et al., 2018) there were CoNLL shared tasks on multilingual UD parsing that attracted a substantial number of participants. While the previous tasks evaluated morphology and prediction of basic dependencies on the UD data, the current task's focus is on predicting enhanced dependency representations. The evaluation was done on datasets covering 17 languages from four language families. The current task was organized as a part of the 16th International Conference on Parsing Technologies[1] (IWPT), collocated with ACL 2020, as a follow-up to stimulate research on parsing natural language into richly annotated structures.

2 Motivation

The basic dependency annotation in the Universal Dependencies format introduces labeled edges between tokens in the input string, where each token is a dependent of exactly one other token, with the exception of the root token. While such an annotation layer supports many downstream tasks, there are also phenomena that are hard to capture using single edges between tokens only. The enhanced dependency layer therefore supports a richer level of annotation, where tokens may have more than one parent, and where additional 'empty' tokens may be added to the input string. The enhanced level can be used to account for a range of linguistic phenomena (see Section 3) and to support downstream applications that require representations that capture more aspects of the semantic interpretation of the input.

There are now a number of treebanks that include enhanced dependency annotation. Furthermore, the recent shared tasks on dependency parsing and subsequent work have shown that considerable progress has been made in multilingual dependency parsing. It remains to be seen, however, whether the same is true for enhanced dependency parsing. The challenge is both formal and practical. First, the enhanced representation is a connected graph, possibly containing cycles, while previous work on dependency parsing mostly dealt with rooted trees. Second, as some dependency labels incorporate the lemma of certain dependents and other additional information, the set of labels to be predicted is much larger and language-dependent.

On the other hand, it has been shown that much of the enhanced annotation can be predicted on the basis of the basic UD annotation (Schuster et al., 2017; Nivre et al., 2018). Moreover, most state of the art work in dependency parsing uses a graph-based approach, where the assumption that the output must form a tree is only used in the final step from predicted links to final output. And finally, work on deep-syntax and semantic parsing has shown that accurate mapping of strings into rich graph representations is possible (Oepen et al., 2014, 2015, 2019) and could even lead to state of the art performance for downstream applications as shown by the results of the Extrinsic Evaluation Parsing shared-task (Oepen et al., 2017).

[1]https://iwpt20.sigparse.org

Proceedings of the 16th International Conference on Parsing Technologies and the IWPT 2020 Shared Task, pages 151–161
Virtual Meeting, July 9, 2020. ©2020 Association for Computational Linguistics

3 Enhanced Universal Dependencies

UD version 2[2] states that apart from the morphological and basic dependency annotation layers, strings may be annotated with an additional, enhanced, dependency layer, where the following phenomena can be captured:

- Gapping. To support a linguistically more satisfying treatment of ellipsis, empty tokens can be introduced into the string to represent missing predicates in gapping constructions.

- Coordination. Dependency relations are propagated from the parent of the coordination structure to each conjunct, and from each conjunct to a shared dependent, e.g., a shared subject or object of coordinate verbs.

- Control and raising constructions. The external subject of `xcomp` dependents, if present, can be explicitly marked.

- Relative clauses. The antecedent noun of a relative clause is annotated as a dependent of a node within the relative clause (thus introducing a cycle) and the relative pronoun is annotated as a `ref` dependent of the antecedent noun.

- Case information. Selected dependents (in particular `obl` and `nmod`), if they are marked by morphological case and/or by an adpositional case dependent, can now be labeled as `obl:marker` or `nmod:marker` where `marker` is the lemma of the case dependent and/or the value of the morphological feature `Case`.

All enhancements are optional, so a UD treebank may contain enhanced graphs with one type of enhancement and still lack the other types.

4 Data

The evaluation was done on 17 languages from 4 language families: Arabic, Bulgarian, Czech, Dutch, English, Estonian, Finnish, French, Italian, Latvian, Lithuanian, Polish, Russian, Slovak, Swedish, Tamil, Ukrainian. The language selection is driven simply by the fact that at least partial enhanced representation is available for the given language.

---

[2] `https://universaldependencies.org/u/overview/enhanced-syntax.html`

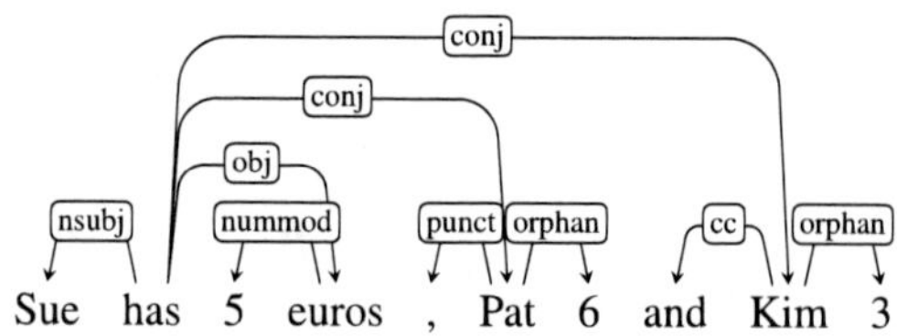

Figure 1: A basic tree of a gapping structure.

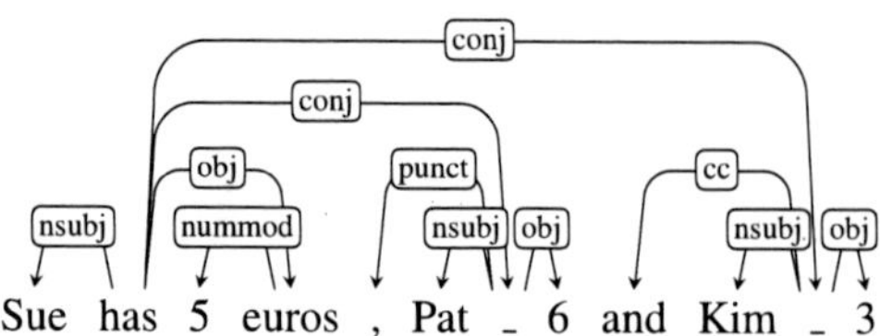

Figure 2: The correct enhanced graph of the gapping structure from Figure 1. "_" are empty nodes.

Training and development data were based on the UD release 2.5 (Zeman et al., 2019) but for several treebanks the enhanced annotation is richer than in UD 2.5. Our goal was to have annotations as uniform and complete as possible. There are only 6 treebanks of 3 languages in UD 2.5 that contain all types of enhancements: Dutch (Alpino and LassySmall), English (EWT and PUD), and Swedish (Talbanken and PUD). For several other languages we obtained new annotations that became part of UD from the next release (2.6) on. For the remaining languages, we applied simple heuristics and added at least some enhancements for the purpose of the shared task, but these annotations are not yet part of the regular UD releases. We only applied our heuristics to the missing enhancement types; we did not attempt to modify the enhancements provided by the data providers. Table 1 gives an overview of enhancements in individual treebanks.

The enhancements differ in how easily and accurately they can be inferred from the basic UD annotation:

- Enhancing relation labels with case information is deterministic. We apply it to the relations `obl`, `nmod`, `advcl` and `acl`. If they have a `case` or `mark` dependent, we add its lowercased lemma (for fixed multiword expressions we glue the lemmas with the "_" character). For `obl` and `nmod` we further examine the `Case` feature and add its lowercased value, if present.

Treebank	UD 2.5	Task	2.6
Arabic PADT	P S	GP S RC	✓
Bulgarian BTB	P SXRC	GP SXRC	
Czech CAC	P S	GP SXRC	✓
Czech FicTree	P S	GP SXRC	✓
Czech PDT	P S	GP SXRC	✓
Czech PUD		GP XRC	✓
Dutch Alpino	GP SXRC	GP SXRC	✓
Dutch LassySmall	GP SXRC	GP SXRC	✓
English EWT	GP SXRC	GP SXRC	✓
English PUD	GP SXRC	GP SXRC	✓
Estonian EDT		GP S RC	(✓)
Estonian EWT	G	GP RC	
Finnish PUD	GP	GP RC	
Finnish TDT	GP SX	GP SXRC	
French FQB		P SX	
French Sequoia		P SX	
Italian ISDT	P SXRC	GP SXRC	
Latvian LVTB	GP SX C	GP SXRC	
Lithuanian ALKS.	P S	GP SXRC	✓
Polish LFG	P SX C	P SXRC	
Polish PDB	P S	GP SXRC	
Polish PUD	P S	GP SXRC	
Russian SynTagRus	G	GP XRC	
Slovak SNK	P S	GP SXRC	✓
Swedish PUD	GP SXRC	GP SXRC	✓
Swedish Talbanken	GP SXRC	GP SXRC	✓
Tamil TTB	P S	P S C	✓
Ukrainian IU	GP SXR	GP SXRC	

Table 1: New annotation for the shared task. Abbreviations: G = gapping; P = parent of coordination; S = shared dependent of coordination; X = external subject of controlled verb; R = relative clause; C = case-enhanced relation label. The check mark in the last column indicates whether the shared task additions also became part of UD 2.6 (only some types for Estonian EDT).

- Linking the parent of coordination to all conjuncts is deterministic.

- Recognizing and transforming relative clauses is easy if relative pronouns can be recognized. This can be tricky in languages where the same pronouns can be used relatively (Figure 3) and interrogatively (Figure 4). We cannot recognize all instances of the latter case reliably; fortunately they do not seem to be too frequent.

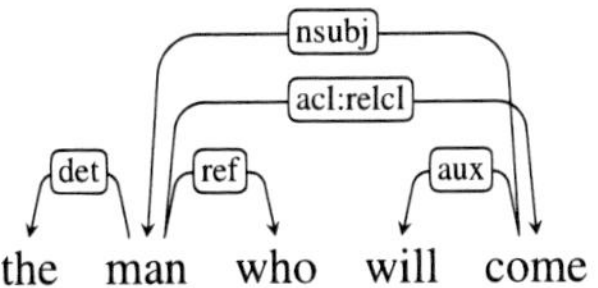

Figure 3: Enhanced graph of a relative clause.

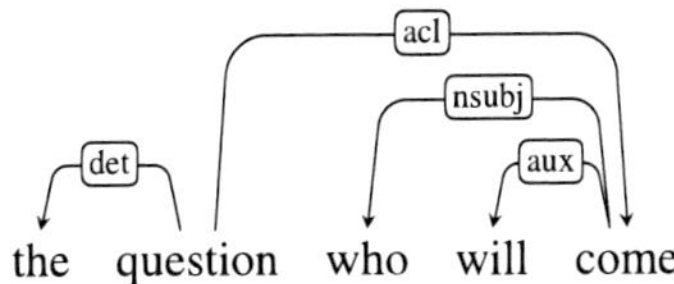

Figure 4: Enhanced graph of an interrogative clause.

- External subjects of xcomp clauses are subjects, objects or oblique dependents of the matrix clause. To find them, we need to know whether the governing verb has subject or object control. We use language-specific verb lists, which can resolve many cases, but not all. If a verb is not on any list, we skip it.

- Gapping can be easily identified by the presence of the orphan relation in the basic tree, insertion of empty nodes is thus trivial. However, we do not know the type of the relation between the empty node and the orphaned dependents. Figure 2 shows a graph where each empty node has one nsubj and one obj dependent. We cannot infer these labels from the basic tree (Figure 1), so we use dep instead.

- Linking conjuncts to shared dependents cannot be done reliably because we cannot know whether a dependent should be shared (this may be sometimes difficult even for a human annotator!) Therefore we do not attempt to add this enhancement to the datasets that do not have it.

Although the UD releases distinguish several different treebanks for some languages, for the purpose of the shared task evaluation we merged all test sets of each language. We wanted to promote robust parsers that are not tightly tied to one particular dataset. Merging treebanks of one language was possible because for almost all languages it holds that treebanks participating in the present task are maintained by the same team, hence no significant treebank-specific annotation decisions are expected. There is one exception, though: Polish. The LFG

Treebank	edeps	% new	% str.n
Arabic PADT	300776	33.88	7.00
Bulgarian BTB	160838	15.30	3.86
Czech CAC	542902	27.61	10.80
Czech FicTree	181370	21.20	9.46
Czech PDT	1612550	24.39	8.20
Czech PUD	20681	26.87	11.42
Dutch Alpino	215595	16.86	4.36
Dutch LassySmall	102130	18.10	4.90
English EWT	267247	17.40	5.17
English PUD	22173	19.58	5.28
Estonian EDT	440974	23.81	1.77
Estonian EWT	29046	26.23	7.52
Finnish PUD	17034	26.27	8.43
Finnish TDT	220061	25.94	9.19
French FQB	24513	2.88	1.55
French Sequoia	73982	6.03	4.70
Italian ISDT	311341	21.39	5.16
Latvian LVTB	238416	23.98	9.56
Lithuanian ALKSNIS	77868	32.25	10.68
Polish LFG	134732	11.17	2.89
Polish PDB	376601	22.82	8.23
Polish PUD	19752	24.61	8.02
Russian SynTagRus	1170014	22.45	6.17
Slovak SNK	111823	20.47	6.12
Swedish PUD	21101	25.25	10.95
Swedish Talbanken	102912	21.19	7.15
Tamil TTB	10408	32.87	7.94
Ukrainian IU	138275	26.48	12.27
total	6945115	23.13	7.09

Table 2: Comparing impact of enhancements in the shared task treebanks where 'edeps' is the number of enhanced dependencies, 'new' is the percentage of edeps that is new when compared to basic UD relations, and 'str.new' are the 'structurally new' dependencies, i.e. dependencies that do not just differ from the basic dependency in having an enhanced dependency label.

treebank uses a different set of relation subtypes than the PDB and PUD treebanks. This is true in the basic trees and it naturally projects to the enhanced graphs. Thus, for example, in LFG the aux relation occurs without a subtype (21%), or subtyped aux:aglt (65%) or aux:pass (14%). In PDB, aux occurs without a subtype (21%), or subtyped aux:clitic (40%), aux:cnd (12%), aux:imp (1%) or aux:pass (26%). A parser can hardly get the subtypes right when we do not tell it what label dialect is used in the gold data. We can thus expect the labeled attachment score

to be less informative in Polish than in the other languages (see Section 6 for alternative evaluation metrics).

Table 2 shows that the effect of enhancements differs quite a bit between the various languages. For instance, the percentage of enhanced dependencies that is 'new', i.e. does not have a corresponding dependency in the basic tree, ranges from 6 to over 30%. Many of these are a consequence of the decision to add the case information to obl and other relations, extensions which are relatively easy to capture using a few simple heuristics. Enhanced dependencies that introduce truly novel edges or labels are rarer. The percentage of 'structurally new' relations, i.e. dependencies that differ from the basic dependency in more than just the enhanced label, varies between 2 and 12%.

There are slight differences in how individual languages implement particular enhancement types. Some languages follow earlier proposals for enhanced relation subtypes that are not supported by the current UD guidelines, e.g., external subjects are labeled nsubj:xsubj, antecedents of relative clauses are nsubj:relsubj or obj:relobj, the "case" information is extended to showing conjunction lemma with conjuncts (conj:and, conj:or etc.) Empty nodes are occasionally used for other ellipsis types than gapping or stripping. A special case is French where diathesis neutralization is encoded in the spirit of Candito et al. (2017).

The data used in the shared task will be permanently available after the shared task at http://hdl.handle.net/11234/1-3238.

5 Task

As in the previous dependency parsing shared tasks, participants were expected to go from raw, untokenized, strings to full dependency annotation. The evaluation focused on the enhanced annotation layer, but the participants were encouraged to predict all annotation layers, and the evaluation of the other layers is available on the shared task website.[3] The task was open, in the sense that participants were allowed to use any additional resources they deemed fit (with the exception of UD 2.5 test data) as long as this was announced in advance and the additional resource was freely available to everybody.

[3]https://universaldependencies.org/iwpt20/

The submitted system outputs had to be valid CoNLL-U files; if a file was invalid, its score would be zero.[4] The official UD validation script[5] was used to check validity, although only at 'level 2', which means that only basic file format was checked and not the annotation guidelines (e.g., an unknown relation label would not render the file invalid). Still, certain aspects of level-2 validity complicate the prediction of the enhanced graphs, and as the participants were not alerted to individual restrictions beforehand, these restrictions were an unwelcome surprise to them. So the relations can be unknown but can only contain characters from a limited set. The enhanced graph can contain cycles, but not self-loops (a node depending on itself). And most crucially, there must be at least one root node and every node must be reachable via a directed path from at least one root node (rootedness and connectedness). When we saw during the test phase that some teams might not be able to comply with these restrictions, we created a quick-fix script that tries to make the submission valid; however, the solution the script provided for unconnected graphs is not optimal.

In addition to CoNLL-U validity, we also required that systems do not alter any non-whitespace characters when processing the input. This is a pre-requisite for the evaluation, where system-predicted tokens must be aligned with gold-standard tokens; files with modified word forms would be rejected.

6   Evaluation Metrics

The main evaluation metric is ELAS (*labeled attachment score on enhanced dependencies*), where ELAS is defined as F1-score over the set of enhanced dependencies in the system output and the gold standard. Complete edge labels are taken into account, i.e. `obl:on` differs from `obl`. A second metric is EULAS, which differs from ELAS in that only the universal part of the dependency relation label is taken into account. Relation subtypes are ignored, i.e., `obl:on`, `obl:auf`, and `obl` are treated as identical.

As is apparent from Table 1, despite our effort to obtain consistent annotation across all treebanks, there are still treebanks that do not include all enhancements listed in the UD guidelines. Therefore,

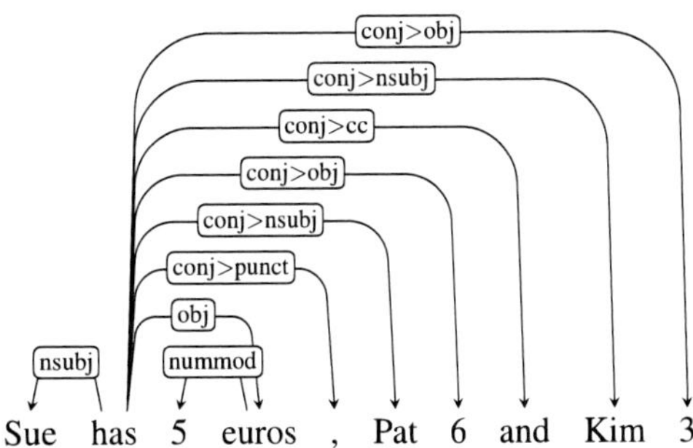

Figure 5: The enhanced graph from Figure 2 after collapsing empty nodes and reflecting the paths in dependency labels.

systems that try to predict all enhancement types for all treebanks might in fact be penalized for predicting more than has been annotated. To give such systems a fair chance, we perform two types of evaluation: 'coarse' and 'qualitative'. In the latter, we ignore dependencies that are specific to enhancement E if the given gold-standard dataset does not include enhancement E. We can trigger individual enhancements on and off separately for each treebank—while the blind input data only distinguishes languages but not treebanks, we still know where each sentence comes from and we can take this information into account during evaluation. The two evaluation methods should give roughly the same result for systems that during training learned to adapt their output to a given treebank, whereas for systems that generally try to predict all possible enhancements, the second method should give more informative results.

A final issue we address is the evaluation of empty nodes. A consequence of the treatment of gapping and ellipsis is that some sentences contain additional nodes (numbered 1.1 etc.). It is not guaranteed that gold and system agree on the position in the string where these should appear, but the information encoded by these additional nodes might nevertheless be identical. Thus, such empty nodes should be considered equal even if their string index differs. To ensure that this is the case, we have opted for a solution that basically compiles the information expressed by empty nodes into the dependency label of its dependents. I.e. if a dependent with dependency label `L2` has an empty node `i2.1` as parent which itself is an `L1` dependent of `i1`, its dependency label will be expanded into a path `i1:L1>L2`. This preserves the infor-

[4] https://universaldependencies.org/format.html

[5] https://universaldependencies.org/release_checklist.html#validation

mation that the dependent was an `L2` dependent of 'something' that was itself an `L1` dependent of `i1`, while at the same time removing the potentially conflicting `i2.1` (Figure 5).[6]

7 Approaches

There is quite a bit of variation in the way various teams have addressed the task. For the initial stages of the analysis (tokenization, lemmatization, POS-tagging) some version of UDPipe[7] (Straka et al., 2016), Udify[8] (Kondratyuk and Straka, 2019), and/or Stanza[9] (Qi et al., 2020) is often involved.

Several teams (Orange (Heinecke, 2020), FAST-PARSE (Dehouck et al., 2020), UNIPI (Attardi et al., 2020), CLASP (Ek and Bernardy, 2020), ADAPT (Barry et al., 2020)) concentrate on parsing into standard UD, and then add hand-written enhancement rules, sometimes in combination with data-driven heuristics to improve robustness. TurkuNLP (Kanerva et al., 2020) transforms EUD into a representation that is compatible with standard UD by combining multiple edges into a single edge with a complex label, and compiling edges involving empty nodes into complex edge labels (as is done by the evaluation script as well). The total number of edge-labels is reduced by de-lexicalising enhanced edge labels and storing a pointer to the dependent from which the lemma of an enhancement originates in the de-lexicalized edge label. A wide range of parsers (graph-based biaffine, transition-based), and pre-trained embeddings (XLM-R or mBERT or language specific BERTs) is used. Finally, several teams (Emory NLP (He and Choi, 2020), ShanghaiTech (Wang et al., 2020), ADAPT, Køpsala (Hershcovich et al., 2020), RobertNLP (Grünewald and Friedrich, 2020)) do not use conversion (or only to restore de-lexicalized labels), but instead use a graph-based parser that can directly produce enhanced dependency graphs. The output of the graph-based parser is often combined with information from a standard UD parser to ensure well-formedness and connectedness of the resulting graph.

8 Results

We include two baseline results:[10] baseline1 was obtained by taking gold basic UD trees and copying these into the enhanced layer without any modifications. Baseline2 uses UDPipe 1.2 trained on UD 2.5 treebanks[11] and again copies basic UD to the enhanced layer. Both baselines give an impression of how much the enhanced layer differs from the basic layer, where baseline1 makes the unrealistic assumption that parsing into basic UD is perfect.

Table 3 shows that the best three submissions achieve ELAS comparable to LAS for multilingual UD parsing (Zeman et al., 2018; Kondratyuk and Straka, 2019; Kulmizev et al., 2019).

If we compare scores for LAS, EULAS, and ELAS, it can be observed that usually there is a small drop in accuracy when going from LAS to EULAS to ELAS, although the drop from LAS/EULAS to ELAS seems to be larger for some of the systems in the lower half of the table. This suggests that predicting the correct label enhancement is problematic for some approaches.

The EULAS and ELAS scores for the qualitative evaluation (which takes into account differences in the enhancement level of treebanks) are only slightly higher than in the coarse evaluation. It should be noted though, that scores cannot be compared directly, as the coarse evaluation is a macro average over languages, whereas most scores in the qualitative evaluation are macro averages over treebanks. This implies that the data is weighted slightly differently in both averages, which plays a role in the LAS scores being generally a bit higher in the qualitative evaluation. When the qualitative ELAS is averaged over languages (the ELAS-l column in Table 3), the scores become similar to coarse ELAS and no general trend is observable.

Difference between coarse and qualitative evaluation is small. This is due to (a) the fact that this makes a difference for 9 of 28 treebanks only and (b) the fact that some of the phenomena that are ignored in the qualitative evaluation are relatively rare in the data (e.g. ellipsis).

Table 4 shows the best ELAS per language. More detailed results (per language, unofficial re-

---

[6]If there are multiple empty nodes in the sentence, we lose the information which orphans were siblings and which were not. Nevertheless, multiple empty nodes in one sentence are extremely rare.

[7]`http://ufal.mff.cuni.cz/udpipe`

[8]`https://github.com/Hyperparticle/udify`

[9]`https://stanfordnlp.github.io/stanza/`

[10]We did not include our baseline3 architecture here due to technical issues that prevented us to parse all languages. Encouraging partial results are however available on the shared task website.

[11]Pretrained models (Straka and Straková, 2019) used with default settings, always using the largest available model for the given language. No pretrained word embeddings.

Team	Coarse			Qualitative			
	LAS	EULAS	ELAS	LAS	EULAS	ELAS-t	ELAS-l
baseline1	100.00	96.37	79.86	100.00	96.22	80.70	79.92
baseline2	75.41	72.97	61.07	76.39	73.80	62.32	60.99
TurkuNLP	87.31	85.83	84.50	87.94	86.36	84.63	84.19
Orange	86.79	84.62	82.60	87.78	85.46	83.07	82.52
Emory NLP	86.14	81.26	79.84	87.20	82.34	80.87	79.64
FASTPARSE	77.57	75.96	74.04	78.63	76.99	74.77	73.95
UNIPI	80.74	78.82	72.76	81.61	79.60	73.48	72.82
ShanghaiTech	0.99	73.01	71.74	1.00	73.77	72.40	71.70
CLASP	82.66	80.18	67.85	83.13	80.60	69.20	68.16
ADAPT	84.09	69.42	67.23	84.73	70.10	67.49	67.17
Køpsala	75.41	64.93	62.91	76.39	65.10	62.67	62.72
RobertNLP	5.11	5.26	5.23	6.21	6.39	6.36	5.24

Table 3: Evaluation results on the test data. LAS is the evaluation of the basic tree, EULAS and ELAS evaluate the enhanced graph. In Coarse, the score is the macro average over languages, in Qualitative, the score for LAS and EULAS is the macro average over treebanks. ELAS-t gives the macro average over treebanks, and ELAS-l the macro average over languages. RobertNLP submitted only the English data.

Language	Team	ELAS
Arabic	TurkuNLP	77.82
Bulgarian	TurkuNLP	90.73
Czech	TurkuNLP	87.51
Dutch	Orange	85.14
English	RobertNLP	88.94
Estonian	TurkuNLP	84.54
Finnish	TurkuNLP	89.49
French	Emory NLP	86.23
Italian	TurkuNLP	91.54
Latvian	TurkuNLP	84.94
Lithuanian	TurkuNLP	77.64
Polish	TurkuNLP	84.64
Russian	TurkuNLP	90.69
Slovak	TurkuNLP	88.56
Swedish	TurkuNLP	85.64
Tamil	Orange	64.23
Ukrainian	TurkuNLP	87.22

Table 4: Best results per language (Coarse).

sults) are available on the results page of the shared task website.[12]

9 Post Shared Task Unofficial Results

A number of teams have submitted runs on the test data after the deadline for the official evaluation, an overview in given in Table 5. In some cases, these

[12]https://universaldependencies.org/iwpt20/Results.html

are runs that fix validation issues and that result in considerably higher scores (i.e., ShanghaiTech). In other cases, these unofficial runs are experiments with various components of the system architecture. The reader should consult the system description papers for further discussion of these results.

10 Conclusions

This shared task was the first attempt at a coordinated evaluation effort on parsing enhanced universal dependencies. While a large part of the methodology could be adopted from the previous CoNLL shared tasks on parsing into UD, a number of issues did require attention.

First, providing training and test data is complicated by the fact that not all treebanks in the UD repository include the same level of enhancements. This makes training a single, multilingual, model, harder than it ought to be, as annotation style differs per treebank. For evaluation, different enhancement levels pose a problem as it is unclear to what extent 'overannotating' data should be considered an error. As Table 1 illustrates, the situation has improved already considerably for UD release 2.6.

Another issue for validation is the status of 'empty' nodes. The position in the string of such nodes is not defined by the guidelines, and therefore one may expect mismatches between gold and system data. Our solution to this issue is described in Section 6. For future tasks, however, it might

Team	Coarse			Qualitative			
	LAS	EULAS	ELAS	LAS	EULAS	ELAS-t	ELAS-l
ShanghaiTech	1.05	86.54	85.06	1.04	87.23	85.63	84.96
ADAPT	84.91	82.25	79.95	85.60	83.12	80.15	79.89
FASTPARSE	79.85	78.27	76.48	80.82	79.20	77.13	76.36
Køpsala	75.41	78.92	76.48	76.39	79.28	76.33	76.28
UNIPI	84.32	82.32	75.92	85.76	83.60	77.16	75.92

Table 5: Post Shared Task evaluation results on the test data.

be worthwhile to investigate whether a different representation of such nodes in the data files or an alternative evaluation strategy is needed.

Several systems struggled with the validation requirements of enhanced UD. While an enhanced graph may contain nodes with more than one parent, may contain cycles, and may have multiple root nodes, there are still constraints that an enhanced UD graph must comply with, such as that the graph must be connected and that there should be one or more 'root' nodes from which all other nodes are reachable. In future tasks, the restrictions should be more carefully described in advance.

The results of the shared task illustrate that there is quite a wide variety in the way that the problem of parsing into enhanced universal dependencies can be approached, with some systems sticking closer to traditional approaches for parsing UD, and dealing with the enhancements in a conversion script, while other systems output a graph directly. The scores indicate that while parsing into enhanced UD is harder than parsing into UD, the drop in performance is minimal for most systems, which suggests that the challenges posed by the annotation format of enhanced UD are not an obstacle for accurate parsing.

Acknowledgments

We heartily thank everyone involved in the development of the Enhanced UD treebanks and who made this shared task possible.
This work has been partially supported by the LUSyD project, grant 20-16819X of the Czech Science Foundation (GAČR). The second author was partly funded by two French National Research Agency projects, PARSITI (ANR-16-CE33-0021) and SoSweet (ANR-15-CE38-0011).

References

Giuseppe Attardi, Daniele Sartiano, and Maria Simi. 2020. Linear neural parsing and hybrid enhancement for Enhanced Universal Dependencies. In *Proceedings of the 16th International Conference on Parsing Technologies and the IWPT 2020 Shared Task on Parsing into Enhanced Universal Dependencies (this volume)*. Association for Computational Linguistics.

James Barry, Joachim Wagner, and Jennifer Foster. 2020. The ADAPT Enhanced Dependency Parser at the IWPT 2020 Shared Task. In *Proceedings of the 16th International Conference on Parsing Technologies and the IWPT 2020 Shared Task on Parsing into Enhanced Universal Dependencies (this volume)*. Association for Computational Linguistics.

Marie Candito, Bruno Guillaume, Guy Perrier, and Djamé Seddah. 2017. Enhanced UD dependencies with neutralized diathesis alternation. In *Proceedings of the Fourth International Conference on Dependency Linguistics (Depling 2017)*, pages 42–53, Pisa, Italy.

Mathieu Dehouck, Mark Anderson, and Carlos Gómez-Rodríguez. 2020. Efficient EUD parsing. In *Proceedings of the 16th International Conference on Parsing Technologies and the IWPT 2020 Shared Task on Parsing into Enhanced Universal Dependencies (this volume)*. Association for Computational Linguistics.

Adam Ek and Jean-Philippe Bernardy. 2020. How much of enhanced UD is contained in UD? In *Proceedings of the 16th International Conference on Parsing Technologies and the IWPT 2020 Shared Task on Parsing into Enhanced Universal Dependencies (this volume)*. Association for Computational Linguistics.

Stefan Grünewald and Annemarie Friedrich. 2020. Robertnlp at the IWPT 2020 Shared Task: Surprisingly Simple Enhanced UD Parsing for English. In *Proceedings of the 16th International Conference on Parsing Technologies and the IWPT 2020 Shared Task on Parsing into Enhanced Universal Dependencies (this volume)*. Association for Computational Linguistics.

Han He and Jinho D. Choi. 2020. Adaptation of Multilingual Transformer Encoder for Robust Enhanced

Universal Dependency Parsing. In *Proceedings of the 16th International Conference on Parsing Technologies and the IWPT 2020 Shared Task on Parsing into Enhanced Universal Dependencies (this volume)*. Association for Computational Linguistics.

Johannes Heinecke. 2020. Hybrid Enhanced Universal Dependencies Parsing. In *Proceedings of the 16th International Conference on Parsing Technologies and the IWPT 2020 Shared Task on Parsing into Enhanced Universal Dependencies (this volume)*. Association for Computational Linguistics.

Daniel Hershcovich, Miryam de Lhoneux, Artur Kulmizev, Elham Pejhan, and Joakim Nivre. 2020. Køpsala: Transition-Based Graph Parsing via Efficient Training and Effective Encoding. In *Proceedings of the 16th International Conference on Parsing Technologies and the IWPT 2020 Shared Task on Parsing into Enhanced Universal Dependencies (this volume)*. Association for Computational Linguistics.

Jenna Kanerva, Filip Ginter, and Sampo Pyysalo. 2020. Turku Enhanced Parser Pipeline: From Raw Text to Enhanced Graphs in the IWPT 2020 Shared Task. In *Proceedings of the 16th International Conference on Parsing Technologies and the IWPT 2020 Shared Task on Parsing into Enhanced Universal Dependencies (this volume)*. Association for Computational Linguistics.

Dan Kondratyuk and Milan Straka. 2019. 75 languages, 1 model: Parsing universal dependencies universally. In *Proceedings of the 2019 Conference on Empirical Methods in Natural Language Processing and the 9th International Joint Conference on Natural Language Processing (EMNLP-IJCNLP)*, pages 2779–2795.

Artur Kulmizev, Miryam de Lhoneux, Johannes Gontrum, Elena Fano, and Joakim Nivre. 2019. Deep contextualized word embeddings in transition-based and graph-based dependency parsing - a tale of two parsers revisited. In *Proceedings of the 2019 Conference on Empirical Methods in Natural Language Processing and the 9th International Joint Conference on Natural Language Processing (EMNLP-IJCNLP)*, pages 2755–2768, Hong Kong, China. Association for Computational Linguistics.

Joakim Nivre, Marie-Catherine de Marneffe, Filip Ginter, Jan Hajič, Christopher D. Manning, Sampo Pyysalo, Sebastian Schuster, Francis Tyers, and Daniel Zeman. 2020. Universal Dependencies v2: An evergrowing multilingual treebank collection. In *Proceedings of the Twelfth International Conference on Language Resources and Evaluation (LREC 2020)*, pages 4027–4036, Paris, France. European Language Resources Association.

Joakim Nivre, Paola Marongiu, Filip Ginter, Jenna Kanerva, Simonetta Montemagni, Sebastian Schuster, and Maria Simi. 2018. Enhancing universal dependency treebanks: A case study. In *Proceedings of the Second Workshop on Universal Dependencies (UDW 2018)*, pages 102–107.

Stephan Oepen, Omri Abend, Jan Hajič, Daniel Hershcovich, Marco Kuhlmann, Tim O'Gorman, Nianwen Xue, Jayeol Chun, Milan Straka, and Zdeňka Urešová. 2019. MRP 2019: Cross-framework meaning representation parsing. In *Proceedings of the Shared Task on Cross-Framework Meaning Representation Parsing at the 2019 Conference on Natural Language Learning*, pages 1–27, Hong Kong. Association for Computational Linguistics.

Stephan Oepen, Jari Björne, Richard Johansson, Emanuele Lapponi, Filip Ginter, Erik Velldal, and Lilja Øvrelid. 2017. The 2017 Shared Task on Extrinsic Parser Evaluation (EPE 2017).

Stephan Oepen, Marco Kuhlmann, Yusuke Miyao, Daniel Zeman, Silvie Cinkova, Dan Flickinger, Jan Hajic, and Zdenka Uresova. 2015. SemEval 2015 task 18: Broad-coverage semantic dependency parsing. In *Proceedings of the 9th International Workshop on Semantic Evaluation (SemEval 2015)*. Association for Computational Linguistics.

Stephan Oepen, Marco Kuhlmann, Yusuke Miyao, Daniel Zeman, Dan Flickinger, Jan Hajic, Angelina Ivanova, and Yi Zhang. 2014. Semeval 2014 task 8: Broad-coverage semantic dependency parsing. In *Proceedings of the 8th International Workshop on Semantic Evaluation (SemEval 2014)*, pages 63–72.

Peng Qi, Yuhao Zhang, Yuhui Zhang, Jason Bolton, and Christopher D. Manning. 2020. Stanza: A Python natural language processing toolkit for many human languages. In *In Association for Computational Linguistics (ACL) System Demonstrations*, Seattle, WA, USA.

Sebastian Schuster, Eric De La Clergerie, Marie Candito, Benoît Sagot, Christopher D. Manning, and Djamé Seddah. 2017. Paris and Stanford at EPE 2017: Downstream evaluation of graph-based dependency representations.

Milan Straka, Jan Hajič, and Jana Straková. 2016. Udpipe: trainable pipeline for processing conll-u files performing tokenization, morphological analysis, pos tagging and parsing. In *Proceedings of the Tenth International Conference on Language Resources and Evaluation (LREC'16)*, pages 4290–4297.

Milan Straka and Jana Straková. 2019. Universal dependencies 2.5 models for UDPipe (2019-12-06). LINDAT/CLARIAH-CZ digital library at the Institute of Formal and Applied Linguistics (ÚFAL), Faculty of Mathematics and Physics, Charles University.

Xinyu Wang, Yong Jiang, and Kewei Tu. 2020. Enhanced Universal Dependency Parsing with Second-Order Inference and Mixture of Training Data. In *Proceedings of the 16th International Conference on Parsing Technologies and the IWPT 2020 Shared Task on Parsing into Enhanced Universal Dependencies (this volume)*. Association for Computational Linguistics.

Daniel Zeman, Jan Hajič, Martin Popel, Martin Potthast, Milan Straka, Filip Ginter, Joakim Nivre, and Slav Petrov. 2018. CoNLL 2018 shared task: Multilingual parsing from raw text to universal dependencies. In *Proceedings of the CoNLL 2018 Shared Task: Multilingual Parsing from Raw Text to Universal Dependencies*, pages 1–21, Brussels, Belgium. Association for Computational Linguistics.

Daniel Zeman, Joakim Nivre, Mitchell Abrams, Noëmi Aepli, Željko Agić, Lars Ahrenberg, Gabrielė Aleksandravičiūtė, Lene Antonsen, Katya Aplonova, Maria Jesus Aranzabe, Gashaw Arutie, Masayuki Asahara, Luma Ateyah, Mohammed Attia, Aitziber Atutxa, Liesbeth Augustinus, Elena Badmaeva, Miguel Ballesteros, Esha Banerjee, Sebastian Bank, Verginica Barbu Mititelu, Victoria Basmov, Colin Batchelor, John Bauer, Sandra Bellato, Kepa Bengoetxea, Yevgeni Berzak, Irshad Ahmad Bhat, Riyaz Ahmad Bhat, Erica Biagetti, Eckhard Bick, Agnė Bielinskienė, Rogier Blokland, Victoria Bobicev, Loïc Boizou, Emanuel Borges Völker, Carl Börstell, Cristina Bosco, Gosse Bouma, Sam Bowman, Adriane Boyd, Kristina Brokaitė, Aljoscha Burchardt, Marie Candito, Bernard Caron, Gauthier Caron, Tatiana Cavalcanti, Gülşen Cebiroğlu Eryiğit, Flavio Massimiliano Cecchini, Giuseppe G. A. Celano, Slavomír Čéplö, Savas Cetin, Fabricio Chalub, Jinho Choi, Yongseok Cho, Jayeol Chun, Alessandra T. Cignarella, Silvie Cinková, Aurélie Collomb, Çağrı Çöltekin, Miriam Connor, Marine Courtin, Elizabeth Davidson, Marie-Catherine de Marneffe, Valeria de Paiva, Elvis de Souza, Arantza Diaz de Ilarraza, Carly Dickerson, Bamba Dione, Peter Dirix, Kaja Dobrovoljc, Timothy Dozat, Kira Droganova, Puneet Dwivedi, Hanne Eckhoff, Marhaba Eli, Ali Elkahky, Binyam Ephrem, Olga Erina, Tomaž Erjavec, Aline Etienne, Wograine Evelyn, Richárd Farkas, Hector Fernandez Alcalde, Jennifer Foster, Cláudia Freitas, Kazunori Fujita, Katarína Gajdošová, Daniel Galbraith, Marcos Garcia, Moa Gärdenfors, Sebastian Garza, Kim Gerdes, Filip Ginter, Iakes Goenaga, Koldo Gojenola, Memduh Gökırmak, Yoav Goldberg, Xavier Gómez Guinovart, Berta González Saavedra, Bernadeta Griciūtė, Matias Grioni, Normunds Grūzītis, Bruno Guillaume, Céline Guillot-Barbance, Nizar Habash, Jan Hajič, Jan Hajič jr., Mika Hämäläinen, Linh Hà Mỹ, Na-Rae Han, Kim Harris, Dag Haug, Johannes Heinecke, Felix Hennig, Barbora Hladká, Jaroslava Hlaváčová, Florinel Hociung, Petter Hohle, Jena Hwang, Takumi Ikeda, Radu Ion, Elena Irimia, Ọlájídé Ishola, Tomáš Jelínek, Anders Johannsen, Fredrik Jørgensen, Markus Juutinen, Hüner Kaşıkara, Andre Kaasen, Nadezhda Kabaeva, Sylvain Kahane, Hiroshi Kanayama, Jenna Kanerva, Boris Katz, Tolga Kayadelen, Jessica Kenney, Václava Kettnerová, Jesse Kirchner, Elena Klementieva, Arne Köhn, Kamil Kopacewicz, Natalia Kotsyba, Jolanta Kovalevskaitė, Simon Krek, Sookyoung Kwak, Veronika Laippala, Lorenzo Lambertino, Lucia Lam, Tatiana Lando, Septina Dian Larasati, Alexei Lavrentiev, John Lee, Phng Lê H`ông, Alessandro Lenci, Saran Lertpradit, Herman Leung, Cheuk Ying Li, Josie Li, Keying Li, KyungTae Lim, Maria Liovina, Yuan Li, Nikola Ljubešić, Olga Loginova, Olga Lyashevskaya, Teresa Lynn, Vivien Macketanz, Aibek Makazhanov, Michael Mandl, Christopher Manning, Ruli Manurung, Cătălina Mărănduc, David Mareček, Katrin Marheinecke, Héctor Martínez Alonso, André Martins, Jan Mašek, Yuji Matsumoto, Ryan McDonald, Sarah McGuinness, Gustavo Mendonça, Niko Miekka, Margarita Misirpashayeva, Anna Missilä, Cătălin Mititelu, Maria Mitrofan, Yusuke Miyao, Simonetta Montemagni, Amir More, Laura Moreno Romero, Keiko Sophie Mori, Tomohiko Morioka, Shinsuke Mori, Shigeki Moro, Bjartur Mortensen, Bohdan Moskalevskyi, Kadri Muischnek, Robert Munro, Yugo Murawaki, Kaili Müürisep, Pinkey Nainwani, Juan Ignacio Navarro Horñiacek, Anna Nedoluzhko, Gunta Nešpore-Bērzkalne, Lng Nguy˜ên Thị, Huy`ên Nguy˜ên Thị Minh, Yoshihiro Nikaido, Vitaly Nikolaev, Rattima Nitisaroj, Hanna Nurmi, Stina Ojala, Atul Kr. Ojha, Adédayọ Olúòkun, Mai Omura, Petya Osenova, Robert Östling, Lilja Øvrelid, Niko Partanen, Elena Pascual, Marco Passarotti, Agnieszka Patejuk, Guilherme Paulino-Passos, Angelika Peljak-Łapińska, Siyao Peng, Cenel-Augusto Perez, Guy Perrier, Daria Petrova, Slav Petrov, Jason Phelan, Jussi Piitulainen, Tommi A Pirinen, Emily Pitler, Barbara Plank, Thierry Poibeau, Larisa Ponomareva, Martin Popel, Lauma Pretkalniņa, Sophie Prévost, Prokopis Prokopidis, Adam Przepiórkowski, Tiina Puolakainen, Sampo Pyysalo, Peng Qi, Andriela Rääbis, Alexandre Rademaker, Loganathan Ramasamy, Taraka Rama, Carlos Ramisch, Vinit Ravishankar, Livy Real, Siva Reddy, Georg Rehm, Ivan Riabov, Michael Rießler, Erika Rimkutė, Larissa Rinaldi, Laura Rituma, Luisa Rocha, Mykhailo Romanenko, Rudolf Rosa, Davide Rovati, Valentin Roșca, Olga Rudina, Jack Rueter, Shoval Sadde, Benoît Sagot, Shadi Saleh, Alessio Salomoni, Tanja Samardžić, Stephanie Samson, Manuela Sanguinetti, Dage Särg, Baiba Saulīte, Yanin Sawanakunanon, Nathan Schneider, Sebastian Schuster, Djamé Seddah, Wolfgang Seeker, Mojgan Seraji, Mo Shen, Atsuko Shimada, Hiroyuki Shirasu, Muh Shohibussirri, Dmitry Sichinava, Aline Silveira, Natalia Silveira, Maria Simi, Radu Simionescu, Katalin Simkó, Mária Šimková, Kiril Simov, Aaron Smith, Isabela Soares-Bastos, Carolyn Spadine, Antonio Stella, Milan Straka, Jana Strnadová, Alane Suhr, Umut Sulubacak, Shingo Suzuki, Zsolt Szántó, Dima Taji, Yuta Takahashi, Fabio Tamburini, Takaaki Tanaka, Isabelle Tellier, Guillaume Thomas, Liisi Torga, Trond Trosterud, Anna Trukhina, Reut Tsarfaty, Francis Tyers, Sumire Uematsu, Zdeňka Urešová, Larraitz Uria, Hans Uszkoreit, Andrius Utka, Sowmya Vajjala, Daniel van Niekerk, Gertjan van Noord, Viktor Varga, Eric Villemonte de la Clergerie, Veronika Vincze, Lars Wallin, Abigail Walsh, Jing Xian Wang, Jonathan North Washington, Maximilan Wendt, Seyi Williams, Mats Wirén, Christian Wittern, Tsegay Woldemariam, Tak-sum Wong, Alina Wróblewska, Mary Yako, Naoki Yamazaki, Chunxiao Yan, Koichi Yasuoka, Marat M. Yavrumyan, Zhuoran Yu, Zdeněk Žabokrtský, Amir Zeldes, Manying Zhang, and Hanzhi Zhu. 2019. Universal dependencies 2.5. LINDAT/CLARIAH-CZ digital library at the Institute of Formal and Applied Linguistics (ÚFAL), Faculty of Mathematics and Physics, Charles University.

Daniel Zeman, Martin Popel, Milan Straka, Jan Hajič, Joakim Nivre, Filip Ginter, Juhani Luotolahti, Sampo Pyysalo, Slav Petrov, Martin Potthast, Francis Tyers, Elena Badmaeva, Memduh Gökırmak, Anna Nedoluzhko, Silvie Cinková, Jan Hajič jr., Jaroslava Hlaváčová, Václava Kettnerová, Zdeňka Urešová, Jenna Kanerva, Stina Ojala, Anna Missilä, Christopher D. Manning, Sebastian Schuster, Siva Reddy, Dima Taji, Nizar Habash, Herman Leung, Marie-Catherine de Marneffe, Manuela Sanguinetti, Maria Simi, Hiroshi Kanayama, Valeria de Paiva, Kira Droganova, Héctor Martínez Alonso, Çağrı Çöltekin, Umut Sulubacak, Hans Uszkoreit, Vivien Macketanz, Aljoscha Burchardt, Kim Harris, Katrin Marheinecke, Georg Rehm, Tolga Kayadelen, Mohammed Attia, Ali Elkahky, Zhuoran Yu, Emily Pitler, Saran Lertpradit, Michael Mandl, Jesse Kirchner, Hector Fernandez Alcalde, Jana Strnadová, Esha Banerjee, Ruli Manurung, Antonio Stella, Atsuko Shimada, Sookyoung Kwak, Gustavo Mendonca, Tatiana Lando, Rattima Nitisaroj, and Josie Li. 2017. Conll 2017 shared task: Multilingual parsing from raw text to universal dependencies. In *Proceedings of the CoNLL 2017 Shared Task: Multilingual Parsing from Raw Text to Universal Dependencies*, pages 1–19, Vancouver, Canada. Association for Computational Linguistics.

Turku Enhanced Parser Pipeline: From Raw Text to Enhanced Graphs in the IWPT 2020 Shared Task

Jenna Kanerva[*]   **Filip Ginter**   **Sampo Pyysalo**
TurkuNLP group, Department of Future Technologies
University of Turku, Finland
`first.last@utu.fi`

Abstract

We present the approach of the TurkuNLP group to the IWPT 2020 shared task on Multilingual Parsing into Enhanced Universal Dependencies. The task involves 28 treebanks in 17 different languages and requires parsers to generate graph structures extending on the basic dependency trees. Our approach combines language-specific BERT models, the UDify parser, neural sequence-to-sequence lemmatization and a graph transformation approach encoding the enhanced structure into a dependency tree. Our submission averaged 84.5% ELAS, ranking first in the shared task. We make all methods and resources developed for this study freely available under open licenses from `https://turkunlp.org`.

1 Introduction

The Universal Dependencies[1] (UD) effort (Nivre et al., 2016, 2020) seeks to create cross-linguistically consistent dependency annotation and has to date produced more than 150 treebanks in 90 languages. UD is a broad and open community effort with more than 300 contributors (Zeman et al., 2019), and the resources they have created have been instrumental in driving progress in dependency parsing in recent years, also serving as the basis of widely attended CoNLL shared tasks on multilingual parsing in 2017 and 2018 (Zeman et al., 2017, 2018). While UD resources, the CoNLL shared tasks, and recent advances in deep learning-based parsing technology (Dozat et al., 2017; Kanerva et al., 2018; Kondratyuk and Straka, 2019) have contributed substantially to accurate dependency parsing using a consistent syntactic representation for a wide range of human languages, these efforts have focused almost exclusively on the *basic* UD dependency trees. UD defines also an

enhanced graph representation, which allows more detailed representation of the sentence. Common types of enhancements include null nodes for elided predicates, propagation of conjuncts for making connections between words more explicit, and augmentation of modifier labels with prepositional or case-marking information. The ability to produce enhanced UD graphs from raw text, previously explored by e.g. Schuster and Manning (2016), Nivre et al. (2018), and Schuster et al. (2018), would represent a further advance over existing tools.

The IWPT 2020 Shared Task on Multilingual Parsing into Enhanced Universal Dependendies[2] (Bouma et al., 2020) is the first shared task evaluation targeting the enhanced UD graph. The task was organized using data from 28 UD treebanks covering 17 languages, representing Baltic, Finnic, Germanic, Romance, Semitic, Slavic, and Southern Dravidian languages. We participated in the IWPT shared task with our parsing pipeline consisting of components for segmentation, part-of-speech and morphological tagging, lemmatization, dependency parsing, and enhanced dependency graph analysis. Our approach builds on custom pre-trained deep language models (Devlin et al., 2018), a deep neural network-based parser (Kondratyuk and Straka, 2019), a character-level sequence-to-sequence lemmatizer (Kanerva et al., 2020), and a custom graph transformation approach encoding an enhanced dependency graph in a labeled tree structure. The parsing pipeline is fully language agnostic, and therefore trainable with any UD treebank. Our submission to IWPT achieved an average enhanced labeled attachment score (ELAS) of 84.5%, the best performance among the 35 evaluated submissions from ten participating groups with an approximately 2% point margin to the second-best submission.

---

[*]Equal contribution by all three authors
[1]`https://universaldependencies.org/`

[2]`https://universaldependencies.org/iwpt20/`

Proceedings of the 16th International Conference on Parsing Technologies and the IWPT 2020 Shared Task, pages 162–173
Virtual Meeting, July 9, 2020. ©2020 Association for Computational Linguistics

2 Shared Task Data

The shared task data invoves 28 UD treebanks for 17 languages, representing the subset of treebanks for which enhanced dependencies are available. The enhanced dependencies fall into five types: gapping, propagation of conjuncts, controlled and raised subjects, relative clause antecedents, and case information. However, not all treebanks have all of these types. While the training data is divided according to individual treebanks, test data is divided on language level through pooling of the individual treebank test sets, without any direct possibility to identify which test set sentence originates from which source treebank. We note that this is a departure from previous UD parsing shared tasks, where the treebank distinction was preserved also in the test data. The training and development data range from less than 10,000 words for Tamil to over a million for Czech. Table 1 gathers statistics of the enhanced dependencies, compared to the base parse trees. We can see that the number of unique relation types increases by an order of magnitude, yet roughly 70-80% of the enhanced dependencies are copied unmodified from the base tree, and roughly 90-95% are a base dependency with its relation type modified.

3 System Overview

We next introduce our system and our approach to predicting enhanced dependencies.

3.1 Segmentation

For tokenization, multiword token expansion and sentence splitting we apply the Stanza toolkit by Qi et al. (2020) and its downloadable models trained on UD version 2.5 treebanks. Stanza implements a neural model that treats segmentation as a tagging problem over sequences of characters, where for a given character the model predicts whether it is the end of a token, the end of a sentence, or the end of a multiword token. Predicted multiword tokens are then expanded using a combination of a dictionary compiled from the training data and a sequence-to-sequence generation model.

3.2 Base Parser

We use the UDify dependency parser introduced by Kondratyuk and Straka (2019). UDify is a multi-task model for part-of-speech and morphological tagging, lemmatization and dependency parsing supporting fine-tuning of pre-trained BERT models

Treebank	Base	Enh	R%	UR%
Arabic-PADT	36	1074	66.1	92.9
Bulgarian-BTB	36	173	84.7	96.1
Czech-CAC	43	639	72.4	89.3
Czech-FicTree	42	295	78.7	90.5
Czech-PDT	43	759	75.6	91.8
Dutch-Alpino	35	416	83.3	95.7
Dutch-LassyS.	35	293	82.2	95.3
English-EWT	49	375	82.3	94.7
Estonian-EDT	38	560	76.1	98.3
Estonian-EWT	39	178	74.1	92.6
Finnish-TDT	45	418	74.1	91.1
French-Sequoia	46	71	93.9	95.3
Italian-ISDT	44	348	78.6	94.8
Latvian-LVTB	40	133	75.9	90.6
Lithuanian-A.	35	194	66.9	88.8
Polish-LFG	40	178	88.8	97.1
Polish-PDB	67	859	77.2	91.8
Russian-SynTag.	40	635	77.5	93.9
Slovak-SNK	41	268	81.0	94.3
Swedish-Talbank.	40	302	79.1	93.2
Tamil-TTB	28	116	69.3	97.3
Ukrainian-IU	57	351	77.5	91.6

Table 1: Statistics of base and enhanced relations from the training sections of the treebanks: *Base* is the number of unique relations in the base tree, *Enh* is the number of unique relations in the enhanced graph, *R%* is the proportion of enhanced dependencies also present in the base tree, and *UR%* is the proportion of unlabelled enhanced dependencies also present in the base tree. The letter R refers to recall.

on UD treebanks. UDify implements a multi-task network where a separate prediction layer for each task is added on top of the pre-trained BERT encoder. Additionally, instead of using only the top encoder layer representation in prediction, UDify adds attention vertically over the 12 layers of BERT, calculating a weighted sum of all intermediate representations of BERT layers for each token. All prediction layers as well as layer-wise attention are trained simultaneously, while also fine-tuning the pre-trained BERT weights.

In our shared task system we use UDify for part-of-speech tagging (UPOS), predicting morphological features (FEATS) as well as for dependency parsing. By contrast to the original UDify work, we train separate language-specific models rather than one model covering all languages.

3.3 Lemmatizer

For lemmatization we use the Universal Lemmatizer by Kanerva et al. (2020) trained on the shared task training data. The lemmatizer casts the task as a sequence-to-sequence rewrite problem where the input token is represented as a sequence of characters followed by a sequence of its part-of-speech and morphological tags, and the desired lemma is then generated a character at time from the input. Following this approach, the contextual information needed for disambiguating between possible lemmas for ambiguous words is obtained directly from the predicted morphological tags, thus creating a compact context representation which generalizes well. In order to obtain predicted tags for lemmatization, we apply the lemmatizer as the final component in our pipeline.

3.4 Enhanced Representation

Since our base parser is only capable of reproducing trees, the enhanced representation needs to either be encoded into the base trees by enriching the set of dependency types, or alternatively introduced in a separate step after base parsing. In our system submission, we chose the former, but have also experimented with the latter approach. The overall approach of encoding the graph into a tree is well-known and has been applied previously, e.g. by a number of teams in the SemEval tasks on semantic dependency parsing (Oepen et al., 2014, 2015).

Our choices adhered to the following principles: (a) the LAS of the base parser must not be compromised, (b) the encoding must be language-independent and applicable to any treebank, and (c) the method must be sufficiently simple to be included in a production-grade parsing pipeline.

3.4.1 Encoding into Base Tree

In order to encode enhanced dependencies into the base tree, we focused on a just four structures, which nevertheless cover the vast majority of the edges in the enhanced representation (see Table 2 below). The four structures and their encoding are shown in Figure 1. In the encoding, the base tree structure does not change; the enhanced relations are encoded into the base tree relations, also recording whether the enhanced dependency goes from or to the head in the base tree, or from or to the head of the head in the base tree. This encoding makes the decoding process straightforward and deterministic, because there can be at most one head and at most one head of head in the parse tree. The downside of this approach is that the number of unique relation types which the parser needs to predict increases substantially. Note that this encoding applies straightforwardly to cases where a token is the head or dependent in several enhanced relations; their encoding is simply concatenated.

The main reason for the increase in the num-

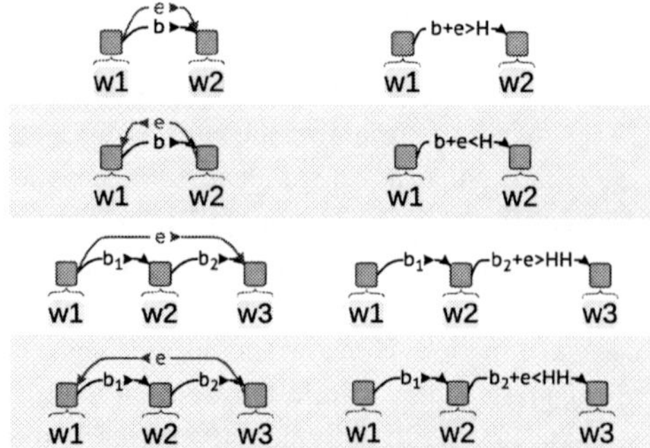

Figure 1: The four enhanced dependency structures currently captured in our encoding. The base (b) and enhanced (e) relations in the left column are encoded in a tree structure as in the right column. In the encoding, the symbol > stands for "relation from", < stands for "relation to", H is the head in the base tree, and HH is the head of the head in the base tree.

ber of unique relation types is the lexicalized relations which encode the lemma of a functional word (e.g. the *case* dependent) into the enhanced relation. To address this issue in a language-independent manner, we scan the enhanced relations for occurrences of a lemma of a dependent of the head or the dependent in the enhanced relation. If one is found, it is replaced with a placeholder encoding which position the lemma occurred at. For instance {*lemma-d-case*} indicates that this placeholder is to be replaced with the lemma of a case dependent of the dependent in this enhanced relation. Similarly, {*lemma-h-case*} indicates that this placeholder is to be replaced with the lemma of a case dependent of the head in this enhanced relation. Such delexicalization is once again straightforward to reverse and in practice deterministic, although not so in theory, since a word can have several dependents of the same type.

The final feature of the enhanced representation that we address is the empty nodes occuring in elliptic constructions. Here, we once again rely on encoding of information into the base tree. The shared task evaluation procedure includes a step whereby empty nodes are removed and encoded in the form of enhanced relations that every two relations (h, e, r_1), (e, d, r_2) produce a new enhanced relation $(h, d, r_1 > r_2)$ which encodes the presence of an empty node. Once all relations of the empty node are encoded in this manner, the empty node is removed. This representation is easy to reverse, and in practice allows one to reconstruct the empty nodes in the enhanced representation except for their position in the sentence, which is not particularly relevant nor evaluated in the shared task. Only cases where a word has several empty node dependents with the same relation type cannot be reconstructed correctly.

The overall procedure for encoding the enhanced representation is:

1. Encode empty nodes as enhanced relations, remove from the graph

2. Replace all recognized function word lemmas with their corresponding placeholders

3. Encode all enhanced relations of the four types using the encoding in Figure 1, discard any other enhanced relations

This sequence of steps produces a tree representation that a standard dependency parser can be trained on. The output of the parser is decoded in the reverse order of the encoding steps, producing the enhanced representation. The decoding must take into account any errors the parser produced which might impair the decoding of the encoded representation, or produce an enhanced graph which does not validate as Universal Dependencies. In particular:

- Any relation headed by the root is given the type *root* regardless of the parser's prediction.

- If a lemma placeholder cannot be reversed (e.g. when a parser predicts a placeholder {*lemma-d-case*} but there is no such dependent in the tree, the enhanced relation is discarded. Note that leads to unconnected words in the enhanced graph.

- Any word that remains unconnected in the enhanced graph is made the dependent of the same head, with the same relation, as in the base tree.

- For any (undirected) connected component that does not include the root node, we identify a word that all other words of the component can be reached from in the directed graph, and make this word a dependent of the root node. If no such word can be found, then the set of words with no incoming edge in the component are made dependents of the root node. This latter condition did not trigger in practice.

The encode-decode procedure can be evaluated by first encoding the enhanced training graphs into

Treebank	Rels	ELAS
Arabic-PADT	1,108	99.28
Bulgarian-BTB	152	99.22
Czech-CAC	939	98.13
Czech-FicTree	355	98.38
Czech-PDT	1,079	98.75
Dutch-Alpino	569	99.16
Dutch-LassySmall	420	99.23
English-EWT	611	98.89
Estonian-EDT	359	99.88
Estonian-EWT	202	99.74
Finnish-TDT	451	97.96
French-Sequoia	79	99.09
Italian-ISDT	561	99.53
Latvian-LVTB	405	97.94
Lithuanian-ALKSNIS	267	98.12
Polish-LFG	146	99.21
Polish-PDB	845	98.34
Russian-SynTagRus	1,119	99.57
Slovak-SNK	281	99.44
Swedish-Talbanken	494	99.16
Tamil-TTB	78	99.79
Ukrainian-IU	363	98.88

Table 2: Number of unique dependency relations after the encoding procedure, and the ELAS value after an encode-decode cycle. The latter number reflects to what extent the original enhanced graphs can be reconstructed after the encoding. The numbers are reported on the training portions of the treebanks.

trees, decoding back, and measuring the ELAS of the decoded data against the original. A lossless representation would result in ELAS of 100%. As shown in Table 2, this value is in the 97.9–99.9% range across all treebanks, meaning the encoding is not far from lossless, and only little gain can be expected from encoding more complex structures. Note, however, that this reflects the comparative structural simplicity of the enhanced relations present in the UD data, rather than the generality of our encoding. Table 2 also reports on the number of unique dependency relations in the training section of each treebank, showing an order of magnitude increase compared to the base tree.

3.4.2 Enhanced Relations as Tagging

The encoding of the enhanced relations into the base tree can also be seen as a tagging task, since every word has exactly one base relation, and therefore also exactly one relation in the encoded tree. It is therefore possible to first parse the sentence with a parser that predicts the base tree, and then subsequently tag the words with tags corresponding to the encoding of the enhanced relations, as introduced earlier, with the base parse tree serving as a source of features. The main advantage of such an approach would be guaranteeing that the

Model	Languages	References
Arabic-BERT	Arabic	`https://github.com/alisafaya/Arabic-BERT`
BERTje	Dutch	`https://github.com/wietsedv/bertje`; (de Vries et al., 2019)
BERT (original)	English	`https://github.com/google-research/bert`; (Devlin et al., 2018)
FinBERT	Finnish	`https://turkunlp.org/FinBERT/`; (Virtanen et al., 2019)
CamemBERT	French	`https://camembert-model.fr/`; (Martin et al., 2020)
Italian BERT	Italian	`https://github.com/dbmdz/berts`
RuBERT	Russian	`https://github.com/deepmipt/deeppavlov/`; (Kuratov and Arkhipov, 2019)
Slavic-BERT	Slavic[1]	`https://github.com/deepmipt/Slavic-BERT-NER`; (Arkhipov et al., 2019)
Swedish BERT	Swedish	`https://github.com/Kungbib/swedish-bert-models`
mBERT	104 lang.	`https://github.com/google-research/bert`

Table 3: Previously released BERT models for shared task languages. [1]Slavic-BERT is trained on Bulgarian, Czech, Polish, and Russian.

base LAS of the parser does not change, while the main disadvantage is the added complexity of an additional step and the possibility of error chaining.

We pursued this alternative approach in parallel to the main line of work. As the results presented in Section 5 show, however, the encoding of the enhanced dependencies does not negatively affect the base LAS, undermining the motivation for a separate tagging approach with its added software complexity. In our preliminary experiments on the development data, the tagging approach resulted in a minimally worse performance than the primary approach, and was therefore not pursued further.

4   Language Models

We apply transfer learning using pre-trained BERT models, using multilingual BERT[3] (mBERT) as a starting point. Based on recent studies introducing language-specific BERT models (Arkhipov et al., 2019; Virtanen et al., 2019; de Vries et al., 2019; Martin et al., 2020), we anticipated that parsing performance could be substantially improved by replacing the multilingual model with dedicated language-specific ones. To identify or create a model that would improve on performance with mBERT for every treebank in the shared task, we adopted a three-stage approach: 1) use previously released models, 2) pre-train a new model on Wikipedia data, and 3) continue pre-training on texts from a web crawl.

4.1   Previously Released Models

We considered the previously released models summarized in Table 3. Based on preliminary experiments, we focused on cased models in cases where both cased and uncased variants are available. We evaluated mBERT for all shared task treebanks, Slavic-BERT for Bulgarian, Czech, Polish, and Russian, and the other models for treebanks for the individual languages that those models target.

4.2   Unannotated Texts

Our primary source of unannotated texts in various languages is Wikipedia. To extract plain text, we processed the full 2020/01/20 Wikipedia database backup dumps[4] for the various languages with WikiExtractor[5]. The basic statistics of extracted Wikipedia texts for the IWPT languages are summarized in Table 9 in the Appendix. We note that the sizes of these unnanotated texts vary greatly between languages, ranging just over 20 million tokens for Latvian to nearly 3 billion for English. In many cases, languages with large Wikipedias also have large annotated treebanks, and vice versa; the language with the smallest amount of annotated training data in the shared task, Tamil, also ranks second from bottom in terms of the available unannotated Wikipedia data. We augmented the collection of unannotated texts for selected languages with texts drawn from OSCAR[6] (Ortiz Suárez et al., 2019), using unshuffled versions provided by the creators of the corpus (see Table 8 in the Appendix). The unshuffled version of the corpus is used since BERT training is carried out on text segments of up to 512 sub-words, far longer than most individual sentences. To reduce the level of noise in the web-crawled texts, we filtered the OSCAR source using 5-gram perplexity with a KenLM[7] language model estimated on Wikipedia data. In brief, we measured the average sentence-level perplexity t and filtered out any document where the average perplexity was greater than t. In terms of tokens, this procedure

---

[3]`https://github.com/google-research/bert/blob/master/multilingual.md`

[4]`https://dumps.wikimedia.org/`

[5]`https://github.com/attardi/wikiextractor`

[6]`https://traces1.inria.fr/oscar/`

[7]`https://github.com/kpu/kenlm`

Treebank	mBERT	Model Language-specific	
Arabic PADT	**83.62**	82.76	(Arabic-BERT)
Bulgarian BTB	90.75	**91.83**	(Slavic-BERT)
Czech CAC	91.80	**92.99**	(Slavic-BERT)
Czech FicTree	92.31	**93.27**	(Slavic-BERT)
Czech PDT	92.58	**93.44**	(Slavic-BERT)
Dutch Alpino	92.58	**93.36**	(BERTje)
Dutch LassySmall	**88.30**	87.69	(BERTje)
English EWT	90.08	**91.82**	(BERT-large)
Estonian EWT	71.27	**73.08**	(WikiBERT-et)
Finnish TDT	87.83	**92.89**	(FinBERT)
French Sequoia	**93.12**	92.99	(CamemBERT)
Italian ISDT	92.75	**93.44**	(Italian BERT)
Latvian LVTB	**86.71**	85.96	(WikiBERT-lv)
Lithuanian ALKSNIS	83.02	**85.26**	(WikiBERT-lt)
Polish LFG	95.34	**96.22**	(Slavic-BERT)
Polish PDB	91.90	**93.37**	(Slavic-BERT)
Russian SynTagRus	92.06	**93.34**	(RuBERT)
Slovak SNK	**92.52**	91.89	(WikiBERT-sk)
Swedish Talbanken	86.96	**90.56**	(Swedish BERT)
Tamil TTB	**69.12**	67.38	(WikiBERT-ta)
Ukrainian IU	89.60	**91.25**	(WikiBERT-uk)
Average	88.30	**89.28**	

Table 4: UDify development set LAS performance with mBERT compared to language-specific BERTs

Treebank	mBERT	Model Language-specific	
Arabic PADT	83.62	**84.79**	(WikiBERT-ar)
Dutch Alpino	92.58	**93.47**	(WikiBERT-nl)
Dutch LassySmall	88.30	**89.23**	(WikiBERT-nl)
French Sequoia	93.12	**93.21**	(WikiBERT-fr)
Average	89.41	**90.18**	

Table 5: UDify development set LAS performance with mBERT compared to additional WikiBERTs

Treebank	mBERT	Model Language-specific	
Latvian LVTB	86.71	**88.47**	(Wiki+OSCAR-BERT-lv)
Slovak SNK	**92.52**	**92.52**	(Wiki+OSCAR-BERT-sk)
Tamil TTB	69.12	**71.02**	(Wiki+OSCAR-BERT-ta)
Average	82.78	**84.00**	

Table 6: UDify development set LAS performance with mBERT compared to Wiki+OSCAR-BERTs

filtered out approx. 10% of the OSCAR data for Latvian and Slovak and 24% for Tamil.

4.3 Pre-training

For pre-training new BERT models, we largely follow the approach used to create the original BERT-base English model by Devlin et al. (2018). Specifically, we adapt the preprocessing pipeline and pre-training process introduced by Virtanen et al. (2019) for creating the Finnish BERT model. In brief, we train BERT-base models for 1M steps, the initial 900K with a maximum sequence length of 128 and the last 100K with 512, using the original BERT software[8] and the same optimizer parameters as Devlin et al. (2018) with the exception of batch size. Due to memory limitations, a batch size of 140 was used with 4 GPUs for the first 900K steps and a batch size of 20 with 8 GPUs for the last 100K steps. Nvidia V100 GPUs with 32 GB memory were used for pre-training. For comprehensive details of the preprocessing and pre-training process, we refer to the documentation of our pipeline.[9]

4.4 Language Model Evaluation

For evaluating pre-trained language models, we trained UDify with the shared task training data for

each language and evaluated on the corresponding development dataset using gold standard tokenization. The standard LAS metric was used to assess model performance.

Table 4 summarizes evaluation results comparing parsing performance with mBERT and language-specific models. As expected, we find that language-specific models outperform the multilingual model in most cases, averaging approximately 1% point higher LAS (~8% reduction in error). There are nevertheless a number of cases where UDify with mBERT outperforms the language-specific model. To address these cases, we introduced additional WikiBERT models for Arabic, Dutch, and French. Results comparing the performance of these models with mBERT are summarized in Table 5. We find that in each case using the WikiBERT model improves on results with mBERT, with absolute differences around 1% point for the Arabic and Dutch treebanks but very limited (~0.1% point) difference for French, averaging 0.8% point higher LAS than mBERT (~7% reduction in error).

Finally, there are three languages for which no previously released language-specific model was available and the WikiBERT failed to improve on performance with mBERT: Latvian, Slovak, and Tamil. For these languages, we continued pre-training with texts from OSCAR for an additional 300,000 steps. Table 6 summarizes performance with these models. For Slovak, the new model improves over the WikiBERT model performance but merely matches the performance with mBERT, while the Latvian and Tamil models outperform

[8]https://github.com/google-research/bert
[9]https://github.com/TurkuNLP/wikibert

Language	adapt	clasp	emory	fastparse	koebsala	orange	robert	shanghai	turku	unipi
						Team				
Arabic	57.19	51.26	67.26	66.92	60.84	70.96	0.0	63.41	**77.82**	57.79
Bulgarian	77.29	84.90	88.19	84.86	68.88	89.42	0.0	78.67	**90.73**	84.93
Czech	66.41	67.13	85.51	77.21	61.11	86.95	0.0	75.43	**87.51**	75.99
Dutch	67.67	78.93	80.72	77.37	62.93	**85.14**	0.0	70.94	84.73	77.62
English	70.44	82.87	85.30	78.45	65.37	85.21	**88.94**	72.34	87.15	83.95
Estonian	61.12	60.44	81.36	74.09	59.07	81.03	0.0	74.91	**84.54**	57.24
Finnish	72.37	65.96	82.96	75.73	67.54	86.24	0.0	75.99	**89.49**	72.13
French	74.74	72.76	**86.23**	77.77	67.93	83.63	0.0	76.99	85.90	78.85
Italian	71.98	87.14	88.52	84.77	69.08	90.83	0.0	73.08	**91.54**	89.14
Latvian	72.41	66.01	79.19	75.57	64.75	82.11	0.0	77.77	**84.94**	68.23
Lithuanian	58.36	52.56	66.12	61.41	56.28	75.89	0.0	66.85	**77.64**	61.06
Polish	65.86	71.22	82.39	74.54	61.34	80.39	0.0	71.01	**84.64**	70.61
Russian	75.27	70.37	88.60	80.35	64.23	89.84	0.0	78.26	**90.69**	76.90
Slovak	68.43	65.16	82.72	73.46	64.08	84.36	0.0	73.14	**88.56**	81.40
Swedish	68.39	71.35	78.19	75.24	64.50	83.27	0.0	69.60	**85.64**	78.73
Tamil	48.47	42.15	54.26	46.99	47.44	**64.23**	0.0	48.20	57.83	48.50
Ukrainian	66.43	63.24	79.69	74.02	64.17	84.64	0.0	72.98	**87.22**	73.90
Average	67.23	67.85	79.84	74.04	62.91	82.60	5.23	71.74	**84.50**	72.76

Table 7: ELAS results for submissions to IWPT 2020 shared task. Team names abbreviated for space: emory = emorynlp, orange = orange_deskin, robert = robertnlp, shanghai = shanghaitech_alibaba, turku = turkunlp.

mBERT with a nearly 2% point absolute difference in LAS. On average, the new models improve on mBERT by 1.2% points, again an approx. 7% reduction in error.

5 Results

For our final submission, we trained a model for each language using the largest treebank (in terms of token count) for the language in the shared task data release. All segmentation, tagging, parsing, and lemmatization models are thus monolingual and trained using only a single treebank. Each UDify model is fine-tuned for 160 epochs using a number of warm-up steps[10] roughly equal to a single pass over the training dataset. For each language the fine-tuning is based on a custom pre-trained BERT model selected as detailed in Section 4.4. Lemmatization models do not require any external resources, and all hyperparameters follow the values used in Kanerva et al. (2020).

The primary evaluation metric in the shared task is ELAS (Labeled Attachment Score on Enhanced dependencies), which calculates F-score over the set of enhanced dependencies in the system output and gold standard.[11] Table 7 summarizes the ELAS results for all ten teams participating the shared task. We note that in addition to achieving

the best average ELAS performance, our system also outperforms all other submissions for 13 out of the 17 individual languages included in the task. For these 13 languages, the largest absolute differences for the second-best result are for Arabic ($\sim$6.9% points), Slovak ($\sim$4.2% points), Estonian, and Finnish (both slightly above 3% points).

For the four languages where our system did not achieve the highest ELAS results, the differences to the highest-performing submission are small (0.3-0.4% points) for Dutch and French, and 1.8% points for English. However, there is a more than 6% point difference to the top result for Tamil, the language with the smallest treebank in the shared task. This difference indicates a tradeoff of our approach in training monolingual models: languages with particularly limited resources do not gain support from annotations in other languages as they would in multilingual training.

Table 10 in the Appendix shows average results for all metrics excepting for XPOS, which due time limitations we decided not to predict, and AllTags, which is not meaningfully defined when not predicting XPOS. We note that our system achieves the best performance for all but two metrics, outperforming other systems in segmentation (Tokens, Words, Sentences), part-of-speech tagging (UPOS), lemmatization (Lemmas) as well as for all but one of the seven dependency attachment score (*AS) metrics. Our system falls behind the best-performing submission (orange_deskin) for the UFeats and MLAS metrics. As MLAS (Morphology-Aware Labeled Attachment Score)

---

[10]During warm-up, the learning rate is gradually increased from zero to its initial value, so as to avoid large changes at the very beginning of the training.

[11]Note that in UD many of the base layer relations are repeated in the enhanced graph, and therefore the ELAS metric evaluates a combination of basic dependencies and enhancements as seen in statistics presented in Table 1.

requires selected features to match, the results for these two metrics likely both reflect performance for morphological features. The absolute difference of our system to the top result for UFeats is 1.2% points, reflecting a 20% relative increase in error and indicating a clear remaining point for improvement in our system.

6 Discussion

Cross-lingual compatibility is a major goal of the UD effort and the ability to train multilingual models where lower-resourced languages can benefit from data in higher-resourced languages a clearly desirable aim in language modeling. While our approach – which trains monolingual models and uses language-specific pre-trained models – can be seen as running counter to these goals, we do nevertheless share them. Our choice to train separate models for each language for the shared task is based in part in awareness of remaining compatibility issues in UD treebanks, even within languages. We hope contrasting results for joint and language-specific models for this shared task will help identify and resolve some of these challenges. Regarding multilingual language models, we note that in aiming to cover more than 100 languages without a corresponding increase in model and vocabulary size, mBERT faces multiple challenges in its capacity, and the model training does not fully balance lower- and higher-resourced languages. While we here found language-specific models to outperform a specific mBERT model, highly multilingual models addressing these challenges might well be competitive with language-specific ones, and the creation of such models would greatly benefit practical parsing efforts targeting a large number of languages.

To study the impact of the language-specific language models in our shared task results, we reproduce our pipeline using exactly same configurations except for replacing all language-specific BERT models with the multilingual mBERT. In this experiment, all languages are using the same multilingual language model as a starting point, later individually fine-tuned for each language while training the language-specific parsing models. When comparing these models to the official submissions of all 10 teams, the average ELAS is approximately 1.7% points below our own primary submission ($\sim$11% increase in error), but still slighty above the second best submission by approximately 0.2%

points. This means that, our pipeline would have reached the highest average ELAS score among the official submissions also without the language-specific BERT models, but only with a very thin margin to the next best team.

7 Conclusions

We have presented the approach of the TurkuNLP group to the IWPT 2020 shared task on Multilingual Parsing into Enhanced Universal Dependencies. Our approach is based on deep transfer learning with language-specific models, the state-of-the-art UDify neural parsing pipeline, sequence-to-sequence lemmatization, and a graph transformation approach to predicting enhanced dependency graphs. Our submission to the shared task achieved the highest performance for the primary evaluation metric (ELAS) both on average as well as for 13 out of the 17 languages involved in the task, also achieving the highest average performance for most other evaluation metrics.

All of the methods and resources developed for this study are made freely available under open licenses from `https://turkunlp.org`.

Acknowledgments

We gratefully acknowledge the support of the Academy of Finland, and CSC — the Finnish IT Center for Science for providing computational resources. We also thank the creators of the OSCAR corpus for making unshuffled versions of their corpus available for this work.

References

Mikhail Arkhipov, Maria Trofimova, Yurii Kuratov, and Alexey Sorokin. 2019. Tuning multilingual transformers for language-specific named entity recognition. In *Proceedings of the 7th Workshop on Balto-Slavic Natural Language Processing*, pages 89–93.

Gosse Bouma, Djamé Seddah, and Daniel Zeman. 2020. Overview of the IWPT 2020 Shared Task on Parsing into Enhanced Universal Dependencies. In *Proceedings of the 16th International Conference on Parsing Technologies and the IWPT 2020 Shared Task on Parsing into Enhanced Universal Dependencies*, Seattle, US. Association for Computational Linguistics.

Jacob Devlin, Ming-Wei Chang, Kenton Lee, and Kristina Toutanova. 2018. Bert: Pre-training of deep bidirectional transformers for language understanding. *arXiv preprint arXiv:1810.04805*.

Timothy Dozat, Peng Qi, and Christopher D Manning. 2017. Stanford's graph-based neural dependency parser at the CoNLL 2017 Shared Task. In *Proceedings of the CoNLL 2017 Shared Task: Multilingual Parsing from Raw Text to Universal Dependencies*, pages 20–30.

Jenna Kanerva, Filip Ginter, Niko Miekka, Akseli Leino, and Tapio Salakoski. 2018. Turku neural parser pipeline: An end-to-end system for the CoNLL 2018 Shared Task. In *Proceedings of the CoNLL 2018 Shared Task: Multilingual parsing from raw text to universal dependencies*, pages 133–142.

Jenna Kanerva, Filip Ginter, and Tapio Salakoski. 2020. Universal Lemmatizer: A sequence to sequence model for lemmatizing Universal Dependencies treebanks. *Natural Language Engineering*. To appear.

Dan Kondratyuk and Milan Straka. 2019. 75 languages, 1 model: Parsing Universal Dependencies universally. In *Proceedings of the 2019 Conference on Empirical Methods in Natural Language Processing and the 9th International Joint Conference on Natural Language Processing (EMNLP-IJCNLP)*, pages 2779–2795, Hong Kong, China. Association for Computational Linguistics.

Yuri Kuratov and Mikhail Arkhipov. 2019. Adaptation of deep bidirectional multilingual transformers for Russian language. *arXiv preprint arXiv:1905.07213*.

Louis Martin, Benjamin Muller, Pedro Javier Ortiz Suárez, Yoann Dupont, Laurent Romary, Éric Villemonte de la Clergerie, Djamé Seddah, and Benoît Sagot. 2020. CamemBERT: a Tasty French Language Model. In *Proceedings of the 58th Annual Meeting of the Association for Computational Linguistics*.

Joakim Nivre, Marie-Catherine De Marneffe, Filip Ginter, Yoav Goldberg, Jan Hajič, Christopher D Manning, Ryan McDonald, Slav Petrov, Sampo Pyysalo, Natalia Silveira, et al. 2016. Universal dependencies v1: A multilingual treebank collection. In *Proceedings of the Tenth International Conference on Language Resources and Evaluation (LREC'16)*, pages 1659–1666.

Joakim Nivre, Marie-Catherine de Marneffe, Filip Ginter, Jan Hajič, Christopher D. Manning, Sampo Pyysalo, Sebastian Schuster, Francis Tyers, and Daniel Zeman. 2020. Universal Dependencies v2: An Evergrowing Multilingual Treebank Collection. In *Proceedings of The 12th Language Resources and Evaluation Conference*, pages 4027–4036. European Language Resources Association.

Joakim Nivre, Paola Marongiu, Filip Ginter, Jenna Kanerva, Simonetta Montemagni, Sebastian Schuster, and Maria Simi. 2018. Enhancing Universal Dependency Treebanks: A Case Study. In *Proceedings of the Second Workshop on Universal Dependencies (UDW 2018)*, pages 102–107. Association for Computational Linguistics.

Stephan Oepen, Marco Kuhlmann, Yusuke Miyao, Daniel Zeman, Silvie Cinková, Dan Flickinger, Jan Hajič, and Zdeňka Urešová. 2015. SemEval 2015 Task 18: Broad-Coverage Semantic Dependency Parsing. In *Proceedings of the 9th International Workshop on Semantic Evaluation (SemEval 2015)*, pages 915–926. Association for Computational Linguistics.

Stephan Oepen, Marco Kuhlmann, Yusuke Miyao, Daniel Zeman, Dan Flickinger, Jan Hajič, Angelina Ivanova, and Yi Zhang. 2014. SemEval 2014 Task 8: Broad-Coverage Semantic Dependency Parsing. In *Proceedings of the 8th International Workshop on Semantic Evaluation (SemEval 2014)*, pages 63–72. Association for Computational Linguistics.

Pedro Javier Ortiz Suárez, Benoît Sagot, and Laurent Romary. 2019. Asynchronous Pipeline for Processing Huge Corpora on Medium to Low Resource Infrastructures. In *7th Workshop on the Challenges in the Management of Large Corpora (CMLC-7)*. Leibniz-Institut für Deutsche Sprache.

Peng Qi, Yuhao Zhang, Yuhui Zhang, Jason Bolton, and Christopher D Manning. 2020. Stanza: A Python Natural Language Processing Toolkit for Many Human Languages. In *Proceedings of the 58th Annual Meeting of the Association for Computational Linguistics (ACL), System Demonstrations*.

Sebastian Schuster and Christopher D. Manning. 2016. Enhanced English Universal Dependencies: An Improved Representation for Natural Language Understanding Tasks. In *Proceedings of the Tenth International Conference on Language Resources and Evaluation (LREC'16)*, pages 2371–2378. European Language Resources Association (ELRA).

Sebastian Schuster, Joakim Nivre, and Christopher D. Manning. 2018. Sentences with Gapping: Parsing and Reconstructing Elided Predicates. In *Proceedings of the 2018 Conference of the North American Chapter of the Association for Computational Linguistics: Human Language Technologies, Volume 1 (Long Papers)*, pages 1156–1168, New Orleans, Louisiana. Association for Computational Linguistics.

Antti Virtanen, Jenna Kanerva, Rami Ilo, Jouni Luoma, Juhani Luotolahti, Tapio Salakoski, Filip Ginter, and Sampo Pyysalo. 2019. Multilingual is not enough: BERT for Finnish. *arXiv preprint arXiv:1912.07076*.

Wietse de Vries, Andreas van Cranenburgh, Arianna Bisazza, Tommaso Caselli, Gertjan van Noord, and Malvina Nissim. 2019. BERTje: A Dutch BERT Model. *arXiv preprint arXiv:1912.09582*.

Daniel Zeman, Jan Hajič, Martin Popel, Martin Potthast, Milan Straka, Filip Ginter, Joakim Nivre, and

Slav Petrov. 2018. CoNLL 2018 shared task: Multilingual parsing from raw text to Universal Dependencies. In *Proceedings of the CoNLL 2018 Shared Task: Multilingual parsing from raw text to universal dependencies*, pages 1–21.

Daniel Zeman, Joakim Nivre, Mitchell Abrams, Noëmi Aepli, Željko Agić, Lars Ahrenberg, Gabrielė Aleksandravičiūtė, Lene Antonsen, Katya Aplonova, Maria Jesus Aranzabe, Gashaw Arutie, Masayuki Asahara, Luma Ateyah, Mohammed Attia, Aitziber Atutxa, Liesbeth Augustinus, Elena Badmaeva, Miguel Ballesteros, Esha Banerjee, Sebastian Bank, Verginica Barbu Mititelu, Victoria Basmov, Colin Batchelor, John Bauer, Sandra Bellato, Kepa Bengoetxea, Yevgeni Berzak, Irshad Ahmad Bhat, Riyaz Ahmad Bhat, Erica Biagetti, Eckhard Bick, Agnė Bielinskienė, Rogier Blokland, Victoria Bobicev, Loïc Boizou, Emanuel Borges Völker, Carl Börstell, Cristina Bosco, Gosse Bouma, Sam Bowman, Adriane Boyd, Kristina Brokaitė, Aljoscha Burchardt, Marie Candito, Bernard Caron, Gauthier Caron, Tatiana Cavalcanti, Gülşen Cebiroğlu Eryiğit, Flavio Massimiliano Cecchini, Giuseppe G. A. Celano, Slavomír Čéplö, Savas Cetin, Fabricio Chalub, Jinho Choi, Yongseok Cho, Jayeol Chun, Alessandra T. Cignarella, Silvie Cinková, Aurélie Collomb, Çağrı Çöltekin, Miriam Connor, Marine Courtin, Elizabeth Davidson, Marie-Catherine de Marneffe, Valeria de Paiva, Elvis de Souza, Arantza Diaz de Ilarraza, Carly Dickerson, Bamba Dione, Peter Dirix, Kaja Dobrovoljc, Timothy Dozat, Kira Droganova, Puneet Dwivedi, Hanne Eckhoff, Marhaba Eli, Ali Elkahky, Binyam Ephrem, Olga Erina, Tomaž Erjavec, Aline Etienne, Wograine Evelyn, Richárd Farkas, Hector Fernandez Alcalde, Jennifer Foster, Cláudia Freitas, Kazunori Fujita, Katarína Gajdošová, Daniel Galbraith, Marcos Garcia, Moa Gärdenfors, Sebastian Garza, Kim Gerdes, Filip Ginter, Iakes Goenaga, Koldo Gojenola, Memduh Gökırmak, Yoav Goldberg, Xavier Gómez Guinovart, Berta González Saavedra, Bernadeta Griciūtė, Matias Grioni, Normunds Grūzītis, Bruno Guillaume, Céline Guillot-Barbance, Nizar Habash, Jan Hajič, Jan Hajič jr., Mika Hämäläinen, Linh Hà Mỹ, Na-Rae Han, Kim Harris, Dag Haug, Johannes Heinecke, Felix Hennig, Barbora Hladká, Jaroslava Hlaváčová, Florinel Hociung, Petter Hohle, Jena Hwang, Takumi Ikeda, Radu Ion, Elena Irimia, Ọlájídé Ishola, Tomáš Jelínek, Anders Johannsen, Fredrik Jørgensen, Markus Juutinen, Hüner Kaşıkara, Andre Kaasen, Nadezhda Kabaeva, Sylvain Kahane, Hiroshi Kanayama, Jenna Kanerva, Boris Katz, Tolga Kayadelen, Jessica Kenney, Václava Kettnerová, Jesse Kirchner, Elena Klementieva, Arne Köhn, Kamil Kopacewicz, Natalia Kotsyba, Jolanta Kovalevskaitė, Simon Krek, Sookyoung Kwak, Veronika Laippala, Lorenzo Lambertino, Lucia Lam, Tatiana Lando, Septina Dian Larasati, Alexei Lavrentiev, John Lee, Phuong Lê H`ông, Alessandro Lenci, Saran Lertpradit, Herman Leung, Cheuk Ying Li, Josie Li, Keying Li, KyungTae Lim, Maria Liovina, Yuan Li, Nikola Ljubešić, Olga Loginova, Olga Lyashevskaya, Teresa Lynn, Vivien Macketanz, Aibek Makazhanov, Michael Mandl, Christopher Manning, Ruli Manurung, Cătălina Mărănduc, David Mareček, Katrin Marheinecke, Héctor Martínez Alonso, André Martins, Jan Mašek, Yuji Matsumoto, Ryan McDonald, Sarah McGuinness, Gustavo Mendonça, Niko Miekka, Margarita Misirpashayeva, Anna Missilä, Cătălin Mititelu, Maria Mitrofan, Yusuke Miyao, Simonetta Montemagni, Amir More, Laura Moreno Romero, Keiko Sophie Mori, Tomohiko Morioka, Shinsuke Mori, Shigeki Moro, Bjartur Mortensen, Bohdan Moskalevskyi, Kadri Muischnek, Robert Munro, Yugo Murawaki, Kaili Müürisep, Pinkey Nainwani, Juan Ignacio Navarro Horñiacek, Anna Nedoluzhko, Gunta Nešpore-Bērzkalne, Luong Nguy~ên Thị, Huy`ên Nguy~ên Thị Minh, Yoshihiro Nikaido, Vitaly Nikolaev, Rattima Nitisaroj, Hanna Nurmi, Stina Ojala, Atul Kr. Ojha, Mai Olúòkun, Adédayọand Omura, Petya Osenova, Robert Östling, Lilja Øvrelid, Niko Partanen, Elena Pascual, Marco Passarotti, Agnieszka Patejuk, Guilherme Paulino-Passos, Angelika Peljak-Łapińska, Siyao Peng, Cenel-Augusto Perez, Guy Perrier, Daria Petrova, Slav Petrov, Jason Phelan, Jussi Piitulainen, Tommi A Pirinen, Emily Pitler, Barbara Plank, Thierry Poibeau, Larisa Ponomareva, Martin Popel, Lauma Pretkalniņa, Sophie Prévost, Prokopis Prokopidis, Adam Przepiórkowski, Tiina Puolakainen, Sampo Pyysalo, Peng Qi, Andriela Rääbis, Alexandre Rademaker, Loganathan Ramasamy, Taraka Rama, Carlos Ramisch, Vinit Ravishankar, Livy Real, Siva Reddy, Georg Rehm, Ivan Riabov, Michael Rießler, Erika Rimkutė, Larissa Rinaldi, Laura Rituma, Luisa Rocha, Mykhailo Romanenko, Rudolf Rosa, Davide Rovati, Valentin Roșca, Olga Rudina, Jack Rueter, Shoval Sadde, Benoît Sagot, Shadi Saleh, Alessio Salomoni, Tanja Samardžić, Stephanie Samson, Manuela Sanguinetti, Dage Särg, Baiba Saulīte, Yanin Sawanakunanon, Nathan Schneider, Sebastian Schuster, Djamé Seddah, Wolfgang Seeker, Mojgan Seraji, Mo Shen, Atsuko Shimada, Hiroyuki Shirasu, Muh Shohibussirri, Dmitry Sichinava, Aline Silveira, Natalia Silveira, Maria Simi, Radu Simionescu, Katalin Simkó, Mária Šimková, Kiril Simov, Aaron Smith, Isabela Soares-Bastos, Carolyn Spadine, Antonio Stella, Milan Straka, Jana Strnadová, Alane Suhr, Umut Sulubacak, Shingo Suzuki, Zsolt Szántó, Dima Taji, Yuta Takahashi, Fabio Tamburini, Takaaki Tanaka, Isabelle Tellier, Guillaume Thomas, Liisi Torga, Trond Trosterud, Anna Trukhina, Reut Tsarfaty, Francis Tyers, Sumire Uematsu, Zdeňka Urešová, Larraitz Uria, Hans Uszkoreit, Andrius Utka, Sowmya Vajjala, Daniel van Niekerk, Gertjan van Noord, Viktor Varga, Eric Villemonte de la Clergerie, Veronika Vincze, Lars Wallin, Abigail Walsh, Jing Xian Wang, Jonathan North Washington, Maximilan Wendt, Seyi Williams, Mats Wirén, Christian Wittern, Tsegay Woldemariam, Tak-sum Wong, Alina Wróblewska, Mary Yako, Naoki Yamazaki, Chunxiao Yan, Koichi Yasuoka, Marat M. Yavrumyan, Zhuoran Yu, Zdeněk Žabokrtský, Amir

Zeldes, Manying Zhang, and Hanzhi Zhu. 2019. Universal Dependencies 2.5. LINDAT/CLARIAH-CZ digital library at the Institute of Formal and Applied Linguistics (ÚFAL), Faculty of Mathematics and Physics, Charles University.

Daniel Zeman, Martin Popel, Milan Straka, Jan Hajič, Joakim Nivre, Filip Ginter, Juhani Luotolahti, Sampo Pyysalo, Slav Petrov, Martin Potthast, Francis Tyers, Elena Badmaeva, Memduh Gokirmak, Anna Nedoluzhko, Silvie Cinkova, Jan Hajič jr., Jaroslava Hlavacova, Václava Kettnerová, Zdenka Uresova, Jenna Kanerva, Stina Ojala, Anna Missilä, Christopher D. Manning, Sebastian Schuster, Siva Reddy, Dima Taji, Nizar Habash, Herman Leung, Marie-Catherine de Marneffe, Manuela Sanguinetti, Maria Simi, Hiroshi Kanayama, Valeria dePaiva, Kira Droganova, Héctor Martínez Alonso, Çağrı Çöltekin, Umut Sulubacak, Hans Uszkoreit, Vivien Macketanz, Aljoscha Burchardt, Kim Harris, Katrin Marheinecke, Georg Rehm, Tolga Kayadelen, Mohammed Attia, Ali Elkahky, Zhuoran Yu, Emily Pitler, Saran Lertpradit, Michael Mandl, Jesse Kirchner, Hector Fernandez Alcalde, Jana Strnadová, Esha Banerjee, Ruli Manurung, Antonio Stella, Atsuko Shimada, Sookyoung Kwak, Gustavo Mendonca, Tatiana Lando, Rattima Nitisaroj, and Josie Li. 2017. CoNLL 2017 Shared Task: Multilingual Parsing from Raw Text to Universal Dependencies. In *Proceedings of the CoNLL 2017 Shared Task: Multilingual Parsing from Raw Text to Universal Dependencies*, pages 1–19. Association for Computational Linguistics.

A   Appendix

Table 8 shows the same statistics for the OSCAR corpora of selected languages, and Table 9 summarizes the basic statistics of extracted Wikipedia texts for the IWPT languages. Table 10 shows average results for various metrics for all submissions to IWPT 2020 shared task.

Language	Docs	Sents	Tokens	Chars
Latvian	1.6M	34M	628M	4.0B
Slovak	5.5M	99M	1.5B	9.1B
Tamil	1.3M	39M	528M	3.8B

Table 8: OSCAR source statistics for selected IWPT 2020 shared task languages

Language	Docs	Sents	Tokens	Chars
Arabic	1.0M	8.0M	184M	889M
Bulgarian	259K	4.1M	71M	397M
Czech	444K	7.9M	143M	804M
Dutch	2.0M	19M	300M	1.7B
English	5.9M	124M	2.7B	14B
Estonian	205K	2.7M	38M	252M
Finnish	477K	7.4M	97M	731M
French	2.2M	34M	858M	4.5B
Italian	1.6M	22M	579M	3.0B
Latvian	99K	1.3M	21M	126M
Lithuanian	196K	2.3M	34M	207M
Polish	1.4M	16M	282M	1.7B
Russian	1.6M	31M	565M	3.5B
Slovak	232K	2.8M	39M	229M
Swedish	3.7M	30M	364M	2.1B
Tamil	132K	1.9M	26M	195M
Ukrainian	979K	15M	260M	1.5B

Table 9: Wikipedia source statistics for IWPT 2020 shared task languages

Metric	adapt	clasp	emory	fastparse	koebsala	orange	robert	shanghai	turku	unipi
					Team					
Tokens	99.54	99.72	99.66	99.66	99.66	99.68	5.85	99.67	**99.74**	99.63
Words	98.96	99.12	99.06	99.06	99.06	99.09	5.85	99.08	**99.13**	99.03
Sentences	89.22	92.34	91.25	91.18	91.25	90.24	5.07	91.97	**92.41**	90.56
UPOS	95.88	95.48	93.63	93.60	93.63	96.69	5.63	0.63	**96.75**	92.78
UFeats	91.36	90.66	87.35	88.11	87.35	**93.98**	5.57	32.84	92.77	86.02
Lemmas	95.40	95.15	92.30	92.23	92.30	95.80	5.62	0.02	**95.96**	91.35
UAS	87.18	86.41	88.95	82.55	79.97	89.45	5.26	13.01	**89.92**	84.90
LAS	84.09	82.66	86.14	77.57	75.41	86.79	5.11	0.99	**87.31**	80.74
CLAS	81.56	79.66	83.81	72.97	71.18	84.42	5.00	1.22	**85.23**	77.42
MLAS	72.57	69.55	67.84	60.82	60.54	**77.75**	4.51	0.01	76.63	62.73
BLEX	78.11	76.00	76.11	66.70	65.38	80.86	4.73	0.00	**81.93**	70.03
EULAS	69.42	80.18	81.26	75.96	64.93	84.62	5.26	73.01	**85.83**	78.82
ELAS	67.23	67.85	79.84	74.04	62.91	82.60	5.23	71.74	**84.50**	72.76

Table 10: Average results for different metrics for submissions to IWPT 2020 shared task. Team names abbreviated for space: emory = emorynlp, orange = orange_deskin, robert = robertnlp, shanghai = shanghaitech_alibaba, turku = turkunlp.

Hybrid Enhanced Universal Dependencies Parsing

Johannes Heinecke

Orange / Data AI / AITT / Deskiñ

2 avenue Marzin

22307 Lannion cedex, France

`johannes.heinecke@orange.com`

Abstract

This paper describes our system to predict enhanced dependencies for Universal Dependencies (UD) treebanks, which ranked 2nd in the Shared Task on Enhanced Dependency Parsing with an average ELAS of 82.60%. Our system uses a hybrid two-step approach. First, we use a graph-based parser to extract a basic syntactic dependency tree. Then, we use a set of linguistic rules which generate the enhanced dependencies for the syntactic tree. The application of these rules is optimized using a classifier which predicts their suitability in the given context. A key advantage of this approach is its language independence, as rules rely solely on dependency trees and UPOS tags which are shared across all languages.

1   Introduction

Parsing Enhanced Universal Dependencies (EUD) (Schuster and Manning, 2016) is an interesting extension of dependency parsing. EUDs provide syntactic information which can be crucial for any NLP processing based on syntactic analysis.

The shared task on EUD parsing (Bouma et al., 2020) provided the platform to develop and compare various systems. Our team participated using a hybrid system (machine learning/rule-based) which came second in both metrics, ELAS (82,6%) and EULAS (84,6%).

1.1   Related Work

Whereas basic dependencies are strict surface syntax trees, enhanced dependencies are implicite syntactic links in constructions like coordinations, raise/control constructions or relative clauses. EUDs also enrich existing basic dependencies such as `obl` and `nmod` relations by adding information about the adposition used and morphological cases. Finally EUDs propose the syntactic annotation of elided words, absent in the actual sentence (Nivre et al., 2018). Even though the basic dependencies tree (apart from the `orphan` relation) is part of the EUD graph, the latter is no longer a tree, since individual tokens can have more than one head. Most of the EUDs can be predicted deterministically (Nivre et al., 2018), others, notably the prediction of EUDs for elided words, are more complex (Schuster et al., 2018).

2   System description

The data of Universal Dependencies treebanks (Nivre et al., 2016)[1] used for the shared task and annotated with enhanced dependencies (other than copied basic dependencies) is small. In total, all training treebanks contain about 5.1 million words, only 5.6% of those have a second enhanced dependency attached to them (the first being the copied basic dependency). Another 7.2% and 8.3% of words have an enhanced dependency like `obl:...` or `nmod:...` which correspond to the basic dependency but also give the adposition and morphological case (if existing in the language in question). In total, only 21.1% or 1 million words have any non basic enhanced dependency.

The enhanced dependencies address specific and well known linguistic phenomena, and are relatively deterministic (Nivre et al., 2018), once the basic dependency tree is available. For this reason, we decided to utilise a hybrid system, using a graph-based parser to produce first a dependency tree and a rule system which uses the generated dependency tree to determin the enhanced dependencies. The latter uses a (learned) filter to control the application of rules in certain contexts. The system functions as a pipeline (cf. Figure 1). Thus errors in earlier parts of the pipeline will impact the results of the following components.

---

[1] https//universaldependencies.org/

Proceedings of the 16th International Conference on Parsing Technologies and the IWPT 2020 Shared Task, pages 174–180

Virtual Meeting, July 9, 2020. ©2020 Association for Computational Linguistics

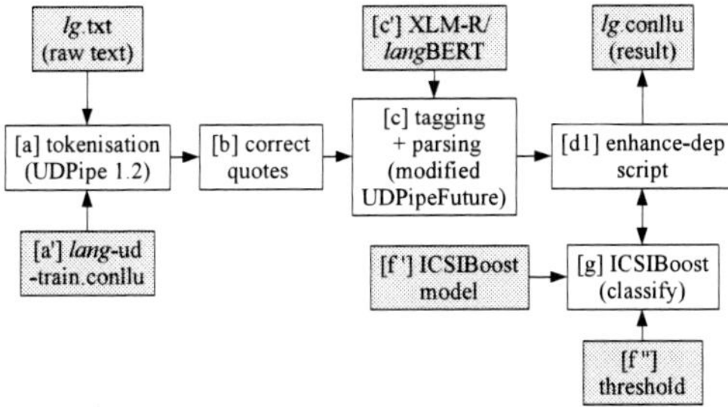

Figure 1: System architecture: gray boxes indicate data, white boxes indicate processing

2.1 Sentence segmentation, tokenisation

For sentence segmentation and tokenisation of the incoming raw text, we use UDPipe 1.2 (Straka and Straková, 2017) ([a] in Figure 1[2]). We trained a tokenizer per language using the training files ([a'] in Fig. 1) of each treebank. For languages with more than one treebank, we chose the one with the largest training file. A python postprocessing script ([b] in Fig. 1) deals with obvious tokenization errors, such as quotes concatenated to letters (e.g. like `word"` , `word″` or `"word`) and separates these tokens into two.

2.2 Tagging and parsing

To tag and parse the texts, we use a special version of UdpipeFuture ([c] in Fig. 1) (Straka, 2018), winner in terms of the Morphology-aware Labeled Attachment Score (MLAS)[3] metric of the shared task on Dependency Parsing in 2018. In our version, we also use contextual embeddings, however instead of using ELMo (Peters et al., 2018), we experimented with a range of contextual embeddings, either multilingual as BERT (Devlin et al., 2019) or XLM-R (Conneau et al., 2019), or language specific models like RoBERTa-large (English, Liu et al. (2019)), CamemBERT (French, Martin et al. (2019)). Experiments with these embeddings on the CoNLL 2018 Shared Task (Zeman et al., 2018) data show that XLM-R outperforms the best score for nearly all treebanks of the 2018 Shared Task. The Content-Word Labeled Attachment Score (CLAS)[4] scores

for these experiments on the treebanks which are used for the Enhanced Dependencies Shared Task are given in Table 1.

treebank	BERT	XLM-R	CoNLL 2018 best score
ar-padt	80.35	**82.43**	74.00
bg-btb	88.49	**90.23**	88.40
cs-cac	89.79	**92.08**	90.06
cs-fictree	87.89	**90.22**	89.61
cs-pdt	90.09	**92.18**	90.53
cs-pud	79.97	79.97	**83.57**
en-ewt	86.89	**87.24**	81.64
en-pud	**87.60**	87.60	85.68
et-edt	83.46	**86.07**	83.74
fi-pud	88.15	**90.00**	88.72
fi-tdt	86.65	**89.90**	87.42
fr-sequoia	90.03	**90.47**	87.26
it-isdt	89.11	**90.01**	88.32
lv-lvtb	79.75	**83.18**	81.17
nl-alpino	85.57	**88.20**	85.23
nl-lassysmall	84.07	**85.18**	81.71
pl-lfg	93.02	**94.28**	93.18
ru-syntagrus	91.60	**93.30**	91.00
sk-snk	87.42	**89.35**	87.01
sv-pud	81.19	**82.25**	79.01
sv-talbanken	86.68	**88.72**	86.94
uk-iu	83.83	**86.97**	85.99

Table 1: Results (CLAS) on CoNLL 2018 Shared Tasks treebanks also present in the IWPT 2020 Shared Task (best values in bold)

Although the CoNLL 2018 Shared Task is based on UD v2.2, we were able to produce similar promising results with the data provided by the current shared task, based on UD v2.5.

To prepare for the shared task, we first merged treebanks of the same language when more than one was available: this was the case for Czech, Dutch, Estonian and Polish. Then, we trained and tested the tagging and parsing using UDPipeFuture with all contextual word embedding models available for the given language (unless the treebank did not provide a dev-file, as e.g. the PUD treebanks). In addition to the multilingual contextual embeddings BERT and XLM-R, we also tested some language-specific transformers such as Arabic BERT[5], CamemBERT[6] (French, Martin et al.

---

[2]Letters in brackets refer to the architecture diagrams shown in Figures 1 and 4. Identical letters refer to the same component.

[3]MLAS is metric inspired by the Content-Word Labeled Attachment Score (CLAS) (Zeman et al., 2018) which takes into account POS tags and morphological features.

[4]CLAS is a variant or the classical Labeled Attachment Score (Nivre and Fang, 2017). It only takes into account dependency reations between content words, in order to be able

to compare parsing results of typologically different languages

[5]https://github.com/alisafaya/Arabic-BERT

[6]https://camembert-model.fr/

(2019)), Finnish BERT[7] (Virtanen et al., 2019), Italian BERT[8], Swedish BERT[9], Slavic BERT[10] (Czech, Bulgarian, Polish, Russian; Arkhipov et al. (2019)) and BERTje[11] (Dutch, Vries et al. (2019)). The results are shown in Table 2.

lang.	XLMR	BERT (ml)	language specific embeddings	
ar	**84.44**	82.86	84.86	Arabic BERT
bg	91.30	90.52	**91.45**	Slavic BERT
cs	**93.95**	92.35	93.29	Slavic BERT
en	**90.56**	89.03	90.11	RoBERTa
et	**89.13**	86.68	(no emb. available)	
fi	90.69	87.96	**90.98**	Finnish BERT
fr	92.70	92.91	**93.43**	CamemBERT
it	93.04	92.46	**93.25**	Italian BERT
lt	**84.92**	81.82	(no emb. available)	
lv	**89.03**	86.14	(no emb. available)	
nl	90.79	90.63	**91.78**	BERTje
pl	**93.16**	91.63	92.47	Slavic BERT
ru	**93.65**	92.04	92.73	Slavic BERT
sk	**90.85**	89.94	88.79	Slavic BERT[12]
sv	87.78	86.46	**89.29**	Swedish BERT
ta	**72.84**	69.44	(no emb. available)	
uk	**90.78**	88.86	85.84	Slavic BERT

Table 2: Parsing test results (LAS) using different contextual word embeddings, best results in bold (train/dev corpora of the shared task)

Evaluations on the development corpora showed that XLM-R gave the best results for nearly all languages, with some exceptions: for Arabic (Arabic BERT), Bulgarian (Slavic BERT), Finnish (Finnish BERT), French (CamemBERT), Italian (Italian BERT) and Dutch (Dutch BERT) the language-specific versions of BERT gave better results in terms of Labeled Attachment Score (LAS) for the parsing.

2.3 Determining enhanced dependencies

To extract enhanced dependencies we implemented a script ([d1] in Figure 1) which interprets the basic dependency tree and applies some linguistic rules. We built the rules by analysing manually the different types of EUDs in all the provided treebanks.

To obtain a language-independent system which can predict enhanced dependencies on any language, we need homogeneous annotations in all the treebanks. Since these annotations, which require time-consuming manual work, are currently missing in many UD treebanks, and the existing annotations are not always homogeneous, we opted for a rule-based system. For example, dep is used frequently as an additional[13] enhanced dependency in the Czech and Arabic treebanks. Other differences stem from language differences, e.g. in Finnish-TDT and Polish-PDB case information is sometimes given with the nmod:poss enhanced dependency, which is absent in other treebanks for languages without morphological case. Similarly, the conj enhanced dependency is enriched with the lemma of the cc relation only in the treebanks of Dutch, English, Italian and Swedish. Similar differences can be observed for relative pronouns or case information for oblique nominals (obl:<prep>:<case>) or nominal modifiers (nmod:<prep>:<case>). The French-Sequoia treebank frequently employs nmod:enh, amod:enh, nsubj:enh and nsubj:passxoxobjenh which are not defined in the guidelines.

Our script takes into account these language specific differences. For example, it discards prepositions and case information in nmod/obl enhanced dependencies for languages where this information has not been annotated. In general, the script mainly exploits basic dependencies and UPOS, i.e. universal information, to determine the enhanced dependencies.

The script first initialises enhanced dependencies by copying all basic dependencies (except orphan). In a second step we look for all words with a obl and nmod relation and check whether they have a case-dependant. If so, we enrich the enhanced dependencies with the lemma of this dependant. If present, we add the Case-feature to obl:<ADP> and nmod:<ADP> as well.

For coordinations of nouns, we simply take the heads of words with a conj-relation (cf. relation (A) in Figure 2) and determine the dependency relation of its head (relation (B) in Fig. 2). With this

---

[7] https://huggingface.co/TurkuNLP/bert-base-finnish-cased-v1

[8] https://huggingface.co/dbmdz/bert-base-italian-cased

[9] https://huggingface.co/KB/bert-base-swedish-cased

[10] https://huggingface.co/DeepPavlov/bert-base-bg-cs-pl-ru-cased

[11] https://huggingface.co/wietsedv/bert-base-dutch-cased

[12] Slavic BERT works nearly as well as XLM-R for Polish and Russian. However, for Ukrainian and Slovak, which are not part of Slavic BERT), the comparatively lower result is not surprising.

[13] I.e. an enhanced dependency which is not a basic dependency.

information we can add the enhanced dependency relation of the coordinated noun to its enhanced head (relation (C) in Fig. 2). We also enrich the `conj`-relation (relation (D) in Fig. 2) using the lemma of the `cc`-dependant (relation (E) in Fig. 2).

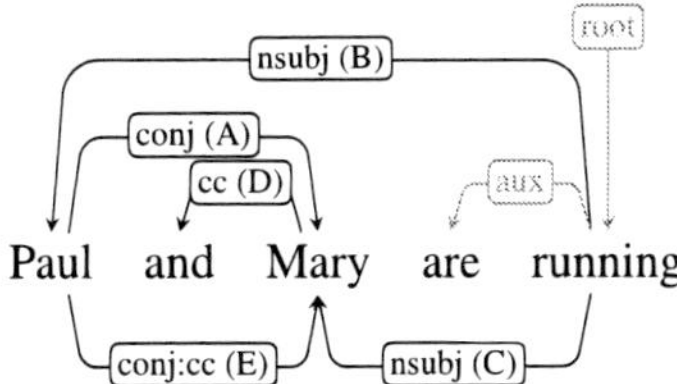

Figure 2: Rule to predict EUDs for coordination: A + B → C and A + D → E

`xcomp` (relation (F) in Fig. 3) relations are processed in a similar way by going through the dependency tree to find the subject (rel. (G) in Fig. 3) of the head of the `xcomp`. We then can add the enhanced dependency relation `nsubj` (rel. (H) in Fig. 3). Referents for relative clauses are processed in an equivalent manner too.

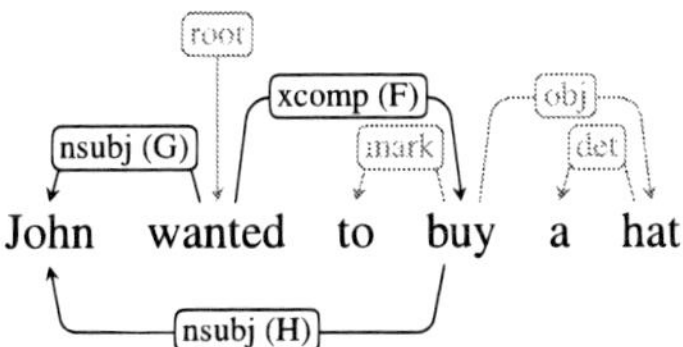

Figure 3: Rule to predict EUDs for `xcomp` subjects: F + G → H

In order to insert elided nodes, we interpret the `orphan` relation. Whereas the insertion itself works fine, we were not able to predict correctly the needed enhanced dependencies for elided nodes and have abandoned this prediction for the shared task.

We validated the rules for enhanced dependency extraction on gold basic dependencies from the validation corpora to avoid the accumulation of errors from the tagging and parsing step. This yielded encouraging results presented in Table 3.

To further improve the performance of the rule-based approach, and to take into account the errors in the tagging/parsing step, we add the ICSIBoost[14] classifier (Favre et al., 2008).

This classifier (cf. [g] in Figures 1 and 4) estimates the probability of success of a given rule in

---

[14]https://github.com/benob/icsiboost

Language	ELAS	EULAS
ar	95.18	96.84
bg	97.84	98.34
cs	94.67	95.79
en	98.04	98.96
et	92.61	95.90
fi	94.40	97.07
fr	96.42	98.21
it	98.41	99.32
lt	94.55	96.61
lv	91.03	95.74
nl	94.40	98.42
pl	91.13	97.23
ru	95.42	96.94
sk	95.44	96.42
sv	96.07	98.38
ta	96.95	99.54
uk	94.58	96.64
Average	**95.13**	**97.43**

Table 3: Enhanced dependencies on gold basic dependencies (development files; without ICSIBoost)

a given context. For this task, we trained a single classifier using the following features:

- rule name
- treebank language
- enhanced dependency label
- UPOS of enhanced dependency head
- (basic) dependency relation of the enhanced dependency head,
- distance (in words) of the basic dependency head
- distance of the enhanced dependency head

To generate the training corpus of ICSIBoost, we ran our enhance-script ([d2] in Fig. 4) on the training CoNLL-U files ([a'] in Fig. 4), with gold UPOS and basic dependencies) of each language to obtain the list of appropriate features and the information whether the rule produced a correct EUD or not within the given context ([d'] in Fig. 4). We then trained ICSIBoosts on this list to obtain a classifier model ([f'] in Fig. 4) which we integrated into the enhance-script ([d3] in Fig. 4) to obtain more accurate predictions.

To get the best threshold for each language, we ran our script ([d3]) on the development CoNLL-U files with various thresholds for each language with UPOS and basic dependencies predicted by UdpipeFuture using contextual embeddings. Rules

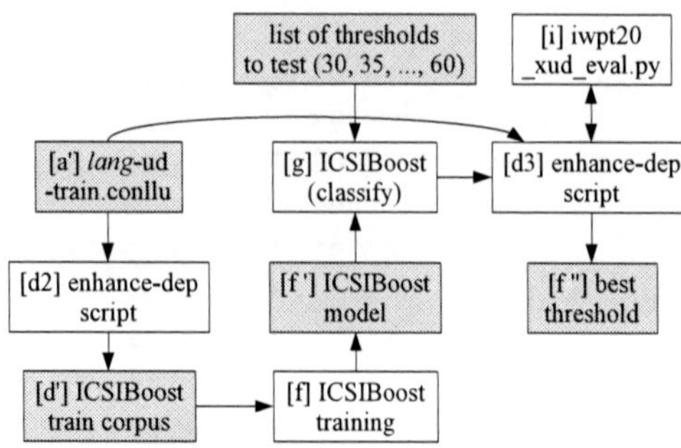

Figure 4: ICSIBoost training

whose score fell below the threshold, in a given context, were not applied. It turned out that thresholds between 30% and 60% gave the best result in terms of ELAS (cf. Table 4). However, the gain from this classification is small for most languages. We observed the biggest increase in ELAS for Estonian, where a threshold of 40% results in 2.13 percent points more than without any filter, whereas for Bulgarian or Italian the difference is only 0.12 or 0.14 points, respectively. On average, the gain is about 0.7 points.

Arabic	40%	Latvian	50%
Bulgarian	55%	Dutch	40%
Czech	40%	Polish	40%
English	55%	Russian	35%
Estonian	40%	Slovak	30%
Finnish	47%	Swedish	40%
French	50%	Tamil	55%
Italian	60%	Ukrainian	50%
Lithuanian	60%		

Table 4: ICSIBoost thresholds to apply a rule in a given context

Running our entire pipeline on gold UPOS and basic dependencies shows that we can predict enhanced dependencies with a very high precision (cf. Table 5).

Applying the entire pipeline on the raw text files provided for the evaluation produced the results shown in Table 6. Since the script which generates the enhanced dependencies depends on basic dependencies and indirectly on the UPOS tags, a lower LAS yields a lower ELAS. By definition, EULAS is always slightly above ELAS. We do not exploit XPOS, since they are too language-specific. Thus the bad results for Finnish XPOS tags do not have an impact on the E(U)LAS score (Table 6). Interestingly the poor sentence segmentation re-

Language	ELAS	EULAS
ar	95.33	97.06
bg	97.74	98.27
cs	94.74	95.88
en	98.19	99.02
et	92.40	96.08
fi	94.94	97.02
fr	97.69	99.10
it	98.18	99.34
lt	93.88	96.10
lv	90.65	95.62
nl	96.36	98.36
pl	88.85	97.08
ru	95.58	97.12
sk	96.00	96.80
sv	95.93	97.86
ta	98.11	99.58
uk	94.82	96.91
Average	**95.26**	**97.48**

Table 5: Predicting enhanced dependencies on gold basic dependencies

sults for Arabic, English and Dutch did not impact the final results since tagging (UPOS) and parsing (LAS) nevertheless gave good results.

3 Conclusion and perspectives

Considering that training data was heterogeneous, partially incomplete, and in general not very voluminous, our hybrid machine-learning (ML)/rule-based approach gave very good results for the shared task. A possible extension would be the processing of elided nodes.

Even if for the long term a purely ML-based approach may prove more efficient, at least our language-independent system can help to pre-annotate existing UD treebanks which, after human validation, can be the basis of an ML approach on predicting enhanced dependencies.

Acknowledgments

We are grateful to two reviewers for constructive comments on the first version of the paper.

References

Mikhail Arkhipov, Maria Trofimova, Yuri Kuratov, and Alexey Sorokin. 2019. Tuning Multilingual Transformers for Language-Specific Named Entity Recognition. In *ACL 2019*, pages 89–93, Florence.

Language	Tokens	Words	Sent.	UPOS	XPOS	Lemmas	UAS	LAS	CLAS	MLAS	EULAS	ELAS
ar	99.97	94.57	81.67	91.87	89.54	90.58	79.39	75.54	72.73	67.43	72.91	70.96
bg	99.89	99.89	93.63	99.17	97.40	98.30	94.46	91.83	89.09	86.11	90.40	89.42
cs	99.85	99.85	92.55	98.98	96.95	98.83	93.93	92.25	91.18	87.16	88.38	86.95
en	99.22	99.22	81.19	96.21	95.47	96.88	89.21	86.94	84.37	78.78	86.02	85.21
et	99.70	99.70	88.02	97.45	98.10	95.18	88.69	86.20	84.96	80.31	84.70	81.03
fi	99.69	99.68	88.52	98.11	56.30	92.12	91.97	90.31	89.07	85.13	87.79	86.24
fr	99.54	99.13	93.27	96.04	99.13	96.53	90.98	86.47	81.11	70.69	85.81	83.63
it	99.90	99.82	96.29	98.46	98.34	98.50	94.74	93.09	89.61	86.84	91.99	90.83
lv	99.34	99.34	98.36	96.69	90.25	96.28	90.69	87.96	85.85	78.45	84.51	82.11
lt	99.94	99.94	87.46	96.57	91.05	94.29	84.91	81.54	79.84	69.95	77.61	75.89
nl	99.71	99.71	77.23	96.75	95.52	97.19	90.57	88.05	83.25	78.73	86.58	85.14
pl	99.33	99.79	96.73	98.58	94.36	98.01	94.26	92.11	90.58	80.97	89.15	80.39
ru	99.48	99.48	97.93	98.80	99.48	98.26	94.41	93.31	92.24	89.93	90.97	89.84
sk	99.99	99.99	84.06	97.16	88.14	96.63	91.20	89.06	87.37	78.03	86.17	84.36
se	99.72	99.72	88.02	97.51	95.64	93.39	88.65	85.91	84.28	69.67	84.36	83.27
ta	99.49	94.96	93.83	87.41	80.36	90.09	71.85	66.23	63.71	54.37	65.68	64.23
uk	99.79	99.75	95.31	98.03	94.69	97.47	90.72	88.59	85.98	79.26	85.46	84.64
Average	**99.68**	**99.09**	**90.24**	**96.69**	**91.81**	**95.80**	**89.45**	**86.79**	**84.42**	**77.75**	**84.62**	**82.60**

Table 6: Official results of our system

Gosse Bouma, Djamé Seddah, and Daniel Zeman. 2020. Overview of the IWPT 2020 Shared Task on Parsing into Enhanced Universal Dependencies. In *Proceedings of the 16th International Conference on Parsing Technologies and the IWPT 2020 Shared Task on Parsing into Enhanced Universal Dependencies*, Seattle, US. Association for Computational Linguistics.

Alexis Conneau, Kartikay Khandelwal, Naman Goyal, Vishrav Chaudhary, Guillaume Wenzek, Francisco Guzmán, Edouard Grace, Myle Ott, Luke Zettlemoyer, and Veselin Stoyanov. 2019. Unsupervised Cross-lingual Representation Learning at Scale. https://arxiv.org/abs/1911.02116.

Jacob Devlin, Ming-Wei Chang Chang, Kenton Lee, and Kristina Toutanova. 2019. BERT: Pre-training of deep bidirectional transformers for language under-standing. In *NAACL*, page 4171–4186, Minneapolis. Association for Computational Linguistics.

Benoît Favre, Dilek Hakkani-Tür, Slav Petrov, and Klein Dan. 2008. Efficient sentence segmentation using syntactic features. In *Spoken Language Technology Workshop*, pages 77–80. IEEE.

Yinhan Liu, Myle Ott, Naman Goyal, Jingfei Du, Mandar Joshi, Danqi Chen, Mike Lewis, Luke Zettlemoyer, and Veselin Stoyanov. 2019. RoBERTa: A Robustly Optimized BERT Pretraining Approach. https://arxiv.org/abs/1907.11692.

Louis Martin, Benjamin Muller, Pedro Javier Ortiz Suárez, Yoann Dupont, Laurent Romary, Éric Villemonte de la Clergerie, Djamé Seddah, and Benoît Sagot. 2019. CamemBERT: a Tasty French Language Model. https://arxiv.org/abs/1911.03894.

Joakim Nivre and Chiao-Ting Fang. 2017. Universal Dependency Evaluation. In *Proceedings of the NoDaLiDa 2017 Workshop on Universal Dependencies*, pages 86–95, Göteborg.

Joakim Nivre, Marie-Catherine de Marneffe, Filip Ginter, Yoav Goldberg, Yoav Goldberg, Jan Hajič, Manning Christopher D., Ryan McDonald, Slav Petrov, Sampo Pyysalo, Natalia Silveira, Reut Tsarfaty, and Daniel Zeman. 2016. Universal Dependencies v1: A Multilingual Treebank Collection. In *the tenth international conference on Language Resources and Evaluation*, pages 23–38, Portorož, Slovenia. European Language Resources Association.

Joakim Nivre, Paola Marongiu, Filip Ginter, Jenna Kanerva, Simonetta Montemagni, Sebastian Schuster, and Maria Simi. 2018. Enhancing Universal Dependency Treebanks: A Case Study. In *Proceedings of the Second Workshop on Universal Dependencies (UDW 2018)*, pages 102–107, Brussels, Belgium. Association for Computational Linguistics.

Matthew E. Peters, Mark Neumann, Mohit Iyyer, Matt Gardner, Christopher Clark, Kendon Lee, and Luke Zettlemoyer. 2018. Deep Contextualized Word Representations. In *NAACL*, page 2227–2237, New Orleans, Louisiana. Association for Computational Linguistics.

Sebastian Schuster and Christopher D. Manning. 2016. Enhanced English Universal Dependencies: An Improved Representation for Natural Language Understanding Tasks. In *the tenth international conference on Language Resources and Evaluation*, pages 2371–2378, Portorož, Slovenia. European Language Resources Association.

Sebastian Schuster, Joachim Nivre, and Christopher D. Manning. 2018. Sentences with Gapping: Parsing and Reconstructing Elided Predicates. In *NAACL*, pages 1156–1168, New Orleans, Louisiana. Association for Computational Linguistics.

Milan Straka. 2018. UDPipe 2.0 Prototype at CoNLL 2018 UD Shared Task. In *Proceedings of the CoNLL 2018 Shared Task: Multilingual Parsing from Raw Text to Universal Dependencies*, pages 197–207,

Brussels. Association for Computational Linguistics.

Milan Straka and Jana Straková. 2017. Tokenizing, POS Tagging, Lemmatizing and Parsing UD 2.0 with UDPipe. In *ACL 2017*, pages 88–99, Vancouver.

Antti Virtanen, Jenna Kanerva, Rami Ilo, Juhani Luotolahti, Tapio Salakoski, Filip Ginter, and Sampo Pyysalo. 2019. Multilingual is not enough: BERT for Finnish. https://arxiv.org/abs/1912.07076.

Wietse de Vries, Andreas van Cranenburgh, Arianna Bisazza, Tommaso Caselli, Gertjan van Noord, and Malvina Nissim. 2019. BERTje: A Dutch BERT Model. https://arxiv.org/abs/1912.09582.

Daniel Zeman, Jan Hajič, Martin Popel, Martin Potthast, Milan Straka, Filip Ginter, Joakim Nivre, and Slav Petrov. 2018. CoNLL 2018 Shared Task: Multilingual Parsing from Raw Text to Universal Dependencies. In *Proceedings of the CoNLL 2018 Shared Task: Multilingual Parsing from Raw Text to Universal Dependencies*, pages 1–21, Brussels. Association for Computational Linguistics.

Adaptation of Multilingual Transformer Encoder for Robust Enhanced Universal Dependency Parsing

Han He
Computer Science
Emory University
Atlanta GA 30322, USA
han.he@emory.edu

Jinho D. Choi
Computer Science
Emory University
Atlanta GA 30322, USA
jinho.choi@emory.edu

Abstract

This paper presents our enhanced dependency parsing approach using transformer encoders, coupled with a simple yet powerful ensemble algorithm that takes advantage of both tree and graph dependency parsing. Two types of transformer encoders are compared, a multilingual encoder and language-specific encoders. Our dependency tree parsing (DTP) approach generates only primary dependencies to form trees whereas our dependency graph parsing (DGP) approach handles both primary and secondary dependencies to form graphs. Since DGP does not guarantee the generated graphs are acyclic, the ensemble algorithm is designed to add secondary arcs predicted by DGP to primary arcs predicted by DTP. Our results show that models using the multilingual encoder outperform ones using the language specific encoders for most languages. Moreover, the ensemble models generally show higher labeled attachment score on enhanced dependencies (ELAS) than the DTP and DGP models. As the result, our best parsing models rank the third place on the macro-average ELAS over 17 languages.

1 Introduction

Dependency parsing can generate computational structures for a wide range of typologically different languages, which provides structural relations that have been found to be useful for various NLP applications. However, these applications often require richer dependency relations carrying on deep semantics, which are missing in traditional dependency trees. Thus, enhanced dependencies emerge to explicitly capture deep semantic relations over surface structures (Schuster and Manning, 2016).

Recently, there has been lots of interests in constructing and parsing advanced graph structures beyond tree representations. Choi (2017) introduce deep dependency graphs that address several limitations in UD tree structures. Schuster et al. (2017)

analyze gapping constructions in the enhanced UD representation. Nivre et al. (2018) evaluate both rule-based and data-driven systems for adding enhanced dependencies to existing treebanks. Apart from syntactic relations, researchers are moving towards semantic dependency parsing (Oepen et al., 2015) for more direct analysis of entities and events. The efforts of treebank construction stimulates the interest of many researchers in improving the performance of semantic parsers (Dozat and Manning, 2018; Du et al., 2015; Almeida and Martins, 2015).

This paper presents our parsing approach to the Shared Task on Enhanced Universal Dependencies at IWPT 2020 (Nivre et al., 2016; Bouma et al.).[1] Our system is a simplified version of the transformer-based dependency parsers presented by He and Choi (2020), which employs the deep biaffine dependency parsing decoder (Dozat and Manning, 2017) over the transformer encoder, BERT (Devlin et al., 2019). We simplify their network by removing the LSTM and fine-tuning their static transformer encoder. In order to effectively predict the enhanced dependencies, we also ensemble the dependency tree parser with an dependency graph parser through a greedy searching algorithm. At last, we perform extensive experiments on the effects of transformer encoders to perform a detailed analysis.

Our experiments show that the multilingual encoder has a substantial advantage over the language-specific encoders. Moreover, our analysis shows that tree parsing model can accurately predict primary dependencies in long sentences, while graph parsing model excels at label prediction. By taking advantages from both sides, our ensemble models outperform individual models in most languages.[2]

---

[1]This work purely focuses on parsing not pre-steps such as sentence split or tokenization, although we recognize that it is important to address the pre-steps to win this competition.

[2]All our resources are available at https://github.

Proceedings of the 16th International Conference on Parsing Technologies and the IWPT 2020 Shared Task, pages 181–191
Virtual Meeting, July 9, 2020. ©2020 Association for Computational Linguistics

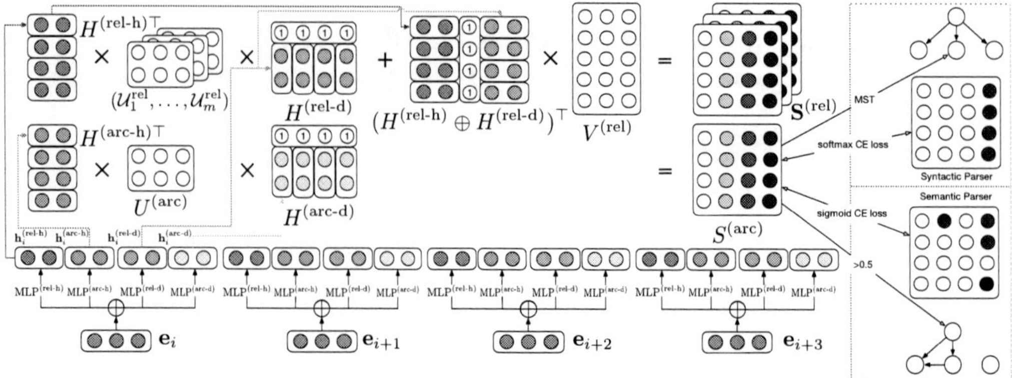

Figure 1: The overview of our transformer-based biaffine dependency parsing model.

2 Approach

2.1 Preprocessing

The data in the training and development sets are already sentence segmented and tokenized. For the test set, UDPipe is used to segment raw input into sentences, where each sentence gets split into a list of tokens (Straka and Straková, 2017). A custom script written by us is used to remove multiwords but retain their splits (e.g., remove *vámonos* but retain *vámos nos*), as well as to collapse empty nodes in the CoNLL-U format.

2.2 Transformer Encoder

Our parsing models use contextualized embeddings generated by transformer encoders such as BERT (Devlin et al., 2019), RoBERTa (Liu et al., 2020) or ALBERT (Lan et al., 2020) that are pretrained on large corpora for language modeling. Each sentence in the preprocessed data by Section 2.1 is fed into a transformer encoder that further splits every token into sub-tokens using SentencePiece (Kudo and Richardson, 2018). The sub-token embeddings from the last layer of the transformer encoder are fed into the biaffine decoder in Section 2.3.

2.3 Biaffine Decoder

Our dependency parsing approach is based on the biaffine decoder that has shown state-of-the-art results on syntactic tree and semantic graph parsing in both English and Chinese (He and Choi, 2020). This model is simplified from the original biaffine parser introduced by Dozat and Manning (2017) such that trainable token embeddings are removed and lemmas are used instead of word forms. This

```
com/emorynlp/iwpt-shared-task-2020
```

section proposes an even more simplified approach that no longer uses embeddings from POS tags, so it can be easily adapted to languages that may not have dedicated POS taggers, and drops the Bidirectional LSTM encoder while integrating the transformer encoder directly into the biaffine decoder to minimize the redundancy of multiple encoders for the generation of contextualized embeddings.

Every token w_i in the input sentence is split into one or more sub-tokens by the transformer encoder (Section 2.2). The contextualized embedding that corresponds to the first sub-token of w_i is treated as the embedding of w_i, say $\mathbf{e}_i$, and fed into four types of multilayer perceptron (MLP) layers to extract features for w_i being a head (*-h) or a dependent (*-d) for the arc relations (arc-*) and the labels (rel-*) (k and l are the dimensions of the arc and label representations, respectively):

$$\mathbf{h}_i^{\text{(arc-h)}} = \text{MLP}^{\text{(arc-h)}}(\mathbf{e}_i) \in \mathbb{R}^{k \times 1}$$
$$\mathbf{h}_i^{\text{(arc-d)}} = \text{MLP}^{\text{(arc-d)}}(\mathbf{e}_i) \in \mathbb{R}^{k \times 1}$$
$$\mathbf{h}_i^{\text{(rel-h)}} = \text{MLP}^{\text{(rel-h)}}(\mathbf{e}_i) \in \mathbb{R}^{l \times 1}$$
$$\mathbf{h}_i^{\text{(rel-d)}} = \text{MLP}^{\text{(rel-d)}}(\mathbf{e}_i) \in \mathbb{R}^{l \times 1}$$

All feature vectors, $\mathbf{h}_1^*, \ldots, \mathbf{h}_n^*$, from each representation are stacked into a matrix (n is the number of tokens in a sentence); these matrices together are used to predict dependency relations among every token pairs. Note that bias terms are appended to the feature vectors $\mathbf{h}_i^{\text{(*-d)}}$ that represent dependent nodes to estimate the likelihood of a certain relation given only the head node:

182

$$H^{\text{(arc-h)}} = (\mathbf{h}_1^{\text{(arc-h)}}, \ldots, \mathbf{h}_n^{\text{(arc-h)}}) \in \mathbb{R}^{k \times n}$$

$$H^{\text{(arc-d)}} = (\mathbf{h}_1^{\text{(arc-d)}}, \ldots, \mathbf{h}_n^{\text{(arc-d)}}) \oplus \mathbf{1} \in \mathbb{R}^{(k+1) \times n}$$

$$H^{\text{(rel-h)}} = (\mathbf{h}_1^{\text{(rel-h)}}, \ldots, \mathbf{h}_n^{\text{(rel-h)}}) \in \mathbb{R}^{l \times n}$$

$$H^{\text{(rel-d)}} = (\mathbf{h}_1^{\text{(rel-d)}}, \ldots, \mathbf{h}_n^{\text{(rel-d)}}) \oplus \mathbf{1} \in \mathbb{R}^{(l+1) \times n}$$

The bilinear and biaffine classifiers are then used for the arc and label predictions respectively, where $U^{\text{(arc)}}$, $U_i^{\text{(rel)}}$ and $V^{\text{(rel)}}$ are trainable parameters, and m is the number of dependency labels. In particular, a separate weight matrix $U_i^{\text{(rel)}}$ is dedicated to the prediction of each label:

$$S^{\text{(arc)}} = H^{\text{(arc-h)}\top} \cdot U^{\text{(arc)}} \cdot H^{\text{(arc-d)}} \in \mathbb{R}^{n \times n}$$

$$\mathcal{U}_i^{\text{(rel)}} = H^{\text{(rel-h)}\top} \cdot U_i^{\text{(rel)}} \cdot H^{\text{(rel-d)}} \in \mathbb{R}^{n \times n}$$

$$S^{\text{(rel)}} = (\mathcal{U}_1^{\text{(rel)}}, \ldots, \mathcal{U}_m^{\text{(rel)}})$$
$$+ (H^{\text{(rel-h)}} \oplus H^{\text{(rel-d)}})^\top \cdot V^{\text{(rel)}} \in \mathbb{R}^{m \times n \times n}$$

2.4 Dependency Tree & Graph Parsing

The arc score matrix $S^{\text{(arc)}}$ and the label score tensor $\mathbf{S}^{\text{(rel)}}$ generated by the bilinear and biaffine classifiers can be used for both dependency tree parsing (DTP) and graph parsing (DGP). For DTP, which takes only the primary dependencies to learn tree structures during training, the Chu-Liu-Edmond's Maximum Spanning Tree (MST) algorithm is applied to $S^{\text{(arc)}}$ for the arc prediction, then the label with largest score in $\mathbf{S}^{\text{(rel)}}$ corresponding to the arc is taken for the label prediction ($\mathcal{A}_{\text{DTP}}$: the list of predicted arcs, $\mathcal{L}_{\text{DTP}}$: the labels predicted for $\mathcal{A}_{\text{DTP}}$, $\mathcal{I}$: the indices of $\mathcal{A}_{\text{DTP}}$ in $\mathbf{S}^{\text{(rel)}}$):

$$\mathcal{A}_{\text{DTP}} = \text{MST}(S^{\text{(arc)}})$$
$$\mathcal{L}_{\text{DTP}} = \text{argmax}(\mathbf{S}^{\text{(rel)}}[\mathcal{I}(\mathcal{A}_{\text{DTP}})])$$

For DGP, which takes the primary as well as the secondary dependencies in the enhanced types to learn graph structures during training, the sigmoid function is applied to $S^{\text{(arc)}}$ instead of the softmax function (Figure 1) so that zero to many heads can be predicted per node by measuring the pairwise losses. Then, the same logic can be used to predict the labels for those arcs as follows:

$$\mathcal{A}_{\text{DGP}} = \text{SIGMOID}(S^{\text{(arc)}})$$
$$\mathcal{L}_{\text{DGP}} = \text{argmax}(\mathbf{S}^{\text{(rel)}}[\mathcal{I}(\mathcal{A}_{\text{DGP}})])$$

It is worth mentioning that the performance of DTP is generally better than the one achieved by DGP

for finding the primary dependencies that form tree structures; however, DTP completely dismisses the secondary dependencies so that DGP outperforms DTP for the overall performance on the enhanced dependencies. Section 2.5 describes our ensemble parsing approach that adapts the best of both worlds by taking the predictions of primary dependencies from DTP and augmenting them with the predictions of secondary dependencies from DGP.

2.5 Ensemble Parsing

The UD guidelines require a graph formed by only primary dependencies to be always a spanning tree, while such a restriction is not applied to graphs with secondary dependencies. We find that the majority of dependency graphs in the training set, however, can be viewed as directed acyclic graphs (DAGs). In fact, all graphs can be transformed into DAGs by removing 0.87% of the secondary dependencies. Therefore, our ensemble parsing method focuses on building maximum spanning DAGs (MSDAGs) by combining arcs from both dependency trees and graphs generated by the DTP and DGP models, respectively (Section 2.4).[3]

Unfortunately, finding MSDAGs from the output of the DGP model is NP-hard (Schluter, 2014). Thus, we design an ensemble approach that finds approximate MSDAGs using a greedy algorithm. Given the score matrices $S_{\text{DTP}}^{\text{(arc)}}$ and $S_{\text{DGP}}^{\text{(arc)}}$ from the DTP and DGP models respectively and the label score tensor $\mathbf{S}_{\text{DGP}}^{\text{(rel)}}$ from the DGP model, Algorithm 1 is applied to compute the MSDAG:

The algorithm begins by initializing scores related to the root in $\mathbf{S}_{\text{DGP}}^{\text{(rel)}}$ (L1$-$3). The label matrix R is created by taking the argmax of every dependent and head pair (d, h) in $\mathbf{S}_{\text{DGP}}^{\text{(rel)}}$ such that each cell contains the most likely label for that pair (L4). Given the arc list $\mathcal{A}_{\text{DTP}}$ from the DTS model (L5), the graph G is generated by taking all arcs in $\mathcal{A}_{\text{DTP}}$ and their corresponding labels in R (L6$-$9).[4] Finally, given the arc list $\mathcal{A}_{\text{DGP}}$ from the DGP model sorted in descending order (L10), arcs in $\mathcal{A}_{\text{DGP}}$ are greedily added to G, as long as they do not create any

---

[3] The motivation behind this DAG approach was to reduce potential confusion in learning caused by cyclic structures, which we later realized may have not been necessary, but we described this approach here for the replicability of our work.

[4] $\mathbf{S}_{\text{DGP}}^{\text{(rel)}}$ is used to find the labels of arcs predicted by both the DTP and DGP models. From our experiments, we find that the DGP model outperforms the DTP model for the label predictions of even primary dependencies, which may be due to the greater number of labels in DGP training data; thus, $\mathbf{S}_{\text{DGP}}^{\text{(rel)}}$ is used for all types of dependencies instead of $\mathbf{S}_{\text{DTP}}^{\text{(rel)}}$.

	AR	BG	CS	EN	ET	FI	FR	IT	LT	LV	NL	PL	RU	SK	SV	TA	UK
TRN	6,075	8,907	102,133	12,543	25,749	12,217	2,231	13,121	2,341	10,156	18,051	31,496	48,814	8,483	4,303	400	5,496
DEV	909	1,115	11,182	2,002	3,125	1,364	412	564	617	1,664	1,394	3,960	6,584	1,060	504	80	672
TST	794	1,112	12,713	2,800	3,588	2,616	2,679	482	652	1,835	1,154	4,923	6,495	1,052	2,258	122	905
> 256	4	0	0	0	2	0	0	0	0	0	2	0	0	0	0	0	0

(a) Sentence counts. The > 256 row shows the number of sentences in the test set whose lengths are greater than 256 tokens.

	AR	BG	CS	EN	ET	FI	FR	IT	LT	LV	NL	PL	RU	SK	SV	TA	UK
TRN	254.3K	124.3K	1783.1K	204.6K	361.8K	163.0K	51.9K	294.4K	47.6K	167.6K	261.0K	388.5K	870.5K	80.6K	66.6K	6.8K	92.4K
DEV	34.2K	16.1K	187.3K	25.1K	44.6K	18.3K	10.3K	12.7K	11.6K	26.0K	22.9K	48.0K	118.5K	12.4K	9.8K	1.4K	12.6K
TST	30.8K	15.7K	220.5K	46.3K	58.7K	36.9K	35.3K	11.2K	10.8K	26.4K	22.6K	65.7K	117.4K	13.0K	39.3K	2.1K	17.1K

(b) Token counts in thousands (K).

Table 1: Statistics of the training (TRN), development (DEV), and test (TST) sets preprocessed by UDPipe. AR: Arabic, BG: Bulgarian, CS: Czech, EN: English, ET: Estonian, FI: Finnish, FR: French, IT: Italian, LT: Lithuanian, LV: Latvian, NL: Dutch, PL: Polish, RU: Russian, SK: Slovak, SV: Swedish, TA: Tamil, UK: Ukrainian.

Algorithm 1: Ensemble parsing algorithm

Input: $S_{\text{DTP}}^{(\text{arc})}$, $S_{\text{DGP}}^{(\text{arc})}$, and $\mathbf{S}_{\text{DGP}}^{(\text{rel})}$

Output: G, that is an approximate MSDAG

1   $r \leftarrow \text{root\_index}(\mathcal{A}_{\text{DTP}})$

2   $\mathbf{S}_{\text{DGP}}^{(\text{rel})}[\text{root}, :, :] \leftarrow -\infty$

3   $\mathbf{S}_{\text{DGP}}^{(\text{rel})}[\text{root}, r, r] \leftarrow +\infty$

4   $R \leftarrow \text{argmax}(\mathbf{S}_{\text{DGP}}^{(\text{rel})}) \in \mathbb{R}^{n \times n}$

5   $\mathcal{A}_{\text{DTP}} \leftarrow \text{MST}(S_{\text{DTP}}^{(\text{arc})})$

6   $G \leftarrow \emptyset$

7   **foreach** arc $(d, h) \in \mathcal{A}_{DTP}$ **do**

8 | $G \leftarrow G \cup \{(d, h, R[d, h]\}$

9   **end**

10   $\mathcal{A}_{\text{DGP}} \leftarrow \text{sorted\_descend}(\text{SIGMOID}(S_{\text{DGP}}^{(\text{arc})}))$

11   **foreach** arc $(d, h) \in \mathcal{A}_{DGP}$ **do**

12 | $G^{(d,h)} \leftarrow G \cup \{(d, h, R[d, h]\}$

13 | **if** is_acyclic$(G^{(d,h)})$ **then**

14 | | $G \leftarrow G^{(d,h)}$

15 | **end**

16   **end**

cycle in G (`L11-16`).

2.6 Postprocessing

As mentioned in Section 2.1, empty nodes in the enhanced dependencies are collapsed before training using the script provided by the UD project.[5] Once dependency structures are generated by any parsing model, empty nodes are restored using our custom script.[6] At last, the postprocessing script provided by the UD project is applied to normalize the Unicode encoding and amend the `SpaceAfter=No` annotation as recommended by the organizers.[7]

3 Experiments

3.1 Datasets

Table 1 shows the statistics of data splits used for our experiments, that are preprocessed by UDPipe trained on UD v2.5 (Straka and Straková, 2017). Training and development sets for treebanks from the same languages are concatenated together. In particular, the following treebanks are merged for Czech, Estonian, and Dutch such that no individual models are developed for those treebanks:

- Czech: `UD_Czech-CAC/FicTree/PDT`

- Estonian: `UD_Estonian-EDT/EWT`

- Dutch: `UD_Dutch-Alpino/LassySmall`

Since transformer encoders usually restrict the input sequence length to be under 512 sub-tokens, our

---

[5] `https://github.com/UniversalDependencies/tools/blob/master/enhanced_collapse_empty_nodes.pl`

[6] `https://gist.github.com/hankcs/776e7d95c19e5ff5da8469fe4e9ab050`

[7] `https://github.com/UniversalDependencies/tools/blob/master/conllu-quick-fix.pl`

	AR	BG	CS	EN	ET	FI	FR	IT	LT	LV	NL	PL	RU	SK	SV	TA	UK
DTP	61.28	79.58	78.37	75.70	68.08	70.37	85.29	75.21	63.91	71.68	71.08	74.33	74.62	70.12	70.92	**54.26**	77.04
DGP	63.56	86.66	79.38	82.31	75.94	72.03	74.35	86.46	61.59	71.58	76.94	70.39	83.19	81.37	77.39	40.10	79.56
ENS	**67.26**	**88.19**	**85.51**	83.24	**81.36**	80.54	81.97	87.83	**66.12**	**79.19**	**80.72**	**82.39**	**88.60**	**82.72**	**78.19**	46.67	**79.69**
DTP	49.38	55.76	71.73	76.99	44.61	72.40	**86.23**	75.50	-	-	70.95	57.35	63.51	30.41	-	-	-
DGP	43.71	45.25	68.47	83.22	43.90	79.38	78.87	86.45	-	-	76.46	51.90	63.44	26.03	-	-	-
ENS	48.02	52.16	51.05	**85.30**	51.82	**82.96**	81.45	**88.52**	-	-	80.02	59.59	71.19	30.08	-	-	-

(a) Labeled attachment score on enhanced dependencies (ELAS) on the test sets.

	AR	BG	CS	EN	ET	FI	FR	IT	LT	LV	NL	PL	RU	SK	SV	TA	UK
DTP	**71.83**	**89.61**	**87.20**	84.61	**82.81**	85.43	87.47	90.49	**73.55**	**81.17**	**83.67**	**88.29**	**89.71**	**86.83**	**81.72**	**58.66**	**85.36**
DGP	65.49	87.31	80.38	82.74	76.42	72.62	75.49	86.98	63.10	71.95	77.37	74.54	83.47	83.39	78.32	41.36	80.18
ENS	69.46	88.84	86.63	83.68	81.98	81.44	83.34	88.35	68.24	79.66	81.21	86.79	88.93	84.73	79.11	48.50	80.34
DTP	56.69	62.27	79.53	**86.24**	53.31	**88.19**	**88.28**	**90.89**	-	-	83.47	67.58	76.05	34.50	-	-	-
DGP	46.75	46.84	69.79	83.67	44.62	80.10	80.12	86.92	-	-	76.97	55.58	64.16	26.82	-	-	-
ENS	51.37	54.01	53.45	85.76	52.74	83.70	82.83	89.04	-	-	80.59	63.82	72.13	31.19	-	-	-

(b) Labeled attachment score on enhanced dependencies where labels are restricted to the UD relation (EULAS).

Table 2: Parsing results on the test sets for all languages. For both (a) and (b), the rows 2-4 show the results by the multilingual encoder and the rows 5-7 show the results by the language-specific encoders if available.

parsing models cannot handle sentences beyond this length. As the distribution of sentence lengths in each dataset is measured, we find out that most sentences consist of fewer than 256 tokens. Thus, we discard sentences beyond 256 tokens from all training and development sets. For such sentences in the test sets, we rely on the parsing outputs from UDPipe; this choice is made due to the negligible numbers of those sentences (Table 1a) although it can be obviously improved.

3.2 Encoder Models

Two types of transformer encoders are used for the development of our models. One is the multilingual BERT (mBERT) pretrained on a mixture of large corpora in 100 languages (Devlin et al., 2019). The mBERT encoder uses one model to generate token embeddings for all languages, which encourages transfer learning in multilingual parsing. The other is language specific encoders that have been made to public by the community. Table 3 shows details about 12 language-specific encoders.[8] More details about the sources of these models are described in Section A.2.

3.3 Development Configuration

Following He and Choi (2020), we use the AdamW optimizer (Loshchilov and Hutter, 2019) with a linear learning rate warm-up and decay for finetuning the pretrained encoders. For the decoder weights, we use the Adam optimizer (Kingma and Ba, 2015) with a learning rate 20 times smaller than the one for finetuning. For the contextualized embeddings, we apply a shared dropout mask for each time step

---

[8]We could not find public models for the other 5 languages.

similar to variational dropout often used for recurrent neural networks (Gal and Ghahramani, 2016).

The KMeans clustering algorithm is adopted to bucket sentences into mini-batches according to their lengths counted by sub-tokens. The NVIDIA RTX GPUs with 24GB memory are used to develop these models. Unfortunately, most of our models cannot be fit into GPUs with smaller memory due to the extensive memory use of both the encoder and the decoder. We will explore innovative ways of reducing our parsing models such as teacher-student learning (Shin et al., 2019).

3.4 Parsing Results

All models are evaluated with 5 metrics, unlabeled attachment score (UAS), labeled attachment score (LAS), content labeled attachment score (CLAS), LAS on enhanced dependencies where labels are restricted to the UD relation (EULAS), and LAS on enhanced dependencies (ELAS). Models with the highest ELAS on the development sets are used to generate the final parse outputs on the test sets. Table 2 shows the ELAS and EULAS on the test sets for all languages. Detailed parsing results evaluated with all 5 metrics are described in Section A.3. For ELAS, our ensemble models (ENS) outperform the other models on 15 out of 17 languages. The only 2 exceptions are French and Tamil; these two languages consist of relatively fewer numbers of multi-head tokens as illustrated in Figure 2. Out of 12 languages with language-specific encoders (Table 3), models using the multilingual encoder outperform 8 of them, indicating the promise of the multilingual encoder to build robust parsing models for low-resource languages. The 4 exceptions

Lang.	Encoder	Corpus	Provider
AR	BERT	8.2 B	Hugging Face
EN	ALBERT	16 GB	Hugging Face
ET	BERT	N/A	TurkuNLP
FR	RoBERTa	138 GB	Hugging Face
FI	BERT	24 B	Hugging Face
IT	BERT	13 GB	Hugging Face
NL	BERT	N/A	Hugging Face
PL	BERT	1.8 B	Hugging Face
SV	BERT	3 B	Hugging Face
BG	BERT	N/A	Hugging Face
CS	BERT	N/A	Hugging Face
SK	BERT	N/A	Hugging Face

Table 3: Language-specific transformer encoders to develop our models. The corpus column shows the corpus size used to pretrain each encoder (B: billion tokens, GB: gigabytes). BERT and RoBERTa adapt the base models whereas ALBERT adapts the large model. Publications and resource links are shown in Table 5.

are English, Finnish, French, and Italian, which either use more advanced encoding methods or their language models are trained on larger corpora.

For EULAS, the multilingual encoding approach still outperforms 8 out of the 12 languages as for ELAS. However, DTP models completely outperform both DGP and ENS models, indicating that the primary and secondary dependencies are not distinguishable by our current DGP approach, which complies with the fact that DGP is trained on enhanced relations rather than the basic dependencies DTP is trained on. We believe the performance of DGP could be improved through ad-hoc strategies to handle enhancement of case and lemma.

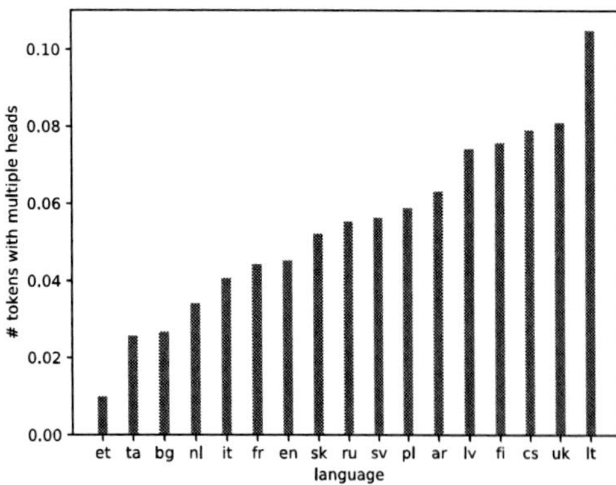

Figure 2: Percentages of tokens with multiple heads.

4 Analysis

This section analyzes factors that affect our models the most, common error made across languages and what possible improvement that can be made.

4.1 Data Size

We use the same hyper-parameters for all datasets, which may have led to possible overfitting (or underfitting). To verify this, we compute the differences between the ELAS scores of our models and that of the highest models from other teams. We then plot the differences as a function of the log training data size and fit the differences to a linear regression model shown in Figure 3.

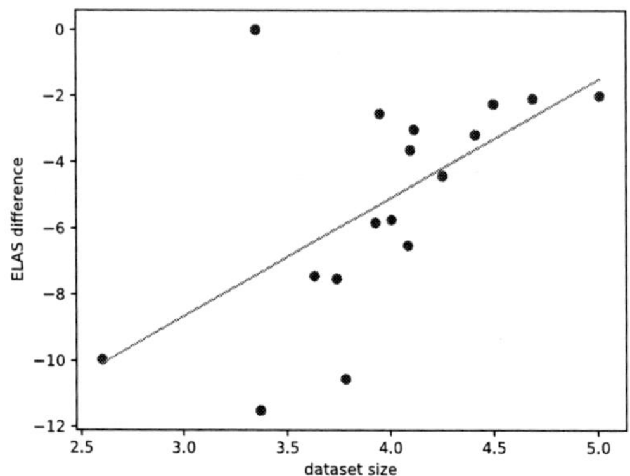

Figure 3: Difference in ELAS between our parser and the top team as a function of dataset size.

We also fit the differences with sentence scores as random effects to another regression model, finding that the p values for sentence scores and dataset sizes are 0.760 and 0.001. It shows that our system performs relatively better on larger datasets while overfits to smaller datasets, suggesting that decreasing model capacity may improve ELAS for languages with less training data.

4.2 OOV

To investigate the performance of each model on Out-Of-Vocabulary (OOV) tokens, we evaluate them on the OOV-only subset of English treebank. As shown in Figure 4, language specific encoder outperforms multilingual encoder in therse model settings, which is not surprising.

4.3 Sentence Length

We evaluate the ELAS of English treebank offline relative to sentence length with gold tokenization and sentence split. As shown in Figure 5, DTP models are very stable on long sentences while the performance of DGP models dramatically drops with the increase of sentence length. Performance of multilingual encoder models tends to drop faster than their language-specific counterparts.

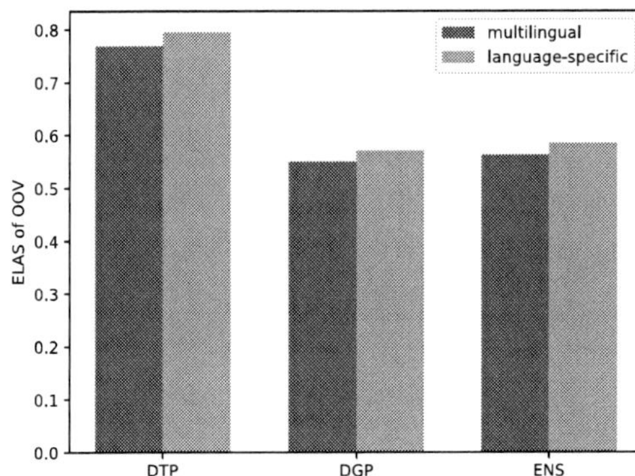

Figure 4: ELAS of Out-Of-Vocabulary tokens.

5 Related Work

Our work in utilizing multilingual Transformers as the encoder for parser model is most closely related to the UDify system (Kondratyuk and Straka, 2019). UDify is a multilingual multi-task model leveraging a multilingual BERT to accurately predict universal part-of-speech, morphological features, lemmas, and dependency trees simultaneously across 75 languages. UDify concatenates all training sets together to encourage knowledge transferring across languages, which benefits low-resource languages the most. In our multilingual BERT approach, each model is trained separately.

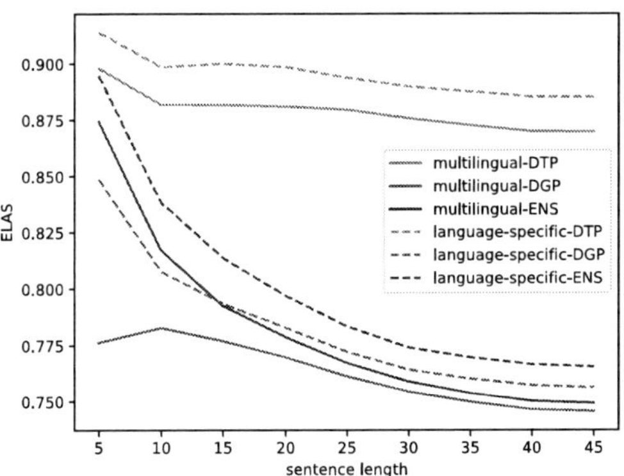

Figure 5: ELAS of the English treebank relative to sentence length.

For the encoder, pre-trained Transformers (Devlin et al., 2019; Liu et al., 2020; Lan et al., 2020) has been shown to be effective in tagging and parsing tasks without heavily engineered decoders(He and Choi, 2020). The encoder representations embed entire syntax trees according to the structural probe (Hewitt and Manning, 2019), encouraging the application of Transformers in parsing task. Not only in the embedding space, syntactic structures are used in the Tree Transformer (Wang et al., 2019), where constituent attention is gradually learned bottom-up layer by layer. Our parser employs pre-trained transformer models in Section 3.2.

For the decoder, the deep biaffine attention (Dozat and Manning, 2017) dominates the graph based approach since its establishment. The top ranked graph-based dependency parser at the CoNLL 2017 Shared Task (Dozat et al., 2017) adopts biaffine attention with rich character level features. With a parsing algorithm other than MST, the biaffine parser is successfully extended to semantic dependency parsing (Dozat and Manning, 2018). The current state-of-the-art dependency parsing records on English Penn Treebank (Marcus et al., 1993) and Chinese Treebank (Xue et al., 2005) are maintained by the Head-Driven Phrase Structure parser (Zhou and Zhao, 2019), which jointly learns constituency parsing and dependency parsing with layers including biaffine attention. Apart from parsing, biaffine attention has also been applied to graph related task including relation extraction (Nguyen and Verspoor, 2019) and coreference resolution (Zhang et al., 2018).

6 Conclusion

This paper describes our parsing approach to enhanced universal dependencies for the IWPT 2020 shared task. We find that the multilingual BERT encoder is able to parse various languages without language specific network design. Our proposed ensemble method is shown to be beneficial for the secondary dependency prediction.

In the future, we will improve the secondary dependency prediction in a more systematic way. We believe our current approach generating dependency graphs satisfying the tree constraint of primary dependencies can be further improved if the constraint can be applied to biaffine attention during training time, and the MSDAGs constraint can be relaxed for better performance. We leave these exciting topics for future work.

Acknowledgments

We gratefully acknowledge the support of the AWS Machine Learning Research Awards (MLRA). Any contents in this material are those of the authors and do not necessarily reflect the views of AWS.

References

Mariana SC Almeida and André FT Martins. 2015. Lisbon: Evaluating turbosemanticparser on multiple languages and out-of-domain data. In *Proceedings of the 9th International Workshop on Semantic Evaluation (SemEval 2015)*, pages 970–973.

Mikhail Arkhipov, Maria Trofimova, Yuri Kuratov, and Alexey Sorokin. 2019. Tuning multilingual transformers for language-specific named entity recognition. In *Proceedings of the 7th Workshop on Balto-Slavic Natural Language Processing*, pages 89–93, Florence, Italy. Association for Computational Linguistics.

Gosse Bouma, Djamé Seddah, and Daniel Zeman. Overview of the IWPT 2020 Shared Task on Parsing into Enhanced Universal Dependencies. In *Proceedings of the 16th International Conference on Parsing Technologies and the IWPT 2020 Shared Task on Parsing into Enhanced Universal Dependencies*. Association for Computational Linguistics.

Jinho D. Choi. 2017. Deep Dependency Graph Conversion in English. In *Proceedings of the 15th International Workshop on Treebanks and Linguistic Theories*, TLT'17, pages 35–62, Bloomington, IN.

Jacob Devlin, Ming-Wei Chang, Kenton Lee, and Kristina Toutanova. 2019. BERT: Pre-training of deep bidirectional transformers for language understanding. In *Proceedings of the 2019 Conference of the North American Chapter of the Association for Computational Linguistics: Human Language Technologies, Volume 1 (Long and Short Papers)*, pages 4171–4186, Minneapolis, Minnesota. Association for Computational Linguistics.

Timothy Dozat and Christopher D. Manning. 2017. Deep Biaffine Attention for Neural Dependency Parsing. In *Proceedings of the 5th International Conference on Learning Representations*, ICLR'17.

Timothy Dozat and Christopher D. Manning. 2018. Simpler but More Accurate Semantic Dependency Parsing. In *Proceedings of the 56th Annual Meeting of the Association for Computational Linguistics*, ACL'18, pages 484–490.

Timothy Dozat, Peng Qi, and Christopher D Manning. 2017. Stanford's graph-based neural dependency parser at the conll 2017 shared task. In *Proceedings of the CoNLL 2017 Shared Task: Multilingual Parsing from Raw Text to Universal Dependencies*, pages 20–30.

Yantao Du, Fan Zhang, Xun Zhang, Weiwei Sun, and Xiaojun Wan. 2015. Peking: Building Semantic Dependency Graphs with a Hybrid Parser. In *Proceedings of the 9th International Workshop on Semantic Evaluation*, SemEval'15, pages 927–931.

Yarin Gal and Zoubin Ghahramani. 2016. A theoretically grounded application of dropout in recurrent neural networks. In *Advances in neural information processing systems*, pages 1019–1027.

Han He and Jinho D. Choi. 2020. Establishing strong baselines for the new decade: Sequence tagging, syntactic and semantic parsing with bert. In *Proceedings of the 33rd International Florida Artificial Intelligence Research Society Conference*, FLAIRS'20.

John Hewitt and Christopher D. Manning. 2019. A structural probe for finding syntax in word representations. In *Proceedings of the 2019 Conference of the North American Chapter of the Association for Computational Linguistics: Human Language Technologies, Volume 1 (Long and Short Papers)*, pages 4129–4138, Minneapolis, Minnesota. Association for Computational Linguistics.

Diederik P. Kingma and Jimmy Ba. 2015. Adam: A Method for Stochastic Optimization. In *Proceedings of the 3rd International Conference for Learning Representations*, ICLR'15.

Dan Kondratyuk and Milan Straka. 2019. 75 languages, 1 model: Parsing universal dependencies universally. In *Proceedings of the 2019 Conference on Empirical Methods in Natural Language Processing and the 9th International Joint Conference on Natural Language Processing (EMNLP-IJCNLP)*, pages 2779–2795, Hong Kong, China. Association for Computational Linguistics.

Taku Kudo and John Richardson. 2018. SentencePiece: A simple and language independent subword tokenizer and detokenizer for neural text processing. In *Proceedings of the 2018 Conference on Empirical Methods in Natural Language Processing: System Demonstrations*, pages 66–71, Brussels, Belgium. Association for Computational Linguistics.

Zhenzhong Lan, Mingda Chen, Sebastian Goodman, Kevin Gimpel, Piyush Sharma, and Radu Soricut. 2020. Albert: A lite bert for self-supervised learning of language representations. In *International Conference on Learning Representations*.

Yinhan Liu, Myle Ott, Naman Goyal, Jingfei Du, Mandar Joshi, Danqi Chen, Omer Levy, Mike Lewis, Luke Zettlemoyer, and Veselin Stoyanov. 2020. Ro{bert}a: A robustly optimized {bert} pretraining approach.

Ilya Loshchilov and Frank Hutter. 2019. Decoupled weight decay regularization. In *International Conference on Learning Representations*.

Mitchell P. Marcus, Mary Ann Marcinkiewicz, and Beatrice Santorini. 1993. Building a Large Annotated Corpus of English: The Penn Treebank. *Computational Linguistics*, 19(2):313–330.

Louis Martin, Benjamin Muller, Pedro Javier Ortiz Suárez, Yoann Dupont, Laurent Romary, Éric Villemonte de la Clergerie, Djamé Seddah, and Benoît Sagot. 2020. Camembert: a tasty french language model. In *Proceedings of the 58th Annual Meeting of the Association for Computational Linguistics*.

Dat Quoc Nguyen and Karin Verspoor. 2019. End-to-end neural relation extraction using deep biaffine attention. In *European Conference on Information Retrieval*, pages 729–738. Springer.

Joakim Nivre, Marie-Catherine De Marneffe, Filip Ginter, Yoav Goldberg, Jan Hajic, Christopher D Manning, Ryan McDonald, Slav Petrov, Sampo Pyysalo, Natalia Silveira, et al. 2016. Universal dependencies v1: A multilingual treebank collection. In *Proceedings of the Tenth International Conference on Language Resources and Evaluation (LREC'16)*, pages 1659–1666.

Joakim Nivre, Paola Marongiu, Filip Ginter, Jenna Kanerva, Simonetta Montemagni, Sebastian Schuster, and Maria Simi. 2018. Enhancing universal dependency treebanks: A case study. In *Proceedings of the Second Workshop on Universal Dependencies (UDW 2018)*, pages 102–107.

Stephan Oepen, Marco Kuhlmann, Yusuke Miyao, Daniel Zeman, Silvie Cinková, Dan Flickinger, Jan Hajic, and Zdenka Uresova. 2015. Semeval 2015 task 18: Broad-coverage semantic dependency parsing. In *Proceedings of the 9th International Workshop on Semantic Evaluation (SemEval 2015)*, pages 915–926.

Natalie Schluter. 2014. On maximum spanning dag algorithms for semantic dag parsing. In *Proceedings of the ACL 2014 Workshop on Semantic Parsing*, pages 61–65.

Sebastian Schuster, Matthew Lamm, and Christopher D Manning. 2017. Gapping constructions in universal dependencies v2. In *Proceedings of the NoDaLiDa 2017 Workshop on Universal Dependencies (UDW 2017)*, pages 123–132.

Sebastian Schuster and Christopher D Manning. 2016. Enhanced english universal dependencies: An improved representation for natural language understanding tasks. In *Proceedings of the Tenth International Conference on Language Resources and Evaluation (LREC'16)*, pages 2371–2378.

Bonggun Shin, Hao Yang, and Jinho D. Choi. 2019. The Pupil Has Become the Master: Teacher-Student Model-Based Word Embedding Distillation with Ensemble Learning. In *Proceedings of the 28th International Joint Conference on Artificial Intelligence*, IJCAI'19, pages 3439–3445.

Milan Straka and Jana Straková. 2017. Tokenizing, pos tagging, lemmatizing and parsing ud 2.0 with udpipe. In *Proceedings of the CoNLL 2017 Shared Task: Multilingual Parsing from Raw Text to Universal Dependencies*, pages 88–99, Vancouver, Canada. Association for Computational Linguistics.

Antti Virtanen, Jenna Kanerva, Rami Ilo, Jouni Luoma, Juhani Luotolahti, Tapio Salakoski, Filip Ginter, and Sampo Pyysalo. 2019. Multilingual is not enough: Bert for finnish. *arXiv preprint arXiv:1912.07076*.

Yaushian Wang, Hung-Yi Lee, and Yun-Nung Chen. 2019. Tree transformer: Integrating tree structures into self-attention. In *Proceedings of the 2019 Conference on Empirical Methods in Natural Language Processing and the 9th International Joint Conference on Natural Language Processing (EMNLP-IJCNLP)*, pages 1061–1070, Hong Kong, China. Association for Computational Linguistics.

Naiwen Xue, Fei Xia, Fu-dong Chiou, and Marta Palmer. 2005. The Penn Chinese TreeBank: Phrase Structure Annotation of a Large Corpus. *Natural Language Engineering*, 11(2):207–238.

Rui Zhang, Cícero Nogueira dos Santos, Michihiro Yasunaga, Bing Xiang, and Dragomir Radev. 2018. Neural coreference resolution with deep biaffine attention by joint mention detection and mention clustering. In *Proceedings of the 56th Annual Meeting of the Association for Computational Linguistics (Volume 2: Short Papers)*, pages 102–107, Melbourne, Australia. Association for Computational Linguistics.

Junru Zhou and Hai Zhao. 2019. Head-driven phrase structure grammar parsing on Penn treebank. In *Proceedings of the 57th Annual Meeting of the Association for Computational Linguistics*, pages 2396–2408, Florence, Italy. Association for Computational Linguistics.

A Supplemental Materials

A.1 Hyperparameters

Table 4 shows the hyperparameters used to train models for all languages.

A.3 Parsing Results

Table 6 shows the parsing results using the 5 evaluation metrics, unlabeled attachment score (UAS), labeled attachment score (LAS), content labeled attachment score (CLAS), LAS on enhanced dependencies where labels are restricted to the UD relation (EULAS), and LAS on enhanced dependencies (ELAS).

Transformer	
Max sequence length	256
Warm up steps	10%
Learning rate	$1e^{-5}$
End learning rate	0
Weight decay rate	0
Adam β_1	0.9
Adam β_2	0.999
Adam ϵ	$1e^{-6}$
Parser	
$\text{MLP}^{(arc)}$	500
$\text{MLP}^{(rel)}$	100
Clip norm	5
Learning rate	$1e^{-3}$
Adam β_1	0.9
Adam β_2	0.9
Adam ϵ	$1e^{-12}$
Anneal factor	0.75
Anneal every	5000
Dropout Rates	
Embeddings	33%
MLP	33%
Optimizer	
Batch size	≈ 150
Train epochs	1000

Table 4: Hyperparameters used for our experiments.

A.2 Language-Specific Encoders

Table 5 shows the authors and the sources of the language-specific transformer decoders used to develop our parsing models.

Lang.	Source	Link
AR	Unknown	huggingface.co/asafaya/bert-base-arabic
EN	Lan et al. (2020)	huggingface.co/albert-xxlarge-v2
ET	Unknown	dl.turkunlp.org/estonian-bert/etwiki-bert/pytorch/
FI	Virtanen et al. (2019)	huggingface.co/TurkuNLP/bert-base-finnish-cased-v1
FR	Liu et al. (2020); Martin et al. (2020)	huggingface.co/dbmdz/bert-base-italian-cased
IT	Unknown	huggingface.co/dbmdz/bert-base-italian-cased
NL	Unknown	huggingface.co/wietsedv/bert-base-dutch-cased
PL	Unknown	huggingface.co/dkleczek/bert-base-polish-uncased-v1
SV	Unknown	huggingface.co/KB/bert-base-swedish-cased
BG	Arkhipov et al. (2019)	huggingface.co/DeepPavlov/bert-base-bg-cs-pl-ru-cased
CS	Arkhipov et al. (2019)	huggingface.co/DeepPavlov/bert-base-bg-cs-pl-ru-cased
SK	Arkhipov et al. (2019)	huggingface.co/DeepPavlov/bert-base-bg-cs-pl-ru-cased

Table 5: The authors and sources of the language specific transformer encoders used to develop our models.

		Multilingual Encoder					Language-Specific Encoder					Rank
		UAS	LAS	CLAS	EULAS	ELAS	UAS	LAS	CLAS	EULAS	ELAS	
AR	DTP	**79.05**	**74.75**	**71.76**	**71.83**	61.28	67.06	58.80	51.77	56.69	49.38	
	DGP	73.51	69.50	65.28	65.49	63.56	59.84	51.99	43.88	46.75	43.71	3
	ENS	79.05	74.75	71.76	69.46	**67.26**	67.06	58.80	51.77	51.37	48.02	
BG	DTP	**94.37**	**91.77**	**89.19**	**89.61**	79.58	70.99	63.54	55.96	62.27	55.76	
	DGP	92.64	90.00	86.44	87.31	86.66	59.45	52.72	41.07	46.84	45.25	3
	ENS	94.37	91.77	89.19	88.84	**88.19**	70.99	63.54	55.96	54.01	52.16	
CS	DEP	**93.72**	**91.91**	**90.74**	**87.20**	78.37	86.83	83.58	80.84	79.53	71.73	
	SDP	85.49	83.81	78.52	80.38	79.38	75.95	72.96	66.06	69.79	68.47	3
	ENS	93.72	91.91	90.74	86.63	**85.51**	86.83	83.58	80.84	53.45	51.05	
EN	DTP	89.37	87.01	84.63	84.61	75.70	**90.94**	**88.70**	**87.01**	**86.24**	76.99	
	DGP	87.17	84.79	81.20	82.74	82.31	87.62	85.43	81.82	83.67	83.22	3
	ENS	89.37	87.01	84.63	83.68	83.24	90.94	88.70	87.01	85.76	**85.30**	
ET	DTP	**87.35**	**84.25**	**82.58**	**82.81**	68.08	62.39	54.23	50.25	53.31	44.61	
	DGP	80.73	78.11	73.93	76.42	75.94	52.39	45.98	39.66	44.62	43.90	2
	ENS	87.35	84.25	82.58	81.98	**81.36**	62.39	54.23	50.25	52.74	51.82	
FI	DEP	91.10	88.95	87.37	85.43	70.37	**93.32**	**91.84**	**90.90**	**88.19**	72.40	
	SDP	78.61	76.71	71.06	72.62	72.03	85.89	84.29	80.89	80.10	79.38	3
	ENS	91.10	88.95	87.37	81.44	80.54	93.32	91.84	90.90	83.70	**82.96**	
FR	DTP	92.32	88.49	84.27	87.47	85.29	**92.52**	**89.33**	**85.53**	**88.28**	**86.23**	
	DGP	82.39	79.07	67.42	75.49	74.35	87.46	84.70	77.91	80.12	78.87	1
	ENS	92.32	88.49	84.27	83.34	81.97	92.52	89.33	85.53	82.83	81.45	
IT	DTP	94.96	93.32	89.88	90.49	75.21	**95.03**	**93.66**	**90.67**	**90.89**	75.50	
	DGP	92.33	90.70	85.30	86.98	86.46	91.38	90.13	83.67	86.92	86.45	4
	ENS	94.96	93.32	89.88	88.35	87.83	95.03	93.66	90.67	89.04	**88.52**	
LT	DTP	**81.97**	**77.63**	**75.27**	**73.55**	63.91	-	-	-	-	-	
	DGP	72.23	68.60	63.21	63.10	61.59	-	-	-	-	-	4
	ENS	81.97	77.63	75.27	68.24	**66.12**	-	-	-	-	-	
LV	DTP	**89.07**	**85.98**	**83.79**	**81.17**	71.68	-	-	-	-	-	
	DGP	78.35	75.92	69.89	71.95	71.58	-	-	-	-	-	3
	ENS	89.07	85.98	83.79	79.66	**79.19**	-	-	-	-	-	
NL	DTP	**88.75**	**86.29**	**81.18**	**83.67**	71.08	88.46	86.02	80.87	83.47	70.95	
	DGP	83.18	80.98	72.41	77.37	76.94	82.80	80.60	72.31	76.97	76.46	3
	ENS	88.75	86.29	81.18	81.21	**80.72**	88.46	86.02	80.87	80.59	80.02	
PL	DTP	**94.27**	**91.88**	**90.35**	**88.29**	74.33	76.45	70.03	64.65	67.58	57.35	
	DGP	80.23	77.88	73.53	74.54	70.39	65.67	60.41	51.18	55.58	51.90	2
	ENS	94.27	91.88	90.35	86.79	**82.39**	76.45	70.03	64.65	63.82	59.59	
RU	DTP	**94.20**	**92.87**	**91.71**	**89.71**	74.62	82.31	78.43	74.97	76.05	63.51	
	DGP	87.18	86.13	81.47	83.47	83.19	71.19	68.04	60.93	64.16	63.44	3
	ENS	94.20	92.87	91.71	88.93	**88.60**	82.31	78.43	74.97	72.13	71.19	
SK	DTP	**92.64**	**90.61**	**89.29**	**86.83**	70.12	46.19	35.72	27.97	34.50	30.41	
	DGP	89.91	87.78	85.48	83.39	81.37	38.37	29.66	20.49	26.82	26.03	3
	ENS	92.64	90.61	89.29	84.73	**82.72**	46.19	35.72	27.97	31.19	30.08	
SV	DTP	**88.29**	**85.23**	**83.63**	**81.72**	70.92	-	-	-	-	-	
	DGP	85.53	82.41	79.58	78.32	77.39	-	-	-	-	-	4
	ENS	88.29	85.23	83.63	79.11	**78.19**	-	-	-	-	-	
TA	DTP	**65.57**	**58.69**	**54.73**	**58.66**	**54.26**	-	-	-	-	-	
	DGP	50.95	45.54	40.35	41.36	40.10	-	-	-	-	-	3
	ENS	65.57	58.69	54.73	48.50	46.67	-	-	-	-	-	
UK	DTP	**91.01**	**88.91**	**86.45**	**85.36**	77.04	-	-	-	-	-	
	DGP	88.50	86.30	82.93	80.18	79.56	-	-	-	-	-	3
	ENS	91.01	88.91	86.45	80.34	**79.69**	-	-	-	-	-	
AVG	DTP	**88.71**	**85.80**	**83.34**	**82.85**	71.87	56.03	52.58	49.49	51.00	44.40	
	DGP	81.70	79.07	74.00	75.36	74.28	40.95	38.22	33.70	36.03	35.25	3
	ENS	88.71	85.80	83.34	80.07	**78.83**	50.92	47.66	44.74	43.95	43.01	

Table 6: Parsing results on the test sets evaluated by the 5 metrics, UAS, LAS, CLAS, EULAS, and ELAS. The Rank column indicates the ranking of our best model for the corresponding language. AR: Arabic, BG: Bulgarian, CS: Czech, EN: English, ET: Estonian, FI: Finnish, FR: French, IT: Italian, NL: Dutch, LT: Lithuanian, LV: Latvian, PL: Polish, RU: Russian, SK: Slovak, SV: Swedish, TA: Tamil, UK: Ukrainian.

Efficient EUD Parsing

Mathieu Dehouck   **Mark Anderson**   **Carlos Gómez-Rodríguez**
Universidade da Coruña, CITIC
FASTPARSE Lab, LyS Research Group,
Departamento de Ciencias de la Computación y Tecnologías de la Información
Campus Elviña, s/n, 15071 A Coruña, Spain
{mathieu.dehouck,m.anderson,carlos.gomez}@udc.es

Abstract

We present the system submission from the FASTPARSE team for the EUD Shared Task at IWPT 2020. We engaged with the task by focusing on efficiency. For this we considered training costs and inference efficiency. Our models are a combination of distilled neural dependency parsers and a rule-based system that projects UD trees into EUD graphs. We obtained an average ELAS of 74.04 for our official submission, ranking 4th overall.

1 Introduction

Latterly, the environmental impact of AI and NLP's dependency on deep neural networks has come under scrutiny (Schwartz et al., 2019; Strubell et al., 2019). This has coincided with a renewed push for efficiency in NLP so as to make systems more easily used in different contexts, be it in hardware impaired conditions, large web-scale applications, or a host of other considerations (Strzyz et al., 2019; Clark et al., 2019; Vilares et al., 2019; Junczys-Dowmunt et al., 2018).

Here we describe our contribution to the Enhanced Universal Dependencies (EUD) Shared Task at IWPT 2020 (Bouma et al., 2020), where we have considered efficiency as well as bare accuracy performance. We combine linguistics and machine learning to develop efficient parsers, both with respect to training and inference. First we curtail the amount of training data we use, second we try distillation to create smaller networks for dependency parsers while maintaining accuracy, and third we develop a rule-based system to cast universal dependency (UD) trees as EUD graphs.

1.1 An aside on enhanced graphs

Certain syntactic phenomena, such as the propagation of conjuncts or coreferences in relative clauses, can only be handled implicitly by Universal Dependency (UD) trees resulting in opaque relations or long paths between related content words. EUD graphs is an enhanced representation which can handle these phenomena explicitly. As nodes are not restricted to a single head, these more complex relations can be more readily represented. While this results in a potentially much more useful and informative representation, it also makes for a more challenging task than vanilla UD parsing.

2 Forest felling

Distillation introduces extra training overheads. To mitigate this and to balance our pursuit of inference efficiency with some semblance of training efficiency and considering recent results using distillation suggest larger treebanks suffer greater (Anderson and Gómez-Rodríguez, 2020), we decided to set a limit to the size of training treebanks.

In order to minimise introducing compounding variables that could affect training efficacy, we renormalise the sampled treebanks to follow the same tree length distribution of the original treebank. Where more than one treebank exists for a given language, we took a sample from each treebank renormalised with respect to that treebank and took a sample size so that the contribution from each treebank would follow the same ratio as the full data for that language.

We evaluated what limit to set by testing on 4 languages spanning 3 language families (Uralic, Afro-Asiatic, and Indo-European). The only family to appear in the shared task training data not covered was Dravidian as the only example from this language, Tamil, has too small a treebank to have been useful for this analysis. We also cover two branches of the Indo-European family. Balto-Slavic is covered by Russian as the treebank is rather large and uses the Cyrillic script. Germanic is covered by Dutch, which we chose

Proceedings of the 16th International Conference on Parsing Technologies and the IWPT 2020 Shared Task, pages 192–205
Virtual Meeting, July 9, 2020. ©2020 Association for Computational Linguistics

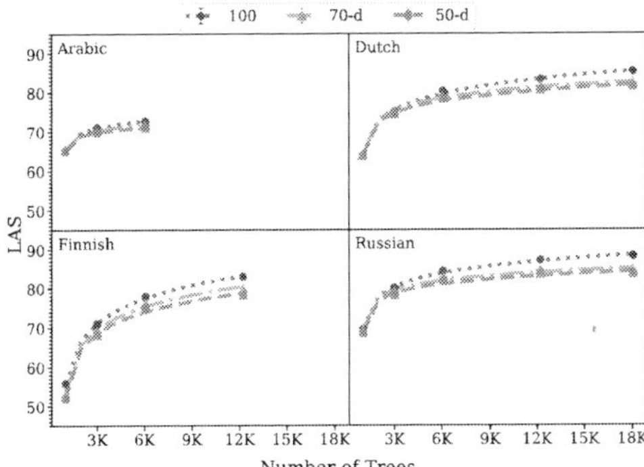

Figure 1: LAS for different models for Arabic, Dutch, Finnish, and Russian development treebanks.

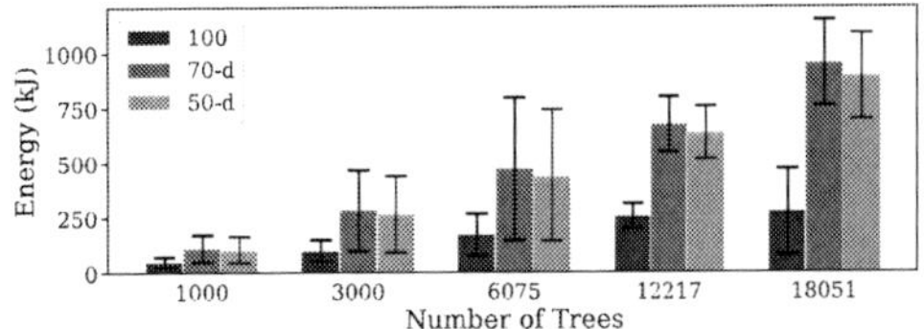

Figure 2: Training energy consumption for different models for different treebank sizes averaged over Arabic, Dutch, Finnish, and Russian.

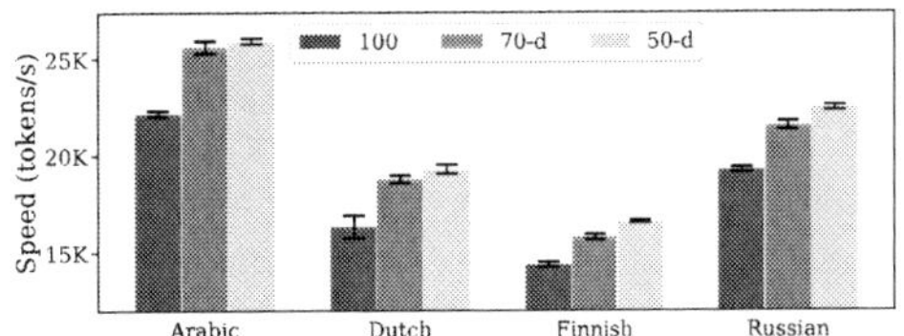

Figure 3: GPU inference speed for different models for treebank 12k (except Arabic which uses its full treebank of 6075 trees) averaged over 5 runs on the development treebanks with batch size 256.

as there are two treebanks which combine to a sizeable number of trees and so would cover the case of combining different treebanks. Finnish was used to cover the Uralic family as we carried this experiment out before the larger Estonian treebank was made available and Arabic was used for Afro-Asiatic. We used sample treebank sizes of 1,000, 3,000, 6,075 (the number of trees in the Arabic treebank), 12,217 (the number of trees in the Finnish treebank), and 18,051 (the combined number of trees in both Dutch treebanks). We created 2 splits where possible (i.e. at 6,075 trees Arabic isn't a sample treebank) as a limited attempt at experimental robustness.

We train a Biaffine parser using the hyperparameters of the original paper, shown in Table 6 in the Appendix (Dozat and Manning, 2017). We then distill (as described in Section 3 and in Appendix A.1) these models to two different network sizes, one which has 70% of the number of nodes in both the BILSTM and MLP layers and one that has 50%. Otherwise the structure of the network is the same as the base model. The LAS averaged over the splits for each sample and model are shown in Figure 1 (similarly for UAS in Figure 8 in Appendix A.1). We are limited by what we can extrapolate from the results for Arabic and Finnish other than they appear to follow a similar trend to Dutch and Russian. For the latter languages we observe the performance levelling at larger treebank sizes, which is neither remarkable nor unexpected, but also a widening between the performance of the full and the distilled models.

As we are concerned with training efficiency, we present the energy consumption for each model type averaged over language and split in Figure 2.

The amount of energy required to distill our models increases significantly with respect to treebank size. However, distilling to a smaller model requires less energy and, as can be seen in Figure 1, the accuracy difference between the two distilled models is nominal.

Figure 3 shows the inference speed (averaged over splits and 5 runs) on GPU using a single CPU core for each language using the models trained with the 12,217 treebanks (for Arabic we use its full treebank). We observe a sizeable increase in speed over the baseline model for both distilled models, but only a small difference between the two distilled models.

From this, we decided to set an upper limit on the treebank size for the main task to 13,121 (the size of the Italian treebank) as this would require the least amount of tampering and was close to the second largest treebank size used here which performed close to the largest. This meant taking a sample of the Czech, Dutch, Estonian, and Polish treebanks and combining them as described above. A sample was taken for the Russian treebank. Some syntactic metrics are given in Table 7 in the Appendix which shows the different breakdown of the training data used for each of these languages and how they are very similar to the full data. Also, we opted to distill to 50% of the original model size. For this analysis, and all subsequent analyses, the CPU used was an Intel Core i7-

7700 and the GPU an Nvidia GeForce GTX 1080.[1]

3 Boiling neural networks in the pot still

Neural network compression is not a new phenomenon. For example, pruning has long been shown to be an effective way to reduce parameters with minimal impact on accuracy and also to help generalisation (LeCun et al., 1990; Hagiwara, 1994; Wan et al., 2009; Han et al., 2015; See et al., 2016). However, pruning isn't overly useful for creating efficient models as they leave networks in irregularly sparse states. Other techniques exist that can recast networks into smaller more efficient ones, but we focus on distillation. For a detailed survey of current neural network compression techniques see Cheng et al. (2018).

Anderson and Gómez-Rodríguez (2020) used *teacher-student* distillation to increase the inference efficiency while only losing marginal accuracy for Universal Dependency (UD) parsing, showing that distilled models outperform models of the same structure and size trained normally. Here we extend that work and use *teacher-student* distillation to obtain efficient dependency parsers as the basis of our enhanched-dependency parser systems. A full description of our implementation can be found in Anderson and Gómez-Rodríguez (2020) but we also offer a condensed version in Appendix A.1.

While we curtailed our training data, we selected our models based on the performance on the full development data for a given language with gold sentence segmentation and tokenisation. We used characters and words as input to our network. The embeddings for both were randomly initialised. The hyperparameters are the same as used above. We also used early stopping to limit unnecessary training time, stopping after 10 epochs without performance improvement.

At inference time we used UDPipe v2.5 models to predict everything except the parse (Straka and Straková, 2019). When a combination of treebanks were being predicted, we used the model which corresponded to the largest of the treebanks.

Table 1 shows the total time to train the full-sized models and the distillation models for all languages. Also, shown is the GPU energy consumption. The costs for distillation include those of the base models.

	Training costs	
	Total time	GPU Energy (kJ)
Base	08h:42m:52.1s	3570.7
Distill	30h:07m:49.6s	9981.8
Rule-based	00h:00m:41.1s	*n/a*

Table 1: Total training time and GPU energy consumption for all treebanks.

Training costs for distillation are more than three times that of the baseline which is hardly surprising. The inference energy cost for all development treebanks (37K trees) for the full model is 2.10 (0.09)kJ (average value over 5 runs for each treebank) whereas the cost for distillation is 1.49 (0.03)kJ. Based on these measurements, we would need to parse 390M sentences to offset the extra cost of distilling models when running on GPU.

	UAS	LAS	ELAS		UAS	LAS	ELAS
Arabic				*Bulgarian*			
full	77.0	72.8	68.4	full	91.5	87.6	85.3
dist	76.5	72.3	67.9	dist	91.6	87.6	85.2
udpipe	72.8	68.1	63.0	udpipe	88.7	84.3	81.9
Czech				*Dutch*			
full	90.0	87.0	82.4	full	87.5	84.0	82.2
dist	89.0	85.3	80.7	dist	86.7	82.9	81.0
udpipe	87.6	84.0	78.4	udpipe	79.3	75.0	73.2
English				*Estonian*			
full	85.6	82.6	81.2	full	85.5	81.5	80.3
dist	84.4	81.2	79.8	dist	84.7	80.2	79.0
udpipe	81.0	77.6	76.3	udpipe	81.5	77.6	76.7
Finnish				*French*			
full	86.2	83.1	79.9	full	88.1	85.5	82.3
dist	85.1	81.3	78.0	dist	88.5	85.8	82.6
udpipe	80.4	76.8	73.7	udpipe	85.2	82.6	79.4
Italian				*Latvian*			
full	91.6	89.3	87.8	full	86.7	83.2	79.3
dist	90.3	87.8	85.9	dist	86.0	81.9	78.2
udpipe	88.5	85.9	84.1	udpipe	79.8	75.4	70.5
Lithuanian				*Polish*			
full	77.6	72.7	68.6	full	90.9	87.2	78.6
dist	78.0	73.0	68.9	dist	90.2	86.0	77.2
udpipe	72.3	64.6	60.9	udpipe	87.1	82.6	74.7
Russian				*Slovak*			
full	90.2	87.3	84.4	full	85.4	81.6	77.0
dist	88.9	85.5	82.5	dist	84.7	80.7	76.1
udpipe	87.4	84.4	81.5	udpipe	81.2	75.9	70.5
Swedish				*Tamil*			
full	85.2	81.4	78.9	full	59.8	52.6	51.2
dist	85.3	81.6	79.0	dist	64.0	56.9	55.5
udpipe	79.5	75.4	73.2	udpipe	60.7	54.1	53.0
Ukrainian				*Average*			
full	87.1	83.2	78.3	full	85.0	81.3	78.0
dist	86.6	82.5	77.5	dist	84.7	80.7	77.3
udpipe	81.6	76.9	72.5	udpipe	80.9	76.5	73.1

Table 2: Attachment scores for both UD trees and EUD graphs for the development treebanks using different dependency parsers: full baseline models (Full), distilled models (dist), and UDPipe v2.5 models (udpipe).

---

[1] Using Python 3.7.0, PyTorch 1.0.0, and CUDA 8.0.

Late in the day we decided to validate the results of Anderson and Gómez-Rodríguez (2020), namely that distilled models outperform models trained normally of equivalent sizes. This highlighted that our distilled models used for our official score had not converged. We trained new distilled models and the results given here are for these new models. Our official results using the partially-trained models are in table 9 in the Appendix. All results, including training costs, in this section are for the full-trained distilled models and unless otherwise stated are using the combined development treebanks for each language.

Table 8 in the Appendix shows the performance for the equivalent-sized models trained normally (small) and the distilled models (dist) with respect to UAS and LAS. For the most part the normal models outperform the distilled models. The main differences between our work and that of Anderson and Gómez-Rodríguez (2020) is we do not use pre-trained word embeddings nor POS tags as features. So perhaps without this extra information distillation is less effective. Also, dropout wasn't used during distillation in the original paper but is here, so perhaps the values used here were too punitive a regularisation. Although we use the same hyperparameters as the original paper, the average LAS for the small normally trained models is 0.4 points less than the large model.

We also evaluated the distilled models against the full baseline model and UDPipe v2.5. These results are shown in Table 2. The distilled models outperform the UDPipe models and are within a point of both UAS and LAS to the full model. The ELAS results for the rule-based system using the predicted dependency trees from each of theses systems are also shown. The performance on ELAS generally follows the dependency scores.

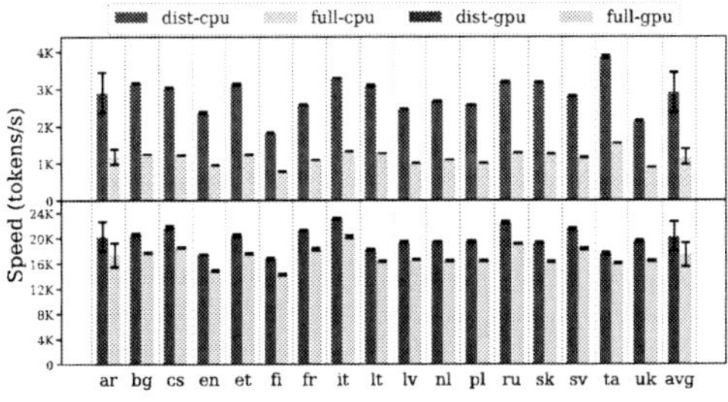

Figure 4: Inference speed for distilled (dist) and full baseline models on CPU (-cpu) and GPU (-gpu) for each development treebank averaged over 5 runs using one CPU core with batch size 256.

Inference speed (token/s)			
CPU		UD parser	Full pipeline
	Base	1194.1 (207.1)	879.0 (123.4)
	Distill	2912.9 (535.1)	1569.9 (238.8)
	UDPipe	3629.4 (584.0)	2220.2 (698.0)
GPU	**Base**	17427.0 (1890.3)	2993.3 (680.2)
	Distill	20321.6 (2348.9)	3073.7 (714.9)

Table 3: Inference speeds for dependency parsers and the full EUD pipeline for different systems run on development treebanks and averaged over 5 runs.

Figure 4 shows the inference speed using GPU and CPU of the full baseline model and the distilled models for each language. These are obtained by running the parser 5 times for each language on the full development data and only using one CPU core. The average speed (token/second) increase was 2.44x (1.17x) on CPU (GPU).

Table 3 shows the inference speeds for the full pipeline and the dependency parser. We also compare UDPipe inference performance as it is a viable candidate for an efficient parser. It is the fastest of the systems compared here, but the full pipeline which used it obtained an average ELAS 4.9 points less than full baseline model whereas the distilled models are only 0.7 points less.

4 Unravelling trees with shrewd rules

Rule-based systems are intrinsically efficient with respect to training time (barely a flash in the pan) and inference time (there is practically none). So we developed a simple rule-based system to enhance the existing dependency tree and reveal hidden dependencies in a cross-lingual setting using as few language specific rules as possible. Beyond the basic enhancement of the original dependencies, there are four main phenomena that create new dependencies: relative clauses, control, conjunction and ellipsis. Since our pipeline does not predict empty nodes, we decided to ignore ellipsis in this system. To deal with each of these phenomena, our algorithm needs to make a number of passes over each sentence.

Pass one - relative clauses and controls: The first pass of the algorithm iterates through each word in the sentence and creates enhanced relations according to the type of the original dependency. When necessary, it adds lemma and case information. If the current word is a relative pronoun/adverb, its antecedent is found by following its path to the root until an `acl:relcl` relation is met. Then a `ref` edge is created between the word and its antecedent and an edge between the antecedent and the governor of the relativiser with the same relation type as the original relation (if the relative pronoun is the object of a verb then the antecedent becomes the object of that verb). If the word is the dependent of an `xcomp` relation, the algorithm looks for a subject amongst its controlling predicate's arguments. If a subject is found, it creates an edge between the subject and the current word of type `nsubj(:xsubj)` (or `csubj` in the case of a clausal argument). If no subject is available, the current word is stored in a separate list for later processing. If the word is the dependent of a `conj` relation, it too is stored in a separate list along with all other conjuncts. Whenever we encounter an argument of the type subject, object or oblique, this information is kept for resolving subjects of controlled predicates.

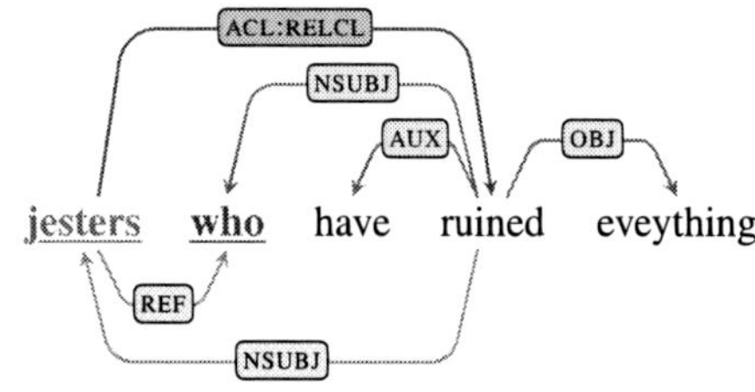

Figure 5: Relative clause example. Pre-existing edges in graph are in magenta and blue. The algorithm observes an `acl:relcl` relation (highlighted in blue) which causes it to generate two new relations (highlighted in green). A `ref` relation is created between *who* and its antecedent, *jesters*. Then a `nsubj` is propagated from the head of *who*, *ruined*, to *jesters*.

Pass two - resolving conjunctions: We have two general functions, one for dependent level conjunctions and one for governor level conjunctions, and a few special cases. The dependent level function propagates the conjunction head's original relation to its conjuncts adapting it if necessary, for example in coordinated `nmod` with different adposition or case. The governor level function propagates the conjunction head's dependents to its conjuncts in the absence of similar dependents and according to morphological agreement. We have a special function that handles subjects of conjuncts because subjects are more diverse than other syntactic functions. In UD at least three relations can mark subjects, namely `nsubj` for nominal subjects, `csubj` for clausal subjects

and `expl` used amongst other for syntactic subjects in non prodrop languages (e.g. *"it rains"*). Subject edges also embed information about their governor, notably information about the voice as `:pass` when relevant. And, subjects can be absent altogether in prodrop languages, so we rely on morphological information to decide to propagate a given subject in these languages.

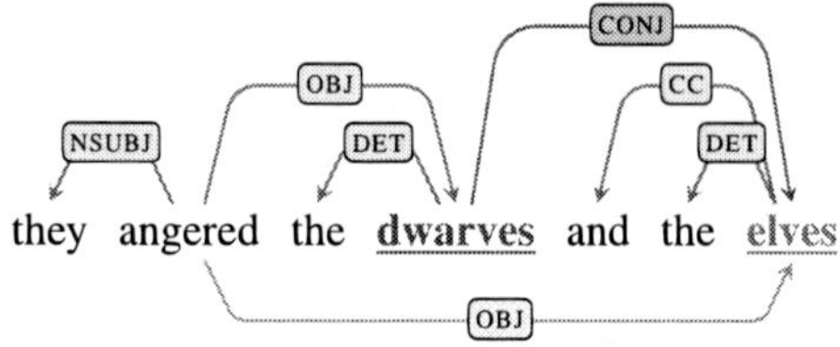

Figure 6: Conjunction example. Magenta and blue edges are those existing in the graph after one pass. During the first pass *elves* is stored as it is the dependent of a `conj` relation (highlighted in blue). On the second pass the `obj` relation of *dwarves*, the head of this `conj` relation, propagates to *elves* generating a new `obj` relation (highlighted in green) from *angered*.

Pass three and onwards - sweeping up controls: Once conjunctions have been resolved and more predicates have their arguments stored, the algorithm iterates over controlled predicates that do not have a subject after the first sentence traversal. Several such iterations may be necessary since the number of times a predicate may be coordinated with a controlled verb itself already coordinated to another controlled verb is not bounded. Like in the sentence *"Sam stood up and wanted to scream and start running."* But in practice one iteration solves the vast majority of missing subjects.

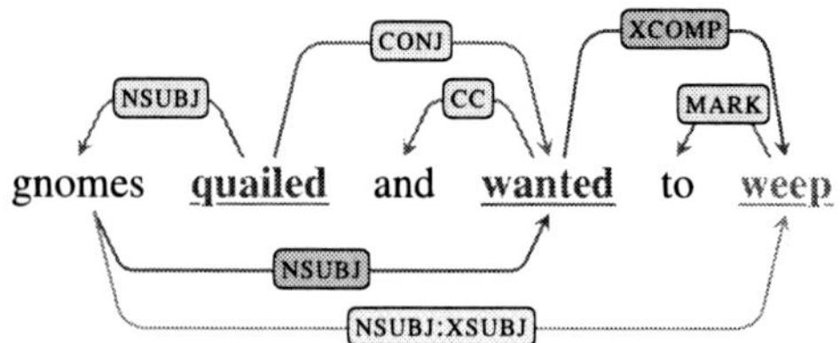

Figure 7: Control example. The edges of the graph after two passes are in magenta and blue. During the first pass *weep* is stored as it is a dependent of a `xcomp` relation (highlighted in blue) but it cannot be resolved until *wanted* is. *wanted* is resolved in the second pass and an `nsubj` relation (shown in blue) is propagated from the head, *gnomes*, of its conjunct, *quailed*. In the third pass this is further propagated to *weep* generating a `nsubj:xsubj` relation (highlighted in green).

4.1 Tuning the rules

A number of enhancements are relation and language specific and some even lexically conditioned such as control, and not all languages include every enhancement type. So the training data is used to tune rules to a given language while keeping the rule definitions as generic as possible.

The first type of information needed regards additional lemmas and cases appearing in edges. For each relation type, the frequency at which `case` is being added to the relation is obtained. Similarly for lemma, the algorithm counts the frequency of relation types between a word and its dependent used for lexicalisation since different relations are augmented with different dependents (`obl` usually uses `case` where `acl` prefers `mark`). Furthermore, for lemmas, when several dependents have the same relation, it checks which is used for lexicalisation. For `conj` though, it only checks if there is anything at all since `conj` is tightly linked to `cc`.

Each language is tested to see if it is prodrop by comparing the number of root verbs with an overt subject to the number of root verbs without an overt subject. Whether `:xsubj` and `:relsubj` should be added to subjects of controlled predicates and relative clauses is also checked.

The algorithm then checks whether each relation propagates to its governor's conjuncts and under which conditions (the conditions are detailed in Appendix A.2.1) and also if it propagates to its own conjuncts. This is mostly relevant since `root` usually does not propagate to conjuncts of the main predicate, but in some treebanks it does.

Morphological features are used for detecting relativisers. For each morphological feature, the number of times it co-occurs with a `ref` enhanced relation is compared to the number of times it co-occurs with another relation. While not an arbitrary choice, it is one of the few cases where an enhanced relation does not depend directly on information in the original tree but on information external to the tree, so in theory we could have chosen other clues such as the lemma of the word instead. These pronouns and adverbs are usually marked with `PronType=Rel` or `PronType=Int,Rel`.

Finally, the controlling profile of controlling predicates is learnt. The system discerns which of the arguments is used as subject of controlled verbs and in which conditions, meaning that we do not count subjects in the absence of other arguments since they become default.

4.2 Problems

While our rule-based system performs remarkably well, as can be seen in Table 4, with the lowest ELAS being 94.9 on the gold development data, it is challenging to improve across languages simultaneously. Besides the expected ambiguity of language, there are several issues which limit us, some easy to fix, some more complicated, some language specific, and some more general.

	ELAS			
	Gold	Full	Dist	UDPipe
Arabic	98.8	68.4	67.9	63.0
Bulgarian	98.6	85.3	85.2	81.9
Czech	97.9	82.4	80.7	78.4
Dutch	98.9	82.2	81.0	73.2
English	99.5	81.2	79.8	76.3
Estonian	99.2	80.3	79.0	76.7
Finnish	97.3	79.9	78.0	73.7
French	98.9	82.3	82.6	79.4
Italian	99.5	87.8	85.9	84.1
Latvian	95.7	79.3	78.2	70.5
Lithuanian	98.8	68.6	68.9	60.9
Polish	94.9	78.6	77.2	74.7
Russian	98.6	84.4	82.5	81.5
Slovak	98.8	77.0	76.1	70.5
Swedish	98.8	78.9	79.0	73.2
Tamil	99.3	51.2	55.5	53.0
Ukrainian	95.8	78.3	77.5	72.5
Average	98.2	78.0	77.3	73.1

Table 4: Enhanced labelled attachment score for EUD graphs when using gold labelled dependency development treebanks (gold), predicted treebanks with full baseline models (Full), distilled models (Dist), and using UDPipe v2.5 models (UDPipe).

On the monolingual front, incomplete, erroneous and inconsistent annotations are the biggest problems. Incomplete annotation can occur both at the enhanced dependency and the lower level of annotation. For example in Dutch Alpino, we miss 515 `ref` relations and thus at least as many enhanced relations from their antecedents, representing two thirds of the missing dependencies. The bulk of these missed references are relative/interrogative pronouns/adverbs that are not annotated with an empty feature column. We wanted to avoid too many language specific rules and ignored them, leading to more than a thousand missing edges. Likewise, in some languages not all relativisers (typically interrogative adverbs) are marked as references when they should be according to UD guidelines.

	Tokens	Words	Sentences	UPOS	XPOS	UFeats	AllTags	Lemmas	UAS	LAS	CLAS	MLAS	BLEX	EULAS	ELAS
Arabic	100.0	94.6	82.1	88.5	84.0	84.2	82.0	88.5	76.5	72.0	68.0	57.0	63.0	70.2	67.8
Bulgarian	99.9	99.9	94.2	97.6	94.3	95.4	93.8	94.6	92.1	88.5	84.5	78.0	77.5	87.3	86.4
Czech	99.9	99.9	93.2	97.8	90.9	90.8	89.7	97.4	88.0	84.1	80.9	70.4	78.6	82.0	79.6
Dutch	99.7	99.7	69.3	92.6	89.9	92.0	89.0	94.4	84.5	80.8	73.7	63.5	68.0	79.3	78.7
English	99.2	99.2	83.8	93.6	92.8	94.1	90.7	95.4	84.8	81.7	77.7	69.0	73.8	80.8	80.1
Estonian	99.7	99.7	90.0	95.0	96.2	92.8	91.0	90.4	82.7	78.2	75.5	67.3	66.2	77.7	76.8
Finnish	99.7	99.7	88.7	94.8	54.5	93.0	51.8	87.1	86.1	82.6	80.0	72.1	67.0	80.8	79.4
French	99.7	99.2	94.3	93.5	99.2	88.8	87.3	94.9	87.8	82.2	74.8	60.5	69.1	81.6	79.5
Italian	99.9	99.8	98.8	97.2	97.0	97.1	96.2	97.4	91.4	89.1	83.8	79.2	80.3	87.6	86.9
Latvian	99.3	99.3	98.7	93.5	84.3	89.5	83.9	92.7	86.0	81.8	78.7	65.9	72.4	79.3	77.8
Lithuanian	99.9	99.9	87.9	90.3	80.7	81.2	79.3	88.8	75.2	69.4	66.0	48.4	56.8	66.6	64.5
Polish	99.4	99.8	97.5	96.4	84.9	83.6	80.3	95.6	90.1	85.9	82.4	62.2	77.8	84.0	77.5
Russian	99.6	99.6	98.8	97.8	99.6	85.3	85.0	96.5	89.3	86.2	83.4	65.5	80.0	84.5	83.3
Slovak	100.0	100.0	85.3	92.9	77.1	80.3	76.7	86.6	85.6	81.5	78.0	56.8	64.8	79.8	76.7
Swedish	99.2	99.2	93.5	93.3	91.0	84.9	83.2	90.0	83.4	79.3	76.0	58.6	67.0	77.9	77.0
Tamil	99.2	94.5	97.5	81.3	76.3	80.5	75.6	84.1	62.5	53.0	48.8	39.9	43.7	53.0	51.7
Ukrainian	99.8	99.8	96.6	94.9	84.0	84.3	83.3	93.6	85.0	81.0	76.4	59.6	70.0	78.4	76.4
Average	99.7	99.1	91.2	93.6	86.9	88.1	83.5	92.2	84.2	79.8	75.8	63.2	69.2	78.3	76.5

Table 5: Test results evaluated through the official submission site and using our updated distilled model. Our official submission results can be seen in Table 9 in the Appendix.

Erroneous annotations can be at lower levels of annotation of the dependency tree, thus when applying rules according to these annotations, erroneous edges are created. For example in English (EWT), there is the sentence *"Let me know if this is the appropriate steps that you would like to see,"* in which *that* which references *steps* is analysed as the object of *like* (*"you would like the steps to see"* vs. *"you would like to see the steps"*) thus the controlling rule for *like* makes *steps* the subject of *see* in place of *you*. Annotation errors can also happen in the enhanced structure. In Russian, for example, a number of nominal modifiers have diverging case information in the feature column and in the enhanced relation one, often `Case=Gen` with `nmod:acc`, so the predicted enhanced relation `nmod:gen` conflicts with the actual annotation.

Latvian offers an example of inconsistent annotation, `nmod` is extended with either the adposition's lemma or the word's case but never both and the selection of lemma or case for any given word is seemingly arbitrary. So it is impossible to devise a rule to address this issue.

However, most of these problems are easily rectified with a system such as ours by checking the agreement of case and lemma information in enhanced relations assuming valid annotation of the underlying data.

On the cross-lingual front, the biggest problem is lack of consistency in annotation conventions. Leaving incomplete annotation aside, there are a number of clear divergences. The most striking example is the way subjects of passive verbs and more generally enhanced relations are handled in French Sequoia. These relations receive an extra `(:)enh` to differentiate them from canonical relations directly taken from the tree, the presence of the column depends mostly on the number of columns in the relation type, if it is a simple relation then a column is used but when it is already a sub-type with a column between the main type and extra information then no column is added. Not only is this unique to this treebank, but it is also redundant since this information can be directly retrieved by looking at the original tree. There are also a number of more subtle inconsistencies. For example, in languages that add lemma information to `conj` relations, when the coordinating conjunction is a symbol (& or /), most languages just ignore them and keep the bare `conj` relation. However, Swedish uses the special `conj:sym` relation.

Beyond these issues, there remain genuine linguistic difficulties. A difficulty common to all languages is the scope of conjunctions and whether to propagate dependents amongst conjuncts or not. This is particularly clear with adverbials and obliques that modify verbs. Due to their broad semantic range, adverbials can propagate from conjunction heads to dependent conjuncts even if they already have other adverbials, as long as they do not conflict semantically. Currently in UD, there is no hierarchy amongst dependents of a word, but there could be a form of scope indexing to distinguish a word's direct dependents from dependents of the whole conjunction attached to its head.

Another difficulty is subject selection in prodrop languages. Fortunately, the prodrop languages in this shared task have personal and number agreement at least on finite verbs which helps testing the compatibility of the overt subject of a verb with its coordinated verbs or verbs in relative clauses that lack an overt subject. However, there are prodrop languages that do not mark personal agreement on verbs and do not use relativisers either (e.g. Japanese). In this case, finding the semantic subject of verbs may be much more challenging.

5   Results and Discussion

Despite focusing on efficiency, our official submission obtained an average ELAS of 74.04 which was the fourth best system (out of 9 full submissions). Our improved score after training distilled models to convergence (or closer to convergence) obtained an average score of 76.14. The full breakdown of these results are shown in Table 5 and Table 9 in the Appendix.

Our system is competitive mainly by the grace of our rule-based system which obtains an average 98.20 ELAS when used on the gold development treebanks. And for the most part its performance echoes the quality of the predicted dependencies and tags used by the system as is seen in Table 2. Having a rule-based system that can perform so well on gold data means that improving the dependency predictions it is based on for a full pipeline will almost always increase ELAS scores. It also means it could be used to generate new data. Although this would be restricted to generating data for pre-existing UD treebanks. Furthermore, it could be used to highlight annotation inconsistencies in a given treebank and between different treebanks for the same language.

We also demonstrated that smaller networks can be competitive, even if in this context distillation does not perform as well as previously observed for UD parsing. And beyond that, we show that it is possible to train competitive models with less data and by doing so lowering the energy cost of training parsers. One potentially interesting result is that Tamil performs noticeably better with distillation than either the full baseline model or the small model of the same size trained normally. It has the smallest training treebank out of all the treebanks used in the shared task. The other smaller treebanks also perform better with distillation, e.g the next three smallest treebanks French, Lithuanian, and Swedish all follow this trend but the increase in performance is less pronounced. Perhaps smaller treebanks benefit from what is essentially ensemble training as it tempers a network's penchant for over-fitting.

Acknowledgments

This work has received funding from the European Research Council (ERC), under the European Union's Horizon 2020 research and innovation programme (FASTPARSE, grant agreement No 714150), from the ANSWER-ASAP project (TIN2017-85160-C2-1-R) from MINECO, and from Xunta de Galicia (ED431B 2017/01, ED431G 2019/01).

References

Mark Anderson and Carlos Gómez-Rodríguez. 2020. Distilling neural networks for greener and faster dependency parsing. In *Proceedings of the 16th International Conference on Parsing Technologies (IWPT 2020) (In press)*.

Jimmy Ba and Rich Caruana. 2014. Do deep nets really need to be deep? In *Advances in Neural Information Processing Systems*, pages 2654–2662.

Gosse Bouma, Djamé Seddah, and Daniel Zeman. 2020. Overview of the IWPT 2020 Shared Task on Parsing into Enhanced Universal Dependencies. In *Proceedings of the 16th International Conference on Parsing Technologies and the IWPT 2020 Shared Task on Parsing into Enhanced Universal Dependencies*, Seattle, US. Association for Computational Linguistics.

Cristian Bucilă, Rich Caruana, and Alexandru Niculescu-Mizil. 2006. Model compression. In *Proceedings of the 12th ACM SIGKDD International Conference on Knowledge Discovery and Data Mining*, pages 535–541. ACM.

Yu Cheng, Duo Wang, Pan Zhou, and Tao Zhang. 2018. Model compression and acceleration for deep neural networks: The principles, progress, and challenges. *IEEE Signal Processing Magazine*, 35(1):126–136.

Kevin Clark, Minh-Thang Luong, Urvashi Khandelwal, Christopher D Manning, and Quoc Le. 2019. BAM! Born-again multi-task networks for natural language understanding. In *Proceedings of the 57th Annual Meeting of the Association for Computational Linguistics*, pages 5931–5937.

Timothy Dozat and Christopher D Manning. 2017. Deep biaffine attention for neural dependency parsing. *Proceedings of the 5th International Conference on Learning Representations*.

Masafumi Hagiwara. 1994. A simple and effective method for removal of hidden units and weights. *Neurocomputing*, 6(2):207–218.

Song Han, Jeff Pool, John Tran, and William Dally. 2015. Learning both weights and connections for efficient neural network. In *Advances in Neural Information Processing Systems*, pages 1135–1143.

Geoffrey Hinton, Oriol Vinyals, and Jeff Dean. 2015. Distilling the knowledge in a neural network. *arXiv preprint arXiv:1503.02531*.

Marcin Junczys-Dowmunt, Roman Grundkiewicz, Tomasz Dwojak, Hieu Hoang, Kenneth Heafield, Tom Neckermann, Frank Seide, Ulrich Germann, Alham Fikri Aji, Nikolay Bogoychev, et al. 2018. Marian: Fast neural machine translation in C++. In *Proceedings of ACL 2018, System Demonstrations*, pages 116–121.

Yoon Kim and Alexander M Rush. 2016. Sequence-level knowledge distillation. In *Proceedings of EMNLP*, pages 1317–1327.

Adhiguna Kuncoro, Miguel Ballesteros, Lingpeng Kong, Chris Dyer, and Noah A. Smith. 2016. Distilling an ensemble of greedy dependency parsers into one MST parser. In *Proceedings of the 2016 Conference on Empirical Methods in Natural Language Processing*, pages 1744–1753, Austin, Texas. Association for Computational Linguistics.

Yann LeCun, John S Denker, and Sara A Solla. 1990. Optimal brain damage. In *Advances in neural information processing systems*, pages 598–605.

Yijia Liu, Wanxiang Che, Huaipeng Zhao, Bing Qin, and Ting Liu. 2018. Distilling knowledge for search-based structured prediction. In *Proceedings of the 56th Annual Meeting of the Association for Computational Linguistics (Volume 1: Long Papers)*, pages 1393–1402, Melbourne, Australia. Association for Computational Linguistics.

Liang Lu, Michelle Guo, and Steve Renals. 2017. Knowledge distillation for small-footprint highway networks. In *2017 IEEE International Conference on Acoustics, Speech and Signal Processing (ICASSP)*, pages 4820–4824. IEEE.

Roy Schwartz, Jesse Dodge, Noah A Smith, and Oren Etzioni. 2019. Green AI. *arXiv preprint arXiv:1907.10597*.

Abigail See, Minh-Thang Luong, and Christopher D Manning. 2016. Compression of neural machine translation models via pruning. In *Proceedings of The 20th SIGNLL Conference on Computational Natural Language Learning*, pages 291–301.

Milan Straka and Jana Straková. 2019. Universal dependencies 2.5 models for UDPipe (2019-12-06). LINDAT/CLARIAH-CZ digital library at the Institute of Formal and Applied Linguistics (ÚFAL), Faculty of Mathematics and Physics, Charles University.

Emma Strubell, Ananya Ganesh, and Andrew McCallum. 2019. Energy and policy considerations for deep learning in NLP. *Proceedings of the 56th Annual Meeting of the Association for Computational Linguistics*.

Michalina Strzyz, David Vilares, and Carlos Gómez-Rodríguez. 2019. Viable dependency parsing as sequence labeling. In *Proceedings of NAACL-HLT*, pages 717–723.

David Vilares, Mostafa Abdou, and Anders Søgaard. 2019. Better, faster, stronger sequence tagging constituent parsers. In *Proceedings of the 2019 Conference of the North American Chapter of the Association for Computational Linguistics: Human Language Technologies, Volume 1 (Long and Short Papers)*, pages 3372–3383.

Weishui Wan, Shingo Mabu, Kaoru Shimada, Kotaro Hirasawa, and Jinglu Hu. 2009. Enhancing the generalization ability of neural networks through controlling the hidden layers. *Applied Soft Computing*, 9(1):404–414.

Seunghak Yu, Nilesh Kulkarni, Haejun Lee, and Jihie Kim. 2018. On-device neural language model based word prediction. In *Proceedings of the 27th International Conference on Computational Linguistics: System Demonstrations*, pages 128–131.

A   Appendix

A.1   Teacher-student distillation

Model distillation is the act of taking one or more models and guiding the training of a single network with these models. It was originally introduced not as a means of creating more efficient models, but as a way of ensemble training with networks (Bucilă et al., 2006; Ba and Caruana, 2014; Hinton et al., 2015; Kuncoro et al., 2016).

Teacher-student distillation, the method used in this work, has been successfully utilised in a number of NLP tasks ranging from machine translation, language modelling, exploring structured linguistic space, and speech recognition (Kim and Rush, 2016; Lu et al., 2017; Liu et al., 2018; Yu et al., 2018).

In *teacher-student* distillation, the *teacher* guides the training of another model, the *student*, which in our experiments is smaller. The *student* explicitly uses the information of the larger model by comparing the probability distribution of the respective model's output layer. We use the Kullback-Leibler divergence to obtain the loss between these two distributions:

$$\mathcal{L}_{KL} = -\sum_{t \in b} \sum_i P(\mathbf{x}_i) \log \frac{P(\mathbf{x}_i)}{Q(\mathbf{x}_i)} \quad (1)$$

where P is the probability distribution from the teacher's softmax layer, Q is the probability distribution from the student's, and $\mathbf{x}_i$ is input vector to the softmax corresponding to token w_i of a given tree t for all trees in batch b.

For our implementation there are two probability distributions as we are using a Biaffine parser, one for head predictions and one for label predictions.[2]

The *student* is also trained directly on the gold heads and labels using a categorical cross entropy loss, e.g. for the loss on head predictions:

$$\mathcal{L}_{CE} = -\sum_{t \in b} \sum_i \log p(h_i | \mathbf{x}_i) \qquad (2)$$

where h_i is the true head position for token w_i, corresponding to the softmax layer input vector $\mathbf{x}_i$, of tree t in batch b.

The total loss is therefore the combination of the Kullback-Leibler loss between the probability distributions of the *teacher* and the *student* for both head and label predictions with the cross entropy loss between the *student* predictions and the gold data:

$$\mathcal{L} = \mathcal{L}_{KL}(T_h, S_h) + \mathcal{L}_{KL}(T_{lab}, S_{lab}) \\ + \mathcal{L}_{CE}(h) + \mathcal{L}_{CE}(lab) \qquad (3)$$

where $\mathcal{L}_{CE}(h)$ is the loss for the student's predicted head positions, $\mathcal{L}_{CE}(lab)$ is the loss for the student's predicted arc label, $\mathcal{L}_{KL}(T_h, S_h)$ is the loss between the teacher's probability distribution for arc predictions and that of the student, and $\mathcal{L}_{KL}(T_{lab}, S_{lab})$ is the loss between label distributions.

A.2 Details of dependency enhancements

In this section we give more details about the enhancement of dependency relations and about the processing subtleties of relative clauses, controlled predicates, and conjunctions.

Most of the original dependencies are kept in the enhanced structure, but they can undergo a number of cosmetic changes. In the simplest case, the relation type t is just appended to the index h of the word's governor to give the relation $h : t$. Sometimes, during the process the relation type is slightly modified. In Estonian (EDT and EWT) some complex relations such as `compound:prt`

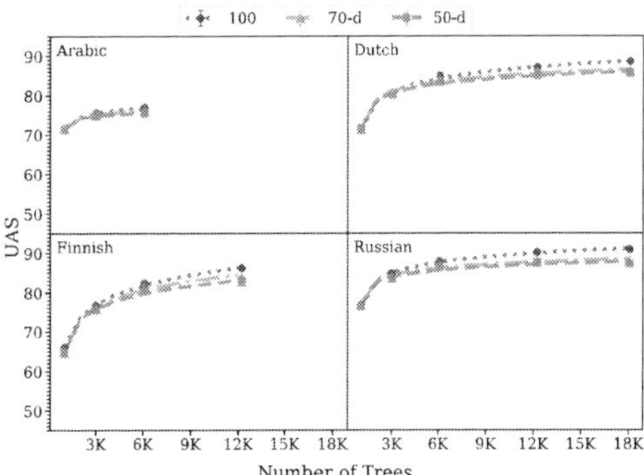

Figure 8: UAS for different models for Arabic, Dutch, Finnish, and Russian development treebanks.

hyperparameter	value
word embedding dimensions	100
char embedding dimensions	32
char BiLSTM dimensions	100
embedding dropout	0.33
BiLSTM dimensions	400 (200)
BiLSTM layers	3
arc MLP dimensions	500 (250)
label MLP dimensions	100 (50)
MLP layers	1
learning rate	0.2
dropout	0.33
momentum	0.9
L2 norm λ	0.9
annealing	$0.75^{(t/5000)}$
ϵ	1×10^{-12}
optimiser	Adam
loss function	cross entropy
epochs	100
min vocab freq.	2

Table 6: Hyperparameters for baseline models. The values in parentheses show the values for the distilled and small models used in the main analysis of the shared task.

or `csubj:cop` are truncated and only the first part is kept. Conversely, in French (Sequoia) some relations receive extra information, such as subjects of passives `nsubj:pass` that are augmented with `xoxobj` stating they are the semantic object of their head.

Some relations receive extra lexical and morphological information. Conjuncts marked with `conj` usually receive the lemma of the coordinating conjunction (`cc`). Likewise, adverbial and adjectival clauses (`advcl` and `acl`) receive the lemma of the word (`mark`) that introduces them. Nominal modifiers and obliques (`nmod` and `obl`) can receive the lemma of the adposition that introduces them (often marked with the `case` re-

	original				sample				
	trees	mL	mDD	NP%	trees	mL	mDD	NP%	2s-KS$_L$
Czech									
-CAC	23478	20.1	3.7	2.5	3016	19.9	3.7	2.5	0.014
-FicTree	10160	13.2	3.6	3.8	1305	13.1	3.6	3.8	0.016
-PDT	68495	17.1	3.7	2.7	8800	17.1	3.7	2.6	0.007
-combined	102133	17.4	3.7	2.7	13121	17.4	3.7	2.7	0.007
Dutch									
-Alpino	12264	15.2	4.0	4.5	8915	15.2	4.0	4.4	0.004
-LassySmall	5787	13.0	3.7	2.0	4206	13.0	3.7	1.9	0.007
-combined	18051	14.5	3.9	3.8	13121	14.5	3.9	3.7	0.004
Estonian									
-EDT	24633	14.0	3.6	0.8	12552	14.1	3.6	0.8	0.010
-EWT	1116	15.4	3.8	1.5	569	15.4	3.8	1.6	0.027
-combined	25749	14.1	3.6	0.9	13121	14.1	3.6	0.8	0.009
Polish									
-LFG	13774	7.6	2.8	0.3	5738	7.6	2.8	0.3	0.006
-PDB	17722	15.9	3.4	1.4	7383	15.9	3.4	1.5	0.008
-combined	31496	12.3	3.3	1.1	13121	12.3	3.3	1.2	0.003
Russian									
-SynTagRus	48814	17.8	3.6	1.6	13121	17.8	3.6	1.6	0.004

Table 7: Analysis of renormalised treebank samples: 2s-KS is the two-sample Kolmogorov-Smirnov test comparing the sentence-length distributions of the original and the sample treebanks (where values close to 0 suggest samples are not from different distributions, and values approaching 1 suggest otherwise); trees is the number of trees; mL is the mean sentence length; mDD the mean dependency distance; and NP% is the percentage of non-projective arcs. Where we use the combined sample (or just the sample for Russian-SynTagRus) for training.

lation). Furthermore `nmod` and `obl` can also receive case information about the word itself. When the introducing marker is not a word but a fixed expression such as *"as well as"* then the *long lemma* composed of the lemmas of each word in the expression (marked by the `fixed` relation) is used, for example `conj:as_well_as`.

Relative clauses The only relations from the original tree that are not kept in the enhanced structure are those whose dependent is an anaphoric pronoun or adverb used to introduce a relative clause. Instead, the dependent (pronoun or adverb) is linked to its antecedent by an edge labelled `ref`. A new edge is then added between the original head of the reference and its antecedent of the same type as the original relation in order to show the argument structure of the clause. Thus, relative clauses are the first phenomenon that creates edges that are not present in the original tree. Their structure is however relatively simple since they can at most create one extra edge and replace one.

There are nonetheless two subtleties with relative clauses. First, in some languages, such as English, relative pronouns are not necessary. In these cases, while there are restrictions on the role the antecedent can fill, we need to infer its actual role from the sentence. Second, there may be sev-

	UAS	LAS		UAS	LAS
Arabic			**Bulgarian**		
small	76.9	72.5	small	91.6	87.6
dist	76.5	72.3	dist	91.6	87.6
Czech			**Dutch**		
small	89.5	86.0	small	87.2	83.3
dist	89.0	85.3	dist	86.7	82.9
English			**Estonian**		
small	85.0	81.9	small	85.2	80.9
dist	84.4	81.2	dist	84.7	80.2
Finnish			**French**		
small	85.8	82.2	small	88.1	85.5
dist	85.1	81.3	dist	88.5	85.8
Italian			**Latvian**		
small	91.3	89.0	small	86.3	82.4
dist	90.3	87.8	dist	86.0	81.9
Lithuanian			**Polish**		
small	76.7	71.5	small	90.5	86.4
dist	78.0	73.0	dist	90.2	86.0
Russian			**Slovak**		
small	89.5	86.3	small	85.6	81.7
dist	88.9	85.5	dist	84.7	80.7
Swedish			**Tamil**		
small	84.5	80.8	small	63.7	55.7
dist	85.3	81.6	dist	64.0	56.9
Ukrainian			**Average**		
small	86.8	82.6	small	85.0	80.9
dist	86.6	82.5	dist	84.7	80.7

Table 8: Comparison of attachment scores for the development treebanks for distilled (dist) models and models with the same parameters (small) trained normally.

	Tokens	Words	Sentences	UPOS	XPOS	UFeats	AllTags	Lemmas	UAS	LAS	CLAS	MLAS	BLEX	EULAS	ELAS
Arabic	100.0	94.6	82.1	88.5	84.0	84.2	82.0	88.5	75.8	71.2	66.8	56.1	62.0	69.2	66.9
Bulgarian	99.9	99.9	94.2	97.6	94.3	95.4	93.8	94.6	91.1	87.0	82.3	75.8	75.5	85.8	84.9
Czech	99.9	99.9	93.2	97.8	90.9	90.8	89.7	97.4	86.2	81.8	78.1	67.9	75.8	79.6	77.2
Dutch	99.7	99.7	69.3	92.6	89.9	92.0	89.0	94.4	83.4	79.4	71.9	61.9	66.4	78.0	77.4
English	99.2	99.2	83.8	93.6	92.8	94.1	90.7	95.4	83.7	80.1	75.8	67.2	72.1	79.2	78.5
Estonian	99.7	99.7	90.0	95.0	96.2	92.8	91.0	90.4	80.7	75.5	72.7	64.6	63.8	75.0	74.1
Finnish	99.7	99.7	88.7	94.8	54.5	93.0	51.8	87.1	84.1	79.7	76.5	69.0	64.3	77.8	75.7
French	99.7	99.2	94.3	93.5	99.2	88.8	87.3	94.9	87.2	80.6	72.1	58.3	66.7	80.1	77.8
Italian	99.9	99.8	98.8	97.2	97.0	97.1	96.2	97.4	90.2	87.4	81.4	76.8	77.9	85.9	84.8
Latvian	99.3	99.3	98.7	93.5	84.3	89.5	83.9	92.7	84.4	79.7	76.1	63.6	70.0	77.2	75.6
Lithuanian	99.9	99.9	87.9	90.3	80.7	81.2	79.3	88.8	72.9	66.3	62.6	45.9	54.3	63.7	61.4
Polish	99.4	99.8	97.5	96.4	84.9	83.6	80.3	95.6	88.4	83.4	79.4	60.1	75.0	81.4	74.5
Russian	99.6	99.6	98.8	97.8	99.6	85.3	85.0	96.5	86.8	83.2	80.0	62.8	76.7	81.7	80.3
Slovak	100.0	100.0	85.3	92.9	77.1	80.3	76.7	86.6	83.2	78.3	73.9	53.8	61.6	76.5	73.5
Swedish	99.2	99.2	93.5	93.3	91.0	84.9	83.2	90.0	82.2	77.6	73.7	56.8	64.9	76.2	75.2
Tamil	99.2	94.5	97.5	81.3	76.3	80.5	75.6	84.1	59.6	48.8	43.6	35.5	39.6	48.1	47.0
Ukrainian	99.8	99.8	96.6	94.9	84.0	84.3	83.3	93.6	83.4	78.7	73.6	57.8	67.4	76.2	74.0
Average	99.7	99.1	91.2	93.6	86.9	88.1	83.5	92.2	82.5	77.6	73.0	60.8	66.7	76.0	74.0

Table 9: Full test results for our official submission using the shared task's submission site for evaluation.

eral words that look like relativisers in a relative clause even outside conjunction. Often, only one of them is a leaf node, the others introducing further embedded clauses. Only in Finnish (TDT) did we find instances of multiple relative pronouns attaching to the same verb and each being marked as the reference of another word in the sentence.

Control A second phenomenon that creates new dependencies is control, where the subject of an embedded clause is not overt and is provided by one of its governor's arguments. For example in the English sentence *"I want you to go,"* the semantic subject of the verb *go* is the object of the main verb, namely *you*. In such a case, an additional relation is added to the structure to represent the dependency of the word *you* to the embedded predicate *go*. These structures are marked by a xcomp relation between the embedded predicate and its governor in the original tree. The identity of the new subject depends usually on the governing predicate and its argument structure. So it is mostly a matter of knowing the governing profile of each lexical item given their argument structure. For example, the subject of a predicate embedded in a *want to* clause is the object of the *want to* clause if present, its subject otherwise. Control is also quite simple since it has a limited span.

Conjunction The vast majority of new edges are created by conjunctions and is much harder to handle than the two previous phenomena. Contrary to relative clauses and control, conjunction has no direction in the sense that it can occur both at the governor level and at the dependent level. In *"Mary and Sam bought strawberries,"* the conjunction *"Mary and Sam"* occurs at the dependent level and both *Mary* and *Sam* are subject of the verb *bought*. In *"Mary bought strawberries and ate them,"* the conjunction is now at the governor level and *Mary* is the subject of both *bought* and *ate*. So unlike relative clauses where one merely needs to find the relativiser's antecedent higher up in the tree, or control where one needs to look for the controlled subject amongst the arguments of the controlling predicate, conjunctions can have repercussions both higher up and lower down in the structure at the same time.

The easiest case for conjunction is when it occurs at the dependent level. One just needs to propagate the relation existing between the head of the conjunction and its governor to the other conjuncts. In the case of conjunction at the governor level, things are more complicated. While dependents don't tend to propagate up a conjunction chain but only down, they can be blocked by a number of reasons. For example in *"Mary bought and ate strawberries,"* the object *strawberries* should attach to *bought* in the tree and only propagate down to *ate*. But in *"Mary spoke and ate strawberries,"* *strawberries* should attach to *ate* and not propagate up to *spoke*, even though *speak* can also have direct objects. And in *"Mary bought strawberries and ate,"* *strawberries* does not propagate down to *ate* since it appears before it in the sentence. However, the conditions under which certain dependents do or do not propagate to their governor's conjuncts are both language and relation specific. In a given language, objects need not behave like subjects nor like determiners or adverbials. Often if a relation slot (object, subject, determiner) is already filled for a given word, it will block the propagation of the same relation from higher up in the conjunction chain, but it need not always be the case, especially with adverbials. But even an empty slot does not always guarantee propagation, especially in case marking and prodrop languages where morphological consideration play a major role as well. So we need to learn the propagation conditions for each relation type on a per language basis.

In our system, we keep track of dependents of `conj` relations during the first traversal of a sentence and handle them in the second pass. The main reason for not processing conjuncts as soon as they arrive in the sentence is that some of their dependents (objects, adjectives or adverbials) can appear later and thus would require extra processing. For example, in *"Mary bought and ate strawberries,"* the object of both verbs only appears after the conjunct *ate*, so upon first seeing *ate*, *bought* does not have any object to be propagated.

A.2.1 Conjunction propagating conditions

We use two sets of conditions in order to guide the propagation of dependents to their governor's conjuncts. The first is about relation types already attached to these conjuncts. Usually an object or a subject does not attach to a verb that already has these slots filled. So for each relation, we measure three frequencies. The frequency at which it co-occurs with other types under its main governor (in the tree), the frequency at which it co-occurs with other types under its conjunct governors (in the enhanced structure) and the frequency at which it does not co-occur with other types because it does not propagate to its governor's conjunct. Any relation with which it co-occurs under its main governor cannot be blocking propagation. Then if a relation is more often than not associated with conjunct governors to which the current relation did not propagate, it is considered a blocking relation. In practice this means that a `subj` does not propagate to a conjunct of its governor that already has an `expl`, for example.

The second condition is based on matching morphological information. For every relation and morphological category (tense, case, aspect, and so on), we measure how often the value of a category agrees or disagrees between the governor and its conjunct (of the same UPOS tag) when the relation propagates and when it does not. If a category disagrees more often than not between conjuncts which the relation did not propagate, then we assume that the category needs to agree for that relation.

A.3 Curious quibbles and questionable jiggery-pokery

While being above 94.9 ELAS for all languages, our rule-based system could still be improved to better capture enhanced structures. There are three main points for further improvement.

Upon reviewing the code for the rule-based system, we realised that we catch arguments of relative clauses only in presence of a relativiser that receives the `ref` relation. This means that we miss a number of relations involved in relative clauses. It remained unnoticed because of all the languages in the shared task, most use relative pronouns/adverbs to introduce relative clauses. In fact the only language that does not have relative pronouns, Tamil, is not yet annotated with relative clauses and it might not even be relevant. Our methodology here is to look for an antecedent when we have a relative pronoun, but we could do the opposite and look for potential relative pronouns when we have a relative clause. The latter should indeed be more language agnostic and work even when there are no relativisers involved.

A second point of improvement has to do with subject finding in controlled predicates. In our current system, the controlling behaviour of each controlling construction is gathered from the training data, and if we encounter an out of vocabulary construction at prediction time the subject is used by default. But further consideration showed that the object might be a more sensible default option when available. It would, however, be more interesting to learn the default behaviour on a per language basis.

Thirdly, due to the march of time, we hard-coded a number of heuristic thresholds used to fine-tune the system. For example, to see if a language is prodrop, we compare the number of root verbs with overt subjects with the number of root verbs without a subject. If at least a third of root verbs do not have an overt subject then that language was considered prodrop. This is clearly not satisfying since this ratio can greatly vary from language to language and from genre to genre. Furthermore, some languages may not be generally prodrop, but ommit syntactic subjects in impersonal constructions, such as Hebrew, or be prodrop only for certain tenses.

Linear Neural Parsing and Hybrid Enhancement for Enhanced Universal Dependencies

Giuseppe Attardi, Daniele Sartiano, Maria Simi
Department of Computer Science,
University of Pisa
{attardi, sartiano, simi}@di.unipi.it

Abstract

To accomplish the shared task on dependency parsing we explore the use of a linear transition-based neural dependency parser as well as a combination of three of them by means of a linear tree combination algorithm. We train separate models for each language on the shared task data. We compare our base parser with two biaffine parsers and also present an ensemble combination of all five parsers, which achieves an average UAS 1.88 point lower than the top official submission. For producing the enhanced dependencies, we exploit a hybrid approach, coupling an algorithmic graph transformation of the dependency tree with predictions made by a multitask machine learning model.

1 System Overview

The shared task is aimed at performing all the levels of linguistic analysis according to the UD guidelines, starting from raw text all the way to enhanced dependency graphs. All this in a multi-language setting for seventeen languages (Bouma et al., 2020).

In this endeavor, we concentrate on the syntactic parsing and enhancement stages, by exploiting existing tools for tokenization, sentence splitting, POS tagging and morphological analysis.

For syntactic parsing we make experiments exploring different ideas, in an attempt to improve state-of-the-art parsers with linear complexity. A parser combination is then used for our official submission, exploiting the linear tree combination algorithm by Attardi and Dell'Orletta (2009), resulting in an overall linear algorithm.

For the enhancement step, we build on previous work in writing an enhancer for UD, based on algorithmic graph transformation, that was used to produce the Italian version of the enhanced dependencies (Simi and Montemagni, 2018). The script used language specific heuristics and lexical information, achieving a good degree of accuracy for Italian and English. In this multi-language challenge, we have to deal with partial implementations of the expected enhancement types as well as with varying degree of compliance with the guidelines in the different languages. In order to address this additional complexity, we implement a new version of the script for making it modular, parametric, and language independent. For specific enhancement tasks, we integrate the output of machine learning classifiers, in an attempt to learn from the training data and make the heuristics more robust and general.

2 Syntactic parsing

State of the art dependency parsers currently often adopt the graph-based model, based on neural networks for the choice of arcs and labels.

We consider as current SoTA on the English PTB the graph dependency parsers listed in Table 1.

In particular the Bi-LSTM-based deep biaffine neural dependency parser by Dozat and Manning (2017) has been quite popular and used in three out of five of the top submissions to the CoNLL 2018 Shared Task: Multilingual Parsing from Raw Text to Universal Dependencies (Zeman et al., 2018), in particular in the top non-ensemble submission (Kanerva et al., 2018).

The preference for such models leads to systems with high accuracy but possibly slower due to their $O(n^2)$ complexity. For example, the original implementation of the Dozat parser is rated at about 400 sents/sec on GPUs, while for example the neural transition-based parser by Chen and Manning (2014) is rated at 640 sents/sec just on CPUs. Our experiments attempt to find a parser with linear complexity and hence good speed performance. Indeed the linear transition parser that we choose for our experiments (UUParser) is twice as fast as the

Proceedings of the 16th International Conference on Parsing Technologies and the IWPT 2020 Shared Task, pages 206–214
Virtual Meeting, July 9, 2020. ©2020 Association for Computational Linguistics

Parser	UAS	LAS
HPSG (Zhou and Zhao, 2019)	**96.09**	**94.68**
BIST-Graph (Kiperwasser and Goldberg, 2016)	93.10	91.00
Biaffine (Dozat and Manning, 2017)	95.74	94.08
Pointer-TD (Ma et al., 2018)	95.87	94.19
Pointer-LR (Fernández-González and Gómez-Rodríguez, 2019)	**96.04**	**94.43**
UUParser (de Lhoneux et al., 2017)	94.63	92.77
BIST-Transition (Kiperwasser and Goldberg, 2016)	93.9	91.9
CM (Chen and Manning, 2014)	91.80	89.60

Table 1: SoTA dependency parsers, grouped into graph-based (top) and transition-based (bottom).

latest version of the biaffine parser from Stanford (Stanza). However, after submission, we discovered a new implementation of the biaffine parser in PyTorch (Zhang, 2019), which is 5 times faster by better exploiting GPU acceleration.

We trained our own models for each language on the shared task treebanks for UUParser, UDPipe and Zysite, while we used a pretrained multilanguage model for UDify and pretrained individual language models for Stanza.

2.1 UUParser

We choose `UUParser` as our base parser. UUParser (de Lhoneux et al., 2017) is a transition-based parser model, derived from the parser by (Kiperwasser and Goldberg, 2016): the (bidirectional) LSTM's recurrent output vector for each word is concatenated with each possible head's recurrent vector, and the result is used as input to a MLP that scores each resulting arc. The predicted tree structure at training time is the one where each word depends on its highest-scoring head. Labels are generated analogously, with each word's recurrent output vector and its gold or predicted head word's recurrent vector being used in a multi-class MLP. We ported the Kiperwasser parser to Python 3. UUParser was further extended to deal with non-projectivity by means of a swap transition and to support ELMo embeddings as an input to the LSTM.

We further extended UUParser in order to exploit BERT and AlBERT embeddings. Words are first tokenized with their specific tokenizer and then the embeddings for words split into wordpieces obtained as the average of the wordpiece embeddings.

The code for the extended version is available on GitHub[1].

On development experiments, using the English

Treebank	Embeddings	UAS	LAS
en-ewt	BERT	91.24	89.33
en-ewt	AlBERT	91.36	89.39
fr-sequoia	BERT	91.44	89.55
cs-pdt	BERT	93.87	91.94
it-isdt	BERT	94.67	93.11

Table 2: Parser accuracy on the development set.

and Italian train and development sets provided for the task, we obtained the results in Table 2.

For BERT we use the base-uncased model and for AlBERT the large-v2 model, which we keep frozen during training. Given the minor difference between using BERT and AlBERT, in our experiments we choose to use the BERT model.

We explored the idea to provide hints to the parser, obtained from structural syntax probes (Hewitt and Mannings, 2019). We use a syntax probe to estimate the parse tree path distance between two tokens. The transition-based parser needs to decide at each step which transition to apply to the pair of words on the top of the stack (s0) and on the input buffer (b0). The parser computes a distance matrix for each pair of tokens in a sentence. The parser is provided as additional features the estimated distances between b0 and the top k (default 3) tokens on the stack. These distances should help the parser in deciding whether to perform a Shift transition rather than a premature Reduce.

The results we obtained with such an extension on the English development corpus where 92.21 UAS and 90.31 LAS, using ELMo embeddings for word representations and BERT for syntax probes, a small improvement with respect to 91.32 UAS and 89.33 LAS without using these features.

We also tested two biaffine parsers: the implementation by `Zysite` (Zhang, 2019) and `Stanza` (Qi et al., 2020) which augments the bi-

---

[1] https://github.com/attardi/uuparser

Parser	GPU sents/s	CPU sents/s	UAS
UUParser	16.62	0.81	83.93
Stanza	7.77	0.43	84.51
Zysite	**84.82**	**2.11**	**86.67**

Table 3: Speed performance of parsers: average user time on all test set.

affine parser with features to predict the *linearization* order of two words in a given language, and to predict the typical distance in linear order between them.

We report in table 3 the average speed performance on all the 17 test sets of the challenge obtained by the linear parser and the two quadratic biaffine graph parsers.

The `Zysite` biaffine parser turns out to be both the most accurate and the fastest. It is also worth mentioning the significant training time, as for example `Zysite` takes more than 39 hours to train it on the Czech treebank, with 68,495 sentences. The experiments were performed on a Dell server using a single NVIDIA Tesla T4 GPU.

2.2 Tokenization, Tagging

UUParser does not provide tokenization nor tagging capabilities, so we have to rely on another set of tools to accomplish these tasks. We choose to use UDPipe (Straka and Straková, 2017) to perform sentence splitting, tokenization and tagging. This gives us a common tagged representation to use also with alternative parsers.

Some of the parsers tested provide the ability to perform end-to-end parsing from raw text, in particular UDify (Kondratyuk and Straka, 2019) and Stanza. However, they turn out not to be very effective: the pretrained model of UDify does not support all the task languages and Stanza has a weird behavior: for example, it would split a word like "GoogleOS" not just into two tokens, "Google" and "OS", but into two separate sentences.

So eventually we decided to use the same tokenization provided by UDPipe as input to all parsers. This enables us also to produce an ensemble version combining the outputs of three parsers.

2.3 Ensemble of Parsers

In the official submission, we exploit the linear tree combination algorithm by Attardi and Dell'Orletta (2009) to combine the outputs of an ensemble of dependency parsers. The algorithm is greedy and works by combining the trees top down. It has been shown to outperform more complex algorithms based on computing the Maximum Spanning Tree.

The parsers used are UDify, UUParser and UD-Pipe.

In a later unofficial submission labeled comb5, we included also `Zysite` and `Stanza` in the ensemble. Table 7 presents the results of this submission compared to the best performing official submission in the challenge.

These scores are within 1% UAS to the results of the top submission by Jenna Kanerva of the University of Turku, except on the Baltic languages (-3.37% Latvian, -4.91% Lithuanian, -4.98% Estonaian), Finnish (-4.42% UAS) and Arabic (-8.22%) and better on Tamil (+3.63%).

3 Enhanced Dependencies

For producing the enhanced dependencies we follow a "hybrid" approach, using a combination of an algorithmic graph transformation of the syntactic dependency tree coupled with predictions made by three machine learning classifiers. The basic enhancing script is an evolution of the work presented in (Simi and Montemagni, 2018) to bootstrap enhanced dependencies for the Italian treebank, also used for experiments in (Nivre et al. 2018).

One classifier is used to recognize the external subjects in `xcomp` constructions. The second classifier detects when a head should be propagated in conjunctions. The third classifier detects the case of propagation of dependents in conjunctions. The classifiers are trained jointly on the three tasks and produce three binary predictions.

The script that adds the enhanced dependencies is modular, so that it can be adapted to perform just the required analysis depending on the kind of enhanced dependencies present in each language and to bypass those that were not implemented. In addition, the script is parametric with respect to predictions coming from machine learning classifiers, which can be taken into account or ignored. We describe below how the different kinds of enhancements are addressed.

3.1 Controlled/Raised Subjects

This type of enhancement applies to subordinate infinitive clauses introduced by the `xcomp` relation and consists in adding an extra `nsubj` dependency to the embedded or controlled verb. The difficult aspect of this enhancement is to predict the correct subject for the dependent clause among the different dependents of the main verb. In fact, this extra subject can be the subject, object or an oblique complement, as the following examples testify:

1. Mary wants to buy a book. *Mary* is the subject of *buy*.

2. Mary asked John to buy a book. *John*, the object, is the subject of *buy*.

3. Maria ha chiesto a Giovanni di comprare un libro. [Mary asked John to buy a book]. In Italian, the buyer, *Giovanni*, is an indirect complement (`obl`) of the main verb *chiesto*.

We train a neural binary classifier to predict which of the dependents of the main verb should be chosen to play the role of the extra subject for the dependent verb, if any. If more than one token is predicted as an external subject of the subordinate clause, currently all of them are added.

The classifier is applied to tokens that have a sibling in a `xcomp` relation, which are either a noun or a pronoun and whose `deprel` is one of the following: `nsubj, csubj, obj, iobj, obl, nsubj:pass, csubj:pass`.

Such tokens are represented by the following features: the form, the `upos` and the `deprel` of the token, the form, the `upos` and the `deprel` of the token's head, the form of the `xcomp` sibling, the form of the `case` or `mark` which introduces the subordinate phrase. A training example for the first classifier has the features for a token as input and a binary value as output depending on whether the sibling is indeed a `nsubj` for the subordinate clause.

3.2 Propagation over Conjuncts

The classifiers for propagation over conjuncts act in a similar way. We train two distinct classifiers for recognizing candidates for head propagation and for dependents propagation over conjuncts. Candidates for head propagation are conjoined subjects and objects, that should each be attached to their head as in "Paul and Mary are running" or "Paul bought apples and oranges".

Candidates for dependent propagation are subjects, objects and other complements of conjoined verbs, as it is the case of *she* in "She was reading and watching a movie".

The model is trained to predict whether a candidate for propagation should be safely propagated, by making the implicit relations explicit.

3.3 Model Architecture

The three classifiers share the same neural network architecture. The first layer collects the embeddings for each form, upos or deprel in the input vector. The embeddings for the forms are obtained from FastText (Bojanowski et al. 2017). The embeddings for `upos` and `deprel` are learned as vectors of size 20 each.

The second layer of the classifier concatenates the embeddings from the first layer. The third layer is a flatten layer, which is followed by a fully connected layer with a hidden dimension of 100. This is followed by a dropout with a probability of 50% (chosen by tuning experiments) and finally there is a fully connected layer with a sigmoid activation.

The classifiers are trained jointly with a binary cross entropy loss function and an Adam optimizer (Kingma and Ba, 2015) on the training set of each language. The training is run for up to four epochs, even though in most cases the loss stops decreasing after the second epoch. Validation accuracies during training range around 97-98%. The code is written in Keras on a Tensorflow backend.

3.4 Relative Clauses

The treatment of enhancements for relative clauses is quite straightforward. It consists in attaching the relative pronoun to its antecedent with the special `ref` relation and attaching the referred antecedent as an argument to the main predicate of the relative clause. This enhancement may create circularities in the enhanced graph.

3.5 Label Augmentation with Case/Mark Information

The most difficult sub-task turned out to be guessing the right case/mark information for augmenting the relation name of non-core dependents, due to the different interpretations and varying degree of compliance with the guidelines in the various treebanks. Given the high frequency of occurrence of this type of enhancements, doing this task right has high impact on the overall performance.

As it turned out, the differences concern all the following aspects, and their combinations:

1. the type of deprels considered for the augmentation (e.g. `conj` is not specialized in Arabic, Bulgarian, Estonian, Finnish, French, Latvian, Lithuanian, Polish etc.)

2. the case/mark information used (either the lemma or form of the case/mark dependent)

3. the strategy adopted in presence of multiple marks/cases dependents (whether their concatenation or the last one as in English)

4. the strategy adopted when cases/marks are fixed multi-word expressions (whether forms or lemmas are combined)

5. the use or not of morphological case information and to what extent

6. the presence of non canonical keywords in some languages (for example `agentxoxnsubj` and `enh` introduced in the French treebank to encode diathesis normalization as described by Candito et al. (2017)).

In this sense, the inclusion/exclusion of type specialization depending on the language is a too coarse strategy, since it does not account of all these variations; moreover the differences are treebank-wise (as opposed to language-wise) in the sense that different subparts of the test set for a specific language may be coming from different treebanks following different approaches.

In order to address these issues, we adopted a very simplistic data driven approach to adjust the result of a rule-based algorithm, which implements the guidelines. We computed a mapping from the label predicted from our enhancer to the gold label found in the training data set and filtered out correspondences whose frequency was less than a fixed threshold, in order to be tolerant to sporadic errors. As a final "patch", we applied the resulting transformation to produce the final augmented label.

This strategy is far from perfect and clean, but it does take care of systematic differences among languages, such as the use of case features (`gen`, tt nom, `dat`, tt ins etc.) in some of the languages with morphological cases. However, it provides no solution to issues related to non-conventional label completions, nor solves the problem of selecting the correct `mark` or `case` when multiple ones are present (e.g. *about whether*, *along with* in English), or to address the non-canonical use, with respect to the guidelines, of lemma vs form in augmentations[2].

---

[2]For case information the guidelines suggest the use of forms in multi-word expressions and lemmas for single words. English apparently adopts the inverse convention

Language	Parameters
Arabic	-e=4; ml; patch
Bulgarian	ml; patch
Czech	patch
Dutch	ml
English	
Estonian	ml; patch
Finnish	ml; patch
French	-e=156; ml
Italian	
Latvian	patch
Lithuanian	ml
Polish	ml
Russian	-e=3; patch
Slovak	patch
Swedish	
Tamil	-e=145; ml; patch
Ukrainian	patch

Table 4: Parameters resulting form tuning: see the text for their meaning.

3.6 Tuning Parameters

The machine learning modules and the "patch" strategy were not equally effective for all languages. On the basis of the performance on the development set, we selected for each language the best choice of parameters for the enhancement script. These were consistently applied in producing the enhanced version of the parser results in all submissions.

Table 4 summarizes the choice of parameters for the different languages, where the values for the parameters "-e" represent the types of enhancement to be excluded, since not implemented for the language (consistently with the parameters of the evaluation script), `ml` means that we used the predictions from the machine learning classifiers, `patch` means that we used the mappings strategy for fixing label augmentation. The lack of parameters means that only the basic enhancement script was used, and all enhancement types were performed.

4 Results

The official results are those labeled UNIPI-003 in our submission, obtained through the combination of the parsers UDify, UUParser and UDPipe.

Table 5 shows the official results obtained in tokenization and tagging on the test sets. Table 6 shows our team official results on parsing and enhancement.

After the submission deadline, we experimented with the biaffibe parsers Stanza and Zysite.

Stanza improves over UUParser by an average of 0.58 UAS, 0.64 LAS, 1.05 CLAS, 4.26 MLAS, 4.26 BLEX, 0.60 EULAS, 0.42 ELAS, with notable improvements of +16.82 LAS on Estonian, while a decrease of -28.52 LAS on Lithuanian, and -9.95 LAS on Polish is observed.

Zysite improves over UUParser by an average of 1.77 UAS, 1.84 LAS, 1.97 CLAS, 0.27 MLAS, 1.28 BLEX, 1.83 EULAS and 1.63 ELAS, with notable improvements of +17.49 LAS on Estonian, +5.02 on Dutch, +3.23 on Svedish, but with a significant drop of -14.48 LAS on Arabic.

These are encouraging results that show that a transition-based parser can be competitive with graph-based ones.

We then produced a new run `comb5` (UNIPI-comb5), as an ensemble of five parsers: UUParser, UDify, UDPipe, Stanza and Zysite. We report these unofficial results in Table 7.

The improvements on parsing by the ensemble of five parsers with respect to the single parser UUParser are summarized in Table 8.

The most significant improvements from the ensemble combinations are +13.07 UAS on Estonian, +5.31 on Tamil, +5.11 on Dutch, +3.59 on Lithuanian, +4.37 on Finnish.

Estonian, Finnish, Latvian, Lithuanian turned out as the most difficult for our dependency parsers, with a difference between 4.2 and 6.5 points of UAS with respect to the submission by Kanerva and even 10.7 point lower on Arabic.

If we consider the average UAS excluding the Baltic languages, the average UAS of the ensemble parsers is 89.82.

As for the enhancement task, its difficulty, besides what we discussed in section 3.5, seems to be confirmed by a significant drop from our EU-LAS score (restricted to UD relations) to the ELAS score, which also takes into account label enhancements. The average drop is 6.26 points and for some languages more than 10 points. The effectiveness of our 'patch' strategy had been carefully assessed with the development data, but did not provide analogous results on the test set. Our algorithm was poor in predicting the label extended with case information. Perhaps a machine learning approach would have provided better results in this case.

5   Conclusions

We experimented with both linear transition-based parsers and two implementations of graph-based biaffine parsers. All parsers have difficulties with Baltic languages, Finnish and Arabic which somehow we were able to mitigate by combining them into an ensemble, except for Arabic, which remains 8.2 points UAS lower than the top submission. Our enhanced version of UUParser, using BERT embeddings, performs competitively well with respect to the biaffine Zysite parser, except on Estonian, Tamil and Dutch, while it outperforms it by +14 LAS on Arabic. Since all the parsers use the same base model, multilingual uncased of BERT, it might be worthwhile to investigate how such models affect the performance on Baltic languages.

The implementation of the biaffine parser by Zysite was a surprising discovery, since it is capable to outperform in speed all other parsers, possibly due to its use of a more efficient biaffine operation via `torch.einsum()`.

For adding the enhanced relations to the output of the parser we opted for a hybrid approach, where for some languages, which appear to be more conforming to the guidelines, we applied an algorithmic solution, while for the rest we exploited machine learning classifiers.

In principle the algorithmic approach should be sufficient as soon as languages adhere more strictly to the guidelines. In the meanwhile, we wonder whether it is worthwhile to develop techniques which are language specific in order to obtain better results, unless there are ways to devise a language agnostic solution.

Acknowledgments

Simonetta Montemagni contributed to the design of a preliminary version of the enhancement script.

The experiments were run on a Dell server with four NVIDIA Tesla P100 GPUs partly funded through the grant "Grandi Attrezzature 2016" by the University of Pisa.

References

Giuseppe Attardi and Felice Dell'Orletta. 2009. Reverse revision and linear tree combination for dependency parsing. In *Proceedings of Human Language Technologies: The 2009 Annual Conference of the North American Chapter of the Association for Computational Linguistics, Companion Volume: Short*

Language	Tokens	Words	Sentences	UPOS	XPOS	UFeats	AllTags	Lemmas
Arabic	99.98	94.58	82.09	88.53	84.00	84.16	81.97	88.46
Bulgarian	99.91	99.91	94.17	97.62	94.34	95.39	93.78	94.60
Czech	99.88	99.88	93.18	97.83	90.88	90.77	89.71	97.42
Dutch	99.74	99.74	70.64	92.58	89.86	92.02	88.97	94.43
English	99.22	99.22	83.82	93.63	92.77	94.09	90.70	95.41
Estonian	99.37	99.37	76.33	82.96	85.77	78.78	75.43	76.11
Finnish	99.70	99.68	88.65	94.83	54.52	93.02	51.82	87.09
French	99.78	99.36	95.46	93.94	99.36	76.02	73.29	96.07
Italian	99.93	99.84	98.76	97.18	97.04	97.10	96.17	97.38
Latvian	99.33	99.33	98.74	93.48	84.29	89.55	83.93	92.73
Lithuanian	99.91	99.91	87.87	90.33	80.69	81.20	79.33	88.75
Polish	99.40	99.83	97.52	96.43	84.87	83.62	80.35	95.60
Russian	99.60	99.60	98.80	97.78	99.60	85.34	84.97	96.55
Slovak	100.00	100.00	85.28	92.93	77.06	80.34	76.71	86.56
Swedish	98.95	98.95	94.07	90.92	0.00	76.18	0.00	88.16
Tamil	99.16	94.51	97.52	81.31	76.35	80.45	75.59	84.14
Ukrainian	99.85	99.81	96.61	94.91	84.03	84.28	83.32	93.56
Average	**99.63**	**99.03**	**90.56**	**92.78**	**80.91**	**86.02**	**76.83**	**91.35**

Table 5: Official results on tagging the test set, produced by UDPipe.

Papers, pages 261–264, Boulder, Colorado. Association for Computational Linguistics.

Piotr Bojanowski, Edouard Grave, Armand Joulin, and Tomas Mikolov. 2017. Enriching word vectors with subword information. *Transactions of the Association for Computational Linguistics*, 5:135–146.

Gosse Bouma, Djamé Seddah, and Daniel Zeman. 2020. Overview of the IWPT 2020 Shared Task on Parsing into Enhanced Universal Dependencies. In *Proceedings of the 16th International Conference on Parsing Technologies and the IWPT 2020 Shared Task on Parsing into Enhanced Universal Dependencies*, Seattle, US. Association for Computational Linguistics.

Marie Candito, Bruno Guillaume, Guy Perrie, and Djamé Seddah. 2017. Enhanced UD dependencies with neutralized diathesis alternation. In *Proceedings of the Fourth International Conference on Dependency Linguistics (Depling 2017)*, pages 42–53.

Danqi Chen and Christopher Manning. 2014. A fast and accurate dependency parser using neural networks. In *Proceedings of the 2014 Conference on Empirical Methods in Natural Language Processing (EMNLP)*, pages 740–750, Doha, Qatar. Association for Computational Linguistics.

Timothy Dozat and Christopher D. Manning. 2017. Deep biaffine attention for neural dependency parsing. In *5th International Conference on Learning Representations, ICLR 2017, Toulon, France, April 24-26, 2017, Conference Track Proceedings*. OpenReview.net.

Daniel Fernández-González and Carlos Gómez-Rodríguez. 2019. Left-to-right dependency parsing with pointer networks. In *Proceedings of the 2019 Conference of the North American Chapter of the Association for Computational Linguistics: Human Language Technologies, Volume 1 (Long and Short Papers)*, pages 710–716, Minneapolis, Minnesota. Association for Computational Linguistics.

Jenna Kanerva, Filip Ginter, Niko Miekka, Akseli Leino, and Tapio Salakoski. 2018. Turku neural parser pipeline: An end-to-end system for the CoNLL 2018 shared task. In *Proceedings of the CoNLL 2018 Shared Task: Multilingual Parsing from Raw Text to Universal Dependencies*, pages 133–142, Brussels, Belgium. Association for Computational Linguistics.

Diederik P. Kingma and Jimmy Ba. 2015. Adam: A method for stochastic optimization. *CoRR*, abs/1412.6980.

Eliyahu Kiperwasser and Yoav Goldberg. 2016. Simple and accurate dependency parsing using bidirectional LSTM feature representations. *Transactions of the Association for Computational Linguistics*, 4:313–327.

Dan Kondratyuk and Milan Straka. 2019. 75 languages, 1 model: Parsing universal dependencies universally. In *Proceedings of the 2019 Conference on Empirical Methods in Natural Language Processing and the 9th International Joint Conference on Natural Language Processing (EMNLP-IJCNLP)*, pages 2779–2795, Hong Kong, China. Association for Computational Linguistics.

Language	UAS	LAS	CLAS	MLA	BLEX	EULAS	ELAS
Arabic	76.46	71.48	67.41	57.26	62.70	68.66	57.79
Bulgarian	91.66	88.26	84.82	79.11	77.98	86.77	84.93
Czech	91.95	89.64	87.99	76.21	85.25	86.19	75.99
Dutch	84.43	80.53	73.42	65.08	67.75	78.95	77.62
English	88.22	85.10	82.21	73.74	77.79	84.54	83.95
Estonian	70.57	63.18	60.04	46.69	42.79	62.45	57.24
Finnish	85.17	81.25	78.79	72.53	66.33	79.04	72.13
French	88.09	82.58	75.37	41.81	71.93	81.84	78.85
Italian	93.04	90.69	86.57	82.55	83.04	89.77	89.14
Latvian	85.47	81.25	78.25	66.47	72.02	78.44	68.23
Lithuanian	76.99	70.76	67.48	51.75	58.40	67.16	61.06
Polish	90.97	87.53	85.24	64.92	80.26	84.83	70.61
Russian	92.44	90.52	89.20	69.95	85.45	88.34	76.90
Slovak	91.24	88.95	87.02	62.99	71.95	85.93	81.40
Swedish	84.80	80.92	78.63	49.09	66.77	79.90	78.73
Tamil	62.79	54.69	51.62	42.50	45.29	54.59	48.50
Ukrainian	88.96	85.23	82.16	63.78	74.89	82.51	73.90
Average	**84.90**	**80.74**	**77.42**	**62.73**	**70.03**	**78.82**	**72.76**

Table 6: UNIPI Official results on parsing the test set: ensemble of UUParser, UDify and UDPipe.

Miryam de Lhoneux, Sara Stymne, and Joakim Nivre. 2017. Arc-hybrid non-projective dependency parsing with a static-dynamic oracle. In *Proceedings of the 15th International Conference on Parsing Technologies*, pages 99–104, Pisa, Italy. Association for Computational Linguistics.

Xuezhe Ma, Zecong Hu, Jingzhou Liu, Nanyun Peng, Graham Neubig, and Eduard Hovy. 2018. Stack-pointer networks for dependency parsing. In *Proceedings of the 56th Annual Meeting of the Association for Computational Linguistics (Volume 1: Long Papers)*, pages 1403–1414, Melbourne, Australia. Association for Computational Linguistics.

Joakim Nivre, Paola Marongiu, Filip Ginter, Jenna Kanerva, Simonetta Montemagni, Sebastian Schuster, and Maria Simi. 2018. Enhancing universal dependency treebanks: A case study. In *Proceedings of the Second Workshop on Universal Dependencies, UDW@EMNLP 2018, Brussels, Belgium, November 1, 2018*, pages 102–107. Association for Computational Linguistics.

Peng Qi, Yuhao Zhang, Yuhui Zhang, Jason Bolton, and Christopher D. Manning. 2020. Stanza: A python natural language processing toolkit for many human languages. *ArXiv*, abs/2003.07082.

Maria Simi and Simonetta Montemagni. 2018. Bootstrapping Enhanced Universal Dependencies for Italian. In *Proceedings of the Fifth Italian Conference on Computational Linguistics CLiC-it 2018, 10-12 December 2018, Torino*, pages 348–353. Torino: Accademia University Press.

Milan Straka and Jana Straková. 2017. Tokenizing, POS tagging, lemmatizing and parsing UD 2.0 with UDPipe. In *Proceedings of the CoNLL 2017 Shared Task: Multilingual Parsing from Raw Text to Universal Dependencies*, pages 88–99, Vancouver, Canada. Association for Computational Linguistics.

Daniel Zeman, Jan Hajič, Martin Popel, Martin Potthast, Milan Straka, Filip Ginter, Joakim Nivre, and Slav Petrov. 2018. CoNLL 2018 shared task: Multilingual parsing from raw text to universal dependencies. In *Proceedings of the CoNLL 2018 Shared Task: Multilingual Parsing from Raw Text to Universal Dependencies*, pages 1–21, Brussels, Belgium. Association for Computational Linguistics.

Y. Zhang. 2019. A pytorch implementation of "deep biaffine attention for neural dependency parsing".

Junru Zhou and Hai Zhao. 2019. Head-driven phrase structure grammar parsing on Penn treebank. In *Proceedings of the 57th Annual Meeting of the Association for Computational Linguistics*, pages 2396–2408, Florence, Italy. Association for Computational Linguistics.

	UniPI run comb5					University of Turku				
Language	**UAS**	**LAS**	**CLAS**	**MLA**	**BLEX**	**UAS**	**LAS**	**CLAS**	**MLA**	**BLEX**
Arabic	77.14	72.97	69.41	58.22	64.31	85.36	81.17	78.81	72.15	75.60
Bulgarian	93.72	90.73	87.72	81.10	80.36	95.07	92.48	89.94	85.96	87.85
Czech	92.89	90.79	89.35	77.26	86.53	92.94	90.83	89.39	81.25	87.53
Dutch	89.54	86.71	81.57	70.29	74.92	90.02	87.20	82.33	75.95	78.84
English	89.09	86.70	84.14	74.93	79.56	91.13	88.97	87.15	81.45	84.71
Estonian	83.64	80.18	78.88	53.55	53.20	88.62	85.86	84.61	79.01	81.40
Finnish	89.54	86.99	85.20	76.87	70.86	93.96	92.50	91.65	87.11	87.60
French	91.54	87.40	83.09	45.72	78.86	91.26	87.85	82.94	70.36	80.07
Italian	94.47	92.66	89.04	84.09	85.08	94.71	93.31	90.34	86.91	88.45
Latvian	88.01	84.54	82.10	68.75	75.16	91.38	88.53	86.64	77.43	82.86
Lithuanian	80.58	74.88	72.03	53.17	61.65	85.49	81.85	79.88	66.23	74.04
Polish	93.42	90.66	88.79	66.76	83.48	94.38	91.82	90.36	77.36	88.11
Russian	93.86	92.45	91.23	71.35	87.30	94.06	92.74	91.84	88.10	89.97
Slovak	92.65	90.43	88.85	63.80	72.74	93.40	91.57	90.60	77.76	86.76
Swedish	88.16	85.18	83.45	51.43	70.60	90.81	88.31	87.29	71.65	80.37
Tamil	68.10	61.32	58.46	51.39	53.86	64.47	59.66	57.72	47.18	53.84
Ukrainian	90.38	87.71	85.23	65.59	77.67	91.65	89.68	87.41	76.92	84.81
Average	**88.04**	**84.84**	**82.27**	**65.55**	**73.89**	**89.92**	**87.31**	**85.23**	**76.63**	**81.93**

Table 7: Unofficial results on parsing: on the left our submission, on the right the best submission.

Language	**UAS**	**LAS**	**CLAS**	**MLAS**	**BLEX**	**EULAS**	**ELAS**
Arabic	0.68	1.49	2.00	0.96	1.61	1.49	0.95
Bulgarian	2.06	2.47	2.90	1.99	2.38	2.44	2.41
Czech	0.94	1.15	1.36	1.05	1.28	1.10	0.93
Dutch	5.11	6.18	8.15	5.21	7.17	6.08	5.92
English	0.87	1.60	1.93	1.19	1.77	1.61	1.72
Estonian	13.07	17.00	18.84	6.86	10.41	16.72	14.50
Finnish	4.37	5.74	6.41	4.34	4.53	5.60	4.97
French	3.45	4.82	7.72	3.91	6.93	4.89	4.58
Italian	1.43	1.97	2.47	1.54	2.04	2.04	2.09
Latvian	2.54	3.29	3.85	2.28	3.14	3.22	2.53
Lithuanian	3.59	4.12	4.55	1.42	3.25	4.03	3.83
Polish	2.45	3.13	3.55	1.84	3.22	3.14	2.48
Russian	1.42	1.93	2.03	1.40	1.85	1.90	1.52
Slovak	1.41	1.48	1.83	0.81	0.79	1.46	0.97
Swedish	3.36	4.26	4.82	2.34	3.83	4.20	4.42
Tamil	5.31	6.63	6.84	8.89	8.57	6.53	5.53
Ukrainian	1.42	2.48	3.07	1.81	2.78	2.31	2.37
Average	**3.14**	**4.10**	**4.85**	**2.82**	**3.86**	**4.04**	**3.63**

Table 8: Improvements by parser combination on unofficial run.

Enhanced Universal Dependency Parsing with Second-Order Inference and Mixture of Training Data

Xinyu Wang[◇], Yong Jiang[†], Kewei Tu[◇]
◇School of Information Science and Technology, ShanghaiTech University
Shanghai Engineering Research Center of Intelligent Vision and Imaging
†DAMO Academy, Alibaba Group
{wangxy1,tukw}@shanghaitech.edu.cn
yongjiang.jy@alibaba-inc.com

Abstract

This paper presents the system used in our submission to the *IWPT 2020 Shared Task*. Our system is a graph-based parser with second-order inference. For the low-resource Tamil corpus, we specially mixed the training data of Tamil with other languages and significantly improved the performance of Tamil. Due to our misunderstanding of the submission requirements, we submitted graphs that are not connected, which makes our system only rank **6th** over 10 teams. However, after we fixed this problem, our system is 0.6 ELAS higher than the team that ranked **1st** in the official results.

1 Introduction

Based on the Universal Dependencies (UD) (Nivre et al., 2016), the Enhanced Universal Dependencies (EUD) (Bouma et al., 2020)[1] are non-tree graphs with reentrancies, cycles, and empty nodes to deal with the problem that purely rooted trees cannot adequately represent grammatical relations. We found that we can reduce parsing such a graph to parsing bi-lexical structures like semantic dependency parsing (SDP) (Oepen et al., 2015) by reducing reentrancies and empty nodes into new labels. (Wang et al., 2019) is a state-of-the-art approach for the semantic dependency parsing tasks that use second-order inference methods with Mean-Field Variational Inference. We adopt their approach for decoding and encode the sentences with strong pretrained token representations: XLMR (Conneau et al., 2019), Flair (Akbik et al., 2018) and Fast-Text (Bojanowski et al., 2017). Among the datasets, the Tamil language only contains 400 labeled sentences for training, which makes the performance of the model for Tamil low. To further improve

the performance for the low resource language, we propose a new approach that we train the Tamil model with a mixture of datasets with Tamil and a rich resource language. Empirical results show that such an approach can improve 2.44 ELAS on the test set of Tamil. Due to our misconceptions on the submission format, we submitted invalid unconnected graphs to the submission site. Thanks to the help of the organizers, they fixed these graphs with simple scripts, and our system is ranked **6th** over 10 teams in the official results. However, the submitted graphs can be easily connected if we apply tree algorithms in the decoding. In the post-evaluation, we submitted our system outputs again and found that our system is 0.56 ELAS higher than the team ranked **1st** in the official results.

2 System Description

2.1 Data Pre-processing

There are two features in the EUD graphs that do not appear in SDP graphs. One is the reentrancies of the same head and dependent on different labels. We combined these arcs into one and concatenate the labels of these arcs with a symbol '+' representing the combination of two arcs. In the post-processing, we split arcs with the '+' symbol in the corresponding labels into multiple arcs. Another one is the empty nodes that are introduced in the shared task (for example, nodes with id 1.1). We used the official script to collapse graphs through reducing such empty nodes into non-empty nodes and introducing new dependency labels[2]. In the post-process, we add empty nodes according to the dependency labels. As the official evaluation only score the collapsed graphs, such a process does not impact the system performance.

---

[1]https://universaldependencies.org/u/overview/enhanced-syntax.html

[2]For more details, please refer to https://universaldependencies.org/iwpt20/task_and_evaluation.html

215

Proceedings of the 16th International Conference on Parsing Technologies and the IWPT 2020 Shared Task, pages 215–220
Virtual Meeting, July 9, 2020. ©2020 Association for Computational Linguistics

2.2 Approach

We follow the approach of Wang et al. (2019)[3] to build our system which uses the second-order inference algorithm for the arc predictions. Given a sentence with n words $\mathbf{w} = [w_1, w_2, ..., w_n]$, we feed a three-layer BiLSTM with their corresponding token representations.

$$\mathbf{R} = \text{BiLSTM}(\mathbf{E})$$

where $\mathbf{E} = [\mathbf{e}_1, \ldots, \mathbf{e}_n]$ is the concatenation of various embeddings of token (We use different combination of XLMR, Flair and FastText for each language as the token representation.) and $\mathbf{R} = [\mathbf{r}_1, \ldots, \mathbf{r}_n]$ represents the output from the BiLSTM. For the arc predictions, we use the feed-forward network, Biaffine and Trilinear functions to encode unary potentials ψ_u and binary potentials ψ_b:

$$\psi_u(w_i, w_j) = \text{FNN\_Biaffine}^{(\text{arc})}(\mathbf{r}_i, \mathbf{r}_j)$$
$$\psi_b(w_i, w_j, w_k) = \text{FNN\_Trilinear}(\mathbf{r}_i, \mathbf{r}_j, \mathbf{r}_k)$$

where FNN_Biaffine and FNN_Trilinear represent a combination of FNN and Biaffine/Trilinear functions. Then we feed these potentials into a Mean-Field Variational Inference network for the second-order inference.

$$P(\mathbf{Y}|\mathbf{w}) = \text{MFVI}(\psi_u, \psi_p)$$

where $P(\mathbf{Y}|\mathbf{w})$ is a probability matrix representing the probabilities of all potential arcs. We first use tree algorithms like the Eisner's (Eisner, 2000) or MST (McDonald et al., 2005) algorithms to ensure the connectivity of the graph. Then we additionally add arcs for the positions that $P(\mathbf{Y}|\mathbf{w}) > 0.5$. For the label predictions, we use the FNN_Biaffine to score the labels for each potential arc.

$$\mathbf{s}_{ij}^{(\text{label})} = \text{FNN\_Biaffine}^{(\text{label})}(\mathbf{r}_i, \mathbf{r}_j)$$
$$P^{(\text{label})}(y_{ij}|\mathbf{w}) = \text{softmax}(\mathbf{s}_{ij}^{(\text{label})})$$

We select the label with the highest score of each potential arc.

To train the system, we follow the approach of Wang et al. (2019) with the cross entropy loss:

$$\mathcal{L}^{(\text{arc})}(\theta) = -\sum_{i,j} \log(P_\theta(y_{ij}^{\star(\text{arc})}|\mathbf{w}))$$
$$\mathcal{L}^{(\text{label})}(\theta) = -\sum_{i,j} \mathbb{1}(y_{ij}^{\star(\text{arc})}) \log(P_\theta(y_{ij}^{\star(\text{label})}|\mathbf{w}))$$

[3] https://github.com/wangxinyu0922/Second_Order_SDP

where θ is the parameters of our system, $\mathbb{1}(y_{ij}^{\star(\text{arc})})$ denotes the indicator function and equals 1 when edge (i, j) exists in the gold parse and 0 otherwise, and i, j ranges over all the tokens $\mathbf{w}$ in the sentence. The two losses are combined by a weighted average.

$$\mathcal{L} = \lambda\mathcal{L}^{(\text{label})} + (1 - \lambda)\mathcal{L}^{(\text{arc})}$$

2.3 Mixture of Datasets for Tamil Parser Training

Tamil dataset has the fewest training and development sentences over all languages, which contains 400 sentences for training and 80 sentences for development. Therefore we believe that Tamil parser can be easily improved if we use more training data. With the emergence of multilingual contextual embeddings like multilingual BERT (Devlin et al., 2019) and XLMR, training a unified multilingual model with high performances over all languages becomes possible through mixing the training data of multiple languages. However, it does not apply to the shared task as the label set of EUD is distinct in different languages. The arc annotations in the dataset are still helpful for training the Tamil parser. Thus we removed the label annotations in the dataset of other languages so that the label loss of these data cannot be back-propagated. Then we mixed one of the languages with the fully annotated Tamil dataset. To solve the problem of data imbalance in the mixture of the dataset in training, we upsampled the Tamil training set to keep the same data size as that of the other language.

3 Settings and Results

3.1 Experimental Settings

In training, we split the official development set into halves as the development set and test set. We used the development set to select the model based on labeled F1 score which is the metric used in the SDP task and it evaluates the accuracy of predicted labeled arcs. We used the test set to choose the best model architecture. We use a batch size of 2000 tokens with the Adam (Kingma and Ba, 2015) optimizer. The hyper-parameters of our system are shown in Table 1, which are mostly adopted from previous work on dependency parsing. We only use the tokenized words as the model input. For the Tamil Parser, we tried English or Czech datasets to mix with the Tamil dataset. For most of languages, we used freezed XLMR embedding

Hidden Layer	Hidden Sizes
BiLSTM LSTM	3*400
Unary Arc/Label	500
Binary Arc	150
Embedding/LSTM Dropouts	33%
Loss Interpolation (λ)	0.10
Adam β_1	0.9
Adam β_2	0.9
Learning rate	$2e^{-3}$
LR decay	0.5

Table 1: Hyper-parameters for our system.

only as we found that the Flair embeddings and FastText embeddings were not helpful for the task except Tamil. We used a concatenate of XLMR, Flair and FastText embeddings for Tamil parser training. For the sentence and word segmentation, we used Stanza (Qi et al., 2020) models that were trained on treebank with the largest training set for all languages except Lithuanian, because the model trained on the Lithuanian-HSE treebank has an extremely low segmentation performance compared with the model trained on Lithuanian-ALKSNIS.

3.2 Main Results

Table 2 shows the results of official evaluations of all teams, as well as the post-evaluations of our system. In the Official submission, we trained the Tamil Parser with a mixture of English and Tamil datasets ('Ours+en+MST' in the table), and in the post-evaluation, we also tried a mixture of Czech and Tamil datasets ('Ours+cs+MST' in the table) because the Czech dataset contains the largest training data over all languages. In the official results, our system was fixed by the organizers through their simple scripts for the connectivity of graphs, which significantly reduced our system performance. In the post-evaluation, we fixed this issue with MST or Eisner's algorithm and showed that our system performs 0.6 ELAS higher than the best team. For the Tamil parser, mixing the Tamil dataset with the Czech dataset performs 1.7 ELAS better than mixing with the English dataset, which shows that a larger dataset gives better results than the smaller one. Our system with the MST algorithm is 0.2 ELAS stronger than the system with Eisner's algorithm, which shows that the non-projective tree algorithm (MST) is better than the projective tree algorithm (Eisner's) for the EUD task. We built our codes based on PyTorch (Paszke

et al., 2019), and ran our experiments on a single Tesla V100 GPU.

3.3 Comparison of First-Order and Second-Order Inference

Table 3 shows a performance comparison between two kinds of embedding choices, XLMR+Flair+FastText and XLMR, and first-order and second-order inference. The results show that second-order inference is stronger than first-order inference in all languages, and embeddings with XLMR embedding only usually perform better than XLMR+Flair+FastText embeddings. However, the Flair+FastText embedding is helpful for Tamil. Therefore we use XLMR+Flair+FastText embeddings for training the Tamil parser while we use XLMR embedding only for other languages.

3.4 Performance Comparison between Connected Graphs and Non-Connected Graphs

Before the deadline of the shared task, the submission site showed the scores of each treebank separately even the submission graphs were not connected, which unfortunately made us believe that the non-connected graphs are also acceptable for the task. In fact, these graphs are not acceptable and the organizers fixed the issue with some simple scripts, and this results in a significant reduction in the final scores. In section 3.2, we show that appending a tree-parsing algorithm to our system produces connected graphs with high scores. Here we also evaluate the non-connected graphs produced by our original system. We think evaluating non-connected graphs is informative for two reasons. The first is that these results help to understand how different the connected graphs and non-connected graphs performs. The second is that in practice, non-connected graphs can be predicted with a relatively faster speed as the MST and Eisner's algorithms are slow while we can get the non-connected graphs through argmax operations. We compare the performance of connected and non-connected graphs for each treebank and each language in Table 4 and 5. The results show that the non-connected graphs perform slightly better than graphs with the tree algorithms. Therefore generating non-connected trees are more practical in practice if there are no such constraints.

Team Name	ar	bg	cs	nl	en	et	fi	fr	it	lv	lt	pl	ru	sl	sv	ta	uk	Avg.
								Official										
RobertNLP	0.0	0.0	0.0	0.0	**88.9**	0.0	0.0	0.0	0.0	0.0	0.0	0.0	0.0	0.0	0.0	0.0	0.0	5.2
Koebsala	60.8	68.9	61.1	62.9	65.4	59.1	67.5	67.9	69.1	64.8	56.3	61.3	64.2	64.1	64.5	47.4	64.2	62.9
ADAPT	57.2	77.3	66.4	67.7	70.4	61.1	72.4	74.7	72.0	72.4	58.4	65.9	75.3	68.4	68.4	48.5	66.4	67.2
clasp	51.3	84.9	67.1	78.9	82.9	60.4	66.0	72.8	87.1	66.0	52.6	71.2	70.4	65.2	71.4	42.2	63.2	67.9
Ours	63.4	78.7	75.4	70.9	72.3	74.9	76.0	77.0	73.1	77.8	66.9	71.0	78.3	73.1	69.6	48.2	73.0	71.7
Unipi	57.8	84.9	76.0	77.6	84.0	57.2	72.1	78.9	89.1	68.2	61.1	70.6	76.9	81.4	78.7	48.5	73.9	72.8
FASTPARSE	66.9	84.9	77.2	77.4	78.5	74.1	75.7	77.8	84.8	75.6	61.4	74.5	80.4	73.5	75.2	47.0	74.0	74.0
EmoryNLP	67.3	88.2	85.5	80.7	85.3	81.4	83.0	**86.2**	88.5	79.2	66.1	82.4	88.6	82.7	78.2	54.3	79.7	79.8
OrangeDeskin	71.0	89.4	87.0	85.1	85.2	81.0	86.2	83.6	90.8	82.1	75.9	80.4	89.8	84.4	83.3	**64.2**	84.6	82.6
TurkuNLP	**77.8**	90.7	87.5	84.7	87.2	84.5	**89.5**	85.9	91.5	84.9	77.6	**84.6**	90.7	**88.6**	**85.6**	57.8	87.2	84.5
								Post-Evaluation										
Ours+en+MST	77.7	91.5	90.1	86.2	87.1	86.0	89.0	85.3	91.5	87.6	78.9	84.0	92.3	87.6	84.7	56.7	88.0	85.0
Ours+cs+Eis	77.8	91.1	89.5	86.3	87.2	85.7	88.5	85.3	**91.5**	87.3	78.6	83.7	92.3	87.1	84.8	58.4	88.0	84.9
Ours+cs+MST	77.7	**91.5**	**90.1**	**86.2**	87.1	**86.0**	89.0	85.3	91.5	**87.6**	**78.9**	84.0	**92.3**	87.6	84.7	58.4	**88.0**	**85.1**

Table 2: Official evaluations of all systems and post-evaluations of our team in ELAS. We use the ISO 639-1 language code to represent each language. MST and Eis means the MST and Eisner's algorithm that we used for decoding. 'en' and 'cs' represents which dataset we mixed with the Tamil dataset for training the Tamil parser. Note that 'Ours+en+MST' represent the parsed results of parsers that we used in the Official submission.

Approach	ar	bg	cs	nl	en	et	fi	fr	it
XLMR+Flair+FastText+1st-Order	81.66	89.29	91.04	92.55	89.74	88.33	89.40	90.64	91.94
XLMR+Flair+FastText+2nd-Order	81.98	89.43	**91.39**	**92.68**	89.58	**88.69**	89.54	91.08	**91.98**
XLMR+1st-Order	82.02	90.15	90.80	92.43	90.05	88.13	89.51	91.14	91.96
XLMR+2nd-Order	**82.42**	**90.37**	91.21	92.66	**90.26**	88.60	90.35	**91.69**	**91.98**

Approach	lv	lt	pl	ru	sk	sv	ta	uk	Avg.
XLMR+Flair+FastText+1st-Order	88.21	80.21	86.91	92.88	87.28	85.52	66.17	88.26	89.40
XLMR+Flair+FastText+2nd-Order	88.59	81.25	86.46	**93.28**	87.18	85.63	**68.76**	88.04	89.59
XLMR+1st-Order	89.62	81.92	85.73	92.86	88.48	86.36	63.28	88.96	89.57
XLMR+2nd-Order	**89.97**	**83.24**	**87.49**	93.21	**89.07**	**86.85**	64.84	**89.99**	**89.95**

Table 3: A comparison of different word embedding concatenation and first-order and second-order inference approaches on the development set split by ourselves. We report Labeled F1 score (LF1) here.

Graph	ar-PADT	bg-BTB	cs-FicTree	cs-CAC	cs-PDT	cs-PUD	nl-Alpino	nl-LassySmall
Non-Connected	77.74	**91.50**	**90.60**	90.55	**90.65**	**84.26**	**90.11**	82.55
MST	77.73	91.48	90.51	**90.59**	90.63	84.25	90.09	82.51
CRF	**77.75**	91.07	89.85	90.02	90.05	83.70	89.69	**83.10**

Graph	en-EWT	en-PUD	et-EDT	et-EWT	fi-TDT	fi-PUD	fr-Sequoia	fr-FQB
Non-Connected	86.33	**88.05**	**87.36**	**79.62**	**90.00**	87.52	89.67	84.11
MST	86.30	**88.05**	87.34	79.61	89.97	**87.52**	89.66	84.09
CRF	**86.40**	88.04	87.07	79.42	89.44	86.97	**89.73**	**84.12**

Graph	it-ISDT	lv-LVTB	lt-ALKSNIS	pl-LFG	pl-PDB	pl-PUD	ru-SynTagRus	sl-SNK
Non-Connected	91.50	**87.69**	78.97	**87.65**	**83.23**	**82.96**	**92.62**	**87.56**
MST	91.49	87.64	**78.94**	**87.65**	83.21	82.95	92.31	87.55
CRF	**91.52**	87.29	78.63	87.59	82.90	82.57	92.31	87.14

Graph	sv-Talbanken	sv-PUD	ta-TTB	uk-IU	Average			
Non-Connective	88.35	**80.88**	56.51	88.00	**85.59**			
MST	88.33	80.87	56.56	**88.02**	85.57			
CRF	**88.37**	80.87	**56.71**	88.02	85.37			

Table 4: A performance comparison in ELAS between non-connected graphs and connected graphs over each treebank on the official test sets.

3.5 Analysis of Mixture of Training Data

For a more in-depth comparison of how the combination of different language datasets affects the performance of the Tamil Parser, Table 6 shows that more training data significantly improve the performance of the parser. We leave for future work other language combinations as well as similar studies of other parsers.

Team Name	ar	bg	cs	nl	en	et	fi	fr	it
TurkuNLP	**77.82**	90.73	87.51	84.73	**87.15**	84.54	**89.49**	**85.90**	**91.54**
Ours+en+MST	77.74	91.48	90.09	86.19	87.10	85.97	88.99	85.28	91.49
Ours+en	77.75	**91.50**	**90.11**	**86.22**	87.12	**85.99**	89.01	85.29	91.50

Team Name	lv	lt	pl	ru	sl	sv	ta	uk	Avg.
TurkuNLP	84.94	77.64	**84.64**	90.69	**88.56**	**85.64**	**57.83**	87.22	84.50
Ours+en+MST	87.64	78.94	84.00	92.31	87.55	84.74	56.71	**88.02**	84.96
Ours+en	**87.69**	**78.97**	84.01	**92.62**	87.56	84.75	56.52	88.00	**84.98**

Table 5: A performance comparison in ELAS between non-connected graphs, connected graphs with the MST algorithm and the best system in the official results over each language. Ours+en represents our official submission and evaluated with official evaluation script.

Combination	# Training Sentences	ELAS
Tamil	400	55.39
English+Tamil	12543+12400	56.56
Czech+Tamil	102131+102000	**58.44**

Table 6: A comparison between different dataset combinations for the Tamil parser training. The 12000 and 102000 in the **# Training Sentences** column represents the upsampled value of 400 labeled sentences in Tamil dataset.

4 Conclusion

Our system is a parser with strong contextual embeddings and second-order inference. For the low-resource language, we propose to train the model with a mixture of datasets. Empirical results show that the second-order inference is stronger than the first-order one, and mixing data improves the performance of parser significantly for the low-resource language. After we fix the graph connectivity issue, our system outperforms the system ranked **1st** by 0.56 ELAS in the official results. We also show that the non-connected graphs are practically useful for its higher performance and faster speed. Our code is available at `https://github.com/Alibaba-NLP/MultilangStructureKD`.

References

Alan Akbik, Duncan Blythe, and Roland Vollgraf. 2018. Contextual string embeddings for sequence labeling. In *Proceedings of the 27th International Conference on Computational Linguistics*, pages 1638–1649, Santa Fe, New Mexico, USA. Association for Computational Linguistics.

Piotr Bojanowski, Edouard Grave, Armand Joulin, and Tomas Mikolov. 2017. Enriching word vectors with subword information. *Transactions of the Association for Computational Linguistics*, 5:135–146.

Gosse Bouma, Djamé Seddah, and Daniel Zeman. 2020. Overview of the IWPT 2020 Shared Task on Parsing into Enhanced Universal Dependencies. In *Proceedings of the 16th International Conference on Parsing Technologies and the IWPT 2020 Shared Task on Parsing into Enhanced Universal Dependencies*, Seattle, US. Association for Computational Linguistics.

Alexis Conneau, Kartikay Khandelwal, Naman Goyal, Vishrav Chaudhary, Guillaume Wenzek, Francisco Guzmán, Edouard Grave, Myle Ott, Luke Zettlemoyer, and Veselin Stoyanov. 2019. Unsupervised cross-lingual representation learning at scale. *arXiv preprint arXiv:1911.02116*.

Jacob Devlin, Ming-Wei Chang, Kenton Lee, and Kristina Toutanova. 2019. BERT: Pre-training of deep bidirectional transformers for language understanding. In *Proceedings of the 2019 Conference of the North American Chapter of the Association for Computational Linguistics: Human Language Technologies, Volume 1 (Long and Short Papers)*, pages 4171–4186, Minneapolis, Minnesota. Association for Computational Linguistics.

Jason Eisner. 2000. Bilexical grammars and their cubic-time parsing algorithms. In *Advances in probabilistic and other parsing technologies*, pages 29–61. Springer.

Diederik P Kingma and Jimmy Ba. 2015. Adam: A method for stochastic optimization. In *International Conference on Learning Representations*.

Ryan McDonald, Koby Crammer, and Fernando Pereira. 2005. Online large-margin training of dependency parsers. In *Proceedings of the 43rd Annual Meeting of the Association for Computational Linguistics (ACL'05)*, pages 91–98.

Joakim Nivre, Marie-Catherine de Marneffe, Filip Ginter, Yoav Goldberg, Jan Hajič, Christopher D. Manning, Ryan McDonald, Slav Petrov, Sampo Pyysalo, Natalia Silveira, Reut Tsarfaty, and Daniel Zeman.

2016. Universal dependencies v1: A multilingual treebank collection. In *Proceedings of the Tenth International Conference on Language Resources and Evaluation (LREC 2016)*, pages 1659–1666, Portorož, Slovenia. European Language Resources Association (ELRA).

Stephan Oepen, Marco Kuhlmann, Yusuke Miyao, Daniel Zeman, Silvie Cinková, Dan Flickinger, Jan Hajic, and Zdenka Uresova. 2015. Semeval 2015 task 18: Broad-coverage semantic dependency parsing. In *Proceedings of the 9th International Workshop on Semantic Evaluation (SemEval 2015)*, pages 915–926.

Adam Paszke, Sam Gross, Francisco Massa, Adam Lerer, James Bradbury, Gregory Chanan, Trevor Killeen, Zeming Lin, Natalia Gimelshein, Luca Antiga, et al. 2019. Pytorch: An imperative style, high-performance deep learning library. In *Advances in Neural Information Processing Systems*, pages 8024–8035.

Peng Qi, Yuhao Zhang, Yuhui Zhang, Jason Bolton, and Christopher D Manning. 2020. Stanza: A python natural language processing toolkit for many human languages. *arXiv preprint arXiv:2003.07082*.

Xinyu Wang, Jingxian Huang, and Kewei Tu. 2019. Second-order semantic dependency parsing with end-to-end neural networks. In *Proceedings of the 57th Annual Meeting of the Association for Computational Linguistics*, pages 4609–4618, Florence, Italy. Association for Computational Linguistics.

How much of enhanced UD is contained in UD?

Adam Ek   **Jean Philippe Bernardy**
Centre for Linguistic Theory and Studies in Probability
Department of Philosophy, Linguistics and Theory of Science
University of Gothenburg
{adam.ek, jean-philippe.bernardy}@gu.se

Abstract

In this paper, we present the submission of team CLASP to the IWPT 2020 Shared Task on parsing enhanced universal dependencies (Bouma et al., 2020). We develop a tree-to-graph transformation algorithm based on dependency patterns. This algorithm can transform gold UD trees to EUD graphs with an ELAS score of 81.55 and a EULAS score of 96.70. These results show that much of the information needed to construct EUD graphs from UD trees are present in the UD trees. Coupled with a standard UD parser, the method applies to the official test data and yields and ELAS score of 67.85 and a EULAS score is 80.18.

1 Introduction

Universal Dependencies (UD) is a syntactic annotation schema focusing on representing shallow syntactic dependencies between *words*. One of the goals of UD has been to use it in semantic downstream tasks, such as event extraction (Fares et al., 2018; McClosky et al., 2011) or negation resolution (Fares et al., 2018) among others. In general, UD can be used as a shallow representation of argument structures, which are useful in a wide array of semantic tasks.

However, the UD format restricts the shape of dependencies to a tree structure. This can be limiting because semantics dependencies can in principle exhibit any graph structure. To remedy this situation, the Enhanced Universal Dependencies (EUD) schema was proposed (Schuster and Manning, 2016). The goal of the schema is to make certain implicit dependencies explicit, such as conjoined subjects and objects. The enhanced dependencies include additional edges between words, as well as augmented labels. For example in enhanced dependencies, the conjunction relation also include what type of conjunction is used, e.g. *and, or, but* and so on.

In this paper, we present our submission for the IWPT 2020 Shared Task on parsing enhanced universal dependencies from annotated UD treebanks. The task target treebanks from 17 different languages where the majority of the languages are Indo-European with five notable exceptions, Tamil (Dravidian), Arabic (Semitic), Finnish and Estonian (Uralic). The goal of the task to produce valid EUD graphs, given raw text as input.

In this context, this paper proposes to test the following hypothesis:

(H1) Most of the information provided by the EUD schema is contained in the basic UD schema.

That is, if (H1) holds, then it is possible to map, algorithmically, UD trees to EUD graphs.

Thus, we set out to implement such an algorithm. Concretely, we construct a tree-to-graph transformation, which recognizes patterns in the (basic) universal dependencies to derive enhanced dependencies.

This experiment provides a *lower bound* on the amount of EUD information which can be extracted from raw UD information, for representative inputs. In other words, we measure how much of EUD is contained in UD. This becomes a lower bound, because a better algorithm can always be conceived, and do better.

Conversely, additionally, by running our algorithm after a state-of-the-art basic UD parser, we will provide a baseline for the EUD reconstruction task.

The enhanced dependency parsing is evaluated using two metrics, ELAS and EULAS. ELAS calculate the F_1-score over both enhanced arcs and labels (for example: "and" in the label "conj:and"). EULAS on the other hand disregard label enhancements and calculate the F_1-score over the enhanced

Proceedings of the 16th International Conference on Parsing Technologies and the IWPT 2020 Shared Task, pages 221–226
Virtual Meeting, July 9, 2020. ©2020 Association for Computational Linguistics

edges. To illustrate, given the gold label "conj:and" and a system prediction of "conj:or" (or "conj", i.e. if nothing is appended to the label), ELAS will count this as an error while EULAS won't.

Our results show that (H1) is vindicated: we achieve an ELAS score of 81.55 and EULAS of 96.70 on human-annotated dependency trees. As a baseline for the shared task, our method is also effective, achieving an ELAS score of 67.85 and a EULAS score of 80.18. (Thus losing about 15 percentage points when going through a machine-generation phase to obtain UD trees.)

2   Method

In essence, our method is to apply, as far as possible, the tree-to-graph recipes provided by Schuster and Manning (2016) to transform basic UD *trees* into EUD graphs.

2.1   Procedure

To obtain basic UD trees for our system we use the universal dependency treebanks provided by the shared task organizers. From these we apply our method on basic UD trees from two sources:

- for each language in the test data we use the Stanford Biaffine Dependency Parser (Dozat and Manning, 2016) provided in Stanza (Qi et al., 2020). We used the stanza model trained on the largest treebank of the language.

- the development and gold trees in the tree-banks, *from which we have removed the enhanced dependencies*. Indeed, the gold data comes with plain UD trees as well.

Thus when using the basic UD trees from the Stanford parser we obtain a baseline for the task, and when using the development/gold trees the *lower bound* on EUD information contained in UD.

Then, we apply a tree-matching procedure against the non-enhanced UD trees. The procedure locally inserts enhanced edges or deletes unwanted edges. Additionally (as a special case) the patterns also re-label some edges.

Our system contains several patterns, which are described in the next subsection. We first apply the patterns that modify the edge labels with case information. Then we apply all the other patterns, which add (and sometimes remove) edges from the basic tree. Here, we only apply the patterns on the (relabeled) input trees and not on the graph of EUD made by any other pattern. In this sense, one can say that patterns are applied in parallel. Once this is done, we convert the result back to the (enhanced) CONLLU format.

2.2   Patterns

Perhaps surprisingly, the patterns that we need to recognize are simple, involving only three nodes. The two patterns to recognize are shown in Fig. 5. Essentially, we need to match on three connected nodes. We need to identify two types of patterns. First, two arcs forming a two-step path (Figs. 5a, 5d and 5e). We refer to this style pattern as "Type 1". Second, with two arcs pointing away from a central node (Figs. 5b and 5c), referred to as "Type 2". In both cases, we have additional constraints on the (edge) labels. Together, the constraints on graph topology and labels form patterns that we can recognize and transform. The exhaustive list of patterns and transformations follows.

1. Type 1 pattern, with a relation label, which can be any of "nsubj","obj", "amod", "ad-vcl","obl", "mark", "nmod", followed by a "conj" label. (Fig. 5a.) In this case we add an edge with the relation label to the other conjunct. A full dependency tree containing this pattern can be found in Fig. 1.

2. Type 2 pattern with a a relation label being either "nsubj" or "aux", and a "conj" label (Fig. 5b). We add a relation label to the other conjunct, but only if the conjunct is not itself "nsubj". Indeed, if it were, then we are conjoining two full sentences and then there is no need for an enhanced dependency. A full dependency tree containing this pattern can be found in Fig. 2.

3. Type 2 pattern with "xcomp" and "nsubj". Here we add an "nsubj:xsubj" edge (Fig. 5c).

4. Type 1 pattern, with "acl:relcl" followed by a relation label which can be either "nsubj","obj","obl", "advmod" (Fig. 5e). The target node should also be a *relative* pronoun, ie. it POS is "PRON" and its XPOS either "WP" (who, whom) or "WDT" (that, which). Indeed, this pattern is also found with other type of pronouns, but then it does not correspond to a relative clause. In this case we add a "ref" edge to the pronoun and a (reverse) relation edge between the first and second node.

The original relation edge is deleted. A full dependency tree containing this pattern can be seen in Fig. 4.

5. Type 1 pattern, with a conjunction followed by a case marking (Fig. 5d). Exhaustively, the type of labels are "case" followed by "obl" or "nmod"; "cc" followed by "conj", "mark" followed by "advcl" or "acl". In this case we enhance the label with the lemma of the target node. This pattern can be seen in Fig. 7.

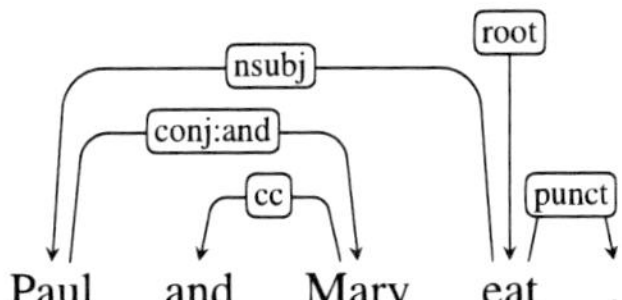

Figure 1: Example sentence for pattern shown in Fig. 5a

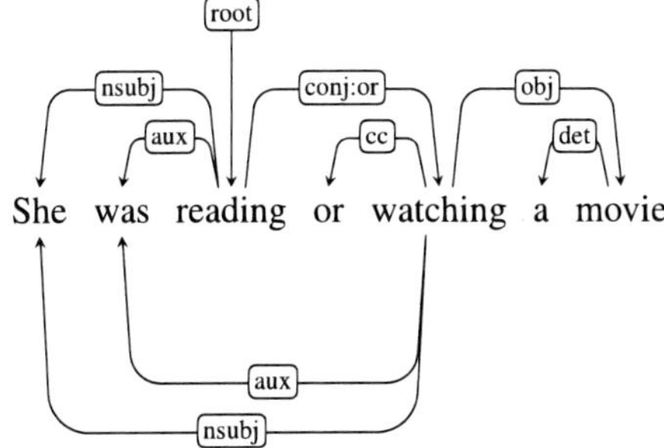

Figure 2: Example sentence for pattern shown in Fig. 5b

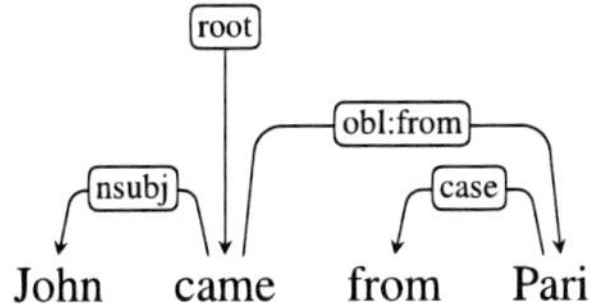

Figure 3: Example sentence for pattern shown in Fig. 5d

2.2.1 Other patterns

For patterns Items 1 and 2, the direction of conjunction dependency could conceptually be inverted, yielding two other patterns (shown in Figs. 6a and 6b). However, we have not implemented these patterns in our system. For the first pattern, the reason is simple: it is not representable as a UD

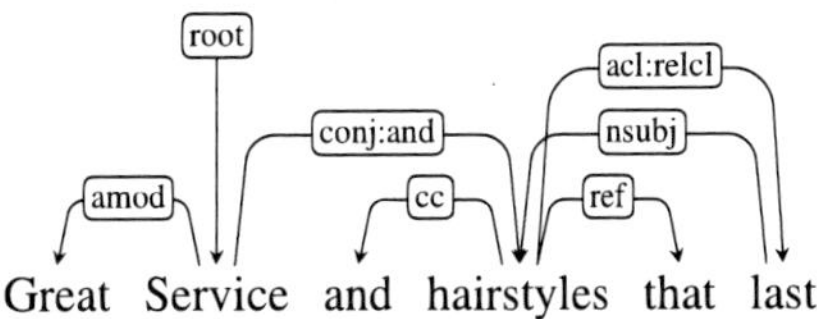

Figure 4: Example sentence for pattern shown in Fig. 5e

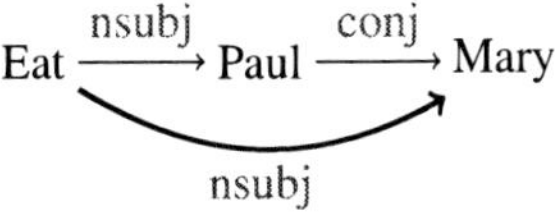

(a) Relation pointing to the conjuncts

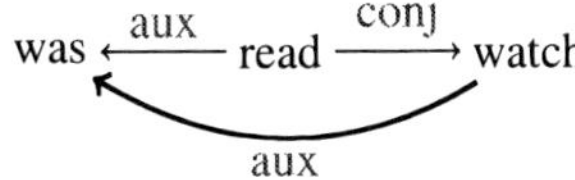

(b) Relation pointing away from the conjuncts.

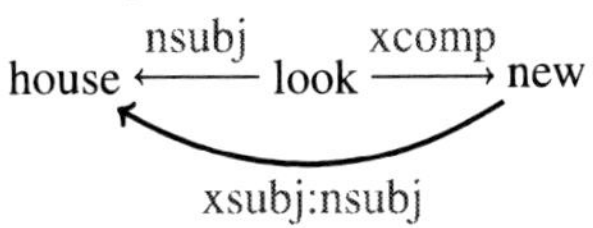

(c) Xcomp special case

from $\xleftarrow{\text{case}}$ Paris $\xrightarrow[\text{obl}]{}$ come

obl:from

(d) Label taken from other word (lemma)

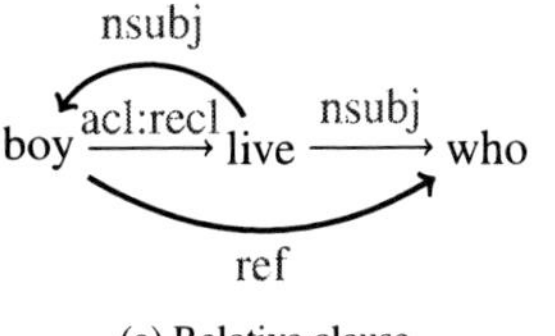

(e) Relative clause

Figure 5: Implemented transformation patterns. Added elements are shown in bold.

tree (a node cannot have two heads). For the second pattern, applying it results in a small loss in performance across the board, and thus it is best left inactive. Aditionally, we have not implemented any pattern for dealing with ellipsis in the current approach. We plan on addressing ellipsis in future work.

3 Results

We present our official results for the shared task in Table 1. The scores are obtained by applying our tree-to-graph transformation to basic dependency trees generated by the Stanford Dependency Parser.

The scoring for unlabeled edges is typically

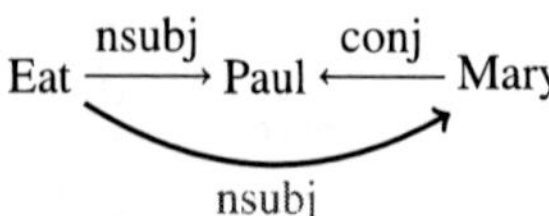

(a) Source pattern not representable in UD format

(b) Transformation pattern leading to a loss in performance

Figure 6: Transformation patterns **not** implemented.

LANG	ELAS	EULAS
ar	51.26	75.62
bg	84.90	87.72
cs	67.13	83.44
en	82.87	83.86
et	60.44	79.43
fi	65.96	83.30
fr	72.76	84.39
it	87.14	88.74
lv	66.01	80.60
nl	78.93	80.20
lt	52.56	67.37
pl	71.22	86.71
ru	70.37	88.02
sk	65.16	83.31
sv	71.35	73.84
ta	42.15	55.32
uk	63.24	81.24
Avg.	**67.85**	**80.18**
Std.	**11.69**	**8.19**

Table 1: Coarse ELAS and EULAS on the languages in the shared task test data.

around 80%. The biggest outlier being Tamil, at 55.32%. The scoring for labeled edges is around 12 points lower, with more variation in scores.

As explained in the introduction, to isolate the accuracy of the tree-to-graph transformation from the performance of the underlying UD parser, we also apply it to the human-annotated dependency trees. We test our approach on both the development and test data. The results from this experiment are shown in Table 2.

The scoring for enhanced edges and unenhanced labels (EULAS) is typically above 95%, with little variation. Tamil is no longer an outlier. The scoring for enhanced edges and labels can be classified into two categories depending on the language. In one

	DEV		TEST	
LANG	ELAS	EULAS	ELAS	EULAS
ar	66.44	96.38	64.14	96.55
bg	94.32	96.95	94.55	97.01
cs	75.65	94.63	76.52	95.12
en	97.57	98.53	97.64	98.65
et	73.35	93.96	72.30	95.53
fi	74.22	95.29	74.40	95.12
fr	83.59	97.93	88.15	99.05
it	96.29	97.61	96.15	97.77
lt	77.50	93.98	72.17	95.49
lv	69.21	96.10	77.47	93.91
nl	96.71	97.55	96.27	97.57
pl	87.03	97.33	80.95	96.49
ru	77.22	96.31	76.72	96.59
sk	72.24	95.82	75.37	96.42
sv	93.85	96.66	94.19	96.67
ta	72.49	99.58	75.04	99.48
uk	75.95	96.04	74.42	96.49
Avg.	**82.97**	**96.53**	**81.55**	**96.70**
Std.	**10.42**	**1.52**	**10.24**	**1.43**

Table 2: Coarse ELAS and EULAS on the gold trees in the development and test data.

category the ELAS is nearly as good as the EULAS case (bg, en, it, nl, sv). Another category scores about 15 points lower (ar, cs, et, fi, lt, lv, ru, sk, ta, uk). French and Polish scores are somewhere in-between.

Comparing Table 1 and Table 2 suggests that the performance of the full pipeline is highly dependent on the underlying parser. In addition to the ELAS and EULAS score being higher, the standard deviation is also much higher for EULAS, 8.19 points in the test versus 1.43 points on the gold data.

To get a further sense on how much our algorithm is sensitive to the quality of the input raw UD trees, we can compare the score that it obtains when fed the gold (raw) UD trees and the trees provided by Stanza for the same text. The results are shown in Table 3.

	Official submission		Stanza trees		Gold trees	
	ELAS	EULAS	ELAS	EULAS	ELAS	EULAS
Avg.	67.85	80.18	66.54	79.91	81.55	96.70

Table 3: Coarse ELAS and EULAS on the test data using our tree-to-graph algorithm on Stanza trees, Stanza trees only and with gold trees.

We find that using our algorithm with stanza trees only marginally increase the performance. Given that we know that our trees are effective for gold trees, this corroborates the suspicion that while having a state-of-the-art performance in dependency parsing, Stanza produces trees that have a significant number of errors for the paths rele-

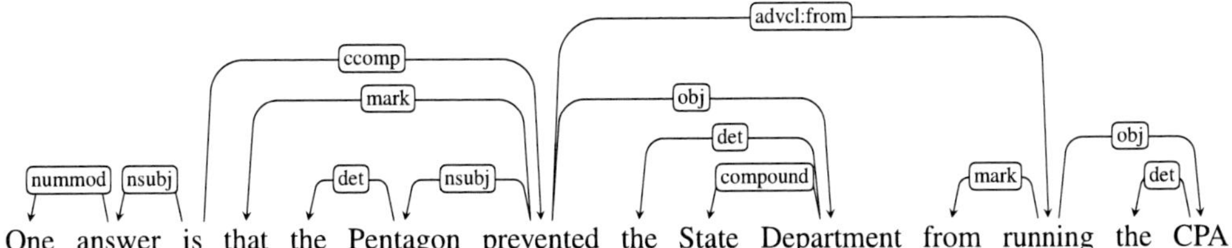

One answer is that the Pentagon prevented the State Department from running the CPA

Figure 7: Example sentence for pattern shown in Fig. 5d

vant to EUD. If the UD trees were of good quality for the parts that are relevant for EUD, we would see a larger increase in performance based on the potential of our algorithm. To some extent, this indicates that when developing a EUD parser, the best approach may be to parse UD and EUD in parallel, and not sequentially. This modus operandi may help the parser to produce fewer UD errors for the parts relevant to EUD.

4 Discussion/Analysis

We can draw the following conclusions from our experiments:

- Our pattern recognizer fails to annotate many enhanced labels for languages where case is expressed by morphological features.

  This is not surprising: we simply did not implement any label rewriting based on such features. (Indeed, the pattern Fig. 5d recognizes case based on a preposition rather than a morphological feature.) This is a shortcoming which we plan to eliminate in future work.

  This shortcoming explains much of the discrepancy between the EULAS and the ELAS scores.

- The performance of the system is heavily dependent on the quality of the UD parser which is used. In other words, our experiments show that, even when using good UD parser, much of the errors are imputable to the UD parser rather than to the algorithmic rewriting step.

- Our tree-to-graph transformation works well on the gold trees, missing less than 4% of the edges, when given gold UD trees as input. Therefore, Broadly speaking, (H1) is vindicated: UD contains most of the information which is necessary to reconstruct EUD graphs.

We note however that (not enhanced) UD is incapable of expressing the difference between the structure of the following two sentences:

(1) She was reading or watching a movie. (Fig. 2)

(2) She was cleaning and eating fruits. (Fig. 8)

In (1) "a movie" is an object of a verb ("watching") which is conjoined with another verb ("reading"), but it applies only to a single verb. In (2), we also have a conjunction between verbs, but "fruits" is the object of both verbs. Yet, the UD structure is the same for both sentences. And thus, our algorithm cannot recognize the difference between the two trees. One solution is to use EUD, but another solution would be to use parse trees, which can make the grouping explicit.

Figuring out which case applies depends on the semantics and pragmatics.

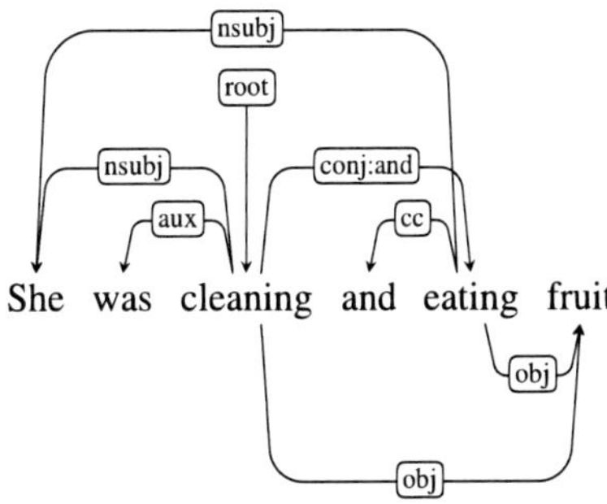

She was cleaning and eating fruit

Figure 8: "She was cleaning and eating fruit"

Even though we have shown that UD contains most information to recover EUD, EUD annotations do have some additional value in certain cases. However, because they have a more rich structure (graph vs. tree), it may be that EUD is more suited as inputs to machine-learning systems. Our systems can help to test this hypothesis by inserting it (or not) in the training pipeline of a state-of-the-art EUD parser. If the EUD parser performs just as well with reconstructed EUD data compared to human-constructed EUD data, then we would know that manual EUD annotations are not necessary. It is likely that we would observe a middle ground situation, where reconstructed EUD data helps, but does not supplant human-constructed EUD. In such a situation, our system can be useful as a bootstrapping tool. (We note however that excellent EUD parsers are not available just yet; in fact they are the purpose of the IWPT task which our system is entering.)

In addition to bootstrapping, a run of our system can provide a baseline for such systems. Indeed, while performing well on gold data, our approach is transparent (only 5 patterns are applied) and efficient, requiring a few seconds to generate enhanced graphs from a treebank.

Future work In addition to the shortcoming about case labeling mentioned above, our system struggles with labels that include multi-word tokens. For example, a valid adverbial clause modifier is *so_that*. Currently our system is not able to identify these. To incorporate this our model would either need to utilize statistical or deep learning methods, or look for children with the "fixed" relation.

Another case that our system is not capable of handling is ellipsis. The problem of ellipsis is difficult, especially in a tree-rewriting approach. We decided not to tackle this problem and instead plan on using a deep learning parser for this task in future work.

Yet our main venue for future work is combining our simple, yet effective method, with deep learning for the problematic cases that are out of reach. These cases include ellipsis, multi-word tokens, objects of conjoined verbs.

Acknowledgments

We would like to thank the reviewers for their helpful comments.The research reported in this paper was supportedby a grant from the Swedish Research Council (VR project 2014-39) for the establishment of the Centre for Linguistic Theory and Studies in Probability (CLASP) at the University of Gothenburg.

References

Gosse Bouma, Djamé Seddah, and Daniel Zeman. 2020. Overview of the IWPT 2020 Shared Task on Parsing into Enhanced Universal Dependencies. In *Proceedings of the 16th International Conference on Parsing Technologies and the IWPT 2020 Shared Task on Parsing into Enhanced Universal Dependencies*, Seattle, US. Association for Computational Linguistics.

Timothy Dozat and Christopher D Manning. 2016. Deep biaffine attention for neural dependency parsing. *arXiv preprint arXiv:1611.01734*.

Murhaf Fares, Stephan Oepen, Lilja Øvrelid, Jari Björne, and Richard Johansson. 2018. The 2018 shared task on extrinsic parser evaluation: on the downstream utility of english universal dependency parsers. In *Proceedings of the CoNLL 2018 Shared Task: Multilingual Parsing from Raw Text to Universal Dependencies*, pages 22–33.

David McClosky, Mihai Surdeanu, and Christopher D Manning. 2011. Event extraction as dependency parsing. In *Proceedings of the 49th Annual Meeting of the Association for Computational Linguistics: Human Language Technologies-Volume 1*, pages 1626–1635. Association for Computational Linguistics.

Peng Qi, Yuhao Zhang, Yuhui Zhang, Jason Bolton, and Christopher D Manning. 2020. Stanza: A python natural language processing toolkit for many human languages. *arXiv preprint arXiv:2003.07082*.

Sebastian Schuster and Christopher D Manning. 2016. Enhanced english universal dependencies: An improved representation for natural language understanding tasks. In *Proceedings of the Tenth International Conference on Language Resources and Evaluation (LREC'16)*, pages 2371–2378.

The ADAPT Enhanced Dependency Parser at the IWPT 2020 Shared Task

James Barry and **Joachim Wagner** and **Jennifer Foster**
ADAPT Centre
School of Computing, Dublin City University, Ireland
`firstname.lastname@adaptcentre.ie`

Abstract

We describe the ADAPT system for the 2020 IWPT Shared Task on parsing enhanced Universal Dependencies in 17 languages. We implement a pipeline approach using UDPipe and UDPipe-future to provide initial levels of annotation. The enhanced dependency graph is either produced by a graph-based semantic dependency parser or is built from the basic tree using a small set of heuristics. Our results show that, for the majority of languages, a semantic dependency parser can be successfully applied to the task of parsing enhanced dependencies.

Unfortunately, we did not ensure a connected graph as part of our pipeline approach and our competition submission relied on a last-minute fix to pass the validation script which harmed our official evaluation scores significantly. Our submission ranked eighth in the official evaluation with a macro-averaged coarse ELAS F1 of 67.23 and a treebank average of 67.49. We later implemented our own graph-connecting fix which resulted in a score of 79.53 (language average) or 79.76 (treebank average), which would have placed fourth in the competition evaluation.

1 Introduction

The 2020 IWPT Shared Task on enhanced dependency parsing (Bouma et al., 2020) requires participants to predict the enhanced dependencies (DEPS column in the CoNLL-U format) in addition to sentence boundaries, tokenisation, lemmata, POS tags, morphological features and the basic dependency tree. We take a pipeline approach using

1. UDPipe for sentence splitting and tokenisation,

2. ensembles of UDPipe-future basic parsers, that also predict lemmata, POS tags and morphological features, with added support for

multi-treebank models (Stymne et al., 2018), and

3. two types of enhancers: *(a)* copying the basic tree and applying a small set of heuristics (baseline system), and *(b)* a graph-based semantic dependency parser (Dozat and Manning, 2018).

To enable reproduction of our results, we make available our helper scripts and modifications of the semantic parser.[1]

Our approach to the task does not guarantee a connected graph – something that we did not account for. Thus, on submission day, we did not have an appropriate solution ready to fix our outputs but were able to provide a valid submission due to some functionality that was added to the `quick-fix` tool provided by the organisers[2] to alter the enhanced graph. The solution was designed primarily to make the files pass validation but in doing so, harms F1-score. In a post-competition run, we addressed the connected graph issue with an alternative solution which increased our macro-averaged ELAS F1-score from 67.23 to 79.53 and the treebank average from 67.49 to 79.76.

2 System Components

2.1 Segmentation

We use UDPipe[3] (Straka and Straková, 2017) with off-the-shelf UD v2.5 models[4] (Straka and Straková, 2019) for the languages of the shared task to split the raw input text into sentences and tokens. In cases where more than one UDPipe model

---

[1]`https://github.com/jbrry/`
`Enhanced-UD-Parsing`
[2]`https://github.com/`
`UniversalDependencies/tools`
[3]`http://ufal.mff.cuni.cz/udpipe`
[4]`http://hdl.handle.net/11234/1-3131`

Proceedings of the 16th International Conference on Parsing Technologies and the IWPT 2020 Shared Task, pages 227–235
Virtual Meeting, July 9, 2020. ©2020 Association for Computational Linguistics

is available for a language, we try all models during development [5] and select for each test language the best overall pipeline according to ELAS on the treebank with the biggest development set for the language.[6]

2.2 Basic Parsing

We choose UDPipe-future (Straka, 2018) for basic parsing and joint prediction of lemmata, POS tags and morphological features so as to not require a separate tagger. We extend UDPipe-future to train multi-treebank models as introduced by (Stymne et al., 2018) with UUParser.[7,8]

Inspired by Straka et al. (2019), we use two types of external word embeddings with UDPipe-future: ELMo contextualised word embeddings (Peters et al., 2018) and FastText character-n-gram-based word embeddings (Bojanowski et al., 2017).[9] For 15 of the 17 test languages, ElmoForManyLangs[10] (Che et al., 2018) provides ELMo models. We train FastText on the raw text provided by the CoNLL'17 shared task for the same 15 languages after shuffling sentences. For the Russian FastText model, we kept getting vectors with large component values even after trying a different machine and a different permutation of sentences, prohibiting effective training of the parser. We then used a model trained on ⅔ of the Russian data for which component values and parser LAS were in the expected range. Furthermore, we train UDPipe-future models using FastText and internal embeddings only.

For Lithuanian and Tamil, we train UDPipe-future without external word embeddings. The parser still uses an internal word embedding covering all words of the training treebank(s) and a word representation obtained with a bidirectional GRU layer over the input characters.

For each target language, we train *(a)* mono-treebank models for each training treebank available with surface strings in UD v2.5, preferring the shared-task version when available, and *(b)* a multi-treebank model for each language using all treebanks for that language for which we also trained mono-treebank models. We train up to seven models with different initialisation for each setting to combine them in ensembles.[11,12] We consider ensembles not just of a single type of model with different initialisation but also combinations of models trained on different treebanks (mono-treebank models) or treebank combinations (multi-treebank models) and in the plain, FastText and ELMo variants.[13] As the number of possible combinations increases exponentially with the number of models, we prune the candidates giving preference to models using all or only one treebank and to models using ELMo. We then test each ensemble on the development data (raw input segmented with UD-Pipe) and pick the best ensembles based on ELAS after applying our heuristic enhancer (Section 2.3) to the basic trees.

To pick the proxy treebank (see description in Footnote 7) for multi-treebank parsing, we use the treebank name in the filename of the raw text during development. However, for final testing, the treebank identifier is unavailable (and if it had been available there would have been cases where

---

[5] Due to a configuration error, we did not try segmentation with UDPipe models trained on `fi_ftb`, `lt_hse` and `sv_lines` in the official submission.

[6] For Czech, we based our decision on results for `cs_cac` instead of `cs_pdt` as we did not have full results available for `cs_pdt`.

[7] Multi-treebank models supply each token with the source treebank ID as additional input with a separate embedding table. Like Stymne et al. (2018), we use a vector size of 12. At test time, a proxy treebank must be chosen when the input sentence does not come from one of the training treebanks or the source is unknown.

[8] `https://github.com/jowagner/UDPipe-Future/tree/multitreebank`

[9] The FastText word embedding is restricted to a fixed vocabulary of one million tokens, not taking advantage of FastText's ability to produce new vectors for OOVs. UDPipe-future does not fine-tune these word embeddings. Instead, the parser trains an additional embedding exclusively for training words and a character-based representation. The latter two are added and the result is concatenated with the two externally provided representations. As far as we understand the code, an all-zero vector is used for OOVs, i. e. words not in the selected one-million-word FastText vocabulary.

[10] `https://github.com/HIT-SCIR/ELMoForManyLangs`

[11] We trained 68 types of models. We trained seven seeds for 34 of these, five seeds for 30 and three seeds for four. Ensembles sizes three, five and seven are considered, including a combination of $(n+1)/2$ models of one type and $(n-1)/2$ models of another type with $n \in \{3, 5, 7\}$.

[12] We use our implementation `https://github.com/jowagner/ud-combination` of the linear combiner of Attardi and Dell'Orletta (2009).

[13] While predicting on development data to facilitate model selection, we temporarily introduced a bug in our system causing it to use the first initialisation seed for all ensemble members only, effectively falling back to a single model when only one model type is used. We fixed this bug before we switched to making test set predictions and tried to account for it in the model selection but, under time pressure, made some hard to explain ad hoc choices, e. g. we used an ensemble of three models for Czech, two mono-treebank models trained on `cs_cac` and one multi-treebank model, even though we also had test set predictions with an ensemble of seven models with the same mixture of model types available. For details, see the reproducibility notes in our code repository.

this treebank is not one of the training treebanks). Given time limits, we decided to simply assign each test set, i. e. each test language, the training treebank with the largest amount of training data as the proxy treebank.[14]

2.3 Heuristic Enhancement

We build a baseline system which concentrates on the two enhanced UD phenomena which are very straightforward to implement using simple heuristic rules, namely, co-reference in relative clauses and modifier relations containing case markers. These rules are applied to the output of the basic parser. We have two versions of the modifier relation rule - one in which the value of the `case` morphological feature is included in the relation label and one without. We also have a rule which adds the lemma of a conjunction to the enhanced label of its head. For each development set, we find the optimal subset of the set of heuristic rules in terms of ELAS among all possible subsets except those combining the two case rules.

This baseline system is clearly suboptimal since it makes no attempt at all to handle those more interesting enhanced UD phenomena which involve the addition or deletion of arcs, i.e. conjunct propagation, ellipsis and control/raising constructions. Nonetheless it is useful as a baseline to check that the main system is performing reasonably and is available as a fall back.

2.4 Semantic Parsing

2.4.1 Modelling Enhanced Dependencies

As our main system to predict the enhanced graph, we follow (Dozat and Manning, 2018) and treat enhanced dependency parsing as a task similar to semantic dependency parsing. In semantic dependency parsing, words may have multiple heads. Thus, Dozat and Manning (2018) apply their deep biaffine graph-based dependency parser (Dozat and Manning, 2017) to the task of semantic dependency parsing but replace the softmax cross-entropy loss with sigmoid cross-entropy loss for edge prediction. The above modification changes the modelling objective such that words are no longer competing with one another to be classified as the appropriate head; rather, the parser chooses whether an edge

exists between each possible pair of words independently. Whether an edge exists between two words is based on a predefined threshold, where a score above this threshold results in an edge being predicted and, subsequently, the edge's label. In our experiments we use an edge prediction threshold of 0.5. If the parser did not predict an edge for a word, we take the edge with the highest probability. As we want to select the label with the highest probability for each chosen edge, standard softmax cross-entropy loss is used for label prediction as in Dozat and Manning (2018).

In order for the semantic dependency parser to be able to model relationships where a word may have multiple heads, we create an adjacency matrix where the ij^{th} entry in the matrix indicates whether an edge exists between tokens i and j with label type k. We also append the dummy *root* token to the adjacency matrix so that an edge can be predicted from the main predicate of the sentence to the dummy *root* token.

Figure 1a shows the enhanced UD graph for the phrase, *Tale of joy and sorrow*. In the enhanced representation, each conjunct in the conjoined noun phrase is attached to the governor of the modifier phrase, e.g. there is an additional *nmod* relation marked in blue between the noun *Tale* and the second conjunct *sorrow*. Note that the lemma of the *case* and *cc* dependents are appended to the enhanced dependency labels of their heads. The corresponding edge-existence probabilities of the semantic parser trained on `en_ewt` are shown in Figure 1b where the parser correctly predicts an edge from *sorrow* to the first conjunct *joy* as well as the head of the modifier phrase *Tale*.

2.4.2 Feature Representations

In our experiments, each word w_i in a sentence $S = (w_0, w_1, \ldots, w_N)$ is converted to its vector representation $\mathbf{x}_i$. We trained different variants of our semantic parser where $\mathbf{x}_i$ is the concatenation of different combinations of the below features:

- **BERT embedding**: The first word-piece embedding of the wordpiece-tokenised input word from BERT (Devlin et al., 2019) $\mathbf{e}_i^{(BERT)} \in \mathbb{R}^{768}$

- **character embedding**: A character embedding obtained by passing the k characters $ch_1, \ldots, ch_k$ of w_i through a BiLSTM: $\text{BiLSTM}(ch_{1:k})$, $\mathbf{e}_i^{(ch)} \in \mathbb{R}^{64}$

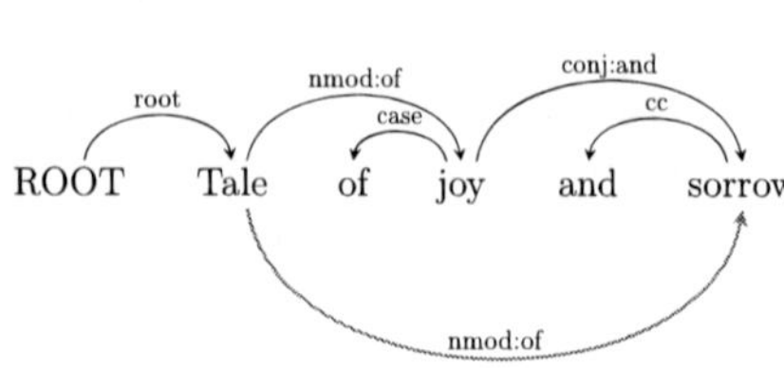

(a) Enhanced UD graph.   (b) Edge-existence probabilities.

Figure 1　The enhanced UD graph and edge-existence probabilities of the semantic parser trained on `en_ewt` for the phrase *Tale of joy and sorrow*.

- **lemma embedding**: The embedding of the word's lemma $\mathbf{e}_i^{(le)} \in \mathbb{R}^{50}$

- **UPOS embedding**: The embedding of the word's universal POS tag $\mathbf{e}_i^{(u)} \in \mathbb{R}^{50}$

- **XPOS embedding**: The embedding of the word's language-specific POS tag $\mathbf{e}_i^{(x)} \in \mathbb{R}^{50}$

- **morphological feature embedding**: The embedding of the word's morphological features $\mathbf{e}_i^{(f)} \in \mathbb{R}^{50}$

- **head-information embedding**: An embedding representing the word's head information from the basic tree $\mathbf{e}_i^{(h)} \in \mathbb{R}^{50}$

- **dependency label embedding**: The embedding of the word's dependency label from the basic tree $\mathbf{e}_i^{(label)} \in \mathbb{R}^{50}$

All model variants use the lexical information of the first BERT word-piece embedding and the character embedding, where ; represents vector concatenation:

$$\mathbf{e}_i^{(l)} = [\mathbf{e}_i^{(BERT)}; \mathbf{e}_i^{(ch)}] \tag{1}$$

The subsequent variation comes from the other types of features used where we experimented with the below feature settings:

$$\mathbf{x}_i = [\mathbf{e}_i^{(l)}; \mathbf{e}_i^{(u)}] \tag{2}$$

$$\mathbf{x}_i = [\mathbf{e}_i^{(l)}; \mathbf{e}_i^{(le)}; \mathbf{e}_i^{(u)}; \mathbf{e}_i^{(f)}] \tag{3}$$

$$\mathbf{x}_i = [\mathbf{e}_i^{(l)}; \mathbf{e}_i^{(le)}; \mathbf{e}_i^{(u)}; \mathbf{e}_i^{(x)}; \mathbf{e}_i^{(f)}] \tag{4}$$

$$\mathbf{x}_i = [\mathbf{e}_i^{(l)}; \mathbf{e}_i^{(le)}; \mathbf{e}_i^{(u)}; \mathbf{e}_i^{(f)}; \mathbf{e}_i^{(b)}] \tag{5}$$

$$\mathbf{x}_i = [\mathbf{e}_i^{(l)}; \mathbf{e}_i^{(le)}; \mathbf{e}_i^{(u)}; \mathbf{e}_i^{(x)}; \mathbf{e}_i^{(f)}; \mathbf{e}_i^{(b)}] \tag{6}$$

For the morphological features, there may be multiple morphological tags $m_1, \ldots, m_t$ for a particular word w_i. Thus, we split the full label into separate features (Hall et al., 2007) and embed each morphological property separately. We then sum the individual embedded representations together and divide by the number of active properties:

$$\mathbf{e}_i^{(f)} = \mathrm{mean}(\mathbf{e}^{(m_{1:t})}) \tag{7}$$

We follow the same process for the head-information embedding $\mathbf{e}_i^{(h)}$. Rather than encoding the head as an integer value, we obtain a *direction* value and a *distance* value: for each head-dependent pair (i, j), we subtract the indices of i, j giving the distance value. If the value is negative it means the head is to the left or if it is positive, to the right. We then take the absolute distance value and define ranges: *short* (1-4), *medium* (5-9), *far* (10-14) and *long-range* (>15). The qualitative direction (*left* or *right*) and distance labels are embedded in the same way as morphological features, e.g. embedded as separate components, summed together and then divided by the number of features (which in this case is always two):

$$\mathbf{e}_i^{(h)} = \mathrm{mean}(\mathbf{e}^{(h_{1:t})}) \tag{8}$$

To encode the basic tree, we then concatenate the head representation and the dependency label embedding:

$$\mathbf{e}_i^{(b)} = [\mathbf{e}_i^{(h)}; \mathbf{e}_i^{(label)}] \tag{9}$$

230

It is worth mentioning that more sophisticated approaches for modelling head distance and direction exist for basic dependency parsing (Qi et al., 2018) but we leave using this approach for enhanced dependency parsing as future work.

2.4.3 Training Details

Our semantic parser predicts edges in a greedy fashion based on local decisions, i. e. we did not make use of any maximum spanning tree algorithm or enforce any global constraints. One property of enhanced dependency graphs is that the graph may contain cycles, therefore, we did not remove any cycles from the graph but observed that this sometimes causes fragments in the graph which are not reachable from the notional ROOT. For graphs with unreachable nodes, we applied our post-processor to attach these (Section 2.5).

We found that this architecture can be easily applied to enhanced dependency parsing given its similar nature to semantic dependency parsing. One caveat is that in enhanced dependency parsing, the label set can be quite large as modifier lemma and case information can be appended to the dependency label which results in very high memory requirements for certain languages such as Arabic. Additionally, modelling all enhanced labels in this fashion means that the parser is limited in its ability to predict labels for rare modifiers. An examination of the semantic parser output on the `en_ewt` development set shows that, although the parser often predicts the correct label, it can sometimes predict the wrong label containing a frequent modifier which is not in the sentence, e.g. *advcl:if* instead of *advcl:as*.

Our semantic parser is built upon the implementation in AllenNLP (Gardner et al., 2018). Due to time constraints, we trained our semantic parsing models on the gold training data released by the organisers as opposed to creating jack-knifed silver data. Hyperparameters are similar to those in Dozat and Manning (2017) as we found the larger network size of Dozat and Manning (2018) to be too restrictive for certain languages with high memory demands. Full hyperparameters of the semantic parser are given in Table 1. We trained for 75 epochs with early-stopping if the development score did not improve after 10 epochs.

Memory Considerations We trained our semantic parsing models on two GPUs: the first was an NVIDIA RTX 2080 Ti with 12GB of VRAM

Semantic Parser Details	
Parameter	**Value**
Char-BiLSTM layers	2
BiLSTM layers	3
BiLSTM size	400
Char-BiLSTM size	64
Arc MLP size	500
Label MLP size	100
Dropout LSTMs	0.33
Dropout MLP	0.33
Dropout embeddings	0.33
Nonlinear act. (MLP)	ELU
Edge prediction threshold	0.5
BERT word-piece embedding	768
Char embedding	64
Tag embedding (all tags)	50
Optimizer	Adam
Learning rate	0.001
beta1	0.9
beta2	0.9
Num. epochs	75
Patience	10
Batch size	16

Table 1 Chosen hyperparameters for our semantic parser. For the tag embedding, we use the same size embedding for all features (lemma, POS, morphological features, head-information and label embeddings) and concatenate them.

where we had to remove very long sentences ($< .03\%$ of sentences overall) from the treebanks: `cs_cac`, `cs_pdt`, `it_isdt`, `ru_syntagrus` and `sv_talbanken` in order to fit a batch into memory. We were also given access to an NVIDIA V100 GPU with 32GB of VRAM which enabled us to process all treebanks except for `ar_padt` without removing long sentences. For `ar_padt`, after removing the longest 75 sentences, the model still required 29GB of VRAM.

2.4.4 BERT Models

For the BERT models, in early development runs we compared multilingual BERT (mBERT) with a language-specific BERT model if there was one available in HuggingFace's (Wolf et al., 2019) models repository.[15] We used a language-specific BERT model for `ar` (Safaya et al., 2020), `bg+cs` (Arkhipov et al., 2019), `en` (Devlin et al., 2019),

---

[15] `https://huggingface.co/models`

fi (Virtanen et al., 2019), it[16], nl (de Vries et al., 2019), pl[17], ru (Kuratov and Arkhipov, 2019) and sv[18] and for the rest of the languages we used mBERT (Devlin et al., 2019). We found that the language-specific variant was always better than mBERT except for pl_lfg. For fr_sequoia, we tried using the CamemBERT model (Martin et al., 2020). As this model uses RoBERTA (Liu et al., 2019) as opposed to BERT, we installed AllenNLP from the master repository which uses HuggingFace's AutoTokenizer module which supports many BERT-like models. We noticed a trend of lower results when using the master branch for some languages but training was also more stable for certain treebanks where we had previously encountered a nan in the loss.[19] Consequently, we include models from the stable release and the bleeding-edge master branch in our development pipeline.

2.5 Connecting the Graph

We had no solution ready to connect fragmented graphs produced by our semantic parser[20] on the system submission day and resorted to using the "connect-to-root" option of the quick-fix tool provided by the shared task organisers, who warned that it had not been thoroughly tested.

After the system submission deadline, we investigated the fragmentation issue. The task is to make all nodes reachable from the notional ROOT[21], where reachability is directional. Adding more edges than necessary harms precision and thus F1-score. We found that the quick-fix tool with the "connect-to-root" option adds edges to every unreachable node. We also noticed a bug in the implementation where certain reachable nodes were being reported as unreachable.

We then implemented an improved tool to connect fragmented graphs trying to minimise the number of edges added to the graph. We repeatedly

---

[16]https://github.com/dbmdz/berts

[17]https://github.com/kldarek/polbert

[18]https://github.com/Kungbib/swedish-bert-models

[19]We incurred a nan loss for cs_cac, cs_pdt, it_isdt and ru_syntagrus using the AllenNLP stable branch 0.9.0 and used the best model from the available epochs.

[20]Between 90.18% (Lithuanian) and 99.51% (Russian) of test sentences in our official submission are not affected, i.e. all nodes are reachable from a root node. This observation excludes Estonian, for which we submitted predictions using our heuristic system.

[21]UD distinguished between the notional ROOT (ID 0) and root nodes. The latter are any nodes that have '0' as a head.

Treebank	ELAS F1	
	sem-frag	heuristic
ar_padt	**70.99**	59.74
bg_btb	**88.09**	86.19
cs_cac	**86.51**	74.41
cs_fictree	**83.23**	77.37
cs_pdt	**79.58**	71.19
en_ewt	**84.71**	82.86
et_edt	62.74	**69.35**
fi_tdt	**83.64**	71.84
fr_sequoia	**88.65**	87.53
it_isdt	**90.13**	88.28
lt_alksnis	**73.63**	57.84
lv_lvtb	**81.82**	71.29
nl_alpino	**89.93**	89.00
nl_lassysmall	79.00	**81.24**
pl_lfg	**94.12**	93.84
pl_pdb	**82.25**	78.27
ru_syntagrus	**88.48**	80.03
sk_snk	**81.30**	75.98
sv_talbanken	**84.54**	81.32
ta_ttb	**55.68**	43.94
uk_iu	**82.41**	76.88

Table 2 Development set ELAS F1 score for the best semantic parser evaluated without connecting fragmented graphs (sem-frag) and for the best combination of heuristic rules (heuristic)

check for each unreachable node how many unreachable nodes can be reached from it. Among the nodes that maximise this number we pick the first node in surface order and make it a child of the notional ROOT, i.e. it becomes an additional root node. This is a rather naive approach which does not try to connect fragments in a sensible manner but, rather, mimics the behaviour of the "connect-to-root" option. Future work could try to show whether our above algorithm adds the minimal number of edges necessary to connect the graph or if a lower optimum exists.

3 Results

Table 2 compares the semantic parser against the heuristic approach on the ELAS F1 metric. The evaluation script was run without connecting fragmented graphs and format validation. For all but two treebanks, the semantic parser performs better than the best heuristic approach. For some lan-

Treebank	ELAS F1		
	subm	frag fix	re-run
Arabic-PADT	57.19	70.08	70.40
Bulgarian-BTB	77.29	89.58	89.60
Czech-FicTree	70.04	80.77	81.63
Czech-CAC	71.72	86.00	86.38
Czech-PDT	65.94	79.03	79.84
Czech-PUD	64.34	77.37	78.08
Dutch-Alpino	71.44	87.61	87.77
Dutch-L.Small	64.03	77.39	77.24
English-EWT	70.61	83.56	83.56
English-PUD	70.25	86.88	87.03
Estonian-EDT	62.29	68.20	68.37
Estonian-EWT	55.70	61.19	60.67
Finnish-TDT	73.02	84.36	84.33
Finnish-PUD	71.58	84.62	84.62
French-Sequoia	77.44	87.58	88.60
French-FQB	74.30	82.68	83.26
Italian-ISDT	71.98	90.24	90.23
Latvian-LVTB	72.41	81.81	82.40
Lithuanian-AL.	58.36	68.76	68.84
Polish-LFG	61.23	70.89	70.71
Polish-PDB	67.68	80.93	82.43
Polish-PUD	65.64	79.77	80.79
Russian-SynT.	75.27	89.21	89.47
Slovak-SNK	68.43	81.63	81.97
Swedish-Talb.	71.86	86.78	86.72
Swedish-PUD	64.70	79.35	79.37
Tamil-TTB	48.47	57.28	57.10
Ukrainian-IU	66.43	79.81	82.92
Average	67.49	79.76	80.15

Table 3 Test set results: subm = submitted, frag fix = using our own fragment connector and quick-fix.pl without connect-to-root, re-run = a re-run with bug fixes, no new models but new model selection

guages, the difference in performance is large. For et_ewt, which does not have a development set, we suspect that we overfitted our semantic parser on the et_ewt training data by allowing it to train for 75 epochs.

Table 3 shows test set ELAS obtained on the shared task submission site for *(a)* our submission fully relying on the organiser's quick-fix tool to fix issues in the output of our system, *(b)* the same predictions post processed by our own fragment connector that aims to minimise the number of root edges added, and *(c)* a re-run of our pipeline using the same models for system components as before but with all bugs fixed during development applied to all predictions and new decisions which models to apply to the test sets. While the quick-fix tool enabled us to make a valid submission in time, its approach of adding edges from the root node to all unreachable tokens has a strong negative impact on precision, e. g. 62.26 ELAS precision on the Czech CAC development set vs. 87.37 without post-processing. Our own post-competition fix avoids this and would have brought us to the top half of the competition.

4 Conclusion

In this system submission, we use a graph-based semantic parser to parse enhanced dependencies and compare to a baseline in which we create enhanced graphs from the basic tree using a very limited set of heuristics. Avenues for future work include:

Post-processing Predict the head and label for edges connecting fragments (as opposed to a dummy "0:root" edge) where this information could come from new edges available from lowering the score threshold or from the basic tree.

Label Prediction The semantic parser performs competitively despite treating enhanced dependency labels containing lemmas and case information as atomic units. However, a more sophisticated approach should still be tried.

Multi-treebank Parsing When randomising the proxy treebank for multi-treebank models, use a different randomisation for each ensemble member. Predict the best proxy treebank for each test sentence or paragraph (Wagner et al., 2020).

Elided Tokens Our semantic parser handles elided tokens by appending the elided token to the adjacency matrix and offsetting the head indices. While we used this approach during training on gold data, we did not predict elided tokens and we wish to explore methods for doing so.

Acknowledgments

This research is supported by Science Foundation Ireland through the ADAPT Centre for Digital Content Technology, which is funded under the SFI Research Centres Programme (Grant 13/RC/2106) and is co-funded under the European Regional Development Fund. We thank the reviewers for their insightful, detailed feedback. We acknowledge Dell for the use of an NVIDIA V100 GPU as part of the Dell AI Ready Bundle with Nvidia.

References

Mikhail Arkhipov, Maria Trofimova, Yuri Kuratov, and Alexey Sorokin. 2019. Tuning multilingual transformers for language-specific named entity recognition. In *Proceedings of the 7th Workshop on Balto-Slavic Natural Language Processing*, pages 89–93, Florence, Italy. Association for Computational Linguistics.

Giuseppe Attardi and Felice Dell'Orletta. 2009. Reverse revision and linear tree combination for dependency parsing. In *Proceedings of Human Language Technologies: The 2009 Annual Conference of the North American Chapter of the Association for Computational Linguistics, Companion Volume: Short Papers*, pages 261–264, Boulder, Colorado. Association for Computational Linguistics.

Piotr Bojanowski, Edouard Grave, Armand Joulin, and Tomas Mikolov. 2017. Enriching word vectors with subword information. *Transactions of the Association for Computational Linguistics*, 5:135–146.

Gosse Bouma, Djamé Seddah, and Daniel Zeman. 2020. Overview of the IWPT 2020 Shared Task on Parsing into Enhanced Universal Dependencies. In *Proceedings of the 16th International Conference on Parsing Technologies and the IWPT 2020 Shared Task on Parsing into Enhanced Universal Dependencies*, Seattle, US. Association for Computational Linguistics.

Wanxiang Che, Yijia Liu, Yuxuan Wang, Bo Zheng, and Ting Liu. 2018. Towards better UD parsing: Deep contextualized word embeddings, ensemble, and treebank concatenation. In *Proceedings of the CoNLL 2018 Shared Task: Multilingual Parsing from Raw Text to Universal Dependencies*, pages 55–64, Brussels, Belgium. Association for Computational Linguistics.

Jacob Devlin, Ming-Wei Chang, Kenton Lee, and Kristina Toutanova. 2019. BERT: Pre-training of deep bidirectional transformers for language understanding. In *Proceedings of the 2019 Conference of the North American Chapter of the Association for Computational Linguistics: Human Language Technologies, Volume 1 (Long and Short Papers)*, pages 4171–4186, Minneapolis, Minnesota. Association for Computational Linguistics.

Timothy Dozat and Christopher D. Manning. 2017. Deep biaffine attention for neural dependency parsing. In *Proceedings of the 5th International Conference on Learning Representations (ICLR 2017)*.

Timothy Dozat and Christopher D. Manning. 2018. Simpler but more accurate semantic dependency parsing. In *Proceedings of the 56th Annual Meeting of the Association for Computational Linguistics (Volume 2: Short Papers)*, pages 484–490, Melbourne, Australia. Association for Computational Linguistics.

Matt Gardner, Joel Grus, Mark Neumann, Oyvind Tafjord, Pradeep Dasigi, Nelson F. Liu, Matthew Peters, Michael Schmitz, and Luke Zettlemoyer. 2018. AllenNLP: A deep semantic natural language processing platform. In *Proceedings of Workshop for NLP Open Source Software (NLP-OSS)*, pages 1–6, Melbourne, Australia. Association for Computational Linguistics.

Johan Hall, Jens Nilsson, Joakim Nivre, Gülşen Eryiğit, Beáta Megyesi, Mattias Nilsson, and Markus Saers. 2007. Single malt or blended? a study in multilingual parser optimization. In *Proceedings of the 2007 Joint Conference on Empirical Methods in Natural Language Processing and Computational Natural Language Learning (EMNLP-CoNLL)*, pages 933–939, Prague, Czech Republic. Association for Computational Linguistics.

Yuri Kuratov and Mikhail Arkhipov. 2019. Adaptation of deep bidirectional multilingual transformers for Russian language. ArXiv 1905.07213.

Yinhan Liu, Myle Ott, Naman Goyal, Jingfei Du, Mandar Joshi, Danqi Chen, Omer Levy, Mike Lewis, Luke Zettlemoyer, and Veselin Stoyanov. 2019. RoBERTa: A robustly optimized BERT pretraining approach. ArXiv 1907.11692.

Louis Martin, Benjamin Muller, Pedro Javier Ortiz Suárez, Yoann Dupont, Laurent Romary, Éric Villemonte de la Clergerie, Djamé Seddah, and Benoît Sagot. 2020. CamemBERT: a tasty French language model. In *Proceedings of the 58th Annual Meeting of the Association for Computational Linguistics (ACL)*. To appear. Also available as ArXiv 1911.03894.

Matthew Peters, Mark Neumann, Mohit Iyyer, Matt Gardner, Christopher Clark, Kenton Lee, and Luke Zettlemoyer. 2018. Deep contextualized word representations. In *Proceedings of the 2018 Conference of the North American Chapter of the Association for Computational Linguistics: Human Language Technologies, Volume 1 (Long Papers)*, pages 2227–2237, New Orleans, Louisiana. Association for Computational Linguistics.

Peng Qi, Timothy Dozat, Yuhao Zhang, and Christopher D. Manning. 2018. Universal dependency parsing from scratch. In *Proceedings of the CoNLL 2018 Shared Task: Multilingual Parsing from Raw Text to Universal Dependencies*, pages 160–170, Brussels, Belgium. Association for Computational Linguistics.

Ali Safaya, Moutasem Abdullatif, and Deniz Yuret. 2020. Kuisail at semeval-2020 task 12: BERT-CNN for offensive speech identification in social media. In *Proceedings of the International Workshop on Semantic Evaluation (SemEval)*. To appear.

Milan Straka. 2018. UDPipe 2.0 prototype at CoNLL 2018 UD shared task. In *Proceedings of the CoNLL 2018 Shared Task: Multilingual Parsing from Raw*

Text to Universal Dependencies, pages 197–207, Brussels, Belgium. Association for Computational Linguistics.

Milan Straka and Jana Straková. 2017. Tokenizing, POS tagging, lemmatizing and parsing UD 2.0 with UDPipe. In *Proceedings of the CoNLL 2017 Shared Task: Multilingual Parsing from Raw Text to Universal Dependencies*, pages 88–99, Vancouver, Canada. Association for Computational Linguistics.

Milan Straka and Jana Straková. 2019. Universal dependencies 2.5 models for UDPipe (2019-12-06). LINDAT/CLARIAH-CZ digital library at the Institute of Formal and Applied Linguistics (ÚFAL), Faculty of Mathematics and Physics, Charles University.

Milan Straka, Jana Straková, and Jan Hajič. 2019. Evaluating contextualized embeddings on 54 languages in POS tagging, lemmatization and dependency parsing. ArXiv 1908.07448.

Sara Stymne, Miryam de Lhoneux, Aaron Smith, and Joakim Nivre. 2018. Parser training with heterogeneous treebanks. In *Proceedings of the 56th Annual Meeting of the Association for Computational Linguistics (Volume 2: Short Papers)*, pages 619–625. Association for Computational Linguistics.

Antti Virtanen, Jenna Kanerva, Rami Ilo, Jouni Luoma, Juhani Luotolahti, Tapio Salakoski, Filip Ginter, and Sampo Pyysalo. 2019. Multilingual is not enough: BERT for Finnish. ArXiv 1912.07076.

Wietse de Vries, Andreas van Cranenburgh, Arianna Bisazza, Tommaso Caselli, Gertjan van Noord, and Malvina Nissim. 2019. BERTje: A Dutch BERT model. Arxiv 1912.09582.

Joachim Wagner, James Barry, and Jennifer Foster. 2020. Treebank embedding vectors for out-of-domain dependency parsing. In *Proceedings of the 58th Annual Meeting of the Association for Computational Linguistics (ACL)*. To appear. Also available as ArXiv 2005.00800.

Thomas Wolf, Lysandre Debut, Victor Sanh, Julien Chaumond, Clement Delangue, Anthony Moi, Pierric Cistac, Tim Rault, Rémi Louf, Morgan Funtowicz, and Jamie Brew. 2019. HuggingFace's transformers: State-of-the-art natural language processing. ArXiv 1910.03771.

Køpsala: Transition-Based Graph Parsing via Efficient Training and Effective Encoding

Daniel Hershcovich[*◇]   Miryam de Lhoneux[*◇]   Artur Kulmizev[♡]
Elham Pejhan[◇]   Joakim Nivre[♡]
◇University of Copenhagen   ♡Uppsala University
{dh, ml, ep}@di.ku.dk,
{artur.kulmizev, joakim.nivre}@lingfil.uu.se

Abstract

We present Køpsala, the Copenhagen-Uppsala system for the Enhanced Universal Dependencies Shared Task at IWPT 2020. Our system is a pipeline consisting of off-the-shelf models for everything but enhanced graph parsing, and for the latter, a transition-based graph parser adapted from Che et al. (2019). We train a single enhanced parser model per language, using gold sentence splitting and tokenization for training, and rely only on tokenized surface forms and multilingual BERT for encoding. While a bug introduced just before submission resulted in a severe drop in precision, its post-submission fix would bring us to 4th place in the official ranking, according to average ELAS. Our parser demonstrates that a unified pipeline is effective for both Meaning Representation Parsing and Enhanced Universal Dependencies.

1 Introduction

The IWPT 2020 Shared Task on Parsing into Enhanced Universal Dependencies (Bouma et al., 2020) involves sentence segmentation, tokenization, lemmatization, part-of-speech tagging, morphological analysis, basic dependency parsing, and finally (for the first time) *enhanced* dependency parsing. The enhancements encode case information, elided predicates, and shared arguments due to conjunction, control, raising and relative clauses (see Figures 1 and 2).

In Universal Dependencies v2 (UD; Nivre et al., 2020), enhanced dependencies (ED) are a separate dependency graph than the *basic* dependency tree (BD). However, ED is *almost* a super-set of BD,[1] and so most previous approaches (Schuster and Manning, 2016; Nivre et al., 2018) have attempted to recover ED from BD using language-specific rules. On the other hand, Hershcovich

---

*Equal contribution

[1]Some BD arcs are deleted in ED, e.g., `orphan` arcs.

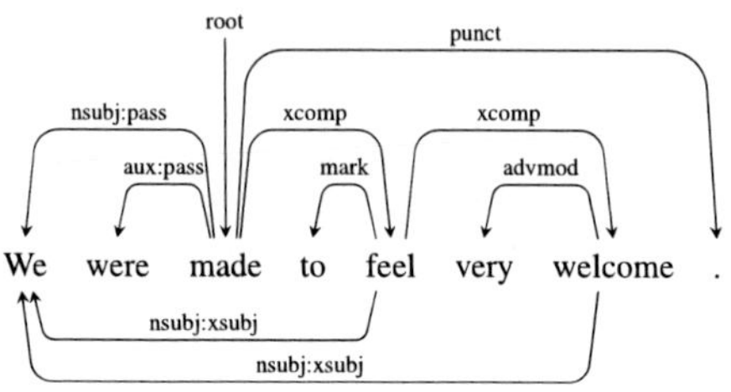

Figure 1: ED for `reviews-077034-0002` from `UD_English-EWT`, containing a control verb (made). Arcs above the sentence are also in BD.

et al. (2018) experimented with TUPA, a transition-based directed acyclic graph (DAG) parser originally designed for parsing UCCA (Abend and Rappoport, 2013), for supervised ED parsing. They converted ED to UCCA-like graphs and did not use pre-trained contextualized embeddings, yielding sub-optimal results. Taking a similar approach, we adapt a transition-based graph parser (Che et al., 2019) designed for Meaning Representation Parsing (Oepen et al., 2019), but parse ED directly and use BERT embeddings (Devlin et al., 2019).

The main contribution of our work is a transition system supporting the graph structures exhibited by ED, including null nodes (meaning this is not a strictly bilexical formalism), cycles and non-crossing graphs (§3.1), as Figure 4 demonstrates for the sentence from Figure 2. We parse ED completely separately from BD, demonstrating the applicability of a full graph parser, starting from only segmented and tokenized text, to ED. Our code is available at `https://github.com/coastalcph/koepsala-parser`.

2 Preprocessing

As the focus of this shared task is ED parsing, we rely on existing systems for preprocessing. Here, we consider two off-the-shelf pipelines: STANZA

Proceedings of the 16th International Conference on Parsing Technologies and the IWPT 2020 Shared Task, pages 236–244
Virtual Meeting, July 9, 2020. ©2020 Association for Computational Linguistics

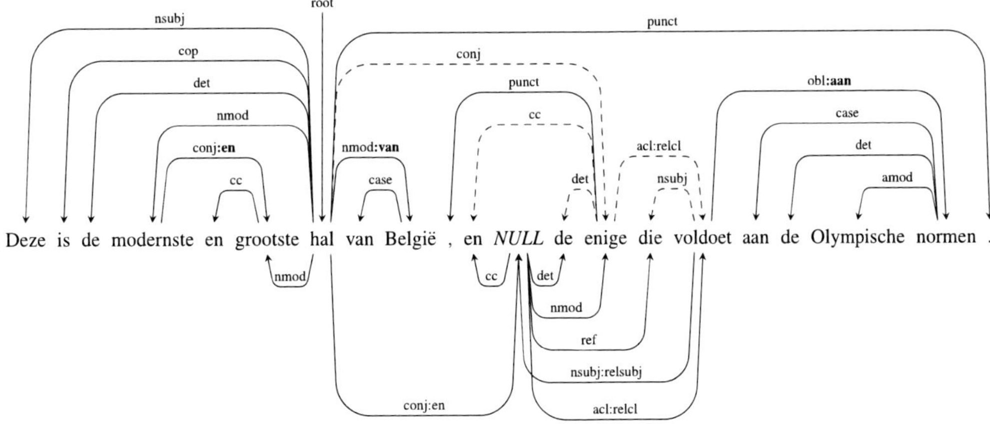

Figure 2: `wiki-3745.p.38.s.5` from `UD_Dutch-LassySmall`, containing a null node *NULL*, not in the original sentence, coordination and case suffixes (`:en`, `:van`, `:aan`), and propagation of conjuncts (hal → grootste). The dashed edges are deleted in ED, and the edges below the sentence are added. Note the cycle *NULL* ↔ voldoet.

(Qi et al., 2020)[2] and UDPIPE 1.2 (Straka and Straková, 2017; Straka et al., 2016),[3] both of which have models pre-trained on UD v2.5 treebanks. We experiment with either pipeline during prediction to process the raw text files for the dev and test sets, eventually selecting UDPIPE for our primary submission. This process entails sentence segmentation, tokenization, lemmatization, part-of-speech tagging, morphological feature tagging, and BD parsing.[4] For training our ED parser (§3), however, we use gold inputs for simplicity. We use the `conllu` Python package[5] to read CoNLL-U files.

Preprocessing model selection. Since the dev and test data do not denote their source treebanks, we simply process the text using the pipeline model trained on the language's largest treebank. To experiment with an alternative method, for languages with more than one treebank, we also train UDPIPE models on combined training treebanks. Table 1 shows the comparison of LAS on the combined dev set, for these models and for the models (pre-)trained on the language's largest treebank. The results show that using the combined training sets does not lead to consistent improvements in terms of LAS, and so we continue using pre-trained

	Language			
	CZECH	DUTCH	ESTONIAN	POLISH
combined	78.88	**76.50**	77.01	**82.96**
largest	**83.97**	74.97	**77.61**	82.59

Table 1: LAS on the combined dev set for UDPIPE models trained on the language's combined training treebanks and the models trained on the language's largest treebank. No consistent trend is observed.

treebank-specific preprocessing models henceforth.

3 Transition-Based Enhanced Dependency Parser

Our system is a transition-based graph parser, based on the HIT-SCIR system (Che et al., 2019), which achieved the highest average score across frameworks (AMR, EDS, UCCA, DM and PSD) in the CoNLL 2019 shared task on Meaning Representation Parsing (MRP; Oepen et al., 2019). It is written in the AllenNLP (Gardner et al., 2018) framework. For training efficiently, it employs stack LSTMs (Dyer et al., 2015), batching operations across sentences. For better encoding, HIT-SCIR fine-tuned BERT (Devlin et al., 2019) while training the parser.

A transition-based parser operates by manipulating a buffer (originally containing the input words provided by the preprocessor, see §2) and a stack (originally containing the root, i.e., word at index 0), to incrementally create the output dependency graph. At each point in the parsing process, a tran-

---

[2]`https://stanfordnlp.github.io/stanza/models.html`

[3]`https://lindat.mff.cuni.cz/repository/xmlui/handle/11234/1-3131`

[4]The preprocessing output, except for segmentation and tokenization, is not used in any way by the ED parser, since it just uses BERT for token representation (§3.2).

[5]`https://github.com/EmilStenstrom/conllu`

sition is selected out of a pre-defined set of possible transitions. A classifier is trained to predict the best transition to apply at each step, by mimicking an oracle during training (see §3.1).

HIT-SCIR used a different transition system per framework (AMR, EDS, UCCA; and one system for DM and PSD), according to the graph properties of each and based on existing framework-specific parsers (Liu et al., 2018; Buys and Blunsom, 2017; Hershcovich et al., 2017; Wang et al., 2018). We construct a transition system for ED using subsets of transitions from two of the HIT-SCIR systems: their system for DM and PSD, as well as their system for UCCA, with some further adaptations specific to ED graphs.

3.1 Transition System

Our system contains the following transitions: {SHIFT, LEFT-EDGE$_l$, RIGHT-EDGE$_l$, REDUCE-0, REDUCE-1, NODE, SWAP and FINISH}. The SHIFT transition pops the first element of the buffer and pushes it onto the stack. The LEFT-EDGE$_l$ and RIGHT-EDGE$_l$ transitions add an arc[6] between the two top items of the stack with label l. We need two different REDUCE transitions to pop the topmost and second topmost items of the stack, which we name REDUCE-0 and a REDUCE-1 respectively. This makes it possible to construct length-2 cycles, which ED allows (and most MRP frameworks do not). The NODE transition inserts a null node as the first element of the buffer, needed to support null nodes. SWAP moves the second-top node of the stack to the buffer, thus swapping the order between the two top nodes of the stack. This is necessary for handling crossing graphs (analogous to non-projective trees). Finally, FINISH terminates the transition sequence. A formal definition of the transition set is shown in Figure 3.

Separate EDGE transitions exist for each edge label. Labels containing coordination or case suffixes (such as `nmod:van`) are treated as any other label and are not split, resulting in a large number of transitions for some languages, shown in Table 2.

NODE transitions, on the other hand, do not se-

---

[6]For consistency, we keep the transition nomenclature using "EDGE", although they create directed dependency *arcs*. Note that in analogous transitions in some transition systems, such as ARCEAGER (Nivre, 2003), the dependent of the transition is also popped out of the stack as part of either of these two transitions. Here, since dependents can have multiple heads and can have arcs with multiple labels, we stick to the EDGE action and use our two REDUCE transitions to pop elements of the stack when necessary.

Language	Total	EDGE	w/ suffix
ARABIC	402	395	345
BULGARIAN	197	191	137
CZECH	768	761	702
DUTCH	393	386	336
ENGLISH	300	293	232
ESTONIAN	445	438	381
FINNISH	266	259	210
FRENCH	112	106	59
ITALIAN	281	274	216
LATVIAN	238	232	161
LITHUANIAN	323	317	263
POLISH	676	669	615
RUSSIAN	944	938	861
SLOVAK	266	259	204
SWEDISH	209	202	153
TAMIL	146	140	103
UKRAINIAN	290	283	225

Table 2: Number of transitions for each language.

lect any label or features, since null nodes are only evaluated with respect to their incoming and outgoing edges. All other information is ignored, and thus not predicted by the parser: predicted null nodes are thus only placeholders.

Constraints. In addition to the modified transition set, we change the constraints for some transitions according to the required graph structure.

Since LEFT-EDGE$_l$ and RIGHT-EDGE$_l$ transitions do not reduce the dependent, we need to ensure that we do not draw the same arc twice. For this reason, these transitions are not allowed if there is already an arc with label l between the two nodes. We also disallow to add an arc with the root as dependent.

To ensure every node gets attached to at least one head, we disallow the REDUCE-0 and REDUCE-1 transitions for nodes that do not have a head yet. We also disallow reducing the root.

For the SWAP transition, we maintain the *generated order* of each node, assigned when the node is shifted (for words) or created (for null nodes). To prevent infinite loops during inference, we only allow swapping nodes whose order in the stack is the same as their generation order.

To limit repeated actions, we arbitrarily constrain NODE transitions such that there are no more null nodes than words (although a lower limit would suffice), and EDGE transitions to limit the

Before Transition				Transition	After Transition					Condition
Stack	Buffer	Nodes	Arcs		Stack	Buffer	Nodes	Arcs	Terminal?	
Σ	$b \mid B$	V	A	SHIFT	$\Sigma \mid b$	B	V	A	$-$	
$\Sigma \mid s_0$	B	V	A	REDUCE-0	Σ	B	V	A	$-$	$s_0 \neq \text{root} \wedge (\cdot, s_0). \in A$
$\Sigma \mid s_1, s_0$	B	V	A	REDUCE-1	$\Sigma \mid s_0$	B	V	A	$-$	$s_1 \neq \text{root} \wedge (\cdot, s_1). \in A$
Σ	B	V	A	NODE	Σ	$b \mid B$	$V \cup \{b\}$	A	$-$	
$\Sigma \mid s_1, s_0$	B	V	A	LEFT-EDGE$_l$	$\Sigma \mid s_1, s_0$	B	V	$A \cup \{(s_0, s_1)_l\}$	$-$	$s_1 \neq \text{root} \wedge (s_0, s_1)_l \notin A$
$\Sigma \mid s_1, s_0$	B	V	A	RIGHT-EDGE$_l$	$\Sigma \mid s_1, s_0$	B	V	$A \cup \{(s_1, s_0)_l\}$	$-$	$(s_1, s_0)_l \notin A$
$\Sigma \mid s_1, s_0$	B	V	A	SWAP	$\Sigma \mid s_0$	$s_1 \mid B$	V	A	$-$	$s_1 \neq \text{root} \wedge i(s_1) < i(s_0)$
[root]	[ ]	V	A	FINISH	[ ]	[ ]	V	A	$+$	

Figure 3: Our transition set. We write the stack with its top to the right and the buffer with its head to the left. $(h, d)_l$ denotes an l-labeled dependency with head h and dependent d. i(x) is the generated order (see §3.1).

number of heads per node to 7.[7]

FINISH is only allowed when the buffer is empty and the stack only contains the root. If no valid transition is available, the sequence is terminated prematurely by applying the FINISH transition, regardless of the FINISH constraints.

Oracle. We use a static oracle similar to HIT-SCIR (a single "gold" transition sequence is given during training, which the parser is forced to follow), but develop one for our transition system.

The oracle deterministically chooses the transition to take given the current configuration. Let s_1 and s_0 be the two top items of the stack and b the first item of the buffer (if these are defined in the current configuration). If the buffer is empty and the stack only contains the root, take a FINISH transition. Otherwise, if there is an arc between s_1 and s_0 with label l that has not yet been constructed, take the necessary RIGHT-EDGE$_l$ or LEFT-EDGE$_l$ action. Otherwise, if s_0 has a node dependent, take a NODE transition. Otherwise, if s_0 has all its heads and dependents, take REDUCE-0, if s_1 has all its heads and dependents, take REDUCE-1. Otherwise, if s_1 and s_0 are in their generated order and s_0 has a head or a dependent in the stack that is not s_1, take a SWAP. Otherwise SHIFT. Figure 4 shows an example transition sequence.

3.2 Classifier

The parser uses BERT (Devlin et al., 2019) for token representation. While Che et al. (2019) used pre-trained English model (`wwm_cased_L-24_H-102416`), we replaced it with a pre-trained multilingual one (`multi_cased_L-12_H-76812`),[8] trained

on 104 languages, including all 17 languages participating in the shared task. As done by Che et al. (2019), we use the `bert-pretrained` text field embedder from AllenNLP, which extracts the first word-piece of each token, applying a scalar mix on all layers of transformer.

The transition classifier is a stack-LSTM (Dyer et al., 2015) with only BERT embedding features for words, as well as a scalar feature denoting the ratio between the number of (null) nodes and the number of words (Hershcovich et al., 2017), as in HIT-SCIR. We do not fine-tune BERT due to memory limitations, though fine-tuning would likely result in improved performance.

3.3 Postprocessing

The enhanced graphs are required to be connected, i.e., every node must be reachable from the root.[9] While the transition constraints ensure that every node has a head, there may be unconnected *cycles* at the end of the parse, resulting in invalid graphs. To fix the problem, at the end of the parse, we iteratively find the unconnected node with the most descendants, and attach it to the predicate (the first dependent of the root) with an `orphan`-labeled arc. In addition to unconnected cycles, this resolves the problem of prematurely terminated transition sequences due to no valid transition being available according to the constraints: instead of resulting in partially-constructed graphs, headless nodes are similarly attached with an `orphan`-labeled arc to the predicate, if it exists, or otherwise to the root.

Parsing tragedy. Our postprocessing procedure to attach unconnected subgraphs had a bug at the time of submission, where many nodes were incorrectly identified as unconnected and thus un-

---

[7]While the observed number of heads per node in the data goes up to 36, in the training data there is only a small minority of cases where a node has more than 7 heads.

[8]`https://github.com/google-research/bert/blob/master/multilingual.md`

[9]This is enforced by the task organizers by running `validate.py --level 2 --lang ud` on the system predictions before evaluation.

	Transition	Stack	Buffer	Arc added
		[ROOT]	[Deze is (…)]	
1-6	SHIFT	[(…) en grootste]	[hal van (…)]	
7	LEFT-EDGE$_{cc}$	[(…) en grootste]	[hal van (…)]	(grootste, en)$_{cc}$
8	REDUCE-1	[(…) modernste grootste]	[hal van (…)]	
9	RIGHT-EDGE$_{conj:en}$	[(…) modernste grootste]	[hal van (…)]	(grootste, modernste)$_{conj:en}$
10	SHIFT	[(…) grootste hal]	[van België (…)]	
11	LEFT-EDGE$_{nmod}$	[(…) grootste hal]	[van België (…)]	(hal, grootste)$_{nmod}$
12	NODE	[(…) grootste hal]	[*NULL* van (…)]	
13-21		Series of LEFT-EDGE and REDUCE-1 transitions		
22	RIGHT-EDGE$_{root}$	[ROOT hal]	[*NULL* van (…)]	(ROOT, hal)$_{root}$
23	SHIFT	[ROOT hal *NULL*]	[van België (…)]	
24	RIGHT-EDGE$_{conj:en}$	[ROOT hal *NULL*]	[van België (…)]	(hal, *NULL*)$_{conj:en}$
25-26	SHIFT	[(…) van België]	[, en (…)]	
27	LEFT-EDGE$_{case}$	[(…) van België]	[, en (…)]	(België, van)$_{case}$
28	REDUCE-1	[(…) *NULL* België]	[, en (…)]	
29	SWAP	[ROOT hal België]	[*NULL* , (…)]	
30	RIGHT-EDGE$_{nmod:van}$	[(…) hal België]	[*NULL* , (…)]	(hal, België)$_{nmod:van}$
31	REDUCE-0	[ROOT hal]	[*NULL* , (…)]	
32-34	SHIFT	[(…) , en]	[de enige (…)]	
35	SWAP	[(…) *NULL* en]	[, de (…)]	
36	RIGHT-EDGE$_{cc}$	[(…) *NULL* en]	[, de (…)]	(*NULL*, en)$_{cc}$
37	REDUCE-0	[ROOT hal *NULL*]	[, de (…)]	
38-39	SHIFT	[(…) , de]	[enige die (…)]	
40	SWAP	[(…) *NULL* de]	[, enige (…)]	
41	RIGHT-EDGE$_{det}$	[(…) *NULL* de]	[, enige (…)]	(*NULL*, de)$_{det}$
42	REDUCE-0	[ROOT hal *NULL*]	[, enige (…)]	
43-44	SHIFT	[(…) , enige]	[die voldoet (…)]	
45	LEFT-EDGE$_{punct}$	[(…) , enige]	[die voldoet (…)]	(enige, ,)$_{punct}$
46	REDUCE-1	[(…) *NULL* enige]	[die voldoet (…)]	
47	RIGHT-EDGE$_{nmod}$	[(…) *NULL* enige]	[die voldoet (…)]	(*NULL*, enige)$_{nmod}$
48	REDUCE-0	[ROOT hal *NULL*]	[die voldoet (…)]	
49	SHIFT	[(…) *NULL* die]	[voldoet aan (…)]	
50	RIGHT-EDGE$_{ref}$	[(…) *NULL* die]	[voldoet aan (…)]	(*NULL*, die)$_{ref}$
51	REDUCE-0	[ROOT hal *NULL*]	[voldoet aan (…)]	
52	SHIFT	[(…) *NULL* voldoet]	[aan de (…)]	
53	RIGHT-EDGE$_{acl:relcl}$	[(…) *NULL* voldoet]	[aan de (…)]	(*NULL*, voldoet)$_{acl:relcl}$
54	LEFT-EDGE$_{nsubj:relsubj}$	[(…) *NULL* voldoet]	[aan de (…)]	(voldoet, *NULL*)$_{nsubj:relsubj}$
55-69		(…)		
70	RIGHT-EDGE$_{punct}$	[ROOT hal .]	[ ]	(hal, .)$_{punct}$
71-72	REDUCE-0	[ROOT]	[ ]	
73	FINISH	[ROOT]	[ ]	

Figure 4: Oracle transition sequence for the sentence from Figure 2. Consecutive SHIFTs grouped for brevity.

necessarily attached to the predicate/root. While this still yielded valid graphs, precision dropped precipitously from before the introduction of the postprocessing procedure. Due to the late stage in the evaluation period at which we made this change, we failed to properly monitor our development scores and could not identify the cause for the drop in time, resulting in low official scores. However, after submission we identified the bug and fixed it,[10] improving our parser's accuracy back to the range we had observed during development.

3.4 Training

For training the ED parser we do *not* simply train it on the largest treebank per language, but rather train it on the concatenated training treebanks per language. In preliminary experiments, this did lead to improvements in terms of combined dev ELAS over treebank-specific models, contrary to our findings in BD parsing for preprocessing (§2). We train our models on an NVIDIA P100 GPU with a batch size of 8. All other hyperparameters can be found in the configuration files in the repository.[11]

Training until convergence took 1h30 (for Tamil,

---

[10]https://github.com/coastalcph/
koepsala-parser/commit/
1b872ad9fc2652649c11eb0a8622c744c92e8cbb

[11]https://github.com/coastalcph/
koepsala-parser/blob/master/config/
transition_eud.jsonnet

the smallest treebank) to up to 2 days (for Arabic, which contains many long sentences). Prediction on the dev set took between 4 minutes (for Tamil) and 55 minutes (for Czech), ranging from 117 words/second (7 sentences/second, for Tamil) to 1300 words/second (81 sentences/second, for Czech), including the model loading time.

3.5 Baselines

In addition to providing validation scores for our trained parsers, we consider three competitive baselines, as provided by the task organizers:

- B1: gold standard dependency trees copied as enhanced graphs. Though this can be technically considered an upper bound, as gold tree information is provided, it should nonetheless provide some idea of how much of the enhanced graph can be derived from the dependency tree.

- B2: predicted trees yielded by UDPipe models trained on UD v2.5 (using the largest treebank where applicable), copied as enhanced graphs. This is more representative than B1 of realistic parsing scenarios, which rely on predictions.

- B3: similar to B2, but applying the Stanford enhancer post-hoc over the predicted trees. Scores for Finnish and Latvian were not provided.

4 Results

Table 3 displays our results on the per-language (not per-treebank) test partitions of the shared task data. As explained in §2, for languages with multiple training treebanks available (Czech, Estonian, Dutch, Polish), we preprocessed the raw text of each treebank using the pipeline trained on the *largest* treebank available for that language (e.g. `alpino` for Dutch). Also, aforementioned in §3.4, we then trained our parsers on the concatenation of each language's treebanks, so that we could parse at the language level (as opposed to treebank). Though we observed scant differences between the two preprocessing pipelines, it was UDPIPE that produced fewer validation errors. As such, we adopted it as the main preprocessor for our official submission.

It is apparent in Table 3 that the unconnected graph issue (described in §3.3) severely affected

Language	Baselines			Ours	
	B1	*B2*	*B3*	*official*	*fixed*
ARABIC	67.35	46.41	45.16	60.84	69.51
BULGARIAN	85.82	73.74	79.9	68.88	84.49
CZECH	78.44	65.31	63.62	61.11	74.79
DUTCH	82.48	62.97	72.65	62.93	76.92
ENGLISH	84.30	66.83	76.16	65.37	81.05
ESTONIAN	76.38	57.53	54.34	59.07	72.38
FINNISH	78.26	61.71	-	67.54	81.58
FRENCH	97.49	71.14	63.31	67.93	82.76
ITALIAN	80.20	70.33	83.03	69.08	84.66
LATVIAN	79.31	59.14	-	64.75	79.12
LITHUANIAN	74.22	46.78	44.84	56.28	69.09
POLISH	81.59	66.38	65.37	61.34	73.89
RUSSIAN	79.63	68.33	67.80	64.23	78.90
SLOVAK	77.60	60.02	58.05	64.08	77.44
SWEDISH	80.98	62.18	71.53	64.50	78.61
TAMIL	76.29	40.71	40.25	47.44	56.85
UKRAINIAN	77.24	58.73	56.92	64.17	78.10
AVERAGE	79.86	61.07	62.90	62.91	76.48

Table 3: Main results for Enhanced Universal Dependencies shared task (ELAS), as evaluated on the provided test sets. *B1, B2, B3* refer to organizer-provided baseline systems. *official* refers to our official submission, prior to fixing the unconnected graph issue (*fixed*).

our official submission to the shared task (observed in the *official* column). After diagnosing and fixing this problem, we observed an improvement of 14.1 ELAS, which is consistent with our scores on the treebanks' development sets. With this in mind, our (fixed) parser tends to perform in a generally stable fashion across languages, with an average ELAS of 76.48 and standard deviation of 6.86. Among our highest scoring languages are Bulgarian, French, and Italian—the former two of which are corroborated by the strong *B1* baseline. Indeed, Tamil is the notable exception among all results, with 56.85 ELAS. We surmise that treebank size is the biggest factor in this degradation of performance, as Tamil has, by far, the smallest treebank at 400 sentences. As such, our parser has comparatively fewer graph samples to train on than it would for some other languages.

When comparing against the organizer-provided baselines, we see a strong improvement in using our system over both *B2* and *B3* systems. This is encouraging, as it demonstrates the benefit of parsing enhanced dependency graphs directly, rather than relying on predicted trees to accurately relay the enhanced structure (*B1*) or employing a heuristic-driven post-processor to derive it (*B2*). Furthermore, though the organizers consider *B1* as an indirect upper bound due to the gold-standard tokenization and dependency structure employed therein, we can nonetheless observe an advantage in using our parser for some languages. These are Arabic (+2.16 ELAS), Finnish (+3.32), Italian (+4.46), and Ukranian (+0.86). Again, this is promising, given that our parser does not rely on any tree structure in order to parse graphs.

4.1 Pre-processing Analysis

Since the test data was provided in a raw, untokenized format, we were interested in the extent of accuracy loss we might observe when relying on off-the-shelf pre-processors. Table 4 displays these results over the development data. It is clear that when we employ predicted segmentation, etc. using either STANZA or UDPIPE pipelines, we observe a slight degradation in accuracy, as compared to the gold data. Omitting Czech, Estonian, Dutch, and Polish (which had several associated treebanks), all other languages degrade by an average of 2.00 ELAS for STANZA and 2.32 for UDPIPE. Though one typically expects such a degradation when evaluating with predicted segmentation, we did observe some unreasonably large gaps in accuracy: namely for Arabic (-4.02, -8.32 for STANZA and UDPIPE, respectively) and Tamil (-12.19, -8.59). The latter can likely be explained via its small training set, which undoubtedly affects all components of the preprocessing pipeline.

When we examine the scores for all multi-treebank languages, we do not notice a large difference between gold and predicted tokenization—which we expect to be different across treebanks. Here, we simply choose the one trained on the largest treebank (`FicTree` for Czech, `EDT` for Estonian, `Alpino` for Dutch, and `LFG` for Polish), as we consider this a simple yet reliable heuristic. However, when generating predictions for the smaller treebanks using the bigger treebank's preprocessing model, we only notice a notable drop in accuracy for Dutch (-2.15, -2.54 for STANZA and UDPIPE, respectively). This indicates that there are likely major differences in the treebanks' domains or how they are respectively segmented or annotated. In general, however, the differences between gold and predicted tokenization is surprisingly not

Language	STANZA	UDPIPE	Gold Tok.
ARABIC	73.66	69.36	77.68
BULGARIAN	83.46	83.17	83.89
CZECH	75.60	75.47	76.00
DUTCH	78.66	78.27	80.81
ENGLISH	80.79	79.80	82.77
ESTONIAN	75.43	75.32	75.81
FINNISH	80.87	80.59	81.89
FRENCH	86.05	85.29	88.97
ITALIAN	85.24	85.04	85.52
LATVIAN	79.00	78.39	79.28
LITHUANIAN	74.92	74.84	75.51
POLISH	71.94	73.22	73.63
RUSSIAN	78.53	78.60	78.87
SLOVAK	77.54	77.33	79.17
SWEDISH	78.26	78.18	78.37
TAMIL	50.66	54.26	62.85
UKRAINIAN	79.70	79.67	79.89
AVERAGE	77.08	76.87	78.88

Table 4: Development ELAS for our *fixed* parser. While in all cases we train the parser on the concatenation of all of a language's gold treebanks (applicable only to Czech, Dutch, Estonian, and Polish), STANZA and UDPIPE refer to generating predictions on the development data preprocessed by the corresponding pipeline. **Gold Tok.** refers to generating predictions over gold development data (tokenization, etc).

as large as we expected.

5 Conclusion

In this paper, we have described the IWPT 2020 Shared Task submission by the Copenhagen-Uppsala team, consisting of graphs predicted by a transition-based neural dependency graph parser with pre-trained multilingual contextualized embeddings. While not ranked among the top submission according to the official scores, the parser architecture proved effective for the type of dependency graphs exhibited by ED, and after fixing a critial bug we found the scores to improve dramatically and agree with the scores we had observed during development.

We expect that with more resources for BERT fine-tuning, hyperparameter tuning, language-specific pre-trained representations and careful pre- and post-processing, our parser will be a competitive system in this task. However, our contribution is a transition system that can directly handle ED, in a unified transition-based parsing system.

Acknowledgments

We thank the anonymous reviewers for their helpful comments. ML is funded by a Google Focused Research Award. We acknowledge the computational resources provided by CSC in Helsinki and Sigma2 in Oslo through NeIC-NLPL (www.nlpl.eu).

References

Omri Abend and Ari Rappoport. 2013. Universal conceptual cognitive annotation (UCCA). In *Proceedings of the 51st Annual Meeting of the Association for Computational Linguistics (Volume 1: Long Papers)*, pages 228–238, Sofia, Bulgaria. Association for Computational Linguistics.

Gosse Bouma, Djamé Seddah, and Daniel Zeman. 2020. Overview of the IWPT 2020 Shared Task on Parsing into Enhanced Universal Dependencies. In *Proceedings of the 16th International Conference on Parsing Technologies and the IWPT 2020 Shared Task on Parsing into Enhanced Universal Dependencies*, Seattle, US. Association for Computational Linguistics.

Jan Buys and Phil Blunsom. 2017. Robust incremental neural semantic graph parsing. In *Proceedings of the 55th Annual Meeting of the Association for Computational Linguistics (Volume 1: Long Papers)*, pages 1215–1226, Vancouver, Canada. Association for Computational Linguistics.

Wanxiang Che, Longxu Dou, Yang Xu, Yuxuan Wang, Yijia Liu, and Ting Liu. 2019. HIT-SCIR at MRP 2019: A unified pipeline for meaning representation parsing via efficient training and effective encoding. In *Proceedings of the Shared Task on Cross-Framework Meaning Representation Parsing at the 2019 Conference on Natural Language Learning*, pages 76–85, Hong Kong. Association for Computational Linguistics.

Jacob Devlin, Ming-Wei Chang, Kenton Lee, and Kristina Toutanova. 2019. BERT: Pre-training of deep bidirectional transformers for language understanding. In *Proceedings of the 2019 Conference of the North American Chapter of the Association for Computational Linguistics: Human Language Technologies, Volume 1 (Long and Short Papers)*, pages 4171–4186, Minneapolis, Minnesota. Association for Computational Linguistics.

Chris Dyer, Miguel Ballesteros, Wang Ling, Austin Matthews, and Noah A. Smith. 2015. Transition-based dependency parsing with stack long short-term memory. In *Proceedings of the 53rd Annual Meeting of the Association for Computational Linguistics and the 7th International Joint Conference on Natural Language Processing (Volume 1: Long Papers)*, pages 334–343, Beijing, China. Association for Computational Linguistics.

Matt Gardner, Joel Grus, Mark Neumann, Oyvind Tafjord, Pradeep Dasigi, Nelson F Liu, Matthew Peters, Michael Schmitz, and Luke Zettlemoyer. 2018. Allennlp: A deep semantic natural language processing platform. In *Proceedings of Workshop for NLP Open Source Software (NLP-OSS)*, pages 1–6.

Daniel Hershcovich, Omri Abend, and Ari Rappoport. 2017. A transition-based directed acyclic graph parser for UCCA. In *Proceedings of the 55th Annual Meeting of the Association for Computational Linguistics (Volume 1: Long Papers)*, pages 1127–1138, Vancouver, Canada. Association for Computational Linguistics.

Daniel Hershcovich, Omri Abend, and Ari Rappoport. 2018. Universal dependency parsing with a general transition-based DAG parser. In *Proceedings of the CoNLL 2018 Shared Task: Multilingual Parsing from Raw Text to Universal Dependencies*, pages 103–112, Brussels, Belgium. Association for Computational Linguistics.

Yijia Liu, Wanxiang Che, Bo Zheng, Bing Qin, and Ting Liu. 2018. An AMR aligner tuned by transition-based parser. In *Proceedings of the 2018 Conference on Empirical Methods in Natural Language Processing*, pages 2422–2430, Brussels, Belgium. Association for Computational Linguistics.

Joakim Nivre. 2003. An efficient algorithm for projective dependency parsing. In *Proceedings of the Eighth International Conference on Parsing Technologies*, pages 149–160, Nancy, France.

Joakim Nivre, Marie-Catherine de Marneffe, Filip Ginter, Jan Hajič, Christopher D Manning, Sampo Pyysalo, Sebastian Schuster, Francis Tyers, and Daniel Zeman. 2020. Universal dependencies v2: An evergrowing multilingual treebank collection. In *Proc. of LREC*.

Joakim Nivre, Paola Marongiu, Filip Ginter, Jenna Kanerva, Simonetta Montemagni, Sebastian Schuster, and Maria Simi. 2018. Enhancing universal dependency treebanks: A case study. In *Proceedings of the Second Workshop on Universal Dependencies (UDW 2018)*, pages 102–107, Brussels, Belgium. Association for Computational Linguistics.

Stephan Oepen, Omri Abend, Jan Hajic, Daniel Hershcovich, Marco Kuhlmann, Tim O'Gorman, Nianwen Xue, Jayeol Chun, Milan Straka, and Zdenka Uresova. 2019. MRP 2019: Cross-framework meaning representation parsing. In *Proceedings of the Shared Task on Cross-Framework Meaning Representation Parsing at the 2019 Conference on Natural Language Learning*, pages 1–27, Hong Kong. Association for Computational Linguistics.

Peng Qi, Yuhao Zhang, Yuhui Zhang, Jason Bolton, and Christopher D. Manning. 2020. Stanza: A Python natural language processing toolkit for many human languages. In *Proceedings of the 58th Annual Meeting of the Association for Computational Linguistics: System Demonstrations*.

Sebastian Schuster and Christopher D. Manning. 2016. Enhanced English Universal Dependencies: An improved representation for natural language understanding tasks. In *Proc. of LREC*. ELRA.

Milan Straka, Jan Hajic, and Jana Straková. 2016. Udpipe: trainable pipeline for processing conll-u files performing tokenization, morphological analysis, pos tagging and parsing. In *Proceedings of the Tenth International Conference on Language Resources and Evaluation (LREC'16)*, pages 4290–4297.

Milan Straka and Jana Straková. 2017. Tokenizing, pos tagging, lemmatizing and parsing ud 2.0 with udpipe. In *Proceedings of the CoNLL 2017 Shared Task: Multilingual Parsing from Raw Text to Universal Dependencies*, pages 88–99, Vancouver, Canada. Association for Computational Linguistics.

Mingxuan Wang, Jun Xie, Zhixing Tan, Jinsong Su, Deyi Xiong, and Chao Bian. 2018. Neural machine translation with decoding history enhanced attention. In *Proceedings of the 27th International Conference on Computational Linguistics*, pages 1464–1473, Santa Fe, New Mexico, USA. Association for Computational Linguistics.

RobertNLP at the IWPT 2020 Shared Task:
Surprisingly Simple Enhanced UD Parsing for English

Stefan Grünewald[1,2]   **Annemarie Friedrich**[2]

[1]Institut für Maschinelle Sprachverarbeitung, University of Stuttgart
[2]Bosch Center for Artificial Intelligence, Renningen, Germany
`stefan.gruenewald|annemarie.friedrich@de.bosch.com`

Abstract

This paper presents our system at the *IWPT 2020 Shared Task on Parsing into Enhanced Universal Dependencies*. Using a biaffine classifier architecture (Dozat and Manning, 2017) which operates directly on fine-tuned RoBERTa embeddings, our parser generates enhanced UD graphs by predicting the best dependency label (or absence of a dependency) for each pair of tokens in the sentence. We address label sparsity issues by replacing lexical items in relations with placeholders at prediction time, later retrieving them from the parse in a rule-based fashion. In addition, we ensure structural graph constraints using a simple set of heuristics. On the English blind test data, our system achieves a very high parsing accuracy, ranking 1st out of 10 with an ELAS F1 score of 88.94 %.

1 Introduction

Enhanced Universal Dependencies are an extension of the widely used Universal Dependencies (UD) framework for syntactic dependency annotation (de Marneffe et al., 2014). Designed with shallow natural language understanding tasks in mind, enhanced UD extends basic UD trees by including a number of additional dependencies between tokens in order to make relations between content words more explicit, especially in the presence of linguistic phenomena such as coordination, raising/control, and relative clauses (Schuster and Manning, 2016). While there is evidence for the utility of enhanced dependencies in downstream applications (Schuster et al., 2017), adding these relations means that dependency structures are not generally constrained to trees any more, which makes parsing them a different problem with its own set of challenges.

Research on UD parsing has so far mostly focused on producing syntax trees according to the basic UD specification (e.g., in the CoNLL 2017 and 2018 Shared Tasks). Prior work on inducing enhanced UD graphs (Nyblom et al., 2013; Simi and Montemagni, 2018; Nivre et al., 2018) infers enhanced UD representations by first parsing text into basic UD trees and then adding enhanced relations by applying rule-based or machine-learning modules. This approach has the disadvantage of propagating errors in the basic layer to the enhanced parse. For our submission to the IWPT 2020 Shared Task (Bouma et al., 2020), we follow an alternative approach. We do not distinguish between the basic UD tree and the enhanced part of the graph, instead treating all types of dependencies equally and extracting them jointly.

Following the approach of Dozat and Manning (2018), we use a biaffine classifier architecture in which we predict the most likely dependency label (or absence of a dependency) for each pair of tokens in the sentence, forming a dependency graph from the union of these predictions. Similar to Kondratyuk and Straka (2019), we extract the inputs for the biaffine classifier directly from fine-tuned contextualized word embeddings, RoBERTa (Liu et al., 2019b) in our case, using a scalar mixture of hidden layers (Liu et al., 2019a). We overcome the problem of sparsity issues caused by enhanced UD's large lexicalized label set by replacing lexical items with placeholders at prediction time and later retrieving them from the full parse via a set of rules. Surprisingly, this simple approach, combined with a straightforward heuristic ensuring that each node receives a head, results in valid enhanced UD graphs for 99% of all sentences in the English blind test data.

Despite being conceptually simple and easy to implement, our system sets a new state of the art for enhanced UD parsing for English, scoring first out of ten submissions on the blind test data according to the official ELAS evaluation metric. While

Proceedings of the 16th International Conference on Parsing Technologies and the IWPT 2020 Shared Task, pages 245–252
Virtual Meeting, July 9, 2020. ©2020 Association for Computational Linguistics

our system is currently available only for English, adapting it to most other languages should be feasible with relatively little effort.

2 Our Model

This section describes the components of our parser as submitted to the Shared Task.

2.1 Pre-processing

For tokenization and sentence segmentation, we employ the StanfordNLP system (Qi et al., 2018), which achieved state-of-the-art results for these tasks on the English treebanks in the CoNLL 2018 Shared Task.

2.2 Input Token Representation

We use RoBERTa (Liu et al., 2019b) to generate contextualized word embeddings for the tokens of the input sentence, fine-tuning the model while training our parser. We create the wordpiece-tokenized input for RoBERTa by feeding each token as identified by StanfordNLP into the RoBERTa tokenizer. In addition, we prepend a special *[root]* token to each sentence, which serves as an artificial head of the *root* relation, which must be present in every sentence. This token receives a fixed, learned embedding instead of a contextualized RoBERTa embedding, but with the same number of dimensions.

Following Kondratyuk and Straka (2019), our model produces an embedding $\mathbf{r}_i$ for the original token at position i by forming a weighted sum of the hidden layers' embeddings at the positions corresponding to the first wordpiece token of the original token. Weights for this scalar mixture of layers are learned during training. Layers are randomly dropped during training to prevent the model from focusing on only a single layer.

We also experimented with using BERT (Devlin et al., 2019) instead of RoBERTa, but found that this yielded lower parsing accuracy (see Sec. 3).

2.3 Dependency Classification

Figure 1 shows an overview of our neural-network based dependency classifier, which simultaneously predicts relation labels or absence of a relation between pairs of tokens.

Classifier architecture. Our dependency classifier follows the architecture proposed by Dozat and Manning (2018), which is capable of producing general (bi-lexical) dependency graph structures.

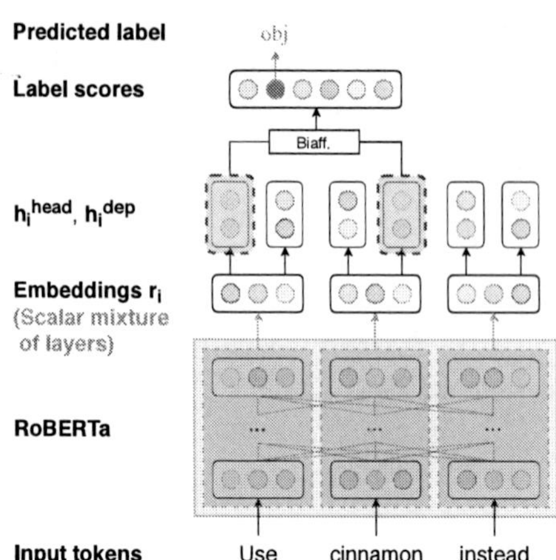

Figure 1: Architecture of neural network predicting dependency relations between pairs of tokens.

The approach works by creating, for each input token embedding $\mathbf{r}_i$, a head representation $\mathbf{h}_i^{head}$ and a dependent representation $\mathbf{h}_i^{dep}$ via two single-layer feedforward networks:

$$\mathbf{h}_i^{head} = \text{FNN}^{head}(\mathbf{r}_i) \qquad (1)$$

$$\mathbf{h}_i^{dep} = \text{FNN}^{dep}(\mathbf{r}_i) \qquad (2)$$

For each ordered pair (i, j) of tokens in the sentence, their respective head and dependent representations are then fed to a biaffine classifier (Eq. 3, Dozat and Manning, 2017), which outputs logits $\mathbf{s}_{i,j}$ over the possible dependency labels.[1] We encode the absence of a dependency relation between two tokens as simply another label ($\varnothing$). This unfactorized approach is in contrast to recent approaches that first predict presence or absence of relations and then use a second classifier to predict labels. It has already been proposed by Dozat and Manning (2018), who found that it performed on par with the factorized approach.

Finally, the most likely label $y_{i,j}$ can then be extracted from these logits:

$$\text{Biaff}(\mathbf{x}_1, \mathbf{x}_2) = \mathbf{x}_1^\top \mathbf{U}\mathbf{x}_2 + W(\mathbf{x}_1 \oplus \mathbf{x}_2) + \mathbf{b} \quad (3)$$

$$\mathbf{s}_{i,j} = \text{Biaff}(\mathbf{h}_i^{head}, \mathbf{h}_j^{dep}) \qquad (4)$$

$$P(y_{i,j}) = \text{softmax}(\mathbf{s}_{i,j}) \qquad (5)$$

$\mathbf{U}$, W and $\mathbf{b}$ in (3) are learned parameters; $\oplus$ denotes the concatenation operation. The model is

---

[1] Note that this means that each pair of tokens is fed to the classifier twice as an ordered pair, once with i as the potential head and j as the potential dependent, and once the other way around.

trained to minimize cross entropy loss w. r. t. the true dependency label between each pair of tokens.

De-lexicalizing dependency labels. Because enhanced UD adds lexical information to certain dependencies (e.g. *obl:instead_of*), the number of dependency labels is huge; the EWT corpus contains 399 unique labels. To avoid sparsity issues, we strip lexical information from labels during training, instead replacing them with placeholders (e.g. *obl:[case]*) indicating where in the dependency graph the lexical information is expected to be found (see Sec. 2.4 for a detailed description of the reconstruction process). This way, we can remove all lexicalized relations from the label vocabulary, instead adding only five new placeholder labels: *nmod:[case]*, *obl:[case]*, *acl:[mark]*, *advcl:[mark]*, and *conj:[cc]*. We keep all other, non-lexicalized subtyped labels (such as *nmod:poss*). This brings the total label count down to 56 (including $\varnothing$).

2.4 Post-processing

The outputs provided by the dependency classifier can be regarded as a 3-dimensional tensor, or in other words, each cell in the matrix as shown in Figure 2 contains the probabilities predicted for the label set with the row label corresponding to the relation's head and the column label corresponding to the relation's dependent. Figure 2 shows the highest-scoring label per entry.

Ensuring graph structure constraints. Using the outputs provided by the dependency classifier, we can assemble a dependency graph by retrieving the highest-scoring dependency (or $\varnothing$, i.e., no relation) for each pair of tokens in the sentence (omitting the diagonal as enhanced UD does not allow links starting and ending at the same node) and forming their union.

Although enhanced UD eliminates the requirement that dependency graphs must be trees, it maintains a set of structural constraints. Specifically, each token needs to have at least one head and must be reachable from at least one of the root(s) of the graph.[2] These global constraints are not automatically adhered to by our simple graph construction method, which operates on pairs of tokens. Nonetheless, we observe that around 99 % of sentences are assigned structurally valid graphs as

	[root]	Use	cinnamon	instead	of	sugar	or	sweetener
[root]	$\varnothing$	*root*	$\varnothing$	$\varnothing$	$\varnothing$	$\varnothing$	$\varnothing$	$\varnothing$
Use	$\varnothing$	$\varnothing$	*obj*	$\varnothing$	$\varnothing$	*obl:[case]*	$\varnothing$	*obl:[case]*
cinnamon	$\varnothing$	$\varnothing$	$\varnothing$	$\varnothing$	$\varnothing$	$\varnothing$	$\varnothing$	$\varnothing$
instead	$\varnothing$	$\varnothing$	$\varnothing$	$\varnothing$	*fixed*	$\varnothing$	$\varnothing$	$\varnothing$
of	$\varnothing$	$\varnothing$	$\varnothing$	$\varnothing$	$\varnothing$	$\varnothing$	$\varnothing$	$\varnothing$
sugar	$\varnothing$	$\varnothing$	$\varnothing$	*case*	$\varnothing$	$\varnothing$	$\varnothing$	*conj:[cc]*
or	$\varnothing$	$\varnothing$	$\varnothing$	$\varnothing$	$\varnothing$	$\varnothing$	$\varnothing$	$\varnothing$
sweetener	$\varnothing$	$\varnothing$	$\varnothing$	$\varnothing$	$\varnothing$	$\varnothing$	*cc*	$\varnothing$

Figure 2: Prediction matrix of the dependency classifier. Cell entries show the highest-scoring label for each ordered pair of tokens, with row/column labels indicating potential heads/dependents respectively.

determined by the official validation script.[3]

To make the graphs of the remaining 1 % sentences structurally valid, we perform the following steps. In the case of tokens lacking a head, the $\varnothing$ label has received the highest score during classification for all possible heads. We now simply retrieve all second-ranked labels and their scores and pick the relation (and corresponding head) that received the highest score across all possible heads.

Further, in order to ensure reachability from the root, in the cases violating this constraint, we fall back to an external dependency tree parse, i.e., a representation of the UD basic layer, for generating candidate links to be added to our graph. We here use the UDify parser (Kondratyuk and Straka, 2019) to predict basic UD trees. We determine the set of nodes V that are not reachable from any root, and for each node $v \in V$ we compute the number of nodes in V that can be reached when starting at v. We then pick the node v_i that can reach the largest number of nodes and check if the head of v_i in the basic layer tree can be when starting at a root in *our* graph. If so, we add the relation between v_i and its head as present in the basic layer tree to our graph, otherwise, we add a *dep* edge from the sentence's first root to v_i. We repeat this procedure until each node in the graph is reachable from at least one root node.

Re-lexicalization of labels. As outlined in Sec. 2.3, lexical information is stripped from dependency labels during training, using the format *base:[placeholder]*. At prediction time, we re-

---

[2]Graphs in enhanced UD may have more than one root.

[3]https://github.com/
UniversalDependencies/tools/blob/master/
validate.py

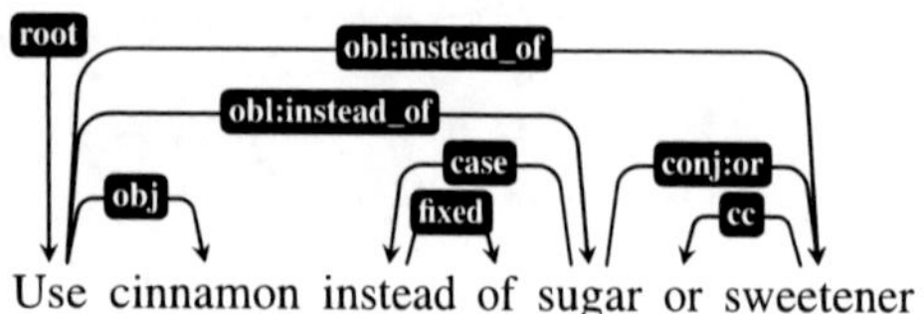
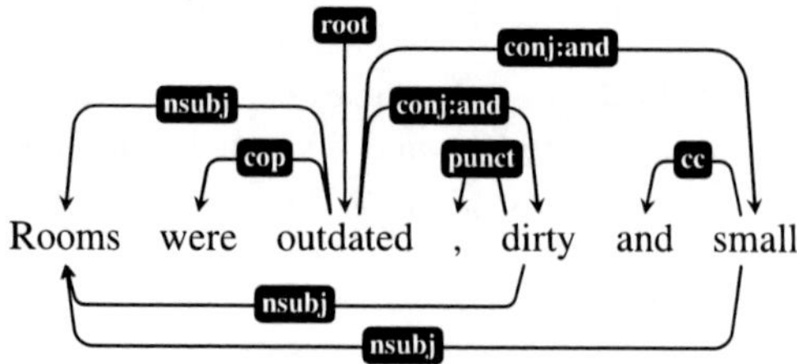

(a) Dependency graph with lexicalization of labels.

(b) Dependency graph with "conjunction siblings."

Figure 3: Re-lexicalization of dependency labels in the presence of conjunctions.

lexicalize predicted placeholder labels using the following set of rules.

First, if the token has a dependent that is attached via the placeholder of the de-lexicalized relation in question, we lexicalize the relation with the token of this dependent. For example, in Figure 3a, our parser predicts *obl:[case]* and we re-lexicalize this relation with the token(s) of the *case* dependents of "sugar." (Multiword expressions, such as "instead of", are handled by concatenating word forms linked by the *fixed* relation.)

If such a dependent does not exist, it may be due to the presence of a *conj* relation. For example, Figure 3a shows a case where for the de-lexicalized link *obl:[case]* ending at "sweetener," no *case* relation starts at this node. This is due to the presence of a *conj* relation, ending at "sweetener." We hence check if the head of the *conj* relation has an incoming lexicalized edge of the same base relation (here *obl*) and if so, re-lexicalize accordingly.

Similarly, *conj* links ending at siblings in coordinate constructions (here "dirty" and "small") are always lexicalized with the same item (in this case "and"). Unlike "small," the dependent "dirty" does not have its own *cc* dependent that could be used to execute the first step, i.e., to replace the placeholder of *conj:[cc]* with a dependent's token. For such nodes, we hence search the graph for siblings that are linked to the common governor via *conj* relations. If we find any, we use the lexicalized label of the corresponding *conj* relation for all siblings.

The above heuristics return a result for 98.9 % of the de-lexicalized relations predicted for the blind test data; in the remaining cases, we simply remove the placeholder without substituting any lexical material. Provided that the underlying base relation was predicted correctly, we are able to retrieve the correct lexical material for 98.4 % of relations.

Removal of relations. In addition, UD contains several relations that empirically only appear on their own, i.e., whose dependent may have only one incoming edge of this type. These relations are *fixed*, *flat*, *goeswith*, *punct*, and *cc*. However, in around 0.4 % of cases our parser erroneously predicts several of these relations for a single token (e.g., punctuation being attached to several tokens at once). In these cases, we remove all but the most confidently predicted dependency.

3 Experiments

This section describes our submission to the Shared Task, as well as a number of additional experiments we conducted to contextualize our results.

3.1 Experimental Settings and Hyperparameters

We use the training and development sections of the EWT corpus for training and validation, respectively. We use gold-tokenized and gold-segmented sentences as input for our system during training.

For hyperparameter settings, we mostly stick with the values used by Kondratyuk and Straka (2019). An exception to this is the training regime, where we found a low batch size, constant learning rate, no gradient clipping, and the AdamW optimizer (Loshchilov and Hutter, 2019) to yield the best results. The final hyperparameters can be found in Table 1.

Our model was trained using a single nVidia Tesla V100 GPU, stopping early when ELAS F1 score on the development set did not improve for 10 epochs. The best model was found after 63 epochs, i.e., 73 training epochs were performed in total, taking ca. 9 hours. Parsing the English blind test set (3077 sentences) takes around 3 minutes in total, i.e. 0.06 seconds per sentence.

RoBERTa embeddings	
Embeddings dimension	1024
Token mask probability	0.15
Layer dropout	0.1
Hidden dropout	0.2
Attention dropout	0.2
Output dropout	0.5
Biaffine classifier	
Hidden size	1024
Dropout	0.33
AdamW Optimizer	
Batch size	5
Learning rate	$5e^{-6}$
β_1, β_2	0.9, 0.999
Weight decay	0.0

Table 1: Hyperparameter values.

Submission	IWPT-all	EWT	PUD
RobertNLP	**88.94**	**88.06**	**89.97**
TurkuNLP	87.15	86.14	88.35
median	83.41	82.04	85.02
Køpsala	65.37	64.18	66.77
UDify + converter	85.67	84.55	87.00

Table 2: Parsing results (ELAS F1) on English blind test data in the IWPT 2020 Shared Task.

3.2 Results of Submission

Table 2 shows the results (in terms of ELAS F1 score) on the blind English test data for our system as well as the highest- and lowest-ranking competing submissions and the median submission. Our system achieves an ELAS F1 score of 88.94 %, ranking first with a margin of more than 1.5 points over the second-ranking submission.

As an additional baseline, we used the state-of-the-art UDify parser (Kondratyuk and Straka, 2019) to predict basic dependencies and then ran the rule-based converter by Schuster and Manning (2016) on the output to extract enhanced relations. This approach achieved an F-Score of 85.67 %, considerably lower than our system, confirming that our end-to-end graph parsing approach is superior to a pipeline model of basic parsing + rule-based conversion.

3.3 Analysis of Results

We here describe several experiments using variations of the setting used in our official submission. These experiments aim at determining the impact of different factors, including choice of pre-trained embeddings, training data, as well as segmentation and tokenization, on model performance. Some of the experiments described in this section were

Embeddings	Train	IWPT-test	EWT-dev
BERT-base	EWT	87.49	87.64
RoBERTa-base	EWT	88.17	88.64
BERT-large	EWT	88.18	88.61
RoBERTa-large	EWT	**88.94**[a]	**89.43**
RoBERTa-large	UD2.5[b]	87.85	88.59

Table 3: Effect of embeddings and training data on model performance (ELAS F1, English blind test data). [a]Official submission. [b]Concatenation of EWT, GUM, LinES, and ParTUT training data.

conducted during the development of our system, others constitute post-evaluation analyses. For consistency, we present results for the blind test data in this section. Most experiments were initially conducted using the development data, showing the same tendencies.

Choice of pre-trained embeddings. We experiment with four different pre-trained embedding models, namely BERT and RoBERTa in their base and large variants respectively. As shown in Table 3, RoBERTa outperforms BERT, and the large variants outperform the base variants, with BERT-large and RoBERTa-base performing roughly equally. The best observed results are achieved by RoBERTa-large (our official submission). The superior performance of RoBERTa may stem from the fact that it was pre-trained on a considerably larger amount of data, and that it dropped the "next sentence prediction" objective, which may be irrelevant or even detrimental for a single-sentence task like syntactic parsing.

Effect of additional training data. While preparing our submission, we experimented with generating additional training data by using the rule-based UD enhancer by Schuster and Manning (2016), which was used to create the gold standard enhanced layers of the EWT and PUD corpora, to build enhanced versions of three other English UD treebanks (GUM, LinES, and ParTUT).

However, we found in preliminary experiments on the dev and test sections of the above mentioned corpora that including this additional training data actually slightly hurts performance if the test data is from a different corpus. This is correlated with the lexical distance between test and training data as computed using the Bhattacharyya distance

$$D_B(p, q) = -\ln \sum_{x \in X} \sqrt{p(x)q(x)} \qquad (6)$$

Corpus	Lex. dist.	ELAS F1
EWT	0.142	88.94
GUM	0.204	87.98
LinES	0.240	88.20
ParTUT	0.248	87.69

Table 4: Lexical (Bhattacharyya) distance and parsing accuracy between the blind test data and the different training corpora. The rightmost column indicates parsing performance on the IWPT test set when adding the respective corpus to the EWT training data. (First line is EWT only.)

between the respective vocabulary probability distributions (Bhattacharya, 1943; Ruder and Plank, 2017).

As the lexical distance of the blind test set and EWT is much smaller than the ones between the test set and the other corpora (see Table 4), our official submission's model was trained only on EWT. Post-evaluation experiments (see rightmost column) confirm that when including corpora with higher lexical distance, parsing accuracy decreases. In addition, parsing results on the blind test set when including all additional data (results see last line in Table 3) confirm this approach. However, if a different test set showed greater similarity to other corpora, including them as training data would likely be beneficial. As one of the anonymous reviewers points out, in addition to lexical similarity, factors such as mean dependency distance or average sentence length may also play a role. In conclusion, our experiments once more highlight that selecting good training corpora for an application domain is a critical factor and an interesting direction for further research.

Effect of segmentation and tokenization. While our parser was trained on gold-tokenized and gold-segmented sentences, the Shared Task required parsing from raw text. In order to determine the extent to which automatic segmentation and tokenization impacts results, we run our parser on the gold-tokenized and gold-segmented version of the test data.

We observe an ELAS F1 score of 90.80, which constitutes an increase of nearly 2 points over the results obtained using automatic segmentation. This indicates that our system is rather sensitive to these kinds of errors and would greatly benefit from improvements in segmentation accuracy. It might also be possible to increase the robustness of our system w. r. t. these errors by training it on system-predicted sentence segmentation.

Performance on basic vs. enhanced relations. We further evaluate how performance of our parser varies between (a) relations that result from enhancements, i. e., relations which are exclusive to the enhanced layer, and (b) relations that occur in the basic layer as well. Because our parser does not differentiate between basic and enhanced relations internally, we can only compute recall for the two classes, but not precision and F1.[4] We perform this evaluation for gold-segmented and gold-tokenized input.

Recall is considerably lower on relations exclusive to the enhanced layer (83.64 %) as opposed to relations that are also present in the basic layer (91.60 %), indicating that predicting the former is indeed a more difficult task compared to predicting the latter, as might be expected. The result further suggests that it might be promising to use our parser architecture in combination with a spanning tree algorithm to predict basic-layer style trees as well (e. g. in a multi-task setting). This would also eliminate the need to rely on external parser input to post-process dependency graphs for the rare cases of invalid graphs.

Performance on individual label types. Finally, while our system achieves a high parsing accuracy overall, we also compute F1-Scores for each individual label type in order to obtain a finer-grained picture of its strengths and weaknesses. Again, we perform this evaluation for gold-segmented and gold-tokenized input. A selection of the results is displayed in Table 5.

As might be expected, the label types on which our parser performs best are highly common functional relations such as *det* and *case*, as well as frequent content word dependencies such as *nsubj* and *amod*. More interestingly, it also performs close to the average on *nsubj:xsubj*, which is not only considerably rarer than the aforementioned relations but also exclusive to the enhanced representation, demonstrating that our joint approach is capable of capturing these dependencies as well.

Somewhat more challenging are the *flat* and *compound* labels (85.53 and 83.51 F-Score, respectively), which are used to annotate multiword ex-

---

[4]We compare to the gold standard which distinguishes between basic and enhanced relations. Our parser does not differentiate between basic and enhanced relations, i.e., the full graph is constructed without internally identifying the subgraph corresponding to the basic syntactic tree.

Label	Freq.	ELAS F1
det	3879	99.04
case	4481	97.16
nsubj	3708	94.78
amod	2552	92.49
(Total/avg.)	48298	90.80
nsubj:xsubj	569	88.22
flat	482	85.53
punct	5519	84.28
compound	2005	83.51
appos	347	66.31
parataxis	301	59.35
list	251	47.72

Table 5: Parsing accuracy (ELAS F1) for a selection of label types. Scores were computed on gold-segmented test data. *Freq.* denotes the number of occurrences of the label in the gold annotations.

pressions. The computational identification and treatment of such expressions is very challenging and constitutes a long-standing research area in itself (Gregoire et al., 2007; Savary et al., 2018, 2019).

The *punct* relation harbors perhaps the greatest potential for improvement, yielding an F-Score of only 84.28 despite being extremely common. This is likely due to the rather complex set of rules that determines which token a piece of punctuation is attached to.[5] However, it might also be the label where improvements are most difficult to achieve, as the gold standard itself contains inconsistencies,[6] leading to a noisy training signal.

Finally, out of all label types which occur more than 200 times in the test data, the worst performance is observed on *appos*, *parataxis*, and *list*. While their low frequency is almost certainly part of the reason for this, it is also worth noting that these dependencies are unusual in that they represent "side-by-side" relations between words rather than more obviously hierarchical structures (as is the case for most other label types). Investigating parser performance on these kinds of constructions in greater detail may present a promising avenue for future work.

4 Discussion and Conclusion

With our submission to the IWPT 2020 Shared Task, we have demonstrated a conceptually simple,

yet highly effective method for parsing Enhanced Universal Dependencies from English text.

Although we have focused on English in our submission, we believe that our system should in principle be easily adaptable to other languages as the only language-specific part of out model is its handling of lexicalized relations. While certain other languages (e. g., Czech or Estonian) have more complex label inventories including for example case information as well, this should not pose a problem for our delexicalization strategy. However, the adaptation might require a moderate amount of manual work, and it remains to be seen how effective the lexicalization strategy is for other languages, a question that may be addressed in future work.

Acknowledgments

We thank Jonas Kuhn, Heike Adel, Jannik Strötgen, Lukas Lange and the anonymous reviewers for their useful comments regarding this work.

References

Anil Bhattacharya. 1943. On a measure of divergence between two statistical populations defined by their population distributions. In *Bulletin of the Calcutta Mathematical Society*, volume 35, pages 99–109.

Gosse Bouma, Djamé Seddah, and Daniel Zeman. 2020. Overview of the IWPT 2020 Shared Task on Parsing into Enhanced Universal Dependencies. In *Proceedings of the 16th International Conference on Parsing Technologies and the IWPT 2020 Shared Task on Parsing into Enhanced Universal Dependencies*, Seattle, US. Association for Computational Linguistics.

Jacob Devlin, Ming-Wei Chang, Kenton Lee, and Kristina Toutanova. 2019. BERT: Pre-training of deep bidirectional transformers for language understanding. In *Proceedings of the 2019 Conference of the North American Chapter of the Association for Computational Linguistics: Human Language Technologies, Volume 1 (Long and Short Papers)*, pages 4171–4186, Minneapolis, Minnesota. Association for Computational Linguistics.

Timothy Dozat and Christopher D. Manning. 2017. Deep biaffine attention for neural dependency parsing. In *5th International Conference on Learning Representations, ICLR 2017, Toulon, France, April 24-26, 2017, Conference Track Proceedings*. OpenReview.net.

Timothy Dozat and Christopher D. Manning. 2018. Simpler but more accurate semantic dependency

---

[5]See `https://universaldependencies.org/u/dep/punct.html`.

[6]As noted on the treebank's Github page at `https://github.com/UniversalDependencies/UD_English-EWT`.

parsing. In *Proceedings of the 56th Annual Meeting of the Association for Computational Linguistics (Volume 2: Short Papers)*, pages 484–490, Melbourne, Australia. Association for Computational Linguistics.

Nicole Gregoire, Stefan Evert, and Su Nam Kim, editors. 2007. *Proceedings of the Workshop on A Broader Perspective on Multiword Expressions.* Association for Computational Linguistics, Prague, Czech Republic.

Dan Kondratyuk and Milan Straka. 2019. 75 languages, 1 model: Parsing universal dependencies universally. In *Proceedings of the 2019 Conference on Empirical Methods in Natural Language Processing and the 9th International Joint Conference on Natural Language Processing (EMNLP-IJCNLP)*, pages 2779–2795, Hong Kong, China. Association for Computational Linguistics.

Nelson F. Liu, Matt Gardner, Yonatan Belinkov, Matthew E. Peters, and Noah A. Smith. 2019a. Linguistic knowledge and transferability of contextual representations. In *Proceedings of the 2019 Conference of the North American Chapter of the Association for Computational Linguistics: Human Language Technologies, Volume 1 (Long and Short Papers)*, pages 1073–1094, Minneapolis, Minnesota. Association for Computational Linguistics.

Yinhan Liu, Myle Ott, Naman Goyal, Jingfei Du, Mandar Joshi, Danqi Chen, Omer Levy, Mike Lewis, Luke Zettlemoyer, and Veselin Stoyanov. 2019b. Roberta: A robustly optimized bert pretraining approach. *arXiv preprint arXiv:1907.11692.*

Ilya Loshchilov and Frank Hutter. 2019. Decoupled weight decay regularization. In *International Conference on Learning Representations.*

Marie-Catherine de Marneffe, Timothy Dozat, Natalia Silveira, Katri Haverinen, Filip Ginter, Joakim Nivre, and Christopher D. Manning. 2014. Universal Stanford dependencies: A cross-linguistic typology. In *Proceedings of the Ninth International Conference on Language Resources and Evaluation (LREC'14)*, pages 4585–4592, Reykjavik, Iceland. European Language Resources Association (ELRA).

Joakim Nivre, Paola Marongiu, Filip Ginter, Jenna Kanerva, Simonetta Montemagni, Sebastian Schuster, and Maria Simi. 2018. Enhancing universal dependency treebanks: A case study. In *Proceedings of the Second Workshop on Universal Dependencies (UDW 2018)*, pages 102–107, Brussels, Belgium. Association for Computational Linguistics.

Jenna Nyblom, Samuel Kohonen, Katri Haverinen, Tapio Salakoski, and Filip Ginter. 2013. Predicting conjunct propagation and other extended Stanford dependencies. In *Proceedings of the Second International Conference on Dependency Linguistics (DepLing 2013)*, pages 252–261, Prague, Czech Republic. Charles University in Prague, Matfyzpress, Prague, Czech Republic.

Peng Qi, Timothy Dozat, Yuhao Zhang, and Christopher D. Manning. 2018. Universal dependency parsing from scratch. In *Proceedings of the CoNLL 2018 Shared Task: Multilingual Parsing from Raw Text to Universal Dependencies*, pages 160–170, Brussels, Belgium. Association for Computational Linguistics.

Sebastian Ruder and Barbara Plank. 2017. Learning to select data for transfer learning with Bayesian optimization. In *Proceedings of the 2017 Conference on Empirical Methods in Natural Language Processing*, pages 372–382, Copenhagen, Denmark. Association for Computational Linguistics.

Agata Savary, Carla Parra Escartín, Francis Bond, Jelena Mitrović, and Verginica Barbu Mititelu, editors. 2019. *Proceedings of the Joint Workshop on Multiword Expressions and WordNet (MWE-WN 2019).* Association for Computational Linguistics, Florence, Italy.

Agata Savary, Carlos Ramisch, Jena D. Hwang, Nathan Schneider, Melanie Andresen, Sameer Pradhan, and Miriam R. L. Petruck, editors. 2018. *Proceedings of the Joint Workshop on Linguistic Annotation, Multiword Expressions and Constructions (LAW-MWE-CxG-2018).* Association for Computational Linguistics, Santa Fe, New Mexico, USA.

Sebastian Schuster, Éric Villemonte de La Clergerie, Marie Candito, Benoît Sagot, Christopher Manning, and Djamé Seddah. 2017. Paris and Stanford at EPE 2017: Downstream evaluation of graph-based dependency representations. In *Proceedings of the 2017 Shared Task on Extrinsic Parser Evaluation (EPE 2017)*, pages 47–59.

Sebastian Schuster and Christopher D. Manning. 2016. Enhanced English universal dependencies: An improved representation for natural language understanding tasks. In *Proceedings of the Tenth International Conference on Language Resources and Evaluation (LREC'16)*, pages 2371–2378, Portorož, Slovenia. European Language Resources Association (ELRA).

Maria Simi and Simonetta Montemagni. 2018. Bootstrapping enhanced universal dependencies for Italian. In *5th Italian Conference on Computational Linguistics, CLiC-it 2018*, volume 2253. CEUR-WS.